CONTENTS

RATINGS & PRICES

Ratings

Our rating system does not tell you – as most guides do – that expensive restaurant are often better than cheap ones! What we do is compare each restaurant's performance – as judged by the average ratings awarded by reporters in the survey – with other similarly-priced restaurants. This approach has the advantage that it helps you find – whatever your budget for any particular meal – where you will get the best 'bang for your buck'.

The following qualities are assessed:

F — Food
S — Service
A — Ambience

The rating indicates that, ***in comparison with other restaurants in the same price-bracket***, performance is...

❶ — Exceptional
❷ — Very good
❸ — Good
④ — Average
⑤ — Poor

Prices

The price shown for each restaurant is the cost for one (1) person of an average three-course dinner with half a bottle of house wine and coffee, any cover charge, service and VAT. Lunch is often cheaper. With BYO restaurants, we have assumed that two people share a £6 bottle of off-licence wine.

Telephone number – *all numbers are '020' numbers.*

Map reference – *shown immediately after the telephone number.*

Full postcodes – *for non-group restaurants, the first entry in the 'small print' at the end of each listing, so you can set your sat-nav.*

Website – *shown in the small print, where applicable.*

Last orders time – *listed after the website (if applicable); Sunday may be up to 90 minutes earlier.*

Opening hours – *unless otherwise stated, restaurants are open for lunch and dinner seven days a week.*

Credit and debit cards – *unless otherwise stated, Mastercard, Visa, Amex and Maestro are accepted.*

Dress – *where appropriate, the management's preferences concerning patrons' dress are given.*

Special menus – *if we know of a particularly good-value set menu we note this (e.g. "set weekday L"), together with its formula price (FP) calculated exactly as in 'Prices' above. Details change, so always check ahead.*

'Rated on Editors' visit' – *indicates ratings have been determined by the Editors personally, based on their visit, rather than derived from the survey.*

SRA Rating – *the sustainability index, as calculated by the Sustainable Restaurant Association –* *see page 8 for more information.*

BlackBerry

iPhone / iPad

London Restaurants 2013

22ND EDITION

Survey driven reviews of over 1,800 restaurants

ISBN 978-1-873721-98-8

British Library Cataloguing-in-Publication data: a catalogue record for this book is available from the British Library.

Printed in Italy by Legoprint

Research assistants: Helen Teschauer, Gilles Talarek, Sarah Ashpole

Harden's Limited
Golden Cross House, 8 Duncannon Street
London WC2N 4JF

Would restaurateurs (and PRs) please address communications to 'Editorial' at the above address, or ideally by email to: editorial@hardens.com

The contents of this book are believed correct at the time of printing. Nevertheless, the publisher can accept no responsibility for errors or changes in or omissions from the details given.

HOW THIS GUIDE IS WRITTEN

Survey

This guide is based on our 22nd annual survey of what 'ordinary' diners-out think of London's restaurants. In 1998, we extended the survey to cover restaurants across the rest of the UK; it is by far the most detailed annual survey of its type. Out-of-town results are published in our UK guide.

This year, the total number of reporters in our combined London/UK survey, conducted mainly online, exceeded 7,500, and, between them, they contributed some 75,000 individual reports.

How we determine the ratings

In the great majority of cases, ratings are arrived at statistically. This essentially involves 'ranking' the average survey rating each restaurant achieves in the survey – for each of food, service and ambience – against the average ratings of the other establishments which fall in the same price-bracket. (This is essentially like football leagues, with the most expensive restaurants going in the top league and the cheaper ones in lower leagues. The restaurant's ranking *within its own particular league* determines its ratings.)

How we write the reviews

The tenor of each review and the ratings are very largely determined by the ranking of the establishment concerned, which we derive as described above. At the margin, we may also pay some regard to the proportion of positive nominations (such as for 'favourite restaurant') compared to negative nominations (such as for 'most overpriced').

To explain why a restaurant has been rated as it has, we extract snippets from survey comments ("enclosed in double quotes"). On larger restaurants, we receive several hundred reports, and a short summary cannot possibly do individual justice to all of them.

What we seek to do – *without any regard to our own personal opinions* – is to illustrate the key themes which have emerged in our analysis of the collective view. The only exception to this is the newest restaurants, where survey views are either few or non-existent, and where we may be obliged to rely on our own opinion. Unless the review carries the small-print note "Rated on Editors' visit", however, the ratings awarded are still our best analysis of the survey view, not our own impression.

Richard Harden

Richard Harden

Peter Harden

Peter Harden

Eat Well

If issues such as climate change, animal welfare and treating people fairly matter to you, look out for the SRA Sustainability Ratings next to restaurant listings.

The Sustainable Restaurant Association (SRA) is a not for profit body helping restaurants achieve greater sustainability. To help diners, it has developed Sustainability Ratings to assess restaurants in 14 key focus areas across three main sustainability categories of Sourcing, Environment and Society.

Harden's has partnered with the SRA to include its Sustainability Ratings, setting a new benchmark for the industry and giving diners the information to identify those restaurants doing great things. For example, sourcing seasonably and supporting local producers is important, as is using high welfare meat and dairy and ensuring fish stocks aren't endangered. Cutting down on food waste and ensuring energy and water efficiency are more ways for restaurants to be sustainable. And the most sustainable restaurants really engage with the communities around them.

Sustainability is an ongoing process: there's always room to improve and there's no final destination. By choosing a sustainable restaurant, you can be sure that your meal isn't costing the earth.

Food connects us with our landscape, our soil, our heritage, our health and what kind of society we are creating for tomorrow. Chefs, restaurateurs and diners can make the difference by embracing sustainable values and in doing so create a better food chain. We hope diners will consider these ideals when choosing to dine out.

Raymond Blanc OBE, President of the SRA

We're proud to support the SRA, and hope that by adding SRA Sustainability Ratings to the restaurants we include, we can help set diners' expectations as to which of their choices will ensure the trade thrives for decades, and hopefully centuries to come.

Harden's

More than 50% = Good Sustainability
More than 60% = Excellent Sustainability
More than 70% = Exceptional Sustainability

SURVEY FAQs

Q. How do you find your reporters?
A. Anyone can take part. Simply register at www.hardens.com. Actually, we find that many people who complete our survey each year have taken part before. So it's really more a question of a very large and ever-evolving panel, or jury, than a random 'poll'.

Q. Wouldn't a random sample be better?
A. That's really a theoretical question, as there is no obvious way, still less a cost-efficient one, by which one could identify a random sample of the guests at each of, say, 5000 establishments across the UK, and get them to take part in any sort of survey. And anyway, which is likely to be more useful: a sample of the views of everyone who's been to a particular place, or the views of people who are interested enough in eating-out to have volunteered their feedback?

Q. What sort of people take part?
A. A roughly 60/40 male/female split, from all adult age-groups. As you might expect – as eating out is not the cheapest activity – reporters tend to have white collar jobs (some at very senior levels). By no means, however, is that always the case.

Q. Do people ever try to stuff the ballot?
A. Of course they do! A rising number of efforts are weeded out every year. But stuffing the ballot is not as trivial a task as some people seem to think: the survey results throw up clear natural voting patterns against which 'campaigns' tend to stand out.

Q. Aren't inspections the best way to run a guide?
A. It is often assumed – even by commentators who ought to know better – that inspections are some sort of 'gold standard'. There is no doubt that the inspection model clearly has potential strengths, but one of its prime weaknesses is that it is incredibly expensive. Take the most famous practitioner of the 'inspection model', Michelin. It doesn't claim to visit each and every entry listed in its guide annually. Even once! And who are the inspectors? Often they are catering professionals, whose likes and dislikes may be very different from the establishment's natural customer base. On any restaurant of note, however, Harden's typically has somewhere between dozens and hundreds of reports each and every year from exactly the type of people the restaurant relies upon to stay in business. We believe that such feedback, carefully analysed, is far more revealing and accurate than an occasional 'professional' inspection.

SURVEY MOST MENTIONED

These are the restaurants which were most frequently mentioned by reporters. (Last year's position is given in brackets.) An asterisk* indicates the first appearance in the list of a recently-opened restaurant.

1 J Sheekey (1)
2 Scott's (2)
3 Chez Bruce (4)
4 Le Gavroche (5)
5 Dinner (24)
6 Clos Maggiore (7)
7 The Ledbury (6)
8 Pollen Street Social*
9 The Wolseley (9)
10 Marcus Wareing (3)

11 Galvin Bistrot de Luxe (7)
12 Les Deux Salons (10)
13 Bleeding Heart (12)
14 La Trompette (16)
15 The Square (14)
16 The Delaunay*
17 Galvin La Chapelle (18)
18 The River Café (23)
19 Terroirs (11)
20 The Cinnamon Club (12)

21 The Ivy (21)
22 Le Caprice (17)
23 Bar Boulud (15)
24 La Poule au Pot (20)
25 Zucca (-)
26= Zuma (26)
26= Bocca di Lupo (24)
26= Medlar*
29 Yauatcha (37)
30 Galvin at Windows (39)

31 Gordon Ramsay (29)
32= Andrew Edmunds (30)
32= MEATLiquor*
34= Amaya (27)
34= Benares (22)
34= Arbutus (38)
37= L'Atelier de Joel Robuchon (32)
37= The Gilbert Scott*
39= Moro (31)
39= Gordon Ramsay at Claridges (32)

SURVEY NOMINATIONS

Top gastronomic experience

1 Dinner (5)
2 The Ledbury (3)
3 Le Gavroche (2)
4 Marcus Wareing (1)
5 Chez Bruce (4)
6 Pollen Street Social*
7 The Square (7)
8 Pied à Terre (8)
9 La Trompette (6)
10 L'Atelier de Joel Robuchon (-)

Favourite

1 Chez Bruce (1)
2 La Trompette (6)
3 J Sheekey (9)
4 Pollen Street Social*
5 Le Gavroche (7)
6 The Wolseley (2)
7 Le Caprice (3)
8 Galvin Bistrot de Luxe (4)
9 Trinity (10)
10 The River Café (-)

Best for business

1 The Wolseley (1)
2 The Square (3)
3 The Don (2)
4 Bleeding Heart (4)
5 Galvin La Chapelle (5)
6 Coq d'Argent (6)
7 The Delaunay*
8 L'Anima (7)
9 Scott's (9)
10 Galvin Bistrot de Luxe (8)

Best for romance

1 Clos Maggiore (1)
2 La Poule au Pot (2)
3 Andrew Edmunds (3)
4 Bleeding Heart (4)
5 Galvin at Windows (6)
6 Chez Bruce (5)
7 Le Gavroche (8)
8 Le Caprice (7)
9 The Ledbury (9)
10 Galvin La Chapelle (-)

RANKED BY THE NUMBER OF REPORTERS' VOTES

Best breakfast/brunch

1 The Wolseley (1)
2 The Delaunay*
3 Roast (2)
4 Cecconi's (4)
5 Riding House Café*
6 Smiths (Ground Floor) (3)
7 Caravan (7)
8 Automat (5)
9 The Modern Pantry (-)
10 Granger & Co*

Best bar/pub food

1 The Anchor & Hope (1)
2 Harwood Arms (2)
3 Bull & Last (3)
4 The Anglesea Arms (7)
5 The Thomas Cubitt (8)
6 Canton Arms (4)
7 The Ladbroke Arms (-)
8 Princess Victoria (-)
9 The Orange (5)
10 The Havelock Tavern (-)

Most disappointing cooking

1 Oxo Tower (Rest') (2)
2 Gordon Ramsay at Claridge's (1)
3 Dinner (-)
4 The Ivy (3)
5 Les Deux Salons (6)
6 The Gilbert Scott*
7 The Wolseley (7)
8 Gordon Ramsay (5)
9 Pollen Street Social*
10 Savoy Grill (-)

Most overpriced restaurant

1 Oxo Tower (Rest') (1)
2 The River Café (5)
3 Gordon Ramsay (3)
4 Gordon Ramsay at Claridge's (2)
5 Cut*
6 Le Gavroche (8)
7 Dinner (-)
8 Alain Ducasse at the Dorchester (7)
9 The Ivy (-)
10 The Gilbert Scott*

SURVEY HIGHEST RATINGS

FOOD	SERVICE
£85+	
1 The Ledbury	1 Le Gavroche
2 One-O-One	2 The Ledbury
3 Le Gavroche	3 Marcus Wareing
4 Marcus Wareing	4 The Square
5 Umu	5 Pétrus
£65-£84	
1 Chez Bruce	1 Chez Bruce
2 Theo Randall	2 Trinity
3 Min Jiang	3 Roganic
4 Trinity	4 The Goring Hotel
5 Roganic	5 Koffmann's
£50-£64	
1 Dinings	1 Oslo Court
2 Hunan	2 La Trompette
3 Michael Nadra	3 Medlar
4 La Trompette	4 Brula
5 Harwood Arms	5 Quilon
£40-£49	
1 Jin Kichi	1 Upstairs Bar
2 Dabbous	2 J Sheekey Oyster Bar
3 Sushi-Say	3 Sushi-Say
4 Sukho Fine Thai Cuisine	4 Indian Zilla
5 Zucca	5 Latium
£39 or less	
1 Pham Sushi	1 Taiwan Village
2 Ragam	2 Kaffeine
3 Mangal 1	3 José
4 Honest Burgers	4 Tinello
5 Taiwan Village	5 Yoshino

SURVEY HIGHEST RATINGS

	AMBIENCE		OVERALL
1	The Ritz Restaurant	1	The Ledbury
2	Le Gavroche	2	Le Gavroche
3	Galvin at Windows	3	Marcus Wareing
4	The Ledbury	4	Pied à Terre
5	Roux at the Landau	5	The Ritz Restaurant
1	Les Trois Garçons	1	Chez Bruce
2	Min Jiang	2	Min Jiang
3	Rules	3	Trinity
4	Criterion	4	J Sheekey
5	Rhodes 24	5	Scott's
1	La Poule au Pot	1	Oslo Court
2	Clos Maggiore	2	La Trompette
3	The Wallace	3	Brula
4	Blueprint Café	4	Clos Maggiore
5	The Wolseley	5	L'Aventure
1	J Sheekey Oyster Bar	1	J Sheekey Oyster Bar
2	Andrew Edmunds	2	Upstairs Bar
3	The Oak	3	Il Bordello
4	St Johns	4	Sushi-Say
5	Il Bordello	5	Corner Room
1	Gordon's Wine Bar	1	José
2	José	2	Kaffeine
3	Kaffeine	3	Tinello
4	Churchill Arms	4	Ganapati
5	Dishoom	5	Taiwan Village

SURVEY BEST BY CUISINE

These are the restaurants which received the best average food ratings (excluding establishments with a small or notably local following).

Where the most common types of cuisine are concerned, we present the results in two price-brackets. For less common cuisines, we list the top three, regardless of price.

For further information about restaurants which are particularly notable for their food, see the cuisine lists starting on page 246. These indicate, using an asterisk*, restaurants which offer exceptional or very good food.

British, Modern

£50 and over		Under £50	
1	The Ledbury	1	Lamberts
2	Chez Bruce	2	The Victoria
3	Trinity	3	The Anglesea Arms
4	Roganic	4	10 Greek Street
5	The Glasshouse	5	The Ladbroke Arms

French

£50 and over		Under £50	
1	Le Gavroche	1	Upstairs Bar
2	Marcus Wareing	2	Brawn
3	Pied à Terre	3	Giaconda Dining Room
4	The Square	4	Terroirs
5	La Trompette	5	Randall & Aubin

Italian/Mediterranean

£50 and over		Under £50	
1	Theo Randall	1	Zucca
2	Assaggi	2	500
3	Olivomare	3	The Oak
4	The River Café	4	Delfino
5	L'Anima	5	Latium

Indian & Pakistani

£50 and over		Under £50	
1	Amaya	1	Ragam
2	Rasoi	2	Indian Zing
3	The Cinnamon Club	3	Babur
4	Benares	4	Roots at N1
5	The Painted Heron	5	Indian Rasoi

Chinese

£50 and over
1 Hunan
2 Min Jiang
3 Yauatcha
4 Hakkasan *Hanway Pl*
5 Shanghai Blues

Under £50
1 Taiwan Village
2 Pearl Liang
3 Four Seasons W2
4 Bar Shu
5 Mandarin Kitchen

Japanese

£50 and over
1 Dinings
2 Defune
3 Umu
4 Zuma
5 Roka W1

Under £50
1 Jin Kichi
2 Pham Sushi
3 Sushi-Say
4 Tsunami SW4
5 Koya

British, Traditional
1 Dinner
2 Scott's
3 St John Bread & Wine

Vegetarian
1 Gate W6
2 Mildreds
3 Vanilla Black

Burgers, etc
1 Honest Burgers
2 MEATLiquor
3 Burgers & Lobster

Pizza
1 Franco Manca
2 The Oak
3 Santa Maria

Fish & Chips
1 Golden Hind
2 Kerbisher & Malt
3 Toff's

Thai
1 Sukho Thai
2 Nahm
3 Patara SW3

Steaks & Grills
1 Hawksmoor WC2
2 Goodman City
3 Hawksmoor E1

Fish & Seafood
1 One-O-One
2 J Sheekey Oyster Bar
3 J Sheekey

Fusion
1 Viajante
2 E&O
3 Providores

Spanish
1 Barrafina
2 José
3 Barrica

Turkish
1 Mangal 1
2 Cyprus Mangal
3 Best Mangal

Lebanese
1 Chez Marcelle
2 Yalla Yalla
3 Maroush II

TOP SPECIAL DEALS

The following menus allow you to eat in the restaurants concerned at a significant discount when compared to their evening à la carte prices.

The prices used are calculated in accordance with our usual formula (i.e. three courses with house wine, coffee and tip).

Special menus are by their nature susceptible to change – please check that they are still available.

Weekday lunch

£70+ The Ritz Restaurant

£65+ Apsleys
Marcus Wareing

£60+ Alain Ducasse
Hibiscus

£55+ L'Atelier de Joel Robuchon
Le Gavroche
The Ledbury
Murano

£50+ Corrigan's Mayfair
Dorchester Grill
Kai Mayfair
Pied à Terre
Roganic
Texture
Viajante

£45+ Bibendum
China Tang
Franco's
Galvin at Windows
Galvin La Chapelle
JW Steakhouse
Koffmann's
One-O-One
Rib Room
Savoy Grill
The Square

£40+ L'Autre Pied
Babylon
Belvedere
The Cinnamon Club
Club Gascon
Criterion
Launceston Place
maze Grill
Orrery
Pearl
Pétrus
Roux at Parliament Square
Seven Park Place
Tamarind

£35+ L'Aventure
Boisdale of Bishopsgate
Chakra
Clos Maggiore
Daphne's
El leven Park Walk
L'Etranger
Galvin Bistrot de Luxe
High Timber
Kiku
Kitchen W8
Little Italy
Lucio
Magdalen
Momo
Odette's
Oxo Tower (Rest')
Pellicano
Ristorante Semplice
Verta

£30+ The Ark
Bradley's
Café des Amis
City Miyama
Les Deux Salons
L'Escargot
Frederick's
Le Garrick Wine Bar
Geales
Haandi
Hereford Road
The Light House
Mint Leaf
Mon Plaisir
Sophie's Steakhouse
Trishna
Verru
Watatsumi

£25+ The Angel & Crown
Carvosso's
Casa Batavia
Chez Patrick
The Forge
The Foundry
Franklins
Fratelli la Bufala
Gastro
Gessler at Daquise
Gilgamesh
The Grove
Grumbles
The Haven
High Road Brasserie
Inaho
Indian Zing
Ishtar
Kew Grill
Mele e Pere
Motcombs
Polish Club

Plane Food
Plateau
Racine
Rebato's
The Salt House
Savoir Faire
XO

£20+ Bumbles
Chowki
Huong-Viet
Lemonia
Loch Fyne
Mill Lane Bistro
Le Petit Normand
La Petite Auberge
The Prince Bonaparte
The Queens Arms
Rising Sun
Seafresh

Soho Japan
Tosa
Yum Yum

£15+ Chettinad
Galicia
Kolossi Grill
El Pirata
El Pirata de Tapas
Sedap
Ten Ten Tei
Toff's
The Water Margin

£10+ Tokyo Diner

Pre/post theatre (and early evening)

£55+ L'Atelier de Joel Robuchon

£50+ Koffmann's

£45+ Le Caprice
Franco's
Morgan M
Savoy Grill
Savoy (River Restaurant)

£40+ L'Autre Pied
Belvedere
The Cinnamon Club
Criterion
Indigo
maze Grill

£35+ The Almeida
Brasserie Joël
Brasserie on St John Street
Clos Maggiore
Daphne's
Dean Street Townhouse
Galvin Bistrot de Luxe
Little Italy
Orso

£30+ Bradley's
Café des Amis
Cape Town Fish Market
Les Deux Salons
Le Deuxième
L'Escargot
The Forge
Frederick's
Gallery Mess
Le Garrick Wine Bar
Harrison's
Joe Allen
The Lawn Bistro
Mele e Pere
Mennula
Quaglino's
Vivat Bacchus
Watasumi

£25+ The Bountiful Cow
Carvosso's
Côte
Grumbles
Ishtar
Kazan
Mela
Mon Plaisir

£20+ Chowki
Ozer
Sofra

£15+ Antepliler

Sunday lunch

40+ Criterion

£35+ Red Fort
Verta

£30+ Polish Club

£20+ Le P'tit Normand

£15+ Galicia

THE RESTAURANT SCENE

Openings very much back to 'normal'!

This year we record 134 openings, some 25% up on last year (107). This figure – the 5th-best ever – brings annual openings well into the top half of the 'normal' range noted in the period 2001-2010 – 120 to 142. Closings, at 74, are marginally up from last year (71), but – again – well within the known-and-usual range. (See lists on pages 22 and 23.)

Indeed if you look at another bellwether – the ratio of the openings we record to the closings – the eerie feeling of return-to-normality is reinforced. The ratio follows a pretty clear cycle, and after last year's low point (1.5:1) it has now rebounded to around the this-millennium average of 1.8:1. Indeed many openings seem notably optimistic in their scale and ambition. Look at *Brasserie Zédel* (a marbled palace with 200 seats), and *Sushisamba/Duck & Waffle* – 38, 39 and 40 floors above the City: with some 250 seats in total, one of the most ambitiously-scaled elevated restaurant complexes to be found anywhere in the world!

We'll take Manhattan

As skycrapers re-shape London's skyline, it's not just the architecture which is becoming more like that of NYC. The top-end retail and leisure 'spaces' – restaurants of course being at the intersection of the two – are becoming ever more like New York's, and especially downtown NYC's.

A US invasion is underway, with the arrival in the last couple of years of such high-profile imports as *Spice Market*, *Bar Boulud* and *Cut*, joined this year by such downtown NYC names as *Standard Grill*, *STK*, and the aforesaid *Sushisamba*.

Then there are the many newcomers which, if not actually rooted across the Pond, draw their inspiration there. Russell Norman (*Polpo* etc) has built a whole empire on Americana, but he is merely the most obvious example of a wider trend. Also ploughing this furrow are the many new openings focussed on individual US-inspired specialities – such as *Bubbledogs*, *Burger & Lobster*, *MEATLiquor*, *Chicken Shop*, *Red Dog Saloon* and *Wishbone*. And that's before we talk about the ongoing, seemingly unstoppable march of the steakhouses – at least half a dozen new establishments (generally charging somewhere round £70 a head) are openings in the latter half of 2012.

Restaurants go East

When we launched our guides, back in 1992, the market for quality dining-out was disproportionately skewed to inner SW London. It was only in the mid-90s that the Mafyair and St James's 'metropolitan dining zone' – as we then called it – emerged, and it took another ten years before the Soho (re-)naissance (and, in due course, Covent Garden's) really got going. The eastward march continues, and now it's the turn of the City and Shoreditch to (re-)emerge. The latter is, of course, London's closest spiritual equivalent to NYC's Meatpacking District, from whence many recent arrivals hail.

Other trends

Shorter-term trends apparent in recent (and impending) openings include the following:

• Though London has been going mad for New York, Paris is having a modest moment too. The style of newcomers such as *Colbert, Brasserie Zédel,* and *Garnier* is *très classique*.

• As the all-conquering-hit that is *Dabbous* tends to confirm, small-plate concepts have now gone entirely mainstream, even for openings of the highest ambition. Indeed, the more fashionable and the more ambitious a restaurant is nowadays, the greater the presumption that it will seek to dazzle with a menu designed to share and 'taste'.

• In keeping with this small-plate revolution, quality Spanish restaurants (*Donostia, José* and *Pizarro*), continue to spread.

• Perhaps inspired by the obvious success of Spanish tapas, Italian-tapas and 'salumeria' openings such as *Briciole, San Carlo Cicchetti* and *Rocco* are getting in on the act too.

• Also benefitting from the small-plate tendency, Japanese (or Japanese-fusion) restaurants are – after a quiet patch – resurgent (*Chrysan, Okku,* the second *Sushinho* and *Sushi Tetsu*).

• Synthesising the American, and Hispanic trends mentioned above and opposite, Latino cuisine continues its growth of recent years, particularly via the discovery of Peru, with openings such as *Lima, Ceviche* and *Tierra Peru.*

• Popularised by the 'food truck' phenomenon (yet another recent US import), and often drawing on simple, essentially American protein-led dishes (see opposite), London is continuing to see much-improved provision of relatively inexpensive, quality options, particularly in the centre of town (*Burger & Lobster, MEATLiquor* and *Pitt Cue Co.*)

So just as the world is supposed to be looking eastwards, our culinary focus is largely moving to the west!

Every year, we select what seem to us personally to be the ten most significant openings of the preceding 12 months. This year, our selection is as follows:

Brasserie Zédel	MEATLiquor
Burger & Lobster	Pitt Cue Co
Dabbous	Sushi Tetsu
The Delaunay	Sushisamba
Lima	10 Greek Street

The quality of openings is as high as it has ever been.

Prices

The average price of dinner for one at establishments listed in the guide is £46.55 (compared to £45.01 last year). Prices have risen by 3.5% in the past 12 months. This increase is ahead of consumer prices more generally over the period. This lead, though, is only marginal – a welcome return to normality, after prices raced ahead last year.

OPENINGS AND CLOSURES

Openings (134)

Abbeville Kitchen
The Angel & Crown
Angler
Antico
Baku
The Balcon
Banca
Barrafina *(WC2)*
Beard to Tail
Ben's Canteen
Bianco43
Big Easy *(WC2)*
Bincho *(EC1)*
Bistro Union
Blue Elephant
La Bodega Negra
Brasserie Blanc *(x7)*
Brasserie Zédel
Briciole
The Bright Courtyard
The Brown Cow
Bubba Gump Shrimp Company
Bubbledogs
Burger & Lobster *(W1 x2, EC1)*
Caravan *(N1)*
Casa Batavia
Ceviche
Chakra
Chettinad
Chicken Shop
Chipotle *(W1,WC2)*
Chisou *(W4)*
Chrysan
Cinnamon Soho
Colbert
Colchis
Copita
Cotidie
Dabbous
De La Panza
The Delaunay
The Deli West One
Donostia
Downtown Mayfair
Duck & Waffle
Ducksoup
Elliot's Cafe
The Fish Market
Fortnum & Mason (Diamond Jubilee Tea Salon)
40 Maltby Street
The Foundry
Franco Manca *(E20)*
Galvin Demoiselle
Garnier
The Gate *(EC1)*
Goode & Wright
Goodman *(E14)*
Granger & Co
Green Man & French Horn
Guglee *(NW6)*
The Hampshire Hog
Hawksmoor *(W1)*
Hix Belgravia
Hix at the Tramshed
Honest Burgers *(W1)*
HKK
The Jugged Hare
Hush *(WC1)*
Kaosarn *(SW11)*
Karpo
The Lady Ottoline
Lardo
The Lawn Bistro
Lima
The Lord Northbrook
Mango Tree *(Harrods)*
Mari Vanna
The Markham Inn
MASH Steakhouse
Mazi
MEATLiquor
Mele e Pere
Mishkin's
Morgan M *(EC1)*
Naamyaa Café
New Street Grill
Okku
One Blenheim Terrace
Orchard
Otto's
Outlaw's Seafood & Grill
Pentolina
Pitt Cue Co
Pizza East *(NW5)*
Polpo *(EC1)*

Openings (cont'd)

Potli
Relais de Venise L'Entrecote *(E14)*
Rocco
Roti Chai
Sacro Cuore
San Carlo Cicchetti
Sapori Sardi
Shrimpy's
Soif
The Standard Grill
Sticks'n'Sushi
STK Steakhouse
Suda
The Surprise
Sushi Tetsu
Tapasia
The 10 Cases
10 Greek Street
Thirty Six
3 South Place
Tierra Peru
Tonkotsu
Tramontana Brindisa
Le Troquet
28-50 *(W1)*
Union Jacks *(all branches)*
Upstairs at the Ten Bells
Vinoteca *(Beak St W1)*
Wabi
Wishbone
Yipin China

Closures (74)

A La Cruz
Acorn House
Ambassador
Awana
Bar Battu
Benja
Bennett Oyster Bar & Brasserie
Bertorelli *(all branches)*
Bistro du Vin *(W1, EC1)*
Bouchon Breton
Blue Jade
Brasserie James
Brasserie Roux
Café Emm
Café Luc
Cafe Strudel
The Capital
Caponata
Cavallino
Chez Gérard *(all branches)*
Cocorino *(W1 x2)*
Colony
Costa's Grill
Curve
Eagle Bar Diner
Edokko
English Pig *(EC1)*
Il Falconiere
54 Farringdon Road
5 Pollen Street
The Gallery
Galoupet
Geeta
Guerilla Burgers
Ilia
Incognico
kare kare
Kiasu
Larder
Livebait *(WC2, SE1)*
Lolo Rojo *(SW6)*
Manchurian Legends
Manson
Morgan M *(N7)*
Mrs Marengos
Napket *(all branches)*
New Culture Revolution *(W11)*
Peninsula
Piccolino *(SW19)*
Polpetto
Le Querce *(SE3)*
Rasa Samudra *(Charlotte St W1)*
Roussillon
S & M Café *(N1, E1)*
Saf *(EC2)*
Saki
Sapori
Scarpetta
Soseki
The Terrace in the Fields

Closures (continued)

Toto's
Vanilla
Venosi
Walnut
Zilli Fish
Zilli Green

EATING IN LONDON FAQs

'How should I use this guide?

You will often wish to use this guide in a practical way. At heart, the issue will usually be geographical – where can we eat near…? To answer such questions, the Maps (from page 300) and Area Overviews (from page 262) are the place to start. The latter tell you all the key facts about the restaurants – perhaps dozens of 'em – in a particular area in the space of a couple of pages. These Area Overviews are unique, so please do spend a second to have a look!

This section, though, is about seeking out new places when you want to be inspired to make a culinary adventure for its own sake, or you need to find a venue for a special event.

What makes London special?

Cosmopolitanism and quality! As one of the world's great 'melting pots', London has long offered incredibly diverse dining-out possibilities, but there was not always a particular emphasis on delivering the very best quality. In recent years, however, standards have improved by leaps and bounds. This has inspired much greater excitement – among both locals and visitors – which, of course, has provided a fertile environment for those wishing to launch new concepts. A virtous circle has ensued.

It is the growth of this excitement factor – especially among younger and less 'traditionally'-minded diners – which has addressed what has arguably in recent years been London's main shortcoming, especially when compared to the more advanced dining scene in New York.

We'll give you some ideas for places and concepts particularly worth exploring on the following two pages, but first let's dispose of that hoary old chestnut…

Which is London's best restaurant?

As the restaurant scene gets more diverse and interesting, it's more and more difficult to give a meaningful single answer to this question. If you're looking for the full grand package in the traditional Gallic mould, the safest choice is in fact the oldest – *Le Gavroche*. London's original grand restaurant of the modern era remains the very best place of the more traditional variety to eat in the centre of town.

The most obvious alternative contender – *The Ledbury* – is interesting because it's everything Le Gavroche is not. The chef is an Aussie, not French, and it is in Notting Hill, not Mayfair. But it is still a classy operation in a fundamentally traditional mould. For something more truly revolutionary, you would have to look to a recent arrival, *Dabbous*… but you'd have to book months ahead! For other truly tip-top suggestions, please use the lists on pages 14-15.

What about something a little more reasonably priced?

Looking for a really good dinner, without a second mortgage? Here are some top suggestions, which, though not cheap, don't involve 'silly' money. For obvious reasons, they tend not to be right in the centre of town.

Most notable in this category is the group formed around 'London's favourite restaurant' (for the 8th successive year), *Chez Bruce* (Wandsworth), plus its siblings *La Trompette* (Chiswick) and the *Glasshouse* (Kew). (It also, incidentally, includes the Ledbury, mentioned on the previous page.) Other hidden jewels out in Zones 2 and 3 include *Trinity* (Clapham), *Bistro Aix* (Crouch End) and a wonderful '70s period-piece, *Oslo Court* (St John's Wood).

What about some really good suggestions in the heart of the West End?

It used to be really difficult to find good-quality 'traditional' (Anglo-French) cooking in the West End at any reasonable sort of cost. No longer, fortunately, and names to look out for include: *Arbutus*, *Giaconda Dining Room*, *Galvin Bistrot de Luxe*, *Terroirs* and *Wild Honey*. There is also a growing band of superb tapas-style restaurants (see below).

If you want a little more comfort and style, you're unlikely to go far wrong at the restaurant which attracts most survey attention, *J Sheekey*, a fish specialist hidden-away in the heart of Theatreland, or *Scott's*, a celebrity magnet on one of the grandest streets in Mayfair. These last are hardly bargain suggestions, but they do offer all-round value.

For pure theatre, a visitor should probably try to eat at the *Wolseley* – the nation's 'grand café', by the Ritz – at some point. Breakfast or tea provide excellent opportunities! In the heart of Covent Garden, *Clos Maggiore* – 'London's most romantic restaurant', and with an extraordinary wine list too – boasts a notably handy central location.

Small is beautiful

Much of the gastronomic excitement of recent years has come from 'tapas' specialists, not just inspired by Spain but by SW France and beyond. Such concepts have played a large part in bringing sophisticated yet affordable formats to the heart of the West End. Soho (and soon Covent Garden's) *Barrafina* represents the tapas ideal at its most classical, with outfits such as *Bocca di Lupo, Ceviche, Copita, Dehesa, Kopapa, Lima* and *Salt Yard* all offering their own variations on the theme.

Don't forget to lunch!

Lunch in London can be a great bargain: *Le Gavroche*, for example, famously offers a superb-value prix-fixe lunch, including wine. Indeed, it is the grandest restaurants, paradoxically, which often offer the best-value set deals. For further suggestions, see the list on pages 18 and 19.

And for the best of British?

British food has become very fashionable over the past decade. The change all began with the Smithfield restaurant *St John*, whose dedication to old-fashioned (and usually offal-heavy) British cooking has won it international acclaim. The trend perhaps reached its high point with last year's opening of Heston Blumenthal's good-but-pricey *Dinner* (Knightsbridge). Other notable British restaurants often trace their roots back to St John, including *Magdalen* (South Bank), *Great Queen Street* (Covent Garden), *Hereford Road* (Bayswater) and *St John Bread & Wine* (Shoreditch). But a lot of 'British' cooking is taking place in gastropubs…

What are gastropubs?

Essentially, bistros in pub premises. They come in a variety of styles. What many people think of as the original gastropub (*The Eagle*, 1991) still looks very much like a pub with a food counter.

At the other end of the scale, however, the 'pub' element can become almost redundant, and the business is really just a restaurant in premises that once housed a pub. Few of the best gastropubs are particularly central. The handy location of the *Anchor & Hope*, on the South Bank, is no doubt part of the reason for its great popularity. Other stars include the *Bull & Last* (Kentish Town), the *Canton Arms* (Stockwell) and the *Harwood Arms* (Fulham).

Isn't London supposed to be a top place for curry?

Many visitors come to London wanting to 'try Indian', and London – with the possible exception of the Indian subcontinent – is the best place on the planet to do so. Indeed, the choice of 'Indian' – a term including Pakistani and Bangladeshi in this context – restaurants is so great that you then need to decide what sort of Indian you want to try.

You want value? Two top names in the East End (and hence relatively accessible from central London) are almost legendary 'experiences' – the *Lahore Kebab House* and *Tayyabs*. The predominantly veggie *Rasa* group also includes some very good-value options. Or, for an immersive experience, go down to Tooting. and check out a fixture like *Sree Krishna*.

Right at the other end of the scale (and, for the most part, right in the heart of town) are the 'nouvelle Indians', where spicy dishes are presented with a heavy European influence. *Amaya, Benares, The Cinnamon Club, The Painted Heron, Quilon, Rasoi, Trishna, Veeraswamy* and *Zaika* are all examples of plush restaurants just as suited to business (and in many cases romance) as their European price-equivalents.

In fact, wherever you are in London, you should be in reach of an Indian restaurant of more-than-average note – search out the asterisked restaurants in the Indian and Pakistani lists commencing on pages 257 and 259 respectively.

Any money-saving tips?

- The top tip, already noted, is to lunch not dine. If you're a visitor, you'll find that it's better for your wallet, as well as your digestion, to have your main meal in the middle of the day. In the centre of town, it's one of the best ways you can be sure of eating 'properly' at reasonable cost. See the spread on pages 18 and 19.

- Think ethnic – for a food 'experience' at modest cost, you'll almost always be better off going Indian, Thai, Chinese or Vietnamese (to choose four of the most obvious cuisines) than French, English or Italian. The days when there was any sort of assumption that ethnic restaurants were – in terms of comfort, service and décor – in any way inferior to European ones is long gone, but they are still often somewhat cheaper.

- Don't assume the West End is the obvious destination. That's not to say that – armed with this book – you shouldn't be able to eat well in the heart of things, but you'll almost certainly do better in value terms outside the Circle line. Many of the best and cheapest restaurants in this guide are easily accessible by tube. Use the maps at the back of this book to identify restaurants near tube stations on a line that's handy for you.

- If you must dine in the West End, try to find either pre-theatre (generally before 7 pm) or post-theatre (generally after 10 pm) menus. You will generally save at least the cost of a cinema ticket, compared to dining à la carte. Many of the more upmarket restaurants in Theatreland do such deals. For some of our top suggestions, see page 19.

- Use this book! Don't take pot luck, when you can benefit from the pre-digested views of thousands of other diners-out. Choose a place with a ➊ or ➋ for food, and you're very likely to eat much better than if you walk in somewhere 'on spec' – this is good advice anywhere, but is most particularly so in the West End.

- Once you have decided that you want to eat within a particular area, use the Area Overviews (starting on p262) to identify the restaurants that are offering top value. We have gone to a lot of trouble to boil down a huge amount of data into the results which are handily summarised in such lists. Please use them! You are unlikely to regret it.

- Visit our website, www.hardens.com for the latest reviews, and restaurant news, and to sign up for our annual spring survey.

DIRECTORY

Comments in "double quotation-marks" were made by reporters.

Establishments which we judge to be particularly notable have their NAME IN CAPITALS.

F S A

A Cena TW1 **£49** ❸❷❷
418 Richmond Rd 8288 0108 1–4A
Just south of Richmond Bridge, this "charming" Italian has built up an impressive fan club with its "good all-round" standards – these include a "varied" choice of "very appetising" dishes, and "some pretty decent wines too". / TW1 2EB; www.acena.co.uk; 10 pm; closed Mon L & Sun D; booking: max 6, Fri & Sat.

The Abbeville SW4 **£42** ④④❷
67-69 Abbeville Rd 8675 2201 10–2D
"Hearty" scoff from an "ever-changing menu" wins praise for this oddly-configured gastroboozer, which is hailed by Clapham types as "a local gem". / SW4 9JW; www.renaissancepubs.co.uk; 10.30 pm, Sun 9 pm; SRA-56%.

Abbeville Kitchen SW4 NEW **£45** ❷❷❸
47 Abbeville Rd 8772 1110 10–2D
Anchor & Hope graduate Kevin McFadden offers a selection of "inventive" but "unfancy" tapas-style dishes at this new Clapham bistro – universally hailed as "a great addition to the neighbourhood". / SW4 9JX; www.abbevillekitchen.com; 10.30 pm, Sun 9.30 pm.

Abeno **£36** ❸❸④
47 Museum St, WC1 7405 3211 2–1C
17-18 Great Newport St, WC2 7379 1160 4–3B
"Japanese pancake/omelettes stuffed with goodies" ('okonomi-yaki', if you prefer) are the speciality at these "friendly" canteens, where the cooking takes place before your very eyes; they make a handy stand-by for a light meal, but beware queues at busy times. / www.abeno.co.uk; 10 pm-midnight; WC2 no booking.

The Abingdon W8 **£53** ❸❸❸
54 Abingdon Rd 7937 3339 5–2A
A "favourite bolt-hole" – this rather glamorous Kensington pub-conversion has long been a great "neighbourhood" spot; this year, however, its generally "dependable" grub hasn't seemed quite as rock-solid as usual. / W8 6AP; www.theabingdon.co.uk; 10.30 pm, Tue-Fri 10 pm, Sat 11 pm, Sun 10 pm.

Abokado **£17** ④❸④
16 Newman St, W1 7636 9218 2–1B
160 Drury Ln, WC2 7242 5600 4–2D
The Lexington, 40-56 City Rd, EC1 7608 2620 12–1A
63 Cowcross St, EC1 7490 4303 9–1A
33 Fleet St, EC4 7353 8284 9–2A
These "bright, clean and tidy" pit stops make handy stand-bys for a "low-cal and flavoursome" Asian-inspired bite; staff have a "good attitude" too. / www.abokado.com; 7.30 pm; no Amex; no booking.

About Thyme SW1 **£50** ❸❶④
82 Wilton Rd 7821 7504 2–4B
"Refreshingly independent and charming", this "efficient" Pimlico stand-by is highly praised by many reporters for its "delicious Spanish-themed fare"; those who don't quite see the attraction, though, may find it "on the expensive side" for what it is. / SW1V 1DL; www.aboutthyme.co.uk; 10.30 pm; closed Sun.

L'Absinthe NW1 **£40** ❸❶❷
40 Chalcot Rd 7483 4848 8–3B
"A happy experience"; "outrageously French" staff buoy up the "very cheerful" atmosphere of this "romantic" (if "slightly cramped") corner-bistro, in Primrose Hill; it serves up "sensible" Gallic staples "with flair"… though "they could change the menu a bit more often". / NW1 8LS; www.labsinthe.co.uk; 10.30 pm, Sun 9.30 pm; closed Mon.

F S A

Abu Zaad W12 **£24** ❸❷④
29 Uxbridge Rd 8749 5107 7–1C
"Tasty" Syrian cuisine at "cheap-as-chips" prices ensures this "local-favourite" café/take-way, near Shepherd's Bush Market, is always "buzzing" (to the extent it can be "crowded and noisy"). / W12 8LH; www.abuzaad.co.uk; 11 pm; no Amex.

Adams Café W12 **£29** ❸❶❷
77 Askew Rd 8743 0572 7–1B
Frances and Abdul are "perfect hosts", at this Shepherd's Bush greasy spoon; it's "extraordinarily cheap", whether you go by day (perhaps for "the best Full English"), or by night when it morphs into a Tunisian café, serving "tasty" tagines and couscous. / W12 9AH; www.adamscafe.co.uk; 10 pm; closed Sun.

Addie's Thai Café SW5 **£31** ❷❸❸
121 Earl's Court Rd 7259 2620 5–2A
"Cramped" but "fun", and offering "great value" – a "down-to-earth" Thai bistro, "usefully-located" near Earl's Court tube. / SW5 9RL; www.addiesthai.co.uk; 11 pm, Sun 10.30 pm; no Amex.

Admiral Codrington SW3 **£49** ❷❸❸
17 Mossop St 7581 0005 5–2C
A "much-improved menu" – specialising in "perfect" steaks and "fantastic burgers" – provides a new reason to seek out this "reliably fun old-favourite", which has long been a key watering hole for the Chelsea set. / SW3 2LY; www.theadmiralcodrington.co.uk; 11 pm, Sun 9.30 pm.

Afghan Kitchen N1 **£21** ❷⑤④
35 Islington Grn 7359 8019 8–3D
"Hectic", "cramped" and "noisy", and with "surly" service, and "stools that don't encourage lingering"... yet this tiny café, by Islington Green, still delights most reporters overall, thanks to its "small menu" of "delicious and filling" Afghan scoff at "bargain" prices. / N1 8DU; 11 pm; closed Mon & Sun; no credit cards.

Aglio e Olio SW10 **£39** ❸❷❸
194 Fulham Rd 7351 0070 5–3B
"Rough, ready, cramped and noisy" it may be, but everyone loves this "cheerful" Italian café, by Chelsea & Westminster Hospital – an "always-reliable" venue, offering "big portions" of filling pasta and other "simple" fare. / SW10 9PN; 11.30 pm.

Al Duca SW1 **£45** ④④④
4-5 Duke of York St 7839 3090 3–3D
"Taken for granted, but it would be missed if it closed!"; it's hard to get too excited by this low-key Italian, but – especially for a business lunch – it's "dependable" and "very reasonably priced", particularly by St James's standards. / SW1Y 6LA; www.alduca-restaurant.co.uk; 11 pm; closed Sun.

Al Forno **£40** ④❷❷
349 Upper Richmond Rd, SW15 8878 7522 10–2A
2a King's Rd, SW19 8540 5710 10–2B
"Always a fun trip with the family" (or in a group) – these "lively" traditional Italians score highly for their bubbly service; they churn out "dependable" pizza and pasta too, at "acceptable" prices. / SW15 11 pm; SW19 11.30 pm, Sun & Mon 10.30 pm.

F S A

Al Hamra W1 £52 ❸④④
31-33 Shepherd Mkt 7493 1954 3–4B
A "compact" Shepherd Market institution, which fans perennially hail as "still the best Lebanese in town" – that's debatable, but the food is certainly "authentic and fresh", and the al fresco tables are very charming. / W1J 7PT; www.alhamrarestaurant.co.uk; 11.30 pm.

Al Sultan W1 £46 ❸❷④
51-52 Hertford St 7408 1155 3–4B
"The food's always great", says a fan of this "welcoming" Shepherd Market Lebanese; even its fans, though, wouldn't call it an exciting destination. / W1J 7ST; www.alsultan.co.uk; 11 pm.

Al Volo
The Old Truman Brewery E1 £37 ❸❸❸
2 Ely's Yd, Hanbury St 7377 0808 12–2C
Trendy but "reliable", this Brick Lane café offers "well-priced" scoff that's "a few notches up from PizzaExpress and the like". / E1 6QR; www.alvolo.co.uk; 10 pm, Thu-Sat 11 pm.

Al-Waha W2 £45 ❸④④
75 Westbourne Grove 7229 0806 6–1B
This low-key Bayswater Lebanese pleases all who report on it with its "above-average" mezze and grills; that said, even fans who "like it very much" are "slightly surprised by the rave reviews it sometimes garners in the press". / W2 4UL; www.alwaharestaurant.com; 11 pm; no Amex.

Alain Ducasse
Dorchester W1 £120 ❸❸④
53 Park Ln 7629 8866 3–3A
"Not up to 3-star standards!"; "everything that's wrong with the Michelin system" is encapsulated by the top marks awarded to this "formal" Mayfair outpost of the famed Gallic chef; some "sublime" meals are recorded, but far too many reporters just find the place "arrogant" or "overhyped", or simply "seriously disappointing". / W1K 1QA; www.alainducasse-dorchester.com; 10 pm; closed Mon, Sat L & Sun; jacket; set weekday L £62 (FP).

Alba EC1 £46 ❸❷④
107 Whitecross St 7588 1798 12–2A
"Where else would you go post-Barbican?" – this Italian stalwart, "in an unprepossessing side-street", is ideal post-concert, or for a business lunch; it offers "high-quality" (Piedmontese) cooking, "great wines" and "courteous" service, from "a cast of characters". / EC1Y 8JH; www.albarestaurant.com; 10.45 pm; closed Sat & Sun.

Albannach WC2 £53 ④❸❸
66 Trafalgar Sq 7930 0066 2–3C
Right on Trafalgar Square, this "lively" Scottish-themed bar/restaurant seems to be on the up; reports are still few, but they hail its cooking as "simple but effective", with "tasty seafood" a highlight. / WC2N 5DS; www.albannach.co.uk; 10.45 pm, Sun 6 pm; closed Sun D.

Albertine W12 £32 ④❷❷
1 Wood Ln 8743 9593 7–1C
"A better choice than anything in nearby Westfield" – this "fabulous, old-school wine bar" offers "wholesome" food and "top-class, reasonably-priced wine", in a cute "bistro-style" setting. / W12 7DP; 10.30 pm; closed Sat L & Sun; no Amex.

F S A

The Albion N1 **£44** ④④❸
10 Thornhill Rd 7607 7450 8–3D
A "quaint" and "beautiful" Islington boozer where, say fans, the food is "top-quality"; there's a strident minority of critics, though, who just find it "poor" and "overpriced" – "yes, it has an amazing garden… but that's it". / N1 1HW; www.the-albion.co.uk; 10 pm, Sun 9 pm.

Albion E2 **£43** ❸④❷
2-4 Boundary St 7729 1051 12–1B
"Lovely, open, airy and bright" styling helps win praise for Sir Terence Conran's (rather "noisy") Shoreditch café; on the food front, highlights include "good brunch staples", and tempting baked goods at any time. / E2 7DD; www.albioncaff.co.uk; 11 pm.

Ali Baba NW1 **£23** ❸❷❷
32 Ivor Pl 7723 5805 2–1A
"Skip the trip to Cairo!" – this "always-bustling" family-run joint, in a Marylebone living room, is a "completely authentic" Egyptian café/take-away (complete with blaring TV, always on), where the dishes are "fresh and simple"; BYO. / NW1 6DA; midnight; no credit cards.

Alisan HA9 **£35** ❷❷❸
The Junction, Engineers Way, Wembley 8903 3888 1–1A
Opposite Wembley Stadium, a surprisingly good (if sometimes "chaotic") modern Chinese that's worth seeking out for its "hard-to-beat dim sum", and also its "unusual northern-style dishes" (as well as the classic Cantonese ones); "avoid during events". / HA9 0ER; www.alisan.co.uk; 11 pm, Sat 11.30 pm, Sun 10.30 pm.

All Star Lanes **£45** ④❸❷
Victoria Hs, Bloomsbury Pl, WC1 7025 2676 2–1D
Whiteley's, 6 Porchester Gdns, W2 7313 8363 6–1C
Old Truman Brewery, 95 Brick Ln, E1 7426 9200 12–2C
Westfield Stratford City, E20 3167 2434 1–1D **NEW**
For a "fun night out", these "glamorous" bowling alleys, with American bar/diners attached, still have their fans; their culinary attractions, however, are rather beside the point. / www.allstarlanes.co.uk; WC1 10.30 pm, Fri & Sat midnight, Sun 9 pm; E1 10 pm; W2 10.30 pm, Fri-Sun 11 pm; E2 9.30 pm; WC1 & W2 closed L Mon-Thu.

Alloro W1 **£62** ❷❷❸
19-20 Dover St 7495 4768 3–3C
"Utterly reliable and proficient" cooking, "prompt" and "efficient" service, and a "well-spaced" interior combine to make this "upmarket" Mayfair Italian a "perfect business restaurant"; nice cocktail bar too. / W1S 4LU; www.alloro-restaurant.co.uk; 10.30 pm; closed Sat L & Sun.

Alma SW18 **£42** ④④❷
499 Old York Rd 8870 2537 10–2B
A large Wandsworth boozer where the atmosphere is "always lively"; it's not the culinary 'destination' it once was, but most reporters were "pleasantly surprised" by their meals this year. / SW18 1TF; www.thealma.co.uk; 10 pm, Fri-Sat 10.30 pm, Sun 7 pm.

FSA

The Almeida N1 £53 ❸④④

30 Almeida St 7354 4777 8–2D

The "calm" interior arguably "lacks buzz", but the D&D Group's large and quite "traditional" French restaurant, in Islington, is a destination worth knowing about; it's not only "convenient" (especially pre/post theatre), but offers an "Upper Street rarity" – "decent food!" / N1 1AD; www.almeida-restaurant.co.uk; 10.30 pm; closed Mon L & Sun D; set pre theatre £35 (FP); SRA-65%.

Alounak £28 ❷④❸

10 Russell Gdns, W14 7603 1130 7–1D

44 Westbourne Grove, W2 7229 0416 6–1B

"Excellent kebabs at unbelievable prices" inspire much respect for these "reliable" and "always-buzzing" Persian cafés, in Olympia and Bayswater – "the bread alone is worth a detour"; "BYO saves a few quid too". / 11.30 pm; no Amex.

Alyn Williams
Westbury Hotel W1 £73 ❷❷❸

Bond St 7078 9579 3–2C

"Truly outstanding!"; Marcus Wareing's former right-hand-man creates some "incredibly memorable" flavour combinations, at this "elegant" and "well-spaced" (if somewhat "hotel-y") Bond Street yearling; it's also notable for its "very helpful" and "efficient" service. / W1S 2YF; www.westburymayfair.com; 10.30 pm; closed Sun; jacket.

Amaranth SW18 £30 ❸④❷

346 Garratt Ln 8874 9036 10–2B

"Packed every night", this "squashed" BYO Thai, in Earlsfield, remains a "buzzy" outfit, serving "tasty" fare at super-"cheap" prices; the food nowadays is rather "generic", though, and service "so quick you're nearly out before you've started!" / SW18 4ES; 10.30 pm; D only, closed Sun; no Amex.

Amaranto
Four Seasons Hotel W1 £80 ④④④

Hamilton Pl 7319 5206 3–4A

The nightclubby dining room of this luxuriously refurbished Mayfair hotel excites surprisingly little feedback – perhaps because prices are ferocious, and standards too often somewhere between "erratic" and "disappointing". / W1J 7DR; www.fourseasons.com; 10.30 pm; jacket.

Amaya SW1 £69 ❶❷❷

Halkin Arc, 19 Motcomb St 7823 1166 5–1D

"Phenomenal modern twists on subcontinental cuisine", from an "ever-evolving menu", help make this "smart and lively" Belgravian one of London's most all-round-consistent 'nouvelle Indians'. / SW1X 8JT; www.realindianfood.com; 11.30 pm, Sun 10.30 pm.

Amico Bio EC1 £36 ④④❸

43-44 Cloth Fair 7600 7778 9–2B

'Veggie-Italian' sounds like quite a good idea, but this low-key spot, in a Smithfield back lane, splits reporters 50/50 – fans proclaim it "a great find" offering "interesting" dishes, but critics just think the food is "mediocre". / EC1 7JQ; www.amicobio.co.uk; 10.30 pm; closed Sat L & Sun.

Anarkali W6 £33 ❷❸❸

303-305 King St 8748 1760 7–2B

This "high-class" Hammersmith curry "stalwart" has been re-invigorated by a recent revamp; a good performer all-round, it offers "excellent 'traditional' food". / W6 9NH; midnight, Sun 11.30 pm; no Amex.

The Anchor & Hope SE1 £40 ❶❸❸
36 The Cut 7928 9898 9–4A
"Streets ahead" – thanks to its "magnificent", "St John-ish" British cooking, London's No. 1 gastropub, near the Old Vic, is still "infested with foodies"; the no-bookings policy (Sunday lunch excepted) strikes some reporters, though, as "ludicrous" – it's "incredibly difficult to get fed". / SE1 8LP; 10.30 pm; closed Mon L & Sun D; no Amex; no booking.

Andrew Edmunds W1 £42 ❸❷❶
46 Lexington St 7437 5708 3–2D
"The epitome of romance"; this "squished" and "idiosyncratic" candlelit Soho townhouse is a "perennial favourite" for legions of Londoners; its short menu of "straightforward" but "well-thought-out" dishes is twinned with an "epic" wine list – "one of the most interesting 'bargain' selections in England". / W1F 0LW; 10.30 pm; no Amex; booking: max 6.

The Angel & Crown WC2 NEW £44 ❷❸❷
58 St Martin's Ln awaiting tel 4–3B
From Tom and Ed Martin's stable of high-end gastropubs, a characterful new Covent Garden venture, where the traditionally-rooted British cooking is surprisingly ambitious, and – sometimes – "superb". / WC2N 4EA; set weekday L £29 (FP).

Angels & Gypsies
Church Street Hotel SE5 £40 ❷❸❷
29-33 Camberwell Church St 7703 5984 1–3C
"Out-of-the-way", in perennially up-and-coming Camberwell, this "fun" hang-out attracts fans from across the capital with its "divine" tapas, its "delightful" atmosphere and its delicious Iberian wines and sherries. / SE5 8TR; www.angelsandgypsies.com; 10.30 pm, Fri & Sat 11 pm.

Angelus W2 £81 ❸❷❸
4 Bathurst St 7402 0083 6–2D
Thierry Thomasin – owner and sommelier of this "buzzy" and "romantic" pub-conversion, near Lancaster Gate tube – is undoubtedly "the perfect host"; some reporters, though, do fear his "clever" wine list outshines the good but rather "overpriced" Gallic cuisine. / W2 2SD; www.angelusrestaurant.co.uk; 11 pm, Sun 10 pm.

Angler
South Place Hotel EC2 NEW
3 South Pl awaiting tel 12–2A
The rooftop dining room of a new D&D Group hotel, near Liverpool Street, which opens in late-2012; it's to offer a menu specialising in fish and seafood. / EC2M 2AF; www.southplacehotel.com.

The Anglesea Arms W6 £47 ❷❸❷
35 Wingate Rd 8749 1291 7–1B
"A consistently excellent hang-out for Hammersmith's cognoscenti"; it has long been one of London's top gastropubs, thanks to its "always fresh and seasonal" cooking ("amazing, as the kitchen is so minuscule"), "great beer and wine", and "authentic pub feel". / W6 0UR; www.anglesea-arms.co.uk; Mon 10 pm, Tue-Sat 10.30 pm, Sun 9.30 pm; no Amex; no booking.

The Anglesea Arms SW7 £45 ④④❷
15 Selwood Ter 7373 7960 5–2B
"A lively terrace" is the stand-out feature of this "proper and authentically pub-like" haunt, charmingly located in South Kensington; "decent" food too. / SW7 3QG; www.angleseaarms.com; 10 pm, Sun 9.30 pm.

FSA

Anglo Asian Tandoori N16 £36 ❷❷❸
60-62 Stoke Newington Church St 7254 3633 1–1C
"Still holding its own", this "cramped" Stoke Newington stalwart may offer a "rather standard" Indian menu, but its value is hard to beat, and the service "can't be faulted". / N16 0NB; 11.45 pm.

L'Anima EC2 £71 ❷❷❸
1 Snowden St 7422 7000 12–2B
In a "slightly macho, New York sort of way", this "smart" modernist Italian, at the foot of a swanky City-fringe office block, has made itself a "perfect business location", and Francesco Mazzei's "refined" cuisine almost invariably lives up; oddly, though, given the name, the operation can strike critics as "soulless". / EC2A 2DQ; www.lanima.co.uk; 11 pm, Sat 11.30 pm; closed Sat L & Sun.

Annie's £45 ④❸❷
162 Thames Rd, W4 8994 9080 1–3A
36-38 White Hart Ln, SW13 8878 2020 10–1A
There's a hint of the "tart's boudoir" in the decor of these popular locals, in Barnes and Strand on the Green, but the overall effect is "homely" and "very romantic"; the food is "none too exciting", but ideal for a casual brunch (including with kids in tow). / www.anniesrestaurant.co.uk; 10 pm, Sat 10.30 pm, Sun 9.30 pm.

Antelope SW17 £38 ❸❸❷
76 Mitcham Rd 8672 3888 10–2C
"Good for beers, for food even better!" – Tooting locals are all very happy with this "lovely buzzy gastropub", where the dishes are "wholesome" and "freshly-cooked". / SW17 9NG; www.theantelopepub.com; 10.30 pm; closed Mon-Fri L & Sun D; no Amex.

Antepliler £32 ❸④❸
139 Upper St, N1 7226 5441 1–1C
46 Grand Pde, N4 8802 5588 1–1C
"Delicious food at reasonable prices" – the styles of the operations may differ, but reporters' views on both the Newington Green and Islington outlets of this Turkish mini-conglomerate are notably consistent.

The Anthologist EC2 £40 ④④❸
58 Gresham St 465 0101 9–2C
"If you like loud and buzzy", this thoroughly Citified venue may seem to offer an "airy and vibrant" sort of experience, where the menu is "fairly basic, but just the job"; breakfasts, of course, are "calmer". / EC2V 7BB; www.theanthologistbar.co.uk; 10 pm; closed Sat & Sun.

Antico SE1 NEW £43 ❸❷❸
214 Bermondsey St 7407 4682 9–4D
"A great addition to the burgeoning Bermondsey scene", this "bright" new corner-Italian is a good all-rounder, offering "tasty and deceptively simple cooking"; "fab cocktail bar" in the basement too. / SE1 3TQ; www.antico-london.co.uk; 10.30 pm; closed Mon & Sun D.

Antidote W1 £49 ④❸❷
12a Newburgh St 7287 8488 3–2C
Just off Carnaby Street, a very "intimate" and authentically Gallic wine bar, where the food inspires much less comment than the "interesting selection of regional wines". / W1F 7RR; www.antidotewinebar.com; 10.30 pm; closed Sun D.

Antipasto & Pasta SW11 £40 ❸❷❸
511 Battersea Park Rd 7223 9765 10–1C
"Half-price nights are a sure-fire winner", at this long-running Battersea favourite; it's not just the regular special offers that win local acclaim, though – "the food's always tasty, the service excellent and the atmosphere cheerful". / SW11 3BW; 11.30 pm, Sun 11 pm; need 4+ to book.

Apollo Banana Leaf SW17 £15 ❷❷⑤
190 Tooting High St 8696 1423 10–2C
"Deceptively down-market", this Tooting BYO spot serves up Sri Lankan scoff of "ridiculously great quality". / SW17 0SF; 10.30 pm; no Amex.

Apostrophe £18 ④❸❸
Branches throughout London
"An example of a chain doing what it does very well" – these Gallic cafés offer "conspicuously superior" coffee, "interesting sarnies" and "thick hot chocolate to put a smile on your face!" / www.apostropheuk.com; most branches 6 pm, Sat 5.30 pm; no booking.

Applebee's Cafe SE1 £42 ❸❸④
5 Stoney St 7407 5777 9–4C
"Fresh fish from the slab at the front of the shop" is "cooked plainly and well", at this "cramped and very busy" fixture – "being in the heart of bustling Borough Market adds to the atmosphere" too. / SE1 9AA; www.applebeesfish.com; 10 pm, Fri 10.30 pm; closed Mon & Sun; no Amex.

Apsleys Lanesborough Hotel SW1 £102 ④④❸
1 Lanesborough Pl 7333 7254 5–1D
Even those praising the "faultless" cuisine and "gorgeous" setting of this Belgravia outpost of top Roman chef Heinz Beck can baulk at its "elitist" pricing; to critics, though, it's just a "boring" place, offering "pretentious" dishes which have a slightly "by-numbers" quality to them. / SW1X 7TA; www.apsleys.co.uk; 10.30 pm; jacket; booking: max 12; set weekday L £65 (FP).

aqua kyoto W1 £70 ④④❷
240 Regent St (entrance 30 Argyll St) 7478 0540 3–2C
The Japanese section of a nightclubby upper-floor complex, near Oxford Circus; even fans of its "good but extortionately pricey" food say a visit here is "all about the atmosphere" – "have pre-dinner drinks on the terrace if you can". / W1B 3BR; www.aqua-london.com; 10.45 pm, Thu-Sat 11.15 pm; closed Sun D.

aqua nueva W1 £62 ⑤⑤④
240 Regent St (entrance 30 Argyll St) 7478 0540 3–2C
It shares the eye-catching location of its Japanese sibling (see 'aqua kyoto'), but this would-be trendy, sixth-floor Spaniard "doesn't live up" – critics can find it like "a soulless barn", but the real problem is that it's "far too expensive". / W1B 3BR; www.aqua-london.com; 11 pm.

Arbutus W1 £52 ❷❷④
63-64 Frith St 7734 4545 4–2A
"Precise, skilled cuisine" that "doesn't cost silly money" has made a big name for this "casual" and "buzzy" (but "squashed" and slightly "sterile") Soho bistro, which popularised the idea of offering "impressive" wines 'en carafe' (and at "fair prices" too); this year, though, its ratings were under pressure across the board. / W1D 3JW; www.arbutusrestaurant.co.uk; 11 pm, Sat 11.30 pm, Sun 10.30 pm.

Archduke Wine Bar SE1 £52 ⑤⑤④
Concert Hall Approach, South Bank 7928 9370 2–3D
In characterful railway arches, this former wine bar (nowadays part of Black & Blue) has traded on its proximity to the Royal Festival Hall for as long as we can recall; little has changed over the years, apart from the competition – as one reporter drily notes: "nowadays, there are lots of other mediocre places round here too…" / SE1 8XU; www.thearchduke.co.uk; 11 pm.

The Arches NW6 £42 ④❸❷
7 Fairhazel Gdns 7624 1867 8–2A
A wine list "full of curiosities", and "lovely staff" too, win praise for this "real neighbourhood wine bar", in Swiss Cottage; the food ("in pedantic Parisian brasserie style") is "decent" enough, but very much a supporting attraction. / NW6 3QE; 10.30 pm; no Amex.

Archipelago W1 £56 ④④❸
110 Whitfield St 7383 3346 2–1B
With its "ridiculously eclectic" menu (crocodile, ostrich,…) and "barking mad" decor, this tiny Fitzrovian has long made a "fun and interesting" destination, especially "for a date" – although the meat may be "exotic", however, some meals of late have been "very ordinary". / W1T 5ED; www.archipelago-restaurant.co.uk; 10.15 pm; closed Sat L & Sun.

The Ark W8 £60 ④④④
122 Palace Gardens Ter 7229 4024 6–2B
A Kensington site which – with its "cosy" proportions and "varied" menu – "ought to be a charming little neighbourhood Italian"; the few reports it inspires, however are very mixed – all the way from a "hidden gem" to "very ordinary". / W8 4RT; www.ark-restaurant.com; 10.30 pm; closed Mon L & Sun; set weekday L £33 (FP).

Ark Fish E18 £44 ❶❸⑤
142 Hermon Hill 8989 5345 1–1D
"Winkles, whelks, the works, plus deliciously fresh fish too" – the reason to endure the mind-numbing queues at this "brilliant", if "brightly-lit", South Woodford restaurant; "if you could book, I'd go more often". / E18 1QH; www.arkfishrestaurant.co.uk; 9.45 pm, Fri & Sat 10.15 pm, Sun 8.45 pm; closed Mon; no Amex.

L'Art du Fromage SW10 £49 ❸④④
1a Langton St 7352 2759 5–3B
A "quirky" and "friendly" Gallic bistro, at World's End, whose cheese-based offerings are "a nice change from the norm"; "the smell when they're making fondue is incroyable!" / SW10 0JL; www.artdufromage.co.uk; 10.30 pm; closed Mon L & Sun.

Artigiano NW3 £48 ❸❸④
12a Belsize Ter 7794 4288 8–2A
"More down-to-earth than it used to be", this Belsize Park Italian is often hailed as a "reliable stand-by"; its odd three-level layout, though, still contributes to an atmosphere that strikes some as "cold". / NW3 4AX; www.etruscarestaurants.com; 10.30 pm, Sun 10 pm; closed Mon L.

L'Artista NW11 £34 ④❸❸
917 Finchley Rd 8731 7501 1–1B
"Ridiculously huge portions" are served up by "amusing" staff, at this "good-value" pizza 'n' pasta stalwart, under the railway arches by Golder's Green tube; it's "always busy" (and "always noisy" too). / NW11 7PE; www.lartistapizzeria.com; 11.30 pm.

L'Artiste Musclé W1 £41 ④④❸

1 Shepherd Mkt 7493 6150 3–4B

A "hole-in-the-wall", this "classic" bistro, in Mayfair's cute Shepherd Market, certainly offers "nothing gourmet" – it does, however, dish up "solid" and "reasonably-priced" fare, plus "enough Parisian-style ambience to be romantic". / W1J 7PA; 10 pm, Fri-Sun 10.30 pm.

Asadal WC1 £39 ❸④❸

227 High Holborn 7430 9006 2–1D

"The location, under Holborn tube station, is not encouraging", but this "reliable" establishment is surprisingly "pleasant" inside, and the Korean cooking is "varied and interesting". / WC1V 7DA; www.asadal.co.uk; 10.30 pm; closed Sun L.

Asakusa NW1 £35 ❶④④

265 Eversholt St 7388 8533 8–3C

Ignore the "incredibly unpromising exterior" – you are offered "real" Japanese food ("sushi doesn't get much better"), at this "authentic" spot near Euston Station; it's "surprisingly inexpensive" too. / NW1 1BA; 11.30 pm, Sat 11 pm; D only, closed Sun.

Asia de Cuba
St Martin's Lane Hotel WC2 £92 ④④❸

45 St Martin's Ln 7300 5588 4–4C

With its "sexy-glam" (and "very noisy") vibe and its eclectic cuisine, this "designer" West End hang-out is still, for its fans, a plain "phenomenal" destination; even they can find prices "absurd", though, and there are many sceptics who think the food "bizarre" and the establishment "massively over-rated". / WC2N 4HX; www.stmartinslane.com; 11.30 pm, Sun 10.30 pm.

Ask £36 ⑤④④

Branches throughout London

Can this increasingly "disastrous" chain really be under the same ownership as PizzaExpress? – "it's difficult to get excited about the new broader menu", especially when results too often veer between "nothing special" and plain "dreadful". / www.askcentral.co.uk; most branches 11 pm, Fri & Sat 11.30 pm; some booking restrictions apply.

Assaggi W2 £69 ❷❷④

39 Chepstow Pl 7792 5501 6–1B

After a wobble last year, this "outstanding" Italian dining room, over a former Bayswater pub, is back amongst London's best, serving "simple yet interesting dishes of fantastic quality"; it can seem "far too noisy", however, and even fans can find it "very expensive for what it is". / W2 4TS; 11 pm; closed Sun; no Amex.

Les Associés N8 £41 ❸❷④

172 Park Rd 8348 8944 1–1C

"More shabby than chic, nowadays, but quite nostalgic!" – this "very French" bistro of long standing, in a Crouch End front room, still offers quality, seasonal cuisine, "with good cheer". / N8 8JT; www.lesassocies.co.uk; 10 pm; closed Mon, Tue L, Sat L & Sun D; 24 hr notice for L bookings.

F S A

Atari-Ya **£30** ❶④⑤
20 James St, W1 7491 1178 3–1A
1 Station Pde, W5 8896 3175 1–3A
31 Vivian Ave, NW4 8202 2789 1–1B
75 Fairfax Road, London, NW6 7328 5338 8–2A
"Probably the freshest sushi in the UK", and at "great-value" prices too, makes for "phenomenal" but functional meals at these no-frills cafés, which are run by a firm of Japanese food importers. / www.atariya.co.uk; W1 8 pm, NW4 & NW6 10 pm; NW4, NW6 closed Mon.

L'ATELIER DE JOEL ROBUCHON WC2 **£90** ❸❸❷
13-15 West St 7010 8600 4–2B
"Incredible little dishes of divine food" and a "seductive" interior make this "luxurious" Theatreland outpost of a top French chef stand out… but so, sadly, do the "eye-popping" prices. / WC2H 9NQ; www.joelrobuchon.co.uk; 10.45 pm, Sun 10.30 pm; no trainers; set weekday L & pre-theatre £58 (FP).

Athenaeum
Athenaeum Hotel W1 **£77** ❷❷❸
116 Piccadilly 7499 3464 3–4B
"Surprisingly good for a hotel restaurant" – this unsung Mayfair dining room inspires strong support from its small fan club, particularly for its "amazing-value set lunch" and "great afternoon tea". / W1J 7BJ; www.athenaeumhotel.com; 10.30 pm.

The Atlas SW6 **£43** ❷❸❷
16 Seagrave Rd 7385 9129 5–3A
"An impressive combo of authentic pub and outstanding food" – this "cracking" hostelry, "tucked-away near Earl's Court 2", is a "buzzy" spot, offering an "expertly-executed Italianate menu"; there's even "a small but leafy garden". / SW6 1RX; www.theatlaspub.co.uk; 10 pm.

Aubaine **£53** ④④④
4 Heddon St, W1 7440 2510 3–2C
260-262 Brompton Rd, SW3 7052 0100 5–2C
37-45 Kensington High St, W8 7368 0950 5–1A
Only found in fashionable corners of town, these "relaxing" Gallic café/bistros are "best for coffee and a cake", or for breakfast – they're somewhat "expensive", and more substantial dishes can disappoint. / www.aubaine.co.uk; SW3 10 pm; Heddon St 11 pm, Oxford St 9 pm, Sun 6 pm, W8 10 pm, Sun 6 pm, Dover St 10 pm, Sun 9.30 pm; W8 no booking.

Aurelia W1 **£64** ❸❸❸
13-14 Cork St 7409 1370 3–3C
A "great addition to Mayfair", say fans of this "happening" newcomer, who applaud its "slick" style and "astonishingly good" Italian dishes; critics, though, find it "not a patch on its sister, La Petite Maison", and complain about prices which "make even the local art-dealers wince". / W1S 3NS; www.aurelialondon.co.uk; 11.30 pm, Sun 10.30 pm.

Aurora W1 **£48** ④④❷
49 Lexington St 7494 0514 3–2D
"Tiny" but "atmospheric", this Soho spot makes an ideal venue for an "intimate" lunch or dinner, especially on days the "lovely small courtyard" is in use – the food, if not the main point, does nothing to spoil the experience. / W1F 9AP; aurorasoho.co.uk; 10 pm, Wed-Sat 10.30 pm, Sun 9 pm.

Automat W1 £61 ④④❸
33 Dover St 7499 3033 3–3C
"Keen to be seen"? – maybe check out this "always-crowded", "fun" and "noisy" American diner, in Mayfair; food and service-wise, though, even fans can find it "over-rated"; "breakfast is the best time". / W1S 4NF; www.automat-london.com; 11.45 pm, Sat 10.45 pm, Sun 10 pm.

L'Autre Pied W1 £67 ❷❷④
5-7 Blandford St 7486 9696 2–1A
Watch out Pied à Terre! – the "stunning" and "inventive" small plates at its Marylebone spin-off are sometimes said to be "better than the parent"; this is a "cramped" sort of place, though, and the interior can seem "bland" and "uninviting". / W1U 3DB; www.lautrepied.co.uk; 10 pm; closed Sun D; set weekday L & pre-theatre £43 (FP).

Avalon SW12 £42 ❸④❷
16 Balham Hill 8675 8613 10–2C
"A huge garden, ideal for a family Sunday lunch" is the stand-out attraction at this "bustling, light and airy" Balham gastropub; most reports say the food is "a cut above" too. / SW12 9EB; www.theavalonlondon.co.uk; 10.30 pm, Sun 9 pm; SRA-56%.

L'Aventure NW8 £59 ❷❶❶
3 Blenheim Ter 7624 6232 8–3A
"Totally brilliant for romance" ("so long as Madame isn't having a strop!"), Catherine Parisot's "superb all-rounder", in St John's Wood, is a "stylish" sort of place whose "Gallic charm" continues to sweep reporters off their feet. / NW8 0EH; 11 pm; closed Sat L & Sun; set weekday L £38 (FP).

The Avenue SW1 £55 ❸❷❷
7-9 St James's St 7321 2111 3–4D
"A great place for a business lunch" – this very "spacious and modern" St James's brasserie makes a "safe" and "efficient" lunchtime choice, albeit in a style whose attractions are primarily "corporate". / SW1A 1EE; www.theavenue-restaurant.co.uk; 10.30 pm; closed Sat L & Sun.

Axis
One Aldwych Hotel WC2 £60 ④④④
1 Aldwych 7300 0300 2–2D
Despite its "strange basement location", this Covent Garden fixture (under a "classy hotel") is often tipped for a "smart business lunch" or "good post-theatre supper"; its cuisine is "not memorable", however, and at quieter times the ambience can verge on "funereal". / WC2B 4RH; www.onealdwych.com; 10.30 pm; closed Mon, Sat L & Sun.

Azou W6 £38 ❸❷❷
375 King St 8563 7266 7–2B
A "cosy" Hammersmith "gem" – a sweet café, with "always-accommodating" service and "inexpensive" Moroccan food; critics, though, can find the style "a bit amateurish". / W6 9NJ; www.azou.co.uk; 11 pm.

Ba Shan W1 £48 ❷④④
24 Romilly St 7287 3266 4–3A
"Wonderful, chilli-laden Hunanese dishes" – they'll "blow your head off!" – make this Soho corner-café "one of the best Chinese restaurants in town"; indeed, its survey ratings rival its parent, Bar Shu, just over the road. / W1D 5AH; 11 pm, Fri & Sat 11.30 pm.

FSA

Babbo W1 **£80** ④⑤④
39 Albermarle St 3205 1099 3–3C
How this Mayfair Italian is sometimes touted as 'special', it's difficult to see; it's "nice enough", but the food is "not the most inspiring" – "why they charge so much" is something of a mystery. / W1S 4JQ; www.babborestaurant.co.uk; 11 pm; closed Sun.

Babur SE23 **£48** ❶❷❷
119 Brockley Rise 8291 2400 1–4D
"Easily the finest Indian restaurant in SE London", this "superb" Honor Oak Park spot pulls in a huge fan club with its "really top-notch" cuisine (from a menu that "changes often to reflect different regional specialities"). / SE23 1JP; www.babur.info; 11 pm, 10.30 pm.

Babylon
Kensington Roof Gardens W8 **£73** ④④❷
99 Kensington High St 7368 3993 5–1A
Adjoining "magical" rooftop gardens and with "great views" over London, this luxurious and "romantic" eighth-floor Kensington space is undeniably a "unique location"; prices are lofty too, though, and the "well-prepared" cuisine offers "little in the way of innovation". / W8 5SA; www.virgin.com/roofgardens; 10.30 pm; closed Sun D; set weekday L £43 (FP); SRA-54%.

Il Bacio **£42** ❸⑤④
61 Stoke Newington Church St, N16 7249 3833 1–1C
178-184 Blackstock Rd, N5 7226 3339 8–1D
"Enormous and tasty pizzas, with lovely thin and crispy bases" win particular praise for these "child-friendly" north London Sardinians; "surly" service, though, can be a "let-down". / www.ilbaciohighbury.co.uk; 10 pm-11 pm; Mon-Fri L; no Amex.

Back to Basics W1 **£47** ❷❸④
21a Foley St 7436 2181 2–1B
Bringing "a whiff of the Cornish seaside" to Fitzrovia, this "unpretentious" and rather "cramped" corner café serves absolutely "fantastic fish" – "honest" and "great-value". / W1W 6DS; www.backtobasics.uk.com; 10 pm; closed Sun.

Baker & Spice **£42** ❸④④
54-56 Elizabeth St, SW1 7730 5524 2–4A
47 Denyer St, SW3 7225 3417 5–2D
20 Clifton Rd, W9 7289 2499 8–4A
Shame these deli/bakeries are "so eye-wateringly expensive" – "the bread is exceptional" and "the pastries worthy of France"… but "you do have to re-mortgage before you visit". / www.bakerandspice.uk.com; 7 pm, Sun 6 pm; closed D; no Amex; no booking.

Baku SW1 NEW **£58** ④❶❸
164-165 Sloane St 7235 5399 5–1D
"Impeccable" service is often the surprise highlight of a visit to this new occupant of a smart and spacious Knightsbridge site that's become something of a 'graveyard'; the "unfamiliar" Azerbaijani food – if "not cheap" – can be "interesting" too. / SW1X 9QB; www.bakulondon.com; 11 pm, Fri-Sat 11.30 pm, Sun 10 pm.

Balans £46 ⑤④❸
34 Old Compton St, W1 7439 3309 4–3A
60-62 Old Compton St, W1 7439 2183 4–3A
239 Old Brompton Rd, SW5 7244 8838 5–3A
Westfield, Ariel Way, W12 8600 3320 7–1C
214 Chiswick High Rd, W4 8742 1435 7–2A
187 Kensington High St, W8 7376 0115 5–1A
Westfield Stratford, E20 8555 5478 1–1D NEW
Those in search of "simple classics" (especially brunch) in a "fun" environment can still find this diner chain a "great place to hang out"; sadly, though, only the Soho branch is really "so gay" nowadays.
/ www.balans.co.uk; midnight-2 am; 34 Old Compton St 24 hrs, E20 11pm; some booking restrictions apply.

The Balcon
Sofitel St James SW1 NEW £52 ❸❸❸
8 Pall Mall 7968 2900 2–3C
A grand Gallic-brasserie-style newcomer, near Trafalgar Square; fans say it's "a hotel restaurant that can stand on its own two feet", but we're with the doubters, who preferred its predecessor, Brasserie Roux (RIP), and find the new venture "dull and overpriced".
/ SW1Y 5NG; www.thebalconlondon.com; 11 pm, Sun 10 pm.

Bald Faced Stag N2 £45 ❸❸❸
69 High Rd 8442 1201 1–1B
This "superior" East Finchley gastropub is, say fans, "an under-rated eatery in a culinary desert" – presumably why, perhaps to a fault, "it's always busy at weekends". / N2 8AB; www.thebaldfacedstagn2.co.uk; 10.30 pm, Sun 9.30 pm.

The Balham Bowls Club SW12 £39 ❸❷❷
7-9 Ramsden Rd 8673 4700 10–2C
"What a find!"; this large dining room within a "spacious" and "quirky" pub has "nothing at all to do with bowls", but it does offer "quality" food in "generous" portions, and at "reasonable prices" too.
/ SW12 8QX; www.balhambowlsclub.com; 11 pm, Fri & Sat midnight; closed weekday L; no Amex.

Balthazar WC2
4-6 Russell St awaiting tel 4–3D
An offshoot of SoHo (NYC)'s famously buzzy brasserie, set to open, at some point, in Covent Garden's former Theatre Museum; its opening has so long been awaited that we also trailed it this time last year… / WC2E 7BN.

Baltic SE1 £47 ❸④❸
74 Blackfriars Rd 7928 1111 9–4A
"Revitalised" in recent times, this "enjoyable" haunt – a "lovely", if "barn-like", space in a former Borough factory – has been dishing up some "surprisingly good" Polish/Baltic food of late; thanks not least to its "amazing cocktail list", it makes a great option for a "good night out". / SE1 8HA; www.balticrestaurant.co.uk; 11.15 pm, Sun 10.15 pm.

Bam-Bou W1 £48 ❸❷❷
1 Percy St 7323 9130 2–1C
"Superb cocktails" in the "great bar" kick off many a "fun night out", at this colonial-style Fitzrovia townhouse, where the menu offers "Franco/Vietnamese food of a high standard". / W1T 1DB; www.bam-bou.co.uk; midnight; closed Sat L & Sun; booking: max 6.

FSA

The Banana Tree Canteen £34 ❸❸❸
103 Wardour St, W1 7437 1351 3–2D
21-23 Westbourne Grove, W2 7221 4085 6–1C
166 Randolph Ave, W9 7286 3869 8–3A
237-239 West End Ln, NW6 7431 7808 1–1B
75-79 Battersea Rise, SW11 7228 2828 10–2C
412-416 St John St, EC1 7278 7565 8–3D
"A nice surprise, for a chain!" – these "fun, canteen-style places" offer "tasty" pan-Asian fare that comes "very fast and very cheap". / 11 pm, Sun 10.30 pm; booking: min 6.

Banca W1 NEW £85 ❷❷❸
30 North Audley St 7647 2525 3–2A
Newly opened in mid-2012, a very smart Italian, aimed at the Mayfair-international crowd; we didn't find our early-days visit an especially engaging experience, but all-round standards were undoubtedly very high… as, of course, were the prices. / W1K 6HP; Rated on Editors' visit; www.bancarestaurant.com.

Bangalore Express £36 ④④❸
103-107 Waterloo Rd, SE1 7021 0886 9–4A
1 Corbet Ct, EC3 7220 9195 9–3C
Fans like the "unusual" approach of these "buzzy" modern Indians, in the City and Waterloo, and say their food is "tasty" and "great value" – for critics, though, this is "not curry as we know it… and not in a good way". / www.bangaloreexpress.co.uk; 10.30 pm; closed Sun.

Bangkok SW7 £40 ❸❷④
9 Bute St 7584 8529 5–2B
"A favourite for nearly 40 years!"; London's oldest Thai is a "fairly basic" South Kensington canteen – "not exactly authentic, but unbelievably consistent". / SW7 3EY; 10.45 pm; no Amex.

Bank Westminster
St James Court Hotel SW1 £56 ④❷④
45 Buckingham Gate 7630 6644 2–4B
With little competition for the Victoria Street business market, this large restaurant provides an "airy" and "fuss-free" venue for client entertainment; the "wide-ranging" menu plays rather a supporting role. / SW1E 6BS; www.bankrestaurants.com; 11 pm; closed Sat L & Sun.

Banners N8 £45 ④❸❶
21 Park Rd 8348 2930 1–1C
A perennial "Crouch End favourite", that's renowned for its "great breakfasts" ("you name it, they offer it"); thanks to its tasty fodder "with a Caribbean twist" (and in "huge" portions), however, it makes a "fun" destination at any time. / N8 8TE; www.bannersrestaurant.com; 11.30 pm, Fri & Sat midnight, Sun 11 pm; no Amex.

Baozi Inn WC2 £18 ❷④④
25 Newport Ct 7287 6877 4–3B
"It's really all about Sichuan buns, dumplings and noodles", at this "tiny", "no-frills" Chinatown café – "a must-try if you're not afraid of spicy food". / WC2H 7JS; 10 pm, Fri-Sat 10.30 pm; no credit cards; no booking.

Bar Boulud
Mandarin Oriental SW1 £52 ❷❷❷
66 Knightsbridge 7201 3899 5–1D
A "sophisticated" Knightsbridge outpost of a top NYC chef, offering "consistently well-executed comfort food" ("out-of-this-world" burgers a speciality) in a "lively" setting – being a basement, though, it's "best by night". / SW1X 7LA; www.barboulud.com; 10.45 pm, Sun 9.45 pm.

Bar Italia W1 £28 ④❷❶
22 Frith St 7437 4520 4–2A
A "Soho institution" par excellence – this legendary Italian coffee shop is THE place for a late-night espresso, while scoping out the "mad and wonderful street-life". / W1D 4RT; www.baritaliasoho.co.uk; open 24 hours, Sun 4 am; no Amex; no booking.

Bar Trattoria Semplice W1 £49 ❸❸❸
22-23 Woodstock St 7491 8638 3–2B
A casual modern-trattoria-style offshoot of Mayfair's Semplice (a few doors away); reports are a bit up-and-down, but most say it offers "good ordinary Italian food at reasonable prices". / W1C 2AP; www.bartrattoriasemplice.com; 11 pm, Sun 9.30 pm.

Barbecoa EC4 £59 ❸④❸
20 New Change Pas 3005 8555 9–2B
Jamie Oliver's "hangar-like" and "very noisy" City "meat-fest" certainly has a "great buzz", and some of its tables offer "brilliant views of St Paul's"; even fans can find it "pricey for what it is", though, and harsher critics say it just "trades on the proprietor's name". / EC4M 9BP; www.barbecoa.com; 10 pm.

La Barca SE1 £66 ④④❷
80-81 Lower Marsh 7928 2226 9–4A
An Italian of the "really old school" – a "very cosy" place, handily-located for Waterloo and the Old Vic; "the food may be straight out of 1975, and slightly overpriced too, but it's none the worse for that!" / SE1 7AB; www.labarca-ristorante.com; 11.15 pm; closed Sat L & Sun.

Il Baretto W1 £57 ❸④④
43 Blandford St 7486 7340 2–1A
This "noisy" Marylebone basement offers cooking "as good as you'll find outside Italy", say fans; even they can think prices "high" however, and – for a few vociferous critics – the whole performance is plain "awful". / W1U 7HF; www.ilbaretto.co.uk; 10.30 pm, Sun 10 pm.

The Barnsbury N1 £42 ④④❸
209-211 Liverpool Rd 7607 5519 8–2D
This "lovely, cosy pub" boasts many plusses, including a "small but pretty courtyard"; shame about the service, though, which is sometimes "so slow". / N1 1LX; www.thebarnsbury.co.uk; 10 pm; closed Mon, Tue, Wed L, Thu L & Sun D.

Barrafina £35 ❶❶❷
54 Frith St, W1 7813 8016 4–2A
43 Drury Ln, WC2 awaiting tel 4–2D NEW
"A serious rival to Cal Pep for the world's greatest tapas!" – this "high-energy" bar, in the heart of Soho, offers "a true Barcelona experience"; no booking, though, and there are only 23 seats – "you've got to be early or lucky to get in!"; late-2012 sees the opening of a spin-off in Covent Garden. / www.barrafina.co.uk; 11 pm, Sun 10 pm; no booking.

FSA

Barrica W1 £37 ❷❷❷
62 Goodge St 7436 9448 2–1B
"Keeping on upping its game" – this "warm and charming", if "cacophonous", Fitzrovia two-year-old serves an ever more "stunning" array of tapas from an "ever-evolving menu" that's "always full of surprises"; the wine list offers "incredibly good value" too. / W1T 4NE; www.barrica.co.uk; 10.30 pm; closed Sun.

Bar Shu W1 £48 ❶⑤④
28 Frith St 7287 6688 4–3A
"My wife thought she could cope, but she was wrong!" – "beware how you choose", at this Soho café, which is acclaimed for its "eye-watering" Sichuan cuisine; "shame about the robotic service". / W1D 5LF; www.bar-shu.co.uk; 11 pm, Fri-Sat 11.30 pm.

Basilico £32 ❷❸⑤
690 Fulham Rd, SW6 0800 028 3531 10–1B
26 Penton St, N1 0800 093 4224 8–3D
51 Park Rd, N8 8616 0290 1–1C
515 Finchley Rd, NW3 0800 316 2656 1–1B
175 Lavender Hill, SW11 0800 389 9770 10–2C
178 Upper Richmond Rd, SW14 0800 096 8202 10–2B
"Superb thin-crust pizza" – "always delivered hot, with interesting, fresh toppings" – wins raves for these "utterly reliable, very quick dial-out places". / www.basilico.co.uk; 11 pm; no booking.

Bayee Village SW19 £42 ❸❷❷
24 High St 8947 3533 10–2B
Fans love the "great buzz", and staff who "always make you feel special", at this "very busy" Chinese, in the heart of Wimbledon Village; the cooking is consistently well-rated too. / SW19 5DX; www.bayee.co.uk; 10.45 pm.

Beach Blanket Babylon £63 ⑤④❷
45 Ledbury Rd, W11 7229 2907 6–1B
19-23 Bethnal Green Rd, E1 7749 3540 12–1C
"Go for the eye-candy" or the Gaudiesque decor ("like a Russian oligarch's Gothic games room"), and you may enjoy a trip to this long-established Notting Hill hang-out – "the food is definitely not the point"; the Shoreditch spin-off inspires little feedback. / www.beachblanket.co.uk; 10.30 pm; W11 booking advisable Fri-Sat.

Beard to Tail EC2 NEW
77 Curtain Rd awaiting tel 12–1B
Opening around the publication date of this guide, a pig-centric Shoreditch newcomer (formerly a 'pop-up'), from the team behind Callooh Callay – a local cocktail bar that's been a major hit. / EC2A 3BS; www.beardtotail.co.uk.

Bedford & Strand WC2 £40 ④④❸
1a Bedford St 7836 3033 4–4D
"'Hidden-away, just off the Strand", this "surprisingly vibrant" basement wine bar makes a "reliable stand-by" – "after work, for a more formal lunch or dinner, or pre- or post-theatre". / WC2E 9HH; www.bedford-strand.com; 10.30 pm; closed Sun.

Bedlington Café W4 £29 ④❸⑤
24 Fauconberg Rd 8994 1965 7–2A
An "old favourite" for some reporters, this one-time "London pioneer of simple Thai cooking" – a converted greasy spoon in deepest Chiswick – still offers "well-produced" dishes at "value-for-money" prices; BYO. / W4 3JY; 10 pm; closed Sun L; no credit cards.

Beirut Express £40 ❸④④
65 Old Brompton Rd, SW7 7591 0123 5–2B
112-114 Edgware Rd, W2 7724 2700 6–1D
"Love the juices and the reasonably-priced mezze and wraps" – this Lebanese duo, in Bayswater and South Kensington, are great for a "reliable, fast, consistent quality" bite; they have a good "buzz" too. / www.maroush.com; W2 2 am; SW7 midnight.

Beiteddine SW1 £50 ❷❷④
8 Harriet St 7235 3969 5–1D
It's nothing to look at, but this long-standing stalwart, just off Sloane Street, is still an undiscovered "gem"; not only is the Lebanese food "really good", but also "reasonably priced"... well, by Belgravia standards. / SW1X 9JW; www.beiteddinerestaurant.com; midnight.

Bel Canto
Corus Hotel Hyde Park W2 £69 ④❶❶
1 Lancaster Gate 7262 1678 6–2C
An entertaining night out; considering you go to have your dinner "punctuated by professionally-sung operatic arias", the food at this "fun" Bayswater dining room is generally rather better than you might expect. / W2 3LG; www.lebelcanto.com; 11 pm; D only, closed Mon & Sun; set always available £69 (FP).

Belgo £38 ⑤④④
50 Earlham St, WC2 7813 2233 4–2C
67 Kingsway, WC2 7242 7469 2–2D
72 Chalk Farm Rd, NW1 7267 0718 8–2B
44-48 Clapham High Rd, SW4 7720 1118 10–2D
"The only good thing is the lager", say fans of this "tired" and "cavernous" Belgian chain, where moules come every way; for "early supper in a hurry", though, the "fantastic beat-the-clock offer" still has its devotees. / www.belgo-restaurants.co.uk; most branches 10.30 pm-11.30 pm; SW4 midnight, Thu 1 am, Fri & Sat 2 am, Sun 12.30 am.

Bellamy's W1 £70 ❸❷❷
18-18a Bruton Pl 7491 2727 3–2B
Hidden-away in a delightful Mayfair mews, this "comfortable" and "very grown-up" brasserie offers "nothing faddish or over-adventurous" – just "beautifully-presented" traditional dishes, and service that's "attentive but not at all overbearing". / W1J 6LY; www.bellamysrestaurant.co.uk; 10.15 pm; closed Sat L & Sun.

Bellevue Rendez-Vous SW17 £45 ❸❷❷
218 Trinity Rd 8767 5810 10–2C
"An ideal neighbourhood restaurant", near Wandsworth Common; the welcome is "warm and friendly", and there's a short menu of "competitively-priced" Gallic "classics", not least a "phenomenal cheeseboard". / SW17 7HP; www.bellevuerendezvous.com; 10.30 pm; closed Mon L; no Amex.

Belvedere W8 £68 ④④❷
Holland Pk, off Abbotsbury Rd 7602 1238 7–1D
"Unique and magical" – this "beautiful" venue, actually inside Holland Park, is a "delightfully romantic" place, and also much-recommended for Sunday lunch; even fans, though, may concede the cooking "will never set the world on fire", and critics say it's plain "dull". / W8 6LU; www.belvedererestaurant.co.uk; 10.30 pm; closed Sun D; set weekday L & pre-theatre £40 (FP).

Ben's Canteen SW11 NEW £47 ❸④④

140 St John's Hill 7228 3260 10–2C

"A nice place to while away a morning over a hearty brunch" – this instantly-popular new Wandsworth diner wins most praise for its "succulent and juicy burgers". / SW11 1SL; www.benscanteen.com; 10 pm.

Benares W1 £80 ❷❷❸

12a Berkeley Square Hs, Berkeley Sq 7629 8886 3–3B

"Exquisite", "high-end" Indian cooking – whose hallmark is "delicacy, with complexity and strength" – has won a huge fan club for Atul Kochar's heart-of-Mayfair restaurant; only real complaint? – its luxurious but windowless first-floor premises can feel a little "soulless". / W1J 6BS; www.benaresrestaurant.co.uk; 10.30 pm, Sun 10 pm; no trainers.

Bengal Clipper SE1 £38 ❸❸❸

Shad Thames 7357 9001 9–4D

On most accounts, this "large" and spacious South Bank stalwart remains "one of London's better Indians"; service can hit the wrong note, though, and the occasional former fan feels the place is just "going through the motions" nowadays. / SE1 2YR; www.bengalclipper.co.uk; 11.30 pm, Sun 11 pm.

Benihana £63 ④④④

37 Sackville St, W1 7494 2525 3–3D

77 King's Rd, SW3 7376 7799 5–3D

"Teppan-yaki, American-style"; standards at this "cheesy" international chain may be pretty "average", but the staff "go out of their way to keep the kids happy", and the chefs' "theatrical" performances can still make it a good choice "for children and groups". / www.benihana.co.uk; 10.30 pm, Sun 10 pm.

Benito's Hat £23 ❸❷❸

12 Great Castle St, W1 7636 6560 3–1C

56 Goodge St, W1 7637 3732 2–1B

19 New Row, WC2 7240 5815 4–3C

"Holy guacamole!"; these self-service Mexicans "feel a lot fresher than many of their competitors" – they serve "yummy, filling burittos", "delicious tacos", and "great margaritas and home-made drinks". / 10 pm, Thu-Sat 11 pm; Great Castle St closed Sun.

Bentley's W1 £75 ❷❷❷

11-15 Swallow St 7734 4756 3–3D

For "great seafood, cooked simply but effectively", Richard Corrigan's "quintessential British fish restaurant", near Piccadilly Circus, is a "100% reliable" destination; for economy, and to enjoy the impressive al fresco tables, stick to the ground-floor oyster bar. / W1B 4DG; www.bentleys.org; 10.30 pm; no jeans; booking: max 8.

Bento Cafe NW1 £33 ❷❸④

9 Parkway 7482 3990 8–3B

"Yes it lacks atmosphere, and the service is rather variable", but the food at this Camden Town Japanese is "always freshly-prepared", and offers "authentic tastes and variety" – "you'd pay twice as much in the West End!" / NW1 7PG; bentocafe.co.uk; 10.15 pm, Fri-Sat 10.45 pm.

F S A

Benugo £35 ④④❷

14 Curzon St, W1 7629 6246 3–4B
23-25 Gt Portland St, W1 7631 5052 3–1C
V&A Museum, Cromwell Rd, SW7 7581 2159 5–2C
Natural History Museum, Cromwell Rd, SW7 7942 5011 5–2B
Westfield, Unit 1070 Ariel Way, W12 8746 9490 7–1C
St Pancras International, , NW1 7833 0201 8–3C
BFI Southbank, Belvedere Rd, SE1 7401 9000 2–3D
116 St John St, EC1 7253 3499 9–1A
82 City Rd, EC1 7253 1295 12–1A

Two outlets – at the V&A ("lovely") and BFI ("stylish") – stand out among the branches of these "casual" snack bars, where the mainstays are coffee, soups and sarnies; in general, though, the food is "not impressive", and service can be "slapdash" too. / www.benugo.com; 4 pm-10 pm; W1 & EC1 branches closed Sat & Sun; W1 & EC1 branches, no credit cards.

Best Mangal £32 ❷❸❸

619 Fulham Rd, SW6 7610 0009 5–4A
104 North End Rd, W14 7610 1050 7–2D
66 North End Rd, W14 7602 0212 7–2D

"Unbeatable for a regular meatfest!" – these "cramped and busy" Turkish BBQs offer "cheap but high-quality grills", plus "all the usual salads and breads". / www.bestmangal.com; midnight, Sat 1 am; no Amex.

Bevis Marks E1 £62

3 Middlesex St 7247 5474 9–2D

"The best kosher restaurant in central London" moved from its former synagogue-setting to a new City site during 2012; early reports suggest the good-but-pricey standards have been maintained, but feedback so far is too little to justify a rating. / E1A 7AA; www.bevismarkstherestaurant.com; 9 pm; closed Fri D, Sat & Sun.

Beyoglu NW3 £35 ❸❸④

72 Belsize Ln 7435 7733 8–2A

"A great little restaurant, a short walk from Belsize Park tube" – a "reliable" Turkish outfit, where quality is "creditable", "prices are good", and "you certainly can't complain about the portions". / NW3 4XR; www.beyoglu.co.uk; 11 pm; no Amex.

Bianco43 SE10 NEW £41 ❸⑤④

43 Greenwich Church St 8858 2668 1–3D

"Mid-range options in Greenwich just got better!" – this "brilliant" new pizzeria wins local acclaim for its "proper" pizza and other "fresh" Italian fare; it's "cramped", though, and service is "hit-and-miss… with the emphasis on miss". / SE10 9BL; www.bianco43.com; 11.30 pm; no Amex.

Bibendum SW3 £79 ④❸❷

81 Fulham Rd 7581 5817 5–2C

"Tops for lunch on a sunny day" – this "sophisticated" Brompton Cross dining room remains as "light, airy and beautiful" as ever; the wine list is "terrific" too, but the "classical" Gallic cuisine has seemed to be "resting on its laurels" rather heavily of late. / SW3 6RD; www.bibendum.co.uk; 11 pm, Sun 10.30 pm; booking: max 12 at L, 10 at D; set weekday L £49 (FP).

Bibendum Oyster Bar SW3 £57 ❸❷❷

81 Fulham Rd 7589 1480 5–2C

"Perfect for the best fruits-de-mer and a bottle of Chablis" – this luxurious café, in the "splendid" foyer of Brompton Cross's Michelin building, offers a "limited but top-quality menu of mainly cold dishes". / SW3 6RD; www.bibendum.co.uk; 10.30 pm, Sun 10 pm; no booking.

Bibimbap Soho W1 £29 ❸④④

11 Greek St 7287 3434 4–2A

"The prices make you wonder why you bother cooking at home"; this "cheap 'n' cheerful" yearling – named after its staple Korean rice dish (ideally with an egg on top) – has instantly established itself as a handy Soho stand-by. / W1D 4DJ; www.bibimbapsoho.com; 11 pm; closed Sun; no Amex.

Big Easy £49 ❸❸❷

12 Maiden Ln, WC2 awaiting tel 4–3D NEW

332-334 King's Rd, SW3 7352 4071 5–3C

"Colourful", "bustling" and "fun", this "always-noisy" Chelsea surf 'n' turf 'shack' is a "pricey-but-worth-it" operation which not only has a "very good family atmosphere", but does "great cocktails" too; an offshoot opens in Covent Garden in late-2012. / www.bigeasy.uk.com; Mon-Thu 11 pm, Fri-Sat 11.30, Sun 10.30 pm.

Bincho Yakitori £37 ④④❷

16 Old Compton St, W1 7287 9111 4–2A

55 Exmouth Mkt, EC1 7837 0009 9–1A NEW

A tale of two branches – the striking West End flagship of this Japanese-skewer concept is "a good place to try yakitori, even if the bill can stack up… but standards at the new Farringdon sibling tend to "average". / W1 11.30, Sun 10.30; EC1 10.30 pm; EC1 closed Sun D.

The Bingham TW10 £68 ❷❷❷

61-63 Petersham Rd 8940 0902 1–4A

This "gorgeous" Richmond hotel dining room not only has a "very beautiful location, with views over the Thames", but also offers "confident, even ambitious cooking which usually comes off"; critics can find the food a touch "over-rated", though, and the style is rather "formal" for some tastes. / TW10 6UT; www.thebingham.co.uk; 10 pm; closed Sun D; no trainers.

Bistro 1 £21 ④❷④

27 Frith St, W1 7734 6204 4–3A

75 Beak St, W1 7287 1840 3–2D

33 Southampton St, WC2 7379 7585 4–3D

"For a youth/student budget", these "crowded and noisy" canteens are "hard to beat" – the scoff is not art, but it is "plentiful and tasty". / www.bistro1.co.uk; midnight.

Bistro Aix N8 £50 ❷❶❷

54 Topsfield Pde, Tottenham Ln 8340 6346 8–1C

"Capturing the essence of France… but with friendly staff!" – this "romantic" Crouch End "gem" attracts many fans with its "exquisite" food and "lovely" ambience. / N8 8PT; www.bistroaix.co.uk; 11 pm; no Amex; set dinner £29 (FP).

Bistro Union SW4 NEW £40 ❸❸❸

40 Abbeville Rd 7042 6400 10–2D

"An excellent addition to the neighbourhood" – with its "simple, flavoursome dishes", Adam (Trinity) Byatt's "quirky" new Clapham bistro "is already good" (and devotees insist "it will get better once it gets into its stride"). / SW4 9NG; www.bistrounion.co.uk; 10 pm; closed Sun D.

Bistrot Bruno Loubet
The Zetter EC1 £53 ❷❷❸
St John's Square 86-88 Clerkenwell Rd 7324 4455 9–1A
Bruno Loubet's "intensely comforting, and superbly-executed" Gallic-based cuisine – "given an extra edge by experimentation" – again excites huge interest in this "airy", "casual" and "buzzy" (if slightly "sparse") Clerkenwell two-year-old. / EC1M 5RJ; www.thezetter.com; 10.30 pm, Sat & Sun 11 pm; SRA-73%.

Bistrotheque E2 £50 ④④❸
23-27 Wadeson St 8983 7900 1–2D
"Expect men in utilikilts" and "lots of asymmetrical haircuts", if you visit this "upmarket-hipster" Bethnal Green warehouse-conversion; with the former cabaret now just a memory, however, old fans fear the place has "gone totally mainstream"; the food has always been rather incidental. / E2 9DR; www.bistrotheque.com; 10.30 pm, Fri & Sat 11 pm; closed weekday L.

Black & Blue £48 ④❸④
37 Berners St, W1 7436 0451 2–1B
90-92 Wigmore St, W1 7486 1912 3–1A
127 King's Rd, SW3 7351 1661 5–3C
105 Gloucester Rd, SW7 7244 7666 5–2B
215-217 Kensington Church St, W8 7727 0004 6–2B
1-2 Rochester Walk, SE1 7357 9922 9–4C
These "handily-located" grill-restaurants are "solid" and "reliable" venues, say fans, not least for those in search of a "surprisingly high-quality" burger or steak; critics, though, find them plain "average" and "pricey, for what they are" too. / www.blackandbluerestaurant.com; most branches 11 pm, Fri & Sat 11.30 pm; no booking.

BLEEDING HEART EC1 £62 ❷❷❶
Bleeding Heart Yd, Greville St 7242 8238 9–2A
In a secret courtyard, near Hatton Garden, this "discreet" and "Dickensian" warren – combining bistro, tavern and restaurant – is as suited to "a long business lunch" as it is to "impressing a very special date"; service is "charming", and the wine list "hugely impressive" – the "classic" Gallic fare arguably plays rather a supporting rôle. / EC1N 8SJ; www.bleedingheart.co.uk; 10.30 pm; closed Sun.

Blue Elephant SW6 NEW £49 ❸❸❸
The Boulevard 7751 3111 10–1B
This once-celebrated Thai veteran recently re-opened in a smart but "less fun" new home, near Chelsea Harbour; some say it's still "a delight", especially "if you get a waterside table", but critics are far from convinced. / SW6 2UB; www.blueelephant.com; 11.30 pm, Sun 10.30 pm.

Blue Legume £33 ④❸❷
101 Stoke Newington Church St, N16 7923 1303 1–1C
177 Upper St, N1 7226 5858 8–2D
130 Crouch Hill, N8 8442 9282 8–1C
"A great meeting place for those under 12 months old!" – these "bustling" and "good-humoured" north London diners may be "swamped by kids", but they are "fun neighbourhood places" par excellence. / www.thebluelegume.co.uk; 10.30 pm.

FSA

Bluebird SW3 £58 ⑤⑤④

350 King's Rd 7559 1000 5–3C

"I just love the light and airy space", say fans of this "hangar-like" D&D Group Chelsea hang-out, who insist it's "on the up!"; too many reporters, though, are "mystified by its popularity" – they find the interior "daunting", and the food "so disappointing", and "very expensive" too. / SW3 5UU; www.bluebird-restaurant.co.uk; 10.30 pm.

Bluebird Café SW3 £41 ⑤⑤④

350 King's Rd 7559 1000 5–3C

"Really bog-standard" food, "lazy and lacklustre service"... – this prominently-sited D&D Group café appears to rely almost entirely on the attractions of its prominent, largely al fresco Chelsea location. / SW3 5UU; www.bluebird-restaurant.co.uk; 10 pm, Sun 9.30 pm; no reservations; SRA-64%.

Blueprint Café
Design Museum SE1 £51 ❸❸❶

28 Shad Thames, Butler's Wharf 7378 7031 9–4D

It's "worth going for the view alone" (Tower Bridge), but this first-floor South Bank restaurant also offers some pretty "decent" food (seemingly unaffected by the recent departure of high-profile chef Jeremy Lee to Quo Vadis); it is most popular as a lunch destination. / SE1 2YD; www.danddlondon.com; 10.30 pm; closed Sun D; SRA-61%.

Bob Bob Ricard W1 £58 ④❷❶

1 Upper James St 3145 1000 3–2D

"The hilarious decor reminiscent of the Orient Express, the 'Champagne' button, the comfort and privacy of the booths"... – this "eccentric" bar/restaurant "de luxe" certainly makes a "sexy" Soho choice; realisation of the "retro" menu, however, can be rather "random". / W1F 9DF; www.bobbobricard.com; 11.15 pm; closed Mon & Sun; jacket.

Bocca Di Lupo W1 £54 ❷❷❷

12 Archer St 7734 2223 3–2D

The "off-piste" Italian tapas – "like nowhere else in the capital" – are "a revelation", say fans of this "wonderfully laid-back" and "understated" Soho three-year-old, hidden-away near Piccadilly Circus; "try to get one of the bar seats, where you can watch the chefs at work". / W1D 7BB; www.boccadilupo.com; 11 pm, Sun 9.15 pm; booking: max 10.

Al Boccon di'vino TW9 £62 ❷❶❸

14 Red Lion St 8940 9060 1–4A

"You get what Riccardo prepares on the day", at this "delightfully eccentric" and rather old-fashioned "real Italian", in Richmond; "skip lunch and go for a long walk before you eat". / TW9 1RW; www.nonsolovinoltd.co.uk; 8 pm; closed Mon, Tue L & Wed L.

Bodean's £42 ④④❸

10 Poland St, W1 7287 7575 3–1D
4 Broadway Chambers, SW6 7610 0440 5–4A
169 Clapham High St, SW4 7622 4248 10–2D
16 Byward St, EC3 7488 3883 9–3D

"A real taste of Americana" – these "trips to the BBQ heartland" serve "proper US food" (ribs, pulled pork, wings) in a "no-fuss" setting that's great "fun"... "so long as you're into American sports on the TV". / www.bodeansbbq.com; 11 pm, Sun 10.30 pm; 8 or more.

La Bodega Negra W1 NEW £47 ④❸❷
13-17 Moor St 7758 4100 4–2B
"Rather NYC in style", this Soho newcomer – "easily missed" behind its "peep-show façade" – is trying so hard to be "edgy" that cynics detect "a touch of Disney" about it; they think the Mexican cuisine "doesn't quite match up to the trendy decor" either. / W1D 5NQ; www.labodeganegra.com; 1 am, Sun 11.30 pm; D only.

Boisdale SW1 £59 ④④❷
13-15 Eccleston St 7730 6922 2–4B
"You can still smoke a cigar without being ostracised", on the "amazing terrace" of this Belgravia bastion of Scottish Baronial taste, acclaimed by fans for its "splendid" atmosphere, its "top-class" haggis and game and its "excellent" wine and whisky; it can, however, seem "extremely expensive" for what it is. / SW1W 9LX; www.boisdale.co.uk; 11.30 pm; closed Sat L & Sun.

Boisdale of Canary Wharf E14 £56 ④④❷
Cabot Pl 7715 5818 11–1C
"For the Wharf, locations don't get much better!"; Ranald Macdonald's "airy", "pseudo-Scottish" venue – with its regular jazz, "outside cigar bar" and "stunning night-time views" – pleases most reporters, and the food is "decent" too, if "quite pricey" for what it is. / E14 4QT; www.boisdale.co.uk; 11.30 pm; closed Sun.

The Bolingbroke SW11 £43 ④❷❷
174 Northcote Rd 7228 4040 10–2C
It's the "friendly welcome and pleasantly relaxed service" that make this Battersea boozer "special", and ensure it's "always busy"; the cooking is well-rated too, but a tad "variable", and "at the upper-end, price-wise". / SW11 6RE; www.renaissancepubs.co.uk; 10.30 pm, Sun 9 pm; SRA-56%.

Bombay Brasserie SW7 £56 ❸❸④
Courtfield Close, Gloucester Rd 7370 4040 5–2B
Still recovering from its "corporate-canteen" make-over of a few years ago, this vast Indian "staple", by Gloucester Road tube, attracts a mixed bag of reviews; the consensus is that it's a "fairly safe bet", but arguably "not worth the price tag". / SW7 4QH; www.bombaybrasserielondon.com; 11.30 pm, Sun 10.30 pm.

Bombay Palace W2 £53 ❶❶④
50 Connaught St 7723 8855 6–1D
Bayswater's "best-kept-secret"; this real "class act" – having long hidden its light under a bushel – was revamped and relaunched as our survey was coming to a close; an early-days reporter says the food is "as good as ever"… which is to say "among the best of the best" of London Indians. / W2 2AA; www.bombay-palace.co.uk; 11.30 pm.

**Bonds
Threadneedles Hotel EC2** £67 ④④④
5 Threadneedle St 7657 8088 9–2C
This "beautiful and grand" dining room (a converted banking hall) is something of "a City favourite", thanks not least to its hyper-convenient location; its "very rich" cuisine is "well-cooked, but quite standard" and "very expensive" – breakfast is best. / EC2R 8AY; www.theetoncollection.com/restaurants/bonds/; 10 pm; closed Sat & Sun.

Il Bordello E1 £44 ❷❶❷
81 Wapping High St 7481 9950 11–1A
"All the smells and noise of a traditional, friendly Italian restaurant" add life to this "very crowded" Wapping favourite, where "great food" – pizza a speciality – comes in "huge portions", and at "good prices". / E1W 2YN; www.ilbordello.com; 11 pm, Sun 10.30 pm; closed Sat L.

F S A

La Bota N8 £31 ❸④④

31 Broadway Pde 8340 3082 1–1C

"Don't go when Spain or Barcelona are playing!" – otherwise, this "uncomfy" but "characterfully authentic" Crouch End tapas bar is a "totally reliable local", where the grub is "tasty and well-priced". / N8 9DB; www.labota.co.uk; 11 pm, Fri-Sun 11.30 pm; no Amex.

The Botanist SW1 £57 ④④④

7 Sloane Sq 7730 0077 5–2D

Right on Sloane Square, this "handy" hang-out certainly has the 'location, location and location' to ensure it's "always really buzzing" (and "very noisy" too) – the crowd is unlikely to be anything to do with the food ("nothing to write home about") or service ("slow"). / SW1W 8EE; www.thebotanistonsloanesquare.com; 10.30 pm.

La Bottega £16 ❸❷❸

20 Ryder St, SW1 7839 5789 3–4C
25 Eccleston St, SW1 7730 2730 2–4B
65 Lower Sloane St, SW1 7730 8844 5–2D
97 Old Brompton Rd, SW7 7581 6622 5–2B

"Perfect coffee", "good panini" and "tasty daily pasta specials" are among the highlights of these smart SW London Italian snackeries; "usually, the only problem is getting a table". / www.labottega65.com; Lower Sloane St 8 pm, Sat 6 pm, Sun 5 pm; Eccleston St 7 pm; Old Brompton Rd 8 pm; Ryder St closed Sat & Sun; no booking.

La Bouchée SW7 £49 ④④❷

56 Old Brompton Rd 7589 1929 5–2B

"A die-hard South Kensington institution" – this "dark, candlelit, cramped cellar" is "really cute" and "great for a date"; service can be "erratic", though, and the "classic bistro fare" has sometimes seemed a bit "lacklustre" of late. / SW7 3DY; 11 pm, Sun 10.30 pm.

Boudin Blanc W1 £63 ❸④❷

5 Trebeck St 7499 3292 3–4B

"The chaos is surprisingly relaxing!", says one of the many fans of this "cosy" Shepherd Market bistro, which is "very French in its hustle, bustle and brusqueness", and has some "lovely" tables al fresco; its one-time 'bargain' status, however, is now just a memory. / W1J 7LT; www.boudinblanc.co.uk; 11 pm.

Boulevard WC2 £43 ④❸❸

40 Wellington St 7240 2992 4–3D

It looks like a tourist trap, and offers food that's "comforting" going on "unremarkable", but this Covent Garden brasserie is "friendlier and more efficient" than many hereabouts; try hard, and "you could almost imagine you were in Paris!" / WC2E 7BD; www.boulevardbrasserie.co.uk; 11 pm, Fri & Sat 11.30 pm, Sun 10.30 pm.

The Boundary E2 £66 ❸❸❷

2-4 Boundary St 7729 1051 12–1B

"Has Conran got it right for once?"; Sir Tel's "beautifully-designed" basement restaurant, in Shoreditch, is well-reported-on for its "gorgeous" (if "pricey") French fare, and "there's a great roof-top bar" too. / E2 7DD; www.theboundary.co.uk; 10.30 pm; D only, ex Sun L only.

The Bountiful Cow WC1 £48 ❸④④

51 Eagle St 7404 0200 2–1D

"Decent, fairly-priced food in a location offering few alternatives"; "juicy burgers" and "huge steaks" win praise for this "cosy and basic" Bloomsbury basement. / WC1R 4AP; www.thebountifulcow.co.uk; 10.30 pm; closed Sun; set pre theatre £28 (FP).

Bradley's NW3 £54 ④④④

25 Winchester Rd 7722 3457 8–2A

"Tucked away behind Swiss Cottage", this "calm" stalwart is – for its fans – "a top neighbourhood restaurant", and "so handy pre-Hampstead theatre" too; those who remember the old days, though, can find its current performance rather "tired". / NW3 3NR; www.bradleysnw3.co.uk; 11 pm; closed Sat L & Sun D; set weekday L & pre-theatre £34 (FP).

Brady's SW18 £34 ❸❷❸

513 Old York Rd 8877 9599 10–2B

An "entertaining owner" adds life to this "always-packed" Wandsworth fish 'n' chip bistro, which offers "good fresh fish with a wide variety of sauces". / SW18 1TF; www.bradysfish.co.uk; 10 pm; closed Mon-Thu L & Sun; no Amex; no booking.

La Brasserie SW3 £54 ④❸❷

272 Brompton Rd 7581 3089 5–2C

"Vive la France!", say fans of this "old favourite", near Brompton Cross, for whom this is a "fun" establishment that "does what it says on the tin", (and is particularly "a winner for weekend brunch"); it's also "noisy and expensive", though, and sceptics "don't understand its popularity". / SW3 2AW; www.labrasserielondon.co.uk; 11.30 pm; no booking, Sat L & Sun L.

Brasserie Blanc £45 ④❸❸

8 Charlotte St, W1 7636 4975 2–1C NEW
119 Chancery Ln, WC2 7405 0290 2–2D NEW
35 The Mkt, WC2 7379 0666 4–3D NEW
9 Belvedere Rd, SE1 7202 8470 2–3D NEW
60 Threadneedle St, EC2 7710 9440 9–2C
64 Bishopsgate, EC2 7588 1200 9–2D NEW
14 Trinity Sq, EC3 7480 5500 9–3D NEW
1 Watling St, EC4 7213 0540 9–2B NEW

"As Raymond says himself, this is not fine dining", but this "well-run" brasserie chain "cuts the mustard" with its "consistent, good-value package"; it stormed the capital in 2012, with the acquisition of Chez Gérard's former premises (including the brilliant Covent Garden site, with huge terrace). / www.brasserieblanc.com; most branches close between 10 pm & 11 pm; SE1 closed Sun D, most City branches closed Sat & Sun; SRA-64%.

Brasserie Max
Covent Garden Hotel WC2 £65 ④❸❸

10 Monmouth St 7806 1000 4–2B

An attractive hotel brasserie that can make a "lovely, retreat from the hustle and bustle of Covent Garden"; some (but not all) reporters find the food "delicious" too. / WC2; www.coventgardenhotel.co.uk; 11 pm; set always available £47 (FP).

Brasserie on St John Street EC1 £40 ❸❸❸

360-362 St John's St 7837 1199 8–3D

"It offers British food at its best", say fans of this "roughly-furnished" and "deafening" establishment, on the fringe of Clerkenwell; the more critical view is that it is "mainly useful for its proximity to Sadlers Wells". / EC1V 4NR; www.the-brasserie.com; 11 pm, Fri-Sat 11.30 pm, Sun 10.30 pm; closed Mon; set pre theatre £36 (FP).

F S A

Brasserie St Jacques SW1 £57 ❸④❸
33 St James's St 7839 1007 3–4C
A "real French brasserie", just off Piccadilly, which fans find "romantic" and good-value; indeed, even its worst critic says the food is "reasonable", but wonders: "why go here, with so many other great options nearby?" / SW1A 1HD; www.brasseriestjacques.co.uk; 10 pm; closed Sat & Sun; no jeans or trainers.

Brasserie Toulouse-Lautrec SE11 £39 ④❷❶
140 Newington Butts 7582 6800 1–3C
"In Kennington, a taste of France!" – the Régent family brasserie, next door to their longer-established 'Lobster Pot', is of most note for its "attentive" service and jolly ambience, but the food is always at least "competent". / SE11 4RN; www.btlrestaurant.co.uk; 10.30 pm, Sat & Sun 11 pm.

Brasserie Zédel W1 NEW £36 ❸❷❷
20 Sherwood St 7734 4888 3–2D
The latest venture from the Wolseley team, this preposterously grand (1930s) marbled basement, near Piccadilly Circus – once 'The Atlantic' – aims to offer a truly Parisian brasserie experience, and at impressively keen prices; it left us un-moved, but early feedback from the press and many early reports is dazzling. / W1F 7ED; Rated on Editors' visit; www.brasseriezedel.com; midnight.

Brawn E2 £47 ❷❷❷
49 Columbia Rd 7729 5692 12–1C
"Even better than its parent, Terroirs!" – this "buzzy" and "charming" spot is "worth the trip East" to enjoy the "earthy and different" small dishes (with "a heavy emphasis on meat") it offers, plus its "extraordinary wine list, with lots of obscure choices". / E2 7RG; www.brawn.co; 11 pm; closed Mon L, Tue L, Wed L & Sun D; no Amex.

Bread Street Kitchen EC4 £56 ④④④
1 New Change 3030 4050 9–2B
"Gordon gets it right", says a fan of this "industrial-scale" City-mall yearling, which "ticks all the obvious boxes, in a flash, New-Yorkish sort of way"; it can seem pretty "soulless", though, and critics wonder: "how could such a big place possibly do food good enough to measure up to the prices?" / EC4M 9AF; www.breadstreetkitchen.com; 11 pm, Sun 8 pm.

Briciole W1 NEW £38 ❷❷❸
20 Homer St 7723 0040 6–1D
"A good formula from the Latium team" – this "pleasant", "eat-anytime" Italian deli/bistro, in Marylebone, serves "high-quality artisanal meats, cheeses and breads, tapas-style", plus "tasty pasta and interesting specials". / W1H 4NA; Rated on Editors' visit; www.briciole.co.uk; 10.15 pm.

Brick Lane Beigel Bake E1 £7 ❶❷⑤
159 Brick Ln 7729 0616 12–1C
"The best hot salt beef beigels in London… perhaps the world!" are served by "friendly" staff, at this 24/7 East End phenomenon, long renowned for its "stunning value". / E1 6SB; open 24 hours; no credit cards; no booking.

The Bright Courtyard W1 NEW £54 ❸❸④
43-45 Baker St 7486 6998 2–1A
"Watch out Royal China Club" (opposite), this "bright and spacious" new kid on the Marylebone block offers some "very accomplished" Shanghai/Canton menus (and dim sum too); critics, though, find it "dreary and expensive". / W1U 8EW; www.lifefashiongroup.com; 10.45 pm, Thu-Sat 11.15 pm.

Brilliant UB2 £36 ❷❷❸

72-76 Western Rd 8574 1928 1–3A

"The name says it all!" – fans cross town to enjoy the "authentic Punjabi cooking" on offer at this "very large and loud family restaurant, deep in Southall". / UB2 5DZ; www.brilliantrestaurant.com; 11 pm; closed Mon, Sat L & Sun L.

Brinkley's SW10 £51 ⑤④❸

47 Hollywood Rd 7351 1683 5–3B

The food may be "predictable", say fans, but the "outstanding" ("fantastic-value") wine list of this stalwart rendezvous fuels what they claim is "one of the best atmospheres in Chelsea"; for critics, though, the place is just a "car crash" – "the cooking is abysmal, and the customers are worse!" / SW10 9HX; www.brinkleys.com; 11 pm; closed weekday L.

Brinkley's Kitchen SW17 £46 ④④❸

35 Bellevue Rd 8672 5888 10–2C

"Unadventurous dining with affordable wines" – that's John Brinkley's classic formula, and, for most (if not all) reporters, it makes this bistro by Wandsworth Common "a perfect neighbourhood eatery". / SW17 7EF; www.brinkleys.com; 11 pm; closed Mon & Sun D.

Brompton Bar & Grill SW3 £50 ❸❷❷

243 Brompton Rd 7589 8005 5–2C

"Straightforward" Gallic cooking and "smart" service make this "casually elegant" bistro quite a favourite for Knightsbridge types; by local standards, it's quite "good value" too. / SW3 2EP; www.bromptonbarandgrill.com; 10.30 pm, Sun 10 pm.

The Brown Cow SW6 NEW

676 Fulham Rd 7384 9559 10–1B

A new gastropub-style sibling for the Sands End, the former Fulham site of Manson (RIP) is to be relaunched – under unchanged ownership – in late-2012. / SW6 5SA.

The Brown Dog SW13 £45 ❸❸❸

28 Cross St 8392 2200 10–1A

In Barnes's super-cute 'Little Chelsea', a "charming" pub offering, "simple" and "reliably good" food, and extending "a warm welcome to adults, children and, of course, dogs"; outside tables are particularly "lovely". / SW13 0AP; www.thebrowndog.co.uk; 10 pm, Sun 9 pm.

(Hix at Albemarle)
Brown's Hotel W1 £75 ④❸❸

Albemarle St 7518 4004 3–3C

"Lovely wood panelling", "discreet" style, "plenty of space"… – this "old-fashioned" Mayfair dining room is certainly "a safe bet for business", even if the cuisine (overseen by Mark Hix) is "no more than OK". / W1S 4BP; www.thealbemarlerestaurant.com; 11 pm, Sun 10.30 pm.

Browns £43 ⑤⑤④
2 Cardinal Pl, SW1 7821 1450 2–4B
47 Maddox St, W1 7491 4565 3–2C
82-84 St Martin's Ln, WC2 7497 5050 4–3B
9 Islington Grn, N1 7226 2555 8–3D
Butler's Wharf, SE1 7378 1700 9–4D
Hertsmere Rd, E14 7987 9777 11–1C
8 Old Jewry, EC2 7606 6677 9–2C
Though still an "old favourite" chain for many reporters (and occupying a number of beautiful buildings), these "tired" English brasseries too often dish up "really forgettable" meals; maybe stick to cocktails… / www.browns-restaurants.co.uk; most branches 10 pm-11 pm; EC2 closed Sat & Sun; W1 closed Sun D.

Brula TW1 £51 ❷❶❶
43 Crown Rd 8892 0602 1–4A
"First-class in every way", this slightly old-fashioned "neighboorhood bistro", "tucked-away" in St Margaret's, is a "little gem that never disappoints"; it serves "satisfying" Gallic fare, plus "good wines by the glass and bottle". / TW1 3EJ; www.brula.co.uk; 10.30 pm; closed Sun D.

Brunswick House Cafe SW8 £41 ❷④❶
30 Wandsworth Rd 7720 2926 10–1D
"Edgily-located" in the large Georgian house at Vauxhall Cross, a "kooky" operation where you eat amidst an "extraordinary assortment of architectural salvage"; the surprise is that the food is "serious", "imaginative" and "skilful", and "the wine ain't bad either". / SW8 2LG; www.brunswickhousecafe.co.uk; closed Mon D, Tue D, Wed D & Sun D.

Bubba Gump Shrimp Company W1 NEW
7 Coventry St awaiting tel 4–4A
Opening in late-2012, in former Planet Hollywood premises near Piccadilly Circus, the first UK branch of a garish American chain loosely based on the characters in 'Forrest Gump'; if successful, more will follow – you have been warned! / W1D 6DG.

Bubbledogs W1 NEW
70 Charlotte St awaiting tel 2–1C
Opening as this guide goes to press, a Fitzrovia newcomer where a chef with serious credentials has decided to make a speciality of hot dogs (and champagne); there will also be a chef-hosted 'Kitchen Table', serving more traditional set lunch and dinner menus. / W1T 4QG; 9 pm; closed Sun.

Buen Ayre E8 £48 ❷❸❸
50 Broadway Mkt 7275 9900 1–2D
"Busy and trendy", this Hackney 'parilla' is much-lauded for its "authentic" steaks, "lush" chips and other Argentinian fare; a few reports this year, however, were of the "decent-but-unspectacular" variety. / E8 4QJ; www.buenayre.co.uk; 10.30 pm; no Amex.

Buenos Aires Cafe £54 ❷❸❸
86 Royal Hill, SE10 8488 6764 1–3D
17 Royal Pde, SE3 8318 5333 1–4D
"Amazing steaks and lovely wines" please practically all who comment on these "friendly" and "packed-out" Argentinians. / www.buenosairesltd.com; SE3 10.30 pm; SE10 7 pm, Sat & Sun 6 pm; no Amex.

FSA

The Builders Arms SW3 £44 ④④❷

13 Britten St 7349 9040 5–2C

"Cosily tucked-away behind the King's Road and patronised mainly by Chelsea denizens", this local "secret" is a "lovely" gastropub, even if the food does tend to be "routine". / SW3 3TY; www.geronimo-inns.co.uk; 10 pm, Thu-Sat 11 pm, Sun 9 pm; no booking.

Bull & Last NW5 £50 ❷❷❷

168 Highgate Rd 7267 3641 8–1B

"Enjoying years at the top of the north London gastropub league!" – this "pretty faultless" ("apart from the noise levels") Kentish Town hostelry, "nestled right by Hampstead Heath", retains its smash-hit status, thanks to its "fantastic, meaty fare" and its "genuine" service. / NW5 1QS; www.thebullandlast.co.uk; 10 pm, Sun 9 pm.

Bumbles SW1 £38 ❸❷❷

16 Buckingham Palace Rd 7828 2903 2–4B

It looks "a little conventional" and "old-fashioned", but this "cheerful" Victoria bistro is something of a "gem", thanks to its surprisingly "impressive" cooking at notably "reasonable prices". / SW1W 0QP; www.bumbles1950.com; 10 pm; closed Sat L & Sun; set weekday L £22 (FP).

Bumpkin £48 ⑤④④

102 Old Brompton Rd, SW7 7341 0802 5–2B

209 Westbourne Park Rd, W11 7243 9818 6–1B

With their menu of "British comfort food" and their casual style, these "buzzy" pub-conversions in Notting Hill, and South Kensington, would potentially be a "fun" experience… were it not for their "erratic" service, "bad cooking" and bills that can tot up to an "unpleasant surprise". / www.bumpkinuk.com; 11 pm.

Buona Sera £36 ❸❸❶

289a King's Rd, SW3 7352 8827 5–3C

22 Northcote Rd, SW11 7228 9925 10–2C

"Basic, wholesome Italian food is served with gusto", at this "consistently friendly and reliable" Battersea fixture – "always fun, especially with kids"; dating back to the '70s, the raised booths at the Chelsea ('Jam') branch still seem a "cool concept" too. / midnight; SW3 11.30 pm, Sun 10 pm; SW3 closed Mon L.

Burger & Lobster £43 ❷❷❷

29 Clarges St, W1 7409 1699 3–4B **NEW**

36 Dean St, W1 7432 4800 4–2A **NEW**

40 St John St, EC1 awaiting tel 9–1B **NEW**

"A brilliant concept!" – this "sparklingly buzzing and urbane" Mayfair newcomer serves "the most succulent" lobster and "one of the best burgers ever", and at "bargain" prices too; it's "always rammed" – arrive early or be prepared to queue; a Soho branch opened in mid-2012, with one in Clerkenwell set to follow. / www.burgerandlobster.com; 10.30 pm; Clarges St closed Sun D.

FSA

Busaba Eathai £37 ❸❸❷
35 Panton St, SW1 7930 0088 4–4A
106-110 Wardour St, W1 7255 8686 3–2D
8-13 Bird St, W1 7518 8080 3–1A
22 Store St, WC1 7299 7900 2–1C
44 Floral St, WC2 7759 0088 4–2D
358 King's Rd, SW3 7349 5488 5–3B
Westfield, Ariel Way, W12 3249 1919 7–1C
Westfield Stratford, E20 8221 8989 1–1D
313-319 Old St, EC1 7729 0808 12–1B
"Think upmarket Thai Wagamama with better decor" – that's the deal at these "dark" and "beautifully-designed" canteens, where "tangy and varied" curries are served "quickly and cheaply", at communal tables. / www.busaba.co.uk; 11 pm, Fri & Sat 11.30 pm, Sun 10 pm; W1 no booking; WC1 booking: min 10.

Butcher & Grill £47 ④❸❸
39-41 Parkgate Rd, SW11 7924 3999 5–4C
33 High St, SW19 8944 8269 10–2B
"Delicious" brunches win praise for these bistro/butchers in Battersea and Wimbledon, where "simple and well-prepared" grills are the best bet; critics, however, feel the food – particularly in SW19 – is "no better than chain-pub quality". / www.thebutcherandgrill.com; 11 pm, Sun 9 pm; SW11 closed Sun D; SW19 closed Mon L.

Butcher's Hook SW6 £41 ❸❷❸
477 Fulham Rd 7385 4654 5–4A
Opposite Stamford Bridge, this "surprisingly good" gastropub plays a good game – it offers an ever-changing formation of "old favourites", and the players are "very friendly and hard-working" too. / SW6 1HL; www.thebutchershook.co.uk; 10.30 pm; no Amex.

Butlers Wharf Chop House SE1 £59 ④④❸
36e Shad Thames 7403 3403 9–4D
With its "great views", this D&D Group operation, near Tower Bridge, wins praise as a "solid" destination, whose "best-of-British" menu is particularly well-suited to business; critics find it "mediocre", though – those looking for "good value" head for the bar. / SE1 2YE; www.chophouse.co.uk; 10.45 pm, Sun 9.45 pm; SRA-63%.

La Buvette TW9 £40 ❸❷❷
6 Church Walk 8940 6264 1–4A
It may be "cramped", but this "lovely little restaurant, tucked-away in a churchyard" is a "romantic" Richmond "gem"; its bistro fare is "good, rather than outstanding", but "the balance between the overall experience and the price is almost perfect". / TW9 1SN; www.labuvette.co.uk; 10 pm.

Byron £33 ❸❸❸
11 Haymarket, SW1 7925 0276 4–4A
97-99 Wardour St, W1 7297 9390 3–2D
24-28 Charing Cross Rd, WC2 7557 9830 4–4B
33-35 Wellington St, WC2 7420 9850 4–3D
300 King's Rd, SW3 7352 6040 5–3C
242 Earl's Court Rd, SW5 7370 9300 5–2A
75 Gloucester Rd, SW7 7244 0700 5–2B
93-95 Old Brompton Rd, SW7 7590 9040 5–2B
Westfield, Ariel Way, W12 8743 7755 7–1C
222 Kensington High St, W8 7361 1717 5–1A
341 Upper St, N1 7704 7620 8–3D
46 Hoxton Sq, N1 3487 1230 12–1B
22 Putney High St, SW15 8246 4170 10–2B
Cabot Place East, E14 7715 9360 11–1C
7 Upper Cheapside Pas, One New Change, EC2 7246 2580 9–2B

Byron (continued)
"Winner in the burger wars!" ("sorry GBK!") – this "exemplary" chain remains, of all the big multiples, the survey's star performer; the branches are "funky", service is "efficient", and the main event is "top-notch" – even the sides (not least "terribly moreish zucchini fries") are "terrific". / www.byronhamburgers.com; SRA-63%.

C London (formerly Cipriani) W1 **£90** ⑤⑤④
25 Davies St 7399 0500 3–2B
A Z-list Mayfair hang-out notorious for its "see-and-be-seen" crowd, "chaotic" service and "hilarious" prices; "have the people who come here ever had Italian food before?" / W1K 3DE; www.crestaurant.co.uk; 11.45 pm.

C&R Cafe **£25** ❸④⑤
3-4 Rupert Ct, W1 7434 1128 4–3A
52 Westbourne Grove, W2 7221 7979 6–1B
"Tucked away in Chinatown", a "simple" café serving "surprisingly good" Malaysian/Indonesian "street-style" scoff, that's "cheap, quick and hot"; no survey mention, this year, of its Bayswater sibling. / 11 pm.

The Cabin W4 **£44** ④④④
148 Chiswick High Rd 8994 8594 7–2A
"For an informal non-fussy meal", this "cosy" surf 'n' turf diner, in Chiswick, has its fans; there's a suspicion, thought, that it is "good without being special", and "getting a bit pricey for what it is". / W4 1PR; www.cabinrestaurants.co.uk; 10.30 pm, Fri & Sat 11 pm; No toddlers after 6pm.

The Cadogan Arms SW3 **£48** ❸④❸
298 King's Rd 7352 6500 5–3C
On a King's Road corner, a "down-to-earth" member of the Martin brothers' gastropub group; "rather casual" service notwithstanding, it generally hits the spot. / SW3 5UG; www.thecadoganarmschelsea.com; 10.30 pm, Sun 9 pm.

Café 209 SW6 **£23** ④❸❶
209 Munster Rd 7385 3625 10–1B
"Joy's still crazy after all these years", and Fulhamites in search of a "fun" and "amazingly cheap" dinner still often head for her tiny, cheek-by-jowl BYO Thai café. / SW6 6BX; 10.30 pm; D only, closed Sun, closed Dec; no Amex.

Le Café Anglais
Whiteley's W2 **£55** ❸④❸
8 Porchester Gdns 7221 1415 6–1C
Rowley Leigh's "spacious" upper-floor Bayswater brasserie feels "like an old ocean liner", and pleases most (if not quite all) passengers with its all-round charms; a "really useful" oyster bar – serving seafood-and-more at "no-nonsense prices" – has been "a great addition". / W2 4DB; www.lecafeanglais.co.uk; 10.30 pm, Fri & Sat 11 pm, Sun 10pm.

Café Below EC2 **£34** ❸❸❷
St Mary-le-Bow, Cheapside 7329 0789 9–2C
"A fabulous crypt", beneath a Wren church, provides the atmospheric setting for this self-service City café – "a good stop-off for unpretentious, filling, comforting food". / EC2 6AU; www.cafebelow.co.uk; 3 pm; L only, closed Sat & Sun.

Café Bohème W1 £45 ❸❸❷
13 Old Compton St 7734 0623 4–2A
A "cosy" heart-of-Soho café/bar/brasserie that makes an extremely handy West End rendezvous – one reason it's often "extremely busy". / W1 5JQ; www.cafeboheme.co.uk; 2.45 am, Sun midnight; no reservations.

Café del Parc N19 £33 ❷❷❸
167 Junction Road 7281 5684 8–1C
"Cooking up a storm on the fringes of Archway", this "intimate" and "trendy" small café offers a set menu of "inspired" Spanish/Moroccan tapas, from a "minuscule open kitchen". / N19 5PZ; www.delparc.co.uk; 10.30 pm; open D only, Wed-Sun; no Amex.

Café des Amis WC2 £57 ④④④
11-14 Hanover Pl 7379 3444 4–2D
Right by the Royal Opera House, this "busy" Gallic bistro has obvious attractions pre-theatre, and the prix-fixes are "good value" too; à la carte, though, diners can find the whole experience not only "uninspired", but "more expensive than you'd expect". / WC2E 9JP; www.cafedesamis.co.uk; 11.30 pm, Sun 7pm; set weekday L £32 (FP), set pre-theatre £34 (FP).

Café du Marché EC1 £54 ❷❷❶
22 Charterhouse Sq 7608 1609 9–1B
"Down a discreet alley in Smithfield", this "little piece of France" – with its "snowy white table-cloths, bare bricks and wonderful cuisine" – is an "unfailing" and surprisingly "rustic" haven, well suited to a "relaxing" business lunch or a romantic supper. / EC1M 6DX; www.cafedumarche.co.uk; 10 pm; closed Sat L & Sun.

Cafe East SE16 £22 ❸④④
100 Redriff Rd 7252 1212 11–2B
A handy option for a bite in Surrey Quays – this "warehouse-style" operation is usually "full of Vietnamese people", and draws queues at peak times with its "cheap but excellent" grub; service, though, can be "a let-down". / SE16 7LH; www.cafeeast.foodkingdom.com; 10.30 pm, Sun 10 pm; closed Tue.

Café España W1 £31 ❸❸④
63 Old Compton St 7494 1271 4–3A
"Inexpensive tapas in the heart of Soho"; this "efficient" café – "easily missed if you aren't looking for it" – "just goes on and on". / W1D 6HT; 11.30 pm, Fri & Sat midnight.

Café in the Crypt
St Martin's in the Fields WC2 £31 ④❸❷
Duncannon St 7766 1158 2–2C
Right on Trafalgar Square, this self-service canteen, within a large and characterful crypt, is "convenient for a quick bite", and it offers a wide range of inexpensive options. / WC2N 4JJ; www.smitf.org; 8 pm, Thu-Sun 9 pm; no Amex; no booking.

Café Japan NW11 £35 ❶❷④
626 Finchley Rd 8455 6854 1–1B
"The best sushi bar in London"?; unassuming but "very professional" and "reasonably-priced", this café opposite Golder's Green tube draws fans from across town for its "wonderful sushi and sashimi" – there are also "a few hot dishes". / NW11 7RR; 10 pm, Sun 9.30 pm; closed Mon; no Amex; only D.

Café Pacifico WC2 £43 ④④❷

5 Langley St 7379 7728 4–2C

Thanks not least to its "exuberant cocktails", this stalwart Covent Garden cantina can offer a "fun" night out, and its "cheap 'n' cheerful" scoff generally pleases. / WC2 9JA; www.cafepacifico-laperla.com; 11.45 pm, Sun 10.45 pm.

Café Rouge £36 ⑤④④

Branches throughout London

A faux-French bistro chain which "desperately needs some energy"; supporters insist, though, that it's "not that bad" – especially with kids in tow, or for breakfast. / www.caferouge.co.uk; 11 pm, Sun 10.30 pm.

Café Spice Namaste E1 £53 ❷❶④

16 Prescot St 7488 9242 11–1A

Cyrus Todiwala's once path-breaking Indian, on the fringe of the City, is still an "old favourite" for many reporters, thanks to its "smiling" staff, and its "delicious and unusual" cuisine – "the focus really is on the spices"; the decor, though, is becoming rather "tired". / E1 8AZ; www.cafespice.co.uk; 10.30 pm; closed Sat L & Sun; SRA-71%.

Caffè Caldesi W1 £58 ❸❸④

118 Marylebone Ln 7487 0754 2–1A

A "straightforward" and "relaxed" Marylebone Italian, where "excellent pasta" is a highlight; the place can otherwise sometimes seem "a bit expensive for what it is". / W1U 2QF; www.caldesi.com; 10.30 pm; closed Sat L & Sun.

Caffè Nero £13 ④❸❸

Branches throughout London

"True, deep-tasting coffee" wins the most obviously 'Italian' of the major coffee-shop chains impressive support from reporters as one of the best too; their branches are "often open when others are closed". / most branches 7 pm; City branches earlier; most City branches closed all or part of weekend; some branches no credit cards; no booking.

Caffé Vergnano £12 ④❸❸

62 Charing Cross Rd, WC2 7240 3512 4–3B

Royal Festival Hall, SE1 7921 9339 2–3D

2 New Street Sq, EC4 7936 3404 9–2A

An Italian duo of note for "marvellous" coffee; the "buzzy" SE1 branch also does light snacks ("proper pasta" and so on) which, say fans, makes it "a great pit stop post-Festival Hall". / www.caffevergnano.com; EC4 11 pm; SE1 midnight; WC2 8 pm, Fri & Sat midnight; EC4 Sat & Sun; no Amex.

La Cage Imaginaire NW3 £41 ④④❸

16 Flask Walk 7794 6674 8–1A

"Cosy and romantic", or "a little bit uninspiring"? – this intimate Gallic fixture, located in an impossibly cute lane just off Hampstead's high street, continues to evoke both views. / NW3 1HE; www.la-cage-imaginaire.co.uk; 11 pm.

Cah-Chi £35 ❸❶❸

394 Garratt Ln, SW18 8946 8811 10–2B

34 Durham Rd, SW20 8947 1081 10–2B

"Deservedly always busy", these Earlsfield and Raynes Park Koreans offer "above-average" dishes ("including an at-table BBQ"), and at "reasonable prices" too; BYO. / www.cahchi.com; SW20 11 pm; SW18 11 pm, Sat & Sun 11.30 pm; SW20 closed Mon; cash only.

Cambio de Tercio SW5 £58 ❷❷❷
163 Old Brompton Rd 7244 8970 5–2B
"As Spanish as Spanish can be", this "cracking" Earl's Court all-rounder continues to wow reporters with its "evolved" cuisine, "incredible wine" and "authentic" style – if anything, "it seems to have gone up a notch after the recent refurbishment". / SW5 0LJ; www.cambiodetercio.co.uk; 11.15 pm, Sun 11 pm.

Camino N1 £44 ④④❸
3 Varnishers Yd, Regent Quarter 7841 7331 8–3C
Differing views on this "jumping" tapas bar, near King's Cross; most reporters find it a "reasonably authentic" place with a "good list of wine and sherries" – critics, though, fear "its popularity has been its downfall". / N1 9FD; www.camino.uk.com; 11 pm; closed Sun D; SRA-70%.

Cannizaro House SW19 £60 ④④❷
West Side, Wimbledon Common 8879 1464 10–2A
"Delightfully-located", by Wimbledon Common, a country house hotel where the afternoon tea is "the best in the area"; the dining experience, however, is "not as special". / SW19 4UE; www.cannizarohouse.com; 9.30 pm.

Canonbury Kitchen N1 £50 ④❸④
19 Canonbury Ln 7226 9791 8–2D
Overseen by its "kindly" proprietor, the former Cantina Italia (RIP) now trades as a thoroughly British bistro; it perhaps lacks the authentic spark of its predecessor, and "standards can be variable", but it generally pleases. / N1 2AS; www.canonburykitchen.com; 11 pm; closed Mon-Fri L & Sun D; no Amex.

Canta Napoli £36 ❸❸④
9 Devonshire Rd, W4 8994 5225 7–2A
136 High St, TW11 8977 3344 1–4A
"Incredible Neapolitan pizza" and other "excellent" dishes, win high praise for these "bright", "cheerful" and "incredibly friendly" Italians, in Chiswick and Teddington. / 10.30 pm; no Amex.

Canteen £41 ⑤⑤⑤
55 Baker St, W1 0845 686 1122 2–1A
21 Wellington St, WC2 7836 8368 4–3D NEW
Royal Festival Hall, SE1 0845 686 1122 2–3D
Park Pavilion, 40 Canada Sq, E14 0845 686 1122 11–1C
Crispin Pl, Old Spitalf'ds Mkt, E1 0845 686 1122 12–2B
These stark cafés "live up to their name more than perhaps they intend" – on a bad day, the "uninteresting" menu can represent "British catering at its embarrassing worst", and with service that's "distant and/or invisible" too. / www.canteen.co.uk; 11 pm, E14 & W1 Sun 7 pm; no booking weekend L.

Cantina del Ponte SE1 £46 ⑤⑤④
Butler's Wharf Building, 36c Shad Thames 7403 5403 9–4D
"You really go for the view", to this D&D Group Italian restaurant, near Tower Bridge – given the perennially "mediocre" cooking and the "terrible" service, that's probably just as well! / SE1 2YE; www.cantina.co.uk; 11 pm, Sun 10 pm; SRA-62%.

Cantina Laredo WC2 £46 ④❸⑤
10 Upper St Martin's Ln 7420 0630 4–3B
If you can endure the remarkably "corporate" atmosphere, this Covent Garden Mexican (an outpost of a US chain) can impress with its "top-quality margaritas" and great guacamole made at the table ("a thrill for the kids"); critics, though, find the whole show "unconvincing". / WC2H 9FB; www.cantinalaredo.co.uk; 11.30 pm, Sat midnight, Sun 10.30 pm.

Cantina Vinopolis
Vinopolis SE1 £55 ④④④
1 Bank End 7940 8333 9–3C
"One of London's top wine lists" is, as you'd hope, the big draw to the café of this South Bank oenological museum; given its superb setting in railway arches, however, its otherwise iffy performance can make it seem "a waste of a great space". / SE1 9BU; www.cantinavinopolis.com; 10 pm; closed Mon L, Tue L, Wed L & Sun.

Cantinetta SW15 £47 ④④④
162-164 Lower Richmond Rd 8780 3131 10–1A
Putney's former Phoenix restaurant (ownership unchanged) continues to attract few and notably mixed reviews – it does have fans, who find it a "very authentic" modern Italian, but also critics who think the food surprisingly "poor". / SW15 1LY; www.cantinetta.co.uk; 10.30 pm, Fri-Sat 11 pm; closed Mon D & Sun D.

Canton Arms SW8 £40 ❷❷❷
177 South Lambeth Rd 7582 8710 10–1D
"Utterly brilliant", "hearty" dishes "with a twist" – "the sensational sharing plates are the way to go" – has made this "sociable" Stockwell boozer quite a phenomenon… and "unlike its Anchor & Hope sibling, you can book too". / SW8 1XP; www.cantonarms.com; 10 pm; closed Mon L & Sun D; no Amex; no booking.

Cape Town Fish Market W1 £49 ❸❸④
5 & 6 Argyll St 7437 1143 3–1C
By the Palladium, a "busy" outpost of a South African-backed concept, majoring in seafood and sushi; it looks very much a chain outlet, and reports are few – they all suggest, however, that the fish, in particular, is surprisingly good; "excellent-value" pre-theatre. / W1F 7TE; www.ctfm.com; 10.45 pm; set pre theatre £30 (FP).

Capote Y Toros SW5 £43 ④④❸
157 Old Brompton Rd 7373 0567 5–2B
"Fabulous tapas" inspire fans of this "fun and buzzing" year-old offshoot from Cambio de Tercio (nearby); results can be "a bit hit 'n' miss" though, and "it's surprising how quickly a few tapas and glasses of sherry add up to a substantial bill…" / SW5 0LJ; www.cambiodetercio.co.uk; 11.15 pm; D only, closed Mon & Sun.

LE CAPRICE SW1 £70 ❸❶❷
Arlington Hs, Arlington St 7629 2239 3–4C
"Newly refurbished, but still retaining its old charm", this "effortlessly stylish" '80s-minimalist brasserie, behind the Ritz, is "still the best" – "utterly reliable, impeccable, graceful, romantic"… and, for its huge fan club, "just right". / SW1A 1RJ; www.le-caprice.co.uk; midnight, Sun 11 pm; set pre theatre £46 (FP).

Caraffini SW1 £49 ❸❶❷
61-63 Lower Sloane St 7259 0235 5–2D
"Consistent standards" and "sensible" prices make this long-established trattoria, near Sloane Square, an "old favourite" for more mature locals; it's "always full". / SW1W 8DH; www.caraffini.co.uk; 11.30 pm; closed Sun.

FSA

Caravaggio EC3 **£55** ④④⑤
107-112 Leadenhall St 7626 6206 9–2D
A grand but perhaps now rather "faded" Italian, which continues to pack 'em in, though it has always inspired mixed feedback – "it's been seriously overpriced for over a decade", says one reporter, "but still popular, thanks to its prime City location". / EC3A 4DP; www.etruscarestaurants.com; 10 pm; closed Sat & Sun.

Caravan **£44** ❸❸❸
1 Granary Sq, N1 7101 7661 8–3C NEW
11-13 Exmouth Mkt, EC1 7833 8115 9–1A
"Absolutely lip-smacking brunch" is the star turn at this "funky" Antipodean café, in Clerkenwell, whose "divine" coffee is quite a hit too; it makes a "buzzy" and "friendly" hang-out at any time, though, thanks to its "intriguing", "World-fusion" tapas; an offshoot opens in King's Cross as this guide goes to press. / www.caravanonexmouth.co.uk; EC1 10.30 pm, Sun 4 pm; EC1 Sun D.

Carluccio's **£40** ⑤④④
Branches throughout London
"Not the foodie haven the design implies", this "bright and hard-edged" faux-Italian chain, never brilliant, has suffered "a real fall-off in standards" of late – complaints about "shocking" meals, with "pretend" food and "indifferent" service, are louder than ever. / www.carluccios.com; most branches 11 pm, Sun 10.30 pm; no booking weekday L; set weekday L £24 (FP); SRA-51%.

Carob Tree NW5 **£31** ❸❷❸
15 Highgate Rd 7267 9880 8–1B
A "very friendly" family-run Greek, in Dartmouth Park; choose the "mix, match and share" dishes, and it makes a "cheerful" and quite "cheap" destination – the (speciality) grilled fish can be "superb" too, but is relatively "pricey". / NW5 1QX; 10.30 pm, Sun 9 pm; closed Mon; no Amex.

The Carpenter's Arms W6 **£46** ❸④❸
91 Black Lion Ln 8741 8386 7–2B
A tucked-away Hammersmith pub, which pleases all who comment with its overall charm (including a cute garden), and food that's always "reliable". / W6 9BG; 10 pm, Sun 9 pm.

Carvosso's W4 **£46** ⑤④❸
210 Chiswick High Rd 8995 9121 7–2A
"A sunny courtyard" is a big plus of this rambling spot, in Chiswick's former police station; "it has a great atmosphere, but the food's not always good". / W4 1PD; www.carvossosat210.co.uk; 11 pm; set weekday L & pre-theatre £29 (FP).

Casa Batavia W8 NEW **£51** ④❷❸
135 Kensington Church St 7221 7348 6–2B
"An unknown gem" is proclaimed by fans of this ambitious new Kensington Italian, who praise its "wonderful" dishes – critics admit there's "much potential and enthusiasm", but can find the food "too busy". / W8 7LP; www.casabatavia.com; set weekday L £25 (FP).

Casa Brindisa SW7 **£40** ④④④
7-9 Exhibition Rd 7590 0008 5–2C
Part of the Tapas Brindisas empire, this "busy" and "bustling" spot, near South Kensington tube, has struck critics as a bit "tired" and "subdued" of late; fans, though, insist the food is still "superior". / SW7 2HQ; www.casabrindisa.com; 10.45 pm, Sun 9.45 pm.

Casa Malevo W2 £47 ④❸❸
23 Connaught St 7402 1988 6–1D
This "cosy" Argentinian yearling is proving "a useful addition to Bayswater's Connaught Village", thanks to its "simple and authentic menu" of "quality steaks and interesting sauces"; critics, though, are resolute that standards are just "average". / W2 2AY; www.casamalevo.com; 10.30 pm.

Cassis Bistro SW3 £66 ⑤④④
232-236 Brompton Rd 7581 1101 5–2C
Even by Knightsbridge standards, bills at Marlon Abela's pretentiously "beige" bistro yearling strike many reporters as "absurd" – "why go here when you can go to Racine?"; perhaps the recent arrival, from Apsleys, of Massimiliano Blasone can buck things up… / SW3 2BB; 10.30 pm.

Le Cassoulet CR2 £45 ❸④④
18 Selsdon Rd 8633 1818 10–2D
"Classy" Gallic cooking has made Malcolm John's "genuine" city-centre bistro something of an oasis, down Croydon way; its ratings have come off their former highs however – "it can seem expensive, unless you're on an offer". / CR2 6PA; www.lecassoulet.co.uk; 10.30 pm, Sat 11 pm, Sun 10 pm.

Cattle Grid £43 ❷④④
76 Northcote Rd, SW11 7228 4188 10–2C
1 Balham Station Rd, SW12 8673 9099 10–2C
"An excellent range of steaks, ribs and burgers" wins a consistent thumbs-up for this mini-chain's "small and closely-packed" branches. / www.cattlegridrestaurant.com; 10 pm, Fri & Sat 10.30 pm; no Amex.

Cây Tre £38 ❸④④
42-43 Dean St, W1 7317 9118 4–2A
301 Old St, EC1 7729 8662 12–1B
A tiny and "cramped" Vietnamese Shoreditch café, offering fragrant dishes with "amazing" flavours; it is "far superior" to its "sanitised" Soho spin-off. / www.vietnamesekitchen.co.uk; 11 pm, Fri-Sat 11.30 pm, Sun 10.30 pm; no Amex.

Cecconi's W1 £68 ❸❷❶
5a Burlington Gdns 7434 1500 3–3C
"The see-and-be-seen locale for the hedge fund set", this Mayfair Italian has an "amazing buzz" all day long; apart from breakfast, though, the food is ordinary – this is "a fairly average trattoria masquerading as something more impressive". / W1S 3EP; www.cecconis.co.uk; 11.30 pm, Sun 10.30 pm.

Cellar Gascon EC1 £35 ❸④❷
59 West Smithfield Rd 7600 7561 9–2B
"Fantastic" SW France wines and "always-interesting" tapas-y fare ("the cheese is never less than great") drive enthusiasm for this "quiet but pleasant" Farringdon wine bar – an offshoot of nearby Club Gascon; "unbeatable set lunch" too. / EC1A 9DS; www.cellargascon.com; midnight; closed Sat & Sun.

Le Cercle SW1 £54 ❷❷❸
1 Wilbraham Pl 7901 9999 5–2D
"Be sure to get one of the curtained-off booths", if you visit this "moody" Gallic charmer, "hidden-away" in a surprisingly romantic "dungeon", near Sloane Square; most reports on the "tapas-style cuisine" are of "true gastronomy", but even fans have noted the odd 'wobble' in recent times. / SW1X 9AE; www.lecercle.co.uk; 10.45 pm; closed Mon & Sun.

FSA

Ceviche W1 NEW £44 ④❸❸
17 Frith St 7292 2040 4–2A
"The freshest" dishes, "full of zingy flavours", have – say fans – helped make this "jolly" Soho Peruvian an instant hit (and the "good pisco sours" help too); critics, though, can find the food "same-y", or "not particularly good value". / W1D 4RG; www.cevicheuk.com; 11.30 pm, Sun 10.15 pm.

Cha Cha Moon W1 £32 ④④❸
15-21 Ganton St 7297 9800 3–2D
It never lived up to the launch hype, but this highly-styled, if "elbow-knockingly cramped", Chinese noodle-canteen, off Carnaby Street, is still tipped by most reporters as a "quick, cheap eat", and "fuss-free" too. / W1F 9BN; www.chachamoon.com; 10.30 pm, Fri & Sat 11.20 pm, Sun 10.20 pm.

Chabrot Bistrot d'Amis SW1 £54 ❸❷④
9 Knightsbridge Grn 7225 2238 5–1D
Hidden-away in the shadow of Knightsbridge's 'Candy Towers', a "welcoming" little "gem" for those in search of a "quintessentially French" experience; its "hearty" dishes range from "simple" to "intriguing", and they are consistently realised to a "good standard". / SW1X 7QL; www.chabrot.co.uk; 11 pm, Sun 10 pm.

Chakra W11 NEW £65 ❸④④
157-159 Notting Hill Gate 7229 2115 6–2B
"A triumph" or "a joke"? – most reports do agree that the "very high-end cooking" at this "nightclubby" new Notting Hill Indian (from the former chef of Vama, RIP) is "delicious", but there is also quite a lot of flak for "ridiculously tiny" portions, "wince-making" prices, and "random" service. / W11 3LF; www.chakralondon.com; 11 pm, Sun 10.30 pm; set weekday L £39 (FP).

Chamberlain's EC3 £62 ❸❸❸
23-25 Leadenhall Mkt 7648 8690 9–2D
The long-established fish restaurant, at the heart of Leadenhall Market, undoubtedly makes "a good location for a City lunch"; even fans can find it "pricey", though, and critics note that portions are "small". / EC3V 1LR; www.chamberlains.org; 9.15 pm; closed Sat & Sun.

Chamomile NW3 £27 ❸❷❸
45 England's Ln 7586 4580 8–2B
"Service comes with a smile", at this "cosy" and "relaxed" all-day café, in Belsize Park – a "rare independent", serving "top breakfasts" and "wonderful home-made cakes" too. / NW3 4YD; 5.45 pm; L only; no Amex.

Champor-Champor SE1 £48 ❸❸❷
62 Weston St 7403 4600 9–4C
"Tucked out-of-the-way, near London Bridge", this "imaginative" gem has long been a haven of "quirky, boudoir-esqe" style and "excitingly different" SE Asian food; with a change of regime, however, the cuisine is now "mainly Thai" – "not bad, but it's lost its magic". / SE1 3QJ; www.champor-champor.com; 10 pm; D only, closed Sun.

The Chancery EC4 £51 ❷❷④
9 Cursitor St 7831 4000 9–2A
"A little oasis in the barren Midtown landscape"; this "nicely understated" venture is "always packed" – for its (largely legal) following, its "subtle" and "beautifully presented" cuisine and "efficient" service make it "a perfect business lunch venue". / EC4A 1LL; www.thechancery.co.uk; 10.30 pm; closed Sat L & Sun.

Chapters SE3 £47 ④④④

43-45 Montpelier Vale 8333 2666 1–4D

A Blackheath brasserie, right by the common, that's hailed as "reliable local", and a particularly popular destination for a "perfect breakfast"; overall, it's "coasting", though, and the cooking is sometimes notably "ho-hum". / SE3 0TJ; www.chaptersrestaurants.com; 11 pm, Sun 9 pm.

Le Chardon £46 ④④❸

65 Lordship Ln, SE22 8299 1921 1–4D

32 Abbeville Rd, SW4 8673 9300 10–2D

"The old butcher's-shop decor adds to the ambience" of the East Dulwich original branch of this south London bistro duo, praised for its "high-quality, if simple, French fare"; the Clapham offshoot attracts similar – but slightly less enthusiastic – feedback. / www.lechardon.co.uk; 11 pm.

Charles Lamb N1 £40 ❸❷❶

16 Elia St 7837 5040 8–3D

A marvellous "traditional" Islington boozer, where only one detail is out-of-kilter: the "lovely" staff are "authentically French"! – they create a brilliant atmosphere, and serve up "excellent real ale" and a "good wine list", plus "competent, if sometimes oddball, cuisine". / N1 8DE; www.thecharleslambpub.com; 9.30 pm; closed Mon L, Tue L & Sun D; no booking.

Charlotte's Bistro W4 £50 ❸❸❸

6 Turnham Green Ter 8742 3590 7–2A

"Easy-going and laid-back", this Chiswick hang-out won more praise this year; critics still cite "average" results or "erratic" service, but approval of its "excellent modern cooking", "cheerful" approach and "atmospheric bar" is on the rise. / W4 1QP; www.charlottes.co.uk; 10.30 pm, Sun 9 pm; SRA-56%.

Charlotte's Place W5 £48 ❸❷❸

16 St Matthew's Rd 8567 7541 1–3A

A "dependable bistro, overlooking Ealing Common"; its local fan club proclaims "a gem", with "above-average" cooking and "well-judged" service too. / W5 3JT; www.charlottes.co.uk; 10.30 pm, Fri & Sat 11 pm, Sun 9 pm; SRA-56%.

Chella W4 £39 ❸④❸

142 Chiswick High Rd 8994 6816 7–2A

"Interesting" dishes and "reasonable" prices have won a dedicated Chiswick following for this "low-lit" Iranian; ratings awarded, though, tend to indicate satisfaction rather than excitement. / W4 1PU; www.chella-restaurant.co.uk; 11 pm; no Amex.

The Chelsea Brasserie
Sloane Square Hotel SW1 £54 ④④④

7-12 Sloane Sq 7881 5999 5–2D

"Nothing to complain about, but nothing to rave about either" – this hotel brasserie at the centre of the Sloane world makes a very "convenient" rendezvous before the Royal Court/Cadogan Hall, for shoppers or for business. / SW1W 8EG; www.chelsea-brasserie.co.uk; 10.30 pm; no Amex.

Chelsea Bun Diner SW10 £26 ❸④❸

9a Lamont Rd 7352 3635 5–3B

"The longest breakfast menu in London" greets diners at this "noisy" and "fun" World's End greasy spoon, and many reports confirm that its "huge" portions offer "good value" too; to watch the world go by, sit upstairs. / SW10 0HP; www.chelseabun.co.uk; 6 pm; L only; no Amex; no booking, Sat & Sun.

FSA

The Chelsea Kitchen SW10 £28 ④❸❸
451 Fulham Rd 3055 0088 5–3B
"Cheap, for Chelsea"; this ancient, no-nonsense canteen still undercuts most rivals price-wise, even in its smarter new dining room – a pub-conversion at the 'wrong' end of the Royal Borough. / SW10 9UZ; www.chelseakitchen.com; 11.30 pm, Sun 11 pm.

The Chelsea Ram SW10 £39 ❸❸❷
32 Burnaby St 7351 4008 5–4B
Recently re-opened as a Geronimo inn, this smart but "chilled" boozer, at the far end of Chelsea, offers "a good all-round experience", with "delicious" burgers a highlight. / SW10 0PL; www.chelsearam.com; 10 pm; no Amex.

Chettinad W1 NEW £25 ❷❷④
16 Percy St 3556 1229 2–1C
"A welcome addition to central London's Indian choices"; this Fitzrovia newcomer (on the former site of Camerino, RIP) offers veggie cooking where "the different dishes really do taste different"; the set lunch is "a steal". / W1T 1DT; www.chettinadrestaurant.com; set weekday L £17 (FP).

Cheyne Walk Brasserie SW3 £68 ④④❸
50 Cheyne Walk 7376 8787 5–3C
In a "lovely" Chelsea location (with nice Thames-views from the upstairs bar), an attractively-converted pub, whose "light-flooded" dining room is "dominated by an aromatic, wood-fired grill"; sadly, though, the Gallic cuisine is "nothing special", and "horrendously expensive" too. / SW3 5LR; www.cheynewalkbrasserie.com; 10.30 pm; closed Mon L.

CHEZ BRUCE SW17 £68 ❶❶❷
2 Bellevue Rd 8672 0114 10–2C
"The consistent excellence never ceases to amaze", say fans of Bruce Poole's Wandsworth Common-side legend – the Survey's favourite for the 8th year; the cooking is executed "with skill and passion", the wine's "terrific", and staff are "genuinely caring"; post-expansion, the interior is "better, and less crowded" too. / SW17 7EG; www.chezbruce.co.uk; 10 pm, Fri & Sat 10.30 pm, Sun 9.30 pm.

Chez Liline N4 £40 ❶❸⑤
101 Stroud Green Rd 7263 6550 8–1D
Thanks to its "unusual" and "very fresh" fish dishes – with "sensational Mauritian flavours and spicing" – Sylvain Hong's Finsbury Park stalwart is "well worth the journey", even if the ambience is "quietly morbid"; top tip for parties of 4+ – "the all-in menu, which just keeps coming". / N4 3PX; www.chezliline.co.uk; 10.30 pm; closed Mon.

Chez Marcelle W14 £32 ❶⑤⑤
34 Blythe Rd 7603 3241 7–1D
A "hidden gem" of a café, in a backstreet behind Olympia, where "the indefatigable Marcelle" dishes up "superb" Lebanese nosh at "incredibly cheap" prices; "don't go in a hurry", though – the waits are "monstrous". / W14 0HA; 10 pm; closed Mon, Tue-Thu D only, Fri-Sun open L & D; no credit cards.

Chez Patrick W8 £46 ❸❷❸
7 Stratford Rd 7937 6388 5–2A
Genial patron Patrick's "idiosyncratic Gallic style" is the lifeblood of this "cosy" neighbourhood spot, in a "charming corner of Kensington", which is liked by an (older) fan club for its "reliable" and straightforward seafood-centric cuisine. / W8 6RF; www.chez-patrick.co.uk; 10.45 pm; closed Sun D; set weekday L £25 (FP).

Chicken Shop NW5 NEW
79 Highgate Rd awaiting tel 8–1B
Around press time, the trendy Soho House group is set to open this Americana-themed joint, in ever-trendier Kentish Town; on the menu – chicken, chicken or chicken. / NW5 1TL.

Chilango £15 ❷❷❸
76 Chancery Ln, WC2 7430 1231 2–1D
27 Upper St, N1 7704 2123 8–3D
142 Fleet St, EC4 7353 6761 9–2A
"Belt-straining burritos", "zesty salsas", "efficient" service and "fun" styling – these "funky Mexican stand-bys" get a major thumbs-up from reporters. / www.chilango.co.uk; EC4 9 pm; N1 10 pm, Fri & Sat midnight; EC4 closed Sat & Sun; no booking.

Chilli Cool WC1 £29 ❷⑤⑤
15 Leigh St 7383 3135 2–1D
"Wonderful, zingy, mouth-tingling spices" and "lots of lovely offal" – hallmarks of the "cheap and super-hot" Sichuan fare on offer at this "terrific-value" Bloomsbury café. / WC1H 9EW; www.chillicool.com; 10.15 pm.

China Tang
Dorchester Hotel W1 £77 ④④❸
53 Park Ln 7629 9988 3–3A
David Tang's "OTT-opulent" Mayfair basement oriental was rated a little higher than usual this year (and the Peking Duck is a "real tour de force") – critics, though, still find it not only "seriously overpriced" but "very average" too. / W1K 1QA; www.thedorchesterhotel.com; 11.30 pm; set weekday L £47 (FP).

Chinese Cricket Club EC4 £45 ❸❷⑤
19 New Bridge St 7438 8051 9–3A
A "handy venue for business-lunching", in the thin area around Blackfriars – it's an admittedly "soulless" hotel dining room, but offers above-average Chinese cooking and "friendly and efficient" service. / EC4V 6DB; www.chinesecricketclub.com; 10 pm; closed Sun; no Amex.

Chipotle £19 ❸❷⑤
101-103 Baker St, W1 7935 9881 2–1A NEW
181-185 Wardour St, W1 7494 4156 3–1D NEW
114-116 Charing Cross Rd, WC2 7836 8491 4–1A
92-93 St Martin's Ln, WC2 awaiting tel 4–4B NEW
Surprisingly little survey feedback on the London outlets of a Mexican chain that's big news in the US, especially as "ingredients taste fresh", and "portions are generous". / www.chipotle.com.

Chisou £50 ❷❷④
4 Princes St, W1 7629 3931 3–1C
31 Beauchamp Pl, SW3 3155 0005 5–2D
1-4 Barley Mow Pas, W4 8994 3636 7–2A NEW
"Fantastic sushi" and "incredible sakes" are hallmarks of the Mayfair original branch of this "true Japanese", and there is also upbeat, if limited, feedback on the Knightsbridge offshoot;
the newest member of the group is a welcome arrival amongst the chains of Chiswick. / www.chisourestaurant.com; Mon-Sat 10.30 pm, Sun 9.30 pm.

Chiswell Street Dining Rooms EC1 **£60** ④④④
56 Chiswell St 7614 0177 12–2A
The Martin brothers' "noisy" City yearling – a "comfy" pub-conversion – is doing good trade, but inspires decidedly middle-of-the-road feedback; it's "a buzzy, midweek place" and "competent for a business lunch", but the food's a tad "boring" and the ambience "quite pedestrian". / EC1Y 4SA; 11 pm; closed Sat & Sun.

Cho-San SW15 **£41** ❷❷❸
292 Upper Richmond Rd 8788 9626 10–2A
"A slice of real provincial Japan, in a row of shops in Putney" – this authentically "tatty" family-run veteran has a dedicated fan club, who appreciate its "genuine welcome" and "very authentic" cooking – "from nabe to tempura, from soba to yakitori". / SW15 6TH; 10.30 pm; closed Mon.

Chor Bizarre W1 **£55** ❷❸❷
16 Albemarle St 7629 9802 3–3C
Oddly little reported-on, this "stylish and eclectically-decorated" Mayfair Indian is worth seeking out for its "rich", "hot" and "varied" cooking, and a "very interesting" interior too. / W1S 4HW; www.chorbizarre.com; 11.30 pm, Sun 10.30 pm.

Chowki W1 **£36** ❸❸④
2-3 Denman St 7439 1330 3–2D
Looking for a good cheap eat two minutes from Piccadilly Circus? – this "affordable" and "authentic" Indian may well fit the bill; the lunch menu (served till 5pm) is a particular steal. / W1D 7HA; www.chowki.com; 11.30 pm, Sun 10.30 pm; set weekday L £20 (FP), set pre-theatre £21 (FP).

Choys SW3 **£39** ④❷❸
172 King's Rd 7352 9085 5–3C
A Chelsea Chinese that hasn't changed much in 40 years – a "pleasant neighbourhood spot", it offers "reliable, if undemanding, food" and "assured" service. / SW3 4UP; 11 pm.

Christopher's WC2 **£61** ④❸❷
18 Wellington St 7240 4222 4–3D
This grand but "lively" surf 'n' turf American, in a beautiful Covent Garden townhouse, seems to have had a "new lease of life" in recent times; it's still most often recommended as a place for business, brunch, or pre-theatre, but it was consistently much better rated this year. / WC2E 7DD; www.christophersgrill.com; 10.45 pm, Sun 9.15 pm; booking: max 14.

Chrysan EC2 NEW
Snowden St awaiting tel 12–2B
From the same backers as Hakkasan, this ambitious City-fringe Japanese newcomer opens in late-2012, a top chef from Kyoto at the helm. / EC2A 2DQ.

Chuen Cheng Ku W1 **£35** ❸④④
17 Wardour St 7437 1398 4–3A
"You start eating pretty much the second you sit down", when you take weekend dim sum from the trolleys which criss-cross the dining rooms of this "bustling" Chinatown institution – highly recommended for big family groups"; visits at other times are less fun. / W1D 6DJ; www.chuenchengku.co.uk; 11.45 pm.

Churchill Arms W8 £26 ❷❸❶
119 Kensington Church St 7792 1246 6–2B
Behind a "quaint" pub, off Notting Hill Gate, this "rammed" conservatory ("with more pot plants than the Chelsea Flower Show") has long been a major hit, thanks to its basic but "fabulous" Thai scoff at bargain-basement prices. / W8 7LN; 10 pm, 9.30 pm.

Chutney SW18 £32 ❸❸❸
11 Alma Rd 8870 4588 10–2B
The style is "fairly typical", but this Wandsworth spot attracts much praise for its "great curries" and attractive deals – it's "often full". / SW18 1AA; www.chutneyrestaurant.co.uk; 11.30 pm; D only.

Chutney Mary SW10 £55 ❷❷❷
535 King's Rd 7351 3113 5–4B
"Incredibly subtle blends of spices" contribute to the "real originality" of the cuisine of this distant-Chelsea Indian "classic" – a "very professional" operation whose "calm and relaxed" ambience is "best enjoyed in the conservatory". / SW10 0SZ; www.realindianfood.com; 11.45 pm, Sun 10.45 pm; closed weekday L; booking: max 8.

Chutneys NW1 £32 ❸④④
124 Drummond St 7388 0604 8–4C
"Basic" but "always consistent", this veggie Indian, by Euston, remains a handy "cheap 'n' cheerful" option – it's "very busy" at lunch, as "the buffet takes some beating". / NW1 2PA; www.chutneyseuston.co.uk; 11 pm; no Amex; need 5+ to book.

Ciao Bella WC1 £42 ④❸❸
86-90 Lamb's Conduit St 7242 4119 2–1D
"Endearingly old-school", this "rammed" Bloomsbury Italian still pulls in a big following, thanks to its "cheery" buzz; the scoff is "nothing special", but "cheap" – "ideally, stick to the pizza menu". / WC1N 3LZ; www.ciaobellarestaurant.co.uk; 11.30 pm, Sun 10.30 pm.

Cibo W14 £50 ❷❷❸
3 Russell Gdns 7371 6271 7–1D
Perhaps because it's "a bit out-of-the-way", this "slightly '80s" "gem" of an Olympia Italian isn't widely-known nowadays; thanks to its "fresh" and quite "reasonably-priced" cuisine, though, it's still "going strong". / W14 8EZ; www.ciborestaurant.net; 11 pm; closed Sat L & Sun D.

Cicada EC1 £46 ❸❸❸
132-136 St John St 7608 1550 9–1B
"No prizes for romance, but there's good fun and a great buzz", at this "noisy" Clerkenwell haunt, which still hits the spot with its "tasty" pan-Asian tapas; top tip – "divine" ice creams. / EC1V 4JT; www.rickerrestaurants.com; 11 pm; closed Sat L & Sun.

Cigala WC1 £49 ❸④④
54 Lamb's Conduit St 7405 1717 2–1D
A "lively" Spanish venture, on a "quiet" and "increasingly upmarket" Bloomsbury street; standards are a bit "erratic", but "on a good day, the cooking is authentic and enjoyable". / WC1N 3LW; www.cigala.co.uk; 10.45 pm, Sun 9.30 pm.

Le Cigalon WC2 £53 ❷❷❷
115 Chancery Ln 7242 8373 2–2D
An offshoot of Club Gascon, in the heart of legal London, where "bright and fresh" Provençale décor and "genial" service come together to create "a bit of an oasis"; the cuisine is very "competent", and "reasonably-priced" too. / WC2A 1PP; www.cigalon.co.uk/; 10 pm; closed Sat & Sun.

F S A

THE CINNAMON CLUB SW1 £67 ❷❷❷
Old Westminster Library, Great Smith St 7222 2555 2–4C
"Such an amazing twist on curry!" – London's best Indian all-rounder, in a "magnificent" former library by Westminster Abbey, stays at the top of its game, offering its "magical" and "distinctive" cuisine "with flair"; it's "a good place to spot MPs" too… / SW1P 3BU; www.cinnamonclub.com; 10.45 pm; closed Sun; no trainers; set weekday L & pre-theatre £42 (FP); SRA-65%.

Cinnamon Kitchen EC2 £59 ❷❸❸
9 Devonshire Sq 7626 5000 9–2D
The Cinnamon Club's stylish City spin-off delivers a "modern twist on traditional Indian cooking" which leads fans on "an incredible taste-journey"; perhaps inevitably, though, the atmosphere is a mite "corporate", and service can sometimes be "rude" too. / EC2M 4WY; www.cinnamon-kitchen.com; 11 pm; closed Sat L & Sun; SRA-61%.

Cinnamon Soho W1 NEW £43 ❷❷❸
5 Kingly St 7437 1664 3–2D
"Interesting" Indian dishes "with a British twist", and "helpful" service too, make this casual Soho newcomer a worthy 'budget' addition to the Cinnamon Club group. / W1B 5PE; www.cinnamon-kitchen.com/soho-home; 11 pm, Sun 4.30 pm; closed Sun D.

Circus WC2 £61 ④❸❶
27-29 Endell St 7420 9300 4–2C
"Fabulous fun" – this before-your-very-eyes cabaret/restaurant, in Covent Garden, is definitely "somewhere different"; it's hardly a foodie destination, but the food could be much worse. / WC2H 9BA; www.circus-london.co.uk; midnight, Fri-Sat 2 am; closed Sun; no Amex.

City Càphê EC2 £14 ❷❸⑤
17 Ironmonger St no tel 9–2C
"Queues snake daily", outside this tiny Vietnamese joint, on a City side street – "no wonder", given the total deliciousness of its "authentic and tasty" baguettes (báhn mi), soups and spring rolls. / EC2V 8EY; www.citycaphe.com; 3 pm; L only, closed Sat & Sun.

City Miyama EC4 £51 ❸④⑤
17 Godliman St 7489 1937 9–3B
The setting is "drab" and the service "functional", but this "genuine" City basement Japanese "never fails to impress at the sushi bar". / EC4 5BD; www.miyama.co.uk; 9.30 pm; closed Sat & Sun; set weekday L £33 (FP).

Clarke's W8 £67 ❸❷❷
124 Kensington Church St 7221 9225 6–2B
"Charming" service, "elegant" décor and Californian-inspired cuisine that's "full of interest" – fans still find much to like at Sally Clarke's "intimate" Kensington stalwart; even they, though, may wonder if the style "smacks of yesteryear"; avoid the basement. / W8 4BH; www.sallyclarke.com; 10 pm; closed Sun D; booking: max 14.

Clifton E1 £26 ❷❸④
1 Whitechapel Rd 7377 5533 9–2D
A Brick Lane "classic", this "bustling" Indian justifies its "prime location" on the 'strip' – it offers an "excellent range" of dishes, at prices that are "a steal". / E1 6TY; www.cliftonbricklane.com; midnight.

The Clissold Arms N2 £49 ④❸❸
Fortis Grn 8444 4224 1–1C
This attractive Muswell Hill boozer (known for its associations with The Kinks) is still tipped by locals as a very "decent" stand-by, particularly on days you can use the garden; it's "slipped a bit in recent times", though. / N2 9HR; 10 pm, Sat 10.30 pm, Sun 9 pm.

F S A

CLOS MAGGIORE WC2 £60 ❷❶❶

33 King St 7379 9696 4–3C

"The man at the next table proposed!" – London's Romantic No. 1 (for the 2nd year) is an "enchanting" oasis "amidst the hustle of Covent Garden" – try to book in the "magical" conservatory; the cooking is "more than competent" too, although it's out-shone by the "stunning" wine list. / WC2E 8JD; www.closmaggiore.com; 11 pm, Sun 10 pm; set weekday L & pre-theatre £39 (FP).

Club Gascon EC1 £77 ❷❷❸

57 West Smithfield 7796 0600 9–2B

"Unbelievable combinations of flavours" (including "out-of-this-world" foie gras) and some "very interesting regional French wines" have made a big name for this City-fringe haven of "style and sophistication" – an early-days pioneer of the small-plate revolution. / EC1A 9DS; www.clubgascon.com; 10 pm, Fri-Sat 10.30 pm; closed Sat L & Sun; set weekday L £44 (FP).

Cocotte NW3 £45 ④❷④

85b Fleet Rd 7433 3317 8–2A

"Very good for food and value" – this Gallic bistro yearling, by South End Green, pleases locals "not because it's the all-round greatest place, but because it's friendly and genuine". / NW3 2QY; 11 pm; closed Mon, Tue L, Wed L, Thu L & Sun D.

Cocum SW20 £30 ❸❷❷

9 Approach Rd 8540 3250 10–2B

"Far superior to your average curry house"; this Raynes Park Keralan serves "reliable south Indian cooking of a high standard", and the staff are "attentive" and "cheerful" too. / SW20 8BA; www.cocumrestaurant.co.uk; 10.30 pm.

Colbeh W2 £26 ❷④④

6 Porchester Pl 7706 4888 6–1D

A "simple" and "authentic" spot, in Bayswater, offering not just "wonderful meat and typical Persian stews", but also "the best rice in London" to go with it. / W2 2BS; 11 pm.

Colbert SW1 NEW

51 Sloane Sq awaiting tel 5–2D

Sloane Rangers are besides themselves with excitement; can Corbin and King (the 'Wolseley boys') make a hit of their late-2012 re-launch of the former site of the unlamented Oriel (RIP)? – trips to Peter Jones could become such fun! / SW1W 8AX.

Colchis W2 NEW £55 ❷❸❸

39 Chepstow Pl 7221 7620 6–1B

In a former Bayswater boozer (the upstairs dining room of which is Assaggi), an interesting newcomer featuring "really tasty" Georgian specialities, plus some "amazing" Georgian wines. / W2 4TS; www.colchisrestaurant.co.uk; 11 pm, Sun 10 pm; closed Mon.

La Collina NW1 £52 ④④❸

17 Princess Rd 7483 0192 8–3B

"Eating in the garden in summer is quite lovely", say fans of this "hidden-away" Primrose Hill spot; its "unfussy" Piedmontese food can come as "a pleasant surprise" too, but there are also critics – particularly those who remember past standards – who find it "disappointing". / NW1 8JR; 10.30 pm; closed Mon L.

F S A

Le Colombier SW3 **£58** ❸❶❷
145 Dovehouse St 7351 1155 5–2C
"A perfect re-creation of a smaller Parisian brasserie", this Chelsea backstreet "treasure" is "always a pleasant experience" for those of a "traditional" bent, especially on the days when one of London's best terraces comes into play. / SW3 6LB; www.le-colombier-restaurant.co.uk; 10.30 pm, Sun 10 pm.

Como Lario SW1 **£47** ④⑤④
18-22 Holbein Pl 7730 2954 5–2D
"They just don't make 'em like this any more", say fans of this age-old trattoria, near Sloane Square; perhaps that's a good thing – critics complain of "appalling" service, and of "overpriced" food that's "resting on its laurels". / SW1W 8NL; www.comolario.co.uk; 11.30 pm, Sun 10 pm.

Comptoir Gascon EC1 **£44** ❸❸❷
63 Charterhouse St 7608 0851 9–1A
"Terrific duck-burgers" headline a "carnivore's delight" menu – which is twinned with "great wines from SW France" – at this "engaging" and "unpretentious" spin-off from Club Gascon; there seems to have been a "wobble" on the food front this year, but fans find this a "very pleasant" destination nonetheless. / EC1M 6HJ; www.comptoirgascon.com; 10 pm, Thu-Fri 11 pm; closed Mon & Sun.

Comptoir Libanais **£20** ④④❸
65 Wigmore St, W1 7935 1110 3–1A
Westfield, The Balcony, W12 8811 2222 7–1C
"Simple and good" cuisine, "friendly" service and a "buzzy" environment – that's the deal that, for most reporters, makes this Lebanese chain a reliable stand-by. / www.lecomptoir.co.uk; W12 9 pm, Thu & Fri 10 pm, Sun 6 pm; W1 9.30 pm; W12 closed Sun D; no Amex; no bookings.

Constancia SE1 **£45** ❷❷④
52 Tanner St 7234 0676 9–4D
"Just what you'd want in a neighbourhood steakhouse" – this Argentinian, south of Tower Bridge, serves "yummy" steaks, with "simple accompaniments", in "honest surroundings". / SE1 3PH; www.constancia.co.uk; 10.30 pm; D only; no Amex.

Il Convivio SW1 **£61** ❸❷④
143 Ebury St 7730 4099 2–4A
"Can't believe it isn't better-known", say fans of this "traditional" – and, many feel, "delightful" – Belgravia Italian; critics find it on the "expensive" side, though, and "lacking a certain je-ne-sais-quoi". / SW1W 9QN; www.etruscarestaurants.com; 10.45 pm; closed Sun.

Coopers Restaurant & Bar WC2 **£46** ❷❷④
49a Lincolns Inn Fields 7831 6211 2–2D
In an "unprepossessing" building, a "busy" but "very reliable" bistro, which "mostly caters to the local businesses" around Lincoln's Inn Fields – all reports praise its "tremendous value". / WC2A 3PF; www.coopers-restaurant.com; 11 pm; closed Sat & Sun.

Copita W1 NEW **£43** ❷④❷
27 D'Arblay St 7287 7797 3–1D
"Amazing" flavours, albeit on "tiny" plates – often at "less than a fiver a time" – make this "relaxed" Soho newcomer (from the team behind Barrica) "an excellent addition to the tapas scene"; "great wine list" too. / W1F 8EP; www.copita.co.uk; 10.30 pm; closed Sun.

F S A

Coq d'Argent EC2 £66 ④④❸

I Poultry 7395 5000 9–2C

The food is "adequate", prices "sky-high" and the interior "corporate-feeling"; thanks, however, to its "incredible" rooftop gardens and "stunning views of the City", this 6th-floor D&D Group venue is still commended as a top client-entertaining option, especially in summer. / EC2R 8EJ; www.coqdargent.co.uk; 9.45 pm; closed Sat L & Sun D; SRA-65%.

Cork & Bottle WC2 £43 ⑤④❷

44-46 Cranbourn St 7734 7807 4–3B

Seemingly "unchanged since about 1975", this "cramped" basement wine bar, by a Leicester Square tattoo parlour, remains "a lovely hide-away in the middle of the West End"; the "fantastic" wine list, however, is a much greater attraction than the "retro" scoff. / WC2H 7AN; www.corkandbottle.net; 11.30 pm, Sun 10.30 pm; no booking after 6.30 pm.

Corner Room E2 £44 ❶❷❷

Patriot Sq 7871 0461 1–2D

"Not as experimental as Viajante, and a lot more reasonably priced!" – Nuno Mendes's spin-off dining room serves a selection of "exciting" small plates – "for the money, some of the most creative cooking around"; no bookings, though – "arrive early to beat the queues". / E2 9NF; www.viajante.co.uk; 9 pm; Mon-Thu D only, Fri-Sun open L & D.

Corrigan's Mayfair W1 £82 ❸❸❸

28 Upper Grosvenor St 7499 9943 3–3A

Richard Corrigan's "inventive interpretations of the classics" wow fans of his "smart" and "well-spaced" Mayfair HQ; critics, though, say "he's resting on his laurels", and find the ambience too "business-y". / W1K 7EH; www.corrigansmayfair.com; 10.45 pm, Sun 9.30 pm; closed Sat L; booking: max 10; set weekday L £50 (FP).

Côte £40 ④❸④

124-126 Wardour St, W1 7287 9280 3–1D
17-21 Tavistock St, WC2 7379 9991 4–3D
45-47 Parsons Green Ln, SW6 7736 8444 10–1B
98 Westbourne Grove, W2 7792 3298 6–1B
50-54 Turnham Green Ter, W4 8747 6788 7–2A
47 Kensington Ct, W8 7938 4147 5–1A
Hays Galleria, Tooley St, SE1 7234 0800 9–4D
8 High St, SW19 8947 7100 10–2B
26 Ludgate Hill, EC4 7236 4399 9–2A

Richard Caring's "Café Rouge-style operation for the smart(er) set" is still "a cut above", and fans say these "bustling bistros" make "an ideal family venue"; as the chain dashes for growth, though, reporters' ambience ratings have crashed. / www.cote-restaurants.co.uk; 11 pm; set pre theatre £26 (FP).

Cotidie W1 NEW £75 ④⑤④

50 Marylebone High St 7258 9878 2–1A

"A welcome addition to Marylebone", say supporters of Roman chef Bruno Barbieri's ambitious relaunch of the former premises of Café Luc (RIP); "haughty" service is a problem, though, and critics (which include us) say: "there are many better Italians at these sort of prices". / W1U 5HN; www.cotidierestaurant.com; 11.30 pm, Sum 11 pm.

Cottons NW1 £42 ❸❸❶

55 Chalk Farm Rd 7485 8388 8–2B

"A fun Caribbean restaurant, near Camden Lock" – a "lovely little place", it offers "wonderful" cocktails… "and the food is good too". / NW1 8AN; www.cottons-restaurant.co.uk; 11 pm; closed weekday L; set always available £39 (FP).

The Courtauld Gallery Café
The Courtauld Gallery WC2 £30 ④❸❸
Somerset Hs, Strand 7848 2527 2–2D
On a sunny day, the (lower) courtyard al-freso tables at this handy café – located in grand quarters, just off the Strand – are some of the nicest in central London; expect no culinary fireworks, just "tasty snacks at sensible prices". / WC2R 0RN; L only; no Amex.

The Cow W2 £50 ❸④❶
89 Westbourne Park Rd 7221 0021 6–1B
"Very crowded" and "hectic" at peak times, Tom Conran's Irish-style Notting Hill boozer offers good 'craic' and "delicious" seafood; "the ground floor bar's nicer, but the food is better in the upstairs dining room". / W2 5QH; www.thecowlondon.co.uk; 10.30 pm, Sun 10 pm; no Amex.

Crazy Bear W1 £60 ④④❸
26-28 Whitfield St 7631 0088 2–1C
"Funky" and "glittery", this Fitzrovia pan-Asian incorporates a "cool, loungey basement bar", and makes a "fun" place for a party or romance; the food, though, has "gone downhill in recent years". / W1T 2RG; www.crazybeargroup.co.uk; 10.30 pm; closed Sat L & Sun; no shorts.

Criterion W1 £66 ④❸❶
224 Piccadilly 7930 0488 3–3D
"Leave the tacky environs of Eros behind, and enter a world of calm" – this neo-Byzantine chamber, right on Piccadilly Circus, is a "truly wonderful" interior; sadly, though, the food is no more than "OK". / W1J 6NP; www.criterionrestaurant.com; 11.30 pm, Sun 10.30 pm; set weekday L, pre-theatre & Sun L £41 (FP).

The Crooked Well SE5 £45 ❸❷❷
16 Grove Ln 7252 7798 1–3C
"A clever mix of stylish bar, friendly neighbourhood pub, and top-notch restaurant" – this Camberwell gastropub yearling is an "always-welcoming" spot, serving British fare that fans find both "classic" and "inventive"! / SE5 8SY; www.thecrookedwell.com; 10.30 pm; closed Mon L; no Amex.

Crussh £16 ❸❸④
Branches throughout London
"Super value-for-money soups, salads and curries" ("especially for veggies") and "great juices, freshly made" – all stand-out attractions of this small, health-conscious chain. / www.crussh.com; 4.30 pm-8 pm; many branches closed all or part of weekend; no credit cards in many branches.

Cumberland Arms W14 £43 ❷❸❸
29 North End Rd 7371 6806 7–2D
"A surprisingly good pub", in Olympia; "it's not in the most delightful location, but once you're in, you're very well looked after, the menu is excellent, and the ambience pleasingly unfancy". / W14 8SZ; www.thecumberlandarmspub.co.uk; 10 pm, Sun 9.30 pm.

Cut
45 Park Lane W1 £86 ④⑤⑤
45 Park Ln 7493 4545 3–4A
"How much?"; this "glitzy" Mayfair steakhouse (LA restaurateur Wolfgang Puck's first ex-US excursion) may offer some "superb" dishes, but reporters just can't get over the "hideous" prices (particularly of the "gratuitously marked-up" wine); it doesn't help that ambience in this "corridor-like" room is "non-existent". / W1K 1PN; www.45parklane.com; 10.45 pm.

F S A

Cyprus Mangal SW1 £31 ❷❸④
45 Warwick Way 7828 5940 2–4B
"Kebab heaven"; "queues of cabbies and coppers" often mark out this Pimlico charcoal-grill-house, which is a big hit with punters "from all walks of life"; it's all to do with the value it offers, which fans say is "extraordinary". / SW1V 1QS; 10.45 pm, Fri & Sat 11.45 pm.

Da Mario SW7 £42 ❸④❸
15 Gloucester Rd 7584 9078 5–1B
"A popular and bustling spot, convenient for a pre- or post-Albert Hall meal"; a "friendly" place offering "reliable pizzas and pasta dishes", it's "always good with kids" too. / SW7 4PP; www.damario.co.uk; 11.30 pm.

Da Mario WC2 £39 ❸❷❷
63 Endell St 7240 3632 4–1C
"Part of Covent Garden before any of the area's chichi boutiques" – this tiny family-run trattoria serves "honest" scoff in a warm, "welcoming" and "buzzy" setting. / WC2H 9AJ; www.da-mario.co.uk; 11.15 pm; closed Sun.

Dabbous W1 NEW £48 ❶❶❸
39 Whitfield St 7323 1544 2–1C
"For once, the extraordinary hype is justified!"; Ollie Dabbous's "industrial-style" debutant, in Fitzrovia, is "London's best newcomer in years"; the "carefully-crafted" small dishes may look simple, but "OMG… the flavour" he creates from his "brave" (often "Nordic-inspired") combinations; book many months ahead. / W1T 2SF; www.dabbous.co.uk; 11.30 pm; closed Mon & Sun.

Dalchini SW19 £36 ❸④④
147 Arthur Rd 8947 5966 10–2B
"An interesting range of Indo-Chinese Hakka dishes" deliver some "unusual and delicious" flavours, at this friendly little place, opposite Wimbledon Park tube. / SW19 8AB; www.dalchini.co.uk; 10.30 pm, Fri & Sat 11 pm, Sun 10 pm; closed Mon; no Amex.

Dans le Noir EC1 £73 ⑤④④
29 Clerkenwell Grn 7253 1100 9–1A
"Don't go hungry", if you visit this Farringdon venue where "you eat from a surprise menu, in total darkness, led to your table and served by blind waiters" – it can be "fun"… but "the food is horrible!" / EC1R 0DU; www.danslenoir.com; 9.30 pm; D only, closed Sun.

Daphne NW1 £36 ❸❶❷
83 Bayham St 7267 7322 8–3C
"Freshly-cooked" fare (particularly fish) twinned with service that shows "generosity, heart and warmth" ensure this family-run Camden Town stalwart remains an all-round hit; on a summer's evening, the roof terrace can offer a "magical" experience too. / NW1 0AG; 11 pm; closed Sun; no Amex.

Daphne's SW3 £64 ❸❷❷
112 Draycott Ave 7589 4257 5–2C
"You feel terribly special", at this "slick and professional" Chelsea old-favourite Italian – a "romantic" sort of place, with "delightful" décor, where food that's "good not exceptional" plays something of a supporting role. / SW3 3AE; www.daphnes-restaurant.co.uk; 11.30 pm; set weekday L & pre-theatre £38 (FP).

The Dartmouth Arms SE23 £36 ❸❸❸
7 Dartmouth Rd 8488 3117 1–4D
"A gastropub to give gastropubs a good name!"; a "friendly" Forest Hill all-rounder, with "decent" cooking – "the best for miles around". / SE23 3HN; www.thedartmoutharms.com; 10 pm, Sun 9 pm; no Amex.

Daylesford Organic £40 ④⑤④
44b Pimlico Rd, SW1 7881 8060 5–2D
208-212 Westbourne Grove, W11 7313 8050 6–1B
These posh deli/diners – in Pimlico and Notting Hill – offer good Saturday people-watching from their outside tables and, say fans, "the best brunch in town too"; at other times, though, visits can be spoilt by "disappointing" food or "rude" service.
/ www.daylesfordorganic.com; SW1 & W11 7 pm, Sun 4 pm; W1 9 pm, Sun 6.15 pm; W11 no booking L.

De La Panza N1 NEW £44 ❸❸❸
105-107 Southgate Rd 7226 0334 1–2C
"Massive, authentic steaks" inspire upbeat early-days reviews on this out-of-the-way Argentinian steakhouse, near Dalston, universally hailed for its "good value": "book, or risk a long wait". / N1 3JS; www.delapanza.co.uk; 11.30 pm; closed Mon, Tue L, Wed L, Thu L, Fri & Sat D.

Dean Street Townhouse W1 £58 ④❸❷
69-71 Dean St 7434 1775 4–2A
"Totally 'Mad Men'", this "Manhattanite" brasserie makes a perfect destination for those in search of a "vibrant and buzzing" atmosphere, and who want to be at the heart of the "Soho scene" – "superb" breakfasts aside, though, the "comfort food" is very much a side-show. / W1D 3SE; www.deanstreettownhouse.com; 11.30 pm, Fri & Sat midnight, Sun 10.30 pm; set pre theatre £36 (FP).

Defune W1 £60 ❶❸④
34 George St 7935 8311 3–1A
"As near to Japan as you can get… but a plane ticket might be less costly!" – this age-old Marylebone spot may be "ridiculously expensive", and it has "no atmosphere" either, but the sushi and sashimi are "exquisite". / W1U 7DP; 10.15 pm, Sun 10.30 pm.

Dehesa W1 £47 ❷❷❷
25 Ganton St 7494 4170 3–2C
"Cool and buzzing, but somehow still intimate" – this "casual" haunt, off Carnaby Street, is a brilliant all-rounder, serving a "mouth-watering" take on tapas, with "charm and efficiency". / W1F 9BP; www.dehesa.co.uk; 10.45 pm; closed Sun D; SRA-63%.

Del'Aziz £42 ④⑤❸
24-32 Vanston Pl, SW6 7386 0086 5–4A
Westfield, Ariel Way, W12 8740 0666 7–1C
Swiss Cottage Leis' C', Adelaide Rd, NW3 7586 3338 8–2A
11 Bermondsey Sq, SE1 7407 2991 9–4D
5 Canvey St, SE1 7633 0033 9–3B
"Great brunch and buzzing locations" are highlights of this Moroccan-inspired chain; while fans love its "easy-to-enjoy" menu of "simple" dishes, some reporters do encounter poor cooking, and service can be "slow". / www.delaziz.co.uk; SW6 10.30 pm; NW3 9.30 pm; SE1 11 pm; W12 10.45 pm, Sun 9.45 pm; NW3 closed D Sat, Sun.

THE DELAUNAY WC2 NEW £59 ④❷❶
55 Aldwych 7499 8558 2–2D
"Another triumph for Corbin & King!" – with its "clubby" and "imposing" interior, this "memorable" newcomer, on the Aldwych, is "a worthy sibling to the Wolseley"; it similarly owes its "instant popularity" more to "wonderful people-watching" and "celeb-spotting" than to its "slightly ho-hum" (Viennese) cuisine. / WC2B 4BB; www.thedelaunay.com; midnight, Sun 11 pm; SRA-66%.

Delfina SE1 £47 ④④❸
50 Bermondsey St 7357 0244 9–4D
White-walled and "airy", this Bermondsey gallery provides a "stunning" space for lunch; the once-stellar food, however, is merely "fine" nowadays, and service seems increasingly "inattentive". / SE1 3UD; www.thedelfina.co.uk; 10 pm; closed Sun-Thu D, Fri open L & D, closed Sat.

Delfino W1 £48 ❷❸④
121 Mount St 7499 1256 3–3B
"Nothing fancy here, but if it's pizza you want, you won't be disappointed"; this "genuine" Italian bistro, opposite the Connaught, would be handy anywhere, but in "horrifically pricey" Mayfair it's something of a godsend. / W1K 3NW; www.finos.co.uk; 11 pm; closed Sun.

Delhi Grill N1 £33 ❷④❸
21 Chapel Mkt 7278 8100 8–3D
"Themed like a roadside café in India!" (well nearly…) – this "cheap 'n' cheerful" Islingtonian is a "lively" spot, offering "excellent curries" and other "filling and tasty" food, in "Delhi style". / N1 9EZ; www.delhigrill.com; 10.30 pm.

The Deli West One W1 NEW £25 ❷❸④
51 Blandford St 7224 4033 2–1A
"Welcome competition for Reubens!" – this "decent stab at a NY-style Jewish deli" is "small in size", but already winning consistent praise for its "salt beef and chicken soup any mother would be proud of". / W1U 7HJ; www.thedelilondon.com; 10 pm, Fri 4 pm; closed Fri D & Sat.

La Delizia £36 ④❸④
63-65 Chelsea Manor St, SW3 7376 4111 5–3C
314 Trinity Rd, SW18 88759 595 10–2C
"Tucked-away off the Kings Road", the "cramped", long-running original of this Italian duo is "a shoebox of a place", serving pizza that's "thin, crispy and bursting with flavour"; in its trafficky Wandsworth location, the offshoot is pretty good too. / 11 pm, Sun 10.30; no Amex.

Department of Coffee EC1 £15 ❶❶❷
14-16 Leather Ln 7419 6906 9–2A
"Brilliant coffee", "wonderful cakes" ("real", "not synthetically beautiful") and "ultra-friendly staff" inspire a hymn of praise for this "lovely" pit stop, "a stone's throw from the Diamond District". / EC1N 7SU; www.departmentofcoffee.co.uk; 6 pm, Sat-Sun 4 pm; L only.

The Depot SW14 £42 ❸❷❷
Tideway Yd, Mortlake High St 8878 9462 10–1A
"On a sunny evening, there's no better place to be in SW London", say fans, than this "light" and "spacious" brasserie, right on the Thames, near Barnes Bridge; the food, though, is "nothing to get excited about". / SW14 8SN; www.depotbrasserie.co.uk; 10 pm, Sun 9.30 pm.

LES DEUX SALONS WC2 £55 ④④❸

40-42 William IV St 7420 2050 4–4C

"You could be in Paris", say supporters of Will Smith & Anthony Demetre's "gorgeously bustling" brasserie, on the fringe of Covent Garden; but is it "a victim of its own success"? – critics say the food has got "progressively worse" over the first year, with some visits plain "disappointing". / WC2N 4DD; www.lesdeuxsalons.co.uk; 10.45 pm, Sun 10.15 pm; set weekday L & pre-theatre £30 (FP).

Le Deuxième WC2 £52 ④❸⑤

65a Long Acre 7379 0033 4–2D

"The most civilised, reasonably-priced option pre/post-opera" – this small outfit, near the ROH, may suffer from "spare" and sterile decor, but it's a "calm" spot with "consistent" standards, and it offers "wonderful" set deals… all of which also commend it for a business lunch. / WC2E 9JH; www.ledeuxieme.com; midnight, Sun 11 pm; set pre theatre £34 (FP).

dim T £32 ④④④

56-62 Wilton Rd, SW1 7834 0507 2–4B

32 Charlotte St, W1 7637 1122 2–1C

1 Hampstead Ln, N6 8340 8800 8–1B

3 Heath St, NW3 7435 0024 8–2A

Tooley St, SE1 7403 7000 9–4D

This stylish budget pan-Asian chain offers a varied menu realised to a level somewhere between "reliable" and "very average"; its 'crown jewel' feature is its SE1 branch, with "stunning views over the Thames". / www.dimt.co.uk; most branches 11 pm, Sun 10.30 pm.

Diner £32 ④❸❷

18 Ganton St, W1 7287 8962 3–2C

21 Essex Rd, N1 7226 4533 8–3D

64-66 Chamberlayne Rd, NW10 8968 9033 1–2B

2 Jamestown Rd, NW1 7485 5223 8–3B

128 Curtain Rd, EC2 7729 4452 12–1B

"Ensconced in a squashy booth, Bloody Mary in hand"… what's not to like about these "great little American diners", which "seem to have improved of late"? / www.goodlifediner.com; midnight; W1 & NW1 Sun 11.30 pm; EC2 Sun-Wed 11.30 pm, WC2 11 pm, Fri-Sat midnight; booking: max 10.

Dinings W1 £50 ❶❷⑤

22 Harcourt St 7723 0666 8–4A

"Nobu food at a fraction of the price!"; the Marylebone concrete-bunker setting may be "drab" in the extreme, but Tomonari Chiba's "orgasmic" sushi is "hands-down the best in London". / W1H 4HH; www.dinings.co.uk; 10.30 pm; closed Sun.

DINNER MANDARIN ORIENTAL SW1 £92 ❸❸❸

66 Knightsbridge 7201 3833 5–1D

Heston Blumenthal's "genius" menu of "reincarnated olde English recipes" is "a total triumph", say fans of this "slightly cavernous" Knightsbridge dining room (whose best tables have "lovely park views"); shame it was "so hyped", though – an increasing number of doubters ask: "why the fuss?" / SW1X 7LA; www.dinnerbyheston.com; 10 pm.

Dishoom WC2 £35 ❸❸❶

12 Upper St Martins Ln 7420 9320 4–3B

"Delightful" decor ("an imaginative interpretation of a Bombay café") adds considerable va-va-voom to this "interesting concept-Indian" – a "comfy and spacious" set-up, near Covent Garden, serving "yummy bite-sized Indian tapas" (and "brilliant Bombay breakfasts" too); a Shoreditch sibling is to open in late-2012. / WC2H 9FC; www.dishoom.com; 11 pm, Fri & Sat midnight, Sun 10 pm; booking 6+ D.

Diwana Bhel-Poori House NW1 £30 ❸⑤⑤

121-123 Drummond St 7387 5556 8–4C

"Best for its lunch buffet" – this "cramped", "no-nonsense" '60s canteen, near Euston, is "still churning out more-than-acceptable south Indian dishes", at "rock-bottom" prices; BYO. / NW1 2HL; 11.45 pm, Sun 11 pm; no Amex; need 10+ to book.

The Dock Kitchen Portobello Dock W10 £51 ❸❸❶

344 Ladbroke Grove, Portobello Dock 8962 1610 1–2B

"Weirdly located" – by a canal in the backwoods of Notting Hill – Steve Parle's "sophisticated" venue makes a feature of "ever-changing" menus "from around the globe"; fans love all these "fabulous new flavours", but critics sense hype – "it felt like a dinner party, not a restaurant". / W10 5BU; www.dockkitchen.co.uk; 10 pm; closed Sun D.

Dockmaster's House E14 £50 ❸④④

1 Hertsmere Rd 7345 0345 11–1C

"Inventive", "elegant" and "refined", this Docklands spot – in a "charming Georgian building", near Canary Wharf – is "anything but a standard Indian"; even fans, though, can note that it's "quite pricey". / E14 8JJ; www.dockmastershouse.com; 10.30 pm; closed Sat L & Sun.

The Don EC4 £61 ❸❷❷

20 St Swithin's Ln 7626 2606 9–3C

"The best City business spot by far" – this "tucked-away" (but still central) venue offers not only "surprisingly good" Anglo-French fare but also "more atmosphere than you generally find in the Square Mile" (especially in the "cosy" cellar bistro); of late, though, some meals have been rather "ordinary". / EC4N 8AD; www.thedonrestaurant.com; 9.45 pm; closed Sat & Sun; no shorts.

don Fernando's TW9 £42 ④❷④

27f The Quadrant 8948 6447 1–4A

"Efficient and friendly", this large tapas-restaurant, by Richmond station, offers "all the standard dishes well-prepared", and it's "totally dependable" all-round – "great in a group". / TW9 1DN; www.donfernando.co.uk; 11 pm; no Amex; no booking.

Donna Margherita SW11 £41 ❷④④

183 Lavender Hill 7228 2660 10–2C

"Top-quality pizza, and excellent value-for-money too" – the pretty much universal theme of feedback on this "authentic", "easy-going" and "child-friendly" Battersea spot. / SW11 5TE; www.donna-margherita.com; 10.30 pm, Fri-Sat 11 pm; Mon-Thu D only, Fri-Sun open L & D.

Donostia W1 NEW £38 ❷❷❸

10 Seymour Pl 3620 1845 2–2A

Near Marble Arch, a small, bright and friendly new tapas bar/restaurant, which draws its inspiration from San Sebastian – on the food front, an early-days visit encountered many more hits than misses. / W1H 7ND; Rated on Editors' visit; www.donostia.co.uk; 11 pm; closed Mon & Sun.

Dorchester Grill
Dorchester Hotel W1 £92 ❸④❸
53 Park Ln 7629 8888 3–3A
Look out for the set deals, and this "luxurious" and "well-spaced" Mayfair dining room can be a surprisingly "good-value" destination (so long as you go easy on the "astronomically expensive" booze); the "fake Scottish hunting lodge decor" is "memorable" too, if "slightly odd". / W1K 1QA; www.thedorchester.com; 10.45 pm, Sun 10.15 pm; no trainers; set weekday L £53 (FP).

Dose EC1 £13 ❷❷④
70 Long Ln 7600 0382 9–1B
"Amazing flat whites" and "really excellent espressos" make this "lovely" Smithfield coffee shop the "cream of the Antipodean crop" for its small but adoring fan club; "great cakes" too. / EC1A 9EJ; www.dose-espresso.com; L only, closed Sun; no Amex.

Dotori N4 £28 ❷④❸
3 Stroud Green Rd 7263 3562 8–1D
"Brilliant sushi" and a "wide range of really excellent Korean and Japanese dishes" ensure this Finsbury Park joint is always "so busy"; it's "very small, so best to book in advance". / N4 2DQ; 10.30 pm; closed Mon; no Amex.

Downtown Mayfair W1 NEW £88 ④④④
15 Burlington Pl 3056 1001 3–2C
"Eye-watering" prices, "uncomfortable" seating, and a "pretentious" ambience provide plenty of ammunition for those who want to take pot shots at this imposing new Mayfair sibling of 'C London'; even people who don't like it, though, may concede the Italian cuisine is "top-quality". / W1S 2HK; www.downtownmayfair.com; midnight; closed Fri D, Sat D & Sun.

Dragon Castle SE17 £32 ❷④❸
100 Walworth Rd 7277 3388 1–3C
"Worth suffering Elephant & Castle for!" – this "large" and "cavernous" Cantonese "justifies the trek", not just for "brilliant dim sum", but for some "stupendous" other dishes too. / SE17 1JL; www.dragoncastle.eu; 11 pm.

The Drapers Arms N1 £45 ❸❸❷
44 Barnsbury St 7619 0348 8–3D
Improved of late, the "honest" and "flavoursome" cooking at this "real neighbourood gem" of an Islington boozer offers "an interesting take on British classics"; "cute" garden too. / N1 1ER; www.thedrapersarms.com; 10.30 pm; no Amex.

Duck & Waffle EC2 NEW
110 Bishopsgate 3640 7310 9–2D
London's first 24/7 restaurant of ambition of recent times, and 40 floors above the City too! – if it 'works', this upstairs offshoot of Sushisamba should make big waves; it opens as this guide goes to press, so visit hardens.com for our initial review. / EC2N 4AY; www.duckandwaffle.com.

Ducksoup W1 NEW £50 ❸④④
41 Dean St 7287 4599 4–2A
"A fun place… just not as good as everyone says!"; it's a shame "hype" has engulfed this "fashionably scruffy" and "very cramped" Soho newcomer – results from the "biro-scrawled menu" are "decent", but portions are "miserly" and the "gourmet" prices leave you "either starving or broke"! / W1D 4PY; www.ducksoupsoho.co.uk.

FSA

The Duke of Cambridge N1 £53 ❸④❷
30 St Peter's St 7359 3066 1–2C
A "buzzy and airy" all-organic gastropub, in Islington, where "good" dishes – from a seasonal, daily-changing menu – are produced with "top-quality" ingredients; the bill, though, "can be a surprise", and not in a good way. / N1 8JT; www.dukeorganic.co.uk; 10.30 pm, Sun 10 pm; no Amex; SRA-84%.

Duke of Sussex W4 £43 ④④❸
75 South Pde 8742 8801 7–1A
A "charming" dining room sets the tone at this "beautiful" pub, on the Chiswick/Acton borders; fans hail its "successful fusion of Spanish and British dishes", but "the food can sometimes sound better than it tastes". / W4 5LF; 10.30 pm, Sun 9.30 pm.

The Duke of Wellington W1 £48 ④④❸
94a, Crawford St 7723 2790 2–1A
This "convivial" boozer remains "a top Marylebone spot for a chill-out"; even fans, however, feel "the food has fallen some way from the (stellar) heights of its freshman year" – it's a bit "hit-and-miss" nowadays. / W1H 2HQ; www.thedukew1.co.uk; 10 pm, Sun 9 pm.

E&O W11 £51 ❷❷❶
14 Blenheim Cr 7229 5454 6–1A
"Still glamorous after all these years", this "ever-buzzing" Notting Hill hang-out continues to impress with its "tempting" Asian-fusion tapas, its "fab cocktails", and its "fun" style. / W11 1NN; www.rickerrestaurants.com; 11 pm, Sun 10.30 pm; booking: max 6.

El1even Park Walk SW10 £56 ④④④
11 Park Wk 7352 3449 5–3B
Incredibly mixed opinions – from "wonderful" to "very disappointing" – on this smart Chelsea trattoria yearling; the low volume of survey feedback, however, is itself hardly the best advertisement. / SW10 0AJ; www.atozrestaurants.com/11parkwalk; midnight; set weekday L £35 (FP).

The Eagle EC1 £32 ❸⑤❷
159 Farringdon Rd 7837 1353 9–1A
"The original, and never beaten!", say fans of this "boisterous" Clerkenwell boozer – the first, in the early '90s, to earn the modern 'gastropub' label; in truth, it's been upstaged, but it still attracts lots of praise for "consistent peasant cooking at superb prices". / EC1R 3AL; 10.30 pm; closed Sun D; no Amex; no booking.

Earl Spencer SW18 £41 ❸④❸
260-262 Merton Rd 8870 9244 10–2B
"Much better than you might expect at first glance" – this large roadside pub, in Southfields, is a major local destination, thanks to its "interesting, daily-changing menu". / SW18 5JL; www.theearlspencer.co.uk; 10 pm, Sun 9.30 pm; no booking Sun.

The Easton WC1 £40 ❷❸❸
22 Easton St 7278 7608 9–1A
The menu may be "typical", but it's "done really well", at this superior gastroboozer, near trendy Exmouth Market – "the Sunday roasts are perfection!" / WC1X 0DS; 10 pm, Sun 9.30 pm.

Eat £13 ④❸④
Branches throughout London
Fans say "they stole Pret's crown", but these popular pit stops still (slightly) lag their rival in the survey; why quibble, though? – this is clearly "one of the better sarnie chains", and its "attractive range of light bites" includes some "benchmark soups". / www.eat.co.uk; 4 pm-8 pm; most City branches closed all or part of weekend; no credit cards; no booking.

The Ebury SW1 £53
11 Pimlico Rd 7730 6784 5–2D
This large and loungey Pimlico gastroboozer had "gone downhill" in recent times, but some reports suggest it has been "completely rejuvenated" now the original management is back in charge – in the circumstances, we've felt it safest to leave it unrated till the dust settles. / SW1W 8NA; www.theebury.co.uk; 10.30 pm, Sat & Sun 10 pm.

Ebury Restaurant & Wine Bar SW1 £50 ④④❸
139 Ebury St 7730 5447 2–4A
This age-old Belgravia hang-out offers some "very well-priced set menus", and can make a "perfect" destination for lunch (or pre-8pm); à la carte, though, there's a feeling it "doesn't quite deliver". / SW1W 9QU; www.eburyrestaurant.co.uk; 10.15 pm.

Eco SW4 £33 ❸④❸
162 Clapham High St 7978 1108 10–2D
"Still cutting it after all these years"; this once-so-hip Clapham spot still churns out "good thin-crust pizzas", and its tables are still so "crammed-together" that it is difficult to "talk, move or leave"! / SW4 7UG; www.ecorestaurants.com; 11 pm, Fri & Sat 11.30 pm.

Ed's Easy Diner £29 ④❷❷
12 Moor St, W1 7434 4439 4–2A
Trocadero, 19 Rupert St, W1 7287 1951 3–3D
Sedley Pl, 14 Woodstock St, W1 7493 9916 3–2B
Like "a traditional US diner", albeit one "straight out of a Hollywood movie" – these "'50s-kitsch" burger-stops "do what they say on the tin", even if their "tasty and filling" fare is "incidental" to the "fun" overall experience. / www.edseasydiner.co.uk; Rupert St 10.30 pm, Fri & Sat 11.30 pm, Sun 10 pm; Moor St 11.30 pm, Thu-Sat midnight, Sun 10 pm, Sedley Place 9 pm, Thu-Sat 10 pm, NW1 Mon-Sat 10 pm, Sun 9 pm; no Amex; Moor St no booking.

Edera W11 £61 ❷❶❸
148 Holland Park Ave 7221 6090 6–2A
"A Sardinian restaurant with neighbourhood flair" (and "great truffle dishes", in season, too) – the 'hood concerned, though, is Holland Park, so it's no surprise that it's "not the cheapest"! / W11 4UE; www.atozrestaurants.com/edera/; 11 pm, Sun 10 pm.

Eight Over Eight SW3 £56 ❷❸❷
392 King's Rd 7349 9934 5–3B
"Glamorous" and "always buzzing", this World's End hang-out for "Chelsea's bright young things" offers "delicious little morsels" of Asian-fusion tapas – "brilliant whether you're looking for cocktail-nibbles or a sit-down dinner". / SW3 5UZ; www.rickerrestaurants.com; 11 pm, Sun 10.30 pm.

Electric Brasserie W11 £52 ④④❷
191 Portobello Rd 7908 9696 6–1A
For "the best buzziest brunch around" ("book well ahead on weekends"), this social hub for Notting Hillbillies certainly lives up to its name – the food at other times isn't nearly such an attraction, but the place is "always busy" nonetheless. / W11 2ED; www.electricbrasserie.com; 11 pm, Sun 10 pm; max 12.

F S A

Elena's L'Etoile W1 £52 ⑤⑤④
30 Charlotte St 7636 7189 2–1C
Fans of this "faded" Fitzrovia French restaurant (est 1896) say a visit is "still an event", even if "it's not the same since Elena retired"; harsher critics, though, have found it "dead on its feet" of late, citing "ordinary" fare, "dismal" service and an ambience that's simply "forlorn". / W1T 2NG; www.elenasletoile.co.uk; 10.30 pm; closed Sat L & Sun.

Elephant Royale Locke's Wharf E14 £46 ❸④❸
Westferry Rd 7987 7999 11–2C
"One of London's best views" (towards Greenwich) is to be had from the summer terrace of this little-known Isle of Dogs Thai; it's a bit "expensive", so visit on a Sunday for the "good-value buffet deal". / E14 3AN; www.elephantroyale.com; 10.30 pm, Fri & Sat 11 pm, Sun 10 pm.

Elliot's Cafe SE1 NEW £47 ❷❸❸
12 Stoney St 7430 7436 9–4C
"The simple formula of freshly-prepared ingredients" has won a big following for this "nice 'indie' newcomer", near Borough Market. / SE1 9AD; www.elliotscafe.com; 10 pm.

Emile's SW15 £42 ❸❶❸
96-98 Felsham Rd 8789 3323 10–2B
"Hidden-away in the backstreets of Putney", this "reliable", "unpretentious" and "value-for-money" neighbourhood bistro has been a "firm favourite" for as long as anyone can remember, thanks not least to the "friendly" and "welcoming" attentions of the "ebullient" Emile and his team. / SW15 1DQ; www.emilesrestaurant.co.uk; 11 pm; D only, closed Sun; no Amex.

The Empress E9 £43 ❷❸❸
130 Lauriston Rd 8533 5123 1–2D
Recently changed hands, this Victoria Park boozer is now doing "much better food" – a "relaxed" destination, it is now hailed as a "superb" all-rounder. / E9 7LH; www.theempressofindia.com; 10 pm, Sun 9.30 pm.

Empress of Sichuan WC2 £36 ❷❸❷
6 Lisle St 7734 8128 4–3A
"For real foodies, not the faint-hearted!" – this "uncompromising" Sichuanese, off Chinatown's main drag, serves "very good, mouth-numbing cuisine" in superior surroundings (for the area); unexpectedly good wine list too. / WC2H 7BG; 11 pm.

The Engineer NW1 £46 ④④❸
65 Gloucester Ave 7722 0950 8–3B
This famous Primrose Hill gastropub is "a special place in summer, thanks to its lovely beer garden"; to fans, "it's unspoilt by its recent change of ownership"... but equally there is no real sign in reports that the complacency of recent years has been shaken off. / NW1 8JH; www.the-engineer.com; 10.30 pm, Sun 10 pm; no Amex.

Enoteca Turi SW15 £55 ❷❷❸
28 Putney High St 8785 4449 10–2B
A "simply stunning all-Italian wine list" makes Giuseppe and Pamela Turi's "unassuming" jewel, near Putney Bridge, a destination of far more than local interest, and it helps that the food is "very good" too; there's the odd concern, though, that it's "lost its flair" a little of late. / SW15 1SQ; www.enotecaturi.com; 10.30 pm, Fri-Sat 11 pm; closed Sun.

F S A

The Enterprise SW3 £54 ❸❸❷

35 Walton St 7584 3148 5–2C

A hit with "the Chelsea crowd", this "tightly-packed" local haunt is proof of "how well you can do by aiming high, but not too high" – it "never disappoints, but never excels either". / SW3 2HU; www.theenterprise.co.uk; 10 pm, Sat 10.30 pm; no booking, except weekday L.

Entrée SW11 £50 ❸❸❷

2 Battersea Rise 7223 5147 10–2C

"A real buzz, and a piano bar" (downstairs) help this "fantastic local" stand out in the "already-crowded" Battersea restaurant scene; it wins all-round praise for its "understated" styling and its "well-flavoured and creative dishes". / SW11 1ED; www.entreebattersea.co.uk/; 10.30 pm; closed weekday L.

Eriki NW3 £39 ❸❸④

4-6 Northways Pde, Finchley Rd 7722 0606 8–2A

"You don't end up feeling bloated", after a trip to this "upmarket" Indian, in Swiss Cottage, which draws a broadly-based fan club with its cooking that's full of "really authentic flavours"; the interior, though, can seem a trifle "dull". / NW3 5EN; www.eriki.co.uk; 10.45 pm; closed Sat L.

Esarn Kheaw W12 £32 ❸❸⑤

314 Uxbridge Rd 8743 8930 7–1B

It's always looked "dated" in recent times, but this Shepherd's Bush café has long been a 'fave rave' thanks its "top-quality" Northern Thai dishes; worryingly, though, this year also saw some reports of "bog-standard" cooking. / W12 7LJ; www.esarnkheaw.co.uk; 11 pm; closed Sat L & Sun L; no Amex.

L'Escargot W1 £60 ④❷❷

48 Greek St 7439 7474 4–2A

Amidst the "clamour" of Soho, this "refreshingly quiet" veteran makes an unusually "civilised" West End choice; the all-round experience is solid enough, but the food can seen "too safe" nowadays, and critics dismiss the approach as "tired". / W1D 4EF; www.whitestarline.org.uk; 11.15 pm; closed Sat L & Sun; set weekday L & pre-theatre £34 (FP).

Essenza W11 £56 ❸❷④

210 Kensington Park Rd 7792 1066 6–1A

It offers "no bells or whistles", but this little-commented-upon Notting Hill Italian is a "good-value" sort of place, with a "varied" and "honest" menu, and offering a good set lunch too. / W11 1NR; www.essenza.co.uk; 11.30 pm.

L'Etranger SW7 £67 ❸❸④

36 Gloucester Rd 7584 1118 5–1B

A "phenomenal", "one-of-a-kind" wine list is matched up with "novel" Franco/Japanese cuisine to deliver an "interesting spectrum" of flavours, at this "frightfully expensive" (and rather "cold") venture, in South Kensington. / SW7 4QT; www.etranger.co.uk; 11 pm, Sun 10 pm; set weekday L £39 (FP).

Euphorium Bakery N1 £13 ❸❸❸

26a Chapel Mkt 7837 7010 8–3D

With its "delicious cakes and even better biscotti", this Islington café/bakery generally impress; "amazing" coffee too. / N1 9EN; www.euphoriumbakery.com; 6.15 pm; L only; no Amex.

F S A

Everest Inn SE3 **£31** ❷❸❸
41 Montpelier Vale 8852 7872 1–4D
"Fresh-tasting" and "distinctively-flavoured" dishes – with "consistently high standards, year after year" – win a large and enthusiastic local fan club for this "friendly" Blackheath Nepalese/Indian. / SE3 0TJ; www.everestinn.co.uk; midnight, Sun 11 pm.

Eyre Brothers EC2 **£55** ❷❸❸
70 Leonard St 7613 5346 12–1B
With its "sophisticated" cuisine and "sumptuous" wines, this "absolutely first-rate" Iberian restaurant is long established as Shoreditch's business-lunch rendezvous par excellence – "it's better at night", though, "when it metaphorically takes its tie off!" / EC2A 4QX; www.eyrebrothers.co.uk; 10 pm; closed Sat L & Sun.

Faanoos **£26** ④④❸
472 Chiswick High Rd, W4 8994 4217 7–2A
481 Richmond Road, SW14 8878 5738 1–4A
"Excellent breads, straight from the oven", and "simple" grills – plus other Persian fare using "good ingredients" – come together to create a "top cheap 'n' cheerful" experience, at these "straightforward and unpretentious" Sheen and Chiswick joints; BYO. / SW14 11 pm; W4 11 pm; Fri & Sat midnight.

Fabrizio EC1 **£48** ❷❶⑤
30 Saint Cross St 7430 1503 9–1A
"If you want Sicilian food cooked with love, this is the place", and this Diamond District spot is notable for its "wonderful hospitality" too; "more café than restaurant", though, it's "not really smart enough for business". / EC1N 8UH; www.fabriziorestaurant.co.uk; 10 pm; closed Sat L & Sun.

Fairuz W1 **£45** ❸❷❸
3 Blandford St 7486 8108 2–1A
"Reliable", "friendly" and "good-value", this Marylebone Lebanese is an ever-"busy" destination (especially at lunch), but can seem a bit too "cramped" and "noisy". / W1H 3DA; www.fairuz.uk.com; 11 pm, Sun 10.30 pm.

Fakhreldine W1 **£61** ④④④
85 Piccadilly 7493 3424 3–4C
"Great views over Green Park" can make this glitzy first-floor Lebanese a worthwhile sunny-day lunch destination; by night, though, "it charges a lot for kebab-esque food", especially when "nothing makes you go 'wow'!". / W1J 7NB; www.fakhreldine.co.uk; midnight, Sun 11 pm.

La Famiglia SW10 **£57** ④④❸
7 Langton St 7351 0761 5–3B
"A last relic of swinging '60s Italian food culture", this Chelsea trattoria is known for its lovely garden, and can still make a great choice "for a lazy lunch en famille"; most reports find the service "charming", but it can also be a bit "off-hand" too. / SW10 0JL; www.lafamiglia.co.uk; 11.45 pm.

Fat Boy's **£33** ❸④❸
10a-10b Edensor Rd, W4 8742 0249 10–1A
33 Haven Grn, W5 8998 5868 1–2A
201 Upper Richmond Rd, SW14 8876 0644 1–4A
431 Richmond Rd, TW1 8892 7657 1–4A
58 High St, TW8 8569 8481 1–3A
"The Thai food always hits the target", say fans of these "easy neighbourhood diners", in west London; service is "polite" too, if "sometimes slow". / www.fatboysthai.co.uk; 11 pm.

FSA

Faulkner's E8 £29 ❷④④
424-426 Kingsland Rd 7254 6152 1–1D
You can get anything from "amazing take-away fish 'n' chips" to "a huge, whole char-grilled sea bass", to eat in, at this "consistently good" Dalston chippy of long standing. / E8 4AA; 10 pm, Fri-Sun 11 pm; no Amex; need 8+ to book.

The Fellow N1 £43 ④④④
24 York Way 7833 4395 8–3C
By King's Cross, a gastropub that offers "decent grub at realistic prices" – it's nothing remarkable, but perhaps its "popularity with Guardian journalists" tells us something? / N1 9AA; www.thefellow.co.uk; 9.45pm; closed Sun D.

The Fentiman Arms SW8 £43 ❸❸❷
64 Fentiman Rd 7793 9796 10–1D
"A handsome, very friendly pub in a quiet Kennington street", where the "freshly-prepared" food invariably satisfies; "nice garden" too. / SW8 1LA; www.geronimo-inns.co.uk; 10 pm, Sun 9 pm.

Fernandez & Wells £31 ❷❷❶
16a, St Anne's Ct, W1 7494 4242 3–1D
43 Lexington St, W1 7734 1546 3–2D
73 Beak St, W1 7287 8124 3–2D
Somerset Hs, Strand, WC2 7420 9408 2–2D NEW
A "beautiful, airy space" in Somerset House has made a "stunning" recent addition to this group of "casual" but top-quality pit stops – the "funky" Soho branches are, by contrast, "very cosy"; "coffee here is a love affair", the toasted sarnies are "unbeatable", and the cakes are "outstanding". / www.fernandezandwells.com; Lexington St & St Anne's court 10 pm; Beak St 6 pm, Somerset House 11 pm; St Anne's Court closed Sun.

Fez Mangal W11 £16 ❶❸④
104 Ladbroke Grove 7229 3010 6–1A
"A million miles from the normal greasy kebab shop" – this "best-ever" Turkish BBQ, in Ladbroke Grove, serves up "great food from the grill, to eat-in or take away"; BYO. / W11 1PY; www.fezmangal.co.uk; 11.30 pm; no Amex.

Ffiona's W8 £46 ④④❸
51 Kensington Church St 7937 4152 5–1A
"Ffiona is larger than life", and her "cosy" and "romantic" Kensington bistro wins praise from most reporters for its "hearty" British fare (including a "fun and great-value" brunch) – a minority, though, just doesn't 'get' the appeal. / W8 4BA; www.ffionas.com; 11 pm, Sun 10 pm; D only, closed Mon; no Amex.

Fifteen N1 £53 ⑤⑤⑤
15 Westland Pl 3375 1515 12–1A
In mid-2012, the formerly distinct restaurant and trattoria areas at Jamie Oliver's Hoxton training establishment were merged; in both parts, reporters had found "absurd" prices for food that was "just OK". / N1 7LP; www.fifteen.net; 10.45 pm; booking: max 16.

The Fifth Floor Restaurant Harvey Nichols SW1 £68 ④④④
109-125 Knightsbridge 7235 5250 5–1D
For a "leisurely lunch", this "light and airy" (but rather neutral) dining room, over the famous Knightsbridge department store, still has its fans; it inspires very little commentary these days, however, perhaps because standards overall are "average at best". / SW1X 7RJ; www.harveynichols.com; 10.45 pm; closed Sun D; SRA-63%.

Fig N1 £48 ❷❸❷
169 Hemingford Rd 7609 3009 8–3D
"A fabulous neighbourhood restaurant"; "tucked-away in lovely Barnsbury", this "cosy, quiet and candlelit" spot offers "seasonal British dishes, with a bit of Scandinavia thrown in" – a surprisingly happy combination, it seems. / N1 1DA; www.figbistro.co.uk; 10 pm; closed Mon, Tue–Sat D only, Sun open L & D; no Amex.

La Figa E14 £40 ❸❷④
45 Narrow St 7790 0077 11–1B
"A real Limehouse institution", this friendly Italian dishes up pizza (and pasta) plates that are "big enough for two", and "always of good quality"; top tip – "ask for the 'special' wine list". / E14 8DN; www.lafigarestaurant.co.uk; 11 pm, Sun 10.30 pm.

Fino W1 £51 ❷❷❷
33 Charlotte St 7813 8010 2–1C
With its "perfectly-cooked" tapas, "brilliant" Iberian wine and "characterful" staff, the Hart brothers' "clubby" Fitzrovia stalwart is "still going strong"; despite the basement setting, its "large, well-populated bar" helps create "a real buzz". / W1T 1RR; www.finorestaurant.com; 10.30 pm; closed Sat L & Sun; booking: max 12.

Fire & Stone £37 ④④❸
31-32 Maiden Ln, WC2 08443 712550 4–3D
Westfield, Ariel Way, W12 0844 371 2551 7–1C
4 Horner Sq, E1 0844 371 2554 12–2B
"It transformed my love for pizza", say fans of the hallmark range of "quirky" toppings on offer at this small chain; to harsher critics, however, the combinations are "an abomination" – just "so wrong!" / www.fireandstone.com; WC2 11 pm; W12 11.15 pm; E1 11pm, Sun 8 pm.

First Floor W11 £44 ④④❶
186 Portobello Rd 7243 0072 6–1A
A "delightfully quirky", high-ceilinged dining room, overlooking Portobello Market, that's ideal for romance or a party; the food has its ups and downs, but most reports this year were favourable. / W11 1LA; www.firstfloorportobello.co.uk; 10.30 pm.

Fish Central EC1 £29 ❷❷❸
149-155 Central St 7253 4970 12–1A
"They don't muck about", at this "loud and busy" chippy – a "salt-of-the-earth" kind of place where the "superb fresh fish" is "always cooked to order". / EC1V 8AP; www.fishcentral.co.uk; 10.30 pm, Fri & Sat 11 pm; closed Sun.

Fish Club £37 ❷❷④
189 St John's Hill, SW11 7978 7115 10–2C
57 Clapham High St, SW4 7720 5853 10–2D
"The best fish 'n' chips for miles around is the mainstay of these "basic" – but "friendly and helpful" – south London canteens", which offer a "wide-ranging" menu; fish counters attached. / www.thefishclub.com; 10 pm; closed Mon L; no bookings.

Fish in a Tie SW11 £31 ④❷❶
105 Falcon Rd 7924 1913 10–1C
"Good food" at "amazingly low prices" – the simple formula that ensures a constant "lively" crush at this super-budget bistro, "unpromisingly-located" behind Clapham Junction. / SW11 2PF; www.fishinatie.co.uk; midnight, Sun 11 pm; no Amex.

The Fish Market EC2 NEW
16 New St awaiting tel 9–2D
The D&D Group is to launch a new Spitalfields site in late-2012 in the format it might once, in its Conran Restaurants days, have called a 'gastrodrome' – this part of it is apparently to have the slant its name suggests. / EC2M 4TR.

Fish Place SW11 £55 ❷❷④
Vicentia Ct, Bridges Ct 7095 0410 10–1C
"Off the beaten track" – in a Battersea riverside development with "lovely Thames views" – this little-known yearling is highly praised for its "excellent" fish and seafood; even fans can find it "a little expensive", though, and the interior is "ambience-free". / SW11 3GY; www.thefishplace.co.uk; 10.30 pm; closed Mon, Tue L, Wed L, Thu L & Sun D.

fish! SE1 £50 ④④⑤
Cathedral St 7407 3803 9–4C
"Unusually-located", in a glass structure by Borough Market, this clattery fish-brasserie puts in a "curate's egg" performance – fans praise its "succulent" fish (and "piping hot chips"), but "appalling" meals are not unknown. / SE1 9AL; www.fishkitchen.com; 10.45 pm, Sun 10.30 pm.

Fishworks £49 ❸❸④
7-9 Swallow St, W1 7734 5813 3–3D
89 Marylebone High St, W1 7935 9796 2–1A
"A good array of fresh fish" pleases most visitors to these "lively and enjoyable" fishmongers-cum-restaurants, in Mayfair and Marylebone (and also Richmond) – survivors of what was once a national chain. / www.fishworks.co.uk; 10.30 pm.

Fitou's Thai Restaurant W10 £22 ❸❷④
1 Dalgarno Gdns 8968 0558 6–1A
Hidden-away, opposite Little Wormwood Scrubs – a "friendly" BYO café, serving "great Thai food at bargain prices". / W10 5LL; www.fitourestaurant.co.uk; 10.30 pm; closed Sun L.

500 N19 £41 ❶❷④
782 Holloway Rd 7272 3406 8–1C
"Amazing food in an unlikely location!" – this "tiny" and "unassuming" (but now "hugely popular") Italian, "in the darker regions" of Archway, serves "outstanding" Sicilian cooking at "phenomenal-value" prices. / N19 3JH; www.500restaurant.co.uk; 10.30 pm, Sunday 9.30 pm; Mon-Thu D only, Fri-Sun open L & D.

The Flask N6 £40 ④④❸
77 Highgate West Hill 8348 7346 1–1C
Centuries old, this Highgate inn boasts "lots of interesting hidden nooks and corners", and a lovely garden too; the food (including a BBQ) is "simple", but generally "dependable". / N6 6BU; www.theflaskhighgate.com; 10 pm, Sun 9 pm.

Flat White W1 £11 ❸❷❷
17 Berwick St 7734 0370 3–2D
"Fabulous" brews – "made with tenderness and a signature fern leaf" – win continuing respect for this early-wave "trendy little independent" coffee shop, in Soho. / W1F 0PT; www.flat-white.co.uk; L only; no credit cards; No bookings.

Florence SE24 £36 ④④❷
131-133 Dulwich Rd 7326 4987 10–2D
A "gorgeous" Brockwell Park boozer that's "great for a casual meal or a drink" – its "large covered play area" makes it "a very easy place for family dining". / SE24 0NG; www.florencehernehill.com; 10 pm, Sun 9.30 pm.

Floridita W1 £58 ④❸❷

100 Wardour St 7314 4000 3–2D

"A fun night out, but the food should be much better!"; this cavernous Soho basement scores highly for its "live Cuban-style entertainment", but the "music tax" can make the overall package seem far "too expensive" for what it is. / W1F 0TN; www.floriditalondon.com; 11.30 pm; D only, closed Mon & Sun; no trainers; SRA-62%.

Food for Thought WC2 £23 ❷④④

31 Neal St 7836 0239 4–2C

Despite its "bustling, cheek-by-jowl atmosphere, cranky wooden tables and bum-numbing stools", this Covent Garden veggie veteran is always "crammed" – must have something to do with the "scrumptious" food and "great value for money"; BYO. / WC2H 9PR; www.foodforthought-london.co.uk; 8 pm, Sun 5 pm; closed Sun D; no credit cards; no booking.

The Forge WC2 £55 ④④④

14 Garrick St 7379 1432 4–3C

Interestingly housed (in a former Covent Garden stained-glass works), this "solid" Gallic restaurant is a "reliable" pre-theatre choice, and offers a "highly recommended" Sunday deal too; otherwise it can seem "pleasant, but rather dull". / WC2 9BJ; www.theforgerestaurant.co.uk; midnight, Sun 11 pm; set weekday L £28 (FP), set pre-theatre £32 (FP).

Forman's E3 £53 ❸❸④

Stour Rd, Fish Island 8525 2365 1–1D

Overlooking the Olympic Stadium from a canal-side vantage-point, the first-floor dining room of London's only major fish smokery makes a particularly good brunch spot, but it offers decent food at any time – note limited opening hours. / E3 2NH; www.formans.co.uk; 11 pm; Closed Mon-Wed, Thu & Fri D only, Sat open L & D, closed Sun D.

Formosa Dining Room
The Prince Alfred W9 £49 ④④❷

5a Formosa St 7286 3287 6–1C

Attached to a grand and "lovely" Maida Vale tavern (with very distinctive architecture), this "casual" dining room offers "upmarket pub grub" of a dependable standard. / W9 1EE; www.theprincealfred.co.uk; 10 pm, Fri & Sat 11 pm, Sun 9 pm; no Amex.

(The Fountain)
Fortnum & Mason W1 £63 ④❸❸

181 Piccadilly 7734 8040 3–3D

"After some serious shopping", the "old-fashioned plush" atmosphere of the 'buttery' of the Queen's grocer can make a "great place to stop for a while"; reporters' top tip, though, is to start the day here – breakfast is "surprisingly good". / W1A 1ER; www.fortnumandmason.com; 10.45 pm; closed Sun D.

(1707)
Fortnum & Mason W1 £46 ④❸❸

181 Piccadilly 7734 8040 3–3D

"Surprisingly fun for a wine bar in a department store" – this St James's pit stop not only offers an "extensive range by the glass", but you can choose any bottle on sale (1,000+), and pay just retail, plus £10; top food advice – "go for the cheese, which is some of the best in town". / W1A 1ER; www.fortnumandmason.co.uk; 8 pm, Sun 6 pm; closed Sun D.

(The Diamond Jubilee Tea Salon) Fortnum & Mason W1 NEW £54 ❸❷❷
181 Piccadilly 7734 8040 3–3D
Opened by Her Majesty herself, the re-launched 4th-floor restaurant of one's corner shop (previously the St James's Restaurant) is especially worth a visit for its picture-book afternoon teas (complete with tea sommelier); at other times, fare for ladies-who-lunch. / W1A 1ER; Rated on Editors' visit; www.fortnumandmason.com.

Fortune Cookie W2 £28 ❷④⑤
1 Queensway 7727 7260 6–2C
It may be "slightly tired-looking", but this Bayswater Chinese offers some "tasty and intriguing" dishes for those who can successfully navigate its menu. / W2 4QJ; 11 pm.

40 Maltby Street SE1 NEW £40 ❷❷❷
40 Maltby St 7237 9247 9–4D
"A true find!"; this "trendy and hidden-away" wine bar, under railways arches in a Borough foodie enclave, offers not just "amazing" seasonal British food, a "quirky" setting and "knowledgeable" service, but also a splendid range of natural/biodynamic wines. / SE1 3PA; www.40maltbystreet.com; 10 pm; closed Sun- Wed, Thu L, Fri L, Sat D.

The Foundry NW1 NEW £34 ❸❷❷
3-7 Delancey St 7387 5959 8–3B
"A special hide-away, with a superb New York feel"; this relaunch of Camden Town's Caponata (RIP) site is hailed in the (few) early-days report as a bit of a "gem", offering British food that's sometimes "very good". / NW1 7NL; www.foundrycamden.co.uk; set weekday L £28 (FP), set dinner £39 (FP).

Four O Nine SW9 £51 ❸❸❷
409 Clapham Rd 7737 0722 10–1D
Above a pub near Clapham North, a hidden-away room, very highly rated by a small local fan club for its "romantic" decor and "top-notch" food, and at "good-value" prices too. / SW9 9BT; www.fouronine.co.uk; 10.30 pm; closed weekday L.

Four Regions TW9 £42 ❷❷④
102-104 Kew Rd 8940 9044 1–4A
"Good value for money, year-after-year" – the reason to visit this "totally reliable" Chinese, on the Kew/Richmond border; it offers "all the usual suspects", but "will prepare non-menu dishes if you ask". / TW9 2PQ; 11.30 pm, Sun 11 pm.

The Four Seasons £30 ❷④⑤
12 Gerrard St, W1 7494 0870 4–3A
23 Wardour St, W1 7287 9995 4–3A
84 Queensway, W2 7229 4320 6–2C
"The best roast duck in town" is to be had at the "always-busy", decades-old Queensway original branch of this Chinese trio, and also its "amazingly good" Chinatown spin-offs; "you don't go for the ambience". / www.fs-restaurants.co.uk; Queensway 11 pm, Sun 10h45 pm; Gerrard St 1 am; Wardour St 1am, Fri-Sat 3.30 am.

Fox & Grapes SW19 £52 ④④❸
9 Camp Rd 8619 1300 10–2A
Claude Bosi's "jolly" gastropub yearling, by the Common, may offer a nice change from "Wimbledon's chain monotony", but it "doesn't really cut the mustard" – the "expensive" food is rather "variable", and service can be "arrogant and haphazard". / SW19 4UN; foxandgrapeswimbledon.co.uk; 9.30 pm, Sun 8.15 pm; no Amex.

The Fox & Hounds SW11 £40 ❷❷❷

66 Latchmere Rd 7924 5483 10–1C

A "cosy" gastroboozer some Battersea folk proclaim "the best local by far", thanks to its "welcoming" staff and its "seriously yummy" Mediterranean-influenced fare. / SW11 2JU; www.thefoxandhoundspub.co.uk; 10 pm; Mon-Thu D only, Fri-Sun open L & D.

The Fox and Anchor EC1 £46 ❸❸❶

115 Charterhouse St 7250 1300 9–1B

"The real treat of visiting this rare Victorian survivor is the building itself", but this "jewel" of a Smithfield tavern is also renowned for its "enormous breakfasts, served with a pint of stout" (plus other "traditional and hearty" British staples). / EC1M 6AA; www.foxandanchor.com; 9.30 pm.

Foxtrot Oscar SW3 £55 ⑤④⑤

79 Royal Hospital Rd 7352 4448 5–3D

"Exceptionally dull", and "overpriced" too, this Chelsea bistro has lost all its raffish charm of yesteryear, and nowadays gives every impression of "trading on its owner's name" – Gordon Ramsay's worldwide flagship is but a few doors away. / SW3 4HN; www.gordonramsay.com/foxtrotoscar/; 10 pm, Sun 9 pm.

Franco Manca £22 ❶❸❷

144 Chiswick High Rd, W4 8747 4822 7–2A
Unit 4 Market Row, SW9 7738 3021 10–2D
Westfield Stratford, E20 8522 6669 1–1D NEW

"About as good as it gets outside Naples!"; these "always-rammed" pizzerias – in particular the tiny, Brixton market original – are the home of "London's best pizza", and "unbelievably cheap" too; will the formula survive the venture-capital-backed 'roll-out'? – time will tell. / www.francomanca.com; SW9 5 pm; W4 11 pm; E20 9 pm, Thu-Sat 10 pm, Sun 6 pm; SW9 no bookings.

Franco's SW1 £73 ④❸④

61 Jermyn St 7499 2211 3–3C

A "classy" St James's Italian which, say fans, is a "quiet oasis away from the bustle of Piccadilly", serving "superbly-prepared" food; sceptics, though, can find it so "overpriced" as to sap enjoyment. / SW1Y 6LX; www.francoslondon.com; 11 pm; closed Sun; set weekday L & pre-theatre £47 (FP).

Frankie's Italian Bar & Grill SW3 £46 ⑤⑤⑤

3 Yeomans Row 7590 9999 5–2C

Last survivor of MPW and Frankie Dettori's pizza chain – an "underground cavern", decked out with Vegas-style glitz, five minutes from Harrods; fans still say it's a "fun" place with a "wide" menu, but critics report some meals as simply "lousy". / SW3 2AL; www.frankiesitalianbarandgrill.com; 11 pm.

Franklins SE22 £47 ❸❸❸

157 Lordship Ln 8299 9598 1–4D

"Slightly cramped" it may be, but this East Dulwich spot is an "excellent neighbourhood restaurant", offering "carefully-prepared" dishes and a "warm welcome". / SE22 8HX; www.franklinsrestaurant.com; 10.30 pm; set weekday L £29 (FP); SRA-80%.

Frantoio SW10 £52 ④❷❷

397 King's Rd 7352 4146 5–3B

"You're welcomed like a long-lost friend", by the "cheeky" management of this World's End trattoria – it's "more club than restaurant" for its loyal local following, who appreciate its "cheerful" style and "reasonable" prices. / SW10 0LR; www.frantoio.com; 11.15 pm, Sun 10.15 pm.

Frederick's N1 £58 ④❸❷
106 Islington High St 7359 2888 8–3D
"A top place for a special dinner" – this old Islington favourite is a notably "enjoyable" destination, with a "beautiful" and "spacious" interior; its "traditional" cooking is "pleasant" too, though critics do query whether it's worth the prices. / N1 8EG; www.fredericks.co.uk; 11 pm; closed Sun; set weekday L, dinner & pre-theatre £32 (FP).

Freemasons Arms NW3 £41 ⑤⑤❷
32 Downshire Hill 7433 6811 8–2A
"Right on the edge of Hampstead Heath", this "inviting" pub – with its conservatory, garden and "comfy" interior – can feel "really special"; standards are very erratic, though – at worst, service is "very scatty", and the food can be "dreadful". / NW3 1NT; www.freemasonsarms.co.uk; 10 pm, Sat 10.30 pm, Sun 9 pm.

Fresco W2 £25 ❷❷④
25 Westbourne Grove 7221 2355 6–1C
"Great Lebanese food on the go"; "over 20 juice combinations squeezed to order" are the highlight at this Bayswater pit stop. / W2 4UA; www.frescojuices.co.uk; 10.30 pm.

Frizzante at City Farm
Hackney City Farm E2 £29 ❷④④
1a Goldsmiths Row 7729 6381 12–1D
Pleasantly "rough 'n' ready" in style, this "school classroom-style" café, between Columbia Road and Broadway Market, is of particular note for its "delicious" breakfasts; "you'll be surrounded by babies and toddlers", of course. / E2 8QA; www.frizzanteltd.co.uk; D only, closed Mon; no Amex.

Frizzante Cafe
Surrey Docks Farm SE16 £31 ❸❷❸
South Whf, Rotherhithe St 7231 1010 11–2B
A "bustling" little café on a Thames-side working farm, in deepest Rotherhithe; its tiny kitchen dishes up coffees and ices, plus a "surprising variety" of other fare. / SE16 5ET; www.frizzanteltd.co.uk; 4.30 pm; closed Mon, Tue-Sun D; no Amex.

La Fromagerie Café W1 £38 ❷④❷
2-6 Moxon St 7935 0341 3–1A
"For a kick-start to the day", or "an ad-hoc lunch", it's hard to beat the "high-quality light bites" on offer in the café of this famous Marylebone deli/cheese shop; "getting served, however, can be a challenge". / W1U 4EW; www.lafromagerie.co.uk; 7 pm, Sat 6.30 pm, Sun 5.30 pm; L only; no booking.

The Frontline Club W2 £52 ❸❸❸
13 Norfolk Pl 7479 8960 6–1D
"A good find in Paddington" (especially for business); this low-key, professional operation – part of a media club for war reporters, hence the striking photos on the walls – offers "well-combined, flavoursome dishes" which are "reliably good, if perhaps a little expensive for what they are". / W2 1QJ; www.frontlineclub.com; 10.30 pm; closed Sat L & Sun.

Fryer's Delight WC1 £13 ❸④⑤
19 Theobald's Rd 7405 4114 2–1D
The "tatty" décor – "Formica tables" and "glaring strip lights" – will never win prizes, but this "old-fashioned" Bloomsbury spot can still serve up some "wonderful fish 'n' chips". / WC1X 8SL; 10 pm; closed Sun; no credit cards.

Fujiyama SW9 £28 ❸④④
5-7 Vining St 7737 2369 10–2D
For a "cheap 'n' cheerful" snack in Brixton, this "hectic" but "commendable" Japanese canteen is a bit of "a find" – "good for straightforward noodles, but offering excellent sushi too"; it's "very child-friendly". / SW9 8QA; www.newfujiyama.com; 11 pm.

Fulham Wine Rooms SW6 £50 ❸❸❸
871-873 Fulham Rd 7042 9440 10–1B
A "huge range of excellent wines by the glass" – tasted via a "novel wine-card system" – is the signature attraction of this "well-decked-out bar"; with its "enjoyable" cooking, though, it's an all-round "local favourite" – it even has "one of the Fulham Road's few nice terraces". / SW6 5HP; www.greatwinesbytheglass.com; 11 pm.

Fuzzy's Grub £13 ❸❸④
6 Crown Pas, SW1 7925 2791 3–4D
10 Well Ct, EC4 7236 8400 9–2B
62 Fleet St, EC4 7583 6060 9–2A
"Seriously good sarnies" ("roast in a bap, nuff said") and "great breakfasts" continue to win fans for these "top-quality" British-themed diners; why hasn't the formula gone further? / www.fuzzysgrub.co.uk; most branches between 3 pm and 5 pm; closed Sat & Sun; no Amex; no booking.

Gaby's WC2 £34 ❸❸❸
30 Charing Cross Rd 7836 4233 4–3B
"Save Gaby's!"; efforts by the landlord to close this "beloved", if "somewhat tatty", West End pit stop have inspired paeans to its "genuine" attitude, "fabulous falafel" and "the best salt beef in London"; "shame on the Marquess of Salisbury!" / WC2H 0DE; midnight, Sun 10 pm; no Amex.

Gail's Bread £26 ❸❷❸
138 Portobello Rd, W11 7460 0766 6–1B
282 Chiswick High Rd, W4 8995 2266 7–2A
64 Hampstead High St, NW3 7794 5700 8–1A
5 Circus Rd, NW8 7722 0983 8–3A
64 Northcote Rd, SW11 7924 6330 10–2C
33-35 Exmouth Mkt, EC1 7713 6550 9–1A
"Amazing coffee", "legendary" cakes and "excellent breads" all help win strong popularity for this attractive café/bakery chain; even fans, though, can find prices "impressively high". / www.gailsbread.co.uk; W11 7 pm; NW3 & NW6 8 pm, W1 10 pm, SW7 9 pm, Sun 8 pm; no booking.

Galicia W10 £39 ❸④❷
323 Portobello Rd 8969 3539 6–1A
"A real slice of Spain", in North Kensington's Hispanic quarter – this veteran tapas bar is a deeply "unpretentious" sort of place, offering dishes in "home-cooking" style; service though can be "inattentive". / W10 5SY; 11.15 pm; closed Mon; set weekday L £18 (FP), set Sun L £19 (FP).

Gallery Mess
Saatchi Gallery SW3 £50 ④④❸
Duke of Yorks HQ, Kings Rd 7730 8135 5–2D
Near Sloane Square, this spacious gallery-café certainly has a "great location" (not least "for business"), and an impressive terrace too; the food can be a bit "bland", but most reporters still find this a "well-managed" venue all-round. / SW3 4RY; www.saatchigallery.com/gallerymess; 9.30 pm, Sun 6.30 pm; set pre theatre £31 (FP).

FSA

Gallipoli £33 ④❸❷
102 Upper St, N1 7359 0630 8–3D
107 Upper St, N1 7226 5333 8–3D
120 Upper St, N1 7226 8099 8–3D
"An hospitable atmosphere and bargain prices" – key features of these "buzzy" Turkish bistros, in the heart of Islington, where the scoff is "basic" but "fresh" and "filling"; "old folk should avoid on weekend nights!" / *www.cafegallipoli.com; 11 pm, Fri & Sat midnight.*

Galvin at Windows
Park Lane London Hilton Hotel W1 £89 ④❸❶
22 Park Ln 7208 4021 3–4A
The "breathtaking" views at the Galvins' "glamorous" dining room, 28 floors above Mayfair, are sure to "impress your date", and fans say its Gallic fare is "brilliantly-executed" too; prices are "as stratospheric as the location", though, and some meals this year seemed rather "mechanical". / *W1K 1BE; www.galvinatwindows.com; 10.30 pm, Thu-Sat 11 pm; closed Sat L & Sun D; no Maestro; no shorts; set weekday L £49 (FP).*

GALVIN BISTROT DE LUXE W1 £59 ❷❷❷
66 Baker St 7935 4007 2–1A
"A modern interpretation of a Parisian brasserie", the "understatedly classy" Marylebone cradle of the Galvin brothers' empire has won renown with its "slick" service and "superb" bistro-style cuisine; from a stellar starting point, though, ratings slipped a bit this year. / *W1U 7DJ; www.galvinrestaurants.com; 10.30 pm, Thu-Sat 10.45 pm, Sun 9.30 pm; set weekday L £36 (FP), set pre-theatre £38 (FP).*

Galvin Demoiselle
Harrods SW1 NEW £55 ❸❷❸
87-135 Brompton Rd 7730 1234 5–1D
Prices give nothing away, but the Galvin brothers' "friendly" café/bistro, looking down on Harrods' famous fruit 'n' veg hall, does a very superior line in light bites – "top cakes and puds" a highlight. / *SW1X 7XL; www.galvinrestaurants.com; 7.15 pm, Sun 5 pm; closed Fri D, Sat D & Sun D.*

GALVIN LA CHAPELLE E1 £72 ❷❷❶
35 Spital Sq 7299 0400 12–2B
Arguably "the most impressive dining room in London", the Galvins' "glamorous" and "cathedral-like" former school hall, in Spitalfields, makes a brilliant choice "for business or pleasure"; the Gallic cuisine would be "almost incidental"… were it not also "consistently wonderful"! / *E1 6DY; www.galvinrestaurants.com; 10.30 pm, Sun 9.30 pm; set weekday L £45 (FP).*

Ganapati SE15 £38 ❶❷❷
38 Holly Grove 7277 2928 1–4C
"A culinary reason to travel to Peckham" ("and there aren't many of those!") – this "tiny" diner "punches substantially above its weight", offering "subtly-spiced" dishes, with "a true taste of Kerala". / *SE15 5DF; www.ganapatirestaurant.com; 10.30 pm, Sun 10 pm; closed Mon; no Amex.*

Gandhi's SE11 £28 ❸❷❸
347 Kennington Rd 7735 9015 1–3C
An "ever-reliable" Indian "of the old school", in Kennington – "a firm local favourite", with the odd politico of note among its following. / *SE11 4QE; www.gandhis.co.uk; 11.30 pm.*

Garnier SW5 NEW £55 ❸❶❸
314 Earl's Court Rd 7370 4536 5–2A
On a busy Earl's Court location, a solidly bourgeois new French restaurant whose classic style will come as no surprise to those who've followed top maitre d' Eric Garnier since his Racine days; quality is high… but so are prices. / SW5 9BQ; Rated on Editors' visit.

Le Garrick WC2 £41 ④④❸
10-12 Garrick St 7240 7649 4–3C
"A good brasserie, handy for Theatreland", serving classic French dishes at affordable prices; "cramped" but "atmospheric", it inspires only positive reports. / WC2E 9BH; www.garrickrestaurantbar.co.uk; set weekday L & pre-theatre £31 (FP).

Garrison SE1 £46 ❸❸❶
99-101 Bermondsey St 7089 9355 9–4D
"Tiny tables and wobbly chairs" – all part of the "eclectic charm" of this "really nice and bustling pub", in Bermondsey; the scoff is "good but unspectacular". / SE1 3XB; www.thegarrison.co.uk; 10 pm, Fri-Sat 10.30 pm, Sun 9.30 pm.

Garufa N5 £44 ❸❸❸
104 Highbury Pk 7226 0070 8–1D
"Divine BA-style steaks" win fans for this "attractively informal" Argentinian grill, not far from the Emirates Stadium; "it's not cheap", though. / N5 2XE; www.garufa.co.uk; 10.30 pm; no Amex.

Gastro SW4 £42 ⑤⑤❸
67 Venn St 7627 0222 10–2D
Everyone loves the "lively and very authentic French feel" of this café/bistro, by the Clapham Picture House; shame it's so "unreliable", though – on a bad day the food is "hopeless", and service "laughable". / SW4 0BD; midnight; no Amex; set weekday L £27 (FP).

The Gate £41 ❶❸④
51 Queen Caroline St, W6 8748 6932 7–2C
370 St John St, EC1 7278 5483 8–3D NEW
"A great veggie that's stood the test of time" – this "superb" Hammersmith "hidden gem" has long been one of London's top non-meat haunts – it re-opens in late-2012, after a major refurbishment; a spin-off recently opened opposite Sadlers Wells, too late for any survey feedback. / www.thegate.tv; EC1 10.30 pm, W6 10.30, Sat 11 pm; Sat L & Sun.

Gaucho £60 ❸④❸
25 Swallow St, W1 7734 4040 3–3D
60 Charlotte St, W1 7580 6252 2–1C
125 Chancery Ln, WC2 7242 7727 2–2D
89 Sloane Ave, SW3 7584 9901 5–2C
64 Heath St, NW3 7431 8222 8–1A
02 Centre, Peninsular Sq, SE10 8858 7711 11–2D
Tooley St, SE1 7407 5222 9–4D
Tow Path, TW10 8948 4030 1–4A
29 Westferry Circus, E14 7987 9494 11–1B
93a Charterhouse St, EC1 7490 1676 9–1B
5 Finsbury Ave, Broadgate, EC2 7256 6877 12–2B
1 Bell Inn Yd, EC3 7626 5180 9–2C
For its loyal legions of fans, this "understated, classy and cool" Argentinian chain still "does the best steaks", and offers an "exciting" list of reds to go with 'em too; sadly, though, there's also a widespread feeling that it's "seriously overpriced for what it is". / www.gauchorestaurants.co.uk; 11 pm, Fri & Sat 11.30 pm, SE10, Piccadilly midnight, Sun 11 pm; EC3 & EC2 closed Sat & Sun; WC2 7 EC1 closed Sun.

F S A

Gauthier Soho W1 £67 ❷❶❷
21 Romilly St 7494 3111 4–3A
"You ring the bell for entry", at this "romantic" Soho townhouse, where the interior – full of "private nooks and crannies" – "is awkward, yet characterful"; Alexis Gauthier's "very accomplished" seasonally-changing menus include a "winner" of a set lunch.
/ W1D 5AF; www.gauthiersoho.co.uk; 10.30 pm; closed Sun.

LE GAVROCHE W1 £130 ❶❶❷
43 Upper Brook St 7408 0881 3–2A
"The bill could bail out Greece!", but Michel Roux's "rock-solid" Mayfair stalwart is "the real McCoy"; yes, it is "stuffy" and "a little dated", but – with its "opulent" cuisine and "perfect" service – it really does offer "old-school luxury at its finest"; the set lunch, famously, is an "absolute winner" – book well ahead. / W1K 7QR; www.le-gavroche.co.uk; 11 pm; closed Sat L & Sun; jacket required; set weekday L £59 (FP).

Gay Hussar W1 £46 ⑤❸❸
2 Greek St 7437 0973 4–2A
"Socialist luminaries" (both on the walls and at the tables) still adorn this "marvellously retro" Soho Hungarian; it's still hailed by some long-term fans as a "classic", but critics say its hearty scoff is "awful", and that the place "survives on sentiment alone". / W1D 4NB; www.gayhussar.co.uk; 10.45 pm; closed Sun.

Gaylord W1 £46 ❸④④
79-81 Mortimer St 7580 3615 2–1B
North of Oxford Street, a long-established grand Indian; it's "oddly unatmospheric", but reliably serves up grub that's "better than average". / W1W 7SJ; www.gaylordlondon.com; 10.45 pm, Sun 10.30 pm; no Amex.

Gazette £39 ④④❷
79 Sherwood Ct, Chatfield Rd, SW11 7223 0999 10–1C
100 Balham High St, SW12 8772 1232 10–2C
"Typically French" in every sense, these south London bistros are praised by fans for their "fantastic array of no-nonsense fare", at "good-value" prices; critics, though, dismiss them as "dreadful Café Rouge-type places, and twice the price too!"
/ www.gazettebrasserie.co.uk; 11 pm.

Geales £49 ❸④④
1 Cale St, SW3 7965 0555 5–2C
2 Farmer St, W8 7727 7528 6–2B
A "posh chippy", serving "traditional fish 'n' chips" in "a quiet street, off Notting Hill Gate", at decidedly "upmarket" prices; the "more chichi" (but cramped) Chelsea spin-off is "a bit disappointing" in comparison. / www.geales.com; 10.30 pm, Sun 9.30 pm; Mon L; set weekday L £32 (FP).

Gelupo W1 £10 ❶❷❸
7 Archer St 7287 5555 3–2D
"The best gelato in London, hands down" – this "stylish" offshoot of Soho's Bocca di Lupo (opposite) dishes up "heavenly" ice cream "as good as the best in Italy", and "lovely coffee, and a cake-of-the-day too". / W1D 7AU; www.gelupo.com; 11 pm, Thu-Sat 1 am; no Amex; no booking.

Gem N1 £25 ❸❷❷
265 Upper St 7359 0405 8–2D
"Really tasty" mezze and Kurdish grills "at absolute bargain prices" maintain the appeal of this "unspoilt and justifiably bustling" Islington bolthole. / N1 2UQ; www.gemrestaurant.org.uk; 11 pm, Fri-Sat midnight, Sun 10.30 pm; no Amex.

La Genova W1 £58 ④④④
32 North Audley St 7629 5916 3–2A
In very "traditional" style, this long-established Mayfair trattoria is a "polite" and "friendly" sort of place, that can be "good for a business lunch"; to doubters, though, it's just "dated". / W1K 6ZG; www.lagenovarestaurant.com; 11 pm; closed Sun.

George & Vulture EC3 £48 ④❸❷
3 Castle Ct 7626 9710 9–3C
This "proper City chophouse" is certainly "historic" (and much-mentioned in The Pickwick Papers); traditionalists like to feel Dickens himself would recognise its "warm" welcome – the menu would certainly be familiar! / EC3V 9DL; 2.45 pm; L only, closed Sat & Sun.

Gessler at Daquise SW7 £42 ❸❷❷
20 Thurloe St 7589 6117 5–2C
"New owners have done a brilliant job", at this revived Polish bistro, by South Kensington tube, which "has gone up in the world since its days as a '50s café"; "solid, authentic cooking" is served in a "smart" and "understated" setting, at "reasonable prices". / SW7 2LT; www.gessleratdaquise.co.uk; 11 pm; no Amex; set weekday L £26 (FP).

The Giaconda Dining Room WC2 £46
9 Denmark St 7240 3334 4–1A
A "hidden treasure", in the grungy shadow of Centre Point; it's closed at press time for relaunch in late-2012, double the size, and more in the style of a restaurant than the (very cramped) bistro it was. / WC2H 8LS; www.giacondadining.com; 9.15 pm; closed Mon, Sat L & Sun.

Giant Robot EC1 £36 ④④❷
45 Clerkenwell Rd 7065 6810 9–1A
'Bar/café/deli/diner', says the banner, so no wonder the menu at this "fun" Clerkenwell haunt can seem a trifle "confusing for the uninitiated"; the scoff's "tasty" though, as are the cocktails… / EC1M 5RS; www.gntrbt.com; 11 pm.

Gifto's Lahore Karahi UB1 £18 ❷❸④
162-164 The Broadway 8813 8669 1–3A
Large and very well-known, this Indian diner, in Southall, draws weekend queues for its "authentic cuisine, at unbeatable prices". / UB1 1NN; www.gifto.com; 11.30 pm, Sat-Sun midnight.

Gilak N19 £34 ❸❷④
663 Holloway Rd 7272 1692 8–1C
"A hidden gem", in Archway; this "courteous" and "plainly-decorated" spot wins high praise for its "exotic array" of "yummy" and "unusual" North Iranian dishes, and in "big portions" too. / N19 5SE; www.gilakrestaurant.co.uk; 11 pm; no Amex.

Gilbert Scott
St Pancras Renaissance NW1 £62 ④④❸
Euston Rd 7278 3888 8–3C
A chamber of "gorgeous" Victorian grandeur provides the "stunning" setting for Marcus Wareing's brasserie yearling, by St Pancras; "for all the hype", though, reactions are very mixed – tables are "cramped", the "historic" British menu is "cleverer in concept than in execution", and prices can seem "unjustifiably high". / NW1 2AR; www.thegilbertscott.co.uk; 10.30 pm.

Gilgamesh NW1 £62 ❸❸❷

The Stables, Camden Mkt, Chalk Farm Rd 7428 4922 8–3B

This OTT Camden Town venue, with its "beautiful" wood-carvings, has often been dismissed in the past as "style over substance"; most reporters, though, feel it "gets undeserved bad press", and praise it as a "fun" sort of place where the admittedly "pricey" pan-Asian fare is sometimes "fantastic". / NW1 8AH; www.gilgameshbar.com; 11 pm, Fri-Sat 11.30 pm; set weekday L £28 (FP).

Ginger & White £17 ❸❷❷

2 England's Ln, NW3 7722 9944 8–2A

4a-5a, Perrins Ct, NW3 7431 9098 8–2A

"Thank God for a decent coffee in Hampstead!" – this "crowded", "brunch-type place" does a mean brew, plus "decent-to-good" snacks; now also in Belsize Park. / www.gingerandwhite.com; 4.30 pm.

Giraffe £41 ⑤④⑤

120 Wilton Rd, SW1 7233 8303 2–4B

6-8 Blandford St, W1 7935 2333 2–1A

19-21 The Brunswick Centre, WC1 7812 1336 8–4C

120 Holland Park Ave, W11 7229 8567 6–2A

270 Chiswick High Rd, W4 8995 2100 7–2A

7 Kensington High St, W8 7938 1221 5–1A

29-31 Essex Rd, N1 7359 5999 8–3D

196-198 Haverstock Hill, NW3 7431 3812 8–2A

46 Rosslyn Hill, NW3 7435 0343 8–2A

Royal Festival Hall, Riverside, SE1 7928 2004 2–3D

1 Crispin Pl, E1 3116 2000 12–2B

Often, appropriately enough, a "zoo", these "bright and colourfully-decorated" family "havens" are typically full of kids; even some fans concede the 'world-food' repertoire "leaves much to be desired", however, and service is ever more "hit-and-miss". / www.giraffe.net; 10.45 pm, Sun 10.30 pm; no booking, Sat & Sun 9 am-5 pm.

La Giralda HA5 £31 ❸④④

66-68 Pinner Grn 8868 3429 1–1A

"Still going strong", this "old-fashioned" Spanish restaurant, in a suburban parade, may "need freshening up" decor-wise, but its tasty scoff is "always fresh and well-cooked". / HA5 2AB; www.lagiralda.co.uk; 10 pm; closed Mon & Sun D.

The Glasshouse TW9 £65 ❶❶❸

14 Station Pde 8940 6777 1–3A

"Maintaining the same standards as its siblings Chez Bruce and La Trompette", this "bright" (if "oddly-shaped" and "noisy") foodie Mecca, in Kew, wins high esteem for its "exceptional" cuisine ("with a light Asian influence"), "magnificent" wine, and "assured and engaging" service. / TW9 3PZ; www.glasshouserestaurant.co.uk; 10.30 pm, Sun 10 pm.

Gold Mine W2 £32 ❷④④

102 Queensway 7792 8331 6–2C

Roast duck to die for – the star attraction cited in almost all reports on this "reliable" Bayswater Cantonese. / W2 3RR; 11 pm.

Golden Dragon W1 £32 ❸④❸

28-29 Gerrard St 7734 2763 4–3A

"A Chinatown mainstay", and one that looks more "inviting" than most; the main menu is sometimes "very average", but fans say there's a "wide choice of excellently-priced dim sum". / W1 6JD; 11 pm, Fri & Sat 11.30 pm, Sun 10.20 pm.

Golden Hind W1 £26 ❷❷❸
73 Marylebone Ln 7486 3644 2–1A
"Still the best fish 'n' chips in central London!"; a huge number of reports confirm the "terrific" all-round standards maintained by this "cafeteria-style" Marylebone "classic" (recently enlarged); BYO – no corkage. / W1U 2PN; 10 pm; closed Sat L & Sun.

Goldfish NW3 £46 ❷④④
82 Hampstead High St 7794 6666 8–2A
An "original but unalarming" take on Chinese cuisine wins high favour for this "convivial" Hampstead fixture, even if the decor is "uninspiring" and "service can go awry"; its City outpost is no more. / NW3 1RE; www.goldfish-restaurant.co.uk; 10.30 pm, Sat-Sun 11 pm.

Good Earth £53 ❷❸④
233 Brompton Rd, SW3 7584 3658 5–2C
143-145 The Broadway, NW7 8959 7011 1–1B
"A definite cut above" – these civilised Chinese establishments, in Knightsbridge and Mill Hill, "deserve to be as busy as they always are"; "some pain in the wallet department" is, however, to be expected. / www.goodearthgroup.co.uk; 11 pm, Sun 10.30 pm.

Goode & Wright W11 NEW £50 ❸❸④
271 Portobello Rd 7727 5552 6–1A
A "very French" manager works with an English chef to offer good Gallic dishes at this "interesting" newcomer, which is generally (if not quite invariably) hailed as a "welcome addition to the Notting Hill scene". / W11 1LR; www.goodeandwright.co.uk; 10 pm; closed Mon & Sun L.

Goodman £62 ❷❷❸
26 Maddox St, W1 7499 3776 3–2C
3 South Quay, E14 7531 0300 11–1C NEW
11 Old Jewry, EC2 7600 8220 9–2C
"A meat lover's paradise!" – these "NY-style power grill-houses" ("very male-dominated" and "full of suits") serve up not only "divine" steaks ("the best in London"), but also "simply superb burgers", "wonderful truffle chips", and "evilly good lobster mac 'n' cheese". / www.goodmanrestaurants.com; 10.30 pm; W1 & E14 closed Sun; EC2 closed Sat & Sun.

Gopal's of Soho W1 £30 ❸❸④
12 Bateman St 7434 1621 4–2A
It offers no culinary adventure, but – for long-term fans – this curry classic, in a Soho basement, is an "always-enjoyable" destination. / W1D 4AH; www.gopalsofsoho.co.uk; 11.30 pm, Sun 11 pm.

Gordon Ramsay SW3 £126 ❸❸④
68-69 Royal Hospital Rd 7352 4441 5–3D
"Easier to book nowadays, after his battering in the press", but the global TV star's notional home base, in Chelsea, still impresses many reporters, courtesy of Claire Smyth's "fabulous" classic cuisine; over a third of reporters, though, are most impressed by the "rip-off" prices – "come on Michelin, be brave: remove a star… or two!" / SW3 4HP; www.gordonramsay.com; 11 pm; closed Sat & Sun; no jeans or trainers; booking: max 8.

Gordon Ramsay at Claridge's Claridge's Hotel W1 £101 ⑤⑤④
55 Brook St 7499 0099 3–2B
It has its fans, but roughly half the reports on this potentially wonderful Art Deco hotel dining room, in Mayfair, say it's "very average", or "gets worse every year", or is "a total waste of money"; we understand GR's lease is shortly to expire – let's hope the hotel will then at last create an offering that lives up to the location. / W1K 4HR; www.gordonramsay.com; 11 pm, Sun 10 pm; no jeans or trainers; booking: max 8.

Gordon's Wine Bar WC2 £32 ⑤⑤❶
47 Villiers St 7930 1408 4–4D
"Scruffy as hell, but always worth a visit" – this "wonderfully atmospheric dungeon" of a wine bar, by Embankment tube, has a "unique" ambience (and a brilliant, large summer terrace too); on the wine front, "there's an excellent choice by the bottle or glass", accompanied by "basic" dishes. / WC2N 6NE; www.gordonswinebar.com; 10 pm, Sun 9 pm; no booking.

The Goring Hotel SW1 £77 ❸❶❶
15 Beeston Pl 7396 9000 2–4B
"Quintessentially English" and "very civilised", this family-owned Victoria hotel dining room is "always a delight"; it's not just the "exemplary" service that makes it stand out – if you're looking for "proper old-school", "upper-crust" food (breakfast, obviously, a highlight), you won't find it done much better than here. / SW1W 0JW; www.thegoring.com; 10 pm; closed Sat L; no jeans or trainers; table of 8 max.

Gourmet Burger Kitchen £28 ❸④④
Branches throughout London
"You can't beat a GBK burger", say the many fans loyal to this "utilitarian" chain, which – though undoubtedly now "eclipsed by Byron" – still consistently "does what it says on the tin"; its "hefty" and "succulent" burgers are "pepped up with Kiwi culinary flair". / www.gbkinfo.com; most branches close 10.30 pm; no booking.

Gourmet Pizza Company Gabriels Wharf SE1 £32 ④❸❸
56 Upper Ground 7928 3188 9–3A
"Surprisingly good service, and the pizzas aren't bad either", at this "reliable" outfit (now sole survivor of what was once a chain); great views over the Thames too. / SE1 9PP; www.gourmetpizzacompany.co.uk; 10 pm.

Gourmet San E2 £24 ❷⑤⑤
261 Bethnal Green Rd 7729 8388 12–1D
Forget the "basic" setting, "grim" location and "erratic" service – "a wonderful array" of Sichuan dishes, in "enormous portions and at very low prices", has won an impressive following for this "authentic" Bethnal Green spot. / E2 6AH; www.oldplace.co.uk; 11 pm; D only.

Govinda's W1 £14 ❷④④
9 Soho St 7437 4928 4–1A
"A great choice for a cheap 'n' cheerful meal" – the "unchanging" Indian veggie canteen attached to Soho's Radha-Krishna Temple offers fare that's not just "very tasty" but "filling" too. / W1D 3DL; www.iskcon-london.org; 9 pm; closed Sun D; no Amex.

Gow's EC2 £52 ❸❸❸
81 Old Broad St 7920 9645 9–2C
It may seem almost "quaint" nowadays, but this long-established City fish-specialist pleases all who report on it with its "superb oysters", and the "great variety of fish dishes on offer". / EC2M 1PR; www.ballsbrothers.co.uk; 9.30 pm; closed Sat & Sun.

The Gowlett SE15 £31 ❷❸❸
62 Gowlett Rd 7635 7048 1–4C
A Peckham pub that's become quite a local institution, thanks not least to the quality of its "excellent thin-crust pizza". / SE15 4HY; www.thegowlett.com; 10.30 pm, Sun 9 pm; no credit cards.

Goya SW1 £45 ④④④
34 Lupus St 7976 5309 2–4C
"A stand-out in a barren area", this south-Pimlico tapas bar is undoubtedly "popular as an after-work drop-in"… but perhaps more for its wines than for its food, which varies from "great" to "disappointing". / SW1V 3EB; www.goyarestaurant.co.uk; 11.30 pm.

Grace St Paul's EC4 £8 ❷❷❸
8 Creed Ln 821 659 9–2B
"Excellent coffee and home-made sandwiches, soups and snacks", and "lovely" service too – the proposition that inspires all-round satisfaction with this reasonably-priced café, not far from St Paul's. / EC4V 5BR; www.gracestpauls.com; 4 pm; L only, closed Sat & Sun; no credit cards.

Gran Paradiso SW1 £46 ④❸④
52 Wilton Rd 7828 5818 2–4B
"I first visited in 1972, and I swear the menu hasn't changed a bit!" – this Pimlico "old favourite" continues to seduce its (older) following with its "calm" style, "comfort-food" cuisine, and "personal" service; to critics, though, it's "living on past glories". / SW1V 1DE; 10.45 pm; closed Sat L & Sun.

The Grand Imperial
Guoman Grosvenor Hotel SW1 £52 ❸❸❸
101 Buckingham Palace Rd 7821 8898 2–4B
The lofty main dining room of Victoria's station-hotel is a Chinese restaurant nowadays; some reporters find it a "class act" (with bargain dim sum an undoubted highlight), but there are also complaints of "high prices" and "inconsistent" results. / SW1W 0SJ; www.grandimperiallondon.com; 10.30 pm.

Granger & Co W11 NEW £44 ⑤④❸
175 Westbourne Grove 7229 9111 6–1B
"Much hype" has enveloped the opening of Aussie chef Bill Granger's first Old World outpost, and fans "love the vibe" of this "cheerful", "'50s-chic" Notting Hill spot (especially at breakfast); critics however are bewildered – "why on earth are there queues to get in?" / W11 2SB; www.grangerandco.com.

The Grapes E14 £40 ❸❸❷
76 Narrow St 7987 4396 11–1B
This "lovely" Wapping pub "has a wonderful Thames-side setting", and "oozes character"; despite the odd quibble, new management (including Sir Ian McKellen!) seems to have brought little change to its celebrated Sunday roasts, or its upstairs fish-specialist dining room. / E14 8BP; www.thegrapes.co.uk; 9.30 pm; closed Sat L & Sun D.

FSA

Grazing Goat W1 £51 ❸④❸
6 New Quebec St 7724 7243 2–2A
This year-old Thomas Cubitt-group gastropub is "a great addition to the no-man's-land off the Edgware Road"; "book a table in the upstairs dining room, or fight it out in the noisy downstairs bar". / W1H 7RQ; www.thegrazinggoat.co.uk; 10 pm, Sun 9.30 pm; ; SRA-62%.

Great Eastern Dining Room EC2 £43 ❸❷❸
54-56 Great Eastern St 7613 4545 12–1B
"Great Asian-fusion dishes", well-made cocktails and a "lively" vibe still ensure Will Ricker's Shoreditch haunt (one of the area's early pioneers of cool) is a big hit with its fans; ratings are drifting, though – is it starting to show its age? / EC2A 3QR; www.rickerrestaurants.com; 10.45 pm; closed Sat L & Sun.

Great Nepalese NW1 £26 ❸❷⑤
48 Eversholt St 7388 6737 8–3C
A real Euston "stalwart" – this decidedly old-school "institution" continues to offer "a great twist on 'Indian' food" (plus "particularly good" Nepalese specials), served "with pride and pleasure". / NW1 1DA; www.great-nepalese.co.uk; 11.30 pm, Sun 10 pm.

Great Queen Street WC2 £42 ❷❸❸
32 Great Queen St 7242 0622 4–1D
"Quintessentially modern British, seasonal, offally fare" ("rather in the style of St John") has helped make a huge hit of this Covent Garden sibling to the Anchor & Hope – a "dark and plain", "pub-like" space with a "good ambience" (although it can be "astonishingly noisy"). / WC2B 5AA; 10.30 pm; closed Sun D; no Amex.

The Greedy Buddha SW6 £32 ❸❸❸
144 Wandsworth Bridge Rd 7751 3311 10–1B
A "friendly" Fulham subcontinental, of note for "fiery variations on old-favourite dishes", and "some interesting Nepalese options" too; it's also praised for its "non-standard" interior. / SW6 2UH; www.thegreedybuddha.com; 10.30 pm, Fri-Sat 11.30 pm; no Amex.

Green & Blue SE22 £40 ❸❷❷
38 Lordship Ln 8693 9250 1–4D
"The wine is the star, but the dishes complement it perfectly", at this East Dulwich wine store, which "recently up-graded its food offer"; "pick your bottle from the list, or by perusing the shelves". / SE22 8HJ; www.greenandbluewines.com; 10 pm, Fri-Sat 11 pm; closed Sun D; no Amex.

Green Cottage NW3 £40 ❷④⑤
9 New College Pde 7722 5305 8–2A
A Swiss Cottage veteran which is very highly prized by its small but dedicated fan club, thanks not least to the quality of its "consistently delicious" Cantonese fare. / NW3 5EP; 10.30 pm, Sun 9.30 pm; no Amex.

Green Man & French Horn WC2 NEW
54 St Martin's Ln awaiting tel 4–4C
Can the Terroirs team make it four-in-a-row?; this latest offshoot of their bistro empire opens – in an oddly narrow former pub building, a few doors from the Coliseum – in late-2012. / WC2N 4EA.

Green Papaya E8 £31 ❷❷❸
191 Mare St 8985 5486 1–1D
"Tasty Vietnamese food, friendly staff, great value" – that's the deal at this "cheap 'n' cheerful" Hackney spot. / E8 3QE; www.green-papaya.com; 10.30 pm; Closed L, Mon; no Amex.

Green's £63 ❸❸④
36 Duke St, SW1 7930 4566 3–3D
14 Cornhill, EC3 7220 6300 9–2C
"Simple things are done well", at Simon Parker Bowles's "club-like" St James's dining room – ideal for a "very civilised" business meal; its "lifeless" spin-off in a former City banking hall, however, drags down the ratings awarded overall. / www.greens.org.uk; SW1 11 pm; SW1 closed Sun (May-Sep), EC3 closed Sat & Sun.

The Greenhouse W1 £105 ❷❷❸
27a Hays Mews 7499 3331 3–3B
"An outstanding, encyclopaedic wine list with multiple vintages of great wines" remains a particular highlight of a visit to this "tranquil" and business-friendly (and "astronomically expensive") Mayfair stalwart; the cuisine of new chef Arnaud Bignon, however, is "amazing" too. / W1J 5NX; www.greenhouserestaurant.co.uk; 11 pm; closed Sat L & Sun; booking: max 12.

The Grove W6 £37 ④❸④
83 Hammersmith Grove 8748 2966 7–1C
Consistently family-friendly and the food's good too, at this dependable and popular Hammersmith corner-gastroboozer. / W6 0NQ; www.groverestaurants.co.uk; 11 pm; no Amex; set weekday L £27 (FP), set dinner £33 (FP).

Grumbles SW1 £42 ④❷❸
35 Churton St 7834 0149 2–4B
Nearly half a century old, this "cheap 'n' cheerful" Pimlico bistro has a "rough-and-ready" ("very cramped") charm that can still appeal; since it changed hands last year, more of a "personal touch" is in evidence too. / SW1V 2LT; www.grumblesrestaurant.co.uk; 10.45 pm; set weekday L & pre-theatre £26 (FP).

Guglee £29 ❸④④
7 New College Pde, NW3 7722 8–2A
279 West End Ln, NW6 7317 8555 1–1B NEW
"More interesting than your traditional Indian" – these north London spots "try hard to be innovative"; on limited feedback, it seems the new West Hampstead branch is already out-scoring the Swiss Cottage original on that front. / www.guglee.co.uk; 11 pm.

The Guinea Grill W1 £64 ❸❸❸
30 Bruton Pl 7499 1210 3–3B
With its "excellent steaks", "divine steak 'n' kidney pies" and "interesting" wine, this "wonderful, old-fashioned" dining room – at the rear of a pub in a Mayfair mews – can make a "surprisingly good" destination; shame it's "seriously overpriced". / W1J 6NL; www.theguinea.co.uk; 10.30 pm; closed Sat L & Sun; booking: max 8.

The Gun E14 £51 ❸❸❷
27 Coldharbour 7515 5222 11–1C
A real "change from the sterility of Canary Wharf", this "historic" waterside inn – with its well-sourced "pub food", "excellent views" (of the O2) and "the best terrace" – has a large and enthusiastic following; "it's on the expensive side for a gastropub, but lovely all the same". / E14 9NS; www.thegundocklands.com; 10.30 pm, Sun 9.30 pm.

Gung-Ho NW6 £39 ④❷❸
328-332 West End Ln 7794 1444 1–1B
Supporters of this "old-fashioned" West Hampstead Chinese say it's "still solid" and rather "un-sung"; there are quite a few doubters, though, who feel "it seems to be going backwards" nowadays. / NW6 1LN; www.stir-fry.co.uk; 11.30 pm; no Amex.

The Gunmakers EC1 £40 ❷❷❸
13 Eyre Street Hill 7278 1022 9–1A
A small pub, hidden-away in Farringdon; with its good selection of well-cooked food and "great beers on tap" too, it is well worth seeking out. / EC1R 5ET; www.thegunmakers.co.uk; 10 pm; closed Sat & Sun D; no Amex; no booking Fri D.

Haché £36 ❸❸❷
329-331 Fulham Rd, SW10 7823 3515 5–3B
24 Inverness St, NW1 7485 9100 8–3B
"Beating Byron" and "blowing GBK out of the water!" – these "brilliant little joints", in Camden Town and Chelsea, are "cool" places, and offer a great range of "seriously good burgers for a seriously reasonable price", and with loads of "exotic toppings" too. / www.hacheburgers.com; 10.30 pm, Fri-Sat 11 pm, Sun 10 pm.

Hakkasan £83 ❷④❷
17 Bruton St, W1 7907 1888 3–2C
8 Hanway Pl, W1 7927 7000 4–1A
"Full of beautiful people" – these "slick" and "scene-y" Chinese spectacles offer a beguiling mix of "dramatic" decor, "sensational" cooking and "superb" cocktails; staff "could try harder to make you feel valued", though, and prices can seem "exorbitant". / www.hakkasan.com; midnight, Sun 11 pm.

Halepi W2 £44 ❸❶❸
18 Leinster Ter 7262 1070 6–2C
"It may look a bit shabby" nowadays, and it's "not cheap", but this veteran Bayswater taverna is a long-time favourite for older fans, thanks to its "good Greek food", and "staff who make you very welcome". / W2 3ET; www.halepi.co.uk; midnight.

The Hampshire Hog W6 NEW £49 ❸❸❷
227 King St 8748 3391 7–2B
A "terrific" (and "very family-friendly") new gastropub – from a team who left The Engineer – that's brought some unaccustomed style to the strip near Hammersmith Town Hall; it has a notably "cheery" interior, "lovely" garden, and "solid gastro-fare"; cute tea shop too. / W6 9JT; www.thehampshirehog.com; 11 pm; closed Sun D.

Haozhan W1 £48 ❷④⑤
8 Gerrard St 7434 3838 4–3A
"A creative take on Chinese cuisine" wins high praise for this "fusion-style" Chinatown canteen; no prizes for its "basic" interior design, though – "IKEA-on-LSD"? / W1D 5PJ; www.haozhan.co.uk; 11.15 pm, Fri & Sat 11.45 pm, Sun 10.45 pm.

Harbour City W1 £38 ❷④④
46 Gerrard St 7439 7859 4–3B
"It's impossible to spend much", at this "dependable", if "dull"-looking, fixture on Chinatown's main drag; principal attraction – "terrific dim sum, very cheap". / W1D 5QH; 11.30 pm, Fri-Sat midnight, Sun 10 pm.

Hard Rock Café W1 £46 ④④❷
150 Old Park Ln 7629 0382 3–4B
"I've been going for over 30 years – the music seems loud nowadays, but the meat's always good"; the Mayfair original of this worldwide burger-franchise still has more fans than foes, who say it's "consistent" and "great fun", especially with kids. / W1K 1QZ; www.hardrock.com/london; midnight; need 20+ to book.

Hardy's Brasserie W1 **£46** ④❸❸
53 Dorset St 7935 5929 2–1A
"Definitely a locals' favourite"; this "hidden-away" Marylebone wine bar is "a nice, easy-going place" with a "lively" vibe and "accommodating" staff – "great just for a drink, or a full meal". / W1U 7NH; www.hardysbrasserie.co.uk; 10.30 pm; closed Sat & Sun.

Hare & Tortoise **£29** ❸❸④
11-13 The Brunswick, WC1 7278 9799 2–1D
373 Kensington High St, W14 7603 8887 7–1D
38 Haven Grn, W5 8810 7066 1–2A
296-298 Upper Richmond Rd, SW15 8394 7666 10–2B
90 New Bridge St, EC4 7651 0266 9–2A
"It's not hard to see why they're always busy – they're great value!"; these "noisy and bustly" pan-Asian canteens offer "an amazing choice" of dishes, and results are "quick", "fresh" and "so cheap". / www.hareandtortoise-restaurants.co.uk; 10.45 pm, Fri & Sat 11.15 pm; EC4 10 pm; EC4 closed Sun; W14 no bookings.

Harrison's SW12 **£46** ④④❸
15-19 Bedford Hill 8675 6900 10–2C
Sam Harrison's "solid" brasserie is a "favourite local", down Balham way; "perfect for families", it's ideal for "a posh brekkie". / SW12 9EX; www.harrisonsbalham.co.uk; 10.30 pm, Sun 10 pm; set pre theatre £30 (FP); SRA-50%.

Harry Morgan's NW8 **£36** ❸❷❸
31 St John's Wood High St 7722 1869 8–3A
"They're trying harder nowadays" ("they needed to"), at this classic deli, in St John's Wood, which has emerged in recent times as a very consistent all-rounder; highlights – "wonderful salt beef" and "chicken soup like mum used to make". / NW8 7NH; www.harryms.co.uk; 9.30 pm.

Harwood Arms SW6 **£52** ❶❷❷
Walham Grove 7386 1847 5–3A
"Many aspire" but "few deliver" as well as this "unremarkable-looking", yet "audaciously inspirational", corner boozer, in the backwoods of Fulham; a "real class act", its "outstanding" British cuisine ("dominated by game") goes "well beyond pub-standard". / SW6 1QR; www.harwoodarms.com; 9.30 pm, Sun 9 pm; closed Mon L.

Hashi SW20 **£34** ❷❷❸
54 Durham Rd 8944 1888 10–2A
"Why pay West End prices when you can have first-class sushi or sashimi on your doorstop?" – so say Raynes Park fans of this "comfortable" Korean-owned Japanese. / SW20 0TW; 10.30 pm; closed Mon; no Amex.

The Havelock Tavern W14 **£42** ❸④❷
57 Masbro Rd 7603 5374 7–1C
"Vibrant and fun", this "always-busy" Olympia backstreet boozer pulls in a crowd from far 'n' wide; the "simple" food isn't a patch on its standard a few years ago, though, and service is so-so. / W14 0LS; www.havelocktavern.com; 10 pm, Sun 9.30 pm; no booking.

The Haven N20 **£50** ❸④④
1363 High Rd 8445 7419 1–1B
This "closely-packed" neighbourhood spot, in Whetstone, has quite a far-flung fan club, thanks to its "good, if not cheap" cuisine – perhaps that's another way of saying results can sometimes seem rather "average". / N20 9LN; www.haven-bistro.co.uk; 11 pm; set weekday L £28 (FP).

FSA

Hawksmoor £61 ❷❷❸

65 Regent St, W1 awaiting tel 3–3D NEW
11 Langley St, WC2 7420 9390 4–2C
157 Commercial St, E1 7426 4850 12–2B
10-12 Basinghall St, EC2 7397 8120 9–2C
"The ultimate red-meat treat"; these "mega-popular steak-houses win raves for their "glorious" steak (in "overwhelming" portions), "fabulous" chips, "memorable" cocktails and "super" wine; you pay "premium prices", though, and – as the group mushrooms – ratings are under all-round pressure. / www.thehawksmoor.com; 10.30 pm; closed Sun D, EC2 closed Sat-Sun.

Haz £36 ④❸❷

9 Cutler St, E1 7929 7923 9–2D
34 Foster Ln, EC2 7600 4172 9–2B
112 Houndsditch, EC3 7623 8180 9–2D
6 Mincing Ln, EC3 7929 3173 9–3D
"Smart enough for clients, great value with friends" – these "always-buzzing" City operations offer a very "safe" formula of "elegant" decor and "cheerful" service... plus Turkish fare that's "consistent, but never scales the heights". / www.hazrestaurant.co.uk; 11.30 pm; EC3 closed Sun.

Hazev E14 £33 ❸❷④

2 South Quay Sq, Discovery Dock West 7515 9467 11–1C
Looking for a "fresh and simple" bite in Canary Wharf? – this large waterside Turkish restaurant, near Surrey Quays DLR, offers "very good-value" grills, bread and mezze in "hearty portions"; at times, though, it can get "too crowded". / E14 9RT; www.hazev.com; 11.30 pm, Sun 10.30 pm, Mon 11 pm.

Hazuki WC2 £38 ❸④④

43 Chandos Pl 7240 2530 4–4C
"A good-value Japanese, convenient for the Coliseum and Theatreland" – it's "not really an evening-out sort of place" but, as a practical lunchtime or evening option, it invariably hits the spot. / WC2M 4HS; www.hazukilondon.co.uk; 10.30 pm, Sun 9.30 pm; closed Sat L & Sun L.

Hedone W4 £80 ❸❸④

301 Chiswick High Rd 8747 0377 7–2A
Disciples of Mikael Jonsson's "heroic" distant-Chiswick yearling are blown away by his "exciting creativity" and his "painstaking sourcing of ingredients"; there are quite a few critics, though, who find the experience "odd", "overpriced" or "over-hyped", and – worst of all – the place is "full of bloggers taking photos!" / W4 4HH; www.hedonerestaurant.com; 10 pm; closed Mon, Tue L, Wed L, Thu L & Sun.

Hélène Darroze
The Connaught Hotel W1 £112 ④④❸

Carlos Pl 3147 7200 3–3B
"So average, for a top-class hotel"; this Mayfair dining room may have a glorious culinary history behind it, and a Parisian super-chef at its helm, but compliments for Ms Darroze's "technically brilliant (if rich)" cuisine are lost in a haze of complaints about "underwhelming" cooking, "mixed" service and "ridiculous" prices. / W1K 2AL; www.the-connaught.co.uk; 10.30 pm; closed Mon & Sun; jacket & tie.

Hellenic W1 £42
45 Crawford St 7935 1257 6–1D
A decades-old Greek relic, in Marylebone, that moved sites just as our annual survey began; an early report suggests the new incarnation retains its "comforting, familiar, old-fashioned, and uncomplicated" virtues – given the limited feedback, though, we've left it unrated.
/ W1H 1JT; 10.45 pm; closed Sun; no Amex.

The Henry Root SW10 £51 ④④❸
9 Park Walk 7352 7040 5–3B
"A very flexible format" helps make this heart-of-Chelsea hang-out – part bar, part gastropub – a "reliable and very friendly local", short on fireworks as its "comfort-food" formula may be. / SW10 0AJ; www.thehenryroot.com; 10.45 pm, Sun 8.45 pm.

Hereford Road W2 £46 ❷❸④
3 Hereford Rd 7727 1144 6–1B
"Superbly-executed seasonal British food" – "much influenced by St John" – wins high praise for Tom Pemberton's Bayswater bistro; the interior is a tad "chilly and noisy", though, and the occasional critic senses "hype". / W2 4AB; www.herefordroad.org; 10.30 pm, Sun 10 pm; set weekday L £30 (FP).

Hibiscus W1 £111 ④④④
29 Maddox St 7629 2999 3–2C
Claude Bosi's ambitious Mayfair dining room is, say fans, a "calm" and "special" place, delivering "incredible flavours and food-combinations"; prices are "hefty", though, and there are quite a few critics who find the service "pompous", the interior "dull" and the experience "forced". / W1S 2PA; www.hibiscusrestaurant.co.uk; 9.45 pm; closed Sun; set weekday L £60 (FP).

High Road Brasserie W4 £44 ④④❸
162-166 Chiswick High Rd 8742 7474 7–2A
"A good hum", "great street-side seating", "people-watching", a "dependable brunch"... – this "bustling" hang-out, on Chiswick's main drag, certainly has its stylish charms; more objectively, though, standards are "sometimes poor". / W4 1PR; www.brasserie.highroadhouse.co.uk; 10.45 pm, Fri & Sat 11.45 pm, Sun 9.45 pm; set weekday L £28 (FP).

High Timber EC4 £61 ❸❸❸
8 High Timber 7248 1777 9–3B
"Terrific views over the Thames to Tate Modern" and a "superb South African wine list" – highlights of this "low-key" City venue, where "excellent steaks" headline the "uncomplicated" food offer.
/ EC4V 3PA; www.hightimber.com; 10 pm; closed Sat & Sun; set weekday L £39 (FP).

Hilliard EC4 £28 ❷❷❸
26a Tudor St 7353 8150 9–3A
"A haven of foodie focus", by the Temple – this "upmarket" café offers "lovely salads, good hot dishes and interesting sarnies"; it's a legal-land favourite, so "arrive early, or m'learned friends will have scoffed all the best specials!" / EC4Y 0AY; www.hilliardfood.co.uk; 6 pm; L only, closed Sat & Sun; no booking.

Hix W1 £66 ④④④
66-70 Brewer St 7292 3518 3–2D
This "trendy" Soho three-year-old is increasingly "trading on Mark Hix's name"; fans still applaud its "quality, contemporary British food without fuss" and its "lively" style, but it also took a lot of flak this year for "boring" food, and a "soulless" ambience; the basement bar, though, is still as "sexy" as ever. / W1F 9UP; www.hixsoho.co.uk; 10.15 pm.

Hix at The Tramshed EC2 NEW £55 ❸❸❷
32 Rivington St 7749 0478 12–1B
Mark Hix has returned to his Shoreditch roots to create this would-be trendy new steak (and chicken) house, in an impressive post-industrial space (artwork, natch, by Damien Hirst); culinary fireworks were not in evidence on our early-days visit, but the straightforward dishes are very dependably realised. / EC2A 3LX; Rated on Editors' visit; www.chickenandsteak.co.uk.

Hix Belgravia
Belgraves Hotel SW1 NEW £60 ④④❸
20 Chesham St 7858 0100 5–1D
This new '70s-styled boutique-hotel dining room is, say fans, "a great addition to a really dull area"; with its "substandard" food and "drab" atmosphere, though, it simply strikes critics as a "disappointment". / SW1X 8HQ; www.thompsonhotels.com/hotels/london/belgraves; 11 pm, Sun 10.30 pm.

Hix Oyster & Chop House EC1 £57 ❷❸❸
36-37 Greenhill Rents, Cowcross St 7017 1930 9–1A
"A funky place, where the City meets Clerkenwell"; Mark Hix's "homely" eatery, near Smithfield Market, nowadays offers not only "some of the best steaks in town", but also "great oysters and seafood"; it can get "noisy", though. / EC1M 6BN; www.restaurantsetcltd.com; 11 pm, Sun 9 pm; closed Sat L.

HKK EC2 NEW
Snowden St awaiting tel 12–2B
Opening in the City in late-2012, a new Chinese concept from the Hakkasan people; given the location and the backing, we can safely assume it will not be a place to economise… / EC2A 2DQ.

Hole in the Wall W4 £41 ❸❸❸
12 Sutton Lane North 8742 7185 7–2A
A "relaxed" and "above-average" gastropub, hidden-away in Gunnersbury; star feature? – a "lovely" garden. / W4 4LD; 9.45 pm, Sun 9.15 pm; closed Mon L & Tue L.

Holly Bush NW3 £44 ❸④❷
22 Holly Mount 7435 2892 8–1A
"Transporting you to a wonderful Dickensian world" – this "lovely" and "bustling" Hampstead boozer is "no gastropub", but its "pub food" is "excellent" nonetheless ("particularly the Scotch eggs"). / NW3 6SG; fullers.co.uk; 10 pm, Sun 9 pm.

Holy Cow SW11 £25 ❷④❸
166 Battersea Pk Rd 7498 2000 10–1C
"London's best Indian take-away"; this "utterly reliable" Battersea operation attracts a lot of feedback, all to the effect that its "authentic" curries deliver "really great flavours", and at "very good-value prices" too. / SW11 4ND; www.holycowfineindianfood.com; 11 pm, Sun 10.30 pm; D only.

Honest Burgers £21 ❶❸❸
4 Meard St, W1 awaiting tel 4–2A NEW
Brixton Village, Coldharbour Ln, SW9 7733 7963 10–2D
"Knocking spots off everything else", this tiny but "hip" new pit stop, in "trendy" and "bustling" Brixton Market, serves "awesome" burgers (and "oh, the rosemary-salted chips!"), but the queue is "horrible"; a Soho offshoot opened in mid-2012. / www.honestburgers.co.uk; Thu-Sat 10 pm; closed Sun-Wed D.

The Horseshoe NW3 £47 ❸❸④
28 Heath St 7431 7206 8–2A
"Decent food and microbrews" and "smiley" staff make this heart-of-Hampstead local a stand-by worth remembering; "it can be a bit loud and shouty, though". / NW3 6TE; www.thehorseshoehampstead.com; 10pm, Fri-Sat 11 pm.

Hot Stuff SW8 £20 ❷❸④
23 Wilcox Rd 7720 1480 10–1D
Belying its "fairly dubious" Vauxhall location, this "crowded" (despite expansion) BYO Indian has won renown for "brilliant" food that "doesn't cost the earth"; "prices do seem to be running ahead of inflation", though – this is no longer rated the mind-blowing bargain it once was. / SW8 2XA; www.eathotstuff.com; 9.30 pm; no Amex.

The Hoxton Grill EC2 £46 ④❸❷
81 Great Eastern St 7739 9111 12–1B
This "bustling" ("rather noisy") dining area of a "trendy" hotel is adjacent to a "great bar" – it makes a "lively" choice for dinner, and is also popular for "a good breakfast, convenient to the City". / EC2A 3HU; www.hoxtongrill.co.uk; 11.45 pm.

Hudsons SW15 £37 ④④❸
113 Lower Richmond Rd 8785 4522 10–1A
Down in Putney, a "good, solid local bistro", offering an "extensive menu" of "well-prepared" dishes, and "attentive" service; it has quite a name as a breakfast destination. / SW15 1EX; www.hudsonsrestaurant.co.uk; 10 pm, Sun 9.30 pm; closed Tue L.

Hummus Bros £17 ❸④④
88 Wardour St, W1 7734 1311 3–2D
37-63 Southampton Row, WC1 7404 7079 2–1D
128 Cheapside, EC2 7726 8011 9–2B
"Great… if you like hummus!" – these "cafeteria-style" pit stops are just the job for "cheap, tasty, filling and healthy fast food". / www.hbros.co.uk; W1 10 pm, Thu-Sat 11 pm; WC1 9 pm; WC1, EC2 closed Sat & Sun; no booking.

Hunan SW1 £63 ❶❷④
51 Pimlico Rd 7730 5712 5–2D
"Forget the menu, leave it to the boss", when you visit this "unprepossessing" Pimlico stalwart – simply the best Chinese in town; Mr Peng ensures "there's never a dull moment", and the "wonderful food" – a "superb feast" of "exciting, unexpected and eye-opening" dishes – "just keeps coming". / SW1W 8NE; www.hunanlondon.com; 11 pm; closed Sun.

Huong-Viet
An Viet House N1 £34 ④⑤④
12-14 Englefield Rd 7249 0877 1–1C
In a De Beauvoir community centre, this "cheap and cheerful" Vietnamese canteen is still "very friendly", but has it become "too cool for its own good"? – service can be so "slow". / N1 4LS; 11 pm; closed Sun; no Amex; set weekday L £20 (FP).

Hush £57 ❸❸❸
8 Lancashire Ct, W1 7659 1500 3–2B
95-97 High Holborn, WC1 7242 4580 2–1D NEW
Charmingly-located just off Bond Street, a younger Mayfair in-crowd bar/restaurant (with courtyard) that makes a "solid" stand-by for a business lunch – by night, the bar scene is perhaps the greater attraction; a new Holborn sibling opened in mid-2012. / www.hush.co.uk; W1 10.45 pm; WC1 10.30 pm, Sun 9.30 pm; W1 closed Sun.

FSA

Ibérica £43 ❸④❸

195 Great Portland St, W1 7636 8650 2–1B
12 Cabot Sq, E14 7636 8650 11–1C

"High-quality tapas" make this duo of "upmarket" Hispanic ventures worth seeking out; the E14 spin-off seems more "average" and "expensive" than the W1 original, though, and the latter's recent refurbishment struck some reporters as "ill-judged". / 11 pm; W1 closed Sun D.

Ikeda W1 £65 ❷❸⑤

30 Brook St 7629 2730 3–2B

A veteran Mayfair Japanese, which is still "one of the best in town", especially for sushi; "it's very, very expensive", though, and the decor is not so much "retro" as a "dated let-down". / W1K 5DJ; 10.20 pm; closed Sat L & Sun.

Imli W1 £37 ❸❷❷

167-169 Wardour St 7287 4243 3–1D

"Tasty and different Indian tapas" have won quite a following for this large "street-food" operation, in Soho – an excellent choice for a "fast" and "good-value" bite. / W1F 8WR; www.imli.co.uk; 11 pm, Sun 10 pm.

Imperial China WC2 £40 ❸❸❸

25a Lisle St 7734 3388 4–3B

Approached "over a bridge, with fish swimming in a pond", this "spacious" side street spot is "slightly more elegant and comfy than most of Chinatown"; it's best-known for its "superb dim sum", but the food is "decent" at any time. / WC2H 7BA; www.imperial-china.co.uk; 11 pm, Sun 9.30 pm.

Imperial City EC3 £49 ❸❷❸

Royal Exchange, Cornhill 7626 3437 9–2C

"Still, after all these years, my favourite City Chinese" – "dramatically housed" in the cellars of the Royal Exchange, its performance is usually "spot-on". / EC3V 3LL; www.orientalrestaurantgroup.co.uk; 10.15 pm; closed Sat & Sun.

Inaho W2 £39 ❶⑤⑤

4 Hereford Rd 7221 8495 6–1B

"Best sushi in London!" – that's the perennial claim of fans of this very small and "quirky" Bayswater shack; it's certainly not the over-stretched service, or the "dull" and "shabby" ambience, that lures 'em back! / W2 4AA; 11 pm; closed Sat L & Sun; no Amex or Maestro; set weekday L £25 (FP).

Inamo £44 ④④❷

4-12 Regent St, SW1 7484 0500 3–3D
134-136 Wardour St, W1 7851 7051 3–1D

OK, it's a "gimmicky concept", but these West End pan-Asians – where you order off, and play games on, your own interactive tabletop – are "still great fun" (particularly with teenagers). / 11 pm, SW1 12 am.

Indali Lounge W1 £43 ❸❸④

50 Baker St 7224 2232 2–1A

With its "healthy and varied no-ghee cooking", this rather "different" Marylebone Indian can seem "a real find"; its large modern interior does "lacks atmosphere", but "obliging" staff offer consolation. / W1U 7BT; www.indalilounge.com; midnight, Sun 11 pm; closed Sat L.

India Club
Strand Continental Hotel WC2 £25 ❸④⑤
143 Strand 7836 0650 2–2D
"Same as ever!"; this bargain, BYO Indian canteen, near the High Commission, feels "very authentic in every department"; the furniture and decor "look like they were thrown out from a local school hall as unfit-for-service!". / WC2R 1JA; www.strand-continental.co.uk; 10.50 pm; no credit cards; booking: max 6.

Indian Moment SW11 £34 ❸④④
44 Northcote Rd 7223 6575 10–2C
"Delicious, light and flavoursome curries" inspire high local satisfaction with this busy Battersea Indian. / SW11 1NZ; 11.30 pm, Fri & Sat midnight.

Indian Ocean SW17 £28 ❷❷❸
214 Trinity Rd 8672 7740 10–2C
Unaffected by its recent move 'next door', this "great local Indian" continues to please Wandsworth locals with its "old-school but very good" food, and at "reasonable prices" too. / SW17 7HP; www.indianoceanwandsworth.com; 11.30 pm.

Indian Rasoi N2 £36 ❶❷❸
7 Denmark Ter 8883 9093 1–1B
"Setting itself apart from the formulaic norm", this "small but interesting" Muswell Hill Indian offers some "individual" and "exceedingly good" food. / N2 9HG; www.indian-rasoi.co.uk; 10.30 pm; no Amex.

Indian Zilla SW13 £42 ❶❶❷
2-3 Rocks Ln 8878 3989 10–1A
Fans insist "Zilla is better than its parent, Zing", but – notwithstanding the "amazing" quality of its "delicious, well-conceived" cuisine – this Barnes Indian actually only out-scores its stablemate when it comes to its more "luxurious" decor. / SW13 0DB; www.indianzilla.co.uk; 11 pm, Sun 10.30 pm; closed weekday L.

Indian Zing W6 £44 ❶❷❸
236 King St 8748 5959 7–2B
Manoj Vasaikar's "beautiful and sophisticated" cooking, and the "super-friendly" service too, ensures that this "consistently brilliant, high-class Indian" draws fans from Hammersmith and beyond; the room, though, is "squashed-in". / W6 0RS; www.indianzing.co.uk; 11 pm, Sun 10.30 pm; set weekday L £28 (FP).

Indigo
One Aldwych WC2 £66 ④④④
1 Aldwych 7300 0400 2–2D
"Tucked-away above the foyer", the mezzanine of this Theatreland hotel makes a "very comfy" setting for breakfast, for business or for a pre-theatre meal; it's pricey, though, and a number of meals this year were "no more than OK". / WC2B 4BZ; www.onealdwych.com; 11 pm, Sun 10.30 pm; set brunch £40 (FP), set pre-theatre £42 (FP).

Inn the Park SW1 £48 ④⑤❷
St James's Pk 7451 9999 2–3C
"What a location!" – it's hard to beat the setting of this striking modern café in St James's Park, complete with views of the lake; prices are "high", though, the food can be "dull", and service "tends to get overwhelmed in good weather". / SW1A 2BJ; www.peytonandbyrne.co.uk; 8.30 pm; closed Sun D; no Amex.

FSA

Inside SE10 £43 ❷❷④
19 Greenwich South St 8265 5060 1–3D
"Still the best place to go in Greenwich" ("in fact, the only place...") – Guy Awford's "great little restaurant" attracts many reports praising its "adventuresome food" and "good value"; the "austere" ambience, though, "could do with a bit of work". / SE10 8NW; www.insiderestaurant.co.uk; 10.30 pm, Fri-Sat 11 pm; closed Mon & Sun D.

Isarn N1 £56 ❸❸④
119 Upper St 7424 5153 8–3D
A "buzzy" Islington spot that's "a couple of notches up from your standard Thai"; the dining room, though, is "extraordinarily narrow" – "you really need to be very slim to fit in!" / N1 1QP; www.isarn.co.uk; 11 pm, Sun 10 pm; no Amex.

Ishbilia SW1 £51 ❸④④
9 William St 7235 7788 5–1D
Handy for Harvey Nics shoppers, a "busy" Lebanese café with a strong following among arabic customers for its fresh-tasting fare; though last year brought an expansion and refurbishment, reactions to both service and ambience remain mixed. / SW1X 9HL; www.ishbilia.com; 11.30 pm.

Ishtar W1 £45 ❸❷❸
10-12 Crawford St 7224 2446 2–1A
"Either for a quick, cheap lunch or a more leisurely meal", this "well-spaced" Marylebone Turk offers a "top inexpensive dining experience" – "superb-value" set deals in particular. / W1U 6AZ; www.ishtarrestaurant.com; 11 pm, Sun 10.30 pm; set weekday L & pre-theatre £26 (FP).

Isola del Sole SW15 £51 ④④④
16 Lacy Rd 8785 9962 10–2B
"We miss the old Isola!"; this (formerly) "great local Sicilian", in Putney, "has made changes in recent times, and not all to the good" – with some staff departed, "service has suffered", and the food is sometimes only "adequate" nowadays. / SW15 1NL; www.isoladelsole.co.uk; 10.30 pm; closed Sun.

Itsu £31 ④❸④
118 Draycott Ave, SW3 7590 2400 5–2C
100 Notting Hill Gate, W11 7229 4016 6–2B
Level 2, Cabot Place East, E14 7512 5790 11–1C
"Easy to gravitate to", thanks to its "healthy" array of "Japanese fast food" – a "stylish" chain whose branches are often "phenomenally busy"; quibbles? – the cuisine "lacks variety", and it's "tasty but lacking authenticity". / www.itsu.co.uk; 11 pm; E14 10 pm; some are closed Sat & Sun; no booking.

The Ivy WC2 £70 ④❷❷
1-5 West St 7836 4751 4–3B
"Improving" again in recent times, this "discreet" panelled "classic", in the heart of Theatreland, remains, for its army of fans, a simply "awesome" destination; it's still attracting too much flak, though, for food that's "expensive" and "formulaic"; as to celebs? – "they've moved on to the club upstairs". / WC2H 9NQ; www.the-ivy.co.uk; 11.30 pm, Sun 10.30 pm; no shorts; booking: max 6.

Izgara N3 £33 ❸④⑤
11 Hendon Lane 8371 8282 1–1B
"Turkish food in generous portions at reasonable prices" underpins the appeal of this North Finchley café/take-away; "don't expect buzz", though. / N3 1RT; www.izgararestaurant.net; 11.30 pm; no Amex.

F S A

Jai Krishna N4 £19 ❷❷④

161 Stroud Green Rd 7272 1680 8–1D

"Superb south Indian veggie fare" and "friendly" service make this BYO café, in Stroud Green, a stand-by worth knowing about. / N4 3PZ; 10.30 pm; closed Sun; no credit cards.

The Jam Tree £46 ④④❷

541 King's Rd, SW6 3397 3739 5–4B

58 Milson Rd, W14 7371 3999 7–1C

"Tricky to find", in Olympia – a "gem" of a gastropub; it has a pretty well-rated Fulham sibling too, which has a "lovely garden". / W14 11 pm, Sun 10.30 pm; SW6 11 pm, Fri-Sat 2 am.

Jamie's Italian £42 ⑤④④

10-12 Upper St Martin's Ln, WC2 3326 6390 4–3B

Westfield, Ariel Way, W12 8090 9070 7–1C

2 Churchill Pl, E14 3002 5252 11–1C

"For a stress-free meal with kids", Jamie O's "bright and bustling" Italian chain – promising, in its early days – is still tipped as a "fun" option; increasingly, however, it's a case of "all hype and no delivery", with far too many reports nowadays of "absent-minded" staff and "airline-quality" food. / www.jamiesitalian.com; 11.30 pm, Sun 10.30 pm; over 6.

Jenny Lo's Tea House SW1 £33 ❸❸⑤

14 Eccleston St 7259 0399 2–4B

"Very cheap, hot and fast Chinese chow" – the order of the day at this "basic", and often "fiendishly busy", canteen-stalwart, near Victoria. / SW1W 9LT; www.jennylo.co.uk; 9.55 pm; closed Sat & Sun; no credit cards; no booking.

Jin Kichi NW3 £41 ❶❷④

73 Heath St 7794 6158 8–1A

"Homely" and cramped it may be, but this brilliant Hampstead Japanese is "well worth a visit", especially for the "fun" robata bar, where "the grill-master creates the most delicious skewers"; "leave room for the sushi", though. / NW3 6UG; www.jinkichi.com; 11 pm, Sun 10 pm; closed Mon, Tue-Fri D only, Sat & Sun open L & D.

Joanna's SE19 £44 ❸❷❷

56 Westow Hill 8670 4052 1–4D

This "absolute favourite" Crystal Palace local is as suited to a "sophisticated" brunch ("special mention for the pancakes") as it is to a "romantic dinner"; "fantastic City-views" too. / SE19 1RX; www.joannas.uk.com; 10.45 pm, Sun 10.15 pm; set dinner £29 (FP).

Joe Allen WC2 £53 ④④❷

13 Exeter St 7836 0651 4–3D

"Still going strong", this Theatreland basement (which has a NYC doppelgänger) remains an "old favourite" for many fans, thanks not least to its "jolly" ("slightly luvvie") ambience; aside from the "fab burgers" (famously off-menu), though, its "solid" fare is something of a "throwback", and sceptics say the place has plain "lost it". / WC2E 7DT; www.joeallen.co.uk; 12.45 am, Sun 11.45 pm; set dinner & brunch £24 (FP).

Joe's Brasserie SW6 £41 ❸❸❸

130 Wandsworth Bridge Rd 7731 7835 10–1B

"A good-all-round local eatery"; John Brinkley's age-old stand-by, in deepest Fulham, "aims modestly", and succeeds, with its "well-priced" and "wholly reliable" formula – "well above average for the area". / SW6 2UL; www.brinkleys.com; 11 pm.

José SE1 £37 ❶❷❶
104 Bermondsey St 7403 4902 9–4D
"Probably Barrafina's greatest rival" – José Pizarro's "tiny, tiny" Bermondsey corner-bar is "impossible not to love"; thanks to its "perfect" tapas, and its "outstanding" wines and sherries too, it's "mobbed day and night". / SE1 3UB; 10.30 pm, Sun 5.30; closed Fri D, Sat D & Sun D.

Joy King Lau WC2 £34 ❸④④
3 Leicester St 7437 1132 4–3A
Just off Leicester Square, this three-storey stalwart – with its "basic" setting and "simple" food – remains one of Chinatown's most "reliable" options. / WC2H 7BL; www.joykinglau.com; 11.30 pm, Sun 10.30 pm.

The Jugged Hare EC1Y NEW £48 ❸❸❸
49 Chiswell St 7614 0134 12–2A
"Accomplished" cooking and "boutique wines" (served "from a slick Enomatic system") have made this new British bistro, near the Barbican, quite a hit with most (if not quite all) early-days reporters; "it's much better than its nearby sister restaurant, the Chiswell Street Dining Rooms". / EC1Y 4SA; www.etmgroup.co.uk; 11 pm, Thu-Sat midnight, Sun 10.30 pm.

Julie's W11 £59 ④⑤❶
135 Portland Rd 7229 8331 6–2A
"It always delivers for romance" – that's sadly the only reason nowadays to visit this wonderfully seductive, semi-subterranean '70s labyrinth, in Holland Park, where the food is "unimaginative", the service "awful" and the prices "horrendous". / W11 4LW; www.juliesrestaurant.com; 11 pm.

The Junction Tavern NW5 £43 ❸❶❷
101 Fortess Rd 7485 9400 8–2B
"Very welcoming" staff set the tone at this "lively" Kentish Town gastropub, and it has a "lovely garden and conservatory"; food-wise, there's "nothing showy" – "just a short but varied menu of fabulous dishes". / NW5 1AG; www.junctiontavern.co.uk; 10.30 pm, Sun 9.30 pm; Mon-Thu D only, Fri-Sun open L & D; no Amex.

Juniper Dining N5 £40 ❷❸❸
100 Highbury Pk 7288 8716 8–1D
"A cracking local", say Highbury residents, where a "talented chef" produces some "surprisingly imaginative" cooking, which is served with "enthusiasm and friendliness" in a "cosy, modern setting". / N5 2XE; www.juniperdining.co.uk; 9.45 pm; closed Mon & Sun D.

JW Steakhouse
Grosvenor House Hotel W1 £75 ④④④
86 Park Ln 7399 8460 3–3A
"A great range of USDA and British steaks" is on offer at this "airy" Park Lane operation, but the overall experience can still be a tad "lukewarm" – the room's "cavernous", the food can seem "average", and service can be "slow"; "top cheesecake" though. / W1K 7TN; www.jwsteakhouse.co.uk; 10.30 pm, Fri & Sat 11 pm; set weekday L £48 (FP).

K10 EC2 £40 ❷④⑤
20 Copthall Ave 7562 8510 9–2C
"Arrive before the lunchtime rush!"; this City conveyor-Japanese is always "packed" (expect to queue), thanks to its "great array of dishes" – not least "delicious" sushi – all "reasonably-priced"; "shame it's so unattractive". / EC2R 7DN; www.k10.com; L only, closed Sat & Sun; no booking.

Kaffeine W1 £12 ❷❶❶

66 Great Titchfield St 7580 6755 3–1C

They may be "very nerdy about their coffee", but there are some "absolutely amazing" brews to be had at this "cramped" and "bustling" Soho café; "beautiful, freshly-squeezed juices" and "an ever-changing array of sarnies" too. / W1W 7QJ; www.kaffeine.co.uk; L only; no Amex; no bookings.

Kai Mayfair W1 £100 ④④⑤

65 South Audley St 7493 8988 3–3A

"Subtle and extraordinary" cuisine wins many very positive reports on this luxurious Mayfair Chinese… but the "eye-watering expense" is a turn-off for some reporters – "it was nice, but at those prices I should have been raving". / W1K 2QU; www.kaimayfair.co.uk; 10.45 pm, Sun 10.15 pm; set weekday L £52 (FP).

Kaifeng NW4 £61 ❷❷④

51 Church Rd 8203 7888 1–1B

"Finding its feet again, after a tricky patch" – this kosher Chinese, in Hendon, is winning renewed praise for its "consistently good", if "expensive", food; (they also cater for most of the food allergies, even coeliacs). / NW4 4DU; www.kaifeng.co.uk; 10 pm; closed Fri & Sat.

Kaosarn £22 ❶❸④

110 St Johns Hill, SW11 awaiting tel 10–2C NEW

Brixton Village, Coldharbour Ln, SW9 7095 8922 10–2D

"Ask for authentic spicing, and hold on to your hat!" – this "crowded" Thai cafe, in Brixton Village, is "packed daily", thanks to the quality of its "fragrant" and "clear-flavoured" scoff; "the outside tables are nicest"; BYO. / SW9 10 pm, Sun 9 pm.

Karma W14 £38 ❷❶④

44 Blythe Rd 7602 9333 7–1D

This "superb" Olympia "find" inspires many reports – they all confirm that it offers "excellent-value" Keralan cuisine ("with a heavy seafood bias") that's "good enough to travel for"; staff try hard too. / W14 0HA; www.k-a-r-m-a.co.uk; 11 pm; no Amex.

Karpo NW1 NEW £48 ❸❸④

23 Euston Rd 7843 2221 8–3C

"A great little oasis"; it's early days, but this "solid" all-day newcomer – with its "quality, seasonal, tasty" fare – is probably already the best bet for travellers through King's Cross (across the road) and St Pancras. / NW1 2SB; www.karpo.co.uk; 11 pm.

Kateh W9 £42 ❸❸❸

5 Warwick Pl 7289 3393 8–4A

"Shame this always-buzzing local is so cramped" – this "very noisy" Little Venice spot is thriving, thanks to its "interesting and clean-tasting" Persian fare, and its "warm and friendly" service. / W9 2PX; www.katehrestaurant.co.uk; 10.45 pm, Sun 9.30 pm; closed weekday L.

Kazan £43 ❷❷❸

77 Wilton Rd, SW1 7233 8298 2–4B

93-94 Wilton Rd, SW1 7233 7100 2–4B

"Lively and authentic", these "informal and stylish" Turkish operations, a few doors away from one another in Pimlico, are almost always found "reliable and fun" – for a quiet meal, the smaller, more café-style operation is a better bet. / www.kazan-restaurant.com; 10 pm; set pre theatre £27 (FP).

F S A

Ken Lo's Memories SW1 £53 ❷❷❸
65-69 Ebury St 7730 7734 2–4B
"Don't dismiss it for flashier newcomers!"; the Chinese cuisine at this age-old Belgravian "still has zing" – it's "not the cheapest, but it has been consistent over many years". / SW1W 0NZ; www.memoriesofchina.co.uk; 10.45 pm, Sun 10.15 pm.

Ken Lo's Memories of China W8 £51 ❷❷④
353 Kensington High St 7603 6951 7–1D
On the Olympia/Kensington borders, this upscale Chinese "stalwart" is, for the most part, "still well up to scratch" – there's a slight feeling, though, that its consistency has slipped somewhat of late. / W8 6NW; www.memoriesofchina.co.uk; 10.45 pm.

Kennington Tandoori SE11 £45 ❸❷❸
313 Kennington Rd 7735 9247 1–3C
"Top politicos tucking in to a naan" are a common sight at this all-round "above-average" Kennington Indian – a "reliable" establishment, where the curries are "first-class". / SE11 4QE; www.kennningtontandoori.com; 11.30 pm; no Amex.

Kensington Place W8 £49 ❸❷❸
201-209 Kensington Church St 7727 3184 6–2B
"Making a come-back after years in the wilderness"; this nowadays more fish-centric fixture – coincidentally, often likened in looks to a goldfish bowl! – is (re-)establishing itself as a surprisingly good Kensington all-rounder... and from the D&D Group too! / W8 7LX; www.kensingtonplace-restaurant.com; 10.30 pm; closed Mon L & Sun D; SRA-63%.

Kensington Square Kitchen W8 £28 ❸❷❷
9 Kensington Sq 7938 2598 5–1A
"A lovely little neighbourhood place", on a "gorgeous square", off Kensington High Street; top tip is the "home-made brunch" – "great-tasting fry-ups, plus more sophisticated dishes, and the best coffee". / W8 5EP; www.kensingtonsquarekitchen.co.uk; 3.30 pm; L only; no Amex.

The Kensington Wine Rooms W8 £49 ❸❷❷
127-129 Kensington Church St 7727 8142 6–2B
It's not just the "unrivalled choice of wines by the glass" that's made quite a hit of this former boozer, near Notting Hill Gate – it's a "wonderfully relaxed" sort of place where the menu offers "very good value". / W8 7LP; www.greatwinesbytheglass.com; 10.45 pm.

Kentish Canteen NW5 £40 ④④❸
300 Kentish Town Rd 7485 7331 8–2C
"An oasis in the dessert which is Kentish Town" – this "cheap 'n' cheerful" bistro offers "dependable" food, and "decent value-for-money". / NW5 2TG; www.kentishcanteen.co.uk; 10.30 pm.

(Brew House)
Kenwood House NW3 £32 ④❸❷
Hampstead Heath 8341 5384 8–1A
"Perfect after a romp with the dogs on Hampstead Heath" – this self-service café does a "delicious full English", and "great cakes" too; "it's best on a sunny day when you can sit on the large terrace". / NW3 7JR; www.companyofcooks.com; 6 pm (summer), 4 pm (winter); L only.

Kenza EC2 £52 ④④④
10 Devonshire Sq 7929 5533 9–2D
A large Lebanese cellar, near Liverpool Street; it does a "top-value" set lunch, but it's primarily an evening party destination (with belly-dancing) – "if you're sober, it may be of limited interest..." / EC2 4YP; www.kenza-restaurant.com; 10 pm; closed Sat L & Sun.

Kerbisher & Malt W6 £19 ❷❸④

164 Shepherd's Bush Rd 3556 0228 7–1C

"Preserving the dying art of proper fish 'n' chips!" – this artfully retro, white-tiled café/take-away has proved "a great addition" to Brook Green; especially with its metal chairs, however, it's not the warmest place on a winter's evening… / W6 7PB; www.kerbisher.co.uk; 10 pm; closed Mon.

Kettners W1 £49 ④❸❸

29 Romilly St 7734 6112 4–2A

Still not quite recovered from its disastrous refurb a couple of years ago, this "venerable" Soho time warp is a "welcoming" place, particularly the "great champagne bar"; the "very average" food "doesn't match up", but for a posh burger or pizza, you could do worse. / W1D 5HP; www.kettners.com; 11 pm, Fri & Sat 11.30 pm, Sun 9.30 pm.

Kew Grill TW9 £57 ❸❷❷

10b Kew Grn 8948 4433 1–3A

"Delivering what the name promises", AWT's "cosy" steakhouse "has improved significantly since he down-scaled his operations" – many reporters applaud its "lovely steaks". / TW9 3BH; www.awtrestaurants.com; 10.30 pm, Fri-Sat 11 pm, Sun 10 pm; closed Mon L; set weekday L £29 (FP).

Khan's W2 £23 ❸④④

13-15 Westbourne Grove 7727 5420 6–1C

"Not a place for a quiet date!"; this "very busy and rushed" Bayswater Indian veteran, with its "no-frills" service, is "a place you go for the food and nothing else" – "it's consistently good and good value". / W2 4UA; www.khansrestaurant.com; 11.30 pm, Sat-Sun midnight.

Khan's of Kensington SW7 £39 ❸❸④

3 Harrington Rd 7584 4114 5–2B

Fans still find "excellent quality for the price", at this long-established subcontinental, by South Kensington tube; to others, however, "it's simply OK". / SW7 3ES; www.khansofkensington.co.uk; 11.30 pm.

Khoai £31 ❸④④

362 Ballards Ln, N12 8445 2039 1–1B
6 Topsfield Pde, N8 8341 2120 1–1C

"Everything you want from a local Vietnamese" – this no-nonsense duo, in Crouch End and North Finchley, serve "quick, fresh and tasty" scoff at "very reasonable" prices. / 11.30 pm; N12 closed Mon; no booking Fri & Sat after 7.30 pm.

Kiku W1 £55 ❷❸⑤

17 Half Moon St 7499 4208 3–4B

"Divinely fresh sushi and sashimi" win praise for this low-key fixture, in the heart of Mayfair, which is most popular as a lunch destination; it's "unfashionable and plain… just like any good Japanese should be!" / W1J 7BE; www.kikurestaurant.co.uk; 10.15 pm, Sun 9.45 pm; closed Sun L; set weekday L £35 (FP).

Kikuchi W1 £49 ❶④④

14 Hanway St 7637 7720 4–1A

Hidden-away near Tottenham Court Road, a little-known Japanese worth discovering for its "excellent sushi and sashimi". / W1T 1UD; 10.30 pm; closed Sun.

FSA

Kimchee WC1 £36 ❸❸❸

71 High Holborn 7430 0956 2–1D

"Putting Korean cuisine firmly on the map", say fans, this "game-changing" Wagamama-esque yearling wins over most reporters with its "groovy" styling, and its "great-value", "fast-food" formula; critics, though, find standards "rather hit-and-miss". / WC1V 6EA; www.kimchee.uk.com; 10.30 pm.

Kings Road Steakhouse & Grill SW3 £55 ④④④

386 King's Rd 7351 9997 5–3B

Few, and oddly opposing, survey views on Marco Pierre White's "cramped" Chelsea steakhouse – most reporters are "pleasantly surprised" by standards overall, but a vocal minority finds the food "very average and overpriced". / SW3 5UZ; www.kingsroadsteakhouseandgrill.com; 11 pm, Sun 10 pm.

Kipferl N1 £37 ❸④❷

20 Camden Pas 77041 555 8–3D

"The best Sachertorte outside the Ringstraße" – star of the "wonderful baked goods" on offer at this "lovely and homely" café, nowadays removed to Islington; there's also a range of more ambitious and "robust" Austrian fare, plus wines and beers. / N1 8ED; www.kipferl.co.uk; 9 pm, Tue and Sun 5 pm; closed Mon, Tue D & Sun D.

Kiraku W5 £33 ❶❶❸

8 Station Pde 8992 2848 1–3A

"Simply the best-value (and some of the best) Japanese food in town!" – this small, simple-looking café, near Ealing Common tube, offers a "vast" menu (of which "amazing" sushi is just a part), plus "gracious" and "helpful" service. / W5 3LD; www.kiraku.co.uk; 10 pm; closed Mon; no Amex.

Kitchen W8 W8 £61 ❶❷❸

11-13 Abingdon Road 7937 0120 5–1A

"Tucked away off Kensington High Street", this "reassuringly upscale neighbourhood restaurant" – with its "sophisticated and nuanced cooking" (overseen by The Square's Phil Howard) and "charming service" – has made itself quite a destination; "only quibble? – the decor is a bit characterless". / W8 6AH; www.kitchenw8.com; 10.15 pm, Sun 9.15 pm; set weekday L £36 (FP).

Koba W1 £43 ❷❷④

11 Rathbone St 7580 8825 2–1C

"The customers, mostly Korean, seem to have a good time", at this "high-quality" Fitzrovian, which features the traditional table-BBQ – it can get a bit "noisy", but otherwise it's a "really enjoyable" destination. / W1T 1NA; 10.30 pm; closed Sun L.

Koffmann's
The Berkeley SW1 £82 ❷❶❸

The Berkeley, Wilton Pl 7235 1010 5–1D

"Is there better French food in London?" – certainly if you're looking for the "proper old-fashioned" variety, few restaurants out-do the "masterful preparation" characterising this "discreet" and "quietly efficient" Knightsbridge basement, presided over by the legendary Pierre Koffmann; "exceptional-value set lunch". / SW1X 7RL; www.the-berkeley.co.uk/top_restaurants.aspx; 10.30 pm; set weekday L £49 (FP), set pre-theatre £52 (FP).

FSA

Kolossi Grill EC1 £30 ④❷❷

56-60 Rosebery Ave 7278 5758 9–1A

"A throw-back, but rather a charming one" – this '60s taverna, in Farringdon, offers "simple" and inexpensive Greek/Cypriot scoff that generally pleases. / EC1R 4RR; www.kolossigrill.com; 11 pm; closed Sat L & Sun; set weekday L £16 (FP).

Konditor & Cook £26 ❸④④

Curzon Soho, 99 Shaftesbury Ave, W1 854 9367 4–3A
46 Gray's Inn Rd, WC1 854 9365 9–1A
10 Stoney St, SE1 854 9363 9–4C
22 Cornwall Road, SE1 854 9361 9–4A
63 Stamford St, SE1 854 9371 9–4A
30 St Mary Axe, EC3 854 9369 9–2D

"Better baking than anyone else!" – these "joyous" café/take-aways do "scrumptious cakes" and "lovely savouries"; "good salads" too. / www.konditorandcook.com; 6 pm; W1 11 pm; WC1 & EC3 closed Sat & Sun; SE1 branches closed Sun; no booking.

Kopapa WC2 £51 ❸④④

32-34 Monmouth St 7240 6076 4–2B

An "interesting" range of small plates – some of them "absolutely amazing" – has helped Peter Gordon's "clattery" Covent Garden canteen make quite a splash; even fans can find it "pricey", though, and the occasional disaster is not unknown. / WC2H 9HA; www.kopapa.co.uk; 10.30 pm, Sun 9.30 pm.

Koya W1 £32 ❷❷❸

49 Frith St 7434 4463 4–2A

"Brilliant and authentic noodles" ("udon, udon, and more udon") win rave reviews for this "tiny", "stripped-down" and "bustling" Soho two-year-old – "expect queues at lunch, and in the early-evening". / W1D 4SG; www.koya.co.uk; 10.30 pm; no booking.

Kulu Kulu £29 ④⑤⑤

76 Brewer St, W1 7734 7316 3–2D
51-53 Shelton St, WC2 7240 5687 4–2C
39 Thurloe Pl, SW7 7589 2225 5–2C

"The decor is very basic", at this conveyor-sushi mini-chain, and "there's not much ambience" – for fans, though, it offers "perfect fast food", and "very affordably" too. / 10 pm; SW7 10.30 pm; closed Sun; no Amex; no booking.

Kurumaya EC4 £44 ❸❸④

76-77 Watling St 7236 0236 9–2B

With its street-level conveyor-bar, and a "cheerful basement restaurant" too, this "busy" City Japanese makes a "reliable" pit stop, not least for "top-value sushi". / EC4M 9BJ; www.kurumaya.co.uk; 9.30 pm; closed Sat & Sun.

The Ladbroke Arms W11 £46 ❷④❷

54 Ladbroke Rd 7727 6648 6–2B

"Way better than you'd expect pub food to be!" – this "most enjoyable" Notting Hill boozer "continues to surprise", not least with the "twists" it adds to seemingly traditional dishes; arrive early if you want a place on the "sun-trap terrace". / W11 3NW; www.capitalpubcompany.com; 9.30 pm; no booking after 8 pm.

Ladudu NW6 £33 ❸❸❸

152 West End Ln 7372 3217 1–1B

"Cheap, fresh and excellent" – this new, no-booking Vietnamese, in West Hampstead, is going down well with the locals; "expect long waits if you arrive after 8pm". / NW6 1SD; www.ladudu.com; 10.30 pm; closed Tue L.

Ladurée £62 ❷④❸
71-72 Burlington Arc, Piccadilly, W1 7491 9155 3–3C
1 Covent Garden Mkt, WC2 7240 0706 4–3D
"Macarons that melt in your mouth" are the headline attraction of these bijou outposts of the famed Parisian pâtisserie; the Harrods and Covent Garden branches also offer "excellent" (if pricey) sandwiches, omelettes and so on. / www.laduree.com; SW1 8.45 pm, Sun 5.45 pm; W1 6.30 pm, Sun 5 pm; W1 no booking, SW1 no booking 3 pm-6 pm.

The Lady Ottoline WC1 NEW £45 ④④❸
11a, Northington St 7831 0008 2–1D
It's been a "great transformation" of a "handsome" Victorian building, say fans of this Bloomsbury newcomer, who hail the cooking as "delicious"; to critics, though, it's "a gastropub-by-numbers" – a "hit-and-miss" performer, with "disinterested" service and "overpriced" food. / WC1N 2JF; www.theladyottoline.com; 11 pm, Sun 10.30 pm.

Lahore Karahi SW17 £23 ❷④④
1 Tooting High Street, London 8767 2477 10–2C
"The real deal in Tooting!" – this "Formica-tabled" Pakistani café is always "full to bursting", thanks to its "fantastic", "richly-flavoured" dishes at "incredible" prices; "BYO is a bonus". / SW17 0SN; www.lahorekarahi.co.uk; midnight; no Amex.

Lahore Kebab House £23 ❶④④
668 Streatham High Rd, SW16 8765 0771 10–2D
2-10 Umberston St, E1 7488 2551 11–1A
"London's best Indian/Pakistani food" – these "bustling", ultra-"no-frills" canteens offer "awesome lamb chops" and other "brilliantly authentic" fare; the E1 original out-rated its arch-rival, Tayyabs, this year. / midnight.

Lamberts SW12 £46 ❶❶❷
2 Station Pde 8675 2233 10–2C
"A real find in darkest Balham" – this "brilliant" neighbourhood spot draws scores of fans from neighbouring postcodes with its "intimate" style, "friendly and unhurried" service and "consistently excellent" cooking... and all at "outstanding-value" prices too. / SW12 9AZ; www.lambertsrestaurant.com; 10.30 pm, Sun 5 pm; closed Mon, Tue-Fri L & Sun D; no Amex.

(Winter Garden)
The Landmark NW1 £70 ❸❷❶
222 Marylebone Rd 7631 8000 8–4A
The "stunning" atrium of this grand hotel, by Marylebone station, is a "beautiful and special" location; afternoon tea is "very good", but top billing goes to the "excellent, if expensive, Sunday jazz buffet brunch", featuring unlimited champagne – "book well ahead". / NW1 6JQ; www.landmarklondon.co.uk; 10.30 pm; no trainers; booking: max 12.

Langan's Bistro W1 £48 ❸❷❸
26 Devonshire St 7935 4531 2–1A
"Cramped", "cosy" and "old-fashioned", this Marylebone stalwart, is "perfect for romance"; its "rather good retro food" generally pleases too. / W1J 6PH; www.langansrestaurants.co.uk; 11 pm; closed Sat L & Sun.

F S A

Langan's Brasserie W1 £61 ⑤④❸
Stratton St 7491 8822 3–3C
It may be "a bit set in its ways", but fans of this "big and buzzy" Mayfair veteran say "it always impresses out-of-towners" nonetheless; to sceptics, though, it's just a "ghastly" and "raucous" has-been, with food that's "overpriced and out-of-date". / W1J 8LB; www.langansrestaurants.co.uk; 11 pm, Fri & Sat 11.30 pm, Sun 4 pm; closed Sun D.

The Lansdowne NW1 £43 ❸④❷
90 Gloucester Ave 7483 0409 8–3B
A "classic" Primrose Hill boozer that's "always worth a visit", thanks to its "laid-back" and "fun" vibe, and its "expertly-prepared range of pizzas". / NW1 8HX; www.thelansdownepub.co.uk; 10 pm, Sun 9.30 pm; no Amex.

La Lanterna SE1 £41 ④❸④
6-8 Mill St 7252 2420 11–2A
"Hidden-away from the South Bank hordes" – with a "nice terrace for the summer" – this "old-fashioned" Italian offers "huge helpings" of "honest" and "tasty" scoff (not least pizza) at "reasonable prices"; sceptics, though, find it rather "average". / SE1 2BA; www.pizzerialalanterna.co.uk; 11 pm, Sun 10.30 pm; closed Sat L.

Lardo E8 NEW £40
Richmond Rd 8533 8229 1–2D
A former Zucca chef heads up this new Hackney salumeria, which also does a line in pizza; the antecedents are promising, but we didn't have the opportunity to visit before this guide went to press. / E8 3NJ; www.lardo.co.uk.

Latium W1 £48 ❷❶❸
21 Berners St 7323 9123 3–1D
"Discreet and subtle", Maurizio Morelli's low-key business favourite, just north of Oxford Street, offers "terrific" food (including "the best ravioli in town"), wonderfully "professional" service and "a wine list of Italian treasures". / W1T 3LP; www.latiumrestaurant.com; 10.30 pm, Sat 11 pm; closed Sat L & Sun.

Launceston Place W8 £67
1a Launceston Pl 7937 6912 5–1B
In "one of Kensington's loveliest streets", this quiet townhouse is a "hidden gem of romance and intimacy"; after a chef change this year, however, reports are very up-and-down, and we've felt it best to leave it unrated. / W8 5RL; www.launcestonplace-restaurant.co.uk; 10.30 pm; closed Mon L; set weekday L £42 (FP); SRA-63%.

The Lawn Bistro SW19 NEW £52 ❸❸④
67 High St 8947 8278 10–2B
"A godsend in the food desert that is Wimbledon" – this new "high-end bistro" inspires local adulation for its "ambitious" cooking and "smiley" service; the room, though, is "strangely shaped". / SW19 5EE; www.thelawnbistro.co.uk; set pre theatre £31 (FP).

THE LEDBURY W11 £106 ❶❶❷
127 Ledbury Rd 7792 9090 6–1B
"London's culinary No. 1!"; Brett Graham's "unusually independent" culinary style creates "inspired" dishes ("enchantingly presented") at this "calm and confident" Notting Hill superstar – a supremely "classy" operation, but one that's "not too formal". / W11 2AQ; www.theledbury.com; 10.30 pm, Sun 10 pm; closed Mon L; set weekday L £55 (FP).

Lemonia NW1 £41 ⑤❷❷
89 Regent's Park Rd 7586 7454 8–3B
"A certain magic" hangs over this "cheerful" and "homely" Primrose mega-taverna, which is "always full"; we suspect, though, that this sorcery has more to do with the "lovely" service than with the food – "the menu needs a re-fresh". / NW1 8UY; www.lemonia.co.uk; 11.30 pm; closed Sat L & Sun D; no Amex; set weekday L £21 (FP), set dinner £27 (FP).

Leon £22 ④❸❸
275 Regent St, W1 7495 1514 3–1C
35-36 Gt Marlborough St, W1 7437 5280 3–2C
36-38 Old Compton St, W1 7434 1200 4–2A
73-76 The Strand, WC2 7240 3070 4–4D
7 Canvey St, SE1 7620 0035 9–4B
Cabot Place West, E14 7719 6200 11–1C
3 Crispin Pl, E1 7247 4369 12–2B
12 Ludgate Circus, EC4 7489 1580 9–2A
86 Cannon St, EC4 7623 9699 9–3C
By "showing that healthy needn't be boring", this "wholesome" and "quirkily-styled" fast-food chain has won an army of admirers; its food-rating dipped this year however, and critics fear it's becoming rather "formulaic". / www.leonrestaurants.co.uk; 10 pm; W1 8.45 pm; E14 8 pm; EC4 closed Sun; W1 closed Sat & Sun; no booking L.

Leong's Legends £35 ❸④❷
3 Macclesfield St, W1 7287 0288 4–3A
82 Queensway, W2 7221 2280 6–2C
"A great alternative to everyday Chinese" – this Chinatown Taiwanese majors in "delicious Xiao Long Bao" (soup dumplings), served in a setting reminiscent of a budget "opium den"; well-rated Bayswater spin-off too. / www.leongslegend.com; 11 pm, Sat 11.30 pm; no bookings.

Levant W1 £54 ④④❷
Jason Ct, 76 Wigmore St 7224 1111 3–1A
"A great party atmosphere" (complete with occasional belly-dancing) is the prime reason to visit this dimly-lit and "fun" Marylebone basement; fans say the food's "great" too, but doubters say: "if you appreciate good Lebanese cooking, don't go!" / W1U 2SJ; www.levant.co.uk; 9.45pm, Fri-Sat midnight.

The Lido Cafe
Brockwell Lido SE24 £41 ❸❸❷
Dulwich Rd 7737 8183 10–2D
"Epic" breakfasts, in particular, win fans for this "relaxed" café by Brockwell Lido – "a great place all year round, but especially in summer when the terrace is open and the kids can play outside". / SE24 0PA; www.thelidocafe.co.uk; 9.30 pm; closed Sun D; no Amex.

The Light House SW19 £49 ④❸④
75-77 Ridgway 8944 6338 10–2B
"Hard to beat in Wimbledon Village", say fans of this "bare" modern bistro, who praise its buzzy ("very noisy") style and "fresh, seasonal fare" – critics, though, complain of "too many misses", and find the ambience "dull" too. / SW19 4ST; www.lighthousewimbledon.com; 10.30 pm; closed Sun D; set weekday L £31 (FP).

The Lighthouse SW11 £39 ❸❷❷
441 Battersea Park Rd 7223 7721 10–1C
"Lucky to have this as my local!" – Battersea folk are all very up on this "bistro-type pub", where steak is a highlight; nice garden too. / SW11 4LR; www.thelighthousebattersea.com; 10 pm, Fri-Sat midnight, Sun 10.30 pm.

Lima W1 NEW £50 ❷❷❸

31 Rathbone Pl 3002 2640 2–1C

This Fitzrovia Peruvian received instant press acclaim when it opened in mid-2012; our early-days visit found a dazzling array of beautiful-to-behold, über-zesty dishes, served by engaging staff, in a tasteful, but rather noisy, setting. / W1T 1JH; Rated on Editors' visit; www.limalondon.com; 10.30 pm; closed Sun.

Lisboa Pâtisserie W10 £8 ❸❸④

57 Golborne Rd 8968 5242 6–1A

"A Portobello institution" – this "simple, noisy and much-loved" Portuguese café does a mean cup of coffee, and serves "the best pasteis de nata (custard tarts) in the world… even better than in Lisbon!" / W10 5NR; 7 pm; L & early evening only; no booking.

Little Bay £30 ④❷❶

228 Belsize Rd, NW6 7372 4699 1–2B
228 York Rd, SW11 7223 4080 10–2B
171 Farringdon Rd, EC1 7278 1234 9–1A

"How do they do it?" – these splendidly "quirky" and "theatrical" budget bistros (where "regular opera is a bonus") are "always a pleasure", say fans; they offer "good portions" of often-"delicious" food, and all at "bafflingly low prices". / www.little-bay.co.uk; 11.30 pm, Sun 11 pm; no Amex, NW6 no credit cards.

Little Georgia Café E2 £37 ❸④❸

87 Goldsmiths Row 7739 8154 1–2D

"BYO makes this place a bargain", says a fan of this "cute" Georgian café in Bethnal Green; the new Islington offshoot is higher-rated overall, and fans say it has more "space and grace". / E2 8QR; 10 pm; closed Mon D.

LMNT E8 £36 ④❷❶

316 Queensbridge Rd 7249 6727 1–2D

"You can't beat the wacky interior" of this "crazy", pharaoh-kitsch Dalston pub-conversion; "given the low prices", the food's not bad either. / E8 3NH; www.lmnt.co.uk; 10.30 pm; Mon-Thu D only, Fri-Sun open L & D; no Amex.

Lobster Pot SE11 £59 ❸❷❸

3 Kennington Ln 7582 5556 1–3C

"You hear seagulls in the background, as fish swim past the portholes" of this "bizarre" French-family-run stalwart, in deepest Kennington; the big surprise is that its fish and seafood are actually "very good" – "not cheap, but worth it!" / SE11 4RG; www.lobsterpotrestaurant.co.uk; 10.30 pm; closed Mon & Sun; booking: max 8.

Locanda Locatelli Hyatt Regency W1 £72 ❸❸❸

8 Seymour St 7935 9088 2–2A

Exuding "understated style", Giorgio Locatelli's "cool" and "dimly-lit" modern Italian, in Marylebone, dazzles most reporters with its "sensational" cooking; there is a school of thought, however, which finds the food "enjoyable, but not up to the hype". / W1H 7JZ; www.locandalocatelli.com; 11 pm, Thu-Sat 11.30 pm, Sun 10.15 pm; booking: max 8.

Locanda Ottomezzo W8 £69 ❸④❸

2-4 Thackeray St 7937 2200 5–1B

"Real Italian food", "impeccable" wines, "gregarious" staff and a "refreshingly different" approach win praise for this "casual" Kensington café/bistro; prices can seem "out of line", though, and the odd 'bad trip' is not unknown. / W8 5ET; www.locandaottoemezzo.co.uk; 10.30 pm, Fri & Sat 10.45 pm; closed Mon L, Sat L & Sun.

FSA

Loch Fyne **£42** ④④④
2-4 Catherine St, WC2 7240 4999 2–2D
77-78 Gracechurch St, EC3 7929 8380 9–3C
"OK it's a chain", but fans of this national group of busy fish and seafood brasseries tout them as "a good stand-by", albeit offering "fairly unadventurous" food; to critics, however, they are merely "consistently disappointing". / www.lochfyne-restaurants.com; 10 pm; WC2 10.30 pm; set weekday L £24 (FP).

Lola & Simón W6 **£47** ④④❸
278 King St 8563 0300 7–2B
"For an upbeat brunch", locals tip this "stylish" Argentinian/Kiwi café, in Hammersmith; you can dine here too, but – notwithstanding "good steaks" and nice wines – the food offer can seem "limited", and service "erratic". / W6 0SP; www.lolaandsimon.co.uk; 10 pm; no Amex.

Lola Rojo SW11 **£41** ❸④④
78 Northcote Rd 7350 2262 10–2C
"A tapas place which gives the West End a run for its money" – this "trendy" Battersea Spaniard offers some "very interesting takes on classic dishes" ("served with many decibels!"); its lesser-known Fulham outpost is now closed. / SW11 6QL; www.lolarojo.net; 10.30 pm, Sat & Sun 11 pm; no Amex.

Look Mum No Hands! EC1 **£29** ❸④❸
49 Old St 7253 1025 9–1B
"Coffee and a cycle-shop?" – "it may sound like a gimmick", but all reports on this "cheap", "friendly" and "cheerful" Shoreditch café find visits here "a delight"; "why aren't there more places like this?" / EC1V 9HX; www.lookmumnohands.co.uk; 10 pm.

The Lord Northbrook SE12 NEW **£34** ❸❷❷
116 Burnt Ash Rd 8318 1127 1–4D
A recent refurb has "worked wonders" for this "buzzing" and "friendly" Lea Green boozer, praised for its "caring management", "great food" and "good ales"; "hi-viz jackets are banned now, but they will give you water for your dog…" / SE12 8PU; www.thelordnorthbrook.co.uk; 9 pm, Fri-Sat 10 pm.

Lorenzo SE19 **£37** ❸❷④
73 Westow Hill 8761 7485 1–4D
"Always a fun venue", this "reasonably-priced" Upper Norwood Italian is universally hailed for its "reliable" – "mainly pasta 'n' pizza" – cuisine. / SE19 1TX; www.lorenzo.uk.com; 10.30 pm.

Lotus Chinese Floating Restaurant E14 **£40** ④④❸
9 Oakland Quay 7515 6445 11–2C
"A good 'jobbing' Chinese" – the consistent all-round standards of this waterborne restaurant, near Canary Wharf, make it a popular stand-by locally; fans say it offers "the best dim sum in the area" too. / E14 9EA; www.lotusfloating.co.uk; 10.30 pm.

Lucio SW3 **£62** ❸❷❷
257 Fulham Rd 7823 3007 5–3B
"A classic Chelsea Italian", offering "good food and, generally, great service too"; given the "high" dinner prices, the occasional critic senses a "lack of passion" on the culinary front, but lunch is undoubtedly a "bargain". / SW3 6HY; 10.45 pm; set weekday L £36 (FP).

F S A

Lucky Seven W2 **£39** ❸❸❷

127 Westbourne Park Rd 7727 6771 6–1B

"Every detail has been thought out" (including the "cosy booths"), at Tom Conran's "ace" homage to the American diner, on the fringe of Notting Hill; it serves up "excellent" burgers and "great shakes" too. / W2 5QL; www.tomconranrestaurants.com; 10.15 pm, Sun 10 pm; no Amex; no booking.

Lupita WC2 **£37** ❸❷❸

13-15 Villiers St 7930 5355 4–4D

This Mexican café makes an unlikely find in the purlieus of Charing Cross station; OK, it's "crowded and uncomfortable", but it's a "fun" sort of place, and the food is "unusually tasty". / WC2N 6ND; www.lupita.co.uk; 11 pm, Fri-Sat 11.30 pm, Sun 10 pm.

Lutyens EC4 **£65** ④④④

85 Fleet St 7583 8385 9–2A

Undoubtedly "useful" for a business rendezvous (indeed, "something of a canteen for Goldman Sachs types"), Sir Terence Conran's "well-spaced" City brasserie inspires lots of reports... many of which suggest it "lacks warmth and heart"; it's "better for lunch than for dinner". / EC4Y 1AE; www.lutyens-restaurant.com; 10 pm; closed Sat & Sun.

The Luxe E1 **£52** ⑤⑤④

109 Commercial St 7101 1751 12–2B

Ex-Masterchef judge John Torode's "yawn-worthy" Spitalfields two-year-old – "it's priced almost as if for fine dining, but results aren't much better than a gastropub!" / E1 6BG; www.theluxe.co.uk; 10.30 pm; closed Mon D & Sun D; booking: max 10.

Ma Cuisine TW9 **£40** ④❸④

9 Station Approach 8332 1923 1–3A

A "cramped" old-fashioned bistro, with a decent Kew following, thanks not least to its "fair" prices; in the absence of much local competition, though, it does seem to be coasting a bit. / TW9 3QB; www.macuisinekew.co.uk; 10 pm, Fri & Sat 10.30 pm; no Amex.

Ma Goa SW15 **£35** ❷❶❷

242-244 Upper Richmond Rd 8780 1767 10–2B

An "excellent" family-run Indian, in Putney, where the staff "are some of the friendliest in London" – its "magnificent" cuisine "stays true to its Goan roots", and is an "absolute bargain" too. / SW15 6TG; www.ma-goa.com; 11 pm, Sun 10 pm; closed Mon L & Sat L.

Made In Camden Roundhouse NW1 **£35** ❸❸❸

Chalk Farm Rd 7424 8495 8–2B

"Surprisingly excellent" for an eatery attached to a performing venue – this "canteen-like" spot, in the Roundhouse, offers a "distinctive" menu of "inventive small plates", and "helpful" service too. / NW1 8EH; www.madeincamden.com; 10.15 pm; closed Mon L.

Made in Italy **£39** ④④❸

14a, Old Compton St, W1 0011 1214 4–2B
249 King's Rd, SW3 7352 1880 5–3C

"Super" pizza-by-the-metre has made quite a name for this "cosy" (if "high-decibel") and "very Italian" Chelsea fixture; the Soho offshoot, barely commented-on in the survey, is a pale imitation. / www.madeinitalygroup.co.uk; 11 pm, Sun 10 pm; SW3 closed Mon L.

FSA

Madhu's UB1 £33 ❷❷❸

39 South Rd 8574 1897 1–3A

"Worth a trip to Southall, just for the authenticity of its cuisine", this high-street Indian (HQ of a major outside-catering empire) serves some "excellent and unusual" dishes. / UB1 1SW; www.madhusonline.com; 11.30 pm; closed Tue, Sat L & Sun L.

Madsen SW7 £48 ④④④

20 Old Brompton Rd 7225 2772 5–2B

Looking "like a Danish classroom", this South Kensington spot serves up a "limited" seasonal menu, which leads on open sandwiches and "delicious marinated herring"; it's all rather "bland", though, and service can be "slow". / SW7 3DL; www.madsenrestaurant.com; 10 pm, Fri-Sat 10.45 pm; closed Sun D.

Magdalen SE1 £55 ❷❸❸

152 Tooley St 7403 1342 9–4D

"Out-of-the-way, but worth finding" – this "oasis" near City Hall has built a major reputation with its "accomplished" (and offal-heavy) British cuisine, its "well-chosen wine" and its "congenial" ambience. / SE1 2TU; www.magdalenrestaurant.co.uk; 10 pm; closed Sat L & Sun; set weekday L £35 (FP).

Maggie Jones's W8 £52 ④❷❶

6 Old Court Pl 7937 6462 5–1A

This "embracing" candlelit rustic stalwart, near Kensington Gardens, is – for its loyal fans – "the most romantic place in London"; it offers "homely" Anglo/French cuisine which, while "not refined", is still "very satisfying". / W8 4PL; www.maggie-jones.co.uk; 11 pm, Sun 10.30 pm.

Maguro W9 £33 ❷❷❸

5 Lanark Pl 7289 4353 8–4A

"A very good Japanese restaurant, with some excellent and unusual dishes" – this "intimate" but "buzzy" Maida Vale spot makes "a wonderful discovery, down a pedestrian sidestreet"; "it's only small, so you must book". / W9 1BT; www.maguro-restaurant.com; 10.30 pm; no Amex.

Maison Bertaux W1 £16 ❷❸❶

28 Greek St 7437 6007 4–2A

"One of the last remnants of old Soho, not much changed in 60 years!" – this "cosy" ("cramped") café was established in 1871, and is still often "jammed"; the cakes are "thrillingly gooey", and the coffee's not too bad either. / W1D 5DQ; www.maisonbertaux.com; 10.30 pm, Sun 8 pm.

Malabar W8 £43 ❷❷❸

27 Uxbridge St 7727 8800 6–2B

For a "classy" curry, few Indians can match the enduring "commitment to flavour and freshness" of this "stylish" and "accommodating" stalwart, tucked-away near Notting Hill Gate. / W8 7TQ; www.malabar-restaurant.co.uk; 11.30 pm, Sun 10.30 pm.

Malabar Junction WC1 £42 ❸❸❷

107 Gt Russell St 7580 5230 2–1C

Ignore the "nondescript" façade – the interior of this "jolly" Bloomsbury spot is surprisingly "airy", and it's worth seeking out for its "yummy" south Indian food, served by "helpful" (and "unchanging") staff. / WC1B 3NA; www.malabarjunction.com; 11 pm.

The Mall Tavern W8 £42 ❷❷❷
71-73 Palace Gardens Ter 7229 3374 6–2B
"Jesse Dunford Wood's cooking just gets better and more creative", says one of the many fans of this "total gastropub", just off Notting Hill Gate; "book the chef's table for a fun night out!" / W8 4RU; www.themalltavern.com; 10 pm.

Malmaison Brasserie EC1 £51 ❸❷❸
18-21 Charterhouse St 7012 3700 9–1B
The hidden-away but handy location of this "slick" Farringdon hotel brasserie contributes to its attractions as "a good place for business"; culinary highlight – the 'Mal Burger'. / EC1M 6AH; www.malmaison.com; 10.15 pm; closed Sat L.

La Mancha SW15 £42 ❸❸④
32 Putney High St 8780 1022 10–2B
"A long-term Putney stand-by that's maintained its standards"; when busy, it does get "manic", but the tapas are "really well done", and service is "efficient". / SW15 1SQ; www.lamancha.co.uk; 11 pm; need 6+ to book.

Mandalay W2 £27 ❸❸⑤
444 Edgware Rd 7258 3696 8–4A
Overlook the "ghastly interior" of this "idiosyncratic" family-run Burmese, in a converted shop near Edgware Road tube – it offers "interesting" cooking (like a mix of Indian and Chinese) at "bargain prices". / W2 1EG; www.mandalayway.com; 10.30 pm; closed Sun.

Mandarin Kitchen W2 £38 ❷❸⑤
14-16 Queensway 7727 9012 6–2C
"Top-drawer Chinese seafood" – "the lobster noodles are to die for" – has carved out a major reputation for this seemingly "run-down" Bayswater institution; it's still "exceptionally busy", but – for long term fans – "not as outstanding as it once was". / W2 3RX; 11.15 pm.

Mangal I E8 £29 ❶❷④
10 Arcola St 7275 8981 1–1C
"The most authentic Turkish BBQ outside Turkey!"; kebabs "don't come any better" than at this "superb-quality" but "unbelievably inexpensive" Dalston stalwart, which – say fans – is "hands-down the best cheap eat in London". / E8 2DJ; www.mangal1.com; midnight, Sat-Sun 1 am; no credit cards.

Mangal II N16 £36 ❸❸④
4 Stoke Newington Rd 7254 7888 1–1C
"Gilbert & George eat here practically nightly" – the claim to fame of this Dalston Ocakbasi; it's not as highly rated as its elder sibling, but it's a "friendly" place offering "delicious" and "super-cheap" kebabs (and so on). / N16 8BH; www.mangal2.com; 1 am.

Mango & Silk SW14 £34 ④④❸
199 Upper Richmond Rd 8876 6220 1–4A
Udit Sarkhel, the celebrated chef with whom this East Sheen Indian is still often associated, passed on in early-2012 – this is now just a "neighbourhood spot", albeit a "perfectly good" one. / SW14 8QT; www.mangoandsilk.co.uk; 9.30 pm, Fri & Sat 10 pm; closed Mon, Tue–Sat D only, Sun open L & D.

Mango Room NW1 £41 ❸❷❷
10-12 Kentish Town Rd 7482 5065 8–3B
"Laid-back" and "always-buzzy", this Camden Town "Caribbean favourite" is a "very welcoming" sort of place, where the "consistent" food offers some "fantastic flavours"; the atmosphere is often "terrific" too. / NW1 8NH; www.mangoroom.co.uk; 11 pm.

Mango Tree £54 ④④④
46 Grosvenor Pl, SW1 7823 1888 2–4B
Harrods, 87-135 Brompton Rd, SW1 7730 1234 5–1D NEW
These London outposts of an international Thai chain are, say fans, "consistent" performers, offering a "great" all-round experience; for critics, though, they're just "noisy" places with "slow" service – "you almost get the feeling it's policy to have you hanging around in the bar!" / Brompton Rd Mon-Sat 8.30 pm, Sun 7.30 pm; Grosvenor Pl Mon-Wed 11 pm, Thu-Sat 11.30 pm, Sun 10.30 pm.

Mango Tree SE1 £50 ❸④④
5-6 Cromwell Buildings, Redcross Way 7407 0333 9–4C
Tucked-away near Borough Market, and not well known outside the locality – an "above-average" modern Indian; it can get pretty noisy. / SE1 9HR; www.justmangotree.co.uk; 11 pm.

Manicomio £57 ❸④❸
85 Duke of York Sq, SW3 7730 3366 5–2D
6 Gutter Ln, EC2 7726 5010 9–2B
"For a perfect al fresco lunch", these Chelsea and City Italians both boast "fantastic" terraces; the food is "fresh" and "well-executed" too, but those who find prices "OTT" can deem results overall "unimpressive". / www.manicomio.co.uk; SW3 10.30 pm, Sun 10 pm; EC2 10 pm; EC2 closed Sat & Sun.

Manna NW3 £51 ❸④④
4 Erskine Rd 7722 8028 8–3B
A return to "thoughtful", "high-quality" cooking won renewed support this year for this well-worn Primrose Hill veggie café (the UK's longest-established, est 1968); service, though, is "relaxed, to say the least". / NW3 3AJ; www.mannav.com; 10.30 pm; closed Mon, Tue-Fri D only, Sat & Sun open L & D.

Mao Tai SW6 £60 ❸④❸
58 New King's Rd 7731 2520 10–1B
"Incredibly good" or just "incredibly expensive"? – views do differ but, on most accounts, this long-established Parson's Green spot, with its "eclectic menu spanning the Far East", is worth the premium prices. / SW6 4LS; www.maotai.co.uk; 11.30 pm, Sun 10.30 pm; D only, ex Sun open L & D.

Mar I Terra £31 ❸❸❷
17 Air St, W1 7734 1992 3–3D
14 Gambia St, SE1 7928 7628 9–4A
"Hustling and bustling", this ex-pub near Southwark tube is nowadays a "convivial" tapas bar that's highly rated for its "authentic" style and its "very satisfying" dishes; the Soho spin-off is little-known but well-rated. / SE1 10.30 pm; W1 11 pm; SE1 closed Sat L, Sun; W1 closed Sun-Mon & Tue-Sat L.

Marco
Stamford Bridge SW6 £65 ⑤⑤④
Fulham Rd 7915 2929 5–4A
"Nowhere near as good as you'd expect"; Marco Pierre White's restaurant, on the way in to Stamford Bridge, is a "dull" and "expensive" operation, where critics discern all the excitement… "of a glorified Beefeater"! / SW6 1HS; www.marcorestaurant.org; 10.30 pm; D only, closed Mon & Sun.

Marco Pierre White Steakhouse & Grill East India House E1 £60 ④❸④
109-117 Middlesex St 7247 5050 9–2D
Fans of this City-fringe basement praise its "regularly excellent" steak and its "spacious" interior; it is rather "overpriced" however, and, sceptics feel, "a bit lacklustre" too. / E1 7JF; www.mpwsteakandalehouse.org; 10 pm; closed Sat L & Sun.

MARCUS WAREING THE BERKELEY SW1 £116 ❷❷❷
Wilton Pl 7235 1200 5–1D
"Faultless" cuisine "of the highest calibre" maintains Marcus Wareing's "masterful" Belgravia dining room in the top ranks of London's culinary premier league; the setting can sometimes seem a touch "muted", but the more general view is that it is "beautiful and calm". / SW1X 7RL; www.marcus-wareing.com; 11 pm; closed Sat L & Sun; no jeans or trainers; booking: max 8; set weekday L £68 (FP).

Mari Vanna SW1 NEW £70 ④⑤❷
116 Knightsbridge 7581 5920 5–1D
It's undoubtedly "fun", but this "upscale" Russian-rustic newcomer, by Knightsbridge tube, needs to get its act together – food and service are notably "patchy". / SW1X 7PJ; www.marivanna.co.uk; 11.30 pm.

Marine Ices NW3 £34 ④④❸
8 Haverstock Hill 7482 9003 8–2B
"Be sure to leave room for ice cream", at the Manzi family's age-old (1920s) institution, near Chalk Farm tube – a treat for generations of north London kids; "puds are better than mains", but the pizza 'n' pasta are "cheap" and "tasty". / NW3 2BL; www.marineices.co.uk; Sun 10 pm; closed Mon; no Amex.

Market NW1 £46 ④④④
43 Parkway 7267 9700 8–3B
"Simple", "stripped-back" decor sets the "no-frills" tone at this "hard-surfaced" ("noisy") Camden Town bistro; fans applaud its "genuine" British menu, but it can also seem a tad "unmemorable". / NW1 7PN; www.marketrestaurant.co.uk; 10.30 pm, Sun 3.30 pm; closed Sun D.

The Markham Inn SW3 NEW £53 ④❸❸
2 Elystan St 7581 9139 5–2C
Even fans of this "busy" new Chelsea brasserie (on the site of "a forgettable former pub") say it's "nothing racey on the food front"… and even foes admit "it does have a certain lively buzz". / SW3 3NS; www.themarkhaminn.com; 10.45 pm.

Maroush £45 ❸④④
I) 21 Edgware Rd, W2 7723 0773 6–1D
II) 38 Beauchamp Pl, SW3 7581 5434 5–1C
V) 3-4 Vere St, W1 7493 5050 3–1B
VI) 68 Edgware Rd, W2 7224 9339 6–1D
'Garden') 1 Connaught St, W2 7262 0222 6–1D
There's "lots of variety", at this long-established Lebanese chain, which includes not only café/take-aways (part of I, II and VI, offering "super-fresh salads and the best kebabs") but also "rather grand" restaurants of "consistently high quality". / www.maroush.com; most branches close between 12.30 am-5 am.

The Marquess Tavern N1 £44 ❸④❸
32 Canonbury St 7354 2975 8–2D
As imposing a Regency tavern as you'll ever find, this popular gastropub, in leafy Canonbury, wins consistently high ratings, especially for its food. / N1 2TB; www.marquesstavern.com; 10 pm; closed Mon L, Tue L, Wed L, Thu L, Fri L & Sun D.

Masala Zone £30 ❸❸❷

9 Marshall St, W1 7287 9966 3–2D
48 Floral St, WC2 7379 0101 4–2D
147 Earl's Court Rd, SW5 7373 0220 5–2A
583 Fulham Rd, SW6 7386 5500 5–4A
75 Bishop's Bridge Rd, W2 7221 0055 6–1C
80 Upper St, N1 7359 3399 8–3D
25 Parkway, NW1 7267 4422 8–3B

"Reliable as a rock, cheap as chips (if generally healthier), and cheery with it!" – this "high-energy" Indian street food chain offers a "great range" of dishes; "big, yummy thalis" win a particular thumbs-up. / www.realindianfood.com; 11 pm, Sun 10.30 pm; no Amex; booking: min 10.

MASH Steakhouse W1 NEW

81 Brewer St awaiting tel 3–2D

The first Modern American Steak House outside, er, Denmark opens in late-2012, in a huge, gilded basement (neighbour to Brasserie Zédel), near Piccadilly Circus. / W1F 0RH.

**Massimo
Corinthia Hotel SW1** £78

10 Northumberland Ave 7930 8181 2–3D

This "fabulously imposing" new hotel dining room, near Embankment, can certainly dish up some "top-quality fish and seafood" (in particular); Massimo Riccioli (the launch-chef) left in mid-2012, though, so a rating seems inappropriate. / SW1A 2BD; www.massimo-restaurant.co.uk; 10.45 pm; SRA-50%.

Masters Super Fish SE1 £29 ❸④⑤

191 Waterloo Rd 7928 6924 9–4A

"An excellent old-fashioned fish 'n' chip shop, handy for the Old Vic" – recently revamped, it offers "much better value", say fans, "than those trendy places in The Cut". / SE1 8UX; 10.30 pm; closed Sun, Mon L; no Amex; no booking Fri D.

Matsuba TW9 £42 ❷④④

10 Red Lion St 8605 3513 1–4A

"The best Japanese food, down Richmond way"; this "friendly", family-run café offers a consistently high-quality menu – "sashimi, soups, teriyaki and tempura are all excellent". / TW9 1RW; 10.30 pm; closed Sun.

Matsuri SW1 £73 ❸④⑤

15 Bury St 7839 1101 3–3D

This St James's basement houses "London's best teppan-yaki" ("all the food is cooked right in front of you!"), plus a "hidden jewel" of a sushi bar; even fans, though, say it's "expensive", and the setting is "boring" too. / SW1Y 6AL; www.matsuri-restaurant.com; 10.30 pm, Sun 10 pm.

Maxim W13 £38 ❸❷④

153-155 Northfield Ave 8567 1719 1–3A

"At least as good as anything in Chinatown", this Ealing stalwart remains a big local favourite – "it feels a bit cheesy, but the service and food make up for it". / W13 9QT; 11.30 pm, Sun 11 pm.

maze W1 £82 ④④④

10-13 Grosvenor Sq 7107 0000 3–2A

"A mere shadow of its former self" – with its "bland, flavour-mismatched combinations" and its "impersonal" service, Gordon Ramsay's Mayfair tapas-restaurant is nowadays a mere "factory" operation, and a powerfully expensive one too. / W1K 6JP; www.gordonramsay.com/maze; 10.30 pm.

maze Grill W1 £79 ⑤④⑤
10-13 Grosvenor Sq 7495 2211 3–2A
Curiously, it's as an "upmarket place to take the kids" that Ramsay's Mayfair steakhouse is singled out for any real praise – otherwise, it strikes many reporters as an "odd" and "soulless" affair, where "boring" food ("no better than a pub!") comes "way overpriced". / W1K 6JP; www.gordonramsay.com; 11 pm; no shorts; set weekday L & pre-theatre £44 (FP).

Mazi W8 NEW £55
12-14 Hillgate St 7229 3794 6–2B
We didn't get a chance to visit this innovative 'gourmet Greek' establishment, on the Kensington site long known as Costa's Grill (RIP), before this guide went to press – newspaper reviews have generally been upbeat. / W8 7SR; www.mazi.co.uk.

The Meat & Wine Co Westfield W12 £50 ④❸④
Unit 1026 Ariel Way 8749 5914 7–1C
Eye-catchingly sited at the entrance to Westfield, this carnivore's haven (part of a global chain) does have its fans… but it can also seem "characterless, expensive and disappointing". / W12 7GA; www.themeatandwineco.com; 11.30 pm, Sun 10.30 pm; no Maestro.

MEATLiquor W1 NEW £33 ❷④❸
74 Welbeck St 7224 4239 3–1B
"Believe the hype!"; this "raucous", "vandal-chic" newcomer has been one of 2012's smash-hits; "why would anyone queue for an hour outside a multi-storey car park behind Debenhams?" – the "distinctly guilty pleasure" of "the juiciest burger ever", "full of sloppy meaty loveliness". / W1G 0BA; www.meatliquor.com; midnight, Fri-Sat 2 am; closed Sun; no booking.

Mediterraneo W11 £55 ❸❸❷
37 Kensington Park Rd 7792 3131 6–1A
"A true Notting Hill stalwart"; this "chaotic" Italian can still provide "a great experience", combining "cheerful bustle" and "solid" cooking; "it's best in summer, with the doors open to the pavement". / W11 2EU; www.mediterraneo-restaurant.co.uk; 11.30 pm, Sun 10.30 pm; booking: max 10.

Medlar SW10 £60 ❶❷④
438 King's Rd 7349 1900 5–3B
"Magnificent French-leaning cuisine" has made this notable yearling (set up by an ex-Chez Bruce team) "a great addition to distant-Chelsea"; the "narrow premises lack atmosphere", however, and a local notes: "what with the popularity and a recent first-floor expansion, the kitchen sometimes can't cope". / SW10 0LJ; 10.30 pm, Sun 9.30 pm.

Megan's Delicatessen SW6 £43 ❸❸❸
571 Kings Rd 7371 7837 5–4A
"Everything a deli/café should be"; this "rustic" Fulham spot serves a "well-executed, simple menu", in particular "yummy breakfasts and brunch" – it's best in fair weather, when the "terrific" terrace come into its own. / SW6 2EB; www.megansrestaurant.com; 10 pm; closed Sun D; no Amex.

Mekong SW1 £29 ❸❸④
46 Churton St 7630 9568 2–4B
A "cosy" (and cramped) Pimlico stalwart, still sought out by long-terms fans for its "fresh-flavoured" and "good-value" Vietnamese/Thai/Chinese food, and its "kind and solicitous" service. / SW1V 2LP; 10.45 pm, Sun 10 pm.

F S A

Mela WC2 £40 ❸❸④
152-156 Shaftesbury Avenue 7836 8635 4–2B
"Surprisingly good food for a basic West End Indian"; this "reliable" and "so central" curry house, by Cambridge Circus, pleases most reporters; it can get rather "loud". / WC2H 8HL; www.melarestaurant.co.uk; 11.30 pm, Sun 10.30 pm; set pre theatre £27 (FP).

Melati W1 £35 ④④⑤
21 Gt Windmill St 7437 2745 3–2D
A "scruffy" but endearing Soho canteen, whose "authentic" Malaysian/Indonesian scoff shows occasional "flashes of brilliance"; it is always "reasonably-priced". / W1D 7LQ; www.melati.co.uk; 11 pm, Sat-Sun 11.30 pm.

Mele e Pere W1 NEW £48 ④❷④
46 Brewer St 8947 4474 3–2D
Unsettled early-days reports on this large and "noisy" Soho basement bar/restaurant; service is notably "assured", though, and the Italian cooking is generally rated "decent" or better. / W1F 9TF; set weekday L £29 (FP), set pre-theatre £31 (FP).

Mem & Laz N1 £29 ❸❷❷
8 Theberton St 7704 9089 8–3D
"Noisy and overly busy" it may be, but this "cheap 'n' cheerful" operation, near Angel, thrives on its "great-value" formula – an "eclectic" menu of Turkish and Mediterranean dishes, in "huge helpings". / N1 0QX; www.memlaz.com; 11.30 pm, Fri & Sat midnight; no Amex.

Memories of India SW7 £32 ❸❸④
18 Gloucester Rd 7581 3734 5–1B
It's very "standard" in appearance, but this South Kensington stalwart is the epitome of a "reliable local Indian". / SW7 4RB; www.memoriesofindia.com; 11.30 pm, Sun 11 pm.

Memsaheb on Thames E14 £33 ④❸④
65-67 Amsterdam Rd 7538 3008 11–2D
Not far from Canary Wharf, this riverside Indian has its highs and lows, but fans insist it's a "hidden gem". / E14 3UU; www.memsaheb.net; 11 pm; closed Sat L; no Amex.

Menier Chocolate Factory SE1 £44 ⑤❸❸
51-53 Southwark St 7234 9610 9–4B
A quirky adjunct to an "adventurous" South Bank theatre; feedback is mixed, but on a good day, you get "great food, themed to match the performance", and "friendly and attentive" service too. / SE1 1RU; www.menierchocolatefactory.com; 10.45 pm; closed Mon & Sun D.

Mennula W1 £56 ❸④④
10 Charlotte St 7636 2833 2–1C
"A bit chaotic at times, but the food is seriously good" – this "cramped" Fitzrovian is still hailed on most accounts as a "gem", thanks to its "interesting" Sicilian menu and wines; a few reporters though, do bemoan a "loss of sparkle" of late. / W1T 2LT; www.mennula.com; 11 pm, Sun 9.30 pm; closed Sat L & Sun L; set pre theatre £34 (FP).

The Mercer EC2 £53 ❸❷❸
34 Threadneedle St 7628 0001 9–2C
"Refreshingly professional" service, and a menu of "comforting" British classics help makes this heart-of-the-Square-Mile former banking hall a very popular lunching destination. / EC2R 8AY; www.themercer.co.uk; 9.30 pm; closed Sat & Sun.

Le Mercury N1 £28 ④④❸
140a Upper St 7354 4088 8–2D
"Sooooooo cheap" and "usually very cheerful"; this cosy Islington bistro is "such a stalwart", and – notwithstanding the odd let-down – generally churns out "reliably OK" fodder at "unbelievable prices". / N1 1QY; www.lemercury.co.uk; 12.30 am, Sun 11 pm.

Meson don Felipe SE1 £39 ④④④
53 The Cut 7928 3237 9–4A
"Still one of the most authentic Spanish places in London", this "massively popular" bolt hole, near the Old Vic, is "always busy and crowded", and it can get "loud" too (especially when the guitarist gets going); "standard" tapas, but "reliable". / SE1 8LF; www.mesondonfelipe.com; 11 pm; closed Sun; no Amex; no booking after 8 pm.

Mestizo NW1 £41 ⑤④④
103 Hampstead Rd 7387 4064 8–4C
This once path-breaking Mexican, near Warren Street tube, has gone badly off the boil – "nice margaritas" still, but the grub too often seems "formulaic, dull and expensive". / NW1 3EL; www.mestizomx.com; 11 pm, Fri-Sat 11.30 pm, Sun 10 pm.

Mews of Mayfair W1 £62 ④④❸
10 Lancashire Ct, New Bond St 7518 9388 3–2B
The setting is "a haven of calm", off Bond Street, but this "sophisticated" haunt is perhaps most reliably enjoyed for a drink at the bar – the restaurant can be "disappointing", and it's "not the cheapest" either. / W1S 1EY; www.mewsofmayfair.com; 11.30 pm; closed Sun D.

Mezzanine
Royal National Theatre SE1 £50 ④④④
Royal National Theatre, Belvedere Rd 7452 3600 2–3D
"Impersonal", "dull" and offering "unexceptional" cooking… yet the RNT's "reliable" in-house restaurant is still generally thought to be "convenient, before a show". / SE1 9PX; www.nationaltheatre.org.uk; 11 pm; closed Mon L, Fri L & Sun D.

Michael Nadra W4 £51 ❶❸④
6-8 Elliott Rd 8742 0766 7–2A
"London's most under-rated restaurant?" – OK, it may be "squashed", but this side street Chiswick spot has a huge fan club, thanks to its (ex-Trompette) proprietor's "outstanding" and "superbly-presented" food; "get one of the boothed window tables if you can". / W4 1PE; www.restaurant-michaelnadra.co.uk; 10 pm, Fri & Sat 10.30 pm; closed Sun D.

Mien Tay £24 ❷④④
180 Lavender Hill, SW11 7350 0721 10–1C
122 Kingsland Rd, E2 7729 3074 12–1B
"Ignore the décor", and the "sometimes inconsistent service" – it's the "powerfully-flavoured" food at "astounding-value prices" which is the secret of the success of these "somewhat dingy" Vietnamese "gems", in Shoreditch and Battersea. / 11 pm, Fri & Sat 11.30 pm, Sun 10.30 pm; cash only.

Mildreds W1 £40 ❷④❸
45 Lexington St 7494 1634 3–2D
"Who needs meat when you get this much flavour?" – thanks to its "imaginative" and "interesting" cuisine, this "cramped" Soho veggie veteran is "wildly popular"; "don't forget your earplugs", though. / W1F 9AN; www.mildreds.co.uk; 11 pm; closed Sun; no Amex; no booking.

Mill Lane Bistro NW6 £44 ❸❷❸
77 Mill Ln 7794 5577 1–1B
A "super local bistro", in West Hampstead – this Gallic two-year-old is generally praised for its "authentic" style, not least its "small and well-executed" menu. / NW6 1NB; www.milllanebistro.com; 10 pm, Fri-Sat 10.30 pm, Sun 9 pm; closed Mon & Sun D; no Amex; set weekday L £24 (FP).

Mimmo la Bufala NW3 £50 ❸④④
45a South End Rd 7435 7814 8–2B
"Excellent pizza" helps win praise for this "cramped" and "authentically Italian" fixture, occupying "Tardis-like" Hampstead premises; it was recently re-named, from 'Fratelli la Bufala', to distinguish it from the global chain of that name, newly arrived in the capital. / NW3 2QB; www.mimmolabufala.co.uk; 11 pm; Mon-Thu D only, Fri-Sun open L & D; no credit cards; set weekday L £28 (FP).

Min Jiang
The Royal Garden Hotel W8 £73 ❶❷❶
2-24 Kensington High St 7361 1988 5–1A
"Superb food in a superb location"; breaking all the usual rules about rooms-with-views (in this case, of Kensington Gardens and beyond), this "classy" 8th-floor dining room offers "out-of-this-world Chinese haute cuisine" – highlights include "great dim dum" and "awesome duck" (pre-order). / W8 4PT; www.minjiang.co.uk; 10 pm.

Mint Leaf £63 ❸❸❷
Suffolk Pl, Haymarket, SW1 7930 9020 2–2C
Angel Ct, Lothbury, EC2 7600 0992 9–2C
A designer-Indian duo, in a "very dark" basement near Trafalgar Square, and a dramatic space near Bank; the latter – with its "delicious" food, and "even better cocktails" – outscores the former, which recorded a number of "disappointing" meals this year. / www.mintleafrestaurant.com; SW1 11 pm, Sun 10.30 pm; EC2 10.30 pm; SW1 closed Sat & Sun L; EC2 closed Sat & Sun; set weekday L £34 (FP).

Miran Masala W14 £21 ❷❷⑤
3 Hammersmith Rd 7602 4555 7–1D
"Amazing flavours, welcoming staff and good prices" – this Pakistani café, opposite Olympia, doesn't inspire much feedback, but it's all positive; BYO – "two people can walk out having spent less than £25". / W14 8XJ; www.miranmasala.com; 11.30 pm.

Mirch Masala £23 ❷④⑤
171-173 The Broadway, UB1 8867 9222 1–3A
1416 London Rd, SW16 8679 1828 10–2C
213 Upper Tooting Rd, SW17 8767 8638 10–2D
111-113 Commercial Rd, E1 7377 0155 12–2D
For "incredibly tasty food at knock-down prices", pay a visit to these "chaotic", "no-frills" Pakistani canteens… "but don't bother if you're hoping for any ambience or service, still less any booze"; you can, however, BYO. / www.mirchmasalarestaurant.co.uk; midnight.

Mishkin's WC2 NEW £40 ⑤④❷
25 Catherine St 7240 2078 4–3D
"Scratching an itch for those in search of an authentic NYC-style Jewish deli" – Russell Norman's small but "loud" Covent Garden diner has made a "fun, buzzy and stylish" debut; too often, though, the food seems "gimmicky" or "disappointing". / WC2B 5JS; www.mishkins.co.uk; 11.30 pm, 10.30 pm.

F S A

Mitsukoshi SW1 £51 ❷❷⑤

Dorland Hs, 14-20 Lower Regent St 7930 0317 3–3D

"If you're interested in Japanese food and don't mind less fancy decor", it's worth a visit to this "tired-looking" basement, below a department store near Piccadilly Circus – the sushi bar is "one of the best in town". / SW1Y 4PH; www.mitsukoshi-restaurant.co.uk; 10 pm; closed Sun.

Miyama W1 £54 ❷❸⑤

38 Clarges St 7499 2443 3–4B

"Tucked away from the maelstrom of Piccadilly", this "quiet" and "spacious" Japanese may look "sterile" and "a bit dated", but its food is "fabulous", with "heavenly" sushi a high point. / W1J 7EN; www.miyama-restaurant.co.uk; 10.15 pm; closed Sat L & Sun L.

The Modern Pantry EC1 £49 ④④④

47-48 St Johns Sq 7553 9210 9–1A

"Fusion food that really works!"; "interesting-going-on-odd" combinations – an "awesome brunch" in particular – have made a big name for Anna Hansen's "light" (and slightly "cold") Clerkenwell venture; critics, though, find the cooking "confused", and service "inattentive" too. / EC1V 4JJ; www.themodernpantry.co.uk; 10.30 pm, Sun 10 pm; SRA-66%.

Mohsen W14 £25 ❸④⑤

152 Warwick Rd 7602 9888 7–1D

"Delicious freshly-prepared Iranian food" draws fans to this "cramped", "no-fuss" Persian BYO; well, it seems unlikely the location – opposite the Olympia Homebase – is the attraction! / W14 8PS; midnight; no credit cards.

Momo W1 £72 ④④❷

25 Heddon St 7434 4040 3–2C

"Never bad, and sometimes memorable!" – this "lovely" souk-style party-Moroccan, just off Regent Street, makes an "atmospheric" venue for a party or romance; the pricey food is traditionally rather incidental, but there were no particular criticisms in this year's survey. / W1B 4BH; www.momoresto.com; 11.30 pm, Sun 11 pm; closed Sun L; set weekday L £38 (FP).

Mon Plaisir WC2 £55 ❸❸❷

19-21 Monmouth St 7836 7243 4–2B

"Lots of cosy corners" add charm to this classic "old-stager" – "a little bit of France in Covent Garden"; standards may be "a little frayed compared with yesteryear", but the bistro fare is still "reliable", and the pre-theatre menu remains of note for its "excellent value". / WC2H 9DD; www.monplaisir.co.uk; 11.15 pm; closed Sun; set pre-theatre £29 (FP), set weekday L £30 (FP).

Mona Lisa SW10 £28 ④❶❷

417 King's Rd 7376 5447 5–3B

"A great hang-out for toffs and taxi-drivers" – this Italian greasy spoon, in Chelsea, attracts a famously diverse clientèle, thanks not least to its keen prices, and the "excellent service" from the owner and his team. / SW10 0LR; 11 pm, Sun 5.30 pm; closed Sun D; no Amex.

Monmouth Coffee Company £12 ❶❶❷
27 Monmouth St, WC2 7379 3516 4–2B
Arches Northside, Dockley Rd, SE16 7232 3010 9–4D NEW
2 Park St, SE1 7940 9960 9–4C
Cult cafés in Borough and Covent Garden, where "waiting in the queue with other bleary-eyed coffee fanatics is all part of the experience"; their "intense" and "silky" brews remain "the best in London" – "top off your drink with a piece of baguette and some jam". / www.monmouthcoffee.co.uk; 6 pm-6.30 pm; SE16 12 pm; closed Sun; SE16 open Sat only; no Amex; no booking.

Montpeliano SW7 £59 ⑤⑤⑤
13 Montpelier St 7589 0032 5–1C
Even those who say this "very '80s" Knightsbridge trattoria is "a lovely old-fashioned venue" admit "you need to ignore the high prices"; to critics, however, it's just a "conceited" place offering "dull" cooking at "horrific" cost. / SW7 1HQ; www.montpelianorestaurant.com; 11.45 pm, Sun 11.30 pm.

Monty's £33 ❸❸④
692 Fulham Rd, SW6 7371 5971 10–1B
54 Northfield Ave, W13 8567 6281 1–2A
1 The Mall, W5 8567 8122 1–2A
"Interesting Nepalese dishes share a menu with traditional curry-house staples", at these long-established and "welcoming" west London stalwarts; ownership varies by branch, but the formula doesn't change much. / 11 pm.

Mooli's W1 £17 ❷❷④
50 Frith St 7494 9075 4–2A
"Spicy" and "finger-lickin' delicious" wraps with "vibrant chutneys", at "excellent-value prices" is a formula that still "hits the spot" at this Indian-burrito ("sounds strange, but works") pit stop in the heart of Soho; "goat comes highly recommended". / W1D 4SQ; www.moolis.com; 11.30 pm; closed Sun.

The Morgan Arms E3 £44 ❸❸❷
43 Morgan St 8980 6389 1–2D
"Everything a local should be" – this Bow boozer scores well for its "calming" atmosphere, and food that's "not ground-breaking, but consistently good". / E3 5AA; www.capitalpubcompany.com/The-Morgan-Arms; 10 pm, Sun 9 pm.

Morgan M EC1 NEW £68 ❶❷④
50 Long Ln 7609 3560 9–2B
"Now he's moved to Clerkenwell, it's much easier to sample Morgan Meunier's superb cuisine" – "unashamedly French, but often with an outstanding twist"; service is "kind and welcoming" too… but did the new premises' décor really have to be so dismally "uninspired"? / EC1A 9EJ; www.morganm.com; 10.30 pm; closed Sun; set pre theatre £45 (FP).

Morito EC1 £35 ❷❷❷
32 Exmouth Mkt 7278 7007 9–1A
"Moro's equally brilliant little brother" is a "buzzing and bustling" sort of place, where the tapas are "fantastic"; "don't take grandma though!" – it's "cramped" and "basic", and the stools are "uncomfortable". / EC1R 4QE; www.morito.co.uk; 11 pm, Sun 4 pm; closed Sun D; no Amex; no booking for D.

Moro EC1 £52 ❷❷❸
34-36 Exmouth Mkt 7833 8336 9–1A
A "fabulous fusion" of Moorish and Andalucian cuisine, with "passionate" service too, ensures that this "friendly" (but "crowded and noisy") Exmouth Market favourite is "always humming"; has the time now come, though, for "a bit of updating" on the decor front? / EC1R 4QE; www.moro.co.uk; 10.30 pm; closed Sun D.

Mosaica
The Chocolate Factory N22 £46 ❸❷❷
Unit C005, Clarendon Rd 8889 2400 1–1C
"Always a bit of a shock to enter through a semi-abandoned factory!" – in its "out-of-the-way" location, this Wood Green "barn" is certainly "long on wow-factor", and it has a "great buzzy vibe"; the food is "reliably good" too. / N22 6XJ; www.mosaicarestaurants.com; 9.30 pm, Sat 10 pm; closed Sat L & Sun D.

Motcombs SW1 £58 ④❸❷
26 Motcomb St 7235 6382 5–1D
Currently on pretty good form, this "accommodating" wine bar (plus "posher" basement restaurant) keeps the flag of 'old Belgravia' flying; its corner location adds to the appeal – amusing people-watching from the al fresco tables. / SW1X 8JU; www.motcombs.co.uk; 11 pm; closed Sun D; set weekday L £29 (FP).

Moti Mahal WC2 £54 ❷❷❸
45 Gt Queen St 7240 9329 4–2D
"A surprise in a touristy area"; this "first-rate" Covent Garden Indian (part of a Delhi-based group) combines "adventurous" cuisine with "very accommodating" service and "stylish" (if perhaps "slightly sterile") decor. / WC2B 5AA; www.motimahal-uk.com; 10.45 pm; closed Sat L & Sun.

Mount Street Deli W1 £26 ④④❸
100 Mount St 7499 6843 3–3A
"Golly it's expensive", but Richard Caring's chichi café/deli, in the heart of Mayfair, is undoubtedly "a nice option for a coffee", and it does offer "lovely home-made-seeming fare using great ingredients". / W1K 2TG; www.themountstreetdeli.co.uk; 6 pm, Sat 5 pm; L only, closed Sun; no bookings.

Mr Chow SW1 £87 ④④④
151 Knightsbridge 7589 7347 5–1D
Fans still vaunt this once mega-fashionable '60s-hang-over, in Knightsbridge, for its "traditional but delicious" Chinese cuisine; it's striking how little feedback it generates nowadays, though, some of it pretty negative. / SW1X 7PA; www.mrchow.com; 11.45 pm; closed Mon L.

Mr Kong WC2 £30 ❸❸④
21 Lisle St 7437 7341 4–3A
"It never fails!"; this "cramped" Chinatown "stalwart" is a long-time "favourite" for many reporters, thanks to its "smiling" service and its "big menu" with "unusually interesting dishes" – "get to know the manager to get the best". / WC2H 7BA; www.mrkongrestaurant.com; 2.45 am, Sun 1.45 am.

Mr Wing SW5 £45 ❸④❸
242-244 Old Brompton Rd 7370 4450 5–2A
Long-time fans fear this "lovely" Earl's Court Chinese "gem" has "lost its sparkle" since the old maître d' retired last year; the "expensive-but-worth-it" food, though, is "still reliable". / SW5 0DE; www.mrwing.com; 11.30 pm.

Mugen EC4 £46 ❸④④
26 King William St 7929 7879 9–3C
"Good-value Japanese cooking – from a budget lunch to the full à la carte" – helps ensure that this "decent" and "efficient" restaurant, by London Bridge, is usually "extremely busy". / EC4R 9AW; 10.30 pm; closed Sat & Sun.

Murano W1 £93 ❸❸④
20-22 Queen St 7495 1127 3–3B
Many "phenomenal" Italianate meals are reported at Angela Hartnett's "classy" and "understated" Mayfair HQ; bizarrely, though, ever since her establishment quit the Ramsay empire, it has seemed more and more to "lack a personal touch", and the ratings slid noticeably this year… again. / W1J 5PP; www.muranolondon.com; 11 pm; closed Sun; set weekday L £55 (FP).

My Old Place E1 £36 ❷⑤⑤
88-90 Middlesex St 7247 2200 9–2D
"Weird, but that's why you went!" – this "slightly shabby" East Ender serves "authentic" Sichuan cuisine that's "cheap" and "hot, hot, hot". / E1 7EZ; www.oldplace.co.uk; 11 pm; no Amex.

Naamyaa Café EC1 NEW
407 St John St awaiting tel 8–3D
Alan Yau – founder, inter alia, of Wagmamama, Hakkasan and Yauatcha – returns to the London market to launch this new 'Bangkok café' formula, initially in Islington, in late-2012; it's under the same management as Busaba Eathai (with which he's still involved). / EC1V 4AB; www.naamyaa.com.

Nahm
Halkin Hotel SW1 £82 ❷❸⑤
5 Halkin St 7333 1234 2–3A
"David Thompson's a star!", and his Thai cooking is "in a class of its own", according to practically all who report on this boutique-hotel dining room, off Belgrave Square; it's totally "let down by the non-existent atmosphere" however, and even supporters can find it "pricey". / SW1X 7DJ; www.nahm.como.bz; 10.30 pm; closed Sat L & Sun L.

Namo E9 £31 ❸❸❷
178 Victoria Park Rd 8533 0639 1–2D
"Fantastic food at great prices" makes this Vietnamese café, near Victoria Park, quite a "local gem"; even supporters, though, can find it a bit "variable". / E9 7HD; www.namo.co.uk; 10.30 pm.

Nando's £29 ④④④
Branches throughout London
"Should I admit to liking it?" – "yes", say many fans of this flame-roasted, peri-peri chicken chain – a "predictable yet relatively healthy option" for a quick "cheap 'n' cheerful" meal, and one that "caters well for kids" too. / www.nandos.co.uk; 11.30 pm, Sun 10.30 pm; no Amex; no booking.

Napulé SW6 £39 ❸❸❸
585 Fulham Rd 7381 1122 5–4A
There's "always a good pizza, and the pasta and meat dishes are OK too", at this attractive, rambling offshoot of the 'Made in Italy' group, near Fulham Broadway. / SW6 5UA; 11.30 pm, Sun 10.30 pm; closed weekday L; no Amex.

The Narrow E14 £48 ⑤⑤④
44 Narrow St 7592 7950 11–1B
"Gordon, get out of the gastropub game!"; this river-view East End boozer is "a perfect example of how not to run a restaurant"… "abysmal"! / E14 8DP; www.gordonramsay.com; 10.30 pm, Sun 10 pm.

The National Dining Rooms
National Gallery WC2 £51 ⑤⑤④
Sainsbury Wing, Trafalgar Sq 7747 2525 2–2C
This large and "slightly gloomy" first-floor dining room may feel "a bit more like a posh canteen than a restaurant", but its "fantastic views" of Trafalgar Square "give it an edge", and – though its fare is "uninspired" and pricey – it has its fans for lunch or tea. / WC2N 5DN; www.thenationaldiningrooms.co.uk; 7 pm; Sat-Thu closed D, Fri open L & D; no Amex.

National Gallery Café
National Gallery WC2 £45 ④❸④
East Wing, Trafalgar Sq 7747 5942 4–4B
"So convenient!" – this "relaxing", panelled café, run by Peyton & Byrne, has an almost Viennese air, and feels surprisingly "secluded" for somewhere slap-bang on Trafalgar Square; "first-class" breakfasts are a highlight of the generally "fair" cuisine. / WC2N 5DN; www.thenationaldiningrooms.co.uk; 11 pm, Sun 6 pm; closed Sun D; no Amex.

Natural Kitchen £34 ❸④❸
77-78 Marylebone High St, W1 3012 2123 2–1A
15-17 New Street Sq, Fetter Ln, EC4 3012 2123 9–2A
These "busy and informal" delis offer "a good selection of dishes", and have attractive interiors too – they're handy "for a sit-down sandwich or a salad" (or even a "veggie breakfast fry-up"). / EC4 9 pm; W1 8 pm, Sat 7 pm, Sun 6 pm; EC4 closed Sat & Sun.

Nautilus NW6 £41 ❷❸⑤
27-29 Fortune Green Rd 7435 2532 1–1B
"The batter is so light, and the fish so fresh", at this "old-school" West Hampstead chippy – a "welcoming", if "functional", place, with an impressively broad following. / NW6 1DU; 10 pm; closed Sun; no Amex.

Navarro's W1 £41 ❷④❷
67 Charlotte St 7637 7713 2–1C
A "beautiful tiled interior" and "extremely tasty" tapas (plus other fare) win high marks for this "picturesque and truly authentic" Fitzrovian; weekday lunches see "the local media crowd" in full cry. / W1T 4PH; www.navarros.co.uk; 10 pm; closed Sat L & Sun.

Nazmins SW18 £35 ④④④
396-398 Garratt Ln 8944 1463 10–2B
A "great-value" curry house, hailed by most – if not quite all – Earlsfield folk as an "institution"; the occasional sceptic, though, is bemused – "why is it so popular?" / SW18 4HP; www.nazmins.com; midnight.

Needoo E1 £26 ❷❸❸
87 New Rd 7247 0648 12–2D
"Not quite up to New Taayabs" (where the chef trained), but the "brilliantly-flavoured grills" at this "harshly-lit" but "buzzing" East End Pakistani come at similarly "fantastic" prices; here, "you can book" too… "but that just puts you at the front of the queue!" / E1 1HH; www.needoogrill.co.uk; 11.30 pm.

New China Boulevard SW18 £40 ❷④❸
1 The Boulevard, Smugglers Way 8871 3881 10–2B
"A best-kept secret"; this Wandsworth Thames-view Cantonese is of particular note for its "weekday lunchtime half-price deals", when the dim sum is "fantastic" value. / SW18 1DE; www.chinaboulevard.com; 11 pm.

New Mayflower W1 £39 ❷❸❸
68-70 Shaftesbury Ave 7734 9207 4–3A
A busy Chinatown-fringe stalwart, typically "packed with Chinese customers"; the cooking's much more "authentic" than most – "it helps to speak Cantonese, but pointing at other diners' dishes seems to work". / W1D 6LY; 4 am; D only; no Amex.

New Street Grill EC2 NEW
16 New St awaiting tel 9–2D
Neighbouring Fish Market (see also), this new Spitalfields warehouse-conversion, from the D&D Group, is to be a steakhouse – a better one, we hope, than its Paternoster Chop House stablemate! / EC2M 4TR.

New World W1 £36 ④④❸
1 Gerrard Pl 7434 2508 4–3A
"Bustling trolleys of steaming dim sum" add to the "very lively" lunchtime ambience of this otherwise "cavernous" stalwart, "in the heart of Chinatown"; "the fun-factor is perhaps better than the food itself". / W1D 5PA; www.newworldlondon.com; 11.45 pm, Sat midnight, Sun 11 pm.

1901
Andaz Hotel EC2 £62 ④④❷
40 Liverpool St 7618 7000 12–2B
Surprisingly little feedback on this grand hotel dining room, by Liverpool Street; food and service don't excite, but the "extraordinary" wine list and "impressive" surroundings certainly contribute to suitability for a business lunch. / EC2M 7QN; www.andazdining.com; 10 pm; closed Sat L & Sun; booking: max 20.

Nizuni W1 £42 ❸❸④
22 Charlotte St 7580 7447 2–1C
"Excellent Japanese food with a Korean tinge" has made quite a hit of this no-nonsense Fitzrovia yearling; it can, however, seem "a bit pricey for what it is". / W1T 2NB; www.nizuni.com; 10.45 pm; closed Sun L.

Nobu
Metropolitan Hotel W1 £85 ❷④❸
19 Old Park Ln 7447 4747 3–4A
"It may not pull the crowds like it did", but this "tired"-looking and "cramped" Mayfair legend still inspires enduring support for its "glorious" Japanese-fusion cuisine, its "eclectic" ambience and the "people-watching" it offers; it remains as "scandalously overpriced" as ever. / W1K 1LB; www.noburestaurants.com; 10.15 pm, Fri & Sat 11 pm, Sun 10 pm.

Nobu W1 £85 ❸④④
15 Berkeley St 7290 9222 3–3C
Like its older namesake, this ever-buzzing Mayfair spot dishes up some "superb" Japanese-inspired cuisine (famously, the "divine black cod"); other similarities – "you pay through the nose for it", service is "a let-down", and the "soulless" setting has "too many tables". / W1J 8DY; www.noburestaurants.com; 11 pm, Sun 9.45 pm; closed Sat L & Sun L.

FSA

Noor Jahan £38 ❷❷❸
2a, Bina Gdns, SW5 7373 6522 5–2B
26 Sussex Pl, W2 7402 2332 6–1D
This "unchanging" stalwart of Earl's Court's "curry corner" – with its "extremely tasty" dishes, "'80s -peach" decor and "brusque" staff – is "a classic, for its smart local crowd"; "tucked-away" in W2, its spin-off offers better food, but less character. / 11.30 pm, Sun 10 pm.

Nopi W1 £55 ❷❸❸
21-22 Warwick St 7494 9584 3–2D
"Zesty, vibrant, a sheer joy!" – Yottam Ottolenghi's "inspired" small plates, featuring "unforgettable" Middle Eastern and Asian flavour combinations, make this "cool" and "electric" Soho yearling a major hit (but "boy, do you pay for it"). / W1B 5NE; www.nopi-restaurant.com; 10.15 pm, Sun 4 pm; closed Sun D.

Nordic Bakery £15 ❸④❸
14a, Golden Sq, W1 3230 1077 3–2D
37b, New Cavendish St, W1 7935 3590 2–1A
"A steaming cinnamon bun" + "Scandinavian aesthetics" + "wonderful coffee" + "great open sandwiches" = "bliss" – so suggest most reports on this small chain. / Golden Square 8 pm, Sat 7 pm, Sun 7 pm; Cavendish Street 6 pm.

The Norfolk Arms WC1 £39 ④❸❸
28 Leigh St 7388 3937 8–4C
Sometimes "puzzlingly inconsistent from meal to meal", this Bloomsbury boozer is nonetheless hailed by most reporters for its "interesting" and "varied" tapas-based menu, and some "great-value wines" too. / WC1H 9EP; www.norfolkarms.co.uk; 10.15 pm.

North China W3 £36 ❷❷❸
305 Uxbridge Rd 8992 9183 7–1A
"Better than many an over-hyped Chinese in the West End" – this "exemplary" family-run Acton stalwart wins strong praise for its "welcoming" approach, and its "delicious, deeply satisfying food". / W3 9QU; www.northchina.co.uk; 11 pm, Fri & Sat 11.30 pm.

The North London Tavern NW6 £44 ❸④❸
375 Kilburn High Rd 7625 6634 1–2B
Near the Tricycle Theatre, a "friendly" Kilburn boozer, with food that's "well above your standard pub dining room grub, but without any real pretensions to being a gastropub". / NW6 7QB; www.northlondontavern.co.uk; 10.30 pm, Sun 9.30 pm.

North Road EC1 £58 ❶❶❸
69-73 St John St 3217 0033 9–1B
"Challenging but worthwhile!" – Christoffer Hruskova's "highly innovative" and "thought-provoking" cuisine offers, say fans, a real dose of "Scandinavian magic"; the interior of his Clerkenwell yearling, though, is "somewhat austere". / EC1M 4AN; www.northroadrestaurant.co.uk; 10.30 pm, Fri-Sat 11 pm; closed Sat L & Sun.

North Sea Fish WC1 £35 ❸❸④
7-8 Leigh St 7387 5892 8–4C
"A blast from the past!" – this "old-fashioned" Bloomsbury chippy is a "very friendly" sort of place, serving "crunchily-battered" fish, plus chips of "championship quality". / WC1H 9EW; www.northseafishrestaurant.co.uk; 10.30 pm; closed Sun; no Amex.

F S A

Northbank EC4 **£50** ④④④
1 Paul's Walk 7329 9299 9–3B
"A really terrific location" – by the Millennium Bridge, with fine Thames views and a big sunny-days terrace – is the high point of this otherwise mid-rank City bar/restaurant; fans do praise "pretty decent" (West Country-inspired) food, but critics can find the whole set-up rather "amateur". / EC4V 3QH; www.northbankrestaurant.co.uk; 10.30 pm; closed Sun.

The Northgate N1 **£42** ❷❷❸
113 Southgate Rd 7359 7392 1–1C
With its "imaginative menu, large portions and very friendly service", this "top-class" De Beauvoir local "does the gastropub thing very well". / N1 3JS; 10.15 pm, Sun 9.15 pm; closed weekday L.

Notes **£18** ④❷❷
31 St Martin's Ln, WC2 7240 0424 4–4C
36 Wellington St, WC2 7240 7899 4–3D
"The locations may seem touristy", but – thanks not least to their "engaging" staff – these handy Covent Garden cafés are strong on "personality"; "fantastic" coffee too – cakes and snacks are less of an attraction. / Wellington St Mon-Wed 10 pm, Thu-Fri 11 pm, Sun 6 pm; St Martin's Ln Mon-Wed 9 pm, Thu-Sat 10 pm, Sun 6 pm.

Notting Hill Brasserie W11 **£77** ④④❸
92 Kensington Park Rd 7229 4481 6–2B
A slick and imposing townhouse venue that – "with its pianist and cosy bar" – feels "like a club"; the food is "perfectly adequate", but – "apart from the eye-watering expense" – "ultimately forgettable". / W11 2PN; www.nottinghillbrasserie.co.uk; 11 pm, Mon & Sun 10.30 pm; closed weekday L.

Noura **£51** ❸④❸
16 Hobart Pl, SW1 7235 9444 2–4B
2 William St, SW1 7235 5900 5–1D
16 Curzon St, W1 7495 1050 3–4B
A "lively" group of brasseries, which please most reporters with their "authentic and enjoyable", if not inexpensive, Lebanese cuisine. / www.noura.co.uk; 11.30 pm, Sun 10 pm; 16 Hobart Place closed Sun.

Novikov (Asian restaurant) W1 NEW **£85** ④④❸
50A Berkeley St 7399 4330 3–3C
"Noisy, boisterous, and full of the surgically-enhanced", this "big and brassy" Russian-backed newcomer is a "fun and glamorous" Mayfair arrival… for those who like that sort of thing; the Asian-fusion fare is "surprisingly good", but "you do need to be an oligarch to endure the eye-watering prices". / W1J 8HD; www.novikovrestaurant.co.uk; 11.15 pm.

Novikov (Italian restaurant) W1 NEW **£85** ❷④❸
50 Berkeley St 7399 4330 3–3C
Less frenetic (and less commented-upon) than the adjacent Asian mêlée – the more "civilised" and "spacious" Italian dining room of this "Eurotrashy" new Mayfair-Muscovite wins praise for its "proper cooking, with top-quality ingredients"; "at the same price, though, you could buy a Range Rover in the showroom opposite…" / W1J 8HD; www.novikovrestaurant.co.uk; 11.30 pm.

Nozomi SW3 £79 ④④④
14-15 Beauchamp Pl 7838 1500 5–1C
The supposed in-crowd charms of this Knightsbridge Japanese continue to elude reporters; it attracts few and very mixed reports, but there is some consensus that it is "expensive" and "noisy" (especially later on). / SW3 1NQ; www.nozomi.co.uk; 11.30 pm, Sun 10.30 pm; closed Mon L.

Numero Uno SW11 £54 ❸❸❷
139 Northcote Rd 7978 5837 10–2C
A "bustling" ambience and "amusing" service underpin the popularity of this "cramped" Nappy Valley Italian; food-wise "it's nothing clever, just excellent at doing the basics". / SW11 6PX; 11.30 pm; no Amex.

Nuovi Sapori SW6 £43 ❸❷④
295 New King's Rd 7736 3363 10–1B
A "fun" Fulham Italian with a "very friendly owner", and offering "delicious" cooking too – no wonder it's usually "buzzing"! / SW6 4RE; 11 pm; closed Sun.

Nusa Kitchen £11 ❷④④
9 Old St, EC1 7253 3135 9–1B
2 Adam's Ct, EC2 7628 1149 9–2C
You get "the best soups in London bar none" – and "great value for money" too – at these City and Farringdon pit stops… "if you can stand the queues". / www.nusakitchen.co.uk; 4 pm; Sat & Sun; no booking.

The Oak W2 £49 ❶❸❶
137 Westbourne Park Rd 7221 3355 6–1B
"Absolutely superb", this Bayswater pub-conversion is not just "an interesting and vibrant" space, but also offers pizzas which are "in a league of their own". / W2 5QL; www.theoaklondon.com; 10.30 pm, Sun 10 pm; closed weekday L; no booking.

Odette's NW1 £57 ❷❸❷
130 Regent's Park Rd 7586 8569 8–3B
"A neighbourhood favourite, firmly back on form" – this "beautiful, classy and quiet" Primrose Hill fixture is a particular romantic hit, thanks to its "intimate" ambience and Bryn Williams's "top-notch" cuisine. / NW1 8XL; www.odettesprimrosehill.com; 10.30 pm; set weekday L £37 (FP).

Odin's W1 £52 ④❶❶
27 Devonshire St 7935 7296 2–1A
"Unhurried and civilised", this Marylebone veteran – adorned with "a superb collection of art", created by the late Peter Langan – is possibly "the calmest restaurant in London"; the term "old-school" may be applied equally to the service and the British cuisine. / W1G 6PL; www.langansrestaurants.co.uk; 11 pm; closed Sat L & Sun; booking: max 12.

Okawari W5 £36 ❸④❸
13 Bond St 8566 0466 1–3A
The "low-down Japanese-style tables may not be to all tastes", but this Ealing café is "a great spot for a simple, cheap, tasty and filling bite". / W5 5AP; www.okawari.co.uk; 11.15 pm, Sun 10.45 pm.

Okku SW1 NEW
16 St James's St awaiting tel 3–4D
Outpost of a concept established in Dubai, this flashy new Japanese is to open in late-2012; the setting is the vast former banking hall formerly occupied by Just St James (RIP), near the Palace of that name. / SW1A 1ER.

F S A

The Old Brewery SE10 £47 ④④❷
The Pepys Building, Old Royal Naval College 3327 1280 1–3D
A "beautiful conversion" of an historic Greenwich site, with a lovely courtyard and offering an "unbeatable selection of beers" from the in-house microbrewery; the "top burger" aside, the food – "sometimes very good, but not entirely consistent" – plays a supporting role. / SE10 9LW; www.oldbrewerygreenwich.com; 10 pm, Fri & Sat 10.30 pm; D only; no Amex.

The Old Bull & Bush NW3 £41 ❸④❸
North End Rd 8905 5456 8–1A
Opposite Golder's Hill Park, a popular local which – with its "always-reasonable" fare and characterful interior – can be "a pleasant surprise"; service, though, "can be a let-down". / NW3 7HE; www.thebullandbush.co.uk; 9.30 pm, Sat 10 pm, Sun 9 pm.

Old Parr's Head W14 £23 ④❸❸
120 Blythe Rd 7371 4561 7–1C
"Excellent Thai-in-a-pub food" at "top-value prices" makes it worth remembering this backstreet Olympia boozer; it has a hidden-away beer garden too. / W14 0HD; www.theoldparrshead.co.uk; 10 pm, Sat & Sun 9.30 pm; no Amex.

The Old White Bear NW3 £48 ❸❷❷
Hampstead 7794 7719 8–1A
"A magical pub, off the Hampstead beaten track", which has been "intelligently shaken up" in recent times, and which most reporters feel is now a "fantastic" all-rounder; not everyone, though, is convinced. / NW3 1LJ; www.theoldwhitebear.co.uk; 10.30 pm, Sun 9.30 pm; closed Mon L.

Oliveto SW1 £50 ❷❸④
49 Elizabeth St 7730 0074 2–4A
"Always heaving with expat Italians", this "buzzy" Belgravia Sardinian offers "fabulous, thin, crispy pizza" that's arguably "the best in town" – book ahead, especially for weekend lunches. / SW1 9PP; www.olivorestaurants.com; 11 pm, Sun 10.30 pm; booking: max 7 at D.

Olivo SW1 £55 ❷❸④
21 Eccleston St 7730 2505 2–4B
The style at this cramped Belgravia Sardinian "hasn't moved on in 15 years", and "the acoustics are terrible" too – "many repeat-customers", however, attest to the quality of the "evergreen" cuisine, and the wine list offers "great value". / SW1 9LX; www.olivorestaurants.com; 10.30 pm; closed Sat L & Sun L.

Olivomare SW1 £60 ❶❸④
10 Lower Belgrave St 7730 9022 2–4B
The "most delicious" fish – "very fresh and light", often with "a twist" – and "lovely off-piste wines" win high popularity for this "consistent" Sardinian, off Eaton Square; the "wacky" '60s-sci-fi-style décor, though, is a touch "cold" and "antiseptic". / SW1W 0LJ; www.olivorestaurants.com; 11 pm, Sun 10.30 pm; booking: max 10.

Olley's SE24 £39 ❸❸❸
65-69 Norwood Rd 8671 8259 10–2D
"Superb fish 'n' chips in a variety of styles" makes this Brockwell Park chippy quite a "south London institution". / SE24 9AA; www.olleys.info; 10 pm, Sun 9.30 pm; closed Mon; no Amex; SRA-70%.

Olympus Fish N3 £33 ❷❷④
140-144 Ballards Ln 8371 8666 1–1B
"Every bit as good as the Two Brothers" – so say fans of this "friendly" Turkish chippy, in Finchley, who rave over its "fresh" and "generous" fish 'n' chips. / N3 2PA; 11 pm; closed Mon.

One Blenheim Terrace NW8 NEW £61 ❸❷④
1 Blenheim Ter 7372 1722 8–3A
This ambitious newcomer aims to bring some "West End style" to sleepy St John's Wood; for most reporters, it succeeds, offering "highly imaginative British cooking" and "fantastic" service to match, but "ambience can be lacking", and prices can seem rather high. / NW8 0EH; www.oneblenheimterrace.co.uk; 10.30 pm, Sun 3 pm; closed Mon.

101 Thai Kitchen W6 £24 ❶❸⑤
352 King St 8746 6888 7–2B
"Leave the location and decor out of account, and this is the perfect Thai!" – a small Hammersmith caff, whose "real north-Thai" cooking inspires raves from all who report on it. / W6 0RX; www.101thaikitchen.com; 10.30 pm, Fri & Sat 11 pm.

1 Lombard Street EC3 £64 ❸❸④
1 Lombard St 7929 6611 9–3C
"A dependable City stalwart"; by the Royal Exchange, this former banking hall certainly has "a handy location for a business lunch", and its fans praise its "surprisingly good" food too (especially at breakfast); the main (brasserie) space is "noisy", though – "while the restaurant is less atmospheric, it's quieter". / EC3V 9AA; www.1lombardstreet.com; 9.30 pm; closed Sat & Sun; 6 max in main restaurant.

One-O-One
Sheraton Park Tower SW1 £90 ❶❸⑤
101 Knightsbridge 7290 7101 5–1D
"One of the best seafood restaurants in Europe"; it's all to do with the "genuine joy" of Pascal Proyart's "inspired" cuisine, though, and "it's too bad" that this "quiet" Knightsbridge chamber is "ugly and lifeless". / SW1X 7RN; www.oneoonerestaurant.com; 10 pm; booking: max 6; set weekday L £47 (FP).

The Only Running Footman W1 £48 ❸④❸
5 Charles St 7499 2988 3–3B
A "useful" Mayfair option – a "real pub but also a gastropub" that's open all-day all-week, and offers a "winning" selection of dishes; "the bar is always packed" – "upstairs less so". / W1J 5DF; www.therunningfootmanmayfair.com; 10 pm.

Opera Tavern WC2 £41 ❷❸❸
23 Catherine St 7836 3680 4–3D
"Terrific mini-burgers and Iberico hams" headline the "innovative tapas" on offer at this "very buzzy" yearling – "a great addition to Covent Garden", from the same stable as Salt Yard; "bills grow quickly", though, and "the bar is more atmospheric than the dining room upstairs". / WC2B 5JS; www.operatavern.co.uk; 11.15 pm; closed Sun D; SRA-63%.

The Orange SW1 £51 ❷❸❷
37 Pimlico Rd 7881 9844 5–2D
"Light and airy", this Pimlico gastropub is more "chilled and less heaving" than its Thomas Cubitt stablemate; it offers a menu including "surprisingly good, thin, crispy pizzas" in a "gorgeous, mellow dining room". / SW1W 8NE; www.theorange.co.uk; 9.30 pm, Sun 9 pm; SRA-62%.

Orange Pekoe SW13 £19 ❸❷❷
3 White Hart Ln 8876 6070 10–1A
"A great Barnes tea room", praised for its "delicious coffee, tea, and cakes, friendly service and tremendous value"; "appetising breakfasts" too. / SW13 0PX; www.orangepekoeteas.com; 5 pm; L only.

FSA

The Orange Tree N20 £42 ④⑤❸

7 Totteridge Ln 8343 7031 1–1B

An "upmarket" Totteridge inn that sometimes seems "too popular for its own good" – it can be a great all-rounder, but at peak times "service struggles", and the food can be "terrible". / N20 8NX; www.theorangetreetotteridge.co.uk; 9.30 pm, Fri-Sat 10.30 pm, Sun 9 pm.

L'Oranger SW1 £84 ❸❸❸

5 St James's St 7839 3774 3–4D

"Flying under the radar", say fans, this "elegant" St James's fixture offers "high-quality" Gallic cuisine in a "quiet and discreet" setting (and with "wonderful courtyard tables" too); overall approval, however, is diluted by those who say that food that's no more than "acceptable" comes at "shocking" prices. / SW1A 1EF; www.loranger.co.uk; 11 pm; closed Sat L & Sun; no jeans or trainers.

Orchard WC1 NEW £40 ❸❷❸

11 Sicilian Ave awaiting Tel 2–1D

"A wonderful change from the area's Identikit culinary offerings" – this "retro-style" Bloomsbury café newcomer attracts consistent praise for its "simple" but "tasty" veggie fare; nice al fresco tables too. / WC1A 2QH.

Orpheus EC3 £41 ❷❷④

26 Savage Gdns 7481 1931 9–3D

Hidden-away near Tower Bridge, a little-known restaurant in a railway arch, hailed by its small fan club for "amazing fresh fish" and "the very best seafood"... all at "surprisingly good prices". / EC3N 2AR; L only, closed Sat & Sun.

Orrery W1 £69 ❸❷❷

55 Marylebone High St 7616 8000 2–1A

Overlooking a Marylebone churchyard, this "light-filled", "understated" and "elegant" D&D Group venue is a "professional" operation, offering "lovely" cooking in a "classic" Gallic mode; as even a fan notes, however, it can be "a bit up-and-down". / W1U 5RB; www.orreryrestaurant.co.uk; 10.30 pm, Fri & Sat 11 pm; set weekday L £43 (FP); SRA-62%.

Orso WC2 £60 ④❸④

27 Wellington St 7240 5269 4–3D

A basement Covent Garden Italian, that's still a "dependable", "satisfying" and "authentic" favourite for many long-terms fans; especially those who remember its '80s heyday, however, can still find it "somewhat in the doldrums". / WC2E 7DB; www.orsorestaurant.co.uk; 11.30 pm; set pre theatre £38 (FP).

Oscar
Charlotte Street Hotel W1 £64 ④④❷

15 Charlotte St 7806 2000 2–1C

A popular haunt for Fitzrovia media types, this "attractive" hotel bar/brasserie is "heaving every weekday lunchtime"; only breakfasts are "great", though – the food is otherwise a bit incidental. / W1T 1RJ; www.charlottestreethotel.com; 10.45 pm, Sun 10 pm.

Oslo Court NW8 £60 ❷❶❶

Charlbert St, off Prince Albert Rd 7722 8795 8–3A

"Straight back to the '70s"; at the foot of a Regent's Park apartment block, this "surreal" spot "really is a time warp", where "some of the most entertaining waiters you'll ever find" dish up "huge helpings" of "delicious" scoff (don't miss the dessert trolley) to a celebratory – usually older – crowd. / NW8 7EN; 11 pm; closed Sun; no jeans or trainers.

Osteria Antica Bologna SW11 £40 ❸❸④
23 Northcote Rd 7978 4771 10–2C
With its "varied, regional Italian food from an oft-changing menu", this "friendly", "bustling" and "closely-packed" stalwart, near Clapham Junction, retains a loyal local fan club. / SW11 1NG; www.osteria.co.uk; 10.30 pm, Sat-Sun 10 pm.

Osteria Basilico W11 £55 ❸❸❷
29 Kensington Park Rd 7727 9957 6–1A
"So cosy and lovely" (albeit "slightly chaotic"), this Notting Hill Italian remains the "fun" linchpin of local life it has been for more than two decades; arrive early if you want a table on the (much nicer) ground floor. / W11 2EU; www.osteriabasilico.co.uk; 11.15 pm, Sun 10.15 pm; no booking, Sat L.

Osteria Dell'Angolo SW1 £54 ❸❷④
47 Marsham St 3268 1077 2–4C
"Classic Tuscan cooking in classic Tuscan surroundings" ("which is to say a bit lacking in atmosphere") – that's the deal at this "excellent" and business-friendly, if rather "antiseptic", Westminster Italian. / SW1P 3DR; www.osteriadellangolo.co.uk; 10.15 pm; closed Sat L & Sun.

Osteria dell'Arancio SW10 £54 ❸❸❸
383 King's Rd 7349 8111 5–3B
"A fascinating collection of regional Italian wines" is the stand-out feature of this "casual" World's End trattoria; the "eclectic regional fare" inspires the odd mixed report, but for hard-core fans this is their "go-to Italian". / SW10 0LP; www.osteriadellarancio.co.uk; 10.30 pm, Sun 9.30 pm; Mon-Thu D only, Fri-Sun open L & D.

Otto Pizza W2 £28 ❷❷❸
6 Chepstow Rd 7792 4088 6–1B
"The cornmeal crust may ruin your appreciation of normal pizza forever", say fans of this "friendly" Bayswater yearling – not only are the pizzas gluten-free, they're "so tasty" too. / W2 5BH; www.ottopizza.com; 11 pm, Sun 10 pm.

Otto's WC1 NEW £48 ❷❷❸
182 Grays Inn Rd 7713 0107 2–1D
"The local French bistro denizens of Gray's Inn Road have longed for!" – this new "hidden gem" lurks behind "an odd exterior that doesn't do it justice", dishing up "high-quality", "traditional" fare in a setting "reminiscent of a quirky antique shop". / WC1X 8EW; www.ottos-restaurant.com; 10 pm; closed Sat L & Sun.

Ottolenghi £48 ❶❸④
13 Motcomb St, SW1 7823 2707 5–1D
63 Ledbury Rd, W11 7727 1121 6–1B
1 Holland St, W8 7937 0003 5–1A
287 Upper St, N1 7288 1454 8–2D
"Extortionate" but "oh-so-delicious"; Yotam Ottolenghi's "zeitgeist-y" delis pack in the "ladies who lunch" with their "food-porn" displays of "zingy" salads and "mind-blowing" cakes; beware "long queues". / www.ottolenghi.co.uk; N1 10.15 pm; W8 & W11 8 pm, Sat 7 pm, Sun 6 pm; N1 closed Sun D; Holland St takeaway only; W11 & SW1 no booking, N1 booking for D only.

**Outlaw's Seafood and Grill
The Capital Hotel SW3** NEW
22-24 Basil St 7589 5171 5–1D
Launching in late-2012, one of the UK's best seafood chefs (HQ, Cornwall) is to oversee the reinvigoration of this small but upscale hotel dining room – it should be a major opening… although the cultural 'fit' between Rock and Knightsbridge is not immediately apparent. / SW3 1AT; www.capitalhotel.co.uk.

(Brasserie)
Oxo Tower SE1 £70 ⑤④❸
Barge House St 7803 3888 9–3A
"You are paying for the view (which is indeed stunning)", when you visit even the cheaper section of this South Bank landmark; the operation itself is "very average". / SE1 9PH; www.harveynichols.com/restaurants/oxo-tower-london; 11 pm, Sun 10 pm.

(Restaurant)
Oxo Tower SE1 £84 ⑤⑤④
Barge House St 7803 3888 9–3A
"Would anyone go if it weren't for the view?" – this top-floor South Bank eyrie is just "a waste of a sublime location", charging "ridiculous" prices for "mediocre rubbish" – "every time I say 'never again'", fumes one reporter… "even though I only ever visit as a guest!" / SE1 9PH; www.harveynichols.com/restaurants/; 11 pm, Sun 10 pm; set weekday L £39 (FP), set always available £56 (FP).

Ozer W1 £44 ❸❷④
5 Langham Pl 7323 0505 3–1C
"The most upmarket of the Sofra restaurants" – this "reliable" Turkish operation, near Broadcasting House, is rather "old-fashioned" in style, but wins praise from all reporters for its "reasonably-priced" cuisine (especially the "very good set deals"). / W1B 3DG; www.sofra.co.uk; 11 pm; set pre-theatre £24 (FP), set always available £25 (FP).

Le P'tit Normand SW18 £41 ❸❷❸
185 Merton Rd 8871 0233 10–2B
"Hidden-away in deepest Southfields", this "intimate" Gallic bistro veteran continues to please the locals with its "interesting" menu; one such counsels summer visits – "in winter, it can seem a bit chilly"! / SW18 5EF; www.leptitnormand.co.uk; 10 pm, Sun 3 pm; closed Mon L, Tue L, Wed L, Sat L & Sun D; set weekday L £20 (FP), set Sun L £22 (FP).

Pacific Oriental EC2 £44 ④❸④
52 Threadneedle St 0871 704 4060 9–2C
A former banking hall provides the "impressive backdrop" for this large City operation, and fans praise its "good" and "relatively inexpensive" pan-Asian food; not everyone's so impressed, though, and reports are few. / EC2R 8AY; www.orientalrestaurantgroup.co.uk; 10.30 pm; closed Sat & Sun; no trainers.

The Paddyfield SW12 £28 ❶❸❸
4 Bedford Hill 8772 1145 10–2C
A "BYO Balham classic" – a "hole-in-the-wall" whose hallmarks are "fantastic Thai/Vietnamese cuisine" and "erratic service with a smile". / SW12 9RG; www.thepaddyfield.co.uk; 11 pm; D only, closed Mon; no credit cards.

Il Pagliaccio SW6 £37 ④❷❶
182-184 Wandsworth Bridge Rd 7371 5253 10–1B
"Excellent pizza" and "entertainers for the kids at weekends" – two key attractions of this "friendly" and "inexpensive" Sands End Italian. / SW6 2UF; www.paggs.co.uk; midnight; no Amex; set always available £20 (FP).

Le Pain Quotidien £35 ④④❷
Branches throughout London
"A delightful Continental scrubbed-tables environment" create a "country-kitchen" vibe at these popular coffee or breakfast stand-bys, which continue to please most reporters. / www.painquotidien.com; most branches close between 7 pm-10 pm; no booking at some branches, especially at weekends.

FSA

The Painted Heron SW10 £53 ❶❷❸
112 Cheyne Walk 7351 5232 5–3B
"Less fussy and pretentious than some of its peers", this "exceptional" but "under-appreciated" nouvelle Indian offers "elegant and impactful" dishes, with "subtle and surprising twists"; it's hidden-away off Chelsea Embankment, though – a location which "doesn't do it any favours". / SW10 0DJ; www.thepaintedheron.com; 10.45 pm; closed weekday L.

The Palm SW1 £80 ⑤④⑤
1 Pont St 7201 0710 5–1D
This "very American" Belgravian does have fans who love its "friendly" style, and who claim its USDA steaks "blow its rivals away"; it "lacks the buzz of the NYC originals", however, and critics say the prices are "abominable". / SW1X 9EJ; www.thepalm.com/london; 11 pm, Sun 10 pm; Mon-Thu D only, Fri-Sun open L & D.

The Palmerston SE22 £44 ❸❸❸
91 Lordship Ln 8693 1629 1–4D
To say this "very solid" neighbourhood spot is "the best gastropub in East Dulwich" is arguably a two-edged compliment; it does, however, serve "classic seasonal British food", realised to a "consistent" standard. / SE22 8EP; www.thepalmerston.net; 10 pm, Sun 9.30 pm.

Palmyra TW9 £40 ❷❷④
277 Sandycombe Rd 8948 7019 1–3A
Unpretentious but "friendly", this Kew Lebanese serves up "great mezze" and "succulent" mains too. / TW9 3LU; www.palmyrarestaurant.co.uk; 11 pm; no Amex.

The Pantechnicon SW1 £58 ❸❸❷
10 Motcomb St 7730 6074 5–1D
The "elegant" upstairs dining room at this "upmarket" Belgravia boozer is more like that of a gentleman's club, and "great for business"; it serves "a good choice" of "well-executed" dishes too, as does the "buzzy" bar below. / SW1X 8LA; www.thepantechnicon.com; 11 pm, Sun 10.30 pm; SRA-62%.

Pantry SW18 £30 ❸❸❷
342 Old York Rd 8871 0713 10–2B
"A lovely, local deli/eatery", in Wandsworth, "run by an excellent team" – it offers "gorgeous home-made lunches", "interesting breakfasts" and "wonderful coffee". / SW18 1SS; www.thepantrylondon.com; L only; no Amex.

Pappa Ciccia £35 ❸❸❸
105 Munster Rd, SW6 7384 1884 10–1B
41 Fulham High St, SW6 7736 0900 10–1B
"Cramped" Fulham Italians, acclaimed by most (if not quite all) reporters as "genuine gems", thanks to their "fun" style, and "authentic Italian fare" (particularly pizza) at "great-value prices". / www.pappaciccia.com; 11 pm, Sat & Sun 11.30 pm; Munster Rd no credit cards.

Paradise by Way of Kensal Green W10 £45 ❷❷❶
19 Kilburn Ln 8969 0098 1–2B
"More than a pub... a super-pub!"; "with its vast warren of rooms and terraces", this perennially hip Kensal Green tavern "takes shabby-chic to a whole new level"; given that "the venue is the star", it's all the more remarkable that "food and service are fantastic" too! / W10 4AE; www.theparadise.co.uk; 10.30 pm, Fri & Sat 11 pm, Sun 9 pm; closed weekday L; no Amex.

Paradise Hampstead NW3 £30 ❷❷④
49 South End Rd 7794 6314 8–2A
Near South End Green, a "classic" Indian, where "all the usual favourites" are realised to "excellent" standards, and "reasonably-priced" too. / NW3 2QB; www.paradisehampstead.co.uk; 10.45 pm.

El Parador NW1 £34 ❷❸❸
245 Eversholt St 7387 2789 8–3C
"Really wonderful tapas" – "a huge variety", and "very authentic" – win lots of fans for this "basic" and "bustling" ("overcrowded" and "noisy") bar, near Mornington Crescent. / NW1 1BA; www.elparadorlondon.com; 11 pm, Fri-Sat 11.30 pm, Sun 9.30 pm; closed Sat L & Sun L; no Amex.

Paramount Centre Point WC1 £62 ④④❶
101-103 New Oxford St 7420 2900 4–1A
"Wow, what a view!" – "the best in London" – from the 32nd floor of Centre Point; it's perhaps better to enjoy it, though, from the "surprisingly well-equipped bar" – those who eat too often encounter "nondescript" food and "inattentive" service. / WC1A 1DD; www.paramount.uk.net; 11 pm.

Pasha SW7 £52 ❸❸❷
1 Gloucester Rd 7589 7969 5–1B
"Privacy in the alcoves" contributes to the "romantic" attractions of this Moroccan 'riad'-style make-over of a grand South Kensington townhouse; "it's not a major gastronomic destination", but has inspired few real complaints of late. / SW7 4PP; www.pasha-restaurant.co.uk; 10.45 pm, Sat & Sun 11.45 pm.

Patara £49 ❷❷❸
15 Greek St, W1 7437 1071 4–2A
7 Maddox St, W1 7499 6008 3–2C
181 Fulham Rd, SW3 7351 5692 5–2C
9 Beauchamp Pl, SW3 7581 8820 5–1C
"Not like a chain, but with the polish of a slick and professional operation"; these "upmarket" Thai oases "always offers a good experience", combining "very refined" cooking, "attentive" service and "tasteful" decor. / www.pataralondon.com; 10.30 pm; Greek St closed Sun.

Paternoster Chop House EC4 £58 ⑤⑤⑤
Warwick Ct, Paternoster Sq 7029 9400 9–2B
This meat-driven D&D Group operation inspires remarkably little feedback for somewhere two minutes walk from St Paul's – something to do, perhaps, with its "indifferent" service, "noisy" interior and "exceptionally poor-value" food? / EC4M 7DX; www.danddlondon.com; 10.30 pm; closed Sat & Sun D; SRA-72%.

Patio W12 £33 ④❶❷
5 Goldhawk Rd 8743 5194 7–1C
"Homely, old-fashioned, and astonishingly cheap", this Shepherd's Bush stalwart – overseen by its "lovely" Polish owner – makes a great party venue; it offers "huge portions of tasty fodder", and an "excellent range of vodkas" too. / W12 8QQ; www.patiolondon.com; 11 pm, Sat & Sun 11.30 pm; closed Sat L & Sun L.

Pâtisserie Valerie £28 ⑤⑤④
Branches throughout London
A once-treasured pâtisserie group that's "growing like Topsy", leaving even the Soho original branch at risk of feeling "chainified"; the "mouth-watering" cakes are "still good", but other fare can be "seriously disappointing", and service is "stretched". / www.patisserie-valerie.co.uk; most branches close between 5 pm-8 pm; no booking except Old Compton St Sun-Thu.

Patogh W1 £21 ❷❸④
8 Crawford Pl 7262 4015 6–1D
As "nightly queues" attest, you get "home-made flatbread and the best kebabs", at this "pokey" but "genuine" Iranian pit stop, just off the Edgware Road. / W1H 5NE; 11 pm; no credit cards.

Patterson's W1 £71 ❸❸④
4 Mill St 7499 1308 3–2C
Shame about the "inert" ambience and slightly "variable" standards of this family-run dining room; for many reporters it's "one of Mayfair's hidden gems", thanks to its "wonderful and creative" cooking and its "very personal" service too. / W1S 2AX; www.pattersonsrestaurant.co.uk; 11 pm; closed Sat L & Sun.

Paul £27 ❸④④
115 Marylebone High St, W1 7224 5615 2–1A
29-30 Bedford St, WC2 7836 3304 4–3C
"Pricier than others, but worth it" – these outposts of France's biggest café/pâtisserie chain impress most reporters with their "wonderful, freshly-made sandwiches", "great salads" and "delicious" pastries and coffee; "daunting" lunchtime queues, though. / www.paul-uk.com; most branches close between 7 pm-8.30 pm; no booking.

Pearl WC1 £80 ❸④④
252 High Holborn 7829 7000 2–1D
Jun Tanaka's "meticulous" cuisine wins high praise from fans of this "impressive" (but slightly soulless) Midtown chamber; even they can deem it "stupidly expensive", though, while critics find service iffy, and say dishes "looked pretty, but lacked taste". / WC1V 7EN; www.pearl-restaurant.com; 10 pm; closed Sat L & Sun; set weekday L £44 (FP).

Pearl Liang W2 £44 ❶❷❸
8 Sheldon Sq 7289 7000 6–1C
"Worth the trek to Paddington Basin"; this "upmarket" basement may "lack the chaotic theatre of Royal China", but its "super-tasty" dim sum is arguably "London's best", and the menu includes some "fantastic seafood" too. / W2 6EZ; www.pearlliang.co.uk; 11 pm.

The Peasant EC1 £45 ❸④❸
240 St John St 7336 7726 8–3D
"Comes and goes, but currently in a good phase" – this cavernous, early-wave Farringdon gastroboozer (an impressive Victorian tavern, with dining room above) doesn't make many ripples nowadays, but its "enterprising" cooking pleases all who comment on it. / EC1V 4PH; www.thepeasant.co.uk; 10.45 pm, Sun 9.30 pm.

Pellicano SW3 £56 ④❷④
19-21 Elystan St 7589 3718 5–2C
A "plain" but "welcoming" Chelsea backstreet Italian that earns praise for its "sympatico" service and "limited but appetising" menu; as ever, though, a few reporters leave "so disappointed" by their visits here. / SW3 3NT; www.pellicanorestaurant.co.uk; 11 pm, Sun 9.30 pm; set weekday L £36 (FP).

F S A

E Pellicci E2 £21 ④❷❶
332 Bethnal Green Rd 7739 4873 12–1D
You get "great East End banter and atmosphere", at this famous Italian greasy spoon, whose Art Deco-style interior is of such architectural note that it's 'listed'. / E2 0AG; 4.15 pm; L only, closed Sun; no credit cards.

Pentolina W14 NEW £40 ❷❷❸
71 Blythe Rd 3010 0091 7–1D
"One minute it wasn't there – the next it was, and it's been full ever since!"; this tiny Olympia newcomer is making a go of a previously tricky site; "it's the kind of high-quality local Italian that every neighbourhood would love to have". / W14 0HP; www.pentolinarestaurant.co.uk; 10 pm; closed Mon & Sun; no Amex.

The Pepper Tree SW4 £27 ❸❷❸
19 Clapham Common S'side 7622 1758 10–2D
"For fast, cheap 'n' cheerful scoff", this "always-packed" canteen, by Clapham South, has long been "an absolute favourite", churning out "really tasty" Thai dishes at "really low prices"; "friendly service too". / SW4 7AB; www.thepeppertree.co.uk; 11 pm, Sun & Mon 10.30 pm; no Amex; no booking at D.

Pescatori £52 ④④④
11 Dover St, W1 7493 2652 3–3C
57 Charlotte St, W1 7580 3289 2–1C
Fans tip the "great fresh fish" on offer at these West End Italians, and praise them as a "safe" option; their ratings were dragged down, however, by a few "terrible" reports. / www.pescatori.co.uk; 11 pm; closed Sat L & Sun.

Petek N4 £31 ❸❷❸
94-96 Stroud Green Rd 7619 3933 8–1D
A "smashing little joint", in Finsbury Park, where "great fresh Turkish food" is "happily served"; "at weekends, make sure you book". / N4 3EN; www.petekrestaurant.co.uk; 11 pm.

Petersham Hotel TW10 £63 ④④❷
Nightingale Ln 8940 7471 1–4A
"There are beautiful views" from this "lovely" (if "slightly stuffy") dining room, overlooking the eponymous Meadows – fans say the vista is "nearly matched by the cooking", but critics feel the prospect is "really the only thing the place has going for it". / TW10 6UZ; www.petershamhotel.co.uk; 9.45 pm, Sun 8.30 pm.

Petersham Nurseries TW10 £70
Church Ln, Off Petersham Rd 8940 5230 1–4A
Being "a bit muddy underfoot" only adds to the "perfect" ("slightly self-conscious") ambience of this "unique and quirky" café; following Skye Gyngell's departure, we've left it unrated, but initial reports of Moroccan Greg Malouf's early days are of uneven results… but at "the normal extortionate prices". / TW10 7AG; www.petershamnurseries.com; L only, closed Mon.

La Petite Maison W1 £78 ❶❷❷
54 Brook's Mews 7495 4774 3–2B
"Provence transported to Mayfair"; this "lively beautiful-people scene" may offer a straightforward menu (based around sharing platters), but its realisation is "simply outstanding" – "so fresh, light, and zingy"; "when the bill arrives… du courage!" / W1K 4EG; www.lpmlondon.co.uk; 11 pm, Sun 10 pm.

Pétrus SW1 £85 ❸❷❷
1 Kinnerton St 7592 1609 5–1D
"Ramsay can still get some things right!"; "you do pay for the pleasure", but – for "classical modern French cuisine at its best", and an outstanding wine list too – this "well-spaced" Belgravian is an impressive destination all-round; there's a "steal" of a set lunch too. / *SW1X 8EA; www.gordonramsay.com/petrus; 10 pm; closed Sun; no trainers; set weekday L £42 (FP).*

Pham Sushi EC1 £35 ❶④④
159 Whitecross St 7251 6336 12–2A
"You wouldn't believe it when you look at it", but you get "the best-value sushi in town", at this "tiny" and "really basic" Japanese pit stop, near the Barbican. / *EC1Y 8JL; www.phamsushi.co.uk; 10 pm; closed Sat L & Sun.*

Pho £33 ❷❷❷
163-165 Wardour St, W1 7434 3938 3–1D
3 Great Titchfield St, W1 7436 0111 3–1C
Westfield, Ariel Way, W12 07824 662320 7–1C
86 St John St, EC1 7253 7624 9–1A
"You can't go wrong", at this impressive chain of "fast", "efficient" and "vibrant" Vietnamese pit stops, whose "interesting" street food is full of "fresh and zingy" flavours. / *www.phocafe.co.uk; EC1 10 pm, Fri & Sat 10.30 pm; W1 10.30 pm; W12 9 pm, Sat 7 pm, Sun 6 pm; EC1 closed Sat L & Sun; W1 closed Sun; no Amex; no booking.*

The Phoenix SW3 £42 ④④❷
23 Smith St 7730 9182 5–2D
It's the "lovely atmosphere" and handy location which make this Chelsea boozer worth seeking out – the "acceptable" food and "slightly shaky" service are no particular attraction in themselves. / *SW3 4EE; www.geronimo-inns.co.uk; 10 pm.*

Phoenix Palace NW1 £46 ❷❸❸
5-9 Glentworth St 7486 3515 2–1A
"Beat the Royal China queues – come here instead!"; "OTT", "glitzy-yet-gloomy", and with a "high proportion of Chinese customers", this "authentically Hong Kong" dim-sum "institution", in Marylebone, offers a menu that's as "unusual" as it is "impressive". / *NW1 5PG; www.phoenixpalace.co.uk; 11.15 pm, Sun 10.30 pm.*

Piccolino £45 ④❸④
21 Heddon St, W1 7287 4029 3–2C
11 Exchange Sq, EC2 7375 2568 12–2B
"Wholesome" food in a "spacious" and "lively" setting – that's the deal that commends these grand (by chain standards) Italians to pretty much all who comment on them. / *www.piccolinorestaurants.co.uk; 11 pm, Sun 10 pm; EC2 closed Sat & Sun.*

PIED À TERRE W1 £98 ❶❷❸
34 Charlotte St 7636 1178 2–1C
"A labour of love, with flashes of genius"; David Moore's long-running Fitzrovia temple of haute cuisine "has shown no dip in standards" since Marcus Eaves replaced Shane Osborn, and it continues to serve "exquisite" dishes with "unstuffy professionalism"; the narrow room, though, can seem a bit "quiet and subdued". / *W1T 2NH; www.pied-a-terre.co.uk; 10.45 pm; closed Sat L & Sun; no Maestro; booking: max 7; set weekday L £51 (FP).*

F S A

The Pig's Ear SW3 £50 ❸④❷
35 Old Church St 7352 2908 5–3C
"You wouldn't know it was a pub!" – the wonderful first-floor dining room of this "handsome" Art Nouveau-themed boozer, hidden-away in Chelsea, offers food that's "well-cooked and interesting" too.
/ SW3 5BS; www.thepigsear.info; 10 pm, Sun 9 pm.

Pinchito EC1 £36 ④④❷
32 Featherstone St 7490 0121 12–1A
"Chilled by day, lively by night" – this "buzzy" haunt is "a great place to unwind", offering "quality tapas" and fabulous cocktails too.
/ EC1Y 8QX; www.pinchito.co.uk; 11 pm; closed Sat L & Sun.

ping pong £32 ④④❸
10 Paddington St, W1 7009 9600 2–1A
29a James St, W1 7034 3100 3–1A
45 Gt Marlborough St, W1 7851 6969 3–2C
48 Eastcastle St, W1 7079 0550 3–1C
74-76 Westbourne Grove, W2 7313 9832 6–1B
Southbank Centre, SE1 7960 4160 2–3D
3-6 Steward St, E1 7422 7650 9–2D
St Katharine Docks, E1 7680 7850 9–3D
3 Appold St, EC2 7422 0780 12–2B
Bow Bells Hs, 1 Bread St, EC4 7651 0880 9–2B
For a "reasonable", "light" and "fun" bite, these "bustling" dim-sum joints are "really not bad at all" – the interiors are "airy", the scoff is "tasty" enough, and the cocktails are "varied and exciting" too.
/ www.pingpongdimsum.com; 10 pm-11.30 pm; EC2 & EC4 closed Sat & Sun; booking: min 8.

El Pirata W1 £38 ④❷❶
5-6 Down St 7491 3810 3–4B
"Cramped tables just add to the happy clamour", at this Mayfair haunt – "one of London's most welcoming restaurants" (but make sure you "go for the ground floor bar rather than the gloomy basement"); the tasty tapas is "sensibly priced" too, especially for somewhere so central. / W1J 7AQ; www.elpirata.co.uk; 11.30 pm; closed Sat L & Sun; set weekday L £18 (FP).

El Pirata de Tapas W2 £35 ❸❸❷
115 Westbourne Grove 7727 5000 6–1B
"Excellent tapas, served cheek-by-jowl" – that's the formula that ensures this "casual" and "lively" Bayswater spot is always "busy".
/ W2 4UP; www.elpiratadetapas.co.uk; 10.45 pm; set weekday L £16 (FP).

Pissarro W4 £45 ④❸❷
Corney Reach Way 8994 3111 10–1A
"A pretty setting on the towpath, with direct views on to the Thames" contributes to the lovely atmosphere at this "romantic" Chiswick fixture – "for maximum intimacy, book a corner table in the conservatory". / W4 2UG; www.pissarro.co.uk; 9.45 pm.

Pitt Cue Co W1 NEW £25 ❶❸❸
1 Newburgh St no tel 3–2D
"Boy, do they do what they do well", at this "authentic" – and notably "cheek-by-jowl" – US-inspired BBQ, off Carnaby Street, which has been one of the foodie world's top hits of 2012; "those bills can rise, though, as you get stuck waiting at the bar…" / W1F 7RB; www.pittcue.co.uk.

F S A

Pizarro SE1 NEW £43 ❷❷❶
194 Bermondsey St 7407 7339 9–4D
"You feel like you're in Barcelona, not Bermondsey", at José P's vibrantly "buzzing" ("loud") newcomer – a "great addition to SE1", whose "slightly unusual" tapas-based cuisine has instantly marked it out as amongst the best Spanish restaurants in town. / SE1 3TQ; www.josepizarro.com/restaurants/pizarro; 11 pm, Sun 10 pm.

Pizza East £46 ❸❸❶
310 Portobello Rd, W10 8969 4500 6–1A
79 Highgate Rd, NW5 awaiting tel 8–1B NEW
56 Shoreditch High St, E1 7729 1888 12–1B
"Shoreditch hipsters are on to a good thing", at this "industrial-style" and "ultra-trendy" Italian, which serves "cracking" pizza; fans say the North Kensington spin-off does "smashing" food too. / www.pizzaeast.com; E1 Sun-Wed 11 pm, Thu 12 am, Fri-Sat 1am; W10 Mon-Thu 11.30 pm, Fri-Sat 12 am, Sun 10.30 pm.

Pizza Metro SW11 £41 ❷❷❸
64 Battersea Rise 7228 3812 10–2C
"Fun" and "vibrant", this Battersea institution is "nearer to a true Neapolitan pizzeria than most"; its year-old Notting Hill offshoot is much less well-known, but also generates enthusiastic feedback. / SW11 1EQ; pizzametropizza.co.uk; 11 pm; closed weekday L; no Amex.

(Ciro's) Pizza Pomodoro SW3 £51 ④④❷
51 Beauchamp Pl 7589 1278 5–1C
Views on the pizzas are mixed (indeed, critics say it's "rubbish"), but everyone agrees you get a "great night out" – "particularly when there's a band" – at this "old-time" Knightsbridge basement. / SW3 1NY; www.pomodoro.co.uk; 1 am; D only.

PizzaExpress £37 ④④❸
Branches throughout London
"The original pizza chain" and still "the best"; this "predictable-in-a-good-way" and "good-value" ("especially if you have vouchers!") multiple is "always a winner", particularly "with kids"; fans say menu "tweaks" – such as the "less piggy 'Legera' pizzas" – have "reinvigorated" its offer. / www.pizzaexpress.co.uk; 11.30 pm-midnight; most City branches closed all or part of weekend; no booking at most branches.

Pizzeria Oregano N1 £39 ❸④④
18-19 St Albans Pl 7288 1123 8–3D
Thanks to its "large portions of tasty food", this "reliable" and family-friendly Islington café is "still holding out against the chains of Upper Street" – "pizzas are often best". / N1 0NX; 11 pm, Fri 11.30 pm, Sun 10.30 pm; closed weekday L.

Pizzeria Pappagone N4 £38 ❸❷❷
131 Stroud Green Rd 7263 2114 8–1D
A "fun, frantic, fully-packed" Italian, in Stroud Green, where "enormous portions" of pizza and pasta come at "bargain" prices. / N4 3PX; www.pizzeriapappagone.co.uk; midnight.

Pizzeria Rustica TW9 £37 ❷❸④
32 The Quadrant 8332 6262 1–4A
A "crammed" and "efficient" venture, offering "lovely thin-crust pizzas with just the right amount of toppings" – not only Richmond locals sing its praises. / TW9 1DN; www.pizzeriarustica.co.uk; 11 pm, Fri & Sat 11.30 pm, Sun 10.30 pm.

PJ's Bar and Grill SW3 £52 ④❷❷
52 Fulham Rd 7581 0025 5–2C
Still "über-trendy" (in the Chelsea Eurotrash sense), this "very American" bar/bistro is something of a "classic" – "an old favourite any day of the week", with "excellent brunches" the highlight. / SW3 6HH; www.pjsbarandgrill.co.uk; 10.30 pm, Sun 10 pm.

Plane Food TW6 £52 ④④④
Heathrow Airport, Terminal 5 8897 4545 1–3A
Gordon Ramsay's "enjoyable" airport-outlet turns out to be one of his more useful ventures – a "calm and efficient oasis" that's "really pretty good value" (especially the "surprisingly good brunch"). / TW6 2GA; www.gordonramsay.com; 9.30 pm; set weekday L £27 (FP).

Plateau E14 £72 ④❸❸
Canada Pl 7715 7100 11–1C
"Stunning views" ("Manhattan-comes-to-London") make this elevated D&D Group venue a Canary Wharf power-lunch rendezvous par excellence; it's no surprise, then, that it's priced "strictly for expense accounts", but food and service – if still "sometimes inconsistent" – have improved in recent times. / E14 5ER; www.plateaurestaurant.co.uk; 10.15 pm; closed Sat L & Sun; set weekday L £28 (FP); SRA-63%.

Plum Valley W1 £38 ❸❸❸
20 Gerrard St 7494 4366 4–3A
"Contemporary" in style (particularly by local standards) – a Chinatown joint that "does the basics beautifully", and at "good-value" prices too. / W1D 6JQ; 11.30 pm.

Pod £14 ❸❷❸
124 High Holborn, WC1 3174 0541 2–1D
Tooley St, SE1 3174 0374 9–4D
10 St Martin's Le Grand, EC1 3174 0399 9–2B
162-163 London Wall, EC2 7256 5506 9–2C
25 Exchange Sq, EC2 3174 0290 12–2B
Devonshire Sq, EC2 3174 0108 9–2D
5 Lloyds Ave, EC3 3174 0038 9–3D
1 Printer St, EC4 3174 0228 9–2A
75 King William St, EC4 7283 7460 9–3C
"Healthy doesn't have to be boring", say fans of these "favourite lunch-stops", who are full of praise for the "quality, freshness and value" (and sometimes "spiciness") of their "quick-bite dishes". / www.podfood.co.uk; 3 pm-4 pm, WC2 7 pm, Sat 8 pm, Sun 5 pm; closed Sat & Sun, St Martin's closed Sun; no Amex.

Poissonnerie de l'Avenue SW3 £68 ❸❸④
82 Sloane Ave 7589 2457 5–2C
A Chelsea "classic"; this "calm" (but tightly-packed) seafood restaurant continues to please its "mature clientele" with its "very old-fashioned" formula – "yes, it is expensive, but where else can you find better turbot?" / SW3 3DZ; www.poissonneriedelavenue.co.uk; 11.30 pm, Sun 11 pm.

(Ognisko Polskie)
The Polish Club SW7 £52 ④④❸
55 Prince's Gate, Exhibition Rd 7589 4635 5–1C
"Pretty good… if you like Polish food", but it's the "relaxed and comfortable" environment of this fadedly-grand South Kensington émigrés' club which is of particular note; pleasant terrace, too, for al fresco dining. / SW7 2PN; www.ognisko.com; 11 pm; no trainers; set weekday L £27 (FP), set Sun L £30 (FP).

POLLEN STREET SOCIAL W1 £72 ❷❸❸
8-10 Pollen St 7290 7600 3–2C
Jason Atherton's "cutting-edge" cuisine (not least a 'dessert bar' that's "heaven on earth") has made this "vibrant" Mayfair yearling one of London's most notable arrivals of recent years; there's no room for complacency, though – the acoustics are "bad", and the style can sometimes seem a bit "impersonal". / W1S 1NQ; www.pollenstreetsocial.com; 10.45 pm; closed Sun.

Polpo £33 ④❸❶
41 Beak St, W1 7734 4479 3–2D
6 Maiden Ln, WC2 7836 8448 4–3D
2-3 Cowcross St, EC1 7250 0034 9–1A NEW
"Always full of trendy types", Russell Norman's "funky" NYC-style hang-outs are always "fun" ("so long as you're prepared for the noise and the squash"); service is increasingly "sporadic", though, and the Venetian tapas ever more give the impression of being prepared "by numbers"; a new EC1 branch opened in mid-2012. / www.polpo.co.uk; W1 & EC1 11 pm; WC2 11 pm, Sun 10.30 pm; W1 & EC1 closed D Sun.

Le Pont de la Tour SE1 £72 ④❸❷
36d Shad Thames 7403 8403 9–4D
"Perfect on a summer's day" – this D&D-group stalwart whose "lovely terrace" enjoys "beautiful" views of the Thames and Tower Bridge; but "it trades on that" of course, and "while the food is good, it doesn't offer the excellence you would expect at the price". / SE1 2YE; www.lepontdelatour.co.uk; 11 pm, Sun 10 pm; no trainers; SRA-59%.

Popeseye £47 ❷❸⑤
108 Blythe Rd, W14 7610 4578 7–1C
277 Upper Richmond Rd, SW15 8788 7733 10–2A
"Forget the new American places, these are the best steaks in London", say fans of these zero-frills bistros, in Olympia and Putney, which "seem not to have been decorated for many years"; "superb" and "well-priced" wines too. / www.popeseye.com; 10.30 pm; D only, closed Sun; no credit cards.

La Porchetta Pizzeria £34 ④❸④
33 Boswell St, WC1 7242 2434 2–1D
141-142 Upper St, N1 7288 2488 8–2D
147 Stroud Green Rd, N4 7281 2892 8–1D
74-77 Chalk Farm Rd, NW1 7267 6822 8–2B
84-86 Rosebery Ave, EC1 7837 6060 9–1A
"Always rammed with happy diners", these noisy north London Italians are known for gigantic pizzas at "unbeatable prices"; reporters seem increasingly nonplussed by their success, though – "the food's ordinary, so is it the jokey staff who pack 'em in?" / www.laporchetta.net; last orders varies by branch; WC1 closed Sat L & Sun; N1 closed Mon-Fri L; N4 closed weekday L, EC1 closed Sat L; no Amex.

Portal EC1 £61 ❸❸❷
88 St John St 7253 6950 9–1B
"Who would think Portuguese could be as good as this?"; with its "creative" cuisine, "lovely conservatory" and "stunning wines", this "elegant" Clerkenwell bar/restaurant is – say fans – "a revelation"; it does have its critics, though, who find it "overpriced and unremarkable". / EC1M 4EH; www.portalrestaurant.com; 10.15 pm; closed Sat L & Sun.

F S A

La Porte des Indes W1 £55 ❸④❷
32 Bryanston St 7224 0055 2–2A
The exterior "gives no hint" of the "astonishing" interior of this "opulent" basement, near Marble Arch; it may be "a bit pricey", but it wins steady praise for its "refined Franco-Indian food", cooked "with a light touch". / W1H 7EG; www.laportedesindes.com; 11.30 pm, Sun 10.30 pm.

Porters English Restaurant WC2 £35 ④❸❸
17 Henrietta St 7836 6466 4–3C
With its (heavy) traditional English theming, Lord Bradford's long-running Covent Garden brasserie can seem rather touristy, but fans of its "tasty pies", "yummy stodgy school puds" and "good-value set menus" say it's "worth a try". / WC2E 8QH; www.porters.uk.com; 11.30 pm, Sun 10.30 pm; no Amex.

Il Portico W8 £46 ❸❶❷
277 Kensington High St 7602 6262 7–1D
"Kensington locals really value this family-run Italian", with its "welcoming" owners and its "old-fashioned" (almost "touristy") decor; the cooking is "good and solid" too (albeit "in the ersatz style of '60s London"). / W8 6NA; www.ilportico.co.uk; 11 pm; closed Sun.

Portobello Ristorante W11 £44 ❷❸❸
7 Ladbroke Rd 7221 1373 6–2B
"Always full, with a loud buzz", a "charming" trattoria, near Notting Hill Gate; "fantastic pizza" is the lead culinary attraction, and there's a "great terrace" out front too; service can get "over-stretched" at busy times. / W11 3PA; www.portobellolondon.co.uk; 11 pm, Sun 10.15 pm.

The Portrait
National Portrait Gallery WC2 £50 ④④❶
St Martin's Pl 7312 2490 4–4B
"Like dining among the chimneys with Dick Van Dyke!" – it's the "unbeatable" views over Trafalgar Square that make this "romantic" rooftop room special, not the "stodgy" cooking or "inattentive" service. / WC2H 0HE; www.searcys.co.uk; Thu-Fri 8.30 pm; Sat-Sun closed L, Sun-Wed closed D.

Potli W6 NEW £37 ❸④④
319-321 King St 8741 4328 7–2B
"A nice addition to the Hammersmith Indians"; this "original" newcomer wins consistent praise from reporters for its "interesting" menu that's "a bit different" from the norm. / W6 9NH; www.potli.co.uk; 10.30 pm, Fri-Sat 11.30 pm.

La Poule au Pot SW1 £57 ❸❸❶
231 Ebury St 7730 7763 5–2D
"Oozing French sex-appeal", this "magical" old Pimlico charmer, with its "hidden corners and candlelight", is "unbeatable for a date"; a menu of "no-nonsense, traditional classics" and staff "with accents as thick as soupe à l'oignon" complete the "rustic" scene. / SW1W 8UT; www.pouleaupot.co.uk; 11 pm, Sun 10 pm.

Pret A Manger £15 ④❷④
Branches throughout London
"Kings of the mass-market sarnie" – this "ubiquitous" chain remains the "benchmark" for those in search of a "fresh and appetising" pit stop; its secret weapon, as ever, is its "preternaturally cheerful" staff. / www.pret.com; generally 4 pm-6 pm; closed Sun (except some West End branches); City branches closed Sat & Sun; no Amex; no booking.

Prince Albert NW1 £38 ④④❸
163 Royal College St 7485 0270 8–3C
A "great local"; this large Camden Town boozer convinces most (if not quite all) reporters of its "friendly", "reliable" and "good-value" charms. / NW1 0SG; www.princealbertcamden.com; 10 pm, Sun 5.30 pm; closed Sun D; no Amex; set always available £21 (FP).

The Prince Bonaparte W2 £42 ❸④❷
80 Chepstow Rd 7313 9491 6–1B
Tucked away in Bayswater, this "bright" and "buzzy" gastroboozer has a "great neighbourhood vibe", and offers food of a "very good standard" too. / W2 5BE; 11 pm; no booking; set weekday L £24 (FP).

The Prince Of Wales SW15 £48 ❸❸❸
138 Upper Richmond Rd 8788 1552 10–2B
"Amazing Scotch eggs" are a highlight at this "always-bustling" gastroboozer, near East Putney station – part of an "inventive" menu, realised to a very "reliable" standard; good beers too. / SW15 2SP; www.princeofwalesputney.co.uk; 10 pm, Sun 9.30 pm.

Princess Garden W1 £59 ❷❷❸
8-10 North Audley St 7493 3223 3–2A
"A peaceful haven, not far from Oxford Street"; this "smart" (slightly "sterile") Mayfair Chinese wins most praise as a lunchtime destination ("truly excellent dim sum"), but it's an "efficient" all-rounder at any time – "everything is good". / W1K 6ZD; www.princessgardenofmayfair.com; 11.45 pm, Sun 10.45 pm.

Princess of Shoreditch EC2 £46 ④❸④
76 Paul St 7729 9270 12–1B
"A favourite of the Shoreditch crowd"; some reporters do feel, though, that the cooking in the "small upstairs dining room" of this trendy gastroboozer is "only average". / EC2A 4NE; www.theprincessofshoreditch.com; 10 pm, Sun 8 pm.

Princess Victoria W12 £46 ❸❸❷
217 Uxbridge Rd 8749 5886 7–1B
This "stunningly-refurbished" gin palace, in distant Shepherd's Bush, is still highly acclaimed for its "lovely" interior, "great gastro-fare" and "stunning wine list"; there were some "off-days" reported this year, though, and prices can seem rather "top-end". / W12 9DH; www.princessvictoria.co.uk; 10.30 pm, Sun 9.30 pm; no Amex.

Princi W1 £27 ❸④❷
135 Wardour St 7478 8888 3–2D
In every sense "a slice of Italy", this recently-enlarged Soho café/bakery is a "chaotic" and "squeezed-in" sort of place offering a "vast array" of "amazing Milanese bread and snacks" (and now pizza too), plus "great people-watching". / W1F 0UT; www.princi.co.uk; midnight, Sun 10 pm; no booking.

Prism EC3 £66 ④❸④
147 Leadenhall St 7256 3875 9–2D
Run by Harvey Nics, this "impressive" banking hall is, say fans, a "slick" all-rounder that's "a good option for a City lunch"; it inspires only limited feedback, though, and critics find it "a disappointingly flat experience", with "mediocre" cooking. / EC3V 4QT; www.harveynichols.com; 9.45 pm; closed Sat & Sun; SRA-51%.

Prix Fixe W1 £35 ④❸❸
39 Dean St 7734 5976 4–2A
"Does what it says on the tin!" – this "fun" and "unpretentious" Soho spot dishes up "a big selection" of "tasty", "bistro-style" fare at "good-value" prices. / W1D 4PU; www.prixfixe.net; 11.30 pm.

FSA

The Providores W1 £66 ❸⑤⑤
109 Marylebone High St 7935 6175 2–1A
Mixed reviews of late on Peter Gordon's "cramped" and "noisy" first-floor dining room, in Marylebone; fans do say it offers "fusion fare at its best", but critics say standards are "slipping", service can be "surly" and that some flavour-combinations just "don't work". / W1U 4RX; www.theprovidores.co.uk; 10.30 pm; SRA-60%.

(Tapa Room)
The Providores W1 £49 ❷④❸
109 Marylebone High St 7935 6175 2–1A
"Jammed" at weekends (with "huge queues out the door and down the street"), Peter Gordon's "cramped" ground-floor Marylebone bar is renowned for its "exciting" brunch fare, and for "exotic" Pacific rim tapas that are "perfect for all-day grazing"; service, though, "could be much better". / W1U 4RX; www.theprovidores.co.uk; 10.30 pm, Sun 10 pm.

Prufrock Coffee EC1 £13 ❸❷❸
23-25 Leather Ln 224 3470 9–2A
"Coffee is elevated to the level of a science", at this Holborn spot, where "lots of love" is evident in both the "rich-tasting" brews and the "interesting" snacks (sandwiches, cakes, lunch plates); you can even train to be a barista! / EC1N 7TE; www.prufrockcoffee.com; 6 pm, Sat 5 pm; L only, closed Sun; no Amex.

The Punch Tavern EC4 £31 ④❸❷
99 Fleet St 7353 6658 9–2A
A "lovely" Victorian tavern, near Ludgate Circus; it offers nothing fancy on the food front, but the fare is "tasty", and "the price is perfect for a daily visit" – "fabulous" Mon-Thu lunch for £5! / EC4Y 1DE; www.punchtavern.com; 10.30 pm, Sat & Sun 6.30 pm.

Quadrato
Four Seasons Hotel E14 £72 ④❸❸
Westferry Circus 7510 1857 11–1B
"An amazing brunch buffet" is the highlight at this smart but corporate-feeling Canary Wharf hotel; on limited feedback, its Italian cuisine seems to be on the up too. / E14 8RS; www.fourseasons.com; 10.30 pm.

Quaglino's SW1 £54 ④④④
16 Bury St 7930 6767 3–3D
Perhaps because locals feel this "huge" D&D Group restaurant, in a St James's basement, is "past the sell-by date" or "for tourists", it generates strikingly few survey reports; some meals of late, however – if still "predictable" – have been "pleasantly surprising". / SW1Y 6AJ; www.quaglinos.co.uk; 10.30 pm, Fri & Sat 11 pm; closed Sun; no trainers; set pre theatre £33 (FP); SRA-62%.

Quantus W4 £40 ❸❷❷
38 Devonshire Rd 8994 0488 7–2A
A "passionate owner" adds life to this "always-buzzing and fun" Chiswick Italian, which is applauded by its local fan club for its "high-quality" menu and "interesting" wines. / W4 2HD; www.quantus-london.com; 11 pm, Sun 10 pm; closed Sat L & Sun L.

Queen's Head W6 £36 ④❷❷
13 Brook Grn 7603 3174 7–1C
A huge, hidden-away garden is the surprise sunny-day attraction of this Brook Green tavern; the food's fine, but not really the point. / W6 7BL; www.fullers.co.uk; 10 pm, Sun 9 pm.

The Queens Arms SW1 £42 ❸④❸
11 Warwick Way 7834 3313 2–4B
"Good", "reliable", "busy", "vibrant", "fun" – a corner boozer which offers "the best pub food in Pimlico" (certainly of the more reasonably-priced variety). / SW1V 1QT; www.thequeensarmspimlico.co.uk; 11 pm, Sun 10.30 pm; set weekday L £23 (FP).

Le Querce SE23 £39 ❶❶❷
66-68 Brockley Rise 8690 3761 1–4D
"The most 'Italian' Italian in town!"; this "charming" Brockley Park hotspot (now minus its Blackheath offshoot) inspires a hymn of praise for its "inspired" Sardinian food – not least "mouth-watering" fish, "super-thin" pizzas, and gorgeous "weird and wacky" ice creams – that "would cost twice as much in the West End". / SE23 1LN; 10 pm, Sun 9 pm; closed Mon & Tue L.

Quilon SW1 £62 ❶❶④
41 Buckingham Gate 7821 1899 2–4B
"Extremely refined" and "subtle" Keralan cuisine has long put this grand Indian, near Buckingham Palace, on the culinary map; the main drawback has always been its "sedate" modern decor – early reporters differ on whether the recent major refurbishment has made it better or worse! / SW1E 6AF; www.quilon.co.uk; 10.45 pm, Sun 10.15 pm.

Quince
The May Fair Hotel W1 £60 ④❸④
Stratton St 7915 3892 3–3C
Celeb chef Silvena Rowe is "much in evidence" at this Ottoman-style Mayfair hotel dining room, where she creates Turkish-inspired dishes fans find "delectable"; they're also "very expensive", though, and critics say the place is "overhyped". / W1J 8LT; www.quincelondon.com; 10.30 pm; closed Sat L.

Quirinale SW1 £60 ❷❸④
North Ct, 1 Gt Peter St 7222 7080 2–4C
"An oasis in the Westminster desert" – this "secret-feeling" basement Italian offers "top-notch" cooking and "discreet" service too; the atmosphere, though, can seem rather "sombre" and "business-like". / SW1P 3LL; www.quirinale.co.uk; 10.30 pm; closed Sat & Sun.

Quo Vadis W1 £55 ❸❷❷
26-29 Dean St 7437 9585 4–2A
"It finally has the menu it deserves!" – "straightforward British food served with aplomb" – says one of the many fans of Jeremy Lee's much-ballyhooed arrival at the Hart brothers' "stylish" Soho landmark; not all reporters, though, are entirely convinced. / W1D 3LL; www.quovadissoho.co.uk; 10.45 pm; closed Sun.

Racine SW3 £62 ❷❷❸
239 Brompton Rd 7584 4477 5–2C
"Earthy and delicious old-fashioned food, albeit at very modern prices" – the formula that wins massive acclaim for Henry Harris's "more-French-than-France" Knightsbridge bistro; long-term fans have gripes though – compared to the place it once was, it can sometimes seem "stiff" and "complacent" nowadays. / SW3 2EP; www.racine-restaurant.com; 10.30 pm, Sun 10 pm; set weekday L £29 (FP), set always available £36 (FP).

Ragam W1 £26 ❶❷⑤
57 Cleveland St 7636 9098 2–1B
Don't be put off by the "rough" decor of this stalwart café, near the Telecom Tower; for value, "it's impossible to beat", thanks to its "terrific" Keralan cooking (including "the best dosas around"), at prices that'll "make you think they've got the bill wrong"; "great for veggies". / W1T 4JN; www.ragam.co.uk; 10.45 pm, Fri-Sun 11.15 pm; essential Fri & Sat.

Randa W8 £45 ❸❷④
23 Kensington Church St 7937 5363 5–1A
"A cut above your standard Lebanese" – this glitzily-converted Kensington pub offers "consistently good" food and "courteous" service. / W8 4LF; www.maroush.com/randa-restaurant; midnight.

Randall & Aubin W1 £49 ❸❸❷
16 Brewer St 7287 4447 3–2D
"Brilliantly lively" (and "loud"), this "excellent" seafood spot, in the sleazy heart of Soho, is "perfect pre/post-theatre, or for an indulgent light lunch"; "don't be put off by the queues – they are all part of the charm!" / W1F 0SG; www.randallandaubin.co.uk; 11 pm, Sat midnight, Sun 10 pm; booking for L only; SRA-58%.

Rani N3 £26 ④④④
7 Long Ln 8349 4386 1–1B
Mixed reports on this Indian veggie veteran, in Finchley – fans say the food's "fresh, cheap and authentic" (with "London's best range of chutneys"), but critics say it's "sadly, not as good as it used to be, and now very bland". / N3 2PR; www.raniuk.com; 10 pm; D only, ex Sun open L & D.

Ranoush £46 ❷❸⑤
22 Brompton Rd, SW1 7584 6999 5–1D
338 King's Rd, SW3 7352 0044 5–3C
43 Edgware Rd, W2 7723 5929 6–1D
86 Kensington High St, W8 7938 2234 5–1A
"The best shawarmas in London" – together with "healthy and fresh" mezze and juices – win praise for this growing chain of "reliable", if "less-than-romantic", Lebanese pit stops. / www.maroush.com; most branches close between 1 am-3 am.

Ransome's Dock SW11 £55 ❸❸❸
35 Parkgate Rd 7223 1611 5–4C
"There's no better wine selection in London", than at Martin and Vanessa Lam's "ungreedily-priced" Battersea stalwart, "tucked-away" near the river; after a tricky period, its "well-sourced" seasonal fare seems to be getting back on track too. / SW11 4NP; www.ransomesdock.co.uk; 11 pm; closed Sun D.

Raoul's Café £40 ④⑤④
105-107 Talbot Rd, W11 7229 2400 6–1B
113-115 Hammersmith Grove, W6 8741 3692 7–1C
13 Clifton Rd, W9 7289 7313 8–4A
"A great place to chillax with the weekend papers" – these Maida Vale and Notting Hill hang-outs are renowned brunch spots, whose "cramped" quarters and "slow" service are worth enduring for "the freshest eggs" and other "wonderful" breakfast treats; shame about W6, though – it's "shocking". / www.raoulsgourmet.com; 10.15 pm, W11 6.15 pm; booking after 5 pm only.

Rasa £36 ❷❷❸
6 Dering St, W1 7637 0222 3–2B NEW
Holiday Inn Hotel, 1 Kings Cross, WC1 7833 9787 8–3D
56 Stoke Newington Church St, N16 7249 1340 1–1C
"Delicate" but "extraordinarily tasty" Keralan cuisine at "attractive" prices again wins much acclaim for these "obliging" spin-offs from Rasa N16; "it's a shame the 'Samudra' branch (speciality: seafood) had to move to Dering Street". / www.rasarestaurants.com; 10.45 pm; WC1 & W1 closed Sun.

Rasa N16 £30 ❶❷❸
55 Stoke Newington Church St 7249 0344 1–1C
"Sublime", "very different", "to die for"… – this Stoke Newington Keralan (the original of the mini-chain) is well "worth the pilgrimage", thanks to its veggie menu of "palate-stimulating surprises", all at "very affordable prices". / N16 0AR; www.rasarestaurants.com; 10.45 pm, Fri & Sat 11.30 pm; closed weekday L.

Rasoi SW3 £100 ❷❸❷
10 Lincoln St 7225 1881 5–2D
"Chef Bhatia is a magician", say fans of this "very impressive" and "private" ("subdued but lovely") Chelsea townhouse; his superbly "inventive" cuisine – with its "tremendous detail and complexity" – is akin to "culinary fantasy", and very arguably makes this London's top Indian. / SW3 2TS; www.rasoirestaurant.co.uk; 10.30 pm, Sun 10 pm; closed Sat L.

The Real Greek £37 ⑤④④
56 Paddington St, W1 7486 0466 2–1A
60-62 Long Acre, WC2 7240 2292 4–2D
Westfield, Ariel Way, W12 8743 9168 7–1C
15 Hoxton Market, N1 7739 8212 12–1B
1-2 Riverside Hs, Southwark Br Rd, SE1 7620 0162 9–3B
6 Horner Sq, E1 7375 1364 12–2B
"Avoid, even with a 50% voucher!" – still the best advice on this unreliable chain; fans do claim its new owners (since mid-2011) "have changed it for the better", but too many dishes are still dismissed as "dismal, cook-by-numbers" affairs. / www.therealgreek.com; 10.45 pm; WC2 10.30 pm, E1 Sun 7 pm; EC1 closed Sun, N1 closed Sun-Mon; WC2 no booking.

Rebato's SW8 £44 ❸❷❸
169 South Lambeth Rd 7735 6388 10–1D
"A little slice of Spain, in Stockwell"; with its "lovely" staff, and "the best tapas in south London" too, this "wonderfully retro" bar and restaurant remains "an old favourite" for almost all who comment on it. / SW8 1XW; www.rebatos.com; 10.45 pm; closed Sat L & Sun; set weekday L £28 (FP).

Red Dog Saloon N1 £36 ④④❸
37 Hoxton Sq 3551 8014 12–1B
"A true slice of Americana!"; "burgers to die for" – plus "the best ribs, wings and all types of food from across the Pond" – win fans for this Hoxton BBQ, which pleases many (if not quite all) of those who comment on it. / N1 6NN; www.reddogsaloon.co.uk.

Red Fort W1 £59 ❷❷❸
77 Dean St 7437 2525 4–2A
This old Soho veteran boasts a "swanky" modern interior nowadays; despite its "fabulous" cooking, it's sometimes "fairly empty" – possibly something to do with the fact that even fans find it "very expensive". / W1D 3SH; www.redfort.co.uk; 11.30 pm; closed Sat L & Sun L; set always available £33 (FP), set Sun L £38 (FP).

F S A

The Red Pepper W9 £44 ❷❸④
8 Formosa St 7266 2708 8–4A
"It's so cramped it's amazing anyone goes"… so the fact that this Maida Vale stalwart is usually "massively busy" must be testament to the "always-excellent" quality of its pizza. / W9 1EE; theredpepper.net; Sat 11 pm, Sun 10.30 pm; closed weekday L; no Amex.

Redhook EC1 £49 ④④④
89-90 Turnmill St 7065 6800 9–1A
"A good choice for steak and seafood fans", say supporters of this "NYC-ish" brasserie, near Farringdon Tube; critics find the food only "so-so", though, and the overall experience "forgettable". / EC1M 5QU; www.redhooklondon.com; midnight, Thu-Sat 1 am; closed Sun.

Refettorio
The Crowne Plaza Hotel EC4 £56 ④❸⑤
19 New Bridge St 7438 8052 9–3A
"It's hard to fault the food" ("even if it is a little pricey") or the "very friendly" service, at this rustic-Italian-inspired dining room, on the fringe of the City; it makes "a decent business option", though the ambience can resemble "an airport lounge on a quiet day". / EC4V 6DB; www.refettorio.com; 10.30 pm, Fri & Sat 10 pm; closed Sat L & Sun.

Refuel
Soho Hotel W1 £68 ④❷❷
4 Richmond Mews 7559 3007 3–2D
It's the "wonderful" bar-scene which creates the "lovely" atmosphere at this upmarket heart-of-Soho hang-out; the food is incidental. / W1D 3DH; www.firmdale.com; midnight, Sun 11 pm.

Le Relais de Venise L'Entrecôte £42 ❷④❸
120 Marylebone Ln, W1 7486 0878 2–1A
18-20 Mackenzie Walk, E14 3475 3331 11–1C NEW
5 Throgmorton St, EC2 7638 6325 9–2C
"It's a pain in the neck queueing, but worth it" – these "no-menu, no-choice, no-hassle" Gallic bistros may "squash you in like sardines", but they offer "brilliant" steak/frites (plus a salad, and a "delicious secret sauce"); "save space for seconds!" / www.relaisdevenise.com; W1 11 pm, Sun 10.30 pm; EC2 10 pm; EC2 closed Sat & Sun; no booking.

Le Rendezvous du Café EC1 £45 ❸❸❸
22 Charterhouse Sq 7336 8836 9–1B
"Really good, for the money"; this cramped offshoot of the Café du Marché is one of London's more authentic Gallic bistros; it makes a very handy Smithfield stand-by. / EC1M 6AA; www.cafedumarche.co.uk; 10 pm; closed Sat L & Sun.

Retsina NW3 £43 ④④④
48-50 Belsize Ln 7431 5855 8–2A
"Teeming by night", this family-run Belsize Park taverna has a big local fan club for its "generous" dishes; critics, however, find its Greek cuisine "lacklustre", and put its success down to a "lack of local competition". / NW3 5AR; www.retsina-london.com; 11 pm; closed Mon L; no Amex.

Reubens W1 £50 ④⑤⑤
79 Baker St 7486 0035 2–1A
Fans may insist it does "the best salt beef sandwiches", but this long-established Marylebone deli/dining room can also disappoint – "it's a real shame to see such easily-cooked Jewish dishes poorly executed". / W1M 1AJ; www.reubensrestaurant.co.uk; 10 pm; closed Fri D & Sat; no Amex.

Rhodes 24 EC2 £80 ❻❸❶
25 Old Broad St 7877 7703 9–2C
"If you can get a window table, the major draw is the view" – that's what provides the "wow", for business or romance, at Gary R's 24th-floor City eyrie; prices can seem "extortionate", but "consistent" standards offer some consolation. / EC2N 1HQ; www.rhodes24.co.uk; 9 pm; closed Sat & Sun; no shorts; booking essential.

Rhodes W1 Restaurant
Cumberland Hotel W1 £68 ④❸❸
Gt Cumberland Pl 7616 5930 2–2A
Fans who vaunt the "masterful" cuisine and "classy" decor of Gary R's fine-dining room, by Marble Arch, feel it is "unfairly overlooked"; critics, though, baulk at its "hotel-like" style, and think prices "sky-high". / W1H 7DL; www.rhodesw1.com; 10 pm; closed Mon, Sat L & Sun; no trainers.

Rib Room
Jumeirah Carlton Tower Hotel SW1 £88 ④④④
Cadogan Pl 7858 7250 5–1D
The "very impressive redecoration" may have given a "new lease of life" to this Belgravia dining room, long known for its beef, but "even though steak is now the big thing in town, they've still not succeeded in rekindling this once-iconic location"; prices, inevitably, are still "too high". / SW1X 9PY; www.jumeirah.com; 10.45 pm, Sun 10.15 pm; set weekday L £46 (FP), set dinner £52 (FP).

RIBA Café
Royal Ass'n of Brit' Architects W1 £40 ④④❷
66 Portland Pl 7631 0467 2–1B
In a "lovely Art Deco building" housing the architects' Marylebone HQ, this airy café occupies a "beautiful, unusual and well-spaced" chamber (and has a "secret gem" of a terrace too); the scoff is "more snack than gourmet", but suits a light business lunch. / W1 4AD; www.riba-venues.com; L only, closed Sat & Sun.

Riccardo's SW3 £42 ⑤④❸
126 Fulham Rd 7370 6656 5–3B
Results at this long-term-favourite Chelsea Italian are "very hit 'n' miss" nowadays; fans still hail it as "a reliable neighbourhood spot", but critics rail against a place which – with its "bog-standard" food and "poor" service – is "well past its prime". / SW3 6HU; www.riccardos.it; 11.30 pm.

Riding House Café W1 £44 ④❸❶
43-51 Great Titchfield St 7927 0840 3–1C
With its "achingly trendy vibe", this "NYC-style" Fitzrovia yearling is a "vibrant" and "versatile" all-day hang-out, most popular as a "delectable" brunch destination; service, though, does "risk becoming a bit too full of itself". / W1W 7PQ; www.ridinghousecafe.co.uk; 11 pm, Sun 10.30 pm.

El Rincón Latino SW4 £33 ④❷❷
148 Clapham Manor St 7622 0599 10–2D
"Nicely rustic" and "friendly" as it is, this Clapham tapas bar seems a little faded nowadays; the top weekend tip, though, is the same as ever – "great-value Spanish fry-ups". / SW4 6BX; www.rinconlatino.co.uk; 10.30 pm, Fri & Sat 11.30 pm; closed Mon-Fri L.

Rising Sun NW7 £38 ❸❷❷
137 Marsh Ln, Highwood Hill 8959 1357 1–1B
"Different from the vast majority of gastropubs"; run by an Italian family, this Mill Hill spot is "a true find" – a "charming" place, serving "a good range of dishes like mamma might make".
/ NW7 4EY; www.therisingsunmillhill.co.uk; 9.30 pm, Sun 8.30 pm; closed Mon L; set weekday L £24 (FP).

Ristorante Semplice W1 £67 ④④④
9-10 Blenheim St 7495 1509 3–2B
Has this "slick" but somewhat "cramped" Mayfair Italian been wrecked by its Michelin star? – the "innovative" and "refined" cuisine still has many fans, but it now has quite a few critics too, who find it "middle-of-the-road", or "nowhere near justifying the prices".
/ W1S 1LJ; www.ristorantesemplice.com; 10.30 pm; closed Sat L & Sun; set weekday L £35 (FP).

(Palm Court)
The Ritz W1 £42 ④❸❶
150 Piccadilly 7493 8181 3–4C
No one really doubts that "afternoon tea at its most romantic" is to be had in this famously grand hotel lounge; even fans, though, may say: "you go for the experience, as the food is run-of-the-mill".
/ W1C 9BR; www.theritzlondon.com; 9.30 pm; jacket & tie.

The Ritz Restaurant
The Ritz W1 £125 ④❷❶
150 Piccadilly 7493 8181 3–4C
"Your partner will be overwhelmed", by this "stunning" Louis XVI-style dining room, overlooking Green Park; after a false dawn in recent years, though, the cuisine is back in its old "not-pushing-any-boundaries" groove, but it can still be "perfect for a special occasion" – on Saturdays, there's dinner-dancing. / W1J 9BR; www.theritzlondon.com; 10 pm; jacket & tie; set weekday L £74 (FP), set dinner £79 (FP).

Riva SW13 £59 ❷❸④
169 Church Rd 8748 0434 10–1A
As ever, the jury divides on Andreas Riva's acclaimed Barnes Italian; fans of its "serene" style, its "simple, seasonal and perfect" food and its "sleek, professional" service say it "never disappoints"… but, to critics, it's just "impersonal", "crowded" and "over-rated".
/ SW13 9HR; 10.30 pm, Sun 9 pm; closed Sat L.

THE RIVER CAFÉ W6 £81 ❷❷❷
Thames Wharf, Rainville Rd 7386 4200 7–2C
Tables are "cramped", volume-levels "high", portions "bijou", service "arrogant", the interior "very '80s" (even post-revamp!) and prices "seriously jaw-dropping"… and yet this world-famous Hammersmith Italian is still "worth it (just about)", thanks to its "incredibly fresh" cuisine; "sublime outside seating in summer" too. / W6 9HA; www.rivercafe.co.uk; 9 pm, Sat 9.15 pm; closed Sun D.

The Riverfront
BFI Southbank SE1 £41 ④④❸
Southbank 7928 0808 2–3D
With its pleasant outside tables, this stylish operation makes a handy option "before visiting one of the South Bank's great temples of culture"; it's the location that makes the place, though – the "perfectly adequate" food plays very much a supporting rôle.
/ SE1 8XT; www.riverfrontbarandkitchen.com; 11.30 pm.

Rivington Grill £51 ④④④

178 Greenwich High Rd, SE10 8293 9270 1–3D
28-30 Rivington St, EC2 7729 7053 12–1B

"Competent", "decent", "straightforward"... – these "laid-back" Shoreditch and Greenwich bar/brasseries offer "simple" British dishes that are short on fireworks but pretty "safe"; the overall impression, though, can be "rather corporate". / www.rivingtongrill.co.uk; 11 pm, Sun 10 pm; SE10 closed Mon, Tue L & Wed L.

Roast SE1 £67 ④④❸

Stoney St 0845 034 7300 9–4C

"A magnificent location in Borough Market" – with "beautiful views" and an "airy" interior – underpins the attraction of this popular venue; "there's no better place for breakfast", but otherwise the "ridiculous" prices tend to restrict the appeal to those on expenses. / SE1 1TL; www.roast-restaurant.com; 10.30 pm, Sun 8.45 pm; SRA-67%.

Rocca Di Papa £32 ④④❸

73 Old Brompton Rd, SW7 7225 3413 5–2B
75-79 Dulwich Village, SE21 8299 6333 1–4D

These "bright and breezy" Italians are "very welcoming to families", and serve "a wide variety of pizza and pasta"; they're so middle-of-the-road, though, that critics see "an opportunity wasted". / SW7 11.30 pm; SE21 11 pm.

Rocco SW5 NEW

254-260 Old Brompton Rd awaiting tel 5–3A

On an Earl's Court site with quite a heritage – it was once Pontevecchio, one of the most fashionable Italians of the '80s, and more recently Langan's Coq d'Or (RIP) – this new trattoria, salumeria and cocktail bar opens as this guide goes to press. / SW5 9HR.

Rochelle Canteen E2 £38 ❸❷❷

Arnold Circus 7729 5677 12–1C

A "shed-like" communal canteen, in a Shoreditch "hidden garden", with quite a name for offering "simple", "fresh" and "seasonal" dishes ("in the school of St John"), at a "very fair price"; BYO – fiver a bottle corkage. / E2 7ES; www.arnoldandhenderson.com; L only, closed Sat & Sun; no Amex.

Rock & Sole Plaice WC2 £34 ❸④④

47 Endell St 7836 3785 4–1C

A "decent" old-fashioned chippy, handy for Covent Garden, and with pleasant al fresco seating too; "it's on the tourist trail", though, and the occasional reporter feels it's 'coasting'. / WC2H 9AJ; 10.30 pm; no Amex; need 4+ to book.

Rock & Rose TW9 £52 ⑤⑤❷

106-108 Kew Rd 8948 8008 1–4A

With its "tongue-in-cheek kitsch", its "faux glamour" and its "great cocktails", this "boudoir-esque" Richmond venue is certainly a "fun" and "romantic" sort of place; "you don't go there for the food" or the service, though – both can be terrible. / TW9 2PQ; www.rockandroserestaurant.co.uk; 10 pm, Fri & Sat 10.30 pm.

Rocket £44 ④❸❸
4 Lancashire Ct, W1 7629 2889 3–2B
2 Churchill Pl, E14 3200 2022 11–1C
201 Bishopsgate, EC2 7377 8863 12–2B NEW
6 Adams Ct, EC2 7628 0808 9–2C
The pizza-and-salads menu may be "unmemorable", but this "reliable" Mayfair fixture (with lesser commented-on City offshoots) is a "buzzy", "bright" and "breezy" place, well worth knowing about as a "relatively inexpensive" stand-by, just off Bond Street.
/ 10.30 pm,Sun 9.30 pm; W1 closed Sun; EC2 closed Sat & Sun; SW15 Mon-Wed D only, Bishopsgate closed Sun D, E14.

Rodizio Rico £45 ⑤④④
11 Jerdan Pl, SW6 7183 6085 5–4A
111 Westbourne Grove, W2 7792 4035 6–1B
77-78 Upper St, N1 7354 1076 8–3D
The 02, Greenwich Peninsular, SE10 8858 6333 11–2D
Opinion divides pretty much 50/50 on these "authentic Brazilian-style BBQs"; fans find 'em "fun", "friendly" and "good value" (especially if you are "a very hungry carnivore") – critics see the potential, but say quality's "too variable", and at worst "really disappointing".
/ www.rodiziorico.com; W2 & N1 midnight, Sun 11 pm; SE10 11 pm, Fri & Sat midnight; W2 & N1 closed weekday L; no Amex, apart from SE10.

The Roebuck W4 £42 ④④❸
122 Chiswick High Rd 8995 4392 7–2A
"The fabulous large garden is jammed in summer", at this "always-buzzy" Chiswick boozer; the food – if not quite as notable as it was – remains "nice, for a pub". / W4 1PU; www.theroebuckchiswick.co.uk; 11 pm, Sun 10.30 pm.

Roganic W1 £80 ❶❶⑤
19 Blandford St 7486 0380 2–1A
Thanks to Simon Rogan's "sublime" small plates – with "incredible textures and flavours" – this two-year pop-up in Marylebone (an offshoot of Cumbria's L'Enclume) offers "some of the best food currently being served in London"; the room, though, is "functional at best" – "it feels like the disused retail outlet it is". / W1U 3DH; www.roganic.co.uk; 9 pm; closed Mon & Sun; set weekday L £51 (FP).

Roka £76 ❶❸❷
37 Charlotte St, W1 7580 6464 2–1C
Unit 4, Park Pavilion, 40 Canada Sq, E14 7636 5228 11–1C
"Sensational", "clean-flavoured" Japanese-fusion fare (majoring in sushi and robata dishes) helps fuel the "vibrant" spirit of these incredibly popular Zuma-siblings; with the help of a "sleepily cool and romantic" basement bar, W1 is rated a touch higher than E14.
/ www.rokarestaurant.com; 11.15 pm, Sun 10.30 pm; booking: max 8.

Roots at N1 N1 £48 ❷❷❸
115 Hemingford Rd 7697 4488 8–3D
"At last, a stylish, upmarket Islington Indian!" – this "amazing" pub-conversion is a "seriously good" place, where "strikingly original" dishes are served, with "charm". / N1 1BZ; www.rootsatn1.com; 10 pm, Sun 9 pm; closed Mon, Tue-Fri D only, Sat & Sun open L & D; no Amex.

Rosa's £36 ❸❷❸
48 Dean St, W1 7494 1638 4–3A
12 Hanbury St, E1 7247 1093 12–2C
"Minimalistic" but attractive, these Thai canteens off Brick Lane and in Soho are worth knowing about for "great curries and stir-fries, at reasonable prices". / www.rosaslondon.com; 10.30 pm, Fri & Sat 11 pm; some booking restrictions apply.

The Rose & Crown N6 £45 ④④④
86 Highgate High St 8340 0770 1–1C
This "pleasant-looking" Highgate two-year-old continues to generate mixed reports – fans praise the cuisine as "creative and delicious", but critics find it "very variable". / N6 5HX; www.roseandcrownhighgate.com; 10 pm, Sun 6 pm; closed Mon L & Sun D; no Amex.

Rossopomodoro £40 ❸④④
50-52 Monmouth St, WC2 7240 9095 4–3B
214 Fulham Rd, SW10 7352 7677 5–3B
184a Kensington Park Rd, W11 7229 9007 6–1A
There's certainly "a feeling of authenticity" to these "rather chaotic" but "friendly" pizzerias – with their HQ in Naples, you'd hope so, but only the "first-class" quality of the pizza really stands out. / www.rossopomodoro.co.uk; 11.30 pm; WC2 Sun 11.30 pm.

Roti Chai W1 NEW £49 ❷❸❸
3 Portman Mews South 7408 0101 3–1A
"Hard-to-find", near Selfridges, this "novel", "proto-chain-feeling" newcomer is widely welcomed as "one of the better additions of the year", thanks not least to its "very different", "properly spicy" Indian street-food, which delivers "great bang for your buck". / W1H 6HS; www.rotichai.com; 11 pm; closed Mon & Sun.

The Rôtisserie £52 ④④④
316 Uxbridge Rd, HA5 8421 2878 1–1A
1288 Whetstone High Rd, N20 8343 8585 1–1B
87 Allitsen Rd, NW8 7722 7444 8–3A
"Reliable but run-of-the-mill…", "predictable but great…", "always the same, always pleasant…" – that's the deal at these local grills, where steak is a highlight. / www.therotisserie.co.uk; 10.30 pm, Sun 9.30 pm; NW6, NW8 & NW20 closed Mon L; no Amex (except HA5).

Rotunda Bar & Restaurant Kings Place N1 £48 ④④❷
90 York Way 7014 2840 8–3C
"Unbeatable on a summer's day", this "interesting" venue in a King's Cross office/arts complex has a "lovely" canal-side location (with many seats al fresco), and fans say the food's "a step up from your usual art-related fare". / N1 9AG; www.rotundabarandrestaurant.co.uk; 10.30 pm, Sun 6.30 pm; closed Sun D.

Roux at Parliament Square RICS SW1 £75 ❸❸④
12 Great George St 7334 3737 2–3C
Fans insist you get "the best food around Westminster", at this rather "antiseptic" Gallic dining room, off Parliament Square; even they can find tastes on the "bland" side, though, and harsher critics think the whole experience rather "dreary". / SW1P 3AD; www.rouxatparliamentsquare.co.uk; 10 pm; closed Sat & Sun; set weekday L £43 (FP).

Roux at the Landau The Langham W1 £86 ❷❸❷
1c, Portland Pl 7965 0165 2–1B
"On the verge of stardom", this "very elegant" and "well-spaced" dining room, opposite Broadcasting House, is a "beautiful" venue offering "the usual, top-class Roux formula", and realised to a very consistent standard too. / W1B 1JA; www.thelandau.com; 10 pm; closed Sat L & Sun; no trainers.

Rowley's SW1 **£63** ④❸❸
113 Jermyn St 7930 2707 3–3D
Tiles inherited from the original Wall's butcher's shop may make this stalwart, near Piccadilly Circus, a "national treasure" architecturally speaking, but views on its cooking are mixed – fans love its "perfect steaks" and "limitless chips" but, to critics, it's "touristy", "unexciting" and "very overpriced". / SW1Y 6HJ; www.rowleys.co.uk; 11 pm.

Royal Academy W1 **£49** ⑤④❸
Burlington Hs, Piccadilly 7300 5608 3–3D
"It's a pity" the "classic British fare" at this civilised café – run by Peyton & Byrne, in the bowels of these Mayfair galleries – is "so average and costly"; it's a venue still sometimes tipped for "elegant tea and delicious cookies". / W1J 0BD; www.royalacademy.org.uk; 11 pm; L only, ex Fri open L & D; no booking at L.

Royal China **£46** ❷④④
24-26 Baker St, W1 7487 4688 2–1A
805 Fulham Rd, SW6 7731 0081 10–1B
13 Queensway, W2 7221 2535 6–2C
30 Westferry Circus, E14 7719 0888 11–1B
"Still setting the benchmark for quality dim sum" – these "garish"-looking Chinese institutions offer a "very authentic" mini-feast that's "great value" too; "curt" service and "huge" queues? – all "part of the experience!" / www.royalchinagroup.co.uk; 10.45 pm, Fri & Sat 11.15 pm, Sun 9.45 pm; no booking Sat & Sun L.

Royal China Club W1 **£57** ❷❸❸
40-42 Baker St 7486 3898 2–1A
Royal China goes 'club class', at this "upmarket" Marylebone outlet; compared to the standard offering, it's clearly an "expensive" upgrade, but many reporters find its "authentic" charms make it worthwhile; "notable dim-sum". / W1U 7AJ; www.royalchinagroup.co.uk; 11 pm, Fri & Sat 11.30 pm, Sun 10.30 pm.

Royal China SW15 **£43** ❸⑤④
3 Chelverton Rd 8780 1520 10–2B
Not actually part of – but with historic links to – the famous chain, this rather dated Putney Chinese offers food that's "largely on a par" with its namesakes (and "very good dim sum" too); shame about the "disinterested" service. / SW15 1RN; www.royalchinaputney.co.uk; 11 pm, Fri-Sat 11.30 pm, Sun 10 pm; only Amex.

The Royal Exchange Grand Café
The Royal Exchange EC3 **£51** ④④❸
The Royal Exchange Bank 7618 2480 9–2C
Oddly-sited in the glorious and "historic" atrium of what's essentially a deluxe shopping mall (by Bank) nowadays, this all-day café provokes limited feedback… presumably because, for somewhere so "expensive", its standards are "decidedly average". / EC3V 3LR; www.royalexchange-grandcafe.co.uk; 10 pm; closed Sat & Sun; SRA-58%.

RSJ SE1 **£50** ❸❸⑤
33 Coin St 7928 4554 9–4A
"The best Loire wine list in the world!" – the stand-out attraction at this South Bank stalwart, near the National Theatre, also praised for its "completely reliable" Gallic cooking; "why don't they refresh the interior", though? – it's so "bleak". / SE1 9NR; www.rsj.uk.com; 11 pm; closed Sat L & Sun.

Rugoletta N2 £37 ❸❸④
59 Church Ln 8815 1743 1–1B
"Caff by day, restaurant by night" – this "cramped" but "reasonably-priced" spot is "the perfect quick local Italian", say East Finchley folk; it's BYO too. / N2 8DR; 10.30 pm; closed Sun.

Rules WC2 £75 ❸❷❶
35 Maiden Ln 7836 5314 4–3D
Your "better class of tourist" is – rightly – wowed by the "lush Edwardiana" of London's oldest restaurant (1798), in Covent Garden; "don't underestimate the place", though – the game and other "meat-heavy traditional fare" is "not cheap, but worth every penny", and service "as polished as the decor". / WC2E 7LB; www.rules.co.uk; 11.30 pm, Sun 10.30 pm; no shorts.

Sabor N1 £42 ❸❶④
108 Essex Rd 7226 5551 8–3D
There's "always a warm welcome", at this lively Latino cantina, in Islington, where "imaginative" and "filling" dishes are served by "very helpful" staff. / N1 8LX; www.sabor.co.uk; 11 pm, Sun 10.30 pm; closed Mon, Tue-Fri D only, Sat & Sun open L & D; no Amex.

Le Sacré-Coeur N1 £37 ④❷❷
18 Theberton St 7354 2618 8–3D
"Our French friends wish they had a local like this!" – an Islington side street bistro that's always "buzzing", thanks not least to the attractions of its "reasonably-priced menu" and its "friendly" staff; nice al fresco seating too. / N1 0QX; www.lesacrecoeur.co.uk; 11 pm, Sat 11.30 pm, Sun 10.30 pm.

Sacro Cuore NW10 NEW
45 Chamberlayne Rd 8579 1462 1–2B
This Kensal Rise outpost of esteemed Ealing pizzeria, Santa Maria, opens as this guide goes to press; given the success of its parent operation, it could be a big local hit. / NW10 3NB.

Sagar £32 ❷❸④
17a, Percy St, W1 7631 3319 3–2B
31 Catherine St, WC2 7836 6377 4–3D
157 King St, W6 8741 8563 7–2C
"Brilliant vegetarian south Indian food", at "ridiculously low prices", helps make these simple cafés "hard to beat for a quick and tasty meal"; "yummy dosas" a highlight. / www.gosagar.com; Sun-Thu 10.45 pm, Fri & Sat 11.30 pm.

Saigon Saigon W6 £40 ❸④❸
313-317 King St 8748 6887 7–2B
An "ever-popular" Hammersmith Vietnamese of long standing, with decor some reporters find "lovely" and others "tired"; the "authentic" cooking is generally acclaimed, but one long-term fan does complain of "growing blandness". / W6 9NH; www.saigon-saigon.co.uk; 11.30 pm, Sun & Mon 10 pm.

St John EC1 £58 ❷❷❸
26 St John St 7251 0848 9–1B
"The daddy of pared-back British cooking"; this famous former Smithfield smokehouse is – for its legion of fans – an "austere but exciting room, where Fergus Henderson dazzles us with his nose-to-tail cuisine"; as ever, though, a sceptical minority just "don't get what all the fuss is about". / EC1M 4AY; www.stjohnrestaurant.com; 11 pm; closed Sat L & Sun D.

St John Bread & Wine E1 £55 ❶❷❸
94-96 Commercial St 7251 0848 12–2C
"Simple" yet "awesome" small plates of "gutsy" British fare (not least the legendary bacon buttie) , with "lovely wines" too, help create the "distinctive ethos" of this "stark" and "laid-back" Shoreditch canteen – not just, say fans, the "best value" of the St John restaurants, but simply "the best". / E1 6LZ; www.stjohnbreadandwine.com; 10.30 pm, Sun 9.30 pm.

St John Hotel WC2 £68 ❸❸④
1 Leicester St 3301 8069 4–3A
"Great to have an offshoot of St John 'up West'", say fans of this "noisy and bustly" dining room on the old Manzi's (RIP) site, by Leicester Square; it's a "cramped" place, though, with "cold" décor, and – "for such simple cooking" – can seem "a bit overpriced". / WC2H 7BL; www.stjohnhotellondon.com; 11.45 pm.

St Johns N19 £43 ❷❷❶
91 Junction Rd 7272 1587 8–1C
"A stunning, high-ceilinged chamber" (a former ballroom) provides the "unexpectedly grand" setting for dinner at this "very atmospheric" Archway tavern – not just a "memorable" and "fun" venue, but one which offers "top-quality" cooking from "well-sourced" produce. / N19 5QU; www.stjohnstavern.com; 11 pm, Sun 9.30 pm; Mon-Thu D only, Fri-Sun open L & D; booking: max 12.

Le Saint Julien EC1 £53 ④❷❸
62-63 Long Ln 7796 4550 9–1B
"Authentic in both food and atmosphere"', this "very French" bistro, by Smithfield Market, is an "efficient" operation in decidedly "classic" style. / EC1A 9EJ; 10 pm; closed Sat & Sun.

St Moritz W1 £55 ❸④❸
161 Wardour St 7734 3324 3–1D
A "convincing Swiss-farmhouse interior" creates a "warm, intimate and cosy" glow, at this "quirky" veteran of "Old Soho"; the "traditional" and "dependably good" cuisine (veal, fondues, Alpine wines…) is entirely in keeping. / W1F 8WJ; www.stmoritz-restaurant.co.uk; 11.30 pm; closed Sat L & Sun.

St Pancras Grand
St Pancras Int'l Station NW1 £51 ⑤⑤④
The Concourse 7870 9900 8–3C
No one seriously expected a riposte to Paris's 'Train Bleu', but good grief… this briefly-glamorous brasserie, near the Eurostar platforms, has quickly become a "ghastly" destination – service is "lackadaisical" and the food "canteen-y and mass-produced". / NW1 2QP; www.stpancrasgrand.com; 10.30 pm.

Sakana-tei W1 £34 ❷❷⑤
11 Maddox St 7629 3000 3–2C
"Shame about the decor", at this "bare" and "basic" Mayfair Japanese – "the sushi and sashimi are to die for". / W1S 2QF; 10 pm; closed Sun.

Sake No Hana SW1 £60 ④④❸
23 St James's St 7925 8988 3–4C
Large and prominently located in St James's, this "expensive" and would-be fashionable Japanese continues to inspire remarkably little survey feedback – perhaps because the consensus is that it is "not memorable". / SW1A 1HA; www.sakenohana.com; 11 pm, Fri-Sat 11.30 pm; closed Sun.

Sakonis HA0 £20 ❸④⑤
127-129 Ealing Rd 8903 9601 1–1A
"You don't need to eat for the rest of the day", having visited the renowned lunchtime buffet at this large no-frills Gujarati canteen, in the boonies of Wembley. / HA0 4BP; www.sakonis.co.uk; 9.30 pm; no Amex.

Sakura W1 £32 ❸❸④
23 Conduit St 7629 2961 3–2C
"Excellent sushi" (with "great prices at lunchtime" too) wins ongoing praise for this "authentic" Mayfair Japanese. / W1S 2XS; 10 pm.

Salaam Namaste WC1 £34 ❷❸④
68 Millman St 7405 3697 2–1D
"Vastly different from the norm" – this Bloomsbury stand-by is a "much better-than-average neighbourhood curry spot", and features some "really well-made regional specials". / WC1N 3EF; www.salaam-namaste.co.uk; 11.30 pm, Sun 11 pm.

Sale e Pepe SW1 £58 ❸❷❷
9-15 Pavilion Rd 7235 0098 5–1D
"A roaring Italian decibel level" and "brilliantly stereotypical service" are all part of the "unchanging" appeal of this "crammed", "time-warp, '70s trattoria", near Harrods; its "reliable, if not thrilling" cooking has bounced back of late. / SW1X 0HD; www.saleepepe.co.uk; 11.30 pm; no shorts.

Salloos SW1 £55 ❷❸⑤
62-64 Kinnerton St 7235 4444 5–1D
"The setting is cramped, the service only OK, and the entrance stairs steep… but the tandoor lamb chops are truly outstanding" – situation normal, then, at this "excellent" (but "very expensive") Pakistani "time warp", in a Belgravia mews. / SW1X 8ER; 11 pm; closed Sun.

The Salt House NW8 £45 ❷❸❷
63 Abbey Rd 7328 6626 8–3A
A "solid neighbourhood spot" with "great atmosphere"; this large St John's Wood gastroboozer, near Abbey Road Studios, is well "worth a visit". / NW8 0AE; www.thesalthouse.co.uk; 11 pm, Fri & Sat midnight; set weekday L £28 (FP).

Salt Yard W1 £40 ❷❷❷
54 Goodge St 7637 0657 2–1B
Not phased by all the new competition, this "cramped" but "buzzy" tapas-pioneer, in Fitzrovia, still turns out "stunning", "varied" and "genuinely innovative" small plates, alongside "some of the most interesting wines from Spain and Italy anywhere in London". / W1T 4NA; www.saltyard.co.uk; 11 pm; closed Sat L & Sun; SRA-63%.

The Salusbury NW6 £43 ❸④❸
50-52 Salusbury Rd 7328 3286 1–2B
A well-established Queen's Park favourite – this cosy gastropub ("with a pizza/deli option and a more formal dining room") serves "an Italian-orientated menu" that's "a touch hit 'n' miss but overall very good". / NW6 6NN; www.thesalusbury.co.uk; 10.30 pm; closed Mon L.

Sam's Brasserie W4 £46 ④❸❸
11 Barley Mow Pas 8987 0555 7–2A
"A great neighbourhood option"; Sam Harrison's "lively" all-day establishment has become a classic Chiswick stand-by for pretty much any occasion; the food's not earth-shattering, but "reliable" and "reasonably priced". / W4 4PH; www.samsbrasserie.co.uk; 10.30 pm, Sun 10 pm; set always available £30 (FP).

FSA

San Carlo Cicchetti W1 NEW £45 ❸❷④
215 Piccadilly 7494 9435 3–3D
Fantastically successful in Manchester, this Italian-small-plate concept tipped up in the capital – at the former premises of La Pigalle (RIP), by Piccadilly Circus – in mid-2012; our early-days visit to its brash and tightly-packed premises suggested it will make a handy stand-by, rather than a 'destination'. / W1J 9HN; Rated on Editors' visit; www.sancarlo.co.uk.

San Daniele del Friuli N5 £41 ④❷❸
72 Highbury Park 7226 1609 8–1D
An "old-favourite" Highbury Park Italian, "much-loved" (including by families) for its "charming" style, and "reliable" and "old-fashioned" dishes, in "generous" portions. / N5 2XE; www.sandanielehighbury.co.uk; 10.30 pm; closed Mon L, Tue L, Wed L & Sun; no Amex.

San Lorenzo SW3 £67 ⑤⑤⑤
22 Beauchamp Pl 7584 1074 5–1C
Once, quite literally, London's top A-List haunt, this Knightsbridge trattoria now generates hardly any feedback; such as there is suggests it is "expensive and uninspiring" / SW3 1NH; 11 pm; closed Sun D.

San Lorenzo Fuoriporta SW19 £46 ④⑤④
38 Wimbledon Hill Rd 8946 8463 10–2B
"Has its ups and downs… recently more downs"; this Wimbledon trattoria-cousin to the once-famous Knightsbridge trattoria looks akin to a posh PizzaExpress; the food can still be "fairly good", but critics say it's "massively overpriced", and service can sometimes be "terrible". / SW19 7PA; www.sanlorenzo.com; 10.40 pm.

The Sands End SW6 £47 ❸❸❷
135 Stephendale Rd 7731 7823 10–1B
Hidden-away it may be, but this Sand's End boozer has become a "vibrant hub" of local life, thanks in part to its "heavenly bar snacks", and other more ambitious dishes too. / SW6 2PR; www.thesandsend.co.uk; 11.30 pm, Thu-Sat midnight.

Santa Lucia SW10 £41 ❸④④
2 Hollywood Rd 7352 8484 5–3B
A buzzing Chelsea pizzeria, which charges by the metre; "it's really fun having the whole table's choices combined into one long pizza". / SW10 9HY; www.madeinitalygroup.co.uk; 11.30 pm, Sun 10.30 pm; closed weekday L.

Santa Maria W5 £30 ❷❸❷
15 St Mary's Rd 8579 1462 1–3A
"Magical" pizza ("super-thin, with lovely toppings") ensures there's "always a queue", at this "amazingly small" but "vibey" yearling – one of the better things to happen in Ealing in many a year. / W5 5RA; www.santamariapizzeria.com; 10.30 pm.

Santa Maria del Sur SW8 £47 ❸④❸
129 Queenstown Rd 7622 2088 10–1C
"Fun", if "crowded", this Argentinian "parilla" (grill), in Battersea, offers steaks fans claim are "the best this side of Cordoba"; a dip in ratings, though, supports those who fear the place "risks becoming a victim of its own success" – "they need to slow down a little!" / SW8 3RH; www.santamariadelsur.co.uk; 10 pm; no Amex.

Santini SW1 £69 ④❸❸
29 Ebury St 7730 4094 2–4B
Little survey commentary on this "time-warp" Belgravia Italian, which "no longer has a real buzz", as once it did; it still has its fans, though, who insist that – with its "smart" style, "reliable" food and "discreet" service – "it hits the spot for business". / SW1W 0NZ; www.santini-restaurant.com; 11 pm, Sun 10 pm; closed Sat L & Sun L.

Santore EC1 £40 ❷❸④
59 Exmouth Mkt 7812 1488 9–1A
In Farringdon, a "lively", "Naples-comes-to-London" outfit, where the pizza is "the real deal". / EC1X 4QL; www.santorerestaurant.co.uk; 11 pm.

Sapori Sardi SW6 NEW £40 ❷❷❸
786 Fulham Rd 7731 0755 10–1B
"Fantastico!" – "small, cosy, friendly and intimate", this "simple" new Fulham Sardinian gets only warm vibes from the locals; it helps that it offers "very good value for money". / SW6 5SL; www.saporisardi.co.uk; 11 pm; closed Mon L.

Sarastro WC2 £45 ⑤⑤④
126 Drury Ln 7836 0101 2–2D
"Drama" and "opulence" – and live operatic arias too – potentially make this "theatrical" Covent Garden fixture a "brilliant" choice for "romance" (or a party); it's become "massively overpriced", though, especially when you consider that the food can be "hideous". / WC2B 5SU; www.sarastro-restaurant.com; 10.30 pm, Fri & Sat 11.15 pm.

Sardo W1 £48 ❸❸④
45 Grafton Way 7387 2521 2–1B
A Fitzrovia Sardinian which impresses most, if not all, reporters with its "unusual" dishes, "interesting" wine and "professional" service; "eat in the front, near the bar", though – "the narrow, neutral dining room feels a little lacklustre". / W1T 5DQ; www.sardo-restaurant.com; 11 pm; closed Sat L & Sun.

Sardo Canale NW1 £49 ④④④
42 Gloucester Ave 7722 2800 8–3B
"More consistent of late", this Primrose Hill Sardinian – which has a terrace, but no view of the 'canale' – can still seem something of a "mixed bag"; fans insist, though, that its "lovely" food "deserves a stronger following". / NW1 8JD; www.sardocanale.com; 11 pm; Mon-Thu D only, Fri-Sun open L & D.

Sarracino NW6 £41 ❷❸④
186 Broadhurst Gdns 7372 5889 1–1B
"Simple Italian classics" (including "genuine Neapolitan-style pizzas", served by the metre) figure in all reports on this sometimes "raucous" trattoria, in West Hampstead. / NW6 3AY; www.sarracinorestaurant.com; 11 pm; closed weekday L.

Sartoria W1 £59 ❸❷❸
20 Savile Row 7534 7000 3–2C
"A spacious setting that is conducive to business" inspires much support for this "crisp and peaceful" Mayfair Italian; it's also praised for its "consistent" cooking and its notably "efficient" service – can this really be a D&D Group restaurant? / W1S 3PR; www.sartoria-restaurant.co.uk; 10.45 pm; closed Sun; SRA-63%.

Satay House W2 £38 ❸④④
13 Sale Pl 7723 6763 6–1D
A veteran Bayswater Malaysian, churning out "excellent food at very reasonable prices"; neither the setting nor the "unchanging menu", however, are likely to set your pulse racing. / W2 1PX; www.satay-house.co.uk; 11 pm.

Satsuma W1 £36 ④❸❸
56 Wardour St 7437 8338 3–2D
In the middle of Soho, this re-launched Japanese canteen has a "bright" and "fun", if rather "hard-surfaced", interior; it has never made a huge culinary impact, but its Bento boxes are pretty "good value". / W1D 4JG; www.osatsuma.com; 10.30 pm, Tue-Thu 11 pm, Fri & Sat midnight; no booking.

Sauterelle
Royal Exchange EC3 £64 ❸❷❸
Bank 7618 2483 9–2C
"The venue is the star, but the food is pretty good too", at this "quiet" and "professional" D&D Group venture, which boasts "splendid" views into the atrium of the Royal Exchange, and is the "great business rendezvous" such a location would suggest. / EC3V 3LR; www.sauterelle-restaurant.co.uk; 9.30 pm; closed Sat & Sun; no trainers; SRA-59%.

Savoir Faire WC1 £41 ❸❷❷
42 New Oxford St 7436 0707 4–1C
A slightly "quirky", "Parisian-bistro-style" spot, in Holborn, praised for its "realistic" prices, and its "caring" service too. / WC1A 1EP; www.savoir.co.uk; 11 pm; set weekday L £26 (FP).

(Savoy Grill)
The Savoy Hotel WC2 £79 ④❸❸
Strand 7592 1600 4–3D
After a decent start, Gordon Ramsay's "sympathetic renovation" of this power-lunch classic quickly ran out of steam – the traditional British fare seems ever more "unexciting and expensive", service is sometimes "second-rate", and even the atmosphere appears to be going "AWOL". / WC2R 0EU; www.gordonramsay.com/thesavoygrill/; 10.45 pm, Sun 10.15 pm; jacket required; set weekday L & pre-theatre £46 (FP).

(River Restaurant)
The Savoy Hotel WC2 £90 ⑤④❸
91 The Strand 7836 4343 4–3D
With its "fussy" food and sometimes surprisingly "poor" service, the "striking" dining room of this world-famous Thames-side hotel too often disappoints, despite its "impressive" decor, and "amazing Thames views" (window tables only). / WC2R 0EU; www.fairmont.com/savoy/; 10.30 pm; no trainers; set always available & pre-theatre £46 (FP).

Scalini SW3 £70 ❸❸❸
1-3 Walton St 7225 2301 5–2C
"Criminally-priced" and "full of Eurotrash" it may be, but this "upscale" Knightsbridge Italian still generally pleases with its "classy but informal" style and "extremely friendly" service; fans say the "simple" cucina is "beautiful" too. / SW3 2JD; www.scalinionline.com; 11.30 pm, Sun 11 pm; no shorts.

Scandinavian Kitchen W1 £14 ❸❸❸
61 Great Titchfield St 7580 7161 2–1B
"All things Scandi, served with a smile!" – that's the deal at this "busy", "home-from-home-style" joint in Fitzrovia ("part of a Nordic grocery store"); "great coffee" is, naturally, a highlight. / W1W 7PP; www.scandikitchen.co.uk; 7 pm, Sat 6 pm, Sun 4 pm; L only; no Maestro; no booking.

F S A

The Scarsdale W8 £38 ④❸❶
23a Edwardes Sq 7937 1811 7–1D
"Cosy" in winter and with a cute garden for the summer, this "proper" Kensington inn is certainly a "fun destination"; the cuisine is very much "pub food", but it generally hits the spot. / W8 6HE; 10 pm, Sun 9.30 pm.

SCOTT'S W1 £78 ❷❶❶
20 Mount St 7495 7309 3–3A
Richard Caring's "electric" Mayfair A-lister is a "cosmopolitan" all-rounder, offering "sublime" fish and seafood ("London's best", say many), and "seamless" service too, in a "luxurious" and rather "old-fashioned" setting. / W1K 2HE; www.scotts-restaurant.com; 10.30 pm, Sun 10 pm; booking: max 6.

The Sea Cow SE22 £29 ❷❷❸
37 Lordship Ln 8693 3111 1–4D
"Pick your fish, get it battered or grilled, and served with chips or salad", at this "superior" East Dulwich chippy – "you share benches and trestle tables, but it's OK given the value". / SE22 8EW; www.theseacow.co.uk; 11 pm, Sun-Mon 10 pm; closed Mon L; no Amex.

Sea Pebbles HA5 £28 ❷❸④
348-352 Uxbridge Rd 8428 0203 1–1A
"Lovely fish 'n' chips at a good price" – the formula that wins consistent praise for this "cheerful and unpretentious" Hatch End chippy. / HA5 4HR; 9.45 pm; closed Sun; debit cards only; need 8+ to book.

Seafresh SW1 £36 ❸④⑤
80-81 Wilton Rd 7828 0747 2–4B
"For fuss-free eating", fans tip this veteran Pimlico chippy, where the "delicious and well-cooked fish" lives up to its name; all other aspects of the operation, though, are very ordinary. / SW1V 1DL; www.seafresh-dining.com; 10.30 pm; closed Sun; set weekday L £21 (FP), set dinner £22 (FP).

Searcy's Brasserie EC2 £56 ④❸❷
Level 2, Barbican Centre 7588 3008 12–2A
"Minuscule portions" are something of a bugbear for reporters on the Barbican Centre's in-house brasserie; it's still handy for business, though – "watching the sun set over London with clients is always a deal-maker!" / EC2Y 8DS; www.searcys.co.uk; 10.30 pm; closed Sat L & Sun.

The Sea Shell NW1 £42 ❸④⑤
49 Lisson Grove 7224 9000 8–4A
The atmosphere is "cheerless", but this famous old Marylebone chippy is still impressively consistent, and its fish 'n' chips are "really delicious". / NW1 6UH; www.seashellrestaurant.co.uk; 10.30 pm; closed Sun L.

Sedap EC1 £28 ❸❷④
102 Old St 7490 0200 12–1A
A "small" and "pretty basic" Malaysian café, not far from Silicon Roundabout, offering "reliable" food at "modest" prices; "hot dishes should be approached with caution!" / EC1V 9AY; www.sedap.co.uk; 10.30 pm; closed Sat L & Sun L; no Amex; set weekday L £16 (FP).

Serafino W1 £58 ❸❷④
8 Mount St 7629 0544 3–3B
"Great value in W1!"; OK, all things are relative but, right by the Connaught, this café-cum-trattoria is a handy place to know about, and the basement makes a "discreet" choice for a not-too-pricey business lunch. / W1K 3NF; www.finos.co.uk; 10.45 pm; closed Sat L & Sun.

FSA

Seven Park Place SW1 £76 ❷❷❸
7-8 Park Pl 7316 1600 3–4C
Particularly at lunch, this "tranquil", if "fragmented", St James's dining room offers some "excellent value", thanks to William Drabble's "incredible, deeply-flavoured" dishes; on most accounts, dinner's a hit too, but – given the prices – sceptics can find results "uninspired". / SW1A 1LP; www.stjameshotelandclub.com; 10 pm; closed Mon & Sun; set weekday L £41 (FP).

Seven Stars WC2 £29 ④④❷
53 Carey St 7242 8521 2–2D
An "olde-worlde" boozer, behind the Royal Courts of Justice, where the pub grub's "a bit hit 'n' miss", but – if you're lucky – spiced up with "mild insults from landlady Roxy Beaujolais". / WC2A 2JB; 9.30 pm.

Seventeen W11 £42 ❸④❷
17 Notting Hill Gate 7985 0006 6–2B
Despite the "strange location", "weird nightclub décor" and sometimes "hapless" service, this two-year-old Chinese – right on Notting Hill Gate – is worth a try; "the food is decent, and you can't help wanting them to succeed". / W11 3JQ; www.seventeen-london.co.uk; 11.15 pm.

Shaka Zulu NW1 £55 ④④④
Stables Mkt 3376 9911 8–3B
Cecil B DeMille would not be ashamed of the ultra-lavish decor of this African-themed venue, in Camden Town; fans proclaim it a "brilliant" place, but critics find prices "way too high", given the "average" fare, "slow" service and "tacky" ambience. / NW1 8AH; www.shaka-zulu.com; 10 pm.

Shampers W1 £44 ❸❷❷
4 Kingly St 7437 1692 3–2D
Thanks not least to its "terrific owner" Simon (a man who "really knows his wines"), this "cosy" '70s survivor is "a Soho institution"; the food is pretty "decent" too. / W1B 5PE; www.shampers.net; 10.45 pm; closed Sun.

Shanghai E8 £34 ❷④❸
41 Kingsland High St 7254 2878 1–1C
Unless karaoke's your thing, "fantastic, cheap dim sum" is the top reason to seek out this Dalston Chinese; "try to sit at the front, in the bit which used to be a pie 'n' eel shop" – the tiling is impressive. / E8 2JS; www.shanghaidalston.co.uk; 11 pm; no Amex.

Shanghai Blues WC1 £62 ❷④❸
193-197 High Holborn 7404 1668 4–1D
"Brilliant" dim sum is a highlight of this "upmarket" (and "pricey") Holborn fixture, which remains one of central London's best-rated Chineses; it occupies an "intriguing" and "beautiful" site (a former library), although "its sheer size can make it feel slightly subdued". / WC1V 7BD; www.shanghaiblues.co.uk; 11.30 pm.

J SHEEKEY WC2 £69 ❷❶❶
28-34 St Martin's Ct 7240 2565 4–3B
"Gorgeous, understated glamour" and "London's top seafood" again propel this "unstuffy Theatreland legend" to No. 1 in the survey's Top 40; "faultless fish pie" headlines an "outstanding" menu, which is served with "finesse" in a "club-like" series of rather "cramped" rooms. / WC2N 4AL; www.j-sheekey.co.uk; midnight, Sun 11 pm; booking: max 6.

J Sheekey Oyster Bar WC2 £48 ❷❶❶
32-34 St Martin's Ct 7240 2565 4–3B
"Just as good as the main restaurant, but with a bit more zip!"; the more "casual" bar adjoining Theatreland's acclaimed fish veteran offers "the perfect at-counter dining experience"… and "the occasional thespian wolfing down plates of oysters adds to that feeling of being in the very heart of London". / WC2N 4AL; www.j-sheekey.co.uk; midnight, Sun 11 pm; booking: max 3.

Shepherd's SW1 £54 ❸❷❸
Marsham Ct, Marsham St 7834 9552 2–4C
"Beloved" by MPs, businessmen and the Westminster press pack, this "quiet" and "welcoming" dining room has never in recent times had much of culinary reputation – rising survey ratings, though, support fans who say its "traditional British cooking" is "on the up". / SW1P 4LA; www.langansrestaurants.co.uk; 10.45 pm; closed Sat & Sun.

Shilpa W6 £30 ❷❸⑤
206 King St 8741 3127 7–2B
"Outside it just looks like an ordinary café/take-away"… and, inside, this "nondescript" Hammersmith Indian doesn't look any better! – it's "a real bargain", nonetheless, thanks to its "superb Keralan food" at "amazingly low prices". / W6 0RA; www.shilparestaurant.co.uk; 11 pm, Thu-Sat midnight.

The Ship SW18 £46 ❸❸❶
41 Jews Row 8870 9667 10–2B
"Always a safe bet on a balmy summer's evening", this popular and "fun" Thames-side boozer, by Wandsworth Bridge, has numerous attractions, not least a good BBQ, and lots of outside seating. / SW18 1TB; www.theship.co.uk; 10 pm; no booking, Sun L.

Shrimpy's N1 NEW £49 ❸❷❷
King's Cross Filling Station, Good's Way 8880 6111 8–3C
A converted petrol station in the depths of the King's Cross development provides the edgy backdrop to this instantly scene-y two-year-pop-up from the hip Bistrotheque team; we enjoyed our early-days visit, but the fish-heavy menu is certainly no particular bargain. / N1C 4UR; Rated on Editors' visit; www.shrimpys.co.uk.

Siam Central W1 £31 ❸❸❸
14 Charlotte St 7436 7460 2–1C
The name says it all about this 'plain vanilla' Fitzrovia Thai, where food that's "always tasty and reliable" comes in "generous" portions, and at "good prices". / W1T 2LX; 10.45 pm, Sun 10.15 pm.

Sichuan Folk E1 £40 ❷❸⑤
32 Hanbury St 7247 4735 12–2C
"Atmosphere nil, and setting very basic"… but it's the "excellent" Sichuan food – "using so many flavours and spices" – which is the draw to this "cheap" East End Chinese; go easy, though – "peppers and chillis abound!" / E1 6QR; www.sichuan-folk.co.uk; 10.30 pm; no Amex.

Signor Sassi SW1 £67 ④④❸
14 Knightsbridge Grn 7584 2277 5–1D
"Slightly off-beat waiters" add to the "fun", at this tightly-packed and "busy" Knightsbridge trattoria; at the price, though, "shouldn't the food be just a bit better?" / SW1X 7QL; www.signorsassi.co.uk; 11.30 pm, Sun 10.30 pm.

Simplicity SE16 £46 ❸❸❸
1 Tunnel Rd 7232 5174 11–2A
"A wonderful local in restaurant-free Rotherhithe!" – it combines "great home-cooked food" with a surprisingly "lovely" atmosphere too… especially for somewhere "on the ground floor of a block of council flats"! / SE16 4JJ; www.simplicityrestaurants.com; 10.30 pm; closed weekday L; no Amex.

Simpson's Tavern EC3 £37 ④④❶
38 1/2 Ball Ct, Cornhill 7626 9985 9–2C
"School dinners for City types"; "thank goodness places like this still exist", say fans of this Dickensian chophouse – still, for those of an antediluvian disposition, "a guilty pleasure". / EC3V 9DR; www.simpsonstavern.co.uk; 3 pm; L only, closed Sat & Sun.

Simpsons-in-the-Strand WC2 £76 ④④④
100 Strand 7836 9112 4–3D
"It's a great trip down Memory Lane to the days of good old roast beef", say fans of this "historic" Covent Garden temple to "traditional" British fare; others, though, say it's been "ruined" – the best (and "less touristy") option is to go for breakfast, which is "fit for a king". / WC2R 0EW; www.simpsonsinthestrand.co.uk; 10.45 pm, Sun 9 pm; no trainers.

Singapore Garden NW6 £40 ❷❷④
83a Fairfax Rd 7624 8233 8–2A
"A great variety of cuisines from Chinese to Malaysian to Singaporean" – all "very well executed" – draw fans from far and wide to this "smart" Swiss Cottage neighbourhood veteran. / NW6 4DY; www.singaporegarden.co.uk; 11 pm, Fri & Sat 11.30 pm.

(Gallery)
Sketch W1 £70 ⑤⑤④
9 Conduit St 7659 4500 3–2C
"Go for brilliant cocktails and a fun crowd", say fans enthralled by the "amazing" decor of this Mayfair fashionista party scene; even they can find the food "horrid" and "scarily expensive", though, and harsher critics think the whole formula is just "silly". / W1S 2XG; www.sketch.uk.com; 11 pm; D only, closed Sun; booking: max 10.

(Lecture Room)
Sketch W1 £90 ④❸❷
9 Conduit St 7659 4500 3–2C
"Better than urban legend might have it!", say fans of the mega-"opulent" first-floor chamber of this Mayfair palazzo, overseen from afar by Parisian super-chef Pierre Gagnaire; from a low base, its ratings did indeed improve this year, but the bill is still nothing short of "terrifying". / W1S 2XG; www.sketch.uk.com; 10.30 pm; closed Mon, Sat L & Sun; no trainers; booking: max 8.

(The Parlour)
Sketch W1 £61 ④④❸
9 Conduit St 7659 4533 3–2C
Arguably the best bit of this hip Mayfair palazzo – a "fun" spot for "fabulous tea in lovely surroundings". / W1S 2XG; www.sketch.uk.com; 10 pm; closed Sun; no booking.

Skipjacks HA3 £38 ❶❷④
268-270 Streatfield Rd 8204 7554 1–1A
"Unbeatable for variety, freshness and taste!"; this Harrow chippy looks "unassuming", but it's prized by the locals for its "absolute quality every time", and "incredible value for money" too. / HA3 9BY; 10.30 pm; closed Sun.

Skylon
South Bank Centre SE1 **£56** ④④❷
Southbank Centre, Belvedere Rd 7654 7800 2–3D
"A magnificent view of the river", through massive plate-glass windows, is the USP of this "iconic" South Bank dining chamber (plus bar and brasserie); it's certainly handy pre-concert, but otherwise there's a feeling it "doesn't really justify the prices".
/ SE1 8XX; www.skylonrestaurant.co.uk; 10.30 pm, Sun 10 pm; no trainers; SRA-64%.

Slurp **£27** ❸④⑤
104-106 Streatham High Rd, SW16 8677 7786 10–2D
138 Merton Rd, SW19 8543 4141 10–2B
"Stacks of choice and great flavours, at bargain prices" – the attraction of the "better-than-Wagamama" menu on offer at these pan-Asian communal-table canteens, in south London.
/ www.slurprestaurant.co.uk; 11 pm; no Amex.

(Top Floor)
Smiths of Smithfield EC1 **£70** ⑤④④
67-77 Charterhouse St 7251 7950 9–1A
"It's a wonderful space" offering "views across London", but this "overpriced" top-floor steakhouse is increasingly "resting on its laurels"; it's still recommended, though, "for business entertaining".
/ EC1M 6HJ; www.smithsofsmithfield.co.uk; 10.45 pm; closed Sat L & Sun D; booking: max 10.

(Dining Room)
Smiths of Smithfield EC1 **£50** ④④④
67-77 Charterhouse St 7251 7950 9–1A
"Not as bad as people say" but "not as good as it should be" either! – the "lively" first floor of this Smithfield warehouse-conversion does win praise for its "great burgers", but other dishes seem "expensive and mediocre" rather too often for comfort. / EC1A 6HJ; www.smithsofsmithfield.co.uk; 10.45 pm; closed Sat L & Sun; booking: max 12.

(Ground Floor)
Smiths of Smithfield EC1 **£30** ④④❸
67-77 Charterhouse St 7251 7950 9–1A
The "noisy" ground floor of this Smithfield warehouse-conversion remains a key weekend hang-out for a "lovely" brunch; at other times, standards are "so-so". / EC1M 6HJ; www.smithsofsmithfield.co.uk; L only; no bookings.

Sofra **£36** ④④❸
1 St Christopher's Pl, W1 7224 4080 3–1A
18 Shepherd St, W1 7493 3320 3–4B
36 Tavistock St, WC2 7240 3773 4–3D
11 Circus Rd, NW8 7586 9889 8–3A
Seats are "packed-in", and service can be "hit-and-miss"... but most reporters still praise the "decent" and "tasty" fare on offer at these "unchanging" and "good-value" Turkish joints, especially the "tremendous" mezze deals. / www.sofra.co.uk; 11 pm-midnight; set pre theatre £23 (FP).

Soho Japan W1 **£42** ❷❸④
52 Wells St 7323 4661 2–1B
It's "a bit chaotic", and looks like the Irish pub it once was, but this "good-quality" haunt, just north of Oxford Street, can be just the job for those in search of "well-priced sushi and sashimi". / W1T 3PR; www.sohojapan.co.uk; 10.30 pm; closed Sat L & Sun; no Amex; set weekday L £21 (FP).

Soif SW11 NEW £43 ❸❸④

27 Battersea Rise 7223 1112 10–2C

"Bustling and noisy", this Battersea spin-off of Terroirs offers an "impressive range of organic wines" and a "sensibly limited menu" of "rustic" small plates; if it's to be a chip off the old block, though, critics do feel it "needs to up its game". / SW11 1HG; 10 pm; closed Mon L, Tue L, Wed L.

Solly's NW11 £44 ④⑤⑤

146-150 Golders Green Rd 8455 0004 1–1B

"It's often full", but this landmark Golder's Green Israeli (with café/take-away downstairs, restaurant above) risks "pricing itself out of the market"; sometimes "arrogant" service offers little in the way of consolation. / NW11 8HE; 10.30 pm; closed Fri D & Sat L; no Amex.

Somerstown Coffee House NW1 £36 ④❸❸

60 Chalton St 7387 7377 8–3C

"An island of civilisation in a featureless area" – this welcoming boozer, between Euston and St Pancras, offers a 'British tapas' formula nowadays, seemingly with a fair degree of success. / NW1 1HS; www.somerstowncoffeehouse.co.uk; 10 pm.

Sông Quê E2 £33 ❸⑤④

134 Kingsland Rd 7613 3222 12–1B

This "no-frills" Vietnamese canteen, in Shoreditch, has "a long-standing reputation for London's best pho", and is still praised for its "fantastic value"; doubters, though, fear it's "slipping" and now "no better or worse than others nearby". / E2 8DY; 11 pm; no Amex.

Sonny's SW13 £51

94 Church Rd 8748 0393 10–1A

Rebecca Mascarenhas's once-brilliant neighbourhood all-rounder was re-launched in mid-2012, with help from Phil ('The Square') Howard, with a view to giving it the Kitchen W8 treatment; we didn't manage to visit before this guide went to press, but newspaper commentary has been broadly positive. / SW13 0DQ; www.sonnys.co.uk; 10.30 pm, Fri & Sat 11 pm; closed Sun D.

La Sophia W10 £52 ❷❸④

46 Golborne Road 8968 2200 6–1A

"Great Middle Eastern/Mediterranean cooking" (plus a "most surprising" wine list) is helping make quite a name locally for this "romantic" North Kensington yearling. / W10 5PR; www.lasophia.co.uk; 9.30 pm, Fri & Sat 10:30 pm, Sun 9 pm; closed Mon L & Tue L.

Sophie's Steakhouse £52 ④④❸

29-31 Wellington St, WC2 7836 8836 4–3D

311-313 Fulham Rd, SW10 7352 0088 5–3B

These "jolly" and "bustling" hang-outs serve "decent" grills and make a "lively" destination that's "fun in a group" (Chelsea, especially); these days, though, "there are better steakhouses around". / www.sophiessteakhouse.com; SW10 11.45 pm, Sun 11.15 pm; WC2 12.45 am, Sun 11 pm; no booking; set weekday L £30 (FP).

Sotheby's Café W1 £57 ④❷❸

34-35 New Bond St 7293 5077 3–2C

Off the foyer of the famous Mayfair auction house, this classy café is nowadays mostly tipped as "an excellent place for tea"; it used to be touted as a superior lunch venue too, but feedback on this score has been muted of late. / W1A 2AA; www.sothebys.com; L only, closed Sat & Sun; booking: max 8.

Spaniard's Inn NW3 £40 ④④❸
Spaniards Rd, Hampstead Heath 8731 8406 8–1A
"Unique, historic surroundings" add something special to a visit to this famous inn, by Hampstead Heath; more pragmatic attractions include "well-cooked pub grub" and a large garden. / NW3 7JJ; www.thespaniardshampstead.co.uk; 10 pm.

Spianata & Co £11 ❷❷❸
Tooley St, SE1 8616 4662 9–4D
41 Brushfield St, E1 7655 4411 12–2B
20 Holborn Viaduct, EC1 7248 5947 9–2A
17 Blomfield St, EC2 7256 9103 9–2C
73 Watling St, EC4 7236 3666 9–2B
A "favourite" small Italian chain, offering "good panini, pasta and salads", and "fantastic coffee" too; "shame they don't have more eat-in tables!" / www.spianata.com; 3.30 pm; EC3 11 pm; closed Sat & Sun; E1 closed Sat; no credit cards; no booking.

Spice Market
W Hotel London W1 £77 ⑤④④
10 Wardour St 7758 1088 4–3A
"After an amazing experience at Spice Market NYC, we thought we were in for a treat, but the food was poles apart"; how top Big Apple chef J-G Vongerichten has managed to botch his "limp" and "arrogant" Leicester Square outpost quite so badly, it's very hard to say. / W1D 6QF; www.spicemarketlondon.co.uk; 11 pm, Thu-Sat 11.30 pm.

The Spread Eagle SE10 £52 ⑤⑤④
1-2 Stockwell St 8853 2333 1–3D
This "fine" Greenwich tavern is potentially a gorgeous destination, but it put in a very poor year, with too many experiences that were "average-to-poor… with the emphasis on poor" – let's hope a recent report of "a return to form under the new chef" is correct! / SE10 9JN; www.spreadeaglerestaurant.co.uk; 10 pm, Fri & Sat 10.30 pm, Sun 9 pm.

Spuntino W1 £40 ❷❸❷
61 Rupert St no tel 3–2D
"Even waiting for a table makes you feel just a little bit hipper", say fans of Russell Norman's "artfully dishevelled" Soho-meets-NYC joint, where "you can gorge yourself silly on small plates" (sliders, burgers, mac 'n' cheese and so on) at "reasonable prices". / W1D 7PW; www.spuntino.co.uk; 11.30 pm, Sun 10.30 pm.

THE SQUARE W1 £104 ❷❷❸
6-10 Bruton St 7495 7100 3–2C
Phil Howard creates some "serious, world-class fine dining" (if "a bit rich" for some tastes), at this "effortlessly classy" Mayfair dining room; with its "mammoth" wine list, it's one of London's surest bets for client-entertaining"… so the feel is inevitably rather "corporate". / W1J 6PU; www.squarerestaurant.com; 9.45 pm, Sat 10.15 pm, Sun 9.30 pm; closed Sun L; booking: max 8; set weekday L £48 (FP).

Sree Krishna SW17 £27 ❷❷❸
192-194 Tooting High St 8672 4250 10–2C
"The first of the Tooting south Indians, and still going strong after 40 years" – this "friendly" veteran still serves up "authentic" food (with "great dosas" a highlight), at "unbelievably good prices". / SW17 0SF; www.sreekrishna.co.uk; 10.45 pm, Fri & Sat 11.45 pm.

The Standard Grill Standard Hotel W1 NEW
Chiltern St awaiting tel 2–1A
In late-2012, high-profile NYC hotelier André Balazs is to open a Marylebone steakhouse with a dining room modelled on the Meatpacking District original – expect much hype. / W1U 7PA.

Star of India SW5 £48 ❷④❸
154 Old Brompton Rd 7373 2901 5–2B
With its "elegant" cooking and rather "classy" decor, the oldest inhabitant of Earl's Court's 'curry corner' broke the standard curry-house mould many years ago; beware "forgetful" service, especially in the "remote"-feeling upstairs room. / SW5 0BE; www.starofindia.eu; 11.45 pm, Sun 11.15 pm.

Stick & Bowl W8 £22 ❸❷❸
31 Kensington High St 7937 2778 5–1A
In pricey Kensington, this grungy Chinese caff is "always packed", as it's just the job "for a quick and delicious meal that doesn't cost the earth"; "arrive early to grab the best dishes!" / W8 5NP; 10.45 pm; no credit cards; no booking.

Sticks'n'Sushi SW19 NEW £40 ❷❷❷
58 Wimbledon Hill Rd 3141 8800 10–2B
Japan meets, er, Denmark at this "really interesting" new concept – a "well-designed" unit in "downtown Wimbledon", with "bubbly" service, and where the sushi (mainly California-style) and 'sticks' (yakitori) are both "very good". / SW19 7PA; www.sticksnsushi.com.

Sticky Fingers W8 £41 ④④❸
1a Phillimore Gdns 7938 5338 5–1A
A "hit with the kids", this "loud" and "lively" Kensington diner – decked-out with Bill Wyman's Stones memorabilia – is "little-changed in two decades"; it can seem "tired and formulaic", but "so long as you know what to expect, you're unlikely to be disappointed". / W8 7QR; www.stickyfingers.co.uk; 10.45 pm.

STK Steakhouse ME by Meliá London WC2 NEW
336-337 The Strand awaiting tel 4–3C
Opening in late-2012, in a new hotel by Aldwych, this new steakhouse is an outpost of an establishment of the same name in NYC's Meatpacking District. / WC2.

Stock Pot £27 ④❷❸
38 Panton St, SW1 7839 5142 4–4A
273 King's Rd, SW3 7823 3175 5–3C
"Cheap 'n' cheerful is an understatement", when it comes to these "bargain" '60s canteens, which dish up "plain and down-to-earth" scoff at "rock-bottom prices"; OK, it's all a bit "school dinners"… but "beggars can't be choosers". / SW1 11.30 pm, Wed-Sat midnight, Sun 11 pm SW3 10.15 pm, Sun 9.45 pm; no Amex.

Story Deli E2 £33 ❷④❸
3 Redchurch St 819 7352 12–2B
Re-located from the Truman Brewery (but still near Brick Lane), this Bohemian spot still serves "fantastic, thin-crust pizza" … and is still good enough to make it worth risking the sometimes "haphazard" service. / E2 7DJ; www.storydeli.com; 10 pm; no credit cards.

F S A

Strada **£39** ⑤④④
Branches throughout London
"It used to be a notch above the other pizza/pasta chains", but this Italian multiple has "gone off the boil" – its standards are "average across the board nowadays", and notably so too. / www.strada.co.uk; 10.30 pm-11 pm; some booking restrictions apply.

Stringray Café **£28** ④④④
36 Highbury Pk, N5 7354 9309 8–2D
135 Fortress Rd, NW5 7482 4855 8–2B
109 Columbia Rd, E2 7613 1141 12–1C
"Bright" and "really friendly", these Italian diners offer "wholesome" dishes (including pizza) at very "reasonable prices"; the best-known outlet is N5 (near the Arsenal ground). / www.stringraycafe.co.uk; 11 pm; no Amex.

Suda WC2 NEW **£39** ④④❸
23 Slingsby Pl, St Martin's Ct 7240 8010 4–3C
In Covent Garden, a large new (presumably chain-prototype) Thai; the food's "above-average", but the "modern" setting can seem "clinical". / WC2E 9AB; www.suda-thai.com; 10.30 pm, Thu-Sat 11 pm.

Sufi W12 **£30** ❸❷④
70 Askew Rd 8834 4888 7–1B
"Simple Persian food" – "lovely grills" and "beautiful breads" from the kiln in the front window – at "good-value" prices, and "friendly" service too, win consistent praise for this homely Shepherd's Bush fixture. / W12 9BJ; www.sufirestaurant.com; 11 pm.

Suk Saran SW19 **£48** ❸④⑤
29 Wimbledon Hill Rd 8947 9199 10–2B
A high-street Thai, near Wimbledon Station, where the food is often "very good", even if it is a tad "pricey"; no prizes for interior design though. / SW19 7NE; www.sukhogroup.com; 11 pm; booking: max 20.

Sukho Fine Thai Cuisine SW6 **£47** ❶❶④
855 Fulham Rd 7371 7600 10–1B
"Absolutely delicious dishes, bursting with exotic flavours", plus service that's "effective and friendly", again win rave reports for this "brilliant" Thai café, in deepest Fulham; downside? – it's "too cramped". / SW6 5HJ; www.sukhogroup.co.uk; 11 pm.

The Summerhouse W9 **£55** ⑤④❷
60 Blomfield Rd 7286 6752 8–4A
"Fab venue, shame about the food" – sadly the majority view on this "unbeatably-located" canal-side restaurant, in Maida Vale, where fans of the "lovely seafood" menu are drowned out by critics of the "indifferent" cooking and "extortionate" pricing. / W9 2PA; www.summerhousebythewaterway.co.uk; 10.30 pm, Sun 10 pm; Mon-Fri closed D, Sat & Sun open L & D; no Amex.

Sumosan W1 **£78** ❸④❸
26b Albemarle St 7495 5999 3–3C
"Similar in concept to Nobu, but without the pulling power"; this lower-profile, but still "fun" Russian-owned Japanese offers "fresh and wonderful" fusion fare; unfortunately, though, it is priced "for oligarchs and their mistresses". / W1S 4HY; www.sumosan.com; 11.30 pm, Sun 10.30 pm; closed Sat L & Sun L.

Le Suquet SW3 £65 ❸❸④
104 Draycott Ave 7581 1785 5–2C
"The best plâteau de fruits-de-mer this side of the Channel" still features on the menu of this nowadays rather overlooked Gallic stalwart, on a quiet Chelsea corner; fans say it's still "a lovely little place", and it offers particularly good value from the set menu. / SW3 3AE; 11.30 pm; set dinner £36 (FP).

The Surprise SW3 NEW £42 ④❸❷
6 Christchurch Ter 7351 6954 5–3D
A "great renovation" of a characterful old boozer has given the Chelsea set this "lovely", "airy" new rendezvous; on the menu, "British tapas" – an "interesting" idea, but the price per mouthful can be a tad daunting. / SW3 4AJ; www.geronimo-inns.co.uk/thesurprise; 10 pm, Sun 9 pm.

Sushi of Shiori NW1 £48 ❶❶④
144 Drummond St 7388 9962 8–4C
"Amazing sushi in the tiniest of spaces"; this "small but perfectly formed" outfit, near Euston, attracts almost universal praise for its "exquisite" Japanese cuisine; "book ahead". / NW1 2PA; www.sushiofshiori.co.uk; 10 pm; closed Mon & Sun; no Amex.

Sushisamba EC2 £80 ④❷❷
Heron Tower, 110 Bishopsgate 3640 7330 9–2D
On the 38th/39th floors of the Heron Tower, a new indoor/outdoor bar/restaurant complex, with breathtaking views, that looks set to become one of 2013's major talking points, and not just for City folk; our 'day one' visit found enjoyably innovative Japanese/South American fare… but at prices as vertigo-inducing as the location. / EC2N 4AY; Rated on Editors' visit.

Sushi Tetsu EC1 NEW £50 ❶❷❸
12 Jerusalem Pas 3217 0090 9–1A
Just 7 seats! – the former Nobu chef who launched this Clerkenwell hole-in-the-wall in mid-2012 must be pretty confident that his simple and authentic sushi is going to attract a steady following; on the evidence of our early-days visit, his confidence may be justified! / EC1V 4JP; Rated on Editors' visit; www.sushitetsu.co.uk.

Sushi-Say NW2 £42 ❶❶❸
33b Walm Ln 8459 7512 1–1A
This "no-frills", family-run fixture, in the "unlikely setting" of Willesden Green, is "one of the best Japaneses in town"; "sublime" sushi and sashimi are part of the formula that makes it "well worth a hike". / NW2 5SH; 10 pm, Sat 10.30 pm, Sun 9.30 pm; closed Mon, Tue, Wed L, Thu L & Fri L; no Amex.

Sushinho £57 ❸④❷
312-314 King's Rd, SW3 7349 7496 5–3C
9a, Devonshire Sq, EC2 awaiting tel 9–2D NEW
"Great flavour combos, and a really unusual menu" (Brazil-meets-Japan) inspire positive vibes for this sleek Chelsea bar/restaurant; its daunting prices feature in practically all comments, but most reporters still say it's "worth it"; an offshoot opens near Liverpool Street in late-2012. / www.sushinho.com.

The Swan W4 £42 ❸❷❷
119 Acton Ln 8994 8262 7–1A
"Definitely worth a visit"; this Chiswick "backwater" gastroboozer – "a pub that, most importantly, still feels like a pub" – offers "amiable" service, "hearty" seasonal food, "cracking real ale" and a "great garden" too. / W4 5HH; theswanchiswick.co.uk; 10 pm, Fri & Sat 10.30 pm, Sun 10 pm; closed weekday L.

Swan & Edgar NW1 **£38** ④④❷
43 Linhope St 7724 6268 2–1A
A "nicely eccentric" little boozer that makes a good bolt-hole for travellers through Marylebone station – the food's somewhere between "good" and "OK", and it's served with "a wide selection of wines by the glass". / NW1 6HL; www.swanandedgar.co.uk; 10 pm, Sun 9 pm; D only, ex Sun open L & D.

The Swan at the Globe SE1 **£49** ④④❷
21 New Globe Walk 7928 9444 9–3B
"As much for the Thames-view as for the food", this "romantic" room, on the first floor of the South Bank landmark, strikes most reporters as a "surprisingly good place… for what looks like a tourist trap"; not everyone, however, is quite convinced. / SE1 9DT; www.swanattheglobe.co.uk; 9.45 pm, Sun 4.45 pm; closed Sun D.

Sweetings EC4 **£58** ❸❸❷
39 Queen Victoria St 7248 3062 9–3B
"Little-changed since it opened in 1889", this City fish "classic" is certainly "a throwback to a distant era", and – for generations of money-men – a "reliable old friend" that's "always full and always fun"; "arrive early". / EC4N 4SA; www.sweetingsrestaurant.com; 3.30 pm; L only, closed Sat & Sun; no booking.

Taberna Etrusca EC4 **£46** ④④④
9 Bow Churchyard 7248 5552 9–2C
"Didn't this sort of Italian go out with the '70s?" – apparently not, and this City stand-by still does quite a trade, thanks to its charming al fresco tables, and its "service with a smile" too. / EC4M 9DQ; www.etruscarestaurants.com; 10 pm; closed Mon D, Sat & Sun.

The Table SE1 **£42** ④④④
83 Southwark St 7401 2760 9–4B
Part of a fashionable architect's HQ near Southwark Bridge, this trendy canteen inspires slightly mixed views – for most reporters it's a "perfect brunch spot" offering "honest and tasty fare" – for critics, though, it's rather too like a "school dining hall". / SE1 0HX; www.thetablecafe.com; 10.30 pm; closed Mon D & Sun D; SRA-64%.

Taiwan Village SW6 **£34** ❶❶❸
85 Lillie Rd 7381 2900 5–3A
"Don't be put of by the location or outward appearance!" – this "incredible-value" Fulham spot is well worth seeking out for its "exemplary" Chinese/Taiwanese fare, and its "friendly service"; choose the "awesome 'chef's choice' menu" – "the food just keeps coming". / SW6 1UD; www.taiwanvillage.com; 11.30 pm; closed weekday L; booking: max 20.

Tajima Tei EC1 **£35** ❶❸④
9-11 Leather Ln 7404 9665 9–2A
Visit this legal-land veteran – "full of Japanese, and westerners in the know" – and you really feel you "could be in Tokyo"; the sushi is "superb", and the set meals offer "good value" too. / EC1N 7ST; www.tajima-tei.co.uk; 10 pm; closed Sat & Sun; no booking, L.

Talad Thai SW15 **£31** ❸❸⑤
320 Upper Richmond Rd 8246 5791 10–2A
"Definitely no frills" are on offer at this "basic" and "cramped" Formica-tabled Thai canteen, in Putney; folks still love it, though, for its "fresh" and "genuine" scoff at "ultra-inexpensive" prices. / SW15 6TL; www.taladthairestaurant.com; 10.30 pm, Sun 9.30 pm; no Amex.

FSA

Tamarind W1 £76 ❸❸❸

20 Queen St 7629 3561 3–3B

"Still good after so many years", this "sophisticated" Mayfair basement remains "one of the top" nouvelle Indians; though "very expensive" and "a little past its best", it still wins consistent praise for its "delectable" cuisine. / W1J 5PR; www.tamarindrestaurant.com; 10.45 pm, Sun 10.30 pm; closed Sat L; set weekday L £41 (FP).

Tandoori Nights SE22 £35 ❷❷❸

73 Lordship Ln 8299 4077 1–4D

"Easily the best curry-house in the area"; the setting may be "rather cramped", but the "freshly-made" fare on offer at this popular East Dulwich spot "never disappoints". / SE22 8EP; www.tandoorinightsdulwich.co.uk; 11.30pm, Fri & Sat midnight; closed weekday L & Sat L.

Tapas Brindisa £40 ❸④❸

46 Broadwick St, W1 7534 1690 3–2D

18-20 Southwark St, SE1 7357 8880 9–4C

"High-quality, interesting ingredients" betray the Spanish-food-importer origins of these "very buzzy, fun and authentic" (and rather "pricey") tapas bars; Soho is "bright" and modern – the Borough original more traditional, and "always rammed" ("with service sometimes suffering as a result"). / 10.45 pm, Sun 10 pm; W1 booking: max 10.

Tapasia W1 NEW £42 ❸❸④

32 Old Compton St 7287 0213 4–2A

A new, very cramped heart-of-Soho venture (more spacious upstairs) from the Tsunami people; on the evidence of our early-days visit, the ambitious pan-Asian small plates formula (or perhaps its prices) needs tweaking if it's to emulate the success of its parent. / W1D 4TP; Rated on Editors' visit.

Taqueria W11 £34 ❸❷❸

139-143 Westbourne Grove 7229 4734 6–1B

"As close as you'll get to Mexican street food" ("I'm Mexican so trust me!"); this "casual" Notting Hill haunt – with its "fresh" and "reasonably-priced" cuisine, zesty home-made drinks, and "delicious" cocktails – is "a must-visit for Latino aficionados". / W11 2RS; www.taqueria.co.uk; 11 pm, Fri & Sat 11.30 pm, Sun 10.30 pm; no Amex; no booking Fri-Sun.

Taro £32 ❸❸❸

10 Old Compton St, W1 7439 2275 4–2B

61 Brewer St, W1 7734 5826 3–2D

"The ever-smiling Mr Taro greets his clients with enthusiasm", at these "cheek-by-jowl" Soho canteens – "a favourite for filling up cheaply and fast". / www.tarorestaurants.co.uk; 10.30 pm, Sun 9.30 pm; no Amex; Brewer St only small bookings.

Tartine SW3 £44 ❸④⑤

114 Draycott Ave 7589 4981 5–2C

"One of the few affordable places in Chelsea!" – this superior snackery, near Brompton Cross, serves an "excellent variety" of posh open sandwiches; the once-chic setting, though, now feels rather "tired". / SW3 3AE; www.tartine.co.uk; 11.30 pm, Thu-Sat midnight, Sun 10.30 pm.

Tas £34 ④❸❸
22 Bloomsbury St, WC1 7637 4555 2–1C
33 The Cut, SE1 7928 2111 9–4A
72 Borough High St, SE1 7403 7200 9–4C
76 Borough High St, SE1 7403 8557 9–4C
37 Farringdon Rd, EC1 7430 9721 9–1A
"Very reliable" and "inexpensive" food and "good, quick service" too – two prime virtues of these "always-crowded" Turkish bistros; the original, near the Old Vic (with its "gorgeous, plant-filled outdoor space") is a particular hit. / www.tasrestaurant.com; 11.30 pm, Sun 10.30 pm.

Tas Pide SE1 £32 ④❷❷
20-22 New Globe Walk 7928 3300 9–3B
"A very useful and reliable location", by Shakespeare's Globe – this "Turkish pizza place" attracts only positive reports for its cosy style, "generous" cuisine, "friendly" service and "cheap" prices. / SE1 9DR; www.tasrestaurant.com/tas_pide; 11.30 pm, Sun 10.30 pm.

(Rex Whistler)
Tate Britain SW1 £52
Millbank 7887 8825 2–4C
"Delightful Whistler murals" and an "astonishing-value wine list" are the twin high points of this "sumptuously-decorated" gallery dining room; currently closed, it re-opens after a major refurbishment – which will give it an independent entrance from Millbank Gardens – in 2013. / SW1 4RG; www.tate.org.uk; L & afternoon tea only.

(Restaurant, Level 7)
Tate Modern SE1 £46 ④④❷
Bankside 7887 8888 9–3B
"Absolutely spectacular views" of the City, across the Thames, are the reason to seek out the "buzzy" ("slightly clinical") top-floor dining room of the world's most-visited modern art gallery; service is "enthusiastic but overworked", and the food "decent but not exciting". / SE1 9TG; www.tate.org.uk; 9.15 pm; Sun-Thu closed D, Fri & Sat open L & D.

(Café, Level 2)
Tate Modern SE1 £39 ④④❸
Bankside 7401 5014 9–3B
The Tate's ground-floor café has good views (from the window seats) and a striking interior; it's the most "family-friendly" option at the venue, and serves a wide variety of "tasty" snacks and cakes. / SE1 9TG; www.tate.org.uk/modern/eatanddrink; Fri 9.30 pm; L & tea only, ex Fri open L & D.

Taylor St Baristas £15 ❷❸❸
22 Brooks Mews, W1 7629 3163 3–2B
Unit 3 Westminster Hs, Kew Rd, TW9 no tel 1–4A
8 South Colonnade, E14 no tel 11–1C
110 Clifton St, EC2 no tel 12–2B
Unit 3, 125 Old Broad St, EC2 no tel 9–2C
"Epic" coffee ("not for the faint-hearted!") wins support for this growing chain; it is "backed up with wholesome, modern Australian snacks". / EC2M 4TP; www.taylor-st.com; All branches 5 pm; Old Broad ST, Clifton St, W1, E14 closed Sat & Sun; New St closed Sat; TW9 closed Sun.

Tayyabs E1 £28 ❶④❸
83 Fieldgate St 7247 9543 9–2D
"Expect a wait, even if you book", at this "manic" East End canteen, whose "daunting" queues are legendary; the draw? – the very "pinnacle" of London's Pakistani cuisine, with "unbeatable" lamb chops and other "no-frills" scoff, all at "shockingly cheap" prices. / E1 1JU; www.tayyabs.co.uk; 11.30 pm.

Telegraph SW15 £39 ④④❷
Telegraph Rd 8788 2011 10–2A
"Accurately describing itself as a 'country pub in London'", this "spacious" Putney Heath boozer has no great culinary ambitions, but is "generally a good all-rounder". / SW15 3TU; www.thetelegraphputney.co.uk; 9 pm, Fri & Sat 9.30 pm.

Tempo W1 £61 ❸④④
54 Curzon St 7629 2742 3–3B
Henry Togna's low-key Mayfair haunt offers an "unusual and enjoyable take on Italian cuisine" which wins over most reporters, even if "it can work out expensive"; hidden-away upstairs, there's a locals' secret bar. / W1J 8PG; www.tempomayfair.co.uk; 10.30 pm; closed Sat L & Sun.

The 10 Cases WC2 NEW £52 ④❶❷
16 Endell St 836 6801 4–2C
It's a "top concept", say fans of this "cramped" Covent Garden newcomer – an "easy-going" place with "cheery" staff and a "quirky" wine offer; views on the food, though, range from "spot-on" to "a bit disappointing". / WC2H 9BD; www.the10cases.co.uk; 11 pm; closed Sun.

10 Greek Street W1 NEW £44 ❷❷❷
10 Greek St 7734 4677 4–2A
"Simple and superb!" – this "squeezed" newcomer is hailed as "a great addition to the Soho scene", thanks to its "clean-flavoured Mediterranean dishes", its "passionate" staff and its "vital" atmosphere, plus an "enthusiast's wine list at fair prices". / W1D 4DH; www.10greekstreet.com; 11.30 pm; closed Sun.

Tendido Cero SW5 £40 ❸❸❷
174 Old Brompton Rd 7370 3685 5–2B
"Designer" tapas and an "always-busy and buzzy" ambience combine to make Cambio de Tercio's younger sibling a good venue for "a really fun night out". / SW5 0BA; www.cambiodetercio.co.uk; 11 pm.

Tendido Cuatro SW6 £40 ❸❷❷
108-110 New King's Rd 7371 5147 10–1B
"A fun restaurant for dinner with friends"; this Fulham sibling to Cambio de Tercio may not quite be at the culinary cutting edge, but its "delicious tapas" are "consistently good". / SW6 4LY; www.cambiodetercio.co.uk; 11 pm.

Tentazioni SE1 £49 ❷❷❸
2 Mill St 7394 5248 11–2A
"People tend to forget this little gem, near Shad Thames!" – seek it out, though, and this "long-term-favourite" Italian offers a "sophisticated" overall experience; only downside – a rather "corridor-like" layout. / SE1 2BD; www.tentazioni.co.uk; 10.45 pm; closed Sat L & Sun.

TERROIRS WC2 £46 ❸❸❷
5 William IV St 7036 0660 4–4C
"A welcome corner of France", near Charing Cross; with its "awesome" (if sometimes "weird") biodynamique wines and its "interestingly earthy" tapas and charcuterie, this "casual and engaging" bistro has won a gigantic following. / WC2N 4DW; www.terroirswinebar.com; 11 pm; closed Sun.

Texture W1 £90 ❷❷❸
34 Portman St 7224 0028 2–2A
"Exciting Scandinavian flavours and textures" (no butter or cream, except in puds) define Agnar Sverrisson's "adventurous" cuisine, at this "upscale yet casual" venture, off Oxford Street – a "sleek" sort of place that's "lovely to look at, but a bit cold". / W1H 7BY; www.texture-restaurant.co.uk; 10.30 pm; closed Mon & Sun; set weekday L £53 (FP).

Thai Corner Café SE22 £21 ❸❸❸
44 North Cross Rd 8299 4041 1–4D
"Cramped" but "fun", this "reassuringly busy" BYO East Dulwich local has been a notably "consistent" performer of late, and fans applaud its "amazing value". / SE22 9EU; www.thaicornercafe.co.uk; 10.30 pm; closed Mon L; no credit cards.

Thai Garden SW11 £30 ❸④④
58 Battersea Rise 7738 0380 10–2C
A "genuinely friendly" stalwart, which "continues to hold its own against the trendier places in nearby Clapham Junction", offering dependable food that's fairly-priced. / SW11 1EG; www.thaigarden.co.uk; 10.30 pm; D only; set dinner £17 (FP).

Thai Pot WC2 £37 ④❸❸
1 Bedfordbury 7379 4580 4–4C
Still, for some reporters, "the go-to Thai in central London", this cramped operation, tucked-away behind the Coliseum, may offer "no surprises on the menu front", but it's great "for a pre-theatre supper". / WC2N 4BP; www.thaipot.biz; 11 pm; closed Sun.

Thai Square £36 ④④❸
21-24 Cockspur St, SW1 7839 4000 2–3C
27-28 St Annes Ct, W1 7287 2000 3–1D
5 Princess St, W1 7499 3333 3–1C
148 The Strand, WC2 7497 0904 2–2D
166-170 Shaftesbury Ave, WC2 7836 7600 4–1B
229-230 Strand, WC2 7353 6980 2–2D
19 Exhibition Rd, SW7 7584 8359 5–2C
347-349 Upper St, N1 7704 2000 8–3D
2-4 Lower Richmond Rd, SW15 8780 1811 10–1A
136-138 Minories, EC3 7680 1111 9–3D
1-7 Great St Thomas Apostle, EC4 7329 0001 9–3B
"A stunning Thames-side location" (SW15) is the only outstanding feature of this "no-thrills Thai chain" – even fans may concede that, generally speaking, it's "not that special". / www.thaisquare.net; 10 pm-11.30 pm; SW1 Fri & Sat 1 am; EC3, EC4 & St Annes Ct closed Sat & Sun, Strand branches and Princess St closed Sun.

Thali SW5 £43 ❷❷④
166 Old Brompton Rd 7373 2626 5–2B
"A world away from most local Indians", this "cosy" (but rather corridor-like) Earl's Court spot wins universal praise for its "really interesting" dishes – "venison bhuna anyone?" / SW5 0BA; www.thali.uk.com; 11.30 pm, Sun 10.30 pm; closed Sun L.

The Thatched House W6 £38 ④❷❸
115 Dalling Rd 8748 6174 7–1B
The team from Wandsworth's Ship have taken over at this attractive Hammersmith gastropub, with cute garden; genuine service was the high point of our early-days visit, but its mid-ranking food seemed no great improvement on the previous regime's. / W6 0ET; Rated on Editors' visit; www.thatchedhouse.com.

Theo Randall
InterContinental Hotel W1 £83 ❶❷④
1 Hamilton Pl 7318 8747 3–4A
"Vying for a place as London's best Italian", this "seriously good" operation, right by Hyde Park Corner attracts a hymn of praise for this somewhat under-sung chef; the only real fault is its "austere" windowless setting. / W1J 7QY; www.theorandall.com; 11.15 pm; closed Sat L & Sun.

34 W1 £74 ④❷❷
34 Grosvenor Sq 3350 3434 3–2A
Richard Caring's "dressy" new grill-house – "a canteen for Mayfair tycoons" – is "a very slick operation" indeed; its "enormously expensive" steaks and so on have, however, yet to rival the standard of the fish at its nearby sibling Scott's – "nothing's wrong, it's just that, at these prices, everything should be better". / W1K 2HD; www.34-restaurant.co.uk; 10.30 pm.

Thirty Six
Duke's Hotel SW1 NEW £88 ❷❷❸
35-36 Saint James's Pl 7491 4840 3–4C
"Still a largely undiscovered gem", this "quiet" and "discreet" St James's basement newcomer offers food that's not just "clever", but "well-priced" too, plus a "short but well-chosen" wine list; service, though, can be a touch "forgetful". / SW1A 1NY; www.dukeshotel.com.

The Thomas Cubitt SW1 £58 ❷❷❷
44 Elizabeth St 7730 6060 2–4A
"An all-round winning formula!"; this "always-buzzing" Belgravia linchpin is one of London's most popular gastropubs, be it for grazing in the ("ear-blastingly noisy") bar, or having "posh nosh" in the "shabby-chic" dining room upstairs. / SW1W 9PA; www.thethomascubitt.co.uk; 10 pm; closed Sat L & Sun D; booking only in restaurant; SRA-62%.

3 South Place
South Place Hotel EC2 NEW
3 South Pl awaiting tel 12–2A
The D&D Group's first venture into hotels opens, near Liverpool Street, in late-2012; the ground-floor main restaurant promises all-day dining. / EC2M 2AF; www.southplacehotel.com.

Tian Fu W12 £32 ❷⑤⑤
37 Bulwer St 8740 4546 7–1C
"The key is to be adventurous and open-minded", if you check out the "hot and numbing" Sichuan cuisine on offer at this otherwise very ordinary-seeming Chinese, near Westfield. / W12 8AR; 11 pm; no Amex.

tibits W1 £33 ❸④④
12-14 Heddon St 7758 4110 3–2C
"The help-yourself veggie buffet is always a delight", say fans of this "clever" and "convenient" operation – the London outpost of a delightfully precise Swiss chain-concept, off Regent Street (where you pay by weight of food consumed). / W1B 4DA; www.tibits.co.uk; 11.30 pm, Sun 10 pm; no Amex; Only bookings for 8+; SRA-61%.

Tierra Peru N1 NEW £42 ❷❷④

164 Essex Rd 7354 5586 8–3D

"Friendly" and "down-to-earth", this new Islington Peruvian has become an "instant favourite", thanks to its "enticingly exotic" dishes. / N1 8LY; www.tierraperu.co.uk; 11 pm; closed weekday L.

Timo W8 £54 ④④④

343 Kensington High St 7603 3888 7–1D

A "high-class" Kensington-fringe Italian, with "a local feel to it", and a reputation for "consistently imaginative cooking"; the volume of feedback is shrinking, though, as complaints rise that "prices now far exceed the quality". / W8 6NW; www.timorestaurant.net; 11 pm; closed Sun; set dinner £35 (FP).

Tinello SW1 £39 ❷❶❶

87 Pimlico Rd 7730 3663 5–2D

In its second year of operation, this "sophisticated" Locatelli-backed Pimlico spot continues to be a big hit, thanks to its "fine", "traditional-at-heart" Tuscan cuisine and "flawless" service; for a vocal minority, though, the place "lacks wow". / SW1W 8PH; www.tinello.co.uk; 10.30 pm; closed Sun.

Toff's N10 £35 ❷❷④

38 Muswell Hill Broadway 8883 8656 1–1B

"Terrific fish 'n' chips", served with "old-fashioned panache", in a "comfy dining room" – that's the unchanging appeal of this "crowded and noisy" Muswell Hill veteran; BYO. / N10 3RT; www.toffsfish.co.uk; 10 pm; closed Sun; set weekday L £18 (FP).

Toku
Japan Centre SW1 £38 ❷❷❷

16 Regent St 3405 1246 3–3D

"Tastes as tasted in Japan" help make this cultural-centre café a hit with all who comment on it; it makes a good West End option for "grabbing a quick lunch". / SW1Y 4PH; 9.45 pm, Sun 8.45 pm; no Amex; no booking Sat.

Tokyo Diner WC2 £26 ④❸④

2 Newport Pl 7287 8777 4–3B

"Reliable", "edible", and "cheap" – this no-nonsense canteen, on the edge of Chinatown, is hard to beat for a "quick noodle-fix", or for some "perfectly good sushi". / WC2H 7JJ; www.tokyodiner.com; 11.30 pm; no Amex; no booking, Fri & Sat; set weekday L £11 (FP).

Tom Aikens SW3 £78 ❷❷④

43 Elystan St 7584 2003 5–2C

"Loving the new look!" – Tom Aikens's relaunch of his Chelsea HQ has revived enthusiasm for his "creative and fabulous" cuisine, and the whole operation works better in a more "casual" style; prices are still "eye-watering", though, and critics can still find the food to be rather on the "fussy" side. / SW3 3NT; www.tomaikens.co.uk; 10.45 pm; closed Sat L & Sun; booking: max 8.

Tom Ilic SW8 £50 ❶❷④

123 Queenstown Rd 7622 0555 10–1C

Tom Ilic's Battersea fixture "deserves to be discovered again and again", say fans of his "marvellous" cuisine, which is full of "bold" flavours (and "Mon-Thu is amazing value, with 50% off"); now if he could just sort the decor out… / SW8 3RH; www.tomilic.com; 10 pm; closed Mon, Tue L & Sun D.

Tom's Deli W11 £33 ❸❸❷
226 Westbourne Grove 7221 8818 6–1B
Tom Conran's Notting Hill deli doesn't inspire the excitement it once did as a brunch Mecca; fans insist, though, that it "still does the best eggs Benedict". / W11 2RH; www.tomsdeli.co.uk; 5.30 pm; L only; no Amex; no booking.

Tom's Kitchen SW3 £63 ④⑤④
27 Cale St 7349 0202 5–2C
Fans do tip Tom Aikens's Chelsea hang-out as a "cool brunch spot"; otherwise, though, it's an "expensive" destination for food that's "bland and boring" rather too often for comfort, and where the service is sometimes "unspeakably awful" too. / SW3 3QP; www.tomskitchen.co.uk; 10.45 pm.

Tom's Terrace Somerset House WC2 £52 ⑤⑤④
150 Strand 7845 4646 2–2D
"Such a waste of a beautiful venue"; Tom Aikens's "Ibiza-style" tented restaurant, on a terrace of Somerset House, offers "a dull menu, realised to a mediocre standard" – "we'd be better off with a Wetherspoons!" / WC2R 1LA; www.tomskitchen.co.uk/somersethouse; 9.30 pm, Sun 4 pm; closed Sun D; no booking.

Tonkotsu W1 NEW £30 ❸❷④
63 Dean St 7437 0071 4–2A
A somewhat cramped and industrial-style Soho noodle-newcomer, whose genuine ramen dishes appear – on an initial inspection – to be a cut above those at that large chain beginning with 'W'. / W1D 4QG; Rated on Editors' visit; www.tonkotsu.co.uk; 10.30 pm, Sun 10 pm.

Tortilla £16 ④④④
6 Market Place, W1 7637 2800 3–1C
6a, King St, W6 8741 7959 7–2C
13 Islington High St, N1 7833 3103 8–3D
106 Southwark St, SE1 7620 0285 9–4B
18 North Colonnade, E14 7719 9160 11–1C
28 Leadenhall Mkt, EC3 7929 7837 9–2D
"Burritos packed to bursting point" provide the affordable fuel at these "cheap 'n' cheerful" Cal-Mex pit stops. / www.tortilla.co.uk; W1 & N1 11 pm, Sun 9 pm, SE1 & E14 9 pm, EC3 7 pm, E14 Sun 7 pm; SE1 & EC3 closed Sat & Sun, N1 closed sun; no Amex.

Tosa W6 £40 ❷④④
332 King St 8748 0002 7–2B
"A great local Japanese"; this Hammersmith café may be a "cramped" place with "straightforward" decor, but wins universal praise for its "beautiful" yakitori and "other excellent dishes", all at very "reasonable prices". / W6 0RR; www.tosauk.com; 10.30 pm; set weekday L £23 (FP).

The Trafalgar Tavern SE10 £47 ⑤⑤④
28 Park Row 8858 2909 1–3D
"Beautifully-located" by the Thames, a "wonderful" and historic Greenwich inn that peddles "middling" food ("simple options are best") at "eye-watering" prices. / SE10 9NW; www.trafalgartavern.co.uk; 10 pm; closed Sun D; no Amex.

Tramontana Brindisa EC2 NEW
152-154 Curtain Rd awaiting tel 12–1B
The fourth restaurant in the Tapas Brindisa empire, opening on the former Shoreditch site of Saf (RIP) as this guide goes to press. / EC2A 3AT.

TRINITY SW4 £66 ➊➊➋

4 The Polygon 7622 1199 10–2D

"A miracle" for Clapham; Adam Byatt's "un-sung star" ("why no Michelin recognition?"), in "a leafy corner of the old town", is "a serious rival to Chez Bruce", turning out "exceptionally interesting" dishes in a "very smart" (but still "neighbourhood") setting. / SW4 0JG; www.trinityrestaurant.co.uk; 10.30 pm; closed Mon L & Sun D.

Triphal SW18 £30 ➋➌④

201 Replingham Rd 8870 0188 10–2B

On the Southfields site that long ago was Sarkhels, this "superb" curry house is, say some locals, "every bit as good" – the menu's "not very large", but its "interesting and unusual" dishes "rarely disappoint". / SW18 5LY; www.triphalindianrestaurant.com; 10 pm; closed Mon; no Amex.

Trishna W1 £51 ➋➌➌

15-17 Blandford St 7935 5624 2–1A

For "foodie fireworks", it's hard to beat the "stunning top-class Indian grub" at this "innovative" Marylebone outpost of the famous Mumbai fish restaurant; for some tastes, the cramped setting still "lacks atmosphere", though, and service can be "patchy". / W1U 3DG; www.trishnalondon.com; 10.45 pm, Sun 9.45 pm; set weekday L £31 (FP).

Les Trois Garçons E1 £70 ➌➌➊

1 Club Row 7613 1924 12–1C

"Brilliant stuffed-animals-in-tiaras and hanging handbags" create "plenty of talking points" for visitors to this "wacky and eclectic" East End pub-conversion; the Gallic fare comes at high prices, but most reporters think that "for a special treat, it's worth it". / E1 6JX; www.lestroisgarcons.com; 10.30 pm; closed Sat L & Sun; need credit card to book £25 deposit.

Trojka NW1 £29 ④④④

101 Regent's Park Rd 7483 3765 8–2B

"More café than restaurant", this Bohemian Primrose Hill haunt dishes up "good and comforting Russian grub" (including some "excellent blinis and pancakes"); "bargain set lunch". / NW1 8UR; www.trojka.co.uk; 10.30 pm; no Amex.

LA TROMPETTE W4 £63 ➊➊➋

5-7 Devonshire Rd 8747 1836 7–2A

"Almost impossible to criticise!"; this "plush" Chiswick all-rounder rivals its sibling Chez Bruce with its "flawless" cuisine, and "consummately professional" staff – not least an "outstanding" sommelier who presides over a "spectacular and formidable" list; OK, there's one gripe – it's a little "tightly-packed". / W4 2EU; www.latrompette.co.uk; 10.30 pm, Sun 9.30 pm; set always available £32 (FP).

Le Troquet SW10 NEW £43 ➋④④

430 King's Rd 7351 5939 5–3B

The old-style 'rustique' décor ("could have been transported from a French village") doesn't delight everyone, but this "friendly" new basement bistro, at World's End, pleases most reporters with its "well-cooked" dishes. / SW10 0LJ; www.letroquet.co.uk; 10.30 pm; closed Mon & Tue.

Troubadour SW5 £42 ④➌➊

263-267 Old Brompton Rd 7370 1434 5–3A

To fans, this brilliantly "Bohemian and relaxed" Earl's Court veteran is still "always special"; critics find the formula a bit "tired" nowadays, but breakfast in the garden is an undoubted "treat". / SW5 9JA; www.troubadour.co.uk; 11 pm.

Truc Vert W1 £55 ❸❸❸
42 North Audley St 7491 9988 3–2A
"Continental in feel", this "spacious" and surprisingly rustic deli/bistro makes a very "convenient" Mayfair destination; "a hedgie favourite for a speedy business lunch", it also does a popular line in "tasty breakfasts". / W1K 6ZR; www.trucvert.co.uk; 10 pm; closed Sun D.

Trullo N1 £45 ❷❷❸
300-302 St Paul's Rd 7226 2733 8–2D
"Amazing rustic Italian food" and "passionate" service have quickly carved out a huge name for Jordan Trullo's Highbury yearling, and it can be "hard to get a table"; critics do wonder if it's a touch "over-rated", though, and the setting is "cosy" to a fault. / N1 2LH; www.trullorestaurant.com; 10.30 pm; closed Sun D.

Tsunami £48 ❷❷❸
93 Charlotte St, W1 7637 0050 2–1C
5-7 Voltaire Rd, SW4 7978 1610 10–1D
"The best black cod in London!" – some would argue the best Japanese food in London full stop – is to be found at this "magnificent" and "sophisticated" (if "crowded") fusion-venue, hidden-away in Clapham; similar – but less ecstatic – praise for its Fitzrovia spin-off. / www.tsunamirestaurant.co.uk; SW4 10.30 pm, Fri & Sat 11 pm, Sun 9.30 pm; W1 11 pm; SW4 closed Mon - Fri L; W1 closed Sat L and Sun; SW4 no Amex.

Tsuru £29 ❸❸④
4 Canvey St, SE1 7928 2228 9–4B
201 Bishopsgate, EC2 7377 1166 12–2B
10 Queen St, EC4 7248 1525 9–2B
"Authentic food at reasonable prices" wins a big thumbs-up for these "very good Japanese locals", in the City and on the South Bank. / www.tsuru-sushi.co.uk; EC2 9 pm; SE1 9 pm, Sat 7 pm, EC4 10 pm; EC2 & EC4 closed Sat & Sun, SE1 closed Sun and Mon D, EC2 closed Mon D; no booking L.

28-50 £50 ❸❷❷
15-17 Marylebone Ln, W1 7486 7922 3–1A NEW
140 Fetter Ln, EC4 7242 8877 9–2A
A "stunning" and "keenly-priced" wine list – with "decent" food playing an honourable supporting role – has made a big name for this "cramped" and "inauspicious" basement, just off Fleet Street; a Marylebone offshoot opened in mid-2012. / www.2850.co.uk; EC4 9.30 pm; W1 Mon-Wed 10 pm, Thu-Sat 10.30 pm, Sun 9.30 pm; EC4 closed Sat-Sun.

2 Amici SW1 £46 ④❸④
48a Rochester Rw 7976 5660 2–4C
In under-provided Westminster, this "neighbourhood Italian" is a "friendly" sort of place, where "good home-made pasta" is a highlight; results can be a bit up-and-down, though, and the setting is "cramped" and "dated". / SW1P 1JU; www.2amici.org; 11 pm; closed Sat L & Sun.

Two Brothers N3 £38 ❸④④
297-303 Regent's Park Rd 8346 0469 1–1B
"Lovely fish 'n' chips" still inspire many very positive reviews for this Finchley institution, where "you queue for a table at busy times"; even fans can find the interior "dreary" however, and sceptics feel it's "very ordinary – "why do people rave?" / N3 1DP; www.twobrothers.co.uk; 10 pm, Sun 8 pm; closed Mon.

202

Nicole Farhi W11 £50 ④❷❸
202 Westbourne Grove 7727 2722 6–1B
Want to hang with the "trendy crowd enjoying a great breakfast" (or light lunch)? – head for this "lively and buzzy" fashion store-cum-bistro, in the heart of Notting Hill. / W11 2RH; 10 pm; closed Mon D & Sun D; only D.

2 Veneti W1 £41 ❸❷❸
10 Wigmore St 7637 0789 3–1B
"Helpful and extremely friendly" staff set the tone at this "comfortable" (but slightly "functional") Italian, near the Wigmore Hall; fans hail the "classy Venetian cooking" as "often very good", but not everyone is convinced. / W1U 2RD; www.2veneti.com; 10.30 pm, Sat 11 pm; closed Sat L & Sun.

Uli W11 £38 ❷❶❷
16 All Saints Rd 7727 7511 6–1B
"Michael makes everyone feel special", at this "lovely, small, homely Asian", discreetly tucked-away in Notting Hill – a "perfect neighbourhood spot", offering "excellent" chow at extremely "good-value" prices. / W11 1HH; www.uli-oriental.co.uk; 10.30 pm; D only, closed Sun; no Amex.

Umu W1 £95 ❷❸❷
14-16 Bruton Pl 7499 8881 3–2C
Marlon Abela's "intimate" Mayfair spot, hidden-away in a cute mews, offers "truly authentic" Kyoto cuisine, to "outstandingly memorable" effect – despite the "ridiculous" prices, this place has a realistic claim to being "London's best Japanese". / W1J 6LX; www.umurestaurant.com; 11 pm; closed Sat L & Sun; no trainers; booking: max 14.

The Union Café W1 £50 ❸④④
96 Marylebone Ln 7486 4860 3–1A
"Low mark-up wine" adds spark to this rather "basic" venue, near Marylebone High Street; even fans concede it's "not very exciting", but they praise it as a "safe", "reliable" and "relaxed" destination nonetheless. / W1U 2QA; www.brinkleys.com; 11 pm; closed Sun D.

Union Jacks £40 ④❸④
4 Central St Giles Piazza, WC2 3597 7888 4–1B NEW
57 The Market, WC2 awaiting tel 4–3D NEW
217-221 Chiswick High Rd, W4 3617 9988 7–2A NEW
"Basically, meat 'n' two veg on a pizza!"; Jamie O's new British flatbread-concept splits opinion into two camps – fans say it's a "spot-on idea that shows Jamie really 'gets' families", whereas critics say the food's "bizarre", and the whole set-up "contrived". / www.unionjacksrestaurants.com; 11 pm, Sun 10.30 pm.

Union Street Café SE1
Harling Hs, Union St awaiting tel 9–4B
Gordon-Ramsay-goes-Southwark-casual – the promise of this very long-awaited, two-floor, 250-seater, finally set to open in late-2012. / SE1 0BS.

Upstairs Bar SW2 £49 ❷❶❶
89b Acre Ln (door on Branksome Rd) 7733 8855 10–2D
"As soon as you ring the bell, you know it's all going to be OK" – this "hidden-away" and "romantic" Brixton gem is a tiny operation, offering "very capable" Gallic cooking and "warm" service too, and all at prices that are "a snip!" / SW2 5TN; www.upstairslondon.com; 9.30 pm, Thu-Sat 10.30 pm; D only, closed Mon & Sun.

FSA

Le Vacherin W4 £52 ❸❷❷
76-77 South Pde 8742 2121 7–1A
"It's an absolute French classic", say fans of Malcolm John's bistro, on the fringe of Chiswick; the menu is a little too "unchanging" for some tastes, though, and the odd critic finds it "an average all-round performance". / W4 5LF; www.levacherin.co.uk; 9.45 pm, Fri & Sat 10.45 pm; closed Mon L.

Vanilla Black EC4 £50 ❸❷❸
17-18 Tooks Ct 7242 2622 9–2A
"Miles away from typical meat-free fare" – this Chancery Lane three-year-old again won praise for its "gourmet" cuisine, "helpful" staff and "tranquil" setting; critics, though, can still find the result "underwhelming". / EC4A 1LB; www.vanillablack.co.uk; 10 pm; closed Sat L & Sun.

Vapiano W1 £25 ❸❸❸
19-21 Great Portland St 7268 0080 3–1C
"Well worth the self-service pain!" – this "efficient" Continental-style food court is "great for a quick cheap eat" near Oxford Circus, thanks to the consistent quality of its "fresh and tasty" pizza, pasta and salads. / W1W 8QB; www.vapiano.co.uk; 11 pm, Sun 10 pm.

Vasco & Piero's Pavilion W1 £58 ❷❷④
15 Poland St 7437 8774 3–1D
"I walked past this restaurant for four years, and at last I tried it!"; this "unassuming"-looking Soho veteran is indeed easy to overlook, but it's well worth discovering for its "very genuinely welcoming" staff and "marvellous, authentically Italian cooking". / W1F 8QE; www.vascosfood.com; 10.30 pm; closed Sat L & Sun.

Veeraswamy W1 £65 ❸❸❷
Victory Hs, 99-101 Regent St 7734 1401 3–3D
With its "colourful" and "beautiful" contemporary decor, London's oldest Indian, near Piccadilly Circus, is a far cry from the tourist-trap you might fear; its "top-end" cuisine is often "amazing" too, though prices do seem to have gone "through the roof" of late. / W1B 4RS; www.realindianfood.com; 10.30 pm, Sun 10 pm; booking: max 12.

El Vergel SE1 £32 ❷❸❷
132 Webber St 7401 2308 9–4B
"A joy!"; this "thriving" Latino lunch-canteen, in Borough, is so much "better than any of the soulless chains that pollute SE1"; the new premises are "a bit less charming than the old", but at least it's now "easier to get a table". / SE1 0QL; www.elvergel.co.uk; 2.45pm, Sat-Sun 3.45 pm; closed D, closed Sun; no Amex.

Verru W1 £51 ❷❸❸
69 Marylebone Ln 7935 0858 2–1A
"Small and cramped" it may be, but this "lovely" Marylebone yearling is making a big name for its "interesting" menu ("with Scandinavian overtones"); service does occasionally hit the wrong note, but otherwise "everything is pretty much faultless" – the value of the set lunch particularly stands out. / W1U 2PH; www.verru.co.uk; 10.30 pm; set weekday L £33 (FP).

Verta SW11 £58 ❸❸④
Bridges Court Rd 7801 3500 10–1C
The food at this "corporate" hotel dining room is, say fans, "surprisingly good"; "why is it always empty?" – perhaps a location convenient only by chopper (50 ft from the Battersea Heliport) has something to do with it? / SW11 3RP; www.hotelverta.com; 10.30 pm, Sun 10 pm; set weekday L £36 (FP), set Sun L £38 (FP).

Vertigo 42
Tower 42 EC2 **£64** ④④❷
25 Old Broad St 7877 7842 9–2C
The stunning panorama creates a "romantic" backdrop to a meal at this 42nd-floor City eyrie – "otherwise it struggles to live up to the price tag". / EC2N 1HQ; www.vertigo42.co.uk; 10.45 pm; closed Sat L & Sun; no shorts; booking essential.

Viajante E2 **£85** ❷❷❸
Patriot Sq 7871 0461 1–2D
"Blows the Fat Duck away!", say fans of Nuno Mendes's slightly "hushed" Bethnal Green venture, where the "amazing modern-molecular" dishes offer an "orgasmic" experience; even the most ardent supporters, though, can feel "some dishes work better than others". / E2 9NF; www.viajante.co.uk; 9.30 pm; Mon-Thu D only, Fri-Sun open L & D; set weekday L £51 (FP).

Il Vicolo SW1 **£48** ④④④
3-4 Crown Passage 7839 3960 3–4D
Hidden-away in a St James's alley, this long-established Sicilian remains quite a local "lunchtime favourite"; by night, it's more in the "good-but-pricey" category, and can be "quiet". / SW1Y 6PP; 10 pm; closed Sat L & Sun.

The Victoria SW14 **£45** ❷❸❷
10 West Temple 8876 4238 10–2A
"Excellently located" near Richmond Park, and with a "lovely dining conservatory", this upscale East Sheen gastropub makes "a most enjoyable and relaxed rendezvous"; with its "emphasis on seasonal fare", owner Paul Merrett's cooking "has been on a high this year" too. / SW14 7RT; www.thevictoria.net; 10 pm, Sat 10 pm; closed Sun D; no Amex.

Viet W1 **£20** ❸④④
34 Greek St 7494 9888 4–3A
"But for the weather, you could be in Saigon!" – such are the "authentic" charms of this "cramped" Soho Vietnamese, where "lovely soups" are a highlight; "be prepared to queue". / W1D 5DJ; 10.30 pm, Fri 11 pm; closed Sun; no Amex; no booking.

Viet Garden N1 **£36** ❸④⑤
207 Liverpool Rd 7700 6040 8–2D
"Stick to the Vietnamese-style dishes", and you can enjoy some "super" and "fresh" flavours at this "funny little place", near Angel (which "seems to get shabbier every year"); the Chinese-style options, though, can be "very average". / N1 1LX; www.vietgarden.co.uk; 11 pm, Sat 11.30 pm; no Amex.

Viet Grill E2 **£37** ❸④❸
58 Kingsland Rd 7739 6686 12–1B
"Extremely busy and bustling", this Shoreditch Vietnamese has made a big name for its "outstanding" scoff; these days, though, "it's no longer such good value for money", and quite a few meals of late have been "disappointing". / E2 8DP; www.vietnamesekitchen.co.uk; 11 pm, Fri & Sat 11.30 pm, Sun 10.30 pm.

Viet Hoa E2 **£32** ④⑤④
70-72 Kingsland Rd 7729 8293 12–1B
"Either they've lost the plot, or they've realised it doesn't matter what you give the hordes before they go clubbing..." – this "busy" Shoreditch Vietnamese is still sometimes praised for its "amazing value", but has "gone downhill since its refurbishment" ("even the atmosphere!"). / E2 8DP; www.viethoarestaurant.co.uk; 11.30 pm.

FSA

Vijay NW6 £30 ❷❷④
49 Willesden Ln 7328 1087 1–1B
No-one cares that this "no-frills" Kilburn "institution" (est 1964) is "so dull" and "dingy" – it's still "packed most nights", thanks to its "gracious" service and "heavenly" south Indian food, all at "very competitive" prices. / NW6 7RF; www.vijayrestaurant.co.uk; 10.45 pm, Fri & Sat 11.45 pm.

Villa Bianca NW3 £55 ④❸❸
1 Perrins Ct 7435 3131 8–2A
"Located in one of Hampstead's cutest streets", this "pretty" Italian is "stuck firmly in a time warp"; fans seem to like it that way – "it ain't broke, so it ain't been fixed", they say. / NW3 1QS; www.villabiancanw3.com; 11.30 pm, Sun 10.30 pm.

Village East SE1 £48 ④④❸
171-173 Bermondsey St 7357 6082 9–4D
This "Manhattan-style hang-out", in Bermondsey railway arches, certainly has "bags of atmosphere", and fans praise its "excellent cocktails", top burgers and "tasty brunches"; the ambience has seemed a bit "loud" of late, though, and service rather hit-and-miss. / SE1 3UW; www.villageeast.co.uk; 10 pm, Sun 9.30 pm.

Villandry W1 £50 ④④④
170 Gt Portland St 7631 3131 2–1B
Adjacent to a "fabulous" Marylebone deli, this could be a "lovely" restaurant… if it weren't for the "ordinary" food and "poor" service, which too often combine to create an "insipid" overall experience. / W1W 5QB; www.villandry.com; 10.30 pm; closed Sat L & Sun.

The Vincent Rooms
Westminster Kingsway College SW1 £31 ❸❸❸
76 Vincent Sq 7802 8391 2–4C
"You're served by the Gordons and Jamies of the future", in this elegant dining room – part of a Westminster catering college; most reporters are thrilled by the "charming, if tentative" service and "top-class food at very reasonable prices"; not everyone, of course, hits lucky… / SW1P 2PD; www.thevincentrooms.com; 7.15 pm; closed Mon D, Tue D, Fri D, Sat & Sun; no Amex.

Vingt-Quatre SW10 £40 ④❷④
325 Fulham Rd 7376 7224 5–3B
An "invaluable stand-by" – this Chelsea café is one of London's still rare 24/7 operations; breakfast is the highlight you might hope – "eggs Benedict is outstanding". / SW10 9QL; www.vingtquatre.co.uk; open 24 hours; no booking.

Vinoteca £40 ❸❷❷
15 Seymour Pl, W1 7724 7288 2–2A
53-55 Beak St, W1 3544 7411 3–2D NEW
7 St John St, EC1 7253 8786 9–1B
An "amazing and eclectic wine list" (and "well-priced" too) is the stand-out feature of these brilliant (and multiplying) "packed-to-the-rafters" wine bars, but the cooking is "very decent". / www.vinoteca.co.uk; 11 pm, Seymour Pl Sun 5 pm; EC1 Sun; Seymour Pl Sun D.

Vivat Bacchus £51 ④❸❸

4 Hay's Ln, SE1 7234 0891 9–4C
47 Farringdon St, EC4 7353 2648 9–2A

"Oooooooh the cheese fridge!" – a perfect combo with the "massive" South African wine cellar at this popular City-fringe wine bar (where other victuals, including "tasty" zebra steaks, play second fiddle); it notably outranks its "competent-at-best" South Bank spin-off. / www.vivatbacchus.co.uk; 9.30 pm; EC4 closed Sat & Sun; SE1 closed Sat L & Sun; set pre theatre £32 (FP).

Vrisaki N22 £35 ④④④

73 Middleton Rd 8889 8760 1–1C

Even if this Greek "old favourite" is now "in a bit of a decline", it's still "one of the few places worth a visit in Bounds Green"; for those wanting a "blow-out", its "never-ending" set menus are still "great value" too – "it's hard to describe just how much food you get!" / N22 8LZ; 11.30 pm, Sun 9 pm.

Wabi WC2 NEW

36-38 Kingsway awaiting tel 2–2D

An ex-Nobu team launches this ambitious newcomer, in an odd Covent Garden-fringe location, in late-2012; let's hope the formula they've refined in Horsham (sic) rises to the challenge! / WC2B 6EY.

Wagamama £34 ④❸④

8 Norris St, SW1 7321 2755 4–4A
Harvey Nichols, Knightsbridge, SW1 7201 8000 5–1D
101a Wigmore St, W1 7409 0111 3–1A
10a Lexington St, W1 7292 0990 3–2D
4a Streatham St, WC1 7323 9223 2–1C
1 Tavistock St, WC2 7836 3330 4–3D
14a Irving St, WC2 7839 2323 4–4B
26a Kensington High St, W8 7376 1717 5–1A
N1 Centre, 37 Parkfield St, N1 7226 2664 8–3D
11 Jamestown Rd, NW1 7428 0800 8–3B
Royal Festival Hall, Southbank Centre, SE1 7021 0877 2–3D
50-54 Putney High St, SW15 8785 3636 10–2B
46-48 Wimbledon Hill Rd, SW19 8879 7280 10–2B
Jubilee Place, 45 Bank St, E14 7516 9009 11–1C
1a Ropemaker St, EC2 7588 2688 12–2A
22 Old Broad St, EC2 7256 9992 9–2C
Tower Pl, EC3 7283 5897 9–3D
109 Fleet St, EC4 7583 7889 9–2A
30 Queen St, EC4 7248 5766 9–3B

Critics say the formula "needs a freshen-up", but – "for a healthy lunch on the run", or one that's "very family-friendly" – these "quick and easy" noodle-canteens still make a "safe" bet for most reporters, thanks to their "welcoming" staff, and "cheap" and "wholesome" fodder. / www.wagamama.com; 10 pm-11 pm; EC4 & EC2 closed Sat & Sun; no booking.

Wahaca £31 ❸❸❷

80-82 Wardour St, W1 7734 0195 3–2D
66 Chandos Pl, WC2 7240 1883 4–4C
Westfield, Ariel Way, W12 8749 4517 7–1C
Unit 4, Park Pavilion, 40 Canada Sq, E14 7516 9145 11–1C

"Thomasina Miers has revolutionised the Mexican restaurant scene", say fans of this really "fun" group, whose "bright, arty decor and feel-good vibe" outclass many independents; the "colourful" street-food is "hardly gourmet", but it's "quick", "fresh" and "zingy", and "great value for money" too. / www.wahaca.com; WC2 & W1 & E14 11 pm, Sun 10.30 pm; W12 11 pm, Sun 10 pm; no booking; SRA-63%.

The Wallace
The Wallace Collection W1 **£56** ④⑤❶
Hertford Hs, Manchester Sq 7563 9505 3–1A
"It looks excellent at first sight", but a visit to the potentially "wonderful" atrium-restaurant of this imposing Marylebone palazzo-museum can quickly descend into a "shambles", as a result of the "average" food and "terrible" service – stick to afternoon tea!
/ W1U 3BN; www.thewallacerestaurant.com; Fri & Sat 9.15 pm; Sun-Thu closed D; no Amex.

The Walmer Castle W11 **£39** ❸❷❶
58 Ledbury Rd 7229 4620 6–1B
Still "part of the trendy Notting Hill set", the "crowded" upstairs dining room at this "cool" and "friendly" boozer has long had a surprise in store for first-timers – "good Thai food". / W11 2AJ; www.walmercastle.co.uk; 11 pm, Fri & Sat midnight, Sun 10.30 pm.

Wapping Food E1 **£51** ❸④❶
Wapping Power Station, Wapping Wall 7680 2080 11–1A
The "amazing and original" setting – a former hydraulic power station – is the key reason to seek out this East End project (part restaurant, part gallery); other attractions include "beautiful" (Oz) wines, and food that "if variable, is well done overall".
/ E1W 3SG; www.thewappingproject.com; 10.45 pm; Mon-Fri D only, Sat open L & D, closed Sun D.

Watatsumi
The Club Quarters Hotel WC2 **£60** ❸④④
7 Northumberland Ave 7036 8520 2–3C
An "imposing" but rather "drab" Edwardian interior doesn't do this Japanese operation, near Trafalgar Square, any favours – the food, though, is very "competent", and lunch and pre-theatre menus offer "good value". / WC2N 5BY; www.watatsumi.co.uk; 11 pm, Sat 11.30 pm, Sun 10.30 pm; closed Sun L; set weekday L £30 (FP), set pre-theatre £32 (FP).

The Water Margin NW11 **£32** ❸④④
96 Golders Green Road 8458 5815 1–1B
A stalwart, if "unglamorous", Golder's Green Chinese, where the food – always reliable – "tastes even better now the place has had a lick of paint"; "Cantonese dishes are best". / NW11 8HB; www.the-water-margin.co.uk; 10.30 pm; no Amex; set weekday L £17 (FP).

Waterloo Bar & Kitchen SE1 **£43** ④④④
131 Waterloo Rd 7928 5086 9–4A
"A busy brasserie, well situated for the Old Vic"; it's a "buzzy" sort of place, and even those who are "not sure it's a destination in itself" generally agree it offers "good dining pre-theatre". / SE1 8UR; www.barandkitchen.co.uk; 10.30 pm.

Waterloo Brasserie SE1 **£42** ⑤❸④
119 Waterloo Rd 7960 0202 9–4A
Bang opposite the station, this busy but rather "average" brasserie seems to rely heavily on its location; with its "quick" service (improved in recent times), though, it can still be "handy before the Old Vic".
/ SE1 8UL; www.waterloobrasserie.co.uk; 11 pm; closed Sun.

The Waterway W9 **£47** ④④❷
54 Formosa St 7266 3557 8–4A
"You can't beat being by the canal in spring or summer", so it gets "very busy" on the terrace of this Maida Vale boozer; "fantastic" BBQs are the top attraction – other fare is "fair" at best. / W9 2JU; www.thewaterway.co.uk; 10.30 pm, Sun 10 pm.

The Wells NW3 £44 ❸❷❷
30 Well Walk 7794 3785 8–1A
"An enviable location by Hampstead Heath" further boosts the appeal of this "superior gastropub"; it inspires a large volume of reports, all of which stand testimony to its "consistent good standards". / NW3 1BX; www.thewellshampstead.co.uk; 10 pm, Sun 9.30 pm.

The Wet Fish Cafe NW6 £45 ❸❷❷
242 West End Ln 7443 9222 1–1B
"Whatever the time of day, you're guaranteed lovely food", at this "cute little restaurant", in West Hampstead (which is named after its ex-fishmonger premises, not its menu); the "buzzy weekend brunch here is a must". / NW6 1LG; www.thewetfishcafe.co.uk; 10 pm; no Amex.

The Wharf TW11 £46 ④❸❶
22 Manor Rd 8977 6333 1–4A
"A lovely setting" – by Teddington Lock and with "great views" – is the reason to seek out this large, modern bar/brasserie, where the fare varies "from good to average". / TW11 8BG; www.thewharfteddington.com; 10 pm.

Wheeler's SW1 £58 ⑤❸④
72-73 St James's St 7408 1440 3–4D
With its "well-spaced" tables, MPW's "quiet" restaurant, by St James's Palace, does have fans who find it a "very professional" operation; it has too many critics, though, who dismiss it as "totally mediocre" – "even for £1, a meal here would be overpriced!" / SW1A 1PH; www.wheelersrestaurant.org; 10.45 pm; closed Sat L & Sun.

White Horse SW6 £43 ④④❸
1-3 Parsons Grn 7736 2115 10–1B
"Less Sloaney than it used to be" (isn't everywhere?), this famous Parson's Green boozer serves up "some interesting dishes" ("some work, some don't"), and a notably "great choice of beers". / SW6 4UL; www.whitehorsesw6.com; 10.30 pm.

The White Swan EC4 £52 ❸❷④
108 Fetter Ln 7242 9696 9–2A
"Above a bustling pub", off Fleet Street, this "high-quality dining room" can come as an "unexpected surprise" to first-time visitors, and it's particularly "excellent for a business lunch"; the occasional meal, though, doesn't live up to expectations. / EC4A 1ES; www.thewhiteswanlondon.com; 10 pm; closed Sat & Sun.

Whitechapel Gallery Dining Room
Whitechapel Gallery E1 £42 ❸❷❸
77-82 Whitechapel High St 7522 7896 12–2C
"Compact and companionable", this gallery dining room, by Aldgate tube, is a handy place in an "out-of-the-way" location, offering "innovative" small plates, and "good wines by the glass" too. / E1 7QX; www.whitechapelgallery.org/dine; 9.30 pm; closed Mon, Tue D & Sun D.

Whits W8 £54 ❸❶❸
21 Abingdon Rd 7938 1122 5–1A
Exceptionally "warm and genuine" service is what really distinguishes this "well-run" Kensington bistro, but most (if not quite all) reporters are very up on the "hearty" Gallic cooking too. / W8 6AH; www.whits.co.uk; 10.30 pm; D only, closed Mon & Sun.

FSA

Wild Honey W1 £62 ❸❸❸

12 St George St 7758 9160 3–2C

With its "quiet booths", this "civilised" Mayfair sibling of Arbutus makes a "pleasantly understated" – perhaps "slightly subdued" – setting in which to enjoy some "unusual" dishes at "good-value" prices, plus a "splendid selection of wines by the 25cl carafe". / W1S 2FB; www.wildhoneyrestaurant.co.uk; 11 pm, Fri & Sat 11.30 pm, Sun 10 pm.

William Curley £17 ❷❸❸

198 Ebury St, SW1 7730 5522 5–2D

10 Paved Ct, TW9 8332 3002 1–4A

"Fantastic" pâtisserie and "fabulous" hot chocolate add to the enticement of these quality chocolatiers, in Belgravia and Richmond. / www.williamcurley.co.uk; 6.30 pm.

Wiltons SW1 £115 ❸❷❷

55 Jermyn St 7629 9955 3–3C

"Antediluvian" it may be, but this bastion of old St James's offers "superb" fish in a "reassuringly traditional" ("rather stuffy") manner; prices, though, are "plain silly" – "I always go on business, as it's hard to justify on my personal account". / SW1Y 6LX; www.wiltons.co.uk; 10.30 pm; closed Sat & Sun; jacket required.

The Windmill W1 £37 ❷④❸

6-8 Mill St 7491 8050 3–2C

"Absolutely legendary pies!" – that's why fans flock to this "old-fashioned" Mayfair boozer, "handily located" on what's effectively the continuation of Savile Row. / W1S 2AZ; www.windmillmayfair.co.uk; 9.30 pm, Sat 4 pm; closed Sat & Sun; no Amex.

The Windsor Castle W8 £34 ❸❸❷

114 Campden Hill Rd 7243 8797 6–2B

Just off Notting Hill Gate, an ancient tavern that's as renowned for its "very pleasant garden" as it is for its "character-filled interior"; it is decidedly "not a gastropub", but its burgers-and-so-on menu is "competently delivered". / W8 7AR; www.thewindsorcastlekensington.co.uk; 10 pm, Sun 9 pm.

Wine Gallery SW10 £45 ④❸❸

49 Hollywood Rd 7352 7572 5–3B

John Brinkley's wine bar has been a Chelsea fixture for over 25 years – its survival has more to do with its gluggable wine at cheapo prices than its OK budget scoff. / SW10 9HX; www.brinkleys.com; 11.30 pm; closed Sun D; booking: max 12.

The Wine Library EC3 £26 ⑤❷❶

43 Trinity Sq 7481 0415 9–3D

"Many an afternoon has been lost", at this hidden-away City cellar; "the food (cheese, bread, pâtés and so on) is nice enough", but it's the "superb and amazingly well-priced wines" which draw the punters in; book. / EC3N 4DJ; www.winelibrary.co.uk; 8 pm, Mon 6 pm; closed Mon D, Sat & Sun.

Wishbone SW9 NEW

Brixton Village, Coldharbour Ln awaiting tel 10–2D

In mega-trendy Brixton Market, a new beer 'n' fried chicken joint, opening as this guide goes to press; it's backed by the MEATLiquor people – expect a zoo! / SW9 8PR.

FSA

Wolfe's WC2 £46 ④④④
30 Gt Queen St 7831 4442 4–1D
Old fans still say this rather '70s, US-style diner, in Covent Garden, does "simply the best burger" – not everyone is convinced, but the location's "convenience for Theatreland" is undoubted. / WC2B 5BB; www.wolfes-grill.net; 10 pm, Fri-Sat 10.30 pm, Sun 9 pm.

THE WOLSELEY W1 £59 ❸❷❶
160 Piccadilly 7499 6996 3–3C
"Yes, that really is Joan Collins at the end of the aisle!" – Corbin & King's "civilised and timeless" metropolitan linchpin, by the Ritz, is peerless in its "sheer buzz" at any time of day; "London's best breakfast" is a particular highlight – otherwise, the brasserie fare is "good but unimaginative". / W1J 9EB; www.thewolseley.com; midnight, Sun 11 pm; SRA-63%.

Wong Kei W1 £29 ④⑤⑤
41-43 Wardour St 7437 8408 4–3A
"The apparent dislike of Western patrons" is all part of the "hilarious" 'charm' of this notorious Chinatown fixture; the reason people go back year-in-year-out, though, probably has more to to do with the "piping-hot and authentic" chow, and the low, low prices. / W1D 6PY; 11.30 pm, Fri & Sat 11.45 pm, Sun 10.30 pm; no credit cards; no booking.

Woodlands £36 ❸❸④
37 Panton St, SW1 7839 7258 4–4A
77 Marylebone Ln, W1 7486 3862 2–1A
102 Heath St, NW3 7794 3080 8–1A
"An appetising selection of well-spiced, light and digestible veggie dishes" – that's the formula that's kept these smart but surprisingly characterless south Indians (part of an international chain) in business for over three decades. / www.woodlandsrestaurant.co.uk; 10 pm; NW3 no L Mon.

Wright Brothers £51 ❷❸❷
13 Kingly St, W1 7434 3611 3–2D
11 Stoney St, SE1 7403 9554 9–4C
"It tastes like you were beside the sea", at this "rough-and-ready" Borough Market oyster bar – an "insanely busy" spot, serving "incredibly fresh" fish and seafood; the Soho spin-off is more "sedate", but inspires similarly high excitement. / 10.30 pm, Sun 9 pm; booking: max 8.

XO NW3 £47 ❸④❸
29 Belsize Ln 7433 0888 8–2A
"A lovely local, tucked-away in Belsize Village", this sibling to E&O serves some "neat" Asian-fusion food; it's perennially "not as vibey" as Will Ricker's other ventures, though, and critics find it rather "overpriced". / NW3 5AS; www.rickerrestaurants.com; 10.30 pm; set weekday L £29 (FP).

Yalla Yalla £31 ❷❸❷
1 Green's Ct, W1 7287 7663 3–2D
12 Winsley St, W1 7637 4748 3–1C
Mezzanine, King's Cross Station, N1 7837 3680 8–3C **NEW**
"Zingy" Lebanese street food – in "large portions" for "small prices" – makes this "fun" and "interesting" chain a hit with all who comment on it; the "vibrant" original, "hidden-away in seedy Soho", is particularly popular – it's "always full". / www.yalla-yalla.co.uk; Green's Court 11 pm, Sun 10 pm; Winsley Street 11.30 pm, Sat 11 pm; W1 Sun.

Yashin W8 £80 ❷❸❸

1a, Argyll Rd 7938 1536 5–1A

"Brilliant, inventive sushi-with-a-twist" create a "sensational" culinary experience at this Manhattan-esque (and quite un-Japanese) Kensington yearling; even fans, though, note that "the prices induce more tears than an overdose of wasabi!" / W8 7DB; www.yashinsushi.com; 10 pm.

Yauatcha W1 £68 ❶④❷

Broadwick Hs, 15-17 Broadwick St 7494 8888 3–2D

"Uniquely divine" dim sum and "amazing" cocktails help fuel the still-"trendy" vibe at this "dark" and "night-clubby" Soho fixture (where service, appropriately enough, can be "too-cool-for-school"); sit downstairs. / W1F 0DL; www.yauatcha.com; 11.15 pm, Sun 10.30 pm.

The Yellow House SE16 £42 ❸❷④

126 Lower Rd 7231 8777 11–2A

"What's this chef doing in SE16, but thank goodness he's here!" – this "brilliant" local "livens up drab Surrey Quays" with its "fabulous" pizza/gastropub menu; "lovely" service too. / SE16 2UE; www.theyellowhouse.eu; 10.30 pm, Sun 9.30 pm; closed Mon, Tue–Sat closed L, Sun open L & D.

Yi-Ban E16 £44 ❸❸⑤

London Regatta Centre, Royal Albert Dock 7473 6699 11–1D

"Exciting views" of London City Airport help justify a trip to this impossible-to-get-to, but often "very busy", concrete shed, deep in Docklands; attracted not least by some "great dim sum", the clientele is "primarily Chinese". / E16 2QT; www.yi-ban.co.uk; 10.45 pm.

Yipin China N1 NEW £41 ❶❷④

70-72 Liverpool Rd 7354 3388 8–3D

"Finally, Islington has a quality Chinese!" – this "welcoming" newcomer is proving a "fantastic addition", thanks to its "very exciting" menu which features "meticulously-flavoured" (if "heavy-on-the-chilli") Hunan and Sichuan dishes; "little atmosphere", though. / N1 0QD; www.yipinchina.co.uk.

Yming W1 £40 ❷❷❸

35-36 Greek St 7734 2721 4–2A

"The default West End Chinese", for many reporters ("certainly now Fung Shing has gone") – this "peaceful" and "slightly old-fashioned" Soho "oasis" inspires a torrent of reports at odds with its small size and low-key appearance, thanks to its "fabulous" cooking, and its "disarmingly charming" service too. / W1D 5DL; www.ymingIondon.com; 11.45 pm.

Yo Sushi £28 ⑤⑤④

Branches throughout London

"The kids love choosing from the coloured plates going round", at this gimmicky conveyor-sushi chain; for too many reporters, though, its "awful" food and "dreadful" service create "a joyless experience", and the novelty "quickly wears off". / www.yosushi.co.uk; 10.30 pm; no booking.

Yoisho W1 £44 ❷④⑤

33 Goodge St 7323 0477 2–1C

With its "terrible decor, OK service and wonderful food", this is "the nearest thing I've found in London to a Tokyo izakaya", opines one reporter – no wonder this Fitzrovia spot is particularly "popular with Japanese customers". / W1; 10.15 pm; closed Sun L.

York & Albany NW1 £53 ④④④
127-129 Parkway 7388 3344 8–3B
Gordon Ramsay's "cool"-looking tavern, in a palatial Victorian building near Regent's Park, has many fans, for the bar in particular; for quite a few critics, though, it's "gone right down the tubes" in recent times – "it feels more like a fall-back dining room in a business hotel!" / NW1 7PS; www.gordonramsay.com; 10.30 pm, Sun 8 pm.

Yoshino W1 £37 ❷❶❸
3 Piccadilly Pl 7287 6622 3–3D
"Tucked-away in a side-alley, off Piccadilly", this "tiny Japanese gem" makes an excellent discovery, thanks to the "extraordinary quality of its sushi", and its "unprecedentedly good" service, all at a "very reasonable" price; its "simple" interior, however, is too low-key for some tastes. / W1J 0DB; www.yoshino.net; 10.30 pm; closed Sun.

Yum Yum N16 £40 ❸❷❷
187 Stoke Newington High St 7254 6751 1–1D
Stoke Newington's huge Thai all-rounder continues to put in an impressive performance; go easy, though – "the food's reasonably-priced, but too many cocktails can push up the bill!" / N16 0LH; www.yumyum.co.uk; 10.30 pm, Fri & Sat 11.30 pm; set weekday L £21 (FP).

Yuzu NW6 £40 ❷❸④
102 Fortune Green Rd 7431 6602 1–1B
"A surprisingly good Japanese local", drawing fans from beyond the environs of West Hampstead. / NW6 1DS; www.yuzu-restaurants.com; 10.30 pm; D only.

Zafferano SW1 £70 ❸❸❸
15 Lowndes St 7235 5800 5–1D
"Still very good, but not what it used to be" – this Belgravia Italian was once renowned as London's best, and although most reports still praise its "subtle and delicate" cooking, "accurate" service and "lovely" interior, nothing really stands out nowadays. / SW1X 9EY; www.zafferanorestaurant.com; 11 pm, Sun 10.30 pm.

Zaffrani N1 £38 ❸❷❸
47 Cross St 7226 5522 8–3D
In Islington, a "very high-quality local Indian", offering "thoughtful" cooking, "attentive" service and a "pleasant" ambience. / N1 2BB; www.zaffrani-islington.co.uk; 10.30 pm.

Zaika W8 £64 ❶❷❸
1 Kensington High St 7795 6533 5–1A
"Surpassing expectations" – this "top-class" spot makes "a great find near the Albert Hall", and deserves more recognition for its "exquisite, French-influenced Indian food"; its "high-ceilinged" premises are "impressive" too, but they do somewhat "lack character". / W8 5NP; www.zaika-restaurant.co.uk; 10.45 pm, Sun 9.45 pm; closed Mon L.

Zayna W1 £46 ❷❷④
25 New Quebec St 7723 2229 2–2A
Near Marble Arch and in need of a "tasty curry"? – look no further than this small and "very friendly" Pakistani outfit. / W1H 7SF; www.zaynarestaurant.co.uk; 11.15 pm, Fri & Sat 11.45 pm.

Zero Degrees SE3 £42 ❸④❸
29-31 Montpelier Vale 8852 5619 1–4D
Thanks to "marvellous beers from the microbrewery", and "distinctive" pizzas too, this "industrial"-style Blackheath venue is regularly "packed to the rafters". / SE3 0TJ; www.zerodegrees.co.uk; midnight, Sun 11.30 pm.

F S A

Ziani's SW3 £48 ❸❷❷

45 Radnor Walk 7351 5297 5–3C

"Unchallenging Italian comfort food" is served by "exceptionally cheerful" staff to customers "squashed in like sardines", at this "noisy" and "characterful" Chelsea stalwart – an experience which most reporters think "great fun". / SW3 4BP; www.ziani.co.uk; 11 pm, Sun 10.30 pm.

Zizzi £44 ④④④

Branches throughout London

The "light and airy style" of these "buzzy" Italians (majoring in pizza, but also serving pasta, risotti and so on) rivals that of its stablemate PizzaExpress; overall, however, it seems more "plain and forgettable". / www.zizzi.co.uk; 11 pm.

Zucca SE1 £42 ❶❷❷

184 Bermondsey St 7378 6809 9–4D

With its "perfectly-executed rustic Italian food" ("River Café quality at a fraction of the price") and its "attractive open feel", this "superlative" Bermondsey two-year-old is "worth booking months in advance for"; "I hate to recommend it, it's already so hard to get a table!" / SE1 3TQ; www.zuccalondon.com; 10 pm; closed Mon & Sun D; no Amex.

Zuma SW7 £79 ❶❸❷

5 Raphael St 7584 1010 5–1C

"Oligarchs and Paris Hilton-look-alikes seem to get all the best tables", at this "hugely buzzing" Knightsbridge scene; the "rocking" ambience (especially in the bar) is not, however, the only attraction – the "superbly original" Japanese-fusion cuisine is arguably "the best in town". / SW7 1DL; www.zumarestaurant.com; 10.45 pm, Sun 10.15 pm; booking: max 8.

INDEXES

BREAKFAST
(with opening times)

Central

Abokado: *WC2 (7.30)*
Al Duca *(9)*
Amaranto *(6.30, Sun 7)*
Apsleys *(7)*
aqua nueva *(Sun brunch 12 pm)*
Asia de Cuba *(7)*
Athenaeum *(7)*
Aubaine: *W1 (8, Sat 10)*
Aurelia *(7.30)*
Automat *(Mon-Fri 7.30)*
Baker & Spice: *SW1 (7)*
Balans: *all central branches (8)*
Bar Italia *(6.30)*
Bentley's *(Mon-Fri 7.30)*
Benugo: *all central branches (7.30)*
Bistro 1: *Beak St W1 (Sun 11)*
Black & Blue: *Berners St W1 (9)*
The Botanist *(8, Sat & Sun 9)*
La Bottega: *Eccleston St SW1 (8, Sat 9); Lower Sloane St SW1 (8, Sat 9, Sun 10)*
Boulevard *(9)*
Brasserie Max *(7)*
Browns (Albemarle) *(7, Sun 7.30)*
Browns: *WC2 (9, 10 Sat & Sun)*
Café Bohème *(8, Sat & Sun 9)*
Café in the Crypt *(Mon-Sat 8)*
Caffé Vergnano: *WC2 (8, Sun 11)*
Canteen: *W1 (8, Sat & Sun 9)*
Cecconi's *(7 am, Sat & Sun 8 am)*
The Chelsea Brasserie *(7)*
Christopher's *(Sat & Sun 11.30)*
The Cinnamon Club *(Mon-Fri 7.30)*
Comptoir Libanais: *W1 (8.30)*
Côte: *W1 (8, Sat & Sun 10)*
The Courtauld Gallery Café *(10)*
Cut *(7am, Sat & Sun 7.30 am)*
Daylesford Organic: *SW1 (8, Sun 10)*
Dean Street Townhouse *(Mon-Fri 7, Sat-Sun 8)*
The Delaunay *(7, Sat 8, Sun 11)*
Diner: *W1 (10, Sat & Sun 9)*
Dishoom *(8, Sat & Sun 10)*
Dorchester Grill *(7, Sat & Sun 8)*
The Duke of Wellington *(Sat 10)*
Ed's Easy Diner: *Sedley Pl, 14 Woodstock St W1 (Sat 9.30 am)*
Fernandez & Wells: *Beak St W1 (7.30, sat& sun 9); Lexington St W1 (7 am); St Anne's Ct W1 (8, sat 10); WC2 (8am, sat-sun 9am)*
Flat White *(8, Sat & Sun 9)*
The Fountain (Fortnum's) *(7.30, Sun 11)*
Franco's *(7, Sat 8)*
La Fromagerie Café *(8, Sat 9, Sun 10)*
Fuzzy's Grub: *SW1 (7)*
Gelupo *(Sat & Sun 12)*
Giraffe: *W1 (7.45, Sat & Sun 9)*
The Goring Hotel *(7, Sun 7.30)*
Grazing Goat *(7.30)*
Hélène Darroze *(Sat 11)*
Hush: *WC1 (8 am)*
Indigo *(6.30)*
Inn the Park *(8, Sat & Sun 9)*
Joe Allen *(8)*
JW Steakhouse *(6.30, Sat & Sun 7)*
Kaffeine *(7.30, Sat 9, Sun 9.30)*
Kazan (Cafe): *Wilton Rd SW1 (8 am, Sun 9 am)*
Konditor & Cook: *WC1 (9.30); W1 (9.30, Sun 10.30)*
Kopapa *(8.30, Sat & Sun 10)*
Ladurée: *W1 (9)*
Leon: *WC2 (7.30, Sat 9, Sun 10); Gt Marlborough St W1 (9.30, Sat & Sun 10.30)*
Maison Bertaux *(8.30, Sun 9)*
maze Grill *(6.45)*
Monmouth Coffee Company: *WC2 (8)*
Mooli's *(9)*
Mount Street Deli *(8, Sat 9)*
The National Dining Rooms *(10)*
National Gallery Café *(8, Sat & Sun 10)*
Natural Kitchen: *W1 (8, Sat 9, Sun 11)*
Nopi *(8, Sat & Sun 10)*
Nordic Bakery: *Golden Sq W1 (Mon-Fri 8, Sat 9, Sun 11)*
Noura: *William St SW1 (8)*
One-O-One *(7)*
The Only Running Footman *(7.30, Sat & Sun 9.30)*
The Orange *(8)*
Oscar *(7, Sun 8)*
Ottolenghi: *SW1 (8, Sun 9)*
Ozer *(8)*
The Pantechnicon *(Sat & Sun 9)*
Paramount *(8)*
Paul: *WC2 (7.30); W1 (7.30, Sat & Sun 8)*
Pearl *(6.30, Sat & Sun 7)*
The Portrait *(10)*
Princi *(8, Sun 8.30)*
Providores (Tapa Room) *(9, Sat & Sun 10)*
Quince *(7)*
Ranoush: *SW1 (9)*
Refuel *(7, Sun 8)*
Rib Room *(7, Sun 8)*
RIBA Café *(8)*
Riding House Café *(7.30, Sat & Sun 9)*
The Ritz Restaurant *(7, Sun 8)*
Roux at the Landau *(7)*
Royal Academy *(10)*
St John Hotel *(8)*
Savoy (River Rest') *(7, Sun 7.30)*
Scandinavian Kitchen *(8, Sat & Sun 10)*
Serafino *(7)*
Simpsons-in-the-Strand *(Mon-Fri 7.30)*
The Sketch (Parlour) *(Mon-Fri 8, Sat 10)*
Sophie's Steakhouse: *all branches (Sat & Sun 11)*
Sotheby's Café *(9.30)*
Spice Market *(7, Sat & Sun 8)*
Stock Pot: *SW1 (9.30)*
Tate Britain (Rex Whistler) *(Sat-Sun 10)*
Taylor St Baristas: *W1 (8 am)*
tibits *(9, Sun 11.30)*
Truc Vert *(7.30, Sat & Sun 9)*
The Union Café *(Sat & Sun 11)*
The Wallace *(10)*
William Curley: *all branches (9.30, Sun 10.30)*
Wolfe's *(9)*
The Wolseley *(7, Sat & Sun 8)*
Yalla Yalla: *Green's Ct W1 (Sat-Sun 10)*

West

Adams Café *(7.30 am)*
Angelus *(10)*
Annie's: *W4 (Tue - Thu 10, Fri & Sat 10.30, Sun 10)*
Aubaine: *SW3 (8, Sun 9); W8 (Mon-Sat 8 am, 9 am Sun)*
Baker & Spice: *all west branches (7, Sun 8)*
Balans West: *SW5, W4, W8 (8)*
Bedlington Café *(8.30)*
Beirut Express: *W2 (7)*
Benugo: *W12 (9)*

Best Mangal: *SW6 (10-12)*
Bluebird Café *(9)*
La Brasserie *(8)*
Bumpkin: *SW7 (11 am)*
The Cabin *(Fri 12, Sat 11, Sun 10)*
Casa Brindisa *(9)*
Chelsea Bun Diner *(7, Sun 9)*
The Chelsea Kitchen *(7, Sun 8)*
Comptoir Libanais: *W12 (9.30)*
Daylesford Organic: *W11 (8, Sun 11)*
Del'Aziz: *W12 (8); SW6 (8 am)*
Electric Brasserie *(8)*
Ffiona's *(Sat & Sun 10)*
Fresco *(8, Sun 9)*
Gail's Bread: *W11 (7, Sat & Sun 8)*
Gallery Mess *(Sat & Sun 10)*
Geales Chelsea Green: *SW3 (9 am Sat & Sun)*
Giraffe: *W4, W8 (7.45, Sat & Sun 9); W11 (8, Sat & Sun 9)*
The Hampshire Hog *(8, Sat& Sun 9)*
The Henry Root *(Sat & Sun 9)*
High Road Brasserie *(7, Sat & Sun 8)*
The Jam Tree: *W14 (10 am Mon-Fri)*
Joe's Brasserie *(Sat & Sun 11)*
Julie's *(10.30 pm, 10 pm Sat & Sun)*
Kensington Square Kitchen *(8, Sun 9.30)*
Lisboa Pâtisserie *(7)*
Lola & Simón *(8, Sat & Sun 9.30)*
Lucky Seven *(Mon noon, Tue-Thu 10, Fri-Sun 9)*
Manson *(Sat 10)*
The Markham Inn *(8, Sat & Sun 9)*
Mona Lisa *(7)*
Ottolenghi: *W11 (8, Sun 8.30)*
Pappa Ciccia: *Fulham High St SW6 (7 am)*
Pizza East Portobello: *W10 (8)*
PJ's Bar and Grill *(Sat & Sun 10)*
Ranoush: *W8 (10); W2 (9); SW3 (noon)*
Raoul's Café & Deli: *W11 (8.30); W9 (8.30 am)*
Sam's Brasserie *(9)*
Sophie's Steakhouse: *all branches (Sat & Sun 11)*
Stock Pot: *SW3 (8)*
Tartine *(11)*
Tom's Deli *(8, Sun 9)*
Tom's Kitchen *(8, Sat & Sun 10)*
Troubadour *(9)*
202 *(Mon & Sun 10, Tue-Sat 8.30)*
Vingt-Quatre *(24 hrs)*
The Waterway *(10 Sat & Sun)*
White Horse *(9.30)*

North

The Almeida *( )*
Banners *(9, Sat & Sun 10)*
Blue Legume: *N16 (9.30)*
Chamomile *(7, Sat 7.30, Sun 8)*
The Clissold Arms *(Mon-Sat 9 am)*
Del'Aziz: *NW3 (8)*
Diner: *N1, NW10 (sat, sun 9)*
The Engineer *(9)*
Euphorium Bakery *(7.30, Sun 9)*
Fifteen *(7.30, Sun 8)*
Fig *(Sun 10)*
Gail's Bread: *NW3 (7, Sat & Sun 8)*
Gallipoli: *Upper St N1, Upper St N1 (10.30)*
Garufa *(10)*
Gilbert Scott *(Sat & Sun 11)*
Ginger & White: *Perrins Ct NW3 (7.30, Sat & Sun 8.30)*
Giraffe: *N1, Rosslyn Hill NW3 (7.45, Sat & Sun 9); Haverstock Hill NW3 (8, Sat & Sun 9)*
Harry Morgan's *(9)*
Juniper Dining *(Sat & Sun 10)*
Kentish Canteen *(10, Sat & Sun 9)*
Kenwood (Brew House) *(9)*
Kipferl *(9, Sun 10)*
Landmark (Winter Gdn) *(7)*
The Lansdowne *(Sat & Sun 10)*
Made In Camden *(Mon-Fri 9.30)*
Ottolenghi: *N1 (8, Sun 9)*
Rugoletta *(10)*
St Pancras Grand *(7, Sun 9)*
Stringray Café: *N5 (11); NW5 (Fri-Sun 11)*
Trojka *(Mon-Fri 8)*
The Wet Fish Cafe *(10)*
York & Albany *(7)*

South

Abbeville Kitchen *(Sat & Sun 9)*
Annie's: *SW13 (Tue-Sun 10)*
The Bingham *(7, Sat-Sun 8)*
The Bolingbroke *(Sat & Sun 10)*
Brasserie Toulouse-Lautrec *(10, Sat & Sun 9)*
Browns: *SE1 (11 am)*
Brunswick House Cafe *(8am, Sat & Sun 10am)*
Buenos Aires Café: *SE10 (7.30 am)*
Butcher & Grill: *SW11 (8.30); SW19 (Sat & Sun 8.30)*
Caffé Vergnano: *SE1 (8, Sat & Sun 11)*
Canteen: *SE1 (8, Sat & Sun 9)*
Chapters *(8, Sun 9)*
Le Chardon: *SW4 (9); SE22 (Sat & Sun 9.30)*
Del'Aziz: *all south branches (8)*
The Depot *(Sat 9.30)*
Elliot's Cafe *(Sat 8)*
Fat Boy's: *TW8 (Mon-Fri 11.30)*
fish! *(Thu-Sat 8, Sun 10)*
Florence *(Sat 11)*
Franklins *(Sat 10)*
Frizzante Cafe *(10)*
Garrison *(8, Sat & Sun 9)*
Gastro *(8)*
Gazette: *SW12 (7); SW11 (8)*
Giraffe: *SE1 (7.45, Sat & Sun 9)*
Green & Blue *(9, Sun 11)*
Harrison's *(Sat & Sun 9)*
Hudsons *(9.30, Sat & Sun 9)*
Joanna's *(10)*
Konditor & Cook: *Cornwall Road SE1, Stoney St SE1 (7.30 am)*
The Lido Cafe *(9)*
Lola Rojo *(Sat & Sun 11)*
Monmouth Coffee Company: *SE1 (7.30)*
Orange Pekoe *(8.30)*
Le P'tit Normand *(Sun 9)*
Pantry *(8, Sat 8.30 & Sun 9.30)*
Petersham Hotel *(Mon-Fri 7, Sat & Sun 8)*
Plane Food *(5.30)*
El Rincón Latino *(Sat & Sun 11)*
The Riverfront *(9, Sun 10)*
Rivington Grill: *SE10 (Thurs-Sun 10)*
Roast *(7, Sat 8)*
San Lorenzo Fuoriporta *(10, Sun 10.30)*
Soif *(Sat & Sun 11)*
Sonny's *(Sat & Sun 10)*
The Table *(8.30, Sat & Sun 9)*
Tapas Brindisa: *SE1 (Fri-Sat 9, Sun 11)*
Tate Modern (Level 2) *(9)*
Taylor St Baristas: *TW9 (7.30 am)*
El Vergel *(8, Sat & Sun 10)*
Verta *(7.00, Sun 12 pm)*

The Victoria *(8.30)*
Waterloo Brasserie *(8)*
William Curley*: all branches (9.30, Sun 10.30)*

East
Albion *(8)*
The Anthologist *(8 am)*
Benugo*: all east branches (7.30)*
Bistrot Bruno Loubet *(7 am, Sat & Sun 7.30 am)*
Bleeding Heart *(Mon-Fri 7.30)*
Bonds *(6.30)*
Bread Street Kitchen *(Mon-Fri 7)*
Brick Lane Beigel Bake *(24 hrs)*
Browns*: E14 (11); EC2 (8)*
Café Below *(7.30)*
Caffé Vergnano*: EC4 (7 am)*
Canteen*: E1 (8, Sat & Sun 9)*
Caravan*: EC1 (8, Sat & Sun 10)*
Cinnamon Kitchen *(7 Mon-Fri)*
Comptoir Gascon *(9)*
Coq d'Argent *(Mon-Fri 7.30)*
Department of Coffee *(7, Sat & Sun 10)*
The Diner*: EC2 (8, Sat & Sun 9)*
Dose *(7, Sat 9)*
The Empress *(Sat & Sun 10 pm)*
Forman's *(Sat 9)*
The Fox and Anchor *(7, Sat & Sun 8.30)*
Fuzzy's Grub*: all east branches (7.30)*
Grace St Paul's *(7)*
Hawksmoor*: E1 (Sat, Sun 11)*
Hazev *(8)*
Hilliard *(8)*
The Hoxton Grill *(7)*
Leon*: Ludgate Circus EC4 (8); E1 (8, Sat 9, Sun 10)*
Little Georgia Café *(9, Sun 10)*
Look Mum No Hands! *(7.30, Sat 9, Sun 10)*
Lutyens *(7.30)*
The Luxe *(8, Sat-Sun 9.30)*
Malmaison Brasserie *(7, Sat & Sun 8)*
Manicomio*: EC2 (Mon-Fri 7)*
The Mercer *(7.30)*
The Modern Pantry *(8, Sat 9, Sun 10)*
Natural Kitchen*: EC4 (8 am)*
Needoo *(9 am)*
1901 *(7 am, Sat & Sun 8 am)*
Nusa Kitchen*: EC2 (7); EC1 (8)*
1 Lombard Street *(7.30)*
E Pellicci *(7)*
Piccolino*: EC2 (9 am)*
Pod*: London Wall EC2, Devonshire Sq EC2, EC3 (6.30); Exchange Sq EC2 (7 am)*
Prufrock Coffee *(8, Sat 10)*
The Punch Tavern *(7.30, Sat & Sun 11)*
Quadrato *(6.30, Sun 8)*
Rivington Grill*: EC2 (Mon-Fri 8)*
Rochelle Canteen *(9)*
Rocket*: Adams Ct EC2 (9); E14 (9.30 am)*
St John Bread & Wine *(9, Sat & Sun 10)*
Simpson's Tavern *(Tues-Fri 8)*
Smiths (Ground Floor) *(7, Sat 10, Sun 9.30)*
Spianata & Co*: E1, EC4 (7.30)*
Taylor St Baristas*: E14, Unit 3, 125 Old Broad St EC2 (7 am); Clifton St EC2 (8 am)*
Tsuru*: EC4 (7.30 am)*
Vivat Bacchus*: EC4 (mon-fri 7)*
Wapping Food *(Sat & Sun 10)*

BRUNCH MENUS

Central
Aubaine*: all branches*
Aurora
Automat
Baker & Spice*: all branches*
Balans*: all branches*
Bar Boulud
Boisdale
Le Caprice
Cecconi's
Christopher's
Daylesford Organic*: all branches*
Dean Street Townhouse
The Delaunay
La Fromagerie Café
Galvin at Windows
Giraffe*: all branches*
Hush*: W1*
Indigo
Inn the Park
The Ivy
Joe Allen
Kopapa
Nordic Bakery*: Golden Sq W1*
Oscar
Ottolenghi*: all branches*
The Providores
Providores (Tapa Room)
RIBA Café
Riding House Café
St John Hotel
Scandinavian Kitchen
Truc Vert
Villandry
The Wolseley

West
The Abingdon
Annie's*: all branches*
Aubaine*: all branches*
Baker & Spice*: all branches*
Balans West*: all branches*
Beach Blanket Babylon*: W11*
Bluebird
Bluebird Café
Bodean's*: SW6*
La Brasserie
The Builders Arms
Bumpkin*: all branches*
The Cabin
Le Café Anglais
Chelsea Bun Diner
Cheyne Walk Brasserie
Daylesford Organic*: all branches*
Del'Aziz*: all branches*
Electric Brasserie
The Enterprise
Ffiona's
First Floor
The Frontline Club
Gail's Bread*: W11*
Giraffe*: all branches*
Granger & Co
High Road Brasserie
Joe's Brasserie
Kensington Square Kitchen
Lola & Simón
Lucky Seven
Notting Hill Brasserie
The Oak
Ottolenghi*: all branches*
PJ's Bar and Grill
Raoul's Café & Deli*: all branches*
Sam's Brasserie

Sophie's Steakhouse: *SW10*
Taqueria
Tartine
Tom's Deli
Tom's Kitchen
Troubadour
202
Vingt-Quatre
Zuma

North
The Arches
Banners
Blue Legume: *N16*
Chamomile
Cottons
Del'Aziz: *all branches*
Diner: *N1*
The Engineer
Fifteen
Gail's Bread: *NW3*
Giraffe: *all branches*
Kenwood (Brew House)
Kipferl
Landmark (Winter Gdn)
Made In Camden
Ottolenghi: *all branches*
The Wet Fish Cafe

South
Alma
Annie's: *all branches*
Bellevue Rendez-Vous
Butcher & Grill: *all branches*
Butlers Wharf Chop House
Canteen: *SE1*
Chapters
Del'Aziz: *all branches*
Garrison
Gastro
Giraffe: *all branches*
Harrison's
Hudsons
Inside
Joanna's
Lamberts
The Lido Cafe
Petersham Hotel
Ransome's Dock
Rivington Grill: *all branches*
Roast
Sonny's
The Table
El Vergel
Village East

East
Balans: *all branches*
Bistrotheque
Canteen: *E1*
Caravan: *EC1*
The Diner: *EC2*
Giant Robot
Giraffe: *all branches*
Hawksmoor: *E1*
The Hoxton Grill
The Modern Pantry
Quadrato
Rivington Grill: *all branches*
St John Bread & Wine
Smiths (Ground Floor)
Wapping Food

BUSINESS

Central
Al Duca
Alain Ducasse
Alloro
Alyn Williams
Amaya
Apsleys
Athenaeum
The Avenue
Axis
The Balcon
Banca
Bank Westminster
Bar Boulud
Bellamy's
Benares
Bentley's
Bob Bob Ricard
Boisdale
Boudin Blanc
Brasserie Blanc: *The Mkt WC2*
Brasserie St Jacques
Browns (Albemarle)
Le Caprice
Cecconi's
The Chelsea Brasserie
China Tang
Christopher's
Le Cigalon
The Cinnamon Club
Clos Maggiore
Corrigan's Mayfair
Dean Street Townhouse
The Delaunay
Les Deux Salons
Le Deuxième
Dinner
Dorchester Grill
Elena's L'Etoile
L'Escargot
Fino
The Forge
Franco's
Galvin at Windows
Galvin Bistrot de Luxe
Gaucho: *all branches*
Le Gavroche
La Genova
Goodman: *all branches*
Gordon Ramsay at Claridge's
The Goring Hotel
Green's: *all branches*
The Greenhouse
The Guinea Grill
Hakkasan: *Hanway Pl W1*
Hawksmoor: *all branches*
Hélène Darroze
Hibiscus
Hush: *all branches*
Indigo
The Ivy
JW Steakhouse
Kai Mayfair
Ken Lo's Memories
Koffmann's
Langan's Brasserie
Latium
Locanda Locatelli
Mango Tree: *Grosvenor Pl SW1*
Marcus Wareing
Massimo
Matsuri
Miyama
Mon Plaisir

Murano
Nobu
Odin's
One-O-One
L'Oranger
Orrery
Oscar
Osteria Dell'Angolo
The Palm
The Pantechnicon
Paramount
Patterson's
Pearl
Pétrus
Pied à Terre
Quilon
Quirinale
Quo Vadis
Refuel
Rhodes W1 Restaurant
Rib Room
RIBA Café
Roka: *all branches*
Roux at Parliament Square
Roux at the Landau
Rules
Santini
Sartoria
Savoy Grill
Savoy (River Rest')
Scott's
Serafino
J Sheekey
Shepherd's
Simpsons-in-the-Strand
The Square
Tamarind
Theo Randall
Thirty Six
Truc Vert
2 Veneti
Veeraswamy
Il Vicolo
The Wallace
Wheeler's
Wild Honey
Wiltons
The Wolseley
Zafferano

West

Bibendum
The Frontline Club
Gaucho: *all branches*
Gordon Ramsay
The Ledbury
Manicomio: *all branches*
Outlaw's Seafood and Grill
Poissonnerie de l'Avenue
Racine
Sam's Brasserie
Tom Aikens
La Trompette
Zuma

North

Frederick's
Gaucho: *all branches*
Landmark (Winter Gdn)
Rotunda Bar & Restaurant
St Pancras Grand

South

Blueprint Café
Butlers Wharf Chop House
Le Cassoulet
Delfina
Gaucho: *all branches*
The Glasshouse
Magdalen
Oxo Tower (Brass')
Oxo Tower (Rest')
Le Pont de la Tour
Roast
Skylon
Vivat Bacchus: *all branches*
Zucca

East

Alba
L'Anima
Barbecoa
Bevis Marks
Bleeding Heart
Boisdale of Canary Wharf
Bonds
Café du Marché
Caravaggio
Chamberlain's
The Chancery
Chinese Cricket Club
Chiswell Street Dining Rms
Cinnamon Kitchen
City Miyama
Club Gascon
Coq d'Argent
Dockmaster's House
The Don
Duck & Waffle
Eyre Brothers
Forman's
The Fox and Anchor
Galvin La Chapelle
Gaucho: *all branches*
Goodman: *all branches*
Gow's
Green's: *all branches*
Hawksmoor: *all branches*
High Timber
The Hoxton Grill
Imperial City
Lutyens
Malmaison Brasserie
Manicomio: *all branches*
The Mercer
Moro
1901
1 Lombard Street
Pacific Oriental
Paternoster Chop House
Plateau
Portal
Prism
Quadrato
Refettorio
Rhodes 24
Roka: *all branches*
The Royal Exchange Grand Café
St John
Sauterelle
Searcy's Brasserie
Smiths (Top Floor)
Smiths (Dining Rm)
Sushisamba
Taberna Etrusca
28-50: *EC4*
Vertigo 42
The White Swan

BYO

(Bring your own wine at no or low – less than £3 – corkage. Note for £5-£15 per bottle, you can normally negotiate to take your own wine to many, if not most, places.)

Central

Food for Thought
Fryer's Delight
Golden Hind
India Club
Patogh
Ragam
Viet

West

Adams Café
Alounak: *all branches*
Bedlington Café
Café 209
Chelsea Bun Diner
Faanoos: *all branches*
Fez Mangal
Fitou's Thai Restaurant
Mirch Masala: *all branches*
Mohsen
Pappa Ciccia: *Munster Rd SW6*

North

Ali Baba
Diwana Bhel-Poori House
Huong-Viet
Jai Krishna
Rugoletta
Toff's
Vijay

South

Amaranth
Apollo Banana Leaf
Cah-Chi: *all branches*
Faanoos: *all branches*
Green & Blue
Hot Stuff
Kaosarn: *SW9*
Lahore Karahi
Lahore Kebab House: *all branches*
Mien Tay: *all branches*
Mirch Masala: *all branches*
The Paddyfield
Sree Krishna
Thai Corner Café

East

Lahore Kebab House: *all branches*
Little Georgia Café
Mangal I
Mien Tay: *all branches*
Mirch Masala: *all branches*
Tayyabs

CHILDREN

(h – high or special chairs
m – children's menu
p – children's portions
e – weekend entertainments
o – other facilities)

Central

Abeno: *WC2 (h); WC1 (hm)*
About Thyme *(hp)*
Al Duca *(hp)*
Al Hamra *(hp)*
Al Sultan *(hp)*
Albannach *(hmp)*
All Star Lanes: *all branches (hm)*
Alloro *(p)*
Alyn Williams *(p)*
Apsleys *(hp)*
Arbutus *(hp)*
Asadal *(h)*
Asia de Cuba *(hp)*
L'Atelier de Joel Robuchon *(hp)*
Athenaeum *(m)*
Aubaine: *all branches (h)*
Aurelia *(h)*
L'Autre Pied *(hp)*
Axis *(hm)*
Babbo *(hp)*
Back to Basics *(hp)*
Baku *(hp)*
Balans: *all central branches (hm)*
Bank Westminster *(hp)*
Bar Boulud *(hp)*
Bar Italia *(hp)*
Bar Trattoria Semplice *(hp)*
Il Baretto *(h)*
Barrica *(p)*
Bar Shu *(h)*
Beiteddine *(p)*
Belgo Centraal: *Earlham St WC2 (hm); Kingsway WC2 (m)*
Bellamy's *(h)*
Benares *(h)*
Benihana: *W1 (hm)*
Benito's Hat: *Goodge St W1 (hp)*
Bentley's *(h)*
Bincho Yakitori: *W1 (hp)*
Bocca Di Lupo *(hp)*
Bodean's: *W1 (ehm)*
The Botanist *(h)*
Boudin Blanc *(hp)*
Boulevard *(hm)*
Brasserie Max *(hmp)*
Briciole *(hp)*
Browns (Albemarle) *(hmp)*
Browns: *W1, WC2 (hm)*
Bumbles *(h)*
Byron: *Wellington St WC2 (hm)*
C London *(hp)*
Café Bohème *(h)*
Café des Amis *(h)*
Café España *(h)*
Café in the Crypt *(hp)*
Café Pacifico *(hm)*
Caffè Caldesi *(hp)*
Caffé Vergnano: *WC2 (p)*
Cantina Laredo *(hm)*
Cape Town Fish Market *(hp)*
Le Caprice *(hp)*
Caraffini *(h)*
Cecconi's *(hp)*
Le Cercle *(p)*
The Chelsea Brasserie *(hm)*
China Tang *(h)*
Chipotle: *Charing Cross Rd WC2 (h)*

West

Poissonnerie de l'Avenue *(h)*
Polish Club *(hp)*
Il Portico *(p)*
Portobello Ristorante *(hmp)*
Potli *(h)*
Princess Victoria *(hp)*
Quantus *(h)*
Queen's Head *(hm)*
Racine *(hp)*
Randa *(hmp)*
Ranoush: *SW3,W8 (hp)*
Raoul's Café & Deli: *W11,W9 (hp)*
The Red Pepper *(p)*
Riccardo's *(hp)*
The River Café *(hp)*
Rocca Di Papa: *SW7 (hp)*
Rodizio Rico: *W2 (h)*
The Roebuck *(hm)*
Rossopomodoro: *SW10 (hp);W11 (p)*
Royal China: *all branches (h)*
Sagar: *W6 (hm)*
Saigon Saigon *(h)*
Sam's Brasserie *(hm)*
San Lorenzo *(hp)*
The Sands End *(hp)*
Santa Lucia *(hp)*
Santa Maria *(hp)*
Satay House *(h)*
Scalini *(hp)*
Seventeen *(p)*
La Sophia *(hp)*
Sophie's Steakhouse: *all branches (hm)*
Sticky Fingers *(ehm)*
Stock Pot: *SW3 (hm)*
Sufi *(hp)*
Sukho Fine Thai Cuisine *(hp)*
The Summerhouse *(hmp)*
The Swan *(h)*
Taiwan Village *(h)*
Taqueria *(hm)*
Tartine *(p)*
Tendido Cuatro *(hp)*
Thali *(p)*
Tian Fu *(h)*
Timo *(p)*
Tom Aikens *(h)*
Tom's Deli *(h)*
Tom's Kitchen *(hp)*
La Trompette *(hp)*
Le Troquet *(hp)*
Troubadour *(hp)*
202 *(p)*
Union Jacks: *W4 (ehm)*
Le Vacherin *(hp)*
Vingt-Quatre *(hp)*
Wagamama: *W8 (hm)*
Wahaca: *W12 (hp)*
The Walmer Castle *(hm)*
The Waterway *(hp)*
White Horse *(hp)*
Wine Gallery *(hp)*
Yashin *(hp)*
Zaika *(hp)*
Zuma *(h)*

North

L'Absinthe *(hm)*
Afghan Kitchen *(h)*
The Albion *(hm)*
Ali Baba *(p)*
Alisan *(h)*
The Almeida *(hm)*
Anglo Asian Tandoori *(h)*
Artigiano *(hm)*
L'Artista *(hp)*
Les Associés *(hmp)*
Atari-Ya: *NW4 (p)*
L'Aventure *(p)*
Il Bacio: *all branches (hmp)*
Bald Faced Stag *(hmp)*
The Banana Tree Canteen: *NW6 (ehm)*
Banners *(ehmp)*
The Barnsbury *(hp)*
Belgo Noord: *NW1 (hm)*
Beyoglu *(hp)*
Bistro Aix *(p)*
Blue Legume: *N16 (hm)*
La Bota *(hp)*
Browns: *N1 (hm)*
Bull & Last *(hmp)*
Byron: *Upper St N1 (hm)*
La Cage Imaginaire *(hp)*
Camino *(hp)*
Canonbury Kitchen *(p)*
Carob Tree *(h)*
Chamomile *(hm)*
Chez Liline *(hp)*
The Clissold Arms *(hm)*
La Collina *(hp)*
Cottons *(h)*
Daphne *(hp)*
Del'Aziz: *NW3 (hmp)*
dim T: *all north branches (hmo)*
The Drapers Arms *(h)*
The Duke of Cambridge *(hp)*
The Engineer *(hm)*
The Fellow *(h)*
Fifteen *(p)*
Fig *(h)*
500 *(hp)*
Frederick's *(hm)*
Freemasons Arms *(hmp)*
Gail's Bread: *NW3 (hmp)*
Gallipoli: *all branches (hp)*
Garufa *(hp)*
Gaucho: *NW3 (hp)*
Gem *(hp)*
Gilak *(hp)*
Gilbert Scott *(hp)*
Gilgamesh *(hp)*
Ginger & White: *Perrins Ct NW3 (hmo)*
Giraffe: *N1, Rosslyn Hill NW3 (ehm)*
La Giralda *(hp)*
Goldfish *(h)*
Good Earth: *NW7 (hp)*
Great Nepalese *(p)*
Haché: *NW1 (h)*
Harry Morgan's *(hmop)*
The Haven *(hm)*
Holly Bush *(hp)*
The Horseshoe *(hp)*
Huong-Viet *(hp)*
Indian Rasoi *(hp)*
Izgara *(hp)*
Jin Kichi *(h)*
The Junction Tavern *(hp)*
Juniper Dining *(hm)*
Kaifeng *(h)*
Kentish Canteen *(hm)*
Kenwood (Brew House) *(hm)*
Khoai Cafe: *all branches (h)*
Kipferl *(hp)*
Ladudu *(hp)*
Landmark (Winter Gdn) *(hmp)*
The Lansdowne *(hp)*
Lemonia *(p)*
The Little Bay: *NW6 (hm)*
Made In Camden *(h)*
Mangal II *(hm)*
Mango Room *(h)*
Manna *(hp)*
Marine Ices *(hp)*
Market *(hp)*

South

Fish Place *(p)*
fish! *(hm)*
Florence *(hmo)*
Four O Nine *(hp)*
Four Regions *(hp)*
Fox & Grapes *(hm)*
The Fox & Hounds *(hp)*
Franklins *(hp)*
Frizzante Cafe *(hm)*
Fujiyama *(h)*
Fulham Wine Rooms *(hp)*
Gandhi's *(m)*
Gastro *(m)*
Gazette*: SW11 (hm); SW12 (hmp)*
Giraffe*: SE1 (ehm)*
The Glasshouse *(hp)*
Gourmet Pizza Company *(h)*
The Gowlett *(hp)*
Green & Blue *(h)*
Hare & Tortoise*: SW15 (h)*
Harrison's *(ehmp)*
Hashi *(hm)*
Hot Stuff *(hp)*
Hudsons *(p)*
Indian Ocean *(h)*
Indian Zilla *(eh)*
Isola del Sole *(hm)*
Joanna's *(hmp)*
Kennington Tandoori *(h)*
Kew Grill *(hm)*
Lahore Karahi *(hmp)*
Lahore Kebab House*: SW16 (hmp)*
Lamberts *(hmp)*
La Lanterna *(hp)*
The Lido Cafe *(hmp)*
The Light House *(hmp)*
The Lighthouse *(ehp)*
Lobster Pot *(hmp)*
Lola Rojo *(h)*
The Lord Northbrook *(hp)*
Ma Cuisine *(hmp)*
Ma Goa *(h)*
Magdalen *(p)*
La Mancha *(h)*
Mango & Silk *(hmp)*
Mar I Terra*: SE1 (hp)*
Masters Super Fish *(h)*
Matsuba *(h)*
Menier Chocolate Factory *(p)*
Mezzanine *(hp)*
Mien Tay*: all branches (h)*
Mirch Masala*: all south branches (h)*
Nazmins *(p)*
China Boulevard *(h)*
Numero Uno *(hp)*
The Old Brewery *(hp)*
Olley's *(ehm)*
Orange Pekoe *(h)*
Osteria Antica Bologna *(hp)*
Oxo Tower (Brass') *(hm)*
Oxo Tower (Rest') *(hm)*
Le P'tit Normand *(hp)*
The Paddyfield *(h)*
The Palmerston *(hp)*
Palmyra *(h)*
Pantry *(hm)*
The Pepper Tree *(hp)*
Petersham Hotel *(hmp)*
Petersham Nurseries *(h)*
Pizarro *(h)*
Pizza Metro *(hp)*
Pizzeria Rustica *(hm)*
Plane Food *(hmp)*
Le Pont de la Tour *(hm)*
The Prince Of Wales *(hp)*
Le Querce *(hop)*
Ransome's Dock *(hp)*
Real Greek*: SE1 (hm)*
Rebato's *(p)*
El Rincón Latino *(hp)*
Riva *(hp)*
The Riverfront *(hp)*
Rivington Grill*: SE10 (hmp)*
Roast *(hmp)*
Rock & Rose *(hmp)*
RSJ *(p)*
San Lorenzo Fuoriporta *(hm)*
Santa Maria del Sur *(h)*
The Sea Cow *(hm)*
The Ship *(hp)*
Simplicity *(m)*
Skylon *(hmp)*
Slurp*: all branches (h)*
Sonny's *(hmp)*
The Spread Eagle *(hp)*
Sree Krishna *(h)*
The Swan at the Globe *(hp)*
The Table *(hp)*
Talad Thai *(h)*
Tandoori Nights *(hp)*
Tas*: The Cut SE1, Borough High St SE1 (h)*
Tas Pide *(hp)*
Tate Modern (Level 7) *(hm)*
Tate Modern (Level 2) *(hmp)*
Telegraph *(hm)*
Tentazioni *(hp)*
Tom Ilic *(hm)*
The Trafalgar Tavern *(hp)*
Trinity *(hp)*
Triphal *(p)*
Tsunami*: SW4 (h)*
Upstairs Bar *(hp)*
El Vergel *(hp)*
Verta *(hm)*
The Victoria *(ehm)*
Wagamama*: SW15, SW19 (hm)*
Waterloo Bar & Kitchen *(hm)*
Waterloo Brasserie *(hm)*
The Wharf *(hm)*
The Yellow House *(hm)*
Zero Degrees *(hp)*
Zucca *(h)*

East

Al Volo *(hp)*
Alba *(hp)*
Albion *(hp)*
All Star Lanes*: all branches (hm)*
Amico Bio *(hp)*
L'Anima *(h)*
Ark Fish *(hm)*
Balans*: E20 (hm)*
Banana Tree Canteen*: EC1 (hm)*
Bangalore Express*: EC3 (m)*
Barbecoa *(hp)*
Beach Blanket Babylon*: all branches (p)*
Bistrot Bruno Loubet *(hp)*
Bistrotheque *(h)*
Bodean's*: EC3 (hp)*
Bonds *(h)*
Il Bordello *(hp)*
The Boundary *(h)*
Brasserie Blanc*: Threadneedle St EC2 (hm)*
Brasserie on St John Street *(hp)*
Brawn *(hp)*
Browns*: all east branches (hm)*
Buen Ayre *(h)*
Café Below *(h)*
Café Spice Namaste *(hp)*
Canteen*: E1 (hmp)*
Caravan*: EC1 (h)*
The Chancery *(p)*
Chinese Cricket Club *(h)*

Chiswell Street Dining Rms *(hp)*
Cinnamon Kitchen *(hp)*
Clifton *(hp)*
Club Gascon *(p)*
Comptoir Gascon *(h)*
Coq d'Argent *(h)*
Dans le Noir *(m)*
The Diner*: EC2 (hmp)*
Dockmaster's House *(hp)*
The Empress *(hp)*
Fabrizio *(hp)*
Faulkner's *(hm)*
La Figa *(hop)*
Fish Central *(hm)*
Forman's *(p)*
The Fox and Anchor *(h)*
Frizzante at City Farm *(hm)*
Galvin La Chapelle *(hmo)*
Gaucho*: E14 (h); EC3 (hp)*
Giant Robot *(h)*
Giraffe*: E1 (ehm)*
Gourmet San *(h)*
Gow's *(p)*
Great Eastern Dining Room *(ehm)*
Green Papaya *(h)*
The Gun *(hp)*
The Gunmakers *(m)*
Hawksmoor*: E1 (hp)*
Haz*: Mincing Ln EC3 (hmp); E1 (hp)*
Hazev *(hp)*
Hilliard *(p)*
Hix Oyster & Chop House *(h)*
The Hoxton Grill *(hm)*
Ibérica*: all branches (p)*
Imperial City *(p)*
Itsu*: E14 (h)*
Kolossi Grill *(p)*
Lahore Kebab House*: E1 (h)*
Leon*: E1 (h)*
The Little Bay*: EC1 (hm)*
Little Georgia Café *(hp)*
Lotus Chinese Floating Restaurant *(h)*
Lutyens *(hp)*
The Luxe *(hp)*
Malmaison Brasserie *(h)*
Mangal 1 *(m)*
Manicomio*: EC2 (p)*
MPW Steakhouse & Grill *(hp)*
Memsaheb on Thames *(h)*
The Mercer *(hp)*
Mien Tay*: all branches (h)*
Mint Leaf*: EC2 (h)*
The Modern Pantry *(hp)*
The Morgan Arms *(hp)*
Morito *(h)*
Moro *(h)*
Namo *(ehm)*
The Narrow *(hp)*
Needoo *(h)*
1901 *(hp)*
Northbank *(h)*
Nusa Kitchen*: all branches (p)*
1 Lombard Street *(p)*
Paternoster Chop House *(hp)*
The Peasant *(hp)*
E Pellicci *(p)*
Pho*: EC1 (hp)*
Piccolino*: EC2 (hp)*
Pizza East*: E1 (hp)*
Plateau *(hmp)*
La Porchetta Pizzeria*: all branches (hp)*
Portal *(hp)*
Princess of Shoreditch *(p)*
Prism *(hp)*
The Punch Tavern *(hp)*
Quadrato *(hm)*
Redhook *(hp)*
Refettorio *(hp)*
Relais de Venise L'Entrecôte*: EC2 (hp)*
Rhodes 24 *(h)*
Rivington Grill*: EC2 (hp)*
Rocket*: Adams Ct EC2 (hp)*
Rosa's*: E1 (p)*
Royal China*: all branches (h)*
St John *(h)*
St John Bread & Wine *(hp)*
Sauterelle *(p)*
Searcy's Brasserie *(h)*
Sedap *(hp)*
Shanghai *(h)*
Sichuan Folk *(h)*
Simpson's Tavern *(m)*
Smiths (Top Floor) *(hp)*
Smiths (Dining Rm) *(hp)*
Smiths (Ground Floor) *(hp)*
Sông Quê *(h)*
Stringray Globe Café*: all branches (hm)*
Sweetings *(p)*
Taberna Etrusca *(h)*
Tas*: EC1 (h)*
Tayyabs *(h)*
Viet Grill *(hop)*
Viet Hoa *(h)*
Vinoteca*: EC1 (p)*
Wagamama*: all east branches (hm)*
Wapping Food *(h)*
The White Swan *(hp)*
Whitechapel Gallery *(hp)*
Yi-Ban *(h)*

ENTERTAINMENT
(Check times before you go)

Central
All Star Lanes*: WC1*
(bowling, DJ Sat)
Bentley's
(pianist, Wed-Sat)
Bincho Yakitori*: W1*
(DJ, Mon; occasional live music, Wed)
Boisdale
(jazz, Mon-Sat)
Café in the Crypt
(jazz, Wed night)
Le Caprice
(pianist, nightly)
Ciao Bella
(pianist, nightly)
Circus
(circus entertainment, nightly, DJ, Sat & Sun)
Crazy Bear
(DJ, Wed-Sat)
Criterion
(live music, Fri & Sat; jazz trio, Wed)
Floridita
(live music, nightly)
Hakkasan*: Hanway Pl W1*
(DJ, nightly)
Hard Rock Café
(regular live music)
Ishtar
(live music, Tue-Sat; belly dancer, Fri & Sat)
Joe Allen
(pianist, Mon-Sat)
Kettners
(pianist, Tue-Sat)
Langan's Brasserie
(jazz, Fri & Sat)
Levant
(belly dancer, nightly)
Maroush*: W1*

(music & dancing, nightly)
Mint Leaf: *SW1*
(DJ, Fri D)
Momo
(live music, Tue)
Notes: *Wellington St WC2*
(jazz, most Wed and Thu evenings)
Noura: *W1*
(belly dancer, Fri & Sat)
L'Oranger
(pianist, Fri & Sat)
Oscar
(film club, Sun)
Pearl
(pianist, Wed-Sat)
Quaglino's
(jazz, Fri & Sat)
Red Fort
(DJ, Fri & Sat)
Refuel
(film club, Sun 3.30 pm)
The Ritz Restaurant
(live music, Fri & Sat)
Roka: *W1*
(DJ, Thu-Sat)
Royal Academy
(jazz, Fri)
Sarastro
(opera, Sun & Mon D)
Savoy Grill
(pianist, nightly)
Savoy (River Rest')
(Jazz, Sun)
Shanghai Blues
(jazz, Fri & Sat)
Simpsons-in-the-Strand
(pianist, nightly)
Sketch (Gallery)
(DJ, Thu-Sat)
Thai Square: *SW1*
(DJ, Fri & Sat)
Tom's Terrace
(DJ, Thu-Fri)
The Windmill
(live music, Mon)

West
All Star Lanes: *W2*
(bowling, DJ Thu-Sat)
Babylon
(nightclub, Fri & Sat; magician, Sun; jazz, Tue)
Beach Blanket Babylon: *all branches*
(DJ, Fri & Sat)
Bel Canto
(opera, nightly)
Belvedere
(pianist, nightly Sat & Sun all day)
Benugo: *Cromwell Rd SW7*
(jazz, Wed)
Big Easy: *SW3*
(live music, nightly)
Brompton Bar & Grill
(jazz, 3rd Fri of the month)
Le Café Anglais
(magician, Sun L)
Cheyne Walk Brasserie
(jazz, first Mon of month)
Del'Aziz: *SW6*
(belly dancer, Thu-Sat, live acoustic music); *W12*
(jazz, Fri-Sat)
Formosa Dining Room
(quiz night, Tue)
Frankie's Italian Bar & Grill
(magician, Sun)
Harwood Arms
(quiz night, Tue)
The Jam Tree: *W14*
(quid night, Wed)
The Markham Inn
(live music, Tue)
Maroush: *I) 21 Edgware Rd W2*
(music & dancing, nightly)
Mr Wing
(jazz, Thu-Sat)
Notting Hill Brasserie
(jazz, nightly, Sun L)
Nozomi
(DJ, nightly)
Okawari
(karaoke)
Old Parr's Head
(quiz night, Mon; poker, Tue)
Il Pagliaccio
(Elvis impersonator, monthly)
Paradise by Way of Kensal Green
(comedy, Wed; Jazz, Fri)
Pasha
(belly dancer, weekends; tarot card reader, special occasions)
(Ciro's) Pizza Pomodoro
(live music, nightly)
Sam's Brasserie
(live music, first and third Sun of month)
Sticky Fingers
(face painter, Sun)
Troubadour
(live music, most nights)
The Waterway
(live music, Thu)

North
Bull & Last
(quiz night, Sun)
Camino
(DJ, Thu-Sat)
Cottons
(live music, Sun; DJ, Fri & Sat)
Del'Aziz: *NW3*
(jazz, Fri & Sat)
The Fellow
(DJ, Fri)
Gilgamesh
(DJ, Fri & Sat)
Landmark (Winter Gdn)
(pianist & musicians, daily)
Mestizo
(DJ, Thu)
The North London Tavern
(jazz, Sun; quiz night, Mon; open mic, Tue; Every third Thu comedy)
Prince Albert
(quiz night, Sun D)
Rotunda Bar & Restaurant
(jazz, Fri)
Shaka Zulu
(live music, bi-weekly; DJ, Fri & Sat)
Thai Square: *N1*
(DJ, Thu-Sat)
Trojka
(Russian music, Fri & Sat)
Villa Bianca
(guitarist, Mon-Thu; pianist, Sat & Sun)
The Wet Fish Cafe
(Spanish soul, occasionally)
York & Albany
(quiz night, Mon)

South
Al Forno: *SW15*
(live music, Sat)

Archduke Wine Bar
(jazz, Mon-Sun)
Avalon
(DJ, Fri & Sat)
Bayee Village
(pianist, Wed & Thu; karaoke)
Bengal Clipper
(pianist, Tue-Sat)
Brasserie Toulouse-Lautrec
(live music, nightly)
Le Chardon: *SW4*
(magician, 1st & 3d Thu of the month); SE22
(magician, Wed)
The Crooked Well
(jazz, Sun D)
Del'Aziz: *Canvey St SE1*
(belly dancing, Fri-Sat); Bermondsey Sq SE1
(jazz, Wed & Sat; belly-dancing Fri)
Entrée
(jazz, Thu-Sat D)
The Fentiman Arms
(quiz night, Tue)
Florence
(play room)
The Gowlett
(DJ, Sun; Lucky 7s, Thu)
The Lighthouse
(live music, occasional)
The Little Bay: *SW11*
(opera, Thu-Sat; piano, Wed & Sun)
Meson don Felipe
(guitarist, nightly)
China Boulevard
(live music)
Oxo Tower (Brass')
(jazz, Sat & Sun L, Sun-Mon D)
Le Pont de la Tour
(pianist, every evening; live jazz trio, Sun L)
The Prince Of Wales
(quiz night, Sun)
Roast
(jazz, Sun)
Santa Maria del Sur
(live music, Mon)
The Ship
(live music, Sun; quiz, Wed)
Tas: *The Cut SE1, Borough High St SE1*
(guitarist, nightly)
Tas Pide
(live music, daily D)
Thai Square: *SW15*
(DJ, Fri & Sat)
The Wharf
(salsa night, first Wed of month)

East

All Star Lanes: *all east branches*
(bowling)
Beach Blanket Babylon: *all branches*
(DJ, Fri & Sat)
Bistrotheque
(regular drag shows and cabarets, piano brunch)
Boisdale of Canary Wharf
(live music, daily)
Café du Marché
(pianist & bass, Mon-Thu; pianist, Fri & Sat)
Cinnamon Kitchen
(DJ, Wed-Fri)
Coq d'Argent
(jazz, Sun L)
Elephant Royale
(live music, Thu-Sat)
Great Eastern Dining Room
(DJ, Fri & Sat)
The Gunmakers
(jazz, Mon)
The Hoxton Grill
(DJ, Thu-Sat)
Kenza
(belly dancers, Mon-Sat; tarot reader, Fri)
The Little Bay: *EC1*
(opera, Thu-Sat)
Mint Leaf: *EC2*
(Jazz, Fri D; DJ, weekends)
The Narrow
(quiz night, Mon; acoustic, Fri)
1 Lombard Street
(DJ, Fri)
Pizza East: *E1*
(DJ, live music, quiz nights, Tue, Thu, Sat)
Portal
(jazz, 2nd and last Tue)
Prism
(pianist, Wed-Fri)
The Punch Tavern
(poker nights, Mon; wine tasting, quiz & comedy nights, monthly)
Le Rendezvous du Café
(jazz, Mon-Sat)
The Royal Exchange Grand Café
(cocktail night, first Wed of month)
Shanghai
(karaoke)
Smiths (Ground Floor)
(DJ, Wed-Sat (summer))
Tas: *EC1*
(guitarist, Tue-Sun)
Thai Square City: *EC3*
(DJ, Fri)
Vivat Bacchus: *EC4*
(jazz, Fri eves)
Yi-Ban
(live smooth jazz, Fri & Sat)

LATE

(open till midnight or later as shown; may be earlier Sunday)

Central

Al Sultan
All Star Lanes: *WC1 (Fri & Sat midnight)*
Balans: *Old Compton St W1 (24 hours); Old Compton St W1 (5 am, Sun 1 am)*
Bam-Bou
Bar Italia *(open 24 hours, Sun 4 am)*
Beiteddine
Bistro 1: *Frith St W1, WC2*
La Bodega Negra *(1 am)*
Brasserie Zédel
Café Bohème *(2.45 am, Sun midnight)*
Café España *(Fri & Sat midnight)*
Cantina Laredo *(Sat midnight)*
Le Caprice
Circus *(midnight, Fri & Sat 2 am)*
Côte: *W1 (Thu-Sat midnight)*
Dean Street Townhouse *(Fri & Sat midnight)*
The Delaunay
Le Deuxième
Diner: *W1 (12.30 am, Sun midnight)*
Dishoom *(Fri & Sat midnight)*
Downtown Mayfair
Ed's Easy Diner: *Rupert St W1, Moor St W1 (midnight, Fri & Sat 1 am)*
Fakhreldine
The Forge
Gaby's
Gelupo *(Thu-Sat 1 am)*

Hakkasan: *Hanway Pl W1 (12.30 am, not Sun)*
Harbour City *(Fri & Sat midnight)*
Hard Rock Café
Inamo: *SW1*
Indali Lounge
Joe Allen *(12.45 am, not Sun)*
Levant *(Fri & Sat midnight)*
Maroush: *W1 (12.30 am)*
MEATLiquor *(midnight, Fri & Sat 2 am)*
Mr Kong *(2.45 am, Sun 1.45 am)*
New Mayflower *(4 am)*
ping pong: *Gt Marlborough St W1, Paddington St W1*
La Porchetta Pizzeria: *WC1 (Sat & Sun midnight)*
Princi
Ranoush: *SW1*
Refuel
Rossopomodoro: *all branches*
Satsuma *(Fri & Sat midnight)*
J Sheekey
J Sheekey Oyster Bar
Sofra: *all branches*
Sophie's Steakhouse: *WC2 (12.45am, not Sun)*
The Wolseley

West

Anarkali
Balans: *W8 ; SW5 (2 am)*
Basilico: *SW6*
Beirut Express: *SW7 ;W2 (2 am)*
Best Mangal: *SW6 ; North End Rd W14 (midnight, Sat 1 am)*
Buona Sera: *all branches*
Chella
Del'Aziz: *W12*
E1 Ieven Park Walk
Gifto's *(Sat & Sun midnight)*
Halepi
Jam Tree: *SW6 (Fri & Sat 2 am)*
Khan's *(Sat & Sun midnight)*
Maroush: *I) 21 Edgware Rd W2 (1.45 am); IV) 68 Edgware Rd W2 (12.30 am); SW3 (3.30 am)*
Mirch Masala: *UB1*
Mohsen
Monty's: *W5*
Il Pagliaccio
ping pong: *W2*
Pizza East Portobello: *W10 (Fri & Sat midnight)*
(Ciro's) Pizza Pomodoro *(1 am)*
Randa
Ranoush: *SW3 ;W8 (1.30 am); W2 (2.30 am)*
Rodizio Rico: *W2*
Rossopomodoro: *all branches*
The Sands End *(Thu-Sat midnight)*
Shilpa *(Thu-Sat midnight)*
Sophie's Steakhouse: *SW10 (12.45 am, not Sun)*
Tartine *(Thu-Sat midnight)*
Vingt-Quatre *(24 hours)*
The Walmer Castle *(Fri & Sat midnight)*

North

Ali Baba
Banners *(Fri & Sat midnight)*
Basilico: *N1, NW3*
Bistro Aix
Chilango: *N1 (Fri & Sat midnight)*
Diner: *N1*
Gallipoli: *all branches (Fri & Sat midnight)*
Gem *(Fri & Sat midnight)*
Mangal II *(1 am)*
Mem & Laz *(Fri & Sat midnight)*
Le Mercury *(12.30 am, not Sun)*
Pizzeria Pappagone
La Porchetta Pizzeria: *NW1 (Fri & Sat midnight); N4 (Sat & Sun midnight); N1 (weekends midnight)*
Rodizio Rico: *N1*
The Salt House *(Fri & Sat midnight)*
Sofra: *all branches*
Yum Yum *(Fri & Sat midnight)*

South

The Balham Bowls Club *(Fri & Sat midnight)*
Basilico: *all south branches*
Belgo: *SW4 (midnight, Thu 1 am, Fri & Sat 2 am)*
Buona Sera: *all branches*
Caffé Vergnano: *SE1*
Cah-Chi: *SW18 (not Sat & Sun)*
Champor-Champor
Everest Inn
Fish in a Tie
Gastro
Green & Blue *(Fri & Sat midnight)*
Indian Moment *(Fri & Sat midnight)*
Lahore Karahi
Lahore Kebab House: *all branches*
The Lighthouse *(Fri & Sat midnight)*
Mirch Masala: *all south branches*
Nazmins
Rodizio Rico: *SE10*
Tandoori Nights *(Fri & Sat midnight)*
Tsunami: *SW4 (Fri-Sun midnight)*
Zero Degrees

East

Brick Lane Beigel Bake *(24 hours)*
Cellar Gascon
Clifton
The Diner: *EC2 (not Sun & Mon)*
Duck&Waffle *(24 hours)*
Elephant Royale *(Fri & Sat midnight)*
Giant Robot
The Jugged Hare *(Thu-Sat midnight)*
Lahore Kebab House: *all branches*
Mangal I *(midnight, Sat-Sun 1 am)*
Mirch Masala: *E1*
Pizza East: *E1 (Thu midnight, Fri & Sat 1 am)*
La Porchetta Pizzeria: *EC1 (Sat & Sun midnight)*
Redhook *(midnight, Thu-Sat 1 am)*
Rocket: *E14*
Wapping Food

OUTSIDE TABLES
(* particularly recommended)

Central

Abokado: *WC2*
Al Duca
Al Hamra
Al Sultan
Amaranto
Andrew Edmunds
Antidote
aqua kyoto*
aqua nueva
Archipelago
L'Artiste Musclé
Atari-Ya: *W1*
Aubaine: *W1*
Aurora

L'Autre Pied
Back to Basics
Baker & Spice: *SW1*
Balans: *Old Compton St W1*
Bam-Bou
Bank Westminster
Bar Italia
Bar Trattoria Semplice
Barrafina: *W1*
Barrica
Benito's Hat: *Goodge St W1*
Bentley's
Benugo: *all central branches*
Bincho Yakitori: *W1*
Bistro 1: *Frith St W1, WC2*
The Botanist
La Bottega: *Lower Sloane St SW1, Eccleston St SW1*
Boudin Blanc
The Bountiful Cow
Brasserie Blanc: *The Mkt WC2**
Busaba Eathai: *WC1*
Café Bohème
Café des Amis
Café España
Caffè Caldesi
Cantina Laredo
Le Caprice
Caraffini
Cecconi's
Cha Cha Moon
The Chelsea Brasserie
Chisou: *W1*
Ciao Bella
Cigala
Comptoir Libanais: *W1*
Côte: *WC2*
The Courtauld Gallery Café
Da Mario
Daylesford Organic: *all branches*
Dean Street Townhouse
Dehesa
Delfino
dim T: *W1*
Diner: *W1*
Dinner
Dishoom
The Duke of Wellington
The Easton
Ed's Easy Diner: *Moor St W1*
Fairuz
Flat White
The Forge
Franco's
Fryer's Delight
Gelupo
Giraffe: *W1*
Golden Hind
Goodman: *W1*
Gordon's Wine Bar*
Goya
Gran Paradiso
Grazing Goat
Great Queen Street
Grumbles
Hard Rock Café
Hardy's Brasserie
Hellenic
Hush: *W1*
Indali Lounge
Inn the Park
Ishbilia
Ishtar
Jenny Lo's Tea House
JW Steakhouse
Kaffeine
Kazan: *all branches*
Kopapa
Ladurée: *W1*
Leon: *Gt Marlborough St W1, WC2*
Levant
Lupita
Maison Bertaux
Mekong
Mennula
Mildreds
Momo
Mooli's
Motcombs
Mount Street Deli
Nizuni
The Norfolk Arms
Olivomare
The Only Running Footman
Opera Tavern
The Orange
L'Oranger
Orrery
Oscar
Ozer
The Pantechnicon
Pescatori: *Charlotte St W1*
La Petite Maison
Piccolino: *W1**
ping pong: *Eastcastle St W1*
El Pirata
La Porchetta Pizzeria: *WC1*
La Poule au Pot
Prix Fixe
Providores (Tapa Room)
The Queens Arms
Quince
Quo Vadis
Le Relais de Venise L'Entrecôte: *W1*
Reubens
RIBA Café*
The Ritz Restaurant
Rock & Sole Plaice
Roka: *W1*
Royal Academy
St John Hotel
Salaam Namaste
Salt Yard
Santini
Sardo
Savoir Faire
Scandinavian Kitchen
Scott's
Serafino
Shampers
J Sheekey
J Sheekey Oyster Bar
Siam Central
The Sketch (Parlour)
Sofra: *Shepherd St W1, WC2*
Soho Japan
Tapas Brindisa Soho: *W1*
Taro: *Brewer St W1*
Tate Britain (Rex Whistler)
Tempo
The Thomas Cubitt
tibits
Toku
Tom's Terrace
Trishna
Truc Vert
Tsunami: *W1*
Union Jacks: *Central St Giles Piazza WC2*
Vapiano
Verru
Villandry
Vinoteca Seymour Place: *Seymour Pl W1*
The Wallace

West

East

PRIVATE ROOMS

(for the most comprehensive listing of venues for functions – from palaces to pubs – visit www.hardens.com/party, or buy *Harden's London Party, Event & Conference Guide*, available in all good bookshops)
*** particularly recommended**

Central

About Thyme *(40)*
Al Hamra *(20)*
Alain Ducasse *(6,10,24)*
Albannach *(20)*
Alloro *(16)*
Alyn Williams *(18,8)*
Amaranto *(8)*
Amaya *(14)*
Antidote *(30)*
Apsleys *(14,14)*
aqua kyoto *(10,16,30)*
aqua nueva *(16)*
L'Artiste Musclé *(25)*
Asadal *(12,12,12)*
Athenaeum *(8,12,60)*
Aurora *(20)*
L'Autre Pied *(16)*
The Avenue *(20)*
Axis *(18)*
Ba Shan *(10)*
Babbo *(14)*
Baku *(22)*
Bam-Bou *(20,30,12,12,9)*
Bank Westminster *(20,20,10)*
Bar Boulud *(20,20)*
Bar Trattoria Semplice *(20)*
Bar Shu *(14)*
Bedford & Strand *(20)*
Belgo Centraal: *Earlham St WC2 (25,30)*
Benares *(16,34,6,10)*
Benihana: *all branches (10)*
Bentley's *(14,60)*
Bincho Yakitori: *W1 (20)*
Bob Bob Ricard *(10)*
Bocca Di Lupo *(32)*
Bodean's: *W1 (10)*
Boisdale *(20,22,45)*
Boudin Blanc *(16)*
Boulevard *(36,70)*
The Bountiful Cow *(45)*
Brasserie Max *(10,12,32)*
Brasserie St Jacques *(18)*
Briciole *(20)*
Browns: *WC2 (35,80,50)*
Bumbles *(40)*
Busaba Eathai: *WC1 (15)*
C London *(40)*
Café des Amis *(24)*
Cantina Laredo *(20)*
Cecconi's *(12)*
Le Cercle *(12,26)*
Chabrot Bistrot d'Amis *(20)*
The Chelsea Brasserie *(10)*
China Tang *(18,16,16)*
Chisou: *W1 (14)*
Chor Bizarre *(30)*
Christopher's *(40)*
Chuen Cheng Ku *(50)*
Cigala *(25)*
Le Cigalon *(8)*
The Cinnamon Club *(60,30)*
Clos Maggiore *(23)*
Como Lario *(28)*
Il Convivio *(14)*
Corrigan's Mayfair *(12,30,26)*
Côte: *W1 (40)*
Cut *(70)*
Defune *(8)*
Dehesa *(13)*
Delfino *(40)*
Les Deux Salons *(10,22)*
dim T: *W1 (20)*
Dinner *(10)*
The Duke of Wellington *(22)*
The Ebury *(50)*
Elena's L'Etoile *(10,14,16,34)*
Empress of Sichuan *(18)*
L'Escargot *(24,60,20)*
Fairuz *(22)*
Fire & Stone: *WC2 (23)*
Floridita *(52)*
The Forge *(22)*
Franco's *(18,60)*
La Fromagerie Café *(12)*
Galvin at Windows *(30)*
Galvin Bistrot de Luxe *(22)*
Gauthier Soho *(6,18)*
Gay Hussar *(12,25)*
Golden Dragon *(14,14)*
Golden Hind *(30)*
Gopal's of Soho *(18)*
Gordon Ramsay at Claridge's *(30,13,10)*
Gordon's Wine Bar *(8)*
The Goring Hotel *(18,14,50,6)*
Goya *(90)*
Gran Paradiso *(30,12)*
The Grand Imperial *(36)*
Grazing Goat *(50)*
Green's: *SW1 (36)*
The Greenhouse *(12)*
Grumbles *(10)*
The Guinea Grill *(28)*
Haozhan *(40)*
Harbour City *(40)*
Hard Rock Café *(200)*
Hardy's Brasserie *(28,16,12,48)*
Hawksmoor: *WC2 (16)*
Hazuki *(25)*
Hellenic *(20)*
Hibiscus *(18)*
Hix *(10)*
Hunan *(20)*
Hush: *WC1 (45); W1 (80)*
Ibérica: *all branches (50)*
Ikeda *(6)*
Imli *(45)*
Imperial China *(12,14,20,25,40,70)*
Inamo: *SW1 (16); W1 (20)*
Indali Lounge *(15)*
India Club *(60)*
Indigo *(25,25,30)*
Ishbilia *(22)*
Ishtar *(8)*
The Ivy *(60)*
Joy King Lau *(50)*
JW Steakhouse *(14)*
Kai Mayfair *(6,12)*
Kazan: *Wilton Rd SW1 (40,80)*
Ken Lo's Memories *(12,14)*
Kettners *(10,12,40,85,55,24,18)*
Kiku *(8)*
Koba *(20)*
Koffmann's *(14)*
Latium *(6)*
Levant *(15,10,12)*
Locanda Locatelli *(60)*
Loch Fyne: *WC2 (50)*
Maison Bertaux *(18)*
Marcus Wareing *(16,8)*
Massimo *(20)*

West

Chez Marcelle *(40)*
Chez Patrick *(30)*
Chutney Mary *(28)*
Cibo *(10,14)*
Clarke's *(40-50)*
Le Colombier *(30)*
The Cow *(32)*
Daphne's *(40)*
Daylesford Organic: *W11 (40)*
Del'Aziz: *SW6 (80)*
The Dock Kitchen *(28)*
E&O *(18)*
El leven Park Walk *(24)*
Edera *(20)*
Eight Over Eight *(18)*
L'Etranger *(20)*
First Floor *(28,40)*
Foxtrot Oscar *(20)*
Frantoio *(12)*
The Frontline Club *(50)*
Gail's Bread: *W11 (15)*
Gallery Mess *(60)*
Geales Chelsea Green: *all branches (14)*
Good Earth: *SW3 (45)*
The Grove *(30)*
The Hampshire Hog *(10,22,22)*
Hedone *(10)*
The Jam Tree: *W14 (20,60)*
Joe's Brasserie *(20,34)*
Julie's *(12,16,24,32,45,60)*
Kateh *(12)*
Kensington Place *(40)*
Kensington Square Kitchen *(20)*
Khan's *(100)*
Kings Road Steakhouse *(20)*
Kiraku *(18)*
Kulu Kulu: *SW7 (8)*
Launceston Place *(10)*
Locanda Ottomezzo *(14,14,18)*
Lucio *(20)*
Made in Italy: *SW3 (40)*
Madhu's *(35)*
Madsen *(10)*
Malabar *(30)*
The Mall Tavern *(15)*
Manicomio: *all branches (30)*
Mao Tai *(30)*
Masala Zone: *SW5 (10)*
The Meat & Wine Co *(14)*
Medlar *(14)*
Memories of India *(30)*
Min Jiang *(20)*
Miran Masala: *W14 (40)*
Monty's: *W5 (50)*
Napulé *(15)*
Noor Jahan: *W2 (10,40)*
North China *(30)*
Notting Hill Brasserie *(44)*
Nozomi *(30,40)*
Nuovi Sapori *(30)*
The Oak *(16)*
Okawari *(25)*
Osteria dell'Arancio *(34)*
Il Pagliaccio *(100)*
Paradise by Way of Kensal Green *(20,50)*
Pasha *(20,2,4,6,6,6)*
Patio *(50)*
Pearl Liang *(45)*
Pellicano *(25)*
Pentolina *(18)*
The Pig's Ear *(35)*
El Pirata de Tapas *(30)*
PJ's Bar and Grill *(30)*
Poissonnerie de l'Avenue *(20)*
Polish Club *(150)*
Portobello Ristorante *(25)*
Potli *(35)*
Princess Victoria *(55)*
Quantus *(15)*
Racine *(20)*
Randa *(50)*
Raoul's Café & Deli: *W11 (22)*
Rasoi *(8,14)*
The Red Pepper *(25)*
Riccardo's *(22)*
The River Café *(18)*
Rossopomodoro: *SW10 (45)*
Royal China: *W2 (20,20)*
Saigon Saigon *(10)*
Sam's Brasserie *(26)*
San Lorenzo *(22,35)*
The Sands End *(24)*
Satay House *(40)*
Scalini *(25)*
La Sophia *(40)*
Star of India *(10,40)*
Le Suquet *(16,25)*
Sushinho: *SW3 (12)*
Taiwan Village *(23,20)*
Tendido Cero *(20)*
Thali *(35)*
The Thatched House *(40)*
Timo *(18)*
Tom Aikens *(12)*
Tom's Kitchen *(22)*
Le Troquet *(30)*
Troubadour *(70,120,16,25)*
Le Vacherin *(30)*
The Walmer Castle *(15)*
White Horse *(20,18)*
Whits *(50)*
Wine Gallery *(18,20,45)*
Zuma *(14,10)*

North

L'Absinthe *(25)*
Alisan *(12)*
The Almeida *(20,10)*
Artigiano *(28,20)*
Il Bacio: *N5 (30)*
Bald Faced Stag *(30)*
Bistro Aix *(30)*
Bull & Last *(60)*
Chutneys *(60,35)*
The Clissold Arms *(80)*
Cocotte *(35)*
La Collina *(15)*
Cottons *(32)*
Daphne *(55)*
The Duke of Cambridge *(60)*
The Engineer *(20,32)*
The Fellow *(12)*
Frederick's *(16,32)*
Freemasons Arms *(40)*
Gaucho: *NW3 (50)*
Gem *(80)*
Gilbert Scott *(10,12)*
Gilgamesh *(100)*
La Giralda *(18,30)*
Goldfish *(50)*
Good Earth: *NW7 (30)*
Great Nepalese *(32)*
The Haven *(70)*
Holly Bush *(15,45)*
Huong-Viet *(25)*
Juniper Dining *(20)*
Kentish Canteen *(40)*
Kenwood (Brew House) *(120)*
The Lansdowne *(55)*
Lemonia *(45)*
Mango Room *(30)*
Manna *(16)*

South

East

ROMANTIC

Central

West

ROOMS WITH A VIEW

Skylon
The Swan at the Globe
Tate Modern (Level 7)
Tate Modern (Level 2)
Thai Square: *SW15*
The Trafalgar Tavern
Upstairs Bar
The Wharf

East

Barbecoa
Coq d'Argent
Duck & Waffle
Elephant Royale
Forman's
The Grapes
The Gun
High Timber
Lotus Chinese Floating Restaurant
Memsaheb on Thames
The Narrow
Northbank
Plateau
Rhodes 24
Searcy's Brasserie
Smiths (Top Floor)
Sushisamba
Vertigo 42
Yi-Ban

NOTABLE WINE LISTS

Central

Alyn Williams
Andrew Edmunds
Antidote
Apsleys
Arbutus
Barrica
Bedford & Strand
Boisdale
Café des Amis
Le Cercle
Cigala
Clos Maggiore
Copita
Cork & Bottle
Dehesa
Ebury Rest' & Wine Bar
L'Escargot
The Fifth Floor Restaurant
Fino
The Fountain (Fortnum's)
1707
La Fromagerie Café
Galvin Bistrot de Luxe
Le Gavroche
Gordon Ramsay at Claridge's
Gordon's Wine Bar
The Greenhouse
Hardy's Brasserie
Hibiscus
The Ivy
Kai Mayfair
Latium
Locanda Locatelli
Marcus Wareing
Olivo
Olivomare
Orrery
Pétrus
Pied à Terre
The Providores
Quo Vadis
The Ritz Restaurant
St Moritz
Salt Yard
Sardo
Savoy Grill
Shampers
Sotheby's Café
The Square
Tate Britain (Rex Whistler)
The 10 Cases
10 Greek Street
Terroirs
Texture
28-50: *all branches*
The Union Café
Vinoteca Seymour Place: *all branches*
Wild Honey
Zafferano

West

Albertine
Angelus
Bibendum
Brinkley's
Brompton Bar & Grill
Cambio de Tercio
Clarke's
Le Colombier
L'Etranger
The Frontline Club
Gordon Ramsay
The Kensington Wine Rooms
The Ledbury
Locanda Ottomezzo
Marco
Osteria dell'Arancio
Popeseye: *all branches*
Princess Victoria
Racine
The River Café
Tendido Cuatro
Tom Aikens
La Trompette
White Horse
Wine Gallery

North

The Arches
La Collina
The Rose & Crown
Swan & Edgar

South

Brinkley's Kitchen
Brula
Cantina Vinopolis
Chez Bruce
Delfina
Emile's
Enoteca Turi
40 Maltby Street
Fulham Wine Rooms
The Glasshouse
Green & Blue
José
Magdalen
Le Pont de la Tour
Popeseye: *all branches*
Ransome's Dock
Riva
RSJ
Soif
Tentazioni
Vivat Bacchus: *all branches*

East

Alba
Bleeding Heart

CUISINES

An asterisk (*) after an entry indicates exceptional or very good cooking

AMERICAN

Central
All Star Lanes *(WC1)*
Automat *(W1)*
Big Easy *(WC2)*
Bodean's *(W1)*
Bubbledogs *(W1)*
Christopher's *(WC2)*
Hard Rock Café *(W1)*
Joe Allen *(WC2)*
Mishkin's *(WC2)*
The Palm *(SW1)*
Pitt Cue Co *(W1)**
Spuntino *(W1)**

West
All Star Lanes *(W2)*
Big Easy *(SW3)*
Bodean's *(SW6)*
Lucky Seven *(W2)*
Sticky Fingers *(W8)*

North
Chicken Shop *(NW5)*
Karpo *(NW1)*
Red Dog Saloon *(N1)*
Shrimpy's *(N1)*

South
Bodean's *(SW4)*
Wishbone *(SW9)*

East
All Star Lanes *(E1, E20)*
Beard to Tail *(EC2)*
Bodean's *(EC3)*
Giant Robot *(EC1)*
The Hoxton Grill *(EC2)*

AUSTRALIAN

West
Granger & Co *(W11)*

BELGIAN

Central
Belgo Centraal *(WC2)*

North
Belgo Noord *(NW1)*

South
Belgo *(SW4)*

BRITISH, MODERN

Central
Alyn Williams *(W1)**
Andrew Edmunds *(W1)*
The Angel & Crown *(WC2)**
Arbutus *(W1)**
Athenaeum *(W1)**
Aurora *(W1)*
The Avenue *(SW1)*
Axis *(WC2)*
Balthazar *(WC2)*
Bank Westminster *(SW1)*
Bellamy's *(W1)*
Bob Bob Ricard *(W1)*
The Botanist *(SW1)*
Brasserie Max *(WC2)*
Canteen *(WC2)*
Le Caprice *(SW1)*
Coopers Restaurant & Bar *(WC2)**
Criterion *(W1)*
Daylesford Organic *(SW1)*
Dean Street Townhouse *(W1)*
Le Deuxième *(WC2)*
Dorchester Grill *(W1)*
Ducksoup *(W1)*
The Duke of Wellington *(W1)*
The Easton *(WC1)**
Ebury Rest' & Wine Bar *(SW1)*
The Fifth Floor Restaurant *(SW1)*
Gordon's Wine Bar *(WC2)*
The Goring Hotel *(SW1)*
Grazing Goat *(W1)*
Hardy's Brasserie *(W1)*
Hix *(W1)*
Hix Belgravia *(SW1)*
Hush *(W1, WC1)*
Indigo *(WC2)*
Inn the Park *(SW1)*
The Ivy *(WC2)*
Kettners *(W1)*
Langan's Brasserie *(W1)*
Mews of Mayfair *(W1)*
The Norfolk Arms *(WC1)*
The Only Running Footman *(W1)*
The Orange *(SW1)**
Oscar *(W1)*
Ozer *(W1)*
The Pantechnicon *(SW1)*
Paramount *(WC1)*
Patterson's *(W1)*
Pollen Street Social *(W1)**
The Portrait *(WC2)*
Quaglino's *(SW1)*
The Queens Arms *(SW1)*
Quo Vadis *(W1)*
Randall & Aubin *(W1)*
Refuel *(W1)*
Rhodes W1 Restaurant *(W1)*
RIBA Café *(W1)*
Roganic *(W1)**
Roux at Parliament Square *(SW1)*
Roux at the Landau *(W1)**
Savoy (River Rest') *(WC2)*
Seven Park Place *(SW1)**
Seven Stars *(WC2)*
1707 *(W1)*
Shampers *(W1)*
Sotheby's Café *(W1)*
Tate Britain (Rex Whistler) *(SW1)*
10 Greek Street *(W1)**
Thirty Six *(SW1)**
The Thomas Cubitt *(SW1)**
Tom's Terrace *(WC2)*
The Union Café *(W1)*
Union Jacks *(WC2)*
Villandry *(W1)*
The Vincent Rooms *(SW1)*
Vinoteca Seymour Place *(W1)*
Wild Honey *(W1)*
The Wolseley *(W1)*

West
The Abingdon *(W8)*
The Anglesea Arms *(W6)**
The Anglesea Arms *(SW7)*
Babylon *(W8)*
Beach Blanket Babylon *(W11)*
Belvedere *(W8)*
Bluebird *(SW3)*
Brinkley's *(SW10)*
Brompton Bar & Grill *(SW3)*

The Builders Arms *(SW3)*
Butcher's Hook *(SW6)*
The Cadogan Arms *(SW3)*
The Carpenter's Arms *(W6)*
Carvosso's *(W4)*
The Chelsea Ram *(SW10)*
Clarke's *(W8)*
The Cow *(W2)*
Daylesford Organic *(W11)*
The Dock Kitchen *(W10)*
Duke of Sussex *(W4)*
Electric Brasserie *(W11)*
The Enterprise *(SW3)*
First Floor *(W11)*
Formosa Dining Room *(W9)*
The Frontline Club *(W2)*
Harwood Arms *(SW6)**
The Havelock Tavern *(W14)*
Hedone *(W4)*
The Henry Root *(SW10)*
High Road Brasserie *(W4)*
Hole in the Wall *(W4)*
Jam Tree *(SW6, W14)*
Joe's Brasserie *(SW6)*
Julie's *(W11)*
Kensington Place *(W8)*
Kensington Square Kitchen *(W8)*
Kitchen W8 *(W8)**
The Ladbroke Arms *(W11)**
Launceston Place *(W8)*
The Ledbury *(W11)**
The Mall Tavern *(W8)**
Marco *(SW6)*
Megan's Delicatessen *(SW6)*
Notting Hill Brasserie *(W11)*
Paradise by Way of Kensal Green *(W10)**
The Phoenix *(SW3)*
Pissarro *(W4)*
The Prince Bonaparte *(W2)*
Princess Victoria *(W12)*
Queen's Head *(W6)*
The Roebuck *(W4)*
Sam's Brasserie *(W4)*
The Sands End *(SW6)*
The Thatched House *(W6)*
Tom Aikens *(SW3)**
Tom's Deli *(W11)*
Tom's Kitchen *(SW3)*
Union Jacks *(W4)*
Vingt-Quatre *(SW10)*
The Waterway *(W9)*
White Horse *(SW6)*
Whits *(W8)*

North

The Albion *(N1)*
Bald Faced Stag *(N2)*
The Barnsbury *(N1)*
Bradley's *(NW3)*
Caravan *(N1)*
Charles Lamb *(N1)*
The Clissold Arms *(N2)*
The Drapers Arms *(N1)*
The Duke of Cambridge *(N1)*
The Engineer *(NW1)*
The Fellow *(N1)*
The Foundry *(NW1)*
Frederick's *(N1)*
Freemasons Arms *(NW3)*
The Haven *(N20)*
The Horseshoe *(NW3)*
The Junction Tavern *(NW5)*
Juniper Dining *(N5)**
Landmark (Winter Gdn) *(NW1)*
The Lansdowne *(NW1)*
Made In Camden *(NW1)*
Mango Room *(NW1)*
Market *(NW1)*
Mosaica *(N22)*
The North London Tavern *(NW6)*
The Northgate *(N1)**
Odette's *(NW1)**
The Old Bull & Bush *(NW3)*
Prince Albert *(NW1)*
Rising Sun *(NW7)*
The Rose & Crown *(N6)*
Rotunda Bar & Restaurant *(N1)*
St Pancras Grand *(NW1)*
Somerstown Coffee House *(NW1)*
The Wells *(NW3)*
The Wet Fish Cafe *(NW6)*

South

The Abbeville *(SW4)*
Abbeville Kitchen *(SW4)**
Alma *(SW18)*
Antelope *(SW17)*
Avalon *(SW12)*
The Balham Bowls Club *(SW12)*
Ben's Canteen *(SW11)*
The Bingham *(TW10)**
Bistro Union *(SW4)*
Blueprint Café *(SE1)*
The Bolingbroke *(SW11)*
The Brown Dog *(SW13)*
Brunswick House Cafe *(SW8)**
Cannizaro House *(SW19)*
Cantina Vinopolis *(SE1)*
Chapters *(SE3)*
Chez Bruce *(SW17)**
The Crooked Well *(SE5)*
The Dartmouth Arms *(SE23)*
The Depot *(SW14)*
Earl Spencer *(SW18)*
Elliot's Cafe *(SE1)**
Emile's *(SW15)*
Entrée *(SW11)*
The Fentiman Arms *(SW8)*
Florence *(SE24)*
40 Maltby Street *(SE1)**
Four O Nine *(SW9)*
Franklins *(SE22)*
Garrison *(SE1)*
The Glasshouse *(TW9)**
Harrison's *(SW12)*
Inside *(SE10)**
Lamberts *(SW12)**
The Lido Cafe *(SE24)*
The Lighthouse *(SW11)*
Magdalen *(SE1)**
Menier Chocolate Factory *(SE1)*
Mezzanine *(SE1)*
The Old Brewery *(SE10)*
Oxo Tower (Rest') *(SE1)*
The Palmerston *(SE22)*
Petersham Hotel *(TW10)*
Petersham Nurseries *(TW10)*
Plane Food *(TW6)*
Le Pont de la Tour *(SE1)*
The Prince Of Wales *(SW15)*
Ransome's Dock *(SW11)*
Rivington Grill *(SE10)*
Rock & Rose *(TW9)*
RSJ *(SE1)*
Simplicity *(SE16)*
Skylon *(SE1)*
Sonny's *(SW13)*
The Swan at the Globe *(SE1)*
The Table *(SE1)*

Tate Modern (Level 7) *(SE1)*
Tom Ilic *(SW8)**
Trinity *(SW4)**
Union Street Café *(SE1)*
Verta *(SW11)*
The Victoria *(SW14)**
Waterloo Bar & Kitchen *(SE1)*
The Wharf *(TW11)*

East
The Anthologist *(EC2)*
Balans *(E20)*
Beach Blanket Babylon *(E1)*
Bevis Marks *(E1)*
Bistrotheque *(E2)*
The Boundary *(E2)*
Brasserie on St John Street *(EC1)*
Bread Street Kitchen *(EC4)*
Café Below *(EC2)*
Caravan *(EC1)*
The Chancery *(EC4)**
Chiswell Street Dining Rms *(EC1)*
The Don *(EC4)*
Duck & Waffle *(EC2)*
The Empress *(E9)**
Gow's *(EC2)*
The Gun *(E14)*
The Gunmakers *(EC1)**
High Timber *(EC4)*
Hilliard *(EC4)**
The Jugged Hare *(EC1Y)*
Malmaison Brasserie *(EC1)*
The Mercer *(EC2)*
The Modern Pantry *(EC1)*
The Morgan Arms *(E3)*
The Narrow *(E14)*
1901 *(EC2)*
North Road *(EC1)**
Northbank *(EC4)*
1 Lombard Street *(EC3)*
The Peasant *(EC1)*
Princess of Shoreditch *(EC2)*
Prism *(EC3)*
The Punch Tavern *(EC4)*
Rhodes 24 *(EC2)*
Rivington Grill *(EC2)*
Rochelle Canteen *(E2)*
Searcy's Brasserie *(EC2)*
Smiths (Ground Floor) *(EC1)*
3 South Place *(EC2)*
Vertigo 42 *(EC2)*
Vinoteca *(EC1)*
Wapping Food *(E1)*
The White Swan *(EC4)*
Whitechapel Gallery *(E1)*

BRITISH, TRADITIONAL

Central
Boisdale *(SW1)*
Browns (Albemarle) *(W1)*
Canteen *(W1)*
Corrigan's Mayfair *(W1)*
Dinner *(SW1)*
The Fountain (Fortnum's) *(W1)*
Fuzzy's Grub *(SW1)*
Great Queen Street *(WC2)**
Green's *(SW1)*
The Guinea Grill *(W1)*
Hardy's Brasserie *(W1)*
The Lady Ottoline *(WC1)*
The National Dining Rooms *(WC2)*
Odin's *(W1)*
Porters English Restaurant *(WC2)*
Rib Room *(SW1)*
Rules *(WC2)*
St John Hotel *(WC2)*
Savoy Grill *(WC2)*
Scott's *(W1)**
Shepherd's *(SW1)*
Simpsons-in-the-Strand *(WC2)*
Wiltons *(SW1)*
The Windmill *(W1)**

West
The Brown Cow *(SW6)*
Bumpkin *(SW7, W11)*
Ffiona's *(W8)*
The Hampshire Hog *(W6)*
Hereford Road *(W2)**
Maggie Jones's *(W8)*
The Markham Inn *(SW3)*
The Surprise *(SW3)*

North
Bull & Last *(NW5)**
Gilbert Scott *(NW1)*
Holly Bush *(NW3)*
Kentish Canteen *(NW5)*
The Marquess Tavern *(N1)*
The Old White Bear *(NW3)*
St Johns *(N19)**

South
The Anchor & Hope *(SE1)**
Butlers Wharf Chop House *(SE1)*
Canteen *(SE1)*
Canton Arms *(SW8)**
Fox & Grapes *(SW19)*
The Lord Northbrook *(SE12)*
The Riverfront *(SE1)*
Roast *(SE1)*

East
Albion *(E2)*
Canteen *(E1, E14)*
The Fox and Anchor *(EC1)*
Fuzzy's Grub *(EC4)*
George & Vulture *(EC3)*
Green's *(EC3)*
Hix Oyster & Chop House *(EC1)**
Paternoster Chop House *(EC4)*
E Pellicci *(E2)*
St John *(EC1)**
St John Bread & Wine *(E1)**
Simpson's Tavern *(EC3)*
Sweetings *(EC4)*

EAST & CENT. EUROPEAN

Central
The Delaunay *(WC2)*
Gay Hussar *(W1)*
The Wolseley *(W1)*

North
Kipferl *(N1)*
Trojka *(NW1)*

FISH & SEAFOOD

Central
Back to Basics *(W1)**
Belgo Centraal *(WC2)*
Bellamy's *(W1)*
Bentley's *(W1)**
Bubba Gump Shrimp Company *(W1)*
Burger & Lobster *(W1)**
Cape Town Fish Market *(W1)*
Fishworks *(W1)*
Green's *(SW1)*
Loch Fyne *(WC2)*

Olivomare *(SW1)**
One-O-One *(SW1)**
The Pantechnicon *(SW1)*
Pescatori *(W1)*
Quaglino's *(SW1)*
Randall & Aubin *(W1)*
Rib Room *(SW1)*
Royal China Club *(W1)**
Scott's *(W1)**
J Sheekey *(WC2)**
J Sheekey Oyster Bar *(WC2)**
Wheeler's *(SW1)*
Wiltons *(SW1)*
Wright Brothers *(W1)**

West
Bibendum Oyster Bar *(SW3)*
Big Easy *(SW3)*
Le Café Anglais *(W2)*
Chez Patrick *(W8)*
The Cow *(W2)*
Geales *(W8)*
Kensington Place *(W8)*
Mandarin Kitchen *(W2)**
Outlaw's Seafood and Grill *(SW3)*
Poissonnerie de l'Avenue *(SW3)*
The Summerhouse *(W9)*
Le Suquet *(SW3)*

North
Belgo Noord *(NW1)*
Bradley's *(NW3)*
Carob Tree *(NW5)*
Chez Liline *(N4)**
Daphne *(NW1)*
Olympus Fish *(N3)**
Sea Pebbles *(HA5)**
Toff's *(N10)**

South
Applebee's Cafe *(SE1)*
Fish Place *(SW11)**
fish! *(SE1)*
Gastro *(SW4)*
Lobster Pot *(SE11)*
Le Querce *(SE23)**
Wright Brothers *(SE1)**

East
Angler *(EC2)*
Burger & Lobster *(EC1)**
Chamberlain's *(EC3)*
Fish Central *(EC1)**
The Fish Market *(EC2)*
Forman's *(E3)*
Gow's *(EC2)*
The Grapes *(E14)*
Hix Oyster & Chop House *(EC1)**
Loch Fyne *(EC3)*
Orpheus *(EC3)**
Redhook *(EC1)*
The Royal Exchange Grand Café *(EC3)*
Sweetings *(EC4)*

FRENCH
Central
Alain Ducasse *(W1)*
Antidote *(W1)*
L'Artiste Musclé *(W1)*
L'Atelier de Joel Robuchon *(WC2)*
L'Autre Pied *(W1)**
The Balcon *(SW1)*
Bar Boulud *(SW1)**
Bellamy's *(W1)*
Boudin Blanc *(W1)*
Boulevard *(WC2)*
Brasserie Blanc *(W1,WC2)*
Brasserie St Jacques *(SW1)*
Brasserie Zédel *(W1)*
Café Bohème *(W1)*
Café des Amis *(WC2)*
Le Cercle *(SW1)**
Chabrot Bistrot d'Amis *(SW1)*
The Chelsea Brasserie *(SW1)*
Le Cigalon *(WC2)**
Clos Maggiore *(WC2)**
Colbert *(SW1)*
Côte *(W1,WC2)*
Les Deux Salons *(WC2)*
The Ebury *(SW1)*
Elena's L'Etoile *(W1)*
L'Escargot *(W1)*
Galvin at Windows *(W1)*
Galvin Bistrot de Luxe *(W1)**
Galvin Demoiselle *(SW1)*
Le Garrick *(WC2)*
Gauthier Soho *(W1)**
Le Gavroche *(W1)**
The Giaconda Dining Room *(WC2)*
Gordon Ramsay at Claridge's *(W1)*
Green Man & French Horn *(WC2)*
The Greenhouse *(W1)**
Hélène Darroze *(W1)*
Hibiscus *(W1)*
Koffmann's *(SW1)**
Langan's Bistro *(W1)*
Marcus Wareing *(SW1)**
maze *(W1)*
Mon Plaisir *(WC2)*
Odin's *(W1)*
L'Oranger *(SW1)*
Orrery *(W1)*
Otto's *(WC1)**
Pearl *(WC1)*
La Petite Maison *(W1)**
Pétrus *(SW1)*
Pied à Terre *(W1)**
La Poule au Pot *(SW1)*
Prix Fixe *(W1)*
Randall & Aubin *(W1)*
Le Relais de Venise L'Entrecôte *(W1)**
The Ritz Restaurant *(W1)*
Savoir Faire *(WC1)*
Savoy Grill *(WC2)*
Savoy (River Rest') *(WC2)*
Sketch (Lecture Rm) *(W1)*
Sketch (Gallery) *(W1)*
The Square *(W1)**
Terroirs *(WC2)*
28-50 *(W1)*
Verru *(W1)**
Villandry *(W1)*
The Wallace *(W1)*

West
Albertine *(W12)*
Angelus *(W2)*
L'Art du Fromage *(SW10)*
Bel Canto *(W2)*
Belvedere *(W8)*
Bibendum *(SW3)*
La Bouchée *(SW7)*
La Brasserie *(SW3)*
Le Café Anglais *(W2)*
Cassis Bistro *(SW3)*
Charlotte's Bistro *(W4)*
Charlotte's Place *(W5)*
Cheyne Walk Brasserie *(SW3)*

Chez Patrick *(W8)*
Le Colombier *(SW3)*
Côte *(SW6, W2, W4, W8)*
Electric Brasserie *(W11)*
L'Etranger *(SW7)*
Garnier *(SW5)*
Goode & Wright *(W11)*
Gordon Ramsay *(SW3)*
Notting Hill Brasserie *(W11)*
The Pig's Ear *(SW3)*
Poissonnerie de l'Avenue *(SW3)*
Quantus *(W4)*
Racine *(SW3)**
La Sophia *(W10)**
Le Suquet *(SW3)*
Tartine *(SW3)*
La Trompette *(W4)**
Le Troquet *(SW10)**
Le Vacherin *(W4)*
Whits *(W8)*

North
L'Absinthe *(NW1)*
The Almeida *(N1)*
Les Associés *(N8)*
L'Aventure *(NW8)**
Bistro Aix *(N8)**
Blue Legume *(N1, N16, N8)*
Bradley's *(NW3)*
La Cage Imaginaire *(NW3)*
Charles Lamb *(N1)*
Cocotte *(NW3)*
Fig *(N1)**
Le Mercury *(N1)*
Mill Lane Bistro *(NW6)*
One Blenheim Terrace *(NW8)*
Oslo Court *(NW8)**
The Rose & Crown *(N6)*
Le Sacré-Coeur *(N1)*
The Wells *(NW3)*

South
Bellevue Rendez-Vous *(SW17)*
Brasserie Blanc *(SE1)*
Brasserie Toulouse-Lautrec *(SE11)*
Brula *(TW1)**
La Buvette *(TW9)*
Le Cassoulet *(CR2)*
Le Chardon *(SE22, SW4)*
Côte *(SE1, SW19)*
Gastro *(SW4)*
Gazette *(SW11, SW12)*
The Lawn Bistro *(SW19)*
Lobster Pot *(SE11)*
Ma Cuisine *(TW9)*
Le P'tit Normand *(SW18)*
Soif *(SW11)*
The Spread Eagle *(SE10)*
Upstairs Bar *(SW2)**
Waterloo Brasserie *(SE1)*

East
Bistrot Bruno Loubet *(EC1)**
Bleeding Heart *(EC1)**
Brasserie Blanc *(EC2, EC3, EC4)*
Brawn *(E2)**
Café du Marché *(EC1)**
Cellar Gascon *(EC1)*
Club Gascon *(EC1)**
Comptoir Gascon *(EC1)*
Coq d'Argent *(EC2)*
Côte *(EC4)*
The Don *(EC4)*
Galvin La Chapelle *(E1)**
Lutyens *(EC4)*
Morgan M *(EC1)**
Plateau *(E14)*
Relais de Venise L'Entrecôte *(E14, EC2)**
Le Rendezvous du Café *(EC1)*
The Royal Exchange Grand Café *(EC3)*
Le Saint Julien *(EC1)*
Sauterelle *(EC3)*
Les Trois Garçons *(E1)*
28-50 *(EC4)*

FUSION
Central
Archipelago *(W1)*
Asia de Cuba *(WC2)*
Kopapa *(WC2)*
Providores (Tapa Room) *(W1)**

West
E&O *(W11)**
Eight Over Eight *(SW3)**
L'Etranger *(SW7)*
Sushinho *(SW3)*

North
XO *(NW3)*

South
Champor-Champor *(SE1)*
Tsunami *(SW4)**
Village East *(SE1)*

East
Caravan *(EC1)*
Sushinho *(EC2)*
Viajante *(E2)**

GAME
Central
Boisdale *(SW1)*
Rules *(WC2)*
Wiltons *(SW1)*

West
Harwood Arms *(SW6)**

North
San Daniele del Friuli *(N5)*

GREEK
Central
Hellenic *(W1)*
Real Greek *(W1, WC2)*

West
Halepi *(W2)*
Mazi *(W8)*
The Real Greek *(W12)*

North
Carob Tree *(NW5)*
Daphne *(NW1)*
Lemonia *(NW1)*
The Real Greek *(N1)*
Retsina *(NW3)*
Vrisaki *(N22)*

South
Real Greek *(SE1)*

East
Kolossi Grill *(EC1)*
Real Greek *(E1)*

HUNGARIAN

Central
Gay Hussar *(W1)*

INTERNATIONAL

Central
Balans *(W1)*
Bedford & Strand *(WC2)*
Boulevard *(WC2)*
Browns *(SW1,W1,WC2)*
Bumbles *(SW1)*
Café in the Crypt *(WC2)*
Cork & Bottle *(WC2)*
The Forge *(WC2)*
Giraffe *(SW1,W1,WC1)*
Gordon's Wine Bar *(WC2)*
Grumbles *(SW1)*
Motcombs *(SW1)*
National Gallery Café *(WC2)*
The Providores *(W1)*
Sarastro *(WC2)*
Stock Pot *(SW1)*
The 10 Cases *(WC2)*
Terroirs *(WC2)*

West
Annie's *(W4)*
Balans West *(SW5,W12,W4,W8)*
Chelsea Bun Diner *(SW10)*
The Chelsea Kitchen *(SW10)*
Foxtrot Oscar *(SW3)*
Gallery Mess *(SW3)*
Giraffe *(W11,W4,W8)*
The Kensington Wine Rooms *(W8)*
Medlar *(SW10)**
Michael Nadra *(W4)**
Mona Lisa *(SW10)*
The Scarsdale *(W8)*
Stock Pot *(SW3)*
202 *(W11)*
The Windsor Castle *(W8)*
Wine Gallery *(SW10)*

North
The Arches *(NW6)*
Banners *(N8)*
Browns *(N1)*
The Flask *(N6)*
Giraffe *(N1, NW3)*
The Haven *(N20)*
The Old Bull & Bush *(NW3)*
The Orange Tree *(N20)*
Petek *(N4)*
Spaniard's Inn *(NW3)*
Swan & Edgar *(NW1)*

South
Annie's *(SW13)*
Brinkley's Kitchen *(SW17)*
Browns *(SE1)*
Delfina *(SE1)*
Giraffe *(SE1)*
Green & Blue *(SE22)*
Hudsons *(SW15)*
Joanna's *(SE19)*
The Light House *(SW19)*
The Riverfront *(SE1)*
The Ship *(SW18)*
Tate Modern (Level 2) *(SE1)*
Telegraph *(SW15)*
The Trafalgar Tavern *(SE10)*
Vivat Bacchus *(SE1)*
The Wharf *(TW11)*
The Yellow House *(SE16)*

East
Browns *(E14, EC2)*
Dans le Noir *(EC1)*
Giraffe *(E1)*
LMNT *(E8)*
The Luxe *(E1)*
Les Trois Garçons *(E1)*
Vivat Bacchus *(EC4)*
The Wine Library *(EC3)*

IRISH

East
Lutyens *(EC4)*

ITALIAN

Central
Al Duca *(SW1)*
Alloro *(W1)**
Amaranto *(W1)*
Apsleys *(SW1)*
Babbo *(W1)*
Banca *(W1)**
Bar Trattoria Semplice *(W1)*
Il Baretto *(W1)*
Bocca Di Lupo *(W1)**
La Bottega *(SW1)*
Briciole *(W1)**
C London *(W1)*
Caffè Caldesi *(W1)*
Caffé Vergnano *(WC2)*
Caraffini *(SW1)*
Cecconi's *(W1)*
Ciao Bella *(WC1)*
Como Lario *(SW1)*
Il Convivio *(SW1)*
Cotidie *(W1)*
Da Mario *(WC2)*
Polpo *(WC2)*
Dehesa *(W1)**
Delfino *(W1)**
Downtown Mayfair *(W1)*
Franco's *(SW1)*
La Genova *(W1)*
Gran Paradiso *(SW1)*
Jamie's Italian *(WC2)*
Latium *(W1)**
Locanda Locatelli *(W1)*
Made in Italy *(W1)*
Mele e Pere *(W1)*
Mennula *(W1)*
Murano *(W1)*
Novikov (Italian restaurant) *(W1)**
Oliveto *(SW1)**
Olivo *(SW1)**
Olivomare *(SW1)**
Opera Tavern *(WC2)**
Orso *(WC2)*
Osteria Dell'Angolo *(SW1)*
Ottolenghi *(SW1)**
Pescatori *(W1)*
Piccolino *(W1)*
Polpo *(W1)*
La Porchetta Pizzeria *(WC1)*
Princi *(W1)*
Quirinale *(SW1)**
Ristorante Semplice *(W1)*
Rossopomodoro *(WC2)*
Sale e Pepe *(SW1)*
Salt Yard *(W1)**
San Carlo Cicchetti *(W1)*
Santini *(SW1)*
Sardo *(W1)*
Sartoria *(W1)*
Serafino *(W1)*
Signor Sassi *(SW1)*

Tempo (W1)
Theo Randall (W1)*
Tinello (SW1)*
2 Amici (SW1)
2 Veneti (W1)
Vapiano (W1)
Vasco & Piero's Pavilion (W1)*
Il Vicolo (SW1)
Zafferano (SW1)

West

Aglio e Olio (SW10)
The Ark (W8)
Assaggi (W2)*
La Bottega (SW7)
Buona Sera (SW3)
Canta Napoli (W4)
Casa Batavia (W8)
Cibo (W14)*
Da Mario (SW7)
Daphne's (SW3)
La Delizia Limbara (SW3)
El Ieven Park Walk (SW10)
Edera (W11)*
Essenza (W11)
La Famiglia (SW10)
Frankie's Italian Bar & Grill (SW3)
Frantoio (SW10)
Jamie's Italian (W12)
Locanda Ottomezzo (W8)
Lucio (SW3)
Made in Italy (SW3)
Manicomio (SW3)
Mediterraneo (W11)
Mona Lisa (SW10)
Montpeliano (SW7)
Napulé (SW6)
Nuovi Sapori (SW6)
The Oak (W2)*
Osteria Basilico (W11)
Osteria dell'Arancio (SW10)
Ottolenghi (W11, W8)*
Il Pagliaccio (SW6)
Pappa Ciccia (SW6)
Pellicano (SW3)
Pentolina (W14)*
Il Portico (W8)
Portobello Ristorante (W11)*
The Red Pepper (W9)*
Riccardo's (SW3)
The River Café (W6)*
Rocco (SW5)
Rossopomodoro (SW10, W11)
San Lorenzo (SW3)
Santa Lucia (SW10)
Scalini (SW3)
Timo (W8)
Ziani's (SW3)

North

Artigiano (NW3)
L'Artista (NW11)
Il Bacio (N16, N5)
Canonbury Kitchen (N1)
La Collina (NW1)
Fifteen (N1)
500 (N19)*
Marine Ices (NW3)
Mimmo la Bufala (NW3)
Ottolenghi (N1)*
Pizzeria Oregano (N1)
Pizzeria Pappagone (N4)
La Porchetta Pizzeria (N1, N4, NW1)
Rugoletta (N2)
The Salt House (NW8)*
The Salusbury (NW6)
San Daniele del Friuli (N5)
Sardo Canale (NW1)
Sarracino (NW6)*
Trullo (N1)*
Villa Bianca (NW3)
York & Albany (NW1)

South

A Cena (TW1)
Al Forno (SW15, SW19)
Antico (SE1)
Antipasto & Pasta (SW11)
La Barca (SE1)
Al Boccon di'vino (TW9)*
Buona Sera (SW11)
Canta Napoli (TW11)
Cantina del Ponte (SE1)
Cantinetta (SW15)
La Delizia (SW18)
Donna Margherita (SW11)*
Enoteca Turi (SW15)*
Frizzante Cafe (SE16)
Isola del Sole (SW15)
La Lanterna (SE1)
Lorenzo (SE19)
Numero Uno (SW11)
Osteria Antica Bologna (SW11)
Pizza Metro (SW11)*
Le Querce (SE23)*
Riva (SW13)*
San Lorenzo Fuoriporta (SW19)
Sapori Sardi (SW6)*
The Table (SE1)
Tentazioni (SE1)*
Zucca (SE1)*

East

Al Volo (E1)
Alba (EC1)
Amico Bio (EC1)
L'Anima (EC2)*
Il Bordello (E1)*
Caravaggio (EC3)
Fabrizio (EC1)*
La Figa (E14)
Frizzante at City Farm (E2)*
Giant Robot (EC1)
Jamie's Italian (E14)
Lardo (E8)
Manicomio (EC2)
E Pellicci (E2)
Piccolino (EC2)
Polpo (EC1)
La Porchetta Pizzeria (EC1)
Quadrato (E14)
Refettorio (EC4)
Santore (EC1)*
Taberna Etrusca (EC4)

MEDITERRANEAN

Central

About Thyme (SW1)
Aurelia (W1)
Bistro 1 (W1, WC2)
Dabbous (W1)*
Hummus Bros (W1, WC1)
Massimo (SW1)
Nopi (W1)*
The Norfolk Arms (WC1)
Quince (W1)
Riding House Café (W1)
Rocket (W1)
Truc Vert (W1)

West
The Atlas *(SW6)**
Cumberland Arms *(W14)**
Del'Aziz *(SW6,W12)*
The Grove *(W6)*
Locanda Ottomezzo *(W8)*
Made in Italy *(SW3)*
Mediterraneo *(W11)*
Raoul's Café *(W9)*
Raoul's Café & Deli *(W11,W6)*
La Sophia *(W10)**
The Swan *(W4)*
Tom's Deli *(W11)*
Troubadour *(SW5)*

North
Blue Legume *(N16)*
Del'Aziz *(NW3)*
The Little Bay *(NW6)*
Mem & Laz *(N1)*
Petek *(N4)*
Stringray Café *(N5, NW5)*

South
Cantina del Ponte *(SE1)*
Cantina Vinopolis *(SE1)*
Del'Aziz *(SE1)*
Fish in a Tie *(SW11)*
The Fox & Hounds *(SW11)**
The Little Bay *(SW11)*
Oxo Tower (Brass') *(SE1)*
The Wharf *(TW11)*

East
Bonds *(EC2)*
The Eagle *(EC1)*
Hummus Bros *(EC2)*
The Little Bay *(EC1)*
Morito *(EC1)**
Portal *(EC1)*
Rocket *(E14)*
Rocket *(EC2)*
Stringray Globe Café *(E2)*
Vinoteca *(EC1)*

ORGANIC
Central
Daylesford Organic *(SW1)*

West
Daylesford Organic *(W11)*

North
The Duke of Cambridge *(N1)*
Holly Bush *(NW3)*

East
Smiths (Dining Rm) *(EC1)*

POLISH
West
Gessler at Daquise *(SW7)*
Polish Club *(SW7)*
Patio *(W12)*

South
Baltic *(SE1)*

PORTUGUESE
West
Lisboa Pâtisserie *(W10)*

East
Corner Room *(E2)**
Eyre Brothers *(EC2)**
The Gun *(E14)*
Portal *(EC1)*

RUSSIAN
Central
Bob Bob Ricard *(W1)*
Mari Vanna *(SW1)*

North
Trojka *(NW1)*

SCANDINAVIAN
Central
Nordic Bakery *(W1)*
Scandinavian Kitchen *(W1)*
Texture *(W1)**
Verru *(W1)**

West
Madsen *(SW7)*

East
North Road *(EC1)**

SCOTTISH
Central
Albannach *(WC2)*
Boisdale *(SW1)*

East
Boisdale of Canary Wharf *(E14)*

SPANISH
Central
aqua nueva *(W1)*
Barrafina *(W1,WC2)**
Barrica *(W1)**
Café España *(W1)*
Cigala *(WC1)*
Copita *(W1)**
Dehesa *(W1)**
Donostia *(W1)**
Fino *(W1)**
Goya *(SW1)*
Ibérica *(W1)*
Mar I Terra *(W1)*
Navarro's *(W1)**
Opera Tavern *(WC2)**
El Pirata *(W1)*
Salt Yard *(W1)**
Tapas Brindisa Soho *(W1)*

West
Cambio de Tercio *(SW5)**
Capote Y Toros *(SW5)*
Casa Brindisa *(SW7)*
Duke of Sussex *(W4)*
Galicia *(W10)*
El Pirata de Tapas *(W2)*
Tendido Cero *(SW5)*
Tendido Cuatro *(SW6)*

North
La Bota *(N8)*
Café del Parc *(N19)**
Camino *(N1)*
La Giralda *(HA5)*
El Parador *(NW1)**

South
Angels & Gypsies *(SE5)**
don Fernando's *(TW9)*
José *(SE1)**

Lola Rojo (SW11)
La Mancha (SW15)
Mar I Terra (SE1)
Meson don Felipe (SE1)
Pizarro (SE1)*
Rebato's (SW8)
El Rincón Latino (SW4)
Tapas Brindisa (SE1)

East
Eyre Brothers (EC2)*
Ibérica (E14)
Morito (EC1)*
Moro (EC1)*
Pinchito (EC1)
Tramontana Brindisa (EC2)

STEAKS & GRILLS

Central
Black & Blue (W1)
Bodean's (W1)
The Bountiful Cow (WC1)
Christopher's (WC2)
Cut (W1)
Gaucho (W1,WC2)
Goodman (W1)*
The Guinea Grill (W1)
Hawksmoor (W1,WC2)*
JW Steakhouse (W1)
MASH Steakhouse (W1)
maze Grill (W1)
The Palm (SW1)
Le Relais de Venise L'Entrecôte (W1)*
Rib Room (SW1)
Rowley's (SW1)
Sophie's Steakhouse (WC2)
The Standard Grill (W1)
STK Steakhouse (WC2)
34 (W1)
Wolfe's (WC2)

West
Admiral Codrington (SW3)*
Black & Blue (SW3, SW7,W8)
Bodean's (SW6)
The Cabin (W4)
Casa Malevo (W2)
Gaucho (SW3)
Haché (SW10)
Kings Road Steakhouse (SW3)
Lola & Simón (W6)
The Meat & Wine Co (W12)
PJ's Bar and Grill (SW3)
Popeseye (W14)*
Sophie's Steakhouse (SW10)

North
De La Panza (N1)
Garufa (N5)
Gaucho (NW3)
Haché (NW1)
Rôtisserie (HA5, N20, NW8)

South
Archduke Wine Bar (SE1)
Black & Blue (SE1)
Bodean's (SW4)
Buenos Aires Café (SE10, SE3)*
Butcher & Grill (SW11, SW19)
Cattle Grid (SW11, SW12)*
Constancia (SE1)*
Gaucho (SE1, SE10,TW10)
Kew Grill (TW9)
Popeseye (SW15)*
Santa Maria del Sur (SW8)

East
Barbecoa (EC4)
Buen Ayre (E8)*
Gaucho (E14, EC1, EC2, EC3)
Goodman (E14)*
Goodman City (EC2)*
Hawksmoor (E1, EC2)*
Hix at The Tramshed (EC2)
Hix Oyster & Chop House (EC1)*
MPW Steakhouse & Grill (E1)
New Street Grill (EC2)
Redhook (EC1)
Relais de Venise L'Entrecôte (E14, EC2)*
Simpson's Tavern (EC3)
Smiths (Top Floor) (EC1)
Smiths (Dining Rm) (EC1)
Smiths (Ground Floor) (EC1)

SWISS

Central
St Moritz (W1)

VEGETARIAN

Central
Chettinad (W1)*
Food for Thought (WC2)*
Govinda's (W1)*
Hummus Bros (W1,WC1)
Malabar Junction (WC1)
Masala Zone (W1)
Mildreds (W1)*
Orchard (WC1)
Ragam (W1)*
Rasa Maricham (WC1)*
Sagar (W1)*
tibits (W1)
Woodlands (SW1,W1)

West
The Gate (W6)*
Masala Zone (SW5, SW6,W2)
Sagar (W6)*

North
Chutneys (NW1)
Diwana Bhel-Poori House (NW1)
Jai Krishna (N4)*
Manna (NW3)
Masala Zone (N1)
Rani (N3)
Rasa (N16)*
Rasa Travancore (N16)*
Sakonis (HA0)
Vijay (NW6)*
Woodlands (NW3)

South
Blue Elephant (SW6)
Cocum (SW20)
Ganapati (SE15)*
Le Pont de la Tour (SE1)
Sree Krishna (SW17)*

East
Amico Bio (EC1)
The Gate (EC1)*
Hummus Bros (EC2)
Vanilla Black (EC4)

AFTERNOON TEA

Central
Athenaeum *(W1)**
The Diamond Jub' Salon (Fortnum's) *(W1)*
The Fountain (Fortnum's) *(W1)*
La Fromagerie Café *(W1)**
Ladurée *(W1,WC2)**
Maison Bertaux *(W1)**
The National Dining Rooms *(WC2)*
National Gallery Café *(WC2)*
Notes *(WC2)*
Oscar *(W1)*
Ritz (Palm Court) *(W1)*
Royal Academy *(W1)*
The Sketch (Parlour) *(W1)*
Villandry *(W1)*
The Wallace *(W1)*
William Curley *(SW1)**
The Wolseley *(W1)*
Yauatcha *(W1)**

North
Kenwood (Brew House) *(NW3)*
Landmark (Winter Gdn) *(NW1)*

South
Cannizaro House *(SW19)*
San Lorenzo Fuoriporta *(SW19)*
William Curley *(TW9)**

BURGERS, ETC

Central
Automat *(W1)*
Bar Boulud *(SW1)**
Black & Blue *(W1)*
The Bountiful Cow *(WC1)*
Burger & Lobster *(W1)**
Byron *(SW1,W1,WC2)*
Diner *(W1)*
Ed's Easy Diner *(W1)*
Goodman *(W1)**
Hard Rock Café *(W1)*
Hawksmoor *(W1,WC2)**
Honest Burgers *(W1)**
Joe Allen *(WC2)*
Kettners *(W1)*
MEATLiquor *(W1)**
Opera Tavern *(WC2)**
Wolfe's *(WC2)*

West
Admiral Codrington *(SW3)**
Big Easy *(SW3)*
Black & Blue *(SW3, SW7, W8)*
Byron *(SW3, SW5, SW7, W12, W8)*
The Chelsea Ram *(SW10)*
Haché *(SW10)*
Lucky Seven *(W2)*
Sticky Fingers *(W8)*
Troubadour *(SW5)*

North
Byron *(N1)*
Diner *(N1, NW1, NW10)*
Haché *(NW1)*
Harry Morgan's *(NW8)*
Red Dog Saloon *(N1)*

South
Ben's Canteen *(SW11)*
Black & Blue *(SE1)*
Byron *(SW15)*
Cattle Grid *(SW11, SW12)**
Honest Burgers *(SW9)**
The Old Brewery *(SE10)*
Village East *(SE1)*

East
Burger & Lobster *(EC1)**
Byron *(E14, EC2)*
Comptoir Gascon *(EC1)*
The Diner *(EC2)*
Goodman *(E14)**
Goodman City *(EC2)**
Hawksmoor *(E1, EC2)**
Malmaison Brasserie *(EC1)*
Smiths (Dining Rm) *(EC1)*

FISH & CHIPS

Central
Fryer's Delight *(WC1)*
Golden Hind *(W1)**
North Sea Fish *(WC1)*
Rock & Sole Plaice *(WC2)*
Seafresh *(SW1)*

West
Geales *(W8)*
Geales Chelsea Green *(SW3)*
Kerbisher & Malt *(W6)**

North
Nautilus *(NW6)**
The Sea Shell *(NW1)*
Skipjacks *(HA3)**
Toff's *(N10)**
Two Brothers *(N3)*

South
Brady's *(SW18)*
Fish Club *(SW11, SW4)**
Masters Super Fish *(SE1)*
Olley's *(SE24)*
The Sea Cow *(SE22)**

East
Ark Fish *(E18)**
Faulkner's *(E8)**

ICE CREAM

Central
Gelupo *(W1)**

North
Marine Ices *(NW3)*

PIZZA

Central
Il Baretto *(W1)*
Delfino *(W1)**
Fire & Stone *(WC2)*
Kettners *(W1)*
Made in Italy *(W1)*
Oliveto *(SW1)**
The Orange *(SW1)**
Piccolino *(W1)*
La Porchetta Pizzeria *(WC1)*
Princi *(W1)*
Rocket *(W1)*
Rossopomodoro *(WC2)*
Union Jacks *(WC2)*

West
Basilico *(SW6)**
Buona Sera *(SW3)*
Canta Napoli *(W4)*
Da Mario *(SW7)*
La Delizia Limbara *(SW3)*

Fire & Stone *(W12)*
Franco Manca *(W4)**
Frankie's Italian Bar & Grill *(SW3)*
Made in Italy *(SW3)*
The Oak *(W2)**
Osteria Basilico *(W11)*
Otto Pizza *(W2)**
Il Pagliaccio *(SW6)*
Pappa Ciccia *(SW6)*
Pizza East Portobello *(W10)*
(Ciro's) Pizza Pomodoro *(SW3)*
Portobello Ristorante *(W11)**
The Red Pepper *(W9)**
Rocca Di Papa *(SW7)*
Rossopomodoro *(SW10,W11)*
Santa Lucia *(SW10)*
Santa Maria *(W5)**
Union Jacks *(W4)*

North

Il Bacio *(N16, N5)*
Basilico *(N1, N8, NW3)**
The Lansdowne *(NW1)*
Marine Ices *(NW3)*
Mimmo la Bufala *(NW3)*
Pizza East *(NW5)*
Pizzeria Oregano *(N1)*
Pizzeria Pappagone *(N4)*
La Porchetta Pizzeria *(N1, N4, NW1)*
Sacro Cuore *(NW10)*
The Salusbury *(NW6)*
Stringray Café *(N5, NW5)*

South

Al Forno *(SW15, SW19)*
Basilico *(SW11, SW14)**
Bianco43 *(SE10)*
Buona Sera *(SW11)*
La Delizia *(SW18)*
Donna Margherita *(SW11)**
Eco *(SW4)*
Franco Manca *(SW9)**
Gourmet Pizza Company *(SE1)*
The Gowlett *(SE15)**
La Lanterna *(SE1)*
Lorenzo *(SE19)*
Pizza Metro *(SW11)**
Pizzeria Rustica *(TW9)**
Rocca Di Papa *(SE21)*
San Lorenzo Fuoriporta *(SW19)*
The Yellow House *(SE16)*
Zero Degrees *(SE3)*

East

Il Bordello *(E1)**
La Figa *(E14)*
Fire & Stone *(E1)*
Franco Manca *(E20)**
Piccolino *(EC2)*
Pizza East *(E1)*
La Porchetta Pizzeria *(EC1)*
Rocket *(E14)*
Rocket *(EC2)*
Story Deli *(E2)**
Stringray Globe Café *(E2)*

SANDWICHES, CAKES, ETC

Central

Abokado *(W1)*
Aubaine *(W1)*
Baker & Spice *(SW1)*
Bar Italia *(W1)*
Benugo *(W1)*
The Courtauld Gallery Café *(WC2)*
Fernandez & Wells *(W1, WC2)**
Flat White *(W1)*
La Fromagerie Café *(W1)**
Fuzzy's Grub *(SW1)*
Kaffeine *(W1)**
Konditor & Cook *(W1, WC1)*
Ladurée *(W1)**
Leon *(W1, WC2)*
Maison Bertaux *(W1)**
Monmouth Coffee Company *(WC2)**
Mount Street Deli *(W1)*
Natural Kitchen *(W1)*
Notes *(WC2)*
Paul *(W1, WC2)*
Pod *(WC1)*
Royal Academy *(W1)*
Scandinavian Kitchen *(W1)*
The Sketch (Parlour) *(W1)*
Taylor St Baristas *(W1)**
William Curley *(SW1)**

West

Aubaine *(SW3, W8)*
Baker & Spice *(SW3, W9)*
Benugo *(SW7, W12)*
Bluebird Café *(SW3)*
Gail's Bakery *(W4)*
Gail's Bread *(W11)*
Lisboa Pâtisserie *(W10)*
Tom's Deli *(W11)*
Troubadour *(SW5)*

North

Benugo *(NW1)*
Chamomile *(NW3)*
Euphorium Bakery *(N1)*
Gail's Bread *(NW3, NW8)*
Ginger & White *(NW3)*
Kenwood (Brew House) *(NW3)*

South

Benugo *(SE1)*
Caffé Vergnano *(SE1)*
Fulham Wine Rooms *(SW6)*
Gail's Bread *(SW11)*
Konditor & Cook *(SE1)*
Leon *(SE1)*
Monmouth Coffee Company *(SE1, SE16)**
Orange Pekoe *(SW13)*
Pantry *(SW18)*
Pod *(SE1)*
Spianata & Co *(SE1)**
Taylor St Baristas *(TW9)**
William Curley *(TW9)**

East

Abokado *(EC1, EC4)*
Benugo *(EC1)*
Brick Lane Beigel Bake *(E1)**
Caffé Vergnano *(EC4)*
Department of Coffee *(EC1)**
Dose *(EC1)**
Fuzzy's Grub *(EC4)*
Gail's Bakery *(EC1)*
Grace St Paul's *(EC4)**
Konditor & Cook *(EC3)*
Leon *(E1, E14, EC4)*
Look Mum No Hands! *(EC1)*
Natural Kitchen *(EC4)*
Nusa Kitchen *(EC1, EC2)**
Pod *(EC1, EC2, EC3, EC4)*
Prufrock Coffee *(EC1)*
Spianata & Co *(E1, EC1, EC2, EC4)**
Taylor St Baristas *(E14, EC2)**

SALADS
Central
Kaffeine *(W1)**
Natural Kitchen *(W1)*

West
Beirut Express *(SW7,W2)*

East
Natural Kitchen *(EC4)*

ARGENTINIAN
Central
Gaucho *(W1,WC2)*

West
Casa Malevo *(W2)*
Gaucho *(SW3)*
Lola & Simón *(W6)*
Quantus *(W4)*

North
Garufa *(N5)*
Gaucho *(NW3)*

South
Buenos Aires Café *(SE10, SE3)**
Constancia *(SE1)**
Gaucho *(SE1, SE10,TW10)*
Santa Maria del Sur *(SW8)*

East
Buen Ayre *(E8)**
Gaucho *(E14, EC1, EC2, EC3)*

BRAZILIAN
West
Rodizio Rico *(SW6,W2)*
Sushinho *(SW3)*

North
Rodizio Rico *(N1)*

South
Rodizio Rico *(SE10)*

East
Sushisamba *(EC2)*

CUBAN
Central
Floridita *(W1)*

MEXICAN/TEXMEX
Central
Benito's Hat *(W1,WC2)*
La Bodega Negra *(W1)*
Café Pacifico *(WC2)*
Cantina Laredo *(WC2)*
Chilango *(WC2)**
Chipotle *(W1,WC2)*
Lupita *(WC2)*
Tortilla *(W1)*
Wahaca *(W1,WC2)*

West
Taqueria *(W11)*
Tortilla *(W6)*
Wahaca *(W12)*

North
Chilango *(N1)**
Mestizo *(NW1)*
Tortilla *(N1)*

South
Tortilla *(SE1)*

East
Chilango *(EC4)**
Tortilla *(E14, EC3)*
Wahaca *(E14)*

PERUVIAN
Central
Ceviche *(W1)*
Lima *(W1)**

North
Tierra Peru *(N1)**

East
Sushisamba *(EC2)*

SOUTH AMERICAN
West
Quantus *(W4)*

North
Sabor *(N1)*

South
El Vergel *(SE1)**

AFRO-CARIBBEAN
North
Cottons *(NW1)*
Mango Room *(NW1)*

MOROCCAN
West
Adams Café *(W12)*
Pasha *(SW7)*

East
Kenza *(EC2)*

NORTH AFRICAN
Central
Momo *(W1)*

West
Azou *(W6)*
Del'Aziz *(SW6)*

East
Kenza *(EC2)*

SOUTH AFRICAN
North
Shaka Zulu *(NW1)*

TUNISIAN
West
Adams Café *(W12)*

AZERBAIJANI
Central
Baku *(SW1)*

EGYPTIAN
North
Ali Baba *(NW1)*

GEORGIAN
West
Colchis *(W2)**

East
Little Georgia Café *(E2)*

ISRAELI
Central
Gaby's *(WC2)*

North
Solly's *(NW11)*

KOSHER
Central
The Deli West One *(W1)**
Reubens *(W1)*

North
Kaifeng *(NW4)**
Solly's *(NW11)*

East
Bevis Marks *(E1)*
Brick Lane Beigel Bake *(E1)**

LEBANESE
Central
Al Hamra *(W1)*
Al Sultan *(W1)*
Beiteddine *(SW1)**
Comptoir Libanais *(W1)*
Fairuz *(W1)*
Fakhreldine *(W1)*
Ishbilia *(SW1)*
Levant *(W1)*
Maroush *(W1)*
Noura *(SW1,W1)*
Ranoush *(SW1)**
Yalla Yalla *(W1)**

West
Al-Waha *(W2)*
Beirut Express *(SW7,W2)*
Chez Marcelle *(W14)**
Comptoir Libanais *(W12)*
Fresco *(W2)**
Maroush *(SW3)*
Maroush Gardens *(W2)*
Pasha *(SW7)*
Randa *(W8)*
Ranoush *(SW3,W2,W8)**

North
Yalla Yalla *(N1)**

South
Palmyra *(TW9)**

East
Kenza *(EC2)*

MIDDLE EASTERN
Central
Patogh *(W1)**

North
Solly's *(NW11)*

East
Morito *(EC1)**

PERSIAN
West
Alounak *(W14,W2)**
Chella *(W4)*
Colbeh *(W2)**
Faanoos *(W4)*
Kateh *(W9)*
Mohsen *(W14)*
Sufi *(W12)*

North
Gilak *(N19)*

South
Faanoos *(SW14)*

SYRIAN
West
Abu Zaad *(W12)*

TURKISH
Central
Cyprus Mangal *(SW1)**
Ishtar *(W1)*
Kazan (Cafe) *(SW1)**
Quince *(W1)*
Sofra *(W1,WC2)*
Tas *(WC1)*

West
Best Mangal *(SW6,W14)**
Fez Mangal *(W11)**

North
Antepliler *(N1,N4)*
Beyoglu *(NW3)*
Gallipoli *(N1)*
Gem *(N1)*
Izgara *(N3)*
Mangal II *(N16)*
Petek *(N4)*
Sofra *(NW8)*

South
Tas (Cafe) *(SE1)*
Tas Pide *(SE1)*

East
Haz *(E1,EC2,EC3)*
Hazev *(E14)*
Mangal I *(E8)**
Tas *(EC1)*

AFGHANI
North
Afghan Kitchen *(N1)**

BURMESE
West
Mandalay *(W2)*

CHINESE
Central
Ba Shan *(W1)**
Baozi Inn *(WC2)**
Bar Shu *(W1)**
The Bright Courtyard *(W1)*
Cha Cha Moon *(W1)*
Chilli Cool *(WC1)**
China Tang *(W1)*
Chuen Cheng Ku *(W1)*
Empress of Sichuan *(WC2)**
The Four Seasons *(W1)**
Golden Dragon *(W1)*

The Grand Imperial *(SW1)*
Hakkasan *(W1)**
Haozhan *(W1)**
Harbour City *(W1)**
Hunan *(SW1)**
Imperial China *(WC2)*
Jenny Lo's Tea House *(SW1)*
Joy King Lau *(WC2)*
Kai Mayfair *(W1)*
Ken Lo's Memories *(SW1)**
Mekong *(SW1)*
Mr Chow *(SW1)*
Mr Kong *(WC2)*
New Mayflower *(W1)**
New World *(W1)*
Plum Valley *(W1)*
Princess Garden *(W1)**
Royal China *(W1)**
Royal China Club *(W1)**
Shanghai Blues *(WC1)**
Wong Kei *(W1)*
Yauatcha *(W1)**
Yming *(W1)**

West
Choys *(SW3)*
Fortune Cookie *(W2)**
The Four Seasons *(W2)**
Gold Mine *(W2)**
Good Earth *(SW3)**
Ken Lo's Memories of China *(W8)**
Mandarin Kitchen *(W2)**
Maxim *(W13)*
Min Jiang *(W8)**
Mr Wing *(SW5)*
North China *(W3)**
Pearl Liang *(W2)**
Royal China *(SW6, W2)**
Seventeen *(W11)*
Stick & Bowl *(W8)*
Taiwan Village *(SW6)**
Tian Fu *(W12)**

North
Alisan *(HA9)**
Goldfish *(NW3)**
Good Earth *(NW7)**
Green Cottage *(NW3)**
Gung-Ho *(NW6)*
Kaifeng *(NW4)**
Phoenix Palace *(NW1)**
Sakonis *(HA0)*
Singapore Garden *(NW6)**
The Water Margin *(NW11)*
Yipin China *(N1)**

South
Bayee Village *(SW19)*
Dalchini *(SW19)*
Dragon Castle *(SE17)**
Four Regions *(TW9)**
China Boulevard *(SW18)**
Royal China *(SW15)*

East
Chinese Cricket Club *(EC4)*
Gourmet San *(E2)**
HKK *(EC2)*
Imperial City *(EC3)*
Lotus Chinese Floating Restaurant *(E14)*
My Old Place *(E1)**
Royal China *(E14)**
Sedap *(EC1)*
Shanghai *(E8)**
Sichuan Folk *(E1)**
Yi-Ban *(E16)*

CHINESE, DIM SUM

Central
The Bright Courtyard *(W1)*
Chuen Cheng Ku *(W1)*
dim T *(W1)*
Golden Dragon *(W1)*
The Grand Imperial *(SW1)*
Hakkasan *(W1)**
Harbour City *(W1)**
Imperial China *(WC2)*
Joy King Lau *(WC2)*
Leong's Legends *(W1)*
New World *(W1)*
ping pong *(W1)*
Princess Garden *(W1)**
Royal China *(W1)**
Royal China Club *(W1)**
Shanghai Blues *(WC1)**
Yauatcha *(W1)**

West
Leong's Legends *(W2)*
Min Jiang *(W8)**
Pearl Liang *(W2)**
ping pong *(W2)*
Royal China *(SW6, W2)**

North
Alisan *(HA9)**
dim T *(N6, NW3)*
Phoenix Palace *(NW1)**

South
dim T *(SE1)*
Dragon Castle *(SE17)**
China Boulevard *(SW18)**
ping pong *(SE1)*
Royal China *(SW15)*

East
Lotus Chinese Floating Restaurant *(E14)*
ping pong *(E1, EC2, EC4)*
Royal China *(E14)**
Shanghai *(E8)**
Yi-Ban *(E16)*

INDIAN

Central
Amaya *(SW1)**
Benares *(W1)**
Chettinad *(W1)**
Chor Bizarre *(W1)**
Chowki *(W1)*
The Cinnamon Club *(SW1)**
Cinnamon Soho *(W1)**
Dishoom *(WC2)*
Gaylord *(W1)*
Gopal's of Soho *(W1)*
Govinda's *(W1)**
Imli *(W1)*
Indali Lounge *(W1)*
India Club *(WC2)*
Malabar Junction *(WC1)*
Masala Zone *(W1, WC2)*
Mela *(WC2)*
Mint Leaf *(SW1)*
Mooli's *(W1)**
Moti Mahal *(WC2)**
La Porte des Indes *(W1)*
Ragam *(W1)**

Red Fort *(W1)**
Roti Chai *(W1)**
Sagar *(W1, WC2)**
Salaam Namaste *(WC1)**
Salloos *(SW1)**
Tamarind *(W1)*
Trishna *(W1)**
Veeraswamy *(W1)*
Woodlands *(SW1, W1)*
Zayna *(W1)**

West
Anarkali *(W6)**
Bombay Brasserie *(SW7)*
Bombay Palace *(W2)**
Brilliant *(UB2)**
Chakra *(W11)*
Chutney Mary *(SW10)**
Gifto's *(UB1)**
The Greedy Buddha *(SW6)*
Indian Zing *(W6)**
Karma *(W14)**
Khan's *(W2)*
Khan's of Kensington *(SW7)*
Madhu's *(UB1)**
Malabar *(W8)**
Masala Zone *(SW5, SW6, W2)*
Memories of India *(SW7)*
Miran Masala *(W14)**
Mirch Masala *(UB1)**
Monty's *(SW6, W13, W5)*
Noor Jahan *(SW5, W2)**
The Painted Heron *(SW10)**
Potli *(W6)*
Rasoi *(SW3)**
Sagar *(W6)**
Star of India *(SW5)**
Thali *(SW5)**
Zaika *(W8)**

North
Anglo Asian Tandoori *(N16)**
Chutneys *(NW1)*
Delhi Grill *(N1)**
Diwana Bhel-Poori House *(NW1)*
Eriki *(NW3)*
Great Nepalese *(NW1)*
Guglee *(NW3, NW6)*
Indian Rasoi *(N2)**
Jai Krishna *(N4)**
Masala Zone *(N1, NW1)*
Paradise Hampstead *(NW3)**
Rani *(N3)*
Roots at N1 *(N1)**
Sakonis *(HA0)*
Vijay *(NW6)**
Woodlands *(NW3)*
Zaffrani *(N1)*

South
Apollo Banana Leaf *(SW17)**
Babur *(SE23)**
Bangalore Express *(SE1)*
Bengal Clipper *(SE1)*
Chutney *(SW18)*
Cocum *(SW20)*
Dalchini *(SW19)*
Everest Inn *(SE3)**
Ganapati *(SE15)**
Gandhi's *(SE11)*
Holy Cow *(SW11)**
Hot Stuff *(SW8)**
Indian Moment *(SW11)*
Indian Ocean *(SW17)**
Indian Zilla *(SW13)**
Kennington Tandoori *(SE11)*
Lahore Karahi *(SW17)**
Lahore Kebab House *(SW16)**
Ma Goa *(SW15)**
Mango & Silk *(SW14)*
Mango Tree *(SE1)*
Mirch Masala *(SW16, SW17)**
Nazmins *(SW18)*
Sree Krishna *(SW17)**
Tandoori Nights *(SE22)**
Triphal *(SW18)**

East
Bangalore Express *(EC3)*
Café Spice Namaste *(E1)**
Cinnamon Kitchen *(EC2)**
Clifton *(E1)**
Dockmaster's House *(E14)*
Lahore Kebab House *(E1)**
Memsaheb on Thames *(E14)*
Mint Leaf *(EC2)*
Mirch Masala *(E1)**
Needoo *(E1)**
Tayyabs *(E1)**

INDIAN, SOUTHERN

Central
India Club *(WC2)*
Malabar Junction *(WC1)*
Quilon *(SW1)**
Ragam *(W1)**
Rasa Maricham *(WC1)**
Rasa Samudra *(W1)**
Sagar *(W1, WC2)**
Woodlands *(SW1, W1)*

West
Sagar *(W6)**
Shilpa *(W6)**

North
Chutneys *(NW1)*
Rani *(N3)*
Rasa *(N16)**
Rasa Travancore *(N16)**
Vijay *(NW6)**
Woodlands *(NW3)*

South
Cocum *(SW20)*
Ganapati *(SE15)**
Sree Krishna *(SW17)**

INDONESIAN

Central
Melati *(W1)*

JAPANESE

Central
Abeno *(WC1, WC2)*
Abokado *(W1, WC2)*
aqua kyoto *(W1)*
Atari-Ya *(W1)**
Benihana *(W1)*
Bincho Yakitori *(W1)*
Chisou *(W1)**
Defune *(W1)**
Dinings *(W1)**
Hazuki *(WC2)*
Ikeda *(W1)**
Kiku *(W1)**
Kikuchi *(W1)**
Koya *(W1)**
Kulu Kulu *(W1, WC2)*

Matsuri (SW1)
Mitsukoshi (SW1)*
Miyama (W1)*
Nizuni (W1)
Nobu (W1)*
Nobu (W1)
Okku (SW1)
Roka (W1)*
Sakana-tei (W1)*
Sake No Hana (SW1)
Sakura (W1)
Satsuma (W1)
Soho Japan (W1)*
Sumosan (W1)
Taro (W1)
Toku (SW1)*
Tokyo Diner (WC2)
Tonkotsu (W1)
Tsunami (W1)*
Umu (W1)*
Wabi (WC2)
Wagamama (SW1, W1, WC1, WC2)
Watatsumi (WC2)
Yoisho (W1)*
Yoshino (W1)*

West
Atari-Ya (W5)*
Benihana (SW3)
Chisou (SW3, W4)*
Inaho (W2)*
Itsu (SW3, W11)
Kiraku (W5)*
Kulu Kulu (SW7)
Maguro (W9)*
Nozomi (SW3)
Okawari (W5)
Sushinho (SW3)
Tosa (W6)*
Wagamama (W8)
Yashin (W8)*
Zuma (SW7)*

North
Asakusa (NW1)*
Atari-Ya (NW4, NW6)*
Bento Cafe (NW1)*
Café Japan (NW11)*
Dotori (N4)*
Jin Kichi (NW3)*
Sushi of Shiori (NW1)*
Sushi-Say (NW2)*
Wagamama (N1, NW1)
Yuzu (NW6)*

South
Cho-San (SW15)*
Fujiyama (SW9)
Hashi (SW20)*
Matsuba (TW9)*
Slurp (SW16, SW19)
Sticks'n'Sushi (SW19)*
Tsunami (SW4)*
Tsuru (SE1)
Wagamama (SE1, SW15, SW19)

East
Abokado (EC1, EC4)
Bincho EC1 (EC1)
Chrysan (EC2)
City Miyama (EC4)
Itsu (E14)
K10 (EC2)*
Kurumaya (EC4)
Mugen (EC4)
Pham Sushi (EC1)*
Roka (E14)*
Sushisamba (EC2)
Sushi Tetsu (EC1)*
Tajima Tei (EC1)*
Tsuru (EC2, EC4)
Wagamama (E14, EC2, EC3, EC4)

KOREAN

Central
Asadal (WC1)
Bibimbap Soho (W1)
Kimchee (WC1)
Koba (W1)*

North
Dotori (N4)*

South
Cah-Chi (SW18, SW20)

MALAYSIAN

Central
C&R Cafe (W1)
Melati (W1)
Spice Market (W1)

West
Satay House (W2)

North
Singapore Garden (NW6)*

South
Champor-Champor (SE1)

East
Sedap (EC1)

PAKISTANI

Central
Salloos (SW1)*

West
Miran Masala (W14)*
Mirch Masala (UB1)*

South
Lahore Karahi (SW17)*
Lahore Kebab House (SW16)*
Mirch Masala (SW16, SW17)*

East
Lahore Kebab House (E1)*
Mirch Masala (E1)*
Needoo (E1)*
Tayyabs (E1)*

PAN-ASIAN

Central
Banana Tree Canteen (W1)
Circus (WC2)
dim T (SW1, W1)
Haozhan (W1)*
Hare & Tortoise (WC1)
Inamo (SW1, W1)
Novikov (Asian restaurant) (W1)
Spice Market (W1)
Tapasia (W1)

West
Banana Tree Canteen (W2, W9)
E&O (W11)*

Eight Over Eight *(SW3)**
Hare & Tortoise *(W14,W5)*
Mao Tai *(SW6)*
Uli *(W11)**

North
The Banana Tree Canteen *(NW6)*
dim T *(N6, NW3)*
Gilgamesh *(NW1)*
XO *(NW3)*

South
The Banana Tree Canteen *(SW11)*
dim T *(SE1)*
Hare & Tortoise *(SW15)*

East
Banana Tree Canteen *(EC1)*
Cicada *(EC1)*
Great Eastern Dining Room *(EC2)*
Hare & Tortoise *(EC4)*
Pacific Oriental *(EC2)*

THAI
Central
Busaba Eathai *(SW1,W1,WC1,WC2)*
C&R Cafe *(W1)*
Crazy Bear *(W1)*
Mango Tree *(SW1)*
Mekong *(SW1)*
Nahm *(SW1)**
Patara *(W1)**
Rosa's Soho *(W1)*
Siam Central *(W1)*
Spice Market *(W1)*
Suda *(WC2)*
Thai Pot *(WC2)*
Thai Square *(SW1,W1,WC2)*

West
Addie's Thai Café *(SW5)**
Bangkok *(SW7)*
Bedlington Café *(W4)*
Busaba Eathai *(SW3,W12)*
C&R Cafe *(W2)*
Café 209 *(SW6)*
Churchill Arms *(W8)**
Esarn Kheaw *(W12)*
Fat Boy's *(W4,W5)*
Fitou's Thai Restaurant *(W10)*
Old Parr's Head *(W14)*
101 Thai Kitchen *(W6)**
Patara *(SW3)**
Sukho Fine Thai Cuisine *(SW6)**
Thai Square *(SW7)*
The Walmer Castle *(W11)*

North
Isarn *(N1)*
Thai Square *(N1)*
Yum Yum *(N16)*

South
Amaranth *(SW18)*
Blue Elephant *(SW6)*
Fat Boy's *(SW14,TW1,TW8)*
Kaosarn *(SW11, SW9)**
The Paddyfield *(SW12)**
The Pepper Tree *(SW4)*
Suk Saran *(SW19)*
Talad Thai *(SW15)*
Thai Corner Café *(SE22)*
Thai Garden *(SW11)*
Thai Square *(SW15)*

East
Busaba Eathai *(E20, EC1)*
Elephant Royale *(E14)*
Naamyaa Café *(EC1)*
Rosa's *(E1)*
Thai Square *(EC4)*
Thai Square City *(EC3)*

VIETNAMESE
Central
Bam-Bou *(W1)*
Cây Tre *(W1)*
Mekong *(SW1)*
Pho *(W1)**
Viet *(W1)*

West
Pho *(W12)**
Saigon Saigon *(W6)*

North
Huong-Viet *(N1)*
Khoai *(N8)*
Khoai Cafe *(N12)*
Ladudu *(NW6)*
Viet Garden *(N1)*

South
Cafe East *(SE16)*
Mien Tay *(SW11)**
The Paddyfield *(SW12)**

East
Cây Tre *(EC1)*
City Càphê *(EC2)**
Green Papaya *(E8)**
Mien Tay *(E2)**
Namo *(E9)*
Pho *(EC1)**
Sông Quê *(E2)*
Viet Grill *(E2)*
Viet Hoa *(E2)*

AREA OVERVIEWS

CENTRAL

Soho, Covent Garden & Bloomsbury (Parts of W1, all WC2 and WC1)

£90+	L'Atelier de Joel Robuchon	*French*	❸❸❷
	Savoy (River Rest')	*"*	⑤④❸
	Asia de Cuba	*Fusion*	④④❸
£80+	Pearl	*French*	❸④④
£70+	The Ivy	*British, Modern*	④❷❷
	Rules	*British, Traditional*	❸❷❶
	Savoy Grill	*"*	④❸❸
	Simpsons-in-the-Strand	*"*	④④④
	aqua kyoto	*Japanese*	④④❷
	Spice Market	*Pan-Asian*	⑤④④
£60+	Christopher's	*American*	④❸❷
	Axis	*British, Modern*	④④④
	Brasserie Max	*"*	④❸❸
	Hix	*"*	④④④
	Indigo	*"*	④④④
	Paramount	*"*	④④❶
	Refuel	*"*	④❷❷
	St John Hotel	*British, Traditional*	❸❸④
	J Sheekey	*Fish & seafood*	❷❶❶
	Clos Maggiore	*French*	❷❶❶
	L'Escargot	*"*	④❷❷
	Gauthier Soho	*"*	❷❶❷
	Orso	*Italian*	④❸④
	aqua nueva	*Spanish*	⑤⑤④
	Gaucho	*Steaks & grills*	❸④❸
	Hawksmoor	*"*	❷❷❸
	Ladurée	*Afternoon tea*	❷④❸
	Shanghai Blues	*Chinese*	❷④❸
	Yauatcha	*"*	❶④❷
	Watatsumi	*Japanese*	❸④④
	Circus	*Pan-Asian*	④❸❶
£50+	Joe Allen	*American*	④④❷
	Arbutus	*British, Modern*	❷❷④
	Bob Bob Ricard	*"*	④❷❶
	Dean Street Townhouse	*"*	④❸❷
	Le Deuxième	*"*	④❸⑤
	Ducksoup	*"*	❸④④
	Hush	*"*	❸❸❸
	The Portrait	*"*	④④❶
	Quo Vadis	*"*	❸❷❷
	Tom's Terrace	*"*	⑤⑤④
	The National Dining Rms	*British, Traditional*	⑤⑤④
	The Delaunay	*East & Cent. European*	④❷❶
	Wright Brothers	*Fish & seafood*	❷❸❷
	Café des Amis	*French*	④④④
	Le Cigalon	*"*	❷❷❷
	Les Deux Salons	*"*	④④❸
	Mon Plaisir	*"*	❸❸❷
	Kopapa	*Fusion*	❸④④

	The Forge	*International*	④④④
	The 10 Cases	*"*	④❶❷
	Bocca Di Lupo	*Italian*	❷❷❷
	Vasco & Piero's Pavilion	*"*	❷❷④
	Nopi	*Mediterranean*	❷❸❸
	Albannach	*Scottish*	④❸❸
	Sophie's Steakhouse	*Steaks & grills*	④④❸
	St Moritz	*Swiss*	❸④❸
	Floridita	*Cuban*	④❸❷
	Moti Mahal	*Indian*	❷❸❸
	Red Fort	*"*	❷❷❸
£40+	All Star Lanes	*American*	④❸❷
	Big Easy	*"*	❸❸❷
	Bodean's	*"*	④④❸
	Mishkin's	*"*	⑤④❷
	Spuntino	*"*	❷❸❷
	Andrew Edmunds	*British, Modern*	❸❷❶
	The Angel & Crown	*"*	❷❸❷
	Aurora	*"*	④④❷
	Canteen	*"*	⑤⑤⑤
	Coopers	*"*	❷❷④
	The Easton	*"*	❷❸❸
	Kettners	*"*	④❸❸
	Shampers	*"*	❸❷❷
	10 Greek Street	*"*	❷❷❷
	Union Jacks	*"*	④❸④
	Vinoteca	*"*	❸❷❷
	Great Queen Street	*British, Traditional*	❷❸❸
	The Lady Ottoline	*"*	④④❸
	Cape Town Fish Market	*Fish & seafood*	❸❸④
	Loch Fyne	*"*	④④④
	J Sheekey Oyster Bar	*"*	❷❶❶
	Antidote	*French*	④❸❷
	Brasserie Blanc	*"*	④❸❸
	Café Bohème	*"*	❸❸❷
	Côte	*"*	④❸④
	Le Garrick	*"*	④④❸
	The Giaconda	*"*	– – –
	Otto's	*"*	❷❷❸
	Randall & Aubin	*"*	❸❸❷
	Savoir Faire	*"*	❸❷❷
	Terroirs	*"*	❸❸❷
	Gay Hussar	*Hungarian*	⑤❸❸
	Balans	*International*	⑤④❸
	Bedford & Strand	*"*	④④❸
	Boulevard	*"*	④❸❸
	Browns	*"*	⑤⑤④
	Cork & Bottle	*"*	⑤④❷
	Giraffe	*"*	⑤④⑤
	National Gallery Café	*"*	④❸④
	Sarastro	*"*	⑤⑤④
	Ciao Bella	*Italian*	④❸❸
	Dehesa	*"*	❷❷❷
	Jamie's Italian	*"*	⑤④④
	Mele e Pere	*"*	④❷④
	San Carlo Cicchetti	*"*	❸❷④
	Cigala	*Spanish*	❸④④

	Copita	"	❷④❷
	Opera Tavern	"	❷❸❸
	Tapas Brindisa Soho	"	❸④❸
	The Bountiful Cow	*Steaks & grills*	❸④④
	Mildreds	*Vegetarian*	❷④❸
	Orchard	"	❸❷❸
	Burger & Lobster	*Burgers, etc*	❷❷❷
	Wolfe's	"	④④④
	Rossopomodoro	*Pizza*	❸④④
	La Bodega Negra	*Mexican/TexMex*	④❸❷
	Café Pacifico	"	④④❷
	Cantina Laredo	"	④❸⑤
	Ceviche	*Peruvian*	④❸❸
	Ba Shan	*Chinese*	❷④④
	Bar Shu	"	❶⑤④
	Imperial China	"	❸❸❸
	Yming	"	❷❷❸
	Cinnamon Soho	*Indian*	❷❷❸
	Malabar Junction	"	❸❸❷
	Mela	"	❸❸④
	Haozhan	*Pan-Asian*	❷④⑤
	Inamo	"	④④❷
	Tapasia	"	❸❸④
	Patara	*Thai*	❷❷❸
£35+	Belgo	*Belgian*	⑤④④
	The Norfolk Arms	*British, Modern*	④❸❸
	Porters	*British, Traditional*	④❸❸
	Brasserie Zédel	*French*	❸❷❷
	Prix Fixe	"	④❸❸
	Real Greek	*Greek*	⑤④④
	Da Mario	*Italian*	❸❷❷
	Made in Italy	"	④④❸
	Barrafina	*Spanish*	❶❶❷
	North Sea Fish	*Fish & chips*	❸❸④
	Fire & Stone	*Pizza*	④④❸
	Lupita	*Mexican/TexMex*	❸❷❸
	Sofra	*Turkish*	④④❸
	Chuen Cheng Ku	*Chinese*	❸④④
	Empress of Sichuan	"	❷❸❷
	Harbour City	"	❷④④
	New Mayflower	"	❷❸❸
	New World	"	④④❸
	Plum Valley	"	❸❸❸
	Leong's Legends	*Chinese, Dim sum*	❸④❷
	Chowki	*Indian*	❸❸④
	Dishoom	"	❸❸❶
	Imli	"	❸❷❷
	Rasa Maricham	*Indian, Southern*	❷❷❸
	Abeno	*Japanese*	❸❸④
	Bincho Yakitori	"	④④❷
	Hazuki	"	❸④④
	Satsuma	"	④❸❸
	Asadal	*Korean*	❸④❸
	Kimchee	"	❸❸❸
	Melati, Gt Windmill St	*Malaysian*	④④⑤
	Busaba Eathai	*Thai*	❸❸❷
	Rosa's Soho	"	❸❷❸

	Suda	"	④④❸
	Thai Pot	"	④❸❸
	Thai Square	"	④④❸
	Cây Tre	*Vietnamese*	❸④④
£30+	Café in the Crypt	*International*	④❸❷
	Gordon's Wine Bar	"	⑤⑤❶
	Polpo	*Italian*	④❸❶
	La Porchetta Pizzeria	"	④❸④
	Café España	*Spanish*	❸❸④
	Mar I Terra	"	❸❸❷
	Byron	*Burgers, etc*	❸❸❸
	Diner	"	④❸❷
	Rock & Sole Plaice	*Fish & chips*	❸④④
	The Courtauld (Café)	*Sandwiches, cakes, etc*	④❸❸
	Fernandez & Wells	"	❷❷❶
	Wahaca	*Mexican/TexMex*	❸❸❷
	Gaby's	*Israeli*	❸❸❸
	Yalla Yalla	*Lebanese*	❷❸❷
	Tas	*Turkish*	④❸❸
	Cha Cha Moon	*Chinese*	④④❸
	The Four Seasons	"	❷④⑤
	Golden Dragon	"	❸④❸
	Joy King Lau	"	❸④④
	Mr Kong	"	❸❸④
	ping pong	*Chinese, Dim sum*	④④❸
	Gopal's of Soho	*Indian*	❸❸④
	Masala Zone	"	❸❸❷
	Sagar	"	❷❸④
	Salaam Namaste	"	❷❸④
	Koya	*Japanese*	❷❷❸
	Taro	"	❸❸❸
	Tonkotsu	"	❸❷④
	Wagamama	"	④❸④
	Banana Tree Canteen	*Pan-Asian*	❸❸❸
	Pho	*Vietnamese*	❷❷❷
£25+	Pitt Cue Co	*American*	❶❸❸
	Seven Stars	*British, Modern*	④④❷
	Princi	*Italian*	❸④❷
	Ed's Easy Diner	*Burgers, etc*	④❷❷
	Bar Italia	*Sandwiches, cakes, etc*	④❷❶
	Konditor & Cook	"	❸④④
	Paul	"	❸④④
	Chilli Cool	*Chinese*	❷⑤⑤
	Wong Kei	"	④⑤⑤
	India Club	*Indian*	❸④⑤
	Kulu Kulu	*Japanese*	④⑤⑤
	Tokyo Diner	"	④❸④
	Bibimbap Soho	*Korean*	❸④④
	Hare & Tortoise	*Pan-Asian*	❸❸④
	C&R Cafe	*Thai*	❸④⑤
£20+	Bistro 1	*Mediterranean*	④❷④
	Food for Thought	*Vegetarian*	❷④④
	Honest Burgers	*Burgers, etc*	❶❸❸
	Leon	*Sandwiches, cakes, etc*	④❸❸
	Benito's Hat	*Mexican/TexMex*	❸❷❸

	Viet	*Vietnamese*	❸④④
£15+	Hummus Bros	*Mediterranean*	❸④④
	Nordic Bakery	*Scandinavian*	❸④❸
	Maison Bertaux	*Afternoon tea*	❷❸❶
	Notes	*Sandwiches, cakes, etc*	④❷❷
	Chilango	*Mexican/TexMex*	❷❷❸
	Chipotle	*"*	❸❷⑤
	Baozi Inn	*Chinese*	❷④④
	Mooli's	*Indian*	❷❷④
	Abokado	*Japanese*	④❸④
£10+	Caffé Vergnano	*Italian*	④❸❸
	Fryer's Delight	*Fish & chips*	❸④⑤
	Gelupo	*Ice cream*	❶❷❸
	Flat White	*Sandwiches, cakes, etc*	❸❷❷
	Monmouth Coffee Co	*"*	❶❶❷
	Pod	*"*	❸❷❸
	Govinda's	*Indian*	❷④④

Mayfair & St James's (Parts of W1 and SW1)

£130+	Le Gavroche	*French*	❶❶❷
£120+	Alain Ducasse	*French*	❸❸④
	The Ritz Restaurant	*"*	④❷❶
£110+	Wiltons	*British, Traditional*	❸❷❷
	Hélène Darroze	*French*	④④❸
	Hibiscus	*"*	④④④
£100+	G Ramsay at Claridges	*French*	⑤⑤④
	The Greenhouse	*"*	❷❷❸
	The Square	*"*	❷❷❸
	Kai Mayfair	*Chinese*	④④⑤
£90+	Dorchester Grill	*British, Modern*	❸④❸
	Sketch (Lecture Rm)	*French*	④❸❷
	C London	*Italian*	⑤⑤④
	Murano	*"*	❸❸④
	Umu	*Japanese*	❷❸❷
£80+	Corrigan's Mayfair	*British, Traditional*	❸❸❸
	Galvin at Windows	*French*	④❸❶
	maze	*"*	④④④
	L'Oranger	*"*	❸❸❸
	Amaranto	*Italian*	④④④
	Babbo	*"*	④⑤④
	Banca	*"*	❷❷❸
	Downtown Mayfair	*"*	④④④
	Novikov (Italian restaurant)	*"*	❷④❸
	Theo Randall	*"*	❶❷④
	Cut	*Steaks & grills*	④⑤⑤
	Hakkasan	*Chinese*	❷④❷
	Benares	*Indian*	❷❷❸
	Nobu, Park Ln	*Japanese*	❷④❸
	Nobu, Berkeley St	*"*	❸④④

	Novikov (Asian restaurant)	*Pan-Asian*	④④❸
£70+	Alyn Williams	*British, Modern*	❷❷❸
	Athenaeum	*"*	❷❷❸
	Bellamy's	*"*	❸❷❷
	Le Caprice	*"*	❸❶❷
	Patterson's	*"*	❸❸④
	Pollen Street Social	*"*	❷❸❸
	Seven Park Place	*"*	❷❷❸
	Browns (Albemarle)	*British, Traditional*	④❸❸
	Bentley's	*Fish & seafood*	❷❷❷
	Scott's	*"*	❷❶❶
	La Petite Maison	*French*	❶❷❷
	Sketch (Gallery)	*"*	⑤⑤④
	Franco's	*Italian*	④❸④
	JW Steakhouse	*Steaks & grills*	④④④
	maze Grill	*"*	⑤④⑤
	34	*"*	④❷❷
	Momo	*North African*	④④❷
	China Tang	*Chinese*	④④❸
	Tamarind	*Indian*	❸❸❸
	Matsuri	*Japanese*	❸④⑤
	Sumosan	*"*	❸④❸
£60+	Automat	*American*	④④❸
	Criterion	*British, Modern*	④❸❶
	Langan's Brasserie	*"*	⑤④❸
	Mews of Mayfair	*"*	④④❸
	Wild Honey	*"*	❸❸❸
	The Fountain (Fortnum's)	*British, Traditional*	④❸❸
	Green's	*"*	❸❸④
	Boudin Blanc	*French*	❸④❷
	Alloro	*Italian*	❷❷❸
	Cecconi's	*"*	❸❷❶
	Ristorante Semplice	*"*	④④④
	Tempo	*"*	❸④④
	Aurelia	*Mediterranean*	❸❸❸
	Gaucho	*Steaks & grills*	❸④❸
	Goodman	*"*	❷❷❸
	The Guinea Grill	*"*	❸❸❸
	Hawksmoor	*"*	❷❷❸
	Rowley's	*"*	④❸❸
	Ladurée	*Afternoon tea*	❷④❸
	The Sketch (Parlour)	*Sandwiches, cakes, etc*	④④❸
	Fakhreldine	*Lebanese*	④④④
	Quince	*Turkish*	④❸④
	Mint Leaf	*Indian*	❸❸❷
	Veeraswamy	*"*	❸❸❷
	Benihana	*Japanese*	④④④
	Ikeda	*"*	❷❸⑤
	Sake No Hana	*"*	④④❸
£50+	The Avenue	*British, Modern*	❸❷❷
	Hush	*"*	❸❸❸
	Quaglino's	*"*	④④④
	Sotheby's Café	*"*	④❷❸
	The Wolseley	*"*	❸❷❶
	Pescatori	*Fish & seafood*	④④④

	Wheeler's	"	⑤❸④
	Brasserie St Jacques	*French*	❸④❸
	La Genova	*Italian*	④④④
	Sartoria	"	❸❷❸
	Serafino	"	❸❷④
	Truc Vert	*Mediterranean*	❸❸❸
	Diamond Jub' Salon (Fortnum's)	*Afternoon tea*	❸❷❷
	Aubaine	*Sandwiches, cakes, etc*	④④④
	Al Hamra	*Lebanese*	❸④④
	Noura	"	❸④❸
	Princess Garden	*Chinese*	❷❷❸
	Chor Bizarre	*Indian*	❷❸❷
	Chisou	*Japanese*	❷❷④
	Kiku	"	❷❸⑤
	Mitsukoshi	"	❷❷⑤
	Miyama	"	❷❸⑤
£40+	Hard Rock Café	*American*	④④❷
	Inn the Park	*British, Modern*	④⑤❷
	The Only Running Footman	"	❸④❸
	1707	"	④❸❸
	Fishworks	*Fish & seafood*	❸❸④
	L'Artiste Musclé	*French*	④④❸
	Brasserie Blanc	"	④❸❸
	Browns	*International*	⑤⑤④
	Al Duca	*Italian*	④④④
	Bar Trattoria Semplice	"	❸❸❸
	Piccolino	"	④❸④
	Il Vicolo	"	④④④
	Rocket	*Mediterranean*	④❸❸
	Ritz (Palm Court)	*Afternoon tea*	④❸❶
	Burger & Lobster	*Burgers, etc*	❷❷❷
	Delfino	*Pizza*	❷❸④
	Royal Academy	*Sandwiches, cakes, etc*	⑤④❸
	Al Sultan	*Lebanese*	❸❷④
	Inamo	*Pan-Asian*	④④❷
	Patara	*Thai*	❷❷❸
£35+	The Windmill	*British, Traditional*	❷④❸
	El Pirata	*Spanish*	④❷❶
	Benugo	*Sandwiches, cakes, etc*	④④❷
	Sofra	*Turkish*	④④❸
	Woodlands	*Indian*	❸❸④
	Rasa Samudra	*Indian, Southern*	❷❷❸
	Toku	*Japanese*	❷❷❷
	Yoshino	"	❷❶❸
	Busaba Eathai	*Thai*	❸❸❷
	Thai Square	"	④④❸
£30+	tibits	*Vegetarian*	❸④④
	Byron	*Burgers, etc*	❸❸❸
	Sakana-tei	*Japanese*	❷❷⑤
	Sakura	"	❸❸④
	Wagamama	"	④❸④
£25+	Stock Pot	*International*	④❷❸
	Ed's Easy Diner	*Burgers, etc*	④❷❷
	Mount Street Deli	*Sandwiches, cakes, etc*	④④❸

£15+	La Bottega	*Italian*	❸❷❸
	Taylor St Baristas	*Sandwiches, cakes, etc*	❷❸❸
£10+	Fuzzy's Grub	*Sandwiches, cakes, etc*	❸❸④

Fitzrovia & Marylebone (Part of W1)

£90+	Pied à Terre	*French*	❶❷❸
	Texture	*Scandinavian*	❷❷❸
£80+	Roganic	*British, Modern*	❶❶⑤
	Roux at the Landau	*"*	❷❸❷
	Hakkasan	*Chinese*	❷④❷
£70+	Cotidie	*Italian*	④⑤④
	Locanda Locatelli	*"*	❸❸❸
	Roka	*Japanese*	❶❸❷
£60+	Oscar	*British, Modern*	④④❷
	Rhodes W1 Restaurant	*"*	④❸❸
	L'Autre Pied	*French*	❷❷④
	Orrery	*"*	❸❷❷
	The Providores	*International*	❸⑤⑤
	Gaucho	*Steaks & grills*	❸④❸
	Defune	*Japanese*	❶❸④
	Crazy Bear	*Thai*	④④❸
£50+	Grazing Goat	*British, Modern*	❸④❸
	The Union Café	*"*	❸④④
	Odin's	*British, Traditional*	④❶❶
	Pescatori	*Fish & seafood*	④④④
	Elena's L'Etoile	*French*	⑤⑤④
	Galvin Bistrot de Luxe	*"*	❷❷❷
	28-50	*"*	❸❷❷
	Villandry	*"*	④④④
	The Wallace	*"*	④⑤❶
	Archipelago	*Fusion*	④④❸
	Il Baretto	*Italian*	❸④④
	Caffè Caldesi	*"*	❸❸④
	Mennula	*"*	❸④④
	Verru	*Scandinavian*	❷❸❸
	Fino	*Spanish*	❷❷❷
	Lima	*Peruvian*	❷❷❸
	Reubens	*Kosher*	④⑤⑤
	Levant	*Lebanese*	④④❷
	The Bright Courtyard	*Chinese*	❸❸④
	Royal China Club	*"*	❷❸❸
	La Porte des Indes	*Indian*	❸④❷
	Trishna	*"*	❷❸❸
	Dinings	*Japanese*	❶❷⑤
£40+	The Duke of Wellington	*British, Modern*	④④❸
	Hardy's Brasserie	*"*	④❸❸
	Ozer	*"*	❸❷④
	RIBA Café	*"*	④④❷
	Vinoteca Seymour Place	*"*	❸❷❷
	Canteen	*British, Traditional*	⑤⑤⑤

	Back to Basics	*Fish & seafood*	❷❸④
	Fishworks	*"*	❸❸④
	Langan's Bistro	*French*	❸❷❸
	Providores (Tapa Room)	*Fusion*	❷④❸
	Hellenic	*Greek*	– – –
	Giraffe	*International*	⑤④⑤
	Latium	*Italian*	❷❶❸
	Sardo	*"*	❸❸④
	2 Veneti	*"*	❸❷❸
	Dabbous	*Mediterranean*	❶❶❸
	Riding House Café	*"*	④❸❶
	Ibérica	*Spanish*	❸④❸
	Navarro's	*"*	❷④❷
	Salt Yard	*"*	❷❷❷
	Black & Blue	*Steaks & grills*	④❸④
	Le Relais de Venise	*"*	❷④❸
	Fairuz	*Lebanese*	❸❷❸
	Maroush	*"*	❸④④
	Ishtar	*Turkish*	❸❷❸
	Royal China	*Chinese*	❷④④
	Gaylord	*Indian*	❸④④
	Indali Lounge	*"*	❸❸④
	Roti Chai	*"*	❷❸❸
	Zayna	*"*	❷❷④
	Kikuchi	*Japanese*	❶④④
	Nizuni	*"*	❸❸④
	Soho Japan	*"*	❷❸④
	Tsunami	*"*	❷❸❸
	Yoisho	*"*	❷④⑤
	Koba	*Korean*	❷❷④
	Bam-Bou	*Vietnamese*	❸❷❷
£35+	Real Greek	*Greek*	⑤④④
	Briciole	*Italian*	❷❷❸
	Barrica	*Spanish*	❷❷❷
	Donostia	*"*	❷❷❸
	Benugo	*Sandwiches, cakes, etc*	④④❷
	La Fromagerie Café	*"*	❷④❷
	Sofra	*Turkish*	④④❸
	Woodlands	*Indian*	❸❸④
£30+	MEATLiquor	*Burgers, etc*	❷④❸
	Natural Kitchen	*Salads*	❸④❸
	Yalla Yalla	*Lebanese*	❷❸❷
	ping pong	*Chinese, Dim sum*	④④❸
	Sagar	*Indian*	❷❸④
	Atari-Ya	*Japanese*	❶④⑤
	Wagamama	*"*	④❸④
	dim T	*Pan-Asian*	④④④
	Siam Central	*Thai*	❸❸❸
	Pho	*Vietnamese*	❷❷❷
£25+	Vapiano	*Italian*	❸❸❸
	Golden Hind	*Fish & chips*	❷❷❸
	Paul	*Sandwiches, cakes, etc*	❸④④
	The Deli West One	*Kosher*	❷❸④
	Chettinad	*Indian*	❷❷④
	Ragam	*"*	❶❷⑤

£20+	Leon	*Sandwiches, cakes, etc*	④❸❸
	Benito's Hat	*Mexican/TexMex*	❸❷❸
	Comptoir Libanais	*Lebanese*	④④❸
	Patogh	*Middle Eastern*	❷❸④
£15+	Nordic Bakery	*Scandinavian*	❸④❸
	Chipotle	*Mexican/TexMex*	❸❷⑤
	Tortilla	*"*	④④④
	Abokado	*Japanese*	④❸④
£10+	Scandinavian Kitchen	*Scandinavian*	❸❸❸
	Kaffeine	*Sandwiches, cakes, etc*	❷❶❶

Belgravia, Pimlico, Victoria & Westminster (SW1, except St James's)

£110+	Marcus Wareing	*French*	❷❷❷
£100+	Apsleys	*Italian*	④④❸
£90+	Dinner	*British, Traditional*	❸❸❸
	One-O-One	*Fish & seafood*	❶❸⑤
£80+	Thirty Six	*British, Modern*	❷❷❸
	Koffmann's	*French*	❷❶❸
	Pétrus	*"*	❸❷❷
	The Palm	*Steaks & grills*	⑤④⑤
	Rib Room	*"*	④④④
	Mr Chow	*Chinese*	④④④
	Nahm	*Thai*	❷❸⑤
£70+	The Goring Hotel	*British, Modern*	❸❶❶
	Roux at Parliament Square	*"*	❸❸④
	Zafferano	*Italian*	❸❸❸
	Massimo	*Mediterranean*	– – –
	Mari Vanna	*Russian*	④⑤❷
£60+	The Fifth Floor Restaurant	*British, Modern*	④④④
	Hix Belgravia	*"*	④④❸
	Olivomare	*Fish & seafood*	❶❸④
	Il Convivio	*Italian*	❸❷④
	Quirinale	*"*	❷❸④
	Santini	*"*	④❸❸
	Signor Sassi	*"*	④④❸
	Hunan	*Chinese*	❶❷④
	Amaya	*Indian*	❶❷❷
	The Cinnamon Club	*"*	❷❷❷
	Quilon	*Indian, Southern*	❶❶④
£50+	Bank Westminster	*British, Modern*	④❷④
	The Botanist	*"*	④④④
	Ebury Rest' & Wine Bar	*"*	④④❸
	The Orange	*"*	❷❸❷
	The Pantechnicon	*"*	❸❸❷
	Tate Britain (Rex Whistler)	*"*	– – –
	The Thomas Cubitt	*"*	❷❷❷
	Shepherd's	*British, Traditional*	❸❷❸

	The Balcon	*French*	❸❸❸
	Bar Boulud	*"*	❷❷❷
	Le Cercle	*"*	❷❷❸
	Chabrot Bistrot d'Amis	*"*	❸❷④
	The Chelsea Brasserie	*"*	④④④
	The Ebury	*"*	– – –
	Galvin Demoiselle	*"*	❸❷❸
	La Poule au Pot	*"*	❸❸❶
	Motcombs	*International*	④❸❷
	Olivo	*Italian*	❷❸④
	Osteria Dell'Angolo	*"*	❸❷④
	Sale e Pepe	*"*	❸❷❷
	About Thyme	*Mediterranean*	❸❶④
	Boisdale	*Scottish*	④④❷
	Oliveto	*Pizza*	❷❸④
	Baku	*Azerbaijani*	④❶❸
	Beiteddine	*Lebanese*	❷❷④
	Ishbilia	*"*	❸④④
	Noura	*"*	❸④❸
	The Grand Imperial	*Chinese*	❸❸❸
	Ken Lo's Memories	*"*	❷❷❸
	Salloos	*Pakistani*	❷❸⑤
	Mango Tree	*Thai*	④④④
£40+	Daylesford Organic	*British, Modern*	④⑤④
	The Queens Arms	*"*	❸④❸
	Browns	*International*	⑤⑤④
	Giraffe	*"*	⑤④⑤
	Grumbles	*"*	④❷❸
	Caraffini	*Italian*	❸❶❷
	Como Lario	*"*	④⑤④
	Gran Paradiso	*"*	④❸④
	Ottolenghi	*"*	❶❸④
	2 Amici	*"*	④❸④
	Goya	*Spanish*	④④④
	Baker & Spice	*Sandwiches, cakes, etc*	❸④④
	Ranoush	*Lebanese*	❷❸⑤
	Kazan	*Turkish*	❷❷❸
£35+	Bumbles	*International*	❸❷❷
	Tinello	*Italian*	❷❶❶
	Seafresh	*Fish & chips*	❸④⑤
£30+	The Vincent Rooms	*British, Modern*	❸❸❸
	Cyprus Mangal	*Turkish*	❷❸④
	Jenny Lo's	*Chinese*	❸❸⑤
	Wagamama	*Japanese*	④❸④
	dim T	*Pan-Asian*	④④④
£25+	Mekong	*Vietnamese*	❸❸④
£15+	La Bottega	*Italian*	❸❷❸
	William Curley	*Afternoon tea*	❷❸❸

WEST

Chelsea, South Kensington, Kensington, Earl's Court & Fulham (SW3, SW5, SW6, SW7, SW10 & W8)

£120+	Gordon Ramsay	*French*	❸❸④
£100+	Rasoi	*Indian*	❷❸❷
£80+	Yashin	*Japanese*	❷❸❸
£70+	Babylon	*British, Modern*	④④❷
	Tom Aikens	*"*	❷❷④
	Bibendum	*French*	④❸❷
	Scalini	*Italian*	❸❸❸
	Min Jiang	*Chinese*	❶❷❶
	Nozomi	*Japanese*	④④④
	Zuma	*"*	❶❸❷
£60+	Clarke's	*British, Modern*	❸❷❸
	Kitchen W8	*"*	❶❷❸
	Launceston Place	*"*	– – –
	Marco	*"*	⑤⑤④
	Tom's Kitchen	*"*	④⑤④
	Poissonnerie de l'Av.	*Fish & seafood*	❸❸④
	Le Suquet	*"*	❸❸④
	Belvedere	*French*	④④❷
	Cassis Bistro	*"*	⑤④④
	Cheyne Walk Bras'	*"*	④④❸
	L'Etranger	*"*	❸❸④
	Racine	*"*	❷❷❸
	Medlar	*International*	❶❷④
	The Ark	*Italian*	④④④
	Daphne's	*"*	❸❷❷
	Lucio	*"*	❸❷❷
	San Lorenzo	*"*	⑤⑤⑤
	Locanda Ottomezzo	*Mediterranean*	❸④❸
	Gaucho	*Steaks & grills*	❸④❸
	Zaika	*Indian*	❶❷❸
	Benihana	*Japanese*	④④④
	Mao Tai	*Pan-Asian*	❸④❸
£50+	The Abingdon	*British, Modern*	❸❸❸
	Bluebird	*"*	⑤⑤④
	Brinkley's	*"*	⑤④❸
	Brompton Bar & Grill	*"*	❸❷❷
	The Enterprise	*"*	❸❸❷
	Harwood Arms	*"*	❶❷❷
	The Henry Root	*"*	④④❸
	Whits	*"*	❸❶❸
	Maggie Jones's	*British, Traditional*	④❷❶
	The Markham Inn	*"*	④❸❸
	Bibendum Oyster Bar	*Fish & seafood*	❸❷❷
	La Brasserie	*French*	④❸❷
	Le Colombier	*"*	❸❶❷
	Garnier	*"*	❸❶❸
	The Pig's Ear	*"*	❸④❷

	Sushinho	*Fusion*	❸④❷
	Mazi	*Greek*	– – –
	Foxtrot Oscar	*International*	⑤④⑤
	Gallery Mess	*"*	④④❸
	Casa Batavia	*Italian*	④❷❸
	Eleven Park Walk	*"*	④④④
	La Famiglia	*"*	④④❸
	Frantoio	*"*	④❷❷
	Manicomio	*"*	❸④❸
	Montpeliano	*"*	⑤⑤⑤
	Osteria dell'Arancio	*"*	❸❸❸
	Pellicano	*"*	④❷④
	Timo	*"*	④④④
	Polish Club	*Polish*	④④❸
	Cambio de Tercio	*Spanish*	❷❷❷
	Kings Road Steakhouse	*Steaks & grills*	④④④
	PJ's Bar and Grill	*"*	④❷❷
	Sophie's Steakhouse	*"*	④④❸
	(Ciro's) Pizza Pomodoro	*Pizza*	④④❷
	Aubaine	*Sandwiches, cakes, etc*	④④④
	Pasha	*Moroccan*	❸❸❷
	Good Earth	*Chinese*	❷❸④
	Ken Lo's Memories	*"*	❷❷④
	Bombay Brasserie	*Indian*	❸❸④
	Chutney Mary	*"*	❷❷❷
	The Painted Heron	*"*	❶❷❸
	Chisou	*Japanese*	❷❷④
	Eight Over Eight	*Pan-Asian*	❷❸❷
£40+	Big Easy	*American*	❸❸❷
	Bodean's	*"*	④④❸
	Sticky Fingers	*"*	④④❸
	The Anglesea Arms	*British, Modern*	④④❷
	The Builders Arms	*"*	④④❷
	Butcher's Hook	*"*	❸❷❸
	The Cadogan Arms	*"*	❸④❸
	Jam Tree	*"*	④④❷
	Joe's Brasserie	*"*	❸❸❸
	Kensington Place	*"*	❸❷❸
	The Mall Tavern	*"*	❷❷❷
	Megan's Delicatessen	*"*	❸❸❸
	The Phoenix	*"*	④④❷
	The Sands End	*"*	❸❸❷
	Vingt-Quatre	*"*	④❷④
	White Horse	*"*	④④❸
	Bumpkin	*British, Traditional*	⑤④④
	Ffiona's	*"*	④④❸
	The Surprise	*"*	④❸❷
	L'Art du Fromage	*French*	❸④④
	La Bouchée	*"*	④④❷
	Chez Patrick	*"*	❸❶❸
	Côte	*"*	④❸④
	Tartine	*"*	❸④⑤
	Le Troquet	*"*	❷④④
	Balans West	*International*	⑤④❸
	Giraffe	*"*	⑤④⑤
	The Kensington Wine Rms	*"*	❸❷❷
	Wine Gallery	*"*	④❸❸

	Da Mario	*Italian*	❸④❸
	Frankie's Italian Bar & Grill	*"*	⑤⑤⑤
	Nuovi Sapori	*"*	❸❶④
	Ottolenghi	*"*	❶❸④
	Il Portico	*"*	❸❶❷
	Riccardo's	*"*	⑤④❸
	Ziani's	*"*	❸❷❷
	The Atlas	*Mediterranean*	❷❸❷
	Del'Aziz	*"*	④⑤❸
	Gessler at Daquise	*Polish*	❸❷❷
	Madsen	*Scandinavian*	④④④
	Capote Y Toros	*Spanish*	④④❸
	Casa Brindisa	*"*	④④④
	Tendido Cero	*"*	❸❸❷
	Tendido Cuatro	*"*	❸❷❷
	Admiral Codrington	*Steaks & grills*	❷❸❸
	Black & Blue	*"*	④❸④
	Geales	*Fish & chips*	❸④④
	Rossopomodoro	*Pizza*	❸④④
	Santa Lucia	*"*	❸④④
	Baker & Spice	*Sandwiches, cakes, etc*	❸④④
	Bluebird Café	*"*	⑤⑤④
	Troubadour	*"*	④❸❶
	Rodizio Rico	*Brazilian*	⑤④④
	Beirut Express	*Lebanese*	❸④④
	Maroush	*"*	❸④④
	Randa	*"*	❸❷④
	Ranoush	*"*	❷❸⑤
	Mr Wing	*Chinese*	❸④❸
	Royal China	*"*	❷④④
	Malabar	*Indian*	❷❷❸
	Star of India	*"*	❷④❸
	Thali	*"*	❷❷④
	Bangkok	*Thai*	❸❷④
	Patara	*"*	❷❷❸
	Sukho Fine Thai Cuisine	*"*	❶❶④
£35+	The Chelsea Ram	*British, Modern*	❸❸❷
	The Scarsdale	*International*	④❸❶
	Aglio e Olio	*Italian*	❸❷❸
	Buona Sera	*"*	❸❸❶
	Made in Italy	*"*	④④❸
	Napulé	*"*	❸❸❸
	Il Pagliaccio	*"*	④❷❶
	Pappa Ciccia	*"*	❸❸❸
	Haché	*Steaks & grills*	❸❸❷
	La Delizia Limbara	*Pizza*	④❸④
	Benugo	*Sandwiches, cakes, etc*	④④❷
	Choys	*Chinese*	④❷❸
	Khan's of Kensington	*Indian*	❸❸④
	Noor Jahan	*"*	❷❷❸
	Busaba Eathai	*Thai*	❸❸❷
	Thai Square	*"*	④④❸
£30+	The Windsor Castle	*International*	❸❸❷
	Byron	*Burgers, etc*	❸❸❸
	Basilico	*Pizza*	❷❸⑤
	Rocca Di Papa	*"*	④④❸

	Best Mangal	*Turkish*	❷❸❸
	Taiwan Village	*Chinese*	❶❶❸
	The Greedy Buddha	*Indian*	❸❸❸
	Masala Zone	*"*	❸❸❷
	Memories of India	*"*	❸❸④
	Monty's	*"*	❸❸④
	Itsu	*Japanese*	④❸④
	Wagamama	*"*	④❸④
	Addie's Thai Café	*Thai*	❷❸❸
£25+	Kensington Square Kitchen	*British, Modern*	❸❷❷
	Chelsea Bun Diner	*International*	❸④❸
	The Chelsea Kitchen	*"*	④❸❸
	Mona Lisa	*"*	④❶❷
	Stock Pot	*"*	④❷❸
	Kulu Kulu	*Japanese*	④⑤⑤
	Churchill Arms	*Thai*	❷❸❶
£20+	Stick & Bowl	*Chinese*	❸❷❸
	Café 209	*Thai*	④❸❶
£15+	La Bottega	*Italian*	❸❷❸

Notting Hill, Holland Park, Bayswater, North Kensington & Maida Vale (W2, W9, W10, W11)

£100+	The Ledbury	*British, Modern*	❶❶❷
£80+	Angelus	*French*	❸❷❸
£70+	Notting Hill Brasserie	*British, Modern*	④④❸
£60+	Beach Blanket Babylon	*British, Modern*	⑤④❷
	Bel Canto	*French*	④❶❶
	Assaggi	*Italian*	❷❷④
	Edera	*"*	❷❶❸
	Chakra	*Indian*	❸④④
£50+	The Cow	*British, Modern*	❸④❶
	The Dock Kitchen	*"*	❸❸❶
	The Frontline Club	*"*	❸❸❸
	Julie's	*"*	④⑤❶
	The Summerhouse	*Fish & seafood*	⑤④❷
	Le Café Anglais	*French*	❸④❸
	Electric Brasserie	*"*	④④❷
	Goode & Wright	*"*	❸❸④
	La Sophia	*"*	❷❸④
	202	*International*	④❷❸
	Essenza	*Italian*	❸❷④
	Mediterraneo	*"*	❸❸❷
	Osteria Basilico	*"*	❸❸❷
	Colchis	*Georgian*	❷❸❸
	Bombay Palace	*Indian*	❶❶④
	E&O	*Pan-Asian*	❷❷❶
£40+	All Star Lanes	*American*	④❸❷

	Granger & Co	*Australian*	⑤④❸
	Daylesford Organic	*British, Modern*	④⑤④
	First Floor	*"*	④④❶
	Formosa Dining Room	*"*	④④❷
	The Ladbroke Arms	*"*	❷④❷
	Paradise, Kensal Green	*"*	❷❷❶
	The Prince Bonaparte	*"*	❸④❷
	The Waterway	*"*	④④❷
	Bumpkin	*British, Traditional*	⑤④④
	Hereford Road	*"*	❷❸④
	Côte	*French*	④❸④
	Halepi	*Greek*	❸❶❸
	Giraffe	*International*	⑤④⑤
	The Oak	*Italian*	❶❸❶
	Ottolenghi	*"*	❶❸④
	Portobello Ristorante	*"*	❷❸❸
	Raoul's Café	*Mediterranean*	④⑤④
	Pizza East Portobello	*Pizza*	❸❸❶
	The Red Pepper	*"*	❷❸④
	Rossopomodoro	*"*	❸④④
	Baker & Spice	*Sandwiches, cakes, etc*	❸④④
	Casa Malevo	*Argentinian*	④❸❸
	Rodizio Rico	*Brazilian*	⑤④④
	Al-Waha	*Lebanese*	❸④④
	Beirut Express	*"*	❸④④
	Maroush	*"*	❸④④
	Ranoush	*"*	❷❸⑤
	Kateh	*Persian*	❸❸❸
	Pearl Liang	*Chinese*	❶❷❸
	Royal China	*"*	❷④④
	Seventeen	*"*	❸④❷
£35+	Lucky Seven	*American*	❸❸❷
	Galicia	*Spanish*	❸④❷
	El Pirata de Tapas	*"*	❸❸❷
	Mandarin Kitchen	*Chinese*	❷❸⑤
	Leong's Legends	*Chinese, Dim sum*	❸④❷
	Noor Jahan	*Indian*	❷❷❸
	Inaho	*Japanese*	❶⑤⑤
	Satay House	*Malaysian*	❸④④
	Uli	*Pan-Asian*	❷❶❷
	The Walmer Castle	*Thai*	❸❷❶
£30+	Tom's Deli	*Sandwiches, cakes, etc*	❸❸❷
	Taqueria	*Mexican/TexMex*	❸❷❸
	The Four Seasons	*Chinese*	❷④⑤
	Gold Mine	*"*	❷④④
	ping pong	*Chinese, Dim sum*	④④❸
	Masala Zone	*Indian*	❸❸❷
	Itsu	*Japanese*	④❸④
	Maguro	*"*	❷❷❸
	Banana Tree Canteen	*Pan-Asian*	❸❸❸
£25+	Otto Pizza	*Pizza*	❷❷❸
	Gail's Bread	*Sandwiches, cakes, etc*	❸❷❸
	Fresco	*Lebanese*	❷❷④
	Alounak	*Persian*	❷④❸
	Colbeh	*"*	❷④④

	Mandalay	*Burmese*	❸❸⑤
	Fortune Cookie	*Chinese*	❷④⑤
	C&R Cafe	*Thai*	❸④⑤
£20+	Khan's	*Indian*	❸④④
	Fitou's Thai Restaurant	*Thai*	❸❷④
£15+	Fez Mangal	*Turkish*	❶❸④
£5+	Lisboa Pâtisserie	*Sandwiches, cakes, etc*	❸❸④

Hammersmith, Shepherd's Bush, Olympia, Chiswick, Brentford & Ealing (W4, W5, W6, W12, W13, W14, TW8)

£80+	Hedone	*British, Modern*	❸❸④
	The River Café	*Italian*	❷❷❷
£60+	La Trompette	*French*	❶❶❷
£50+	Charlotte's Bistro	*French*	❸❸❸
	Le Vacherin	*"*	❸❷❷
	Michael Nadra	*International*	❶❸④
	Cibo	*Italian*	❷❷❸
	The Meat & Wine Co	*Steaks & grills*	④❸④
	Chisou	*Japanese*	❷❷④
£40+	The Anglesea Arms	*British, Modern*	❷❸❷
	The Carpenter's Arms	*"*	❸④❸
	Carvosso's	*"*	⑤④❸
	Duke of Sussex	*"*	④④❸
	The Havelock Tavern	*"*	❸④❷
	High Road Brasserie	*"*	④④❸
	Hole in the Wall	*"*	❸❸❸
	The Jam Tree	*"*	④④❷
	Pissarro	*"*	④❸❷
	Princess Victoria	*"*	❸❸❷
	The Roebuck	*"*	④④❸
	Sam's Brasserie	*"*	④❸❸
	Union Jacks	*"*	④❸④
	The Hampshire Hog	*British, Traditional*	❸❸❷
	Charlotte's Place	*French*	❸❷❸
	Côte	*"*	④❸④
	Annie's	*International*	④❸❷
	Balans	*"*	⑤④❸
	Giraffe	*"*	⑤④⑤
	Jamie's Italian	*Italian*	⑤④④
	Pentolina	*"*	❷❷❸
	Cumberland Arms	*Mediterranean*	❷❸❸
	Del'Aziz	*"*	④⑤❸
	Raoul's Café & Deli	*"*	④⑤④
	The Swan	*"*	❸❷❷
	The Cabin	*Steaks & grills*	④④④
	Popeseye	*"*	❷❸⑤
	The Gate	*Vegetarian*	❶❸④
	Lola & Simón	*Argentinian*	④④❸

	Quantus	*South American*	❸❷❷
	Indian Zing	*Indian*	❶❷❸
	Tosa	*Japanese*	❷④④
	Saigon Saigon	*Vietnamese*	❸④❸
£35+	Queen's Head	*British, Modern*	④❷❷
	The Thatched House	*"*	④❷❸
	The Real Greek	*Greek*	⑤④④
	Canta Napoli	*Italian*	❸❸④
	The Grove	*Mediterranean*	④❸④
	Fire & Stone	*Pizza*	④④❸
	Benugo	*Sandwiches, cakes, etc*	④④❷
	Azou	*North African*	❸❷❷
	Chella	*Persian*	❸④❸
	Maxim	*Chinese*	❸❷④
	North China	*"*	❷❷❸
	Brilliant	*Indian*	❷❷❸
	Karma	*"*	❷❶④
	Potli	*"*	❸④④
	Okawari	*Japanese*	❸④❸
	Busaba Eathai	*Thai*	❸❸❷
£30+	Albertine	*French*	④❷❷
	Patio	*Polish*	④❶❷
	Byron	*Burgers, etc*	❸❸❸
	Santa Maria	*Pizza*	❷❸❷
	Wahaca	*Mexican/TexMex*	❸❸❷
	Chez Marcelle	*Lebanese*	❶⑤⑤
	Sufi	*Persian*	❸❷④
	Best Mangal	*Turkish*	❷❸❸
	Tian Fu	*Chinese*	❷⑤⑤
	Anarkali	*Indian*	❷❸❸
	Madhu's	*"*	❷❷❸
	Monty's	*"*	❸❸④
	Sagar	*"*	❷❸④
	Shilpa	*Indian, Southern*	❷❸⑤
	Atari-Ya	*Japanese*	❶④⑤
	Kiraku	*"*	❶❶❸
	Esarn Kheaw	*Thai*	❸❸⑤
	Fat Boy's	*"*	❸④❸
	Pho	*Vietnamese*	❷❷❷
£25+	Gail's Bakery	*Sandwiches, cakes, etc*	❸❷❸
	Adams Café	*Moroccan*	❸❶❷
	Alounak	*Persian*	❷④❸
	Faanoos	*"*	④④❸
	Mohsen	*"*	❸④⑤
	Hare & Tortoise	*Pan-Asian*	❸❸④
	Bedlington Café	*Thai*	④❸⑤
£20+	Franco Manca	*Pizza*	❶❸❷
	Comptoir Libanais	*Lebanese*	④④❸
	Abu Zaad	*Syrian*	❸❷④
	Mirch Masala	*Pakistani*	❷④⑤
	Old Parr's Head	*Thai*	④❸❸
	101 Thai Kitchen	*"*	❶❸⑤
£15+	Kerbisher & Malt	*Fish & chips*	❷❸④

Tortilla	*Mexican/TexMex*	④④④
Gifto's	*Indian*	❷❸④

NORTH

Hampstead, West Hampstead, St John's Wood, Regent's Park, Kilburn & Camden Town (NW postcodes)

£70+	Landmark (Winter Gdn)	*British, Modern*	❸❷❶
£60+	Gilbert Scott	*British, Traditional*	④④❸
	One Blenheim Terrace	*French*	❸❷④
	Oslo Court	*"*	❷❶❶
	Gaucho	*Steaks & grills*	❸④❸
	Kaifeng	*Chinese*	❷❷④
	Gilgamesh	*Pan-Asian*	❸❸❷
£50+	Bradley's	*British, Modern*	④④④
	Odette's	*"*	❷❸❷
	St Pancras Grand	*"*	⑤⑤④
	Bull & Last	*British, Traditional*	❷❷❷
	L'Aventure	*French*	❷❶❶
	La Collina	*Italian*	④④❸
	Mimmo la Bufala	*"*	❸④④
	Villa Bianca	*"*	④❸❸
	York & Albany	*"*	④④④
	Rôtisserie	*Steaks & grills*	④④④
	Manna	*Vegetarian*	❸④④
	Shaka Zulu	*South African*	④④④
	Good Earth	*Chinese*	❷❸④
£40+	Karpo	*American*	❸❸④
	The Engineer	*British, Modern*	④④❸
	Freemasons Arms	*"*	⑤⑤❷
	The Horseshoe	*"*	❸❸④
	The Junction Tavern	*"*	❸❶❷
	The Lansdowne	*"*	❸④❷
	Market	*"*	④④④
	The North London Tavern	*"*	❸④❸
	The Old Bull & Bush	*"*	❸④❸
	The Wells	*"*	❸❷❷
	The Wet Fish Cafe	*"*	❸❷❷
	Holly Bush	*British, Traditional*	❸④❷
	Kentish Canteen	*"*	④④❸
	The Old White Bear	*"*	❸❷❷
	L'Absinthe	*French*	❸❶❷
	La Cage Imaginaire	*"*	④④❸
	Cocotte	*"*	④❷④
	Mill Lane Bistro	*"*	❸❷❸
	Lemonia	*Greek*	⑤❷❷
	Retsina	*"*	④④④
	The Arches	*International*	④❸❷
	Giraffe	*"*	⑤④⑤
	Spaniard's Inn	*"*	④④❸
	Artigiano	*Italian*	❸❸④
	The Salt House	*"*	❷❸❷
	The Salusbury	*"*	❸④❸
	Sardo Canale	*"*	④④④
	Sarracino	*"*	❷❸④
	Del'Aziz	*Mediterranean*	④⑤❸

	Nautilus	*Fish & chips*	❷❸⑤
	The Sea Shell	*"*	❸④⑤
	Pizza East	*Pizza*	❸❸❶
	Mestizo	*Mexican/TexMex*	⑤④④
	Cottons	*Afro-Caribbean*	❸❸❶
	Mango Room	*"*	❸❷❷
	Solly's	*Israeli*	④⑤⑤
	Goldfish	*Chinese*	❷④④
	Green Cottage	*"*	❷④⑤
	Phoenix Palace	*"*	❷❸❸
	Jin Kichi	*Japanese*	❶❷④
	Sushi of Shiori	*"*	❶❶④
	Sushi-Say	*"*	❶❶❸
	Yuzu	*"*	❷❸④
	Singapore Garden	*Malaysian*	❷❷④
	XO	*Pan-Asian*	❸④❸
£35+	Belgo Noord	*Belgian*	⑤④④
	Made In Camden	*British, Modern*	❸❸❸
	Prince Albert	*"*	④④❸
	Rising Sun	*"*	❸❷❷
	Somerstown Coffee House	*"*	④❸❸
	Daphne	*Greek*	❸❶❷
	Swan & Edgar	*International*	④④❷
	Haché	*Steaks & grills*	❸❸❷
	Harry Morgan's	*Burgers, etc*	❸❷❸
	Skipjacks	*Fish & chips*	❶❷④
	Benugo	*Sandwiches, cakes, etc*	④④❷
	Beyoglu	*Turkish*	❸❸④
	Sofra	*"*	④④❸
	Alisan	*Chinese*	❷❷❸
	Gung-Ho	*"*	④❷❸
	Eriki	*Indian*	❸❸④
	Woodlands	*"*	❸❸④
	Asakusa	*Japanese*	❶④④
	Café Japan	*"*	❶❷④
£30+	The Foundry	*British, Modern*	❸❷❷
	Carob Tree	*Greek*	❸❷❸
	L'Artista	*Italian*	④❸❸
	Marine Ices	*"*	④④❸
	La Porchetta Pizzeria	*"*	④❸④
	The Little Bay	*Mediterranean*	④❷❶
	La Giralda	*Spanish*	❸④④
	El Parador	*"*	❷❸❸
	The Diner	*Burgers, etc*	④❸❷
	Basilico	*Pizza*	❷❸⑤
	Kenwood (Brew House)	*Sandwiches, cakes, etc*	④❸❷
	The Water Margin	*Chinese*	❸④④
	Chutneys	*Indian*	❸④④
	Diwana B-P House	*"*	❸⑤⑤
	Masala Zone	*"*	❸❸❷
	Paradise Hampstead	*"*	❷❷④
	Vijay	*"*	❷❷④
	Atari-Ya	*Japanese*	❶④⑤
	Bento Cafe	*"*	❷❸④
	Wagamama	*"*	④❸④
	The Banana Tree Canteen	*Pan-Asian*	❸❸❸

	dim T	"	④④④
	Ladudu	*Vietnamese*	❸❸❸
£25+	Sea Pebbles	*Fish & seafood*	❷❸④
	Stringray Café	*Mediterranean*	④④④
	Trojka	*Russian*	④④④
	Chamomile	*Sandwiches, cakes, etc*	❸❷❸
	Gail's Bread	"	❸❷❸
	Great Nepalese	*Indian*	❸❷⑤
	Guglee	"	❸④④
£20+	Ali Baba	*Egyptian*	❸❷❷
	Sakonis	*Indian*	❸④⑤
£15+	Ginger & White	*Sandwiches, cakes, etc*	❸❷❷

Hoxton, Islington, Highgate, Crouch End, Stoke Newington, Finsbury Park, Muswell Hill & Finchley (N postcodes)

£50+	The Duke of Cambridge	*British, Modern*	❸④❷
	Frederick's	"	④❸❷
	The Haven	"	❸④④
	The Almeida	*French*	❸④④
	Bistro Aix	"	❷❶❷
	Canonbury Kitchen	*Italian*	④❸④
	Fifteen Trattoria	"	⑤⑤⑤
	Rôtisserie	*Steaks & grills*	④④④
	Isarn	*Thai*	❸❸④
£40+	Shrimpy's	*American*	❸❷❷
	The Albion	*British, Modern*	④④❸
	Bald Faced Stag	"	❸❸❸
	The Barnsbury	"	④④❸
	Caravan	"	❸❸❸
	Charles Lamb	"	❸❷❶
	The Clissold Arms	"	④❸❸
	The Drapers Arms	"	❸❸❷
	The Fellow	"	④④④
	Juniper Dining	"	❷❸❸
	Mosaica	"	❸❷❷
	The Northgate	"	❷❷❸
	The Rose & Crown	"	④④④
	Rotunda Bar & Restaurant	"	④④❷
	The Marquess Tavern	*British, Traditional*	❸④❸
	St Johns	"	❷❷❶
	Chez Liline	*Fish & seafood*	❶❸⑤
	Les Associés	*French*	❸❷④
	Fig	"	❷❸❷
	Banners	*International*	④❸❶
	Browns	"	⑤⑤④
	The Flask	"	④④❸
	Giraffe	"	⑤④⑤
	The Orange Tree	"	④⑤❸
	500	*Italian*	❶❷④
	Ottolenghi	"	❶❸④
	San Daniele	"	④❷❸

	Trullo	"	❷❷❸
	Camino	*Spanish*	④④❸
	De La Panza	*Steaks & grills*	❸❸❸
	Garufa	"	❸❸❸
	Il Bacio	*Pizza*	❸⑤④
	Rodizio Rico	*Brazilian*	⑤④④
	Tierra Peru	*Peruvian*	❷❷④
	Sabor	*South American*	❸❶④
	Yipin China	*Chinese*	❶❷④
	Roots at N1	*Indian*	❷❷❸
	Yum Yum	*Thai*	❸❷❷
£35+	Red Dog Saloon	*American*	④④❸
	Kipferl	*East & Cent. European*	❸④❷
	Le Sacré-Coeur	*French*	④❷❷
	The Real Greek	*Greek*	⑤④④
	Vrisaki	"	④④④
	Pizzeria Oregano	*Italian*	❸④④
	Pizzeria Pappagone	"	❸❷❷
	Rugoletta	"	❸❸④
	Toff's	*Fish & chips*	❷❷④
	Two Brothers	"	❸④④
	Mangal II	*Turkish*	❸❸④
	Anglo Asian Tandoori	*Indian*	❷❷❸
	Indian Rasoi	"	❶❷❸
	Zaffrani	"	❸❷❸
	Rasa Travancore	*Indian, Southern*	❷❷❸
	Thai Square	*Thai*	④④❸
	Viet Garden	*Vietnamese*	❸④⑤
£30+	Olympus Fish	*Fish & seafood*	❷❷④
	Blue Legume	*French*	④❸❷
	La Porchetta Pizzeria	*Italian*	④❸④
	La Bota	*Spanish*	❸④④
	Café del Parc	"	❷❷❸
	Byron	*Burgers, etc*	❸❸❸
	Diner	"	④❸❷
	Basilico	*Pizza*	❷❸⑤
	Yalla Yalla	*Lebanese*	❷❸❷
	Gilak	*Persian*	❸❷④
	Antepliler	*Turkish*	❸④❸
	Gallipoli	"	④❸❷
	Izgara	"	❸④⑤
	Petek	"	❸❷❸
	Delhi Grill	*Indian*	❷④❸
	Masala Zone	"	❸❸❷
	Rasa	*Indian, Southern*	❶❷❸
	Wagamama	*Japanese*	④❸④
	dim T	*Pan-Asian*	④④④
	Huong-Viet	*Vietnamese*	④⑤④
	Khoai	"	❸④④
£25+	Le Mercury	*French*	④④❸
	Mem & Laz	*Mediterranean*	❸❷❷
	Stringray Café	"	④④④
	Gem	*Turkish*	❸❷❷
	Rani	*Indian*	④④④
	Dotori	*Korean*	❷④❸

£20+	Afghan Kitchen	*Afghani*	❷⑤④
£15+	Chilango	*Mexican/TexMex*	❷❷❸
	Tortilla	*"*	④④④
	Jai Krishna	*Indian*	❷❷④
£10+	Euphorium Bakery	*Sandwiches, cakes, etc*	❸❸❸

SOUTH

South Bank (SE1)

Price	Restaurant	Cuisine	Rating
£80+	Oxo Tower (Rest')	*British, Modern*	⑤⑤④
£70+	Le Pont de la Tour	*British, Modern*	④❸❷
	Oxo Tower (Brass')	*Mediterranean*	⑤④❸
£60+	Roast	*British, Traditional*	④④❸
	La Barca	*Italian*	④④❷
	Gaucho	*Steaks & grills*	❸④❸
£50+	Blueprint Café	*British, Modern*	❸❸❶
	Cantina Vinopolis	"	④④④
	Magdalen	"	❷❸❸
	Mezzanine	"	④④④
	RSJ	"	❸❸⑤
	Skylon	"	④④❷
	Butlers W'f Chop-house	*British, Traditional*	④④❸
	fish!	*Fish & seafood*	④④⑤
	Wright Brothers	"	❷❸❷
	Vivat Bacchus	*International*	④❸❸
	Archduke Wine Bar	*Steaks & grills*	⑤⑤④
	Mango Tree	*Indian*	❸④④
£40+	Elliot's Cafe	*British, Modern*	❷❸❸
	40 Maltby Street	"	❷❷❷
	Garrison	"	❸❸❶
	Menier Chocolate Factory	"	⑤❸❸
	The Swan at the Globe	"	④④❷
	The Table	"	④④④
	Tate Modern (Level 7)	"	④④❷
	Waterloo Bar & Kitchen	"	④④④
	The Anchor & Hope	*British, Traditional*	❶❸❸
	Canteen	"	⑤⑤⑤
	The Riverfront	"	④④❸
	Applebee's Cafe	*Fish & seafood*	❸❸④
	Brasserie Blanc	*French*	④❸❸
	Côte	"	④❸④
	Waterloo Brasserie	"	⑤❸④
	Champor-Champor	*Fusion*	❸❸❷
	Village East	"	④④❸
	Browns	*International*	⑤⑤④
	Delfina	"	④④❸
	Giraffe	"	⑤④⑤
	Antico	*Italian*	❸❷❸
	Cantina del Ponte	"	⑤⑤④
	La Lanterna	"	④❸④
	Tentazioni	"	❷❷❸
	Zucca	"	❶❷❷
	Del'Aziz	*Mediterranean*	④⑤❸
	Baltic	*Polish*	❸④❸
	Pizarro	*Spanish*	❷❷❶
	Tapas Brindisa	"	❸④❸
	Black & Blue	*Steaks & grills*	④❸④
	Constancia	*Argentinian*	❷❷④

£35+	Real Greek	*Greek*	⑤④④
	Tate Modern (Level 2)	*International*	④④❸
	José	*Spanish*	❶❷❶
	Meson don Felipe	*"*	④④④
	Benugo	*Sandwiches, cakes, etc*	④④❷
	Bangalore Express	*Indian*	④④❸
	Bengal Clipper	*"*	❸❸❸
£30+	Mar I Terra	*Spanish*	❸❸❷
	Gourmet Pizza Co.	*Pizza*	④❸❸
	El Vergel	*South American*	❷❸❷
	Tas (Cafe)	*Turkish*	④❸❸
	Tas Pide	*"*	④❷❷
	ping pong	*Chinese, Dim sum*	④④❸
	Wagamama	*Japanese*	④❸④
	dim T	*Pan-Asian*	④④④
£25+	Masters Super Fish	*Fish & chips*	❸④⑤
	Konditor & Cook	*Sandwiches, cakes, etc*	❸④④
	Tsuru	*Japanese*	❸❸④
£20+	Leon	*Sandwiches, cakes, etc*	④❸❸
£15+	Tortilla	*Mexican/TexMex*	④④④
£10+	Caffé Vergnano	*Sandwiches, cakes, etc*	④❸❸
	Monmouth Coffee Co	*"*	❶❶❷
	Pod	*"*	❸❷❸
	Spianata & Co	*"*	❷❷❸

Greenwich, Lewisham, Dulwich & Blackheath (All SE postcodes, except SE1)

£60+	Gaucho	*Steaks & grills*	❸④❸
£50+	Rivington Grill	*British, Modern*	④④④
	Lobster Pot	*Fish & seafood*	❸❷❸
	The Spread Eagle	*French*	⑤⑤④
	Buenos Aires Café	*Argentinian*	❷❸❸
£40+	Chapters	*British, Modern*	④④④
	The Crooked Well	*"*	❸❷❷
	Franklins	*"*	❸❸❸
	Inside	*"*	❷❷④
	The Lido Cafe	*"*	❸❸❷
	The Old Brewery	*"*	④④❷
	The Palmerston	*"*	❸❸❸
	Simplicity	*"*	❸❸❸
	Le Chardon	*French*	④④❸
	Green & Blue	*International*	❸❷❷
	Joanna's	*"*	❸❷❷
	The Trafalgar Tavern	*"*	⑤⑤④
	The Yellow House	*"*	❸❷④
	Angels & Gypsies	*Spanish*	❷❸❷
	Bianco43	*Pizza*	❸⑤④
	Zero Degrees	*"*	❸④❸
	Rodizio Rico	*Brazilian*	⑤④④

	Babur	*Indian*	❶❷❷
	Kennington Tandoori	*"*	❸❷❸
£35+	The Dartmouth Arms	*British, Modern*	❸❸❸
	Florence	*"*	④④❷
	Brasserie Toulouse-Lautrec	*French*	④❷❶
	Lorenzo	*Italian*	❸❷④
	Le Querce	*"*	❶❶❷
	Olley's	*Fish & chips*	❸❸❸
	Ganapati	*Indian*	❶❷❷
	Tandoori Nights	*"*	❷❷❸
£30+	The Lord Northbrook	*British, Traditional*	❸❷❷
	Frizzante Cafe	*Italian*	❸❷❸
	The Gowlett	*Pizza*	❷❸❸
	Rocca Di Papa	*"*	④④❸
	Dragon Castle	*Chinese*	❷④❸
	Everest Inn	*Indian*	❷❸❸
£25+	The Sea Cow	*Fish & chips*	❷❷❸
	Gandhi's	*Indian*	❸❷❸
£20+	Thai Corner Café	*Thai*	❸❸❸
	Cafe East	*Vietnamese*	❸④④
£10+	Monmouth Coffee Company	*Sandwiches, cakes, etc*	❶❶❷

Battersea, Brixton, Clapham, Wandsworth Barnes, Putney & Wimbledon (All SW postcodes south of the river)

£60+	Cannizaro House	*British, Modern*	④④❷
	Chez Bruce	*"*	❶❶❷
	Trinity	*"*	❶❶❷
£50+	Entrée	*British, Modern*	❸❸❷
	Four O Nine	*"*	❸❸❷
	Ransome's Dock	*"*	❸❸❸
	Sonny's	*"*	– – –
	Tom Ilic	*"*	❶❷④
	Verta	*"*	❸❸④
	Fox & Grapes	*British, Traditional*	④④❸
	Fish Place	*Fish & seafood*	❷❷④
	The Lawn Bistro	*French*	❸❸④
	Enoteca Turi	*Italian*	❷❷❸
	Isola del Sole	*"*	④④④
	Numero Uno	*"*	❸❸❷
	Riva	*"*	❷❸④
	Fulham Wine Rooms	*Sandwiches, cakes, etc*	❸❸❸
£40+	Bodean's	*American*	④④❸
	The Abbeville	*British, Modern*	④④❷
	Abbeville Kitchen	*"*	❷❷❸
	Alma	*"*	④④❷
	Avalon	*"*	❸④❷
	Ben's Canteen	*"*	❸④④
	Bistro Union	*"*	❸❸❸

	The Bolingbroke	"	④❷❷
	The Brown Dog	"	❸❸❸
	Brunswick House Cafe	"	❷④❶
	The Depot	"	❸❷❷
	Earl Spencer	"	❸④❸
	Emile's	"	❸❶❸
	The Fentiman Arms	"	❸❸❷
	Harrison's	"	④④❸
	Lamberts	"	❶❶❷
	The Prince Of Wales	"	❸❸❸
	The Victoria	"	❷❸❷
	Canton Arms	*British, Traditional*	❷❷❷
	Bellevue Rendez-Vous	*French*	❸❷❷
	Le Cassoulet	"	❸④④
	Le Chardon	"	④④❸
	Côte	"	④❸④
	Gastro	"	⑤⑤❸
	Le P'tit Normand	"	❸❷❸
	Soif	"	❸❸④
	Upstairs Bar	"	❷❶❶
	Annie's	*International*	④❸❷
	Brinkley's Kitchen	"	④④❸
	The Light House	"	④❸④
	The Ship	"	❸❸❶
	Antipasto & Pasta	*Italian*	❸❷❸
	Cantinetta	"	④④④
	Donna Margherita	"	❷④④
	Ost. Antica Bologna	"	❸❸④
	Pizza Metro	"	❷❸❸
	San Lorenzo Fuoriporta	"	④⑤④
	Sapori Sardi	"	❷❷❸
	The Fox & Hounds	*Mediterranean*	❷❷❷
	Lola Rojo	*Spanish*	❸④④
	La Mancha	"	❸❸④
	Rebato's	"	❸❷❸
	Butcher & Grill	*Steaks & grills*	④❸❸
	Cattle Grid	"	❷④④
	Popeseye	"	❷❸⑤
	Al Forno	*Pizza*	④❷❷
	Santa Maria del Sur	*Argentinian*	❸④❸
	Bayee Village	*Chinese*	❸❷❷
	China Boulevard	"	❷④❸
	Royal China	"	❸⑤④
	Indian Zilla	*Indian*	❶❶❷
	Cho-San	*Japanese*	❷❷❸
	Sticks'n'Sushi	"	❷❷❷
	Tsunami	"	❷❸❸
	Blue Elephant	*Thai*	❸❸❸
	Suk Saran	"	❸④⑤
£35+	Belgo	*Belgian*	⑤④④
	Antelope	*British, Modern*	❸❸❷
	The Balham Bowls Club	"	❸❷❷
	The Lighthouse	"	❸❷❷
	Gazette	*French*	④④❷
	Hudsons	*International*	④④❸
	Telegraph	"	④④❷
	Buona Sera	*Italian*	❸❸❶

	Fish Club	*Fish & chips*	❷❷④
	La Delizia	*Pizza*	④❸④
	Dalchini	*Chinese*	❸④④
	Ma Goa	*Indian*	❷❶❷
	Nazmins	*"*	④④④
	Cah-Chi	*Korean*	❸❶❸
	Thai Square	*Thai*	④④❸
£30+	Fish in a Tie	*Mediterranean*	④❷❶
	The Little Bay	*"*	④❷❶
	El Rincón Latino	*Spanish*	④❷❷
	Byron	*Burgers, etc*	❸❸❸
	Brady's	*Fish & chips*	❸❷❸
	Basilico	*Pizza*	❷❸⑤
	Eco	*"*	❸④❸
	Pantry	*Sandwiches, cakes, etc*	❸❸❷
	Chutney	*Indian*	❸❸❸
	Cocum	*"*	❸❷❷
	Indian Moment	*"*	❸④④
	Mango & Silk	*"*	④④❸
	Triphal	*"*	❷❸④
	Hashi	*Japanese*	❷❷❸
	Wagamama	*"*	④❸④
	The Banana Tree Canteen	*Pan-Asian*	❸❸❸
	Amaranth	*Thai*	❸④❷
	Fat Boy's	*"*	❸④❸
	Talad Thai	*"*	❸❸⑤
	Thai Garden	*"*	❸④④
£25+	Gail's Bread	*Sandwiches, cakes, etc*	❸❷❸
	Faanoos	*Persian*	④④❸
	Holy Cow	*Indian*	❷④❸
	Indian Ocean	*"*	❷❷❸
	Sree Krishna	*"*	❷❷❸
	Fujiyama	*Japanese*	❸④④
	Slurp	*"*	❸④⑤
	Hare & Tortoise	*Pan-Asian*	❸❸④
	The Pepper Tree	*Thai*	❸❷❸
	The Paddyfield	*Vietnamese*	❶❸❸
£20+	Honest Burgers	*Burgers, etc*	❶❸❸
	Franco Manca	*Pizza*	❶❸❷
	Hot Stuff	*Indian*	❷❸④
	Lahore Karahi	*Pakistani*	❷④④
	Lahore Kebab House	*"*	❶④④
	Mirch Masala SW16	*"*	❷④⑤
	Kaosarn	*Thai*	❶❸④
	Mien Tay	*Vietnamese*	❷④④
£15+	Orange Pekoe	*Sandwiches, cakes, etc*	❸❷❷
	Apollo Banana Leaf	*Indian*	❷❷⑤

Outer western suburbs
Kew, Richmond, Twickenham, Teddington

£70+	Petersham Nurseries	*British, Modern*	— — —
£60+	The Bingham	*British, Modern*	❷❷❷
	The Glasshouse	*"*	❶❶❸
	Petersham Hotel	*"*	④④❷
	Al Boccon di'vino	*Italian*	❷❶❸
	Gaucho	*Steaks & grills*	❸④❸
£50+	Plane Food	*British, Modern*	④④④
	Rock & Rose	*"*	⑤⑤❷
	Brula	*French*	❷❶❶
	Kew Grill	*Steaks & grills*	❸❷❷
£40+	The Wharf	*British, Modern*	④❸❶
	La Buvette	*French*	❸❷❷
	Ma Cuisine	*"*	④❸④
	A Cena	*Italian*	❸❷❷
	don Fernando's	*Spanish*	④❷④
	Palmyra	*Lebanese*	❷❷④
	Four Regions	*Chinese*	❷❷④
	Matsuba	*Japanese*	❷④④
£35+	Canta Napoli	*Italian*	❸❸④
	Pizzeria Rustica	*Pizza*	❷❸④
£30+	Fat Boy's	*Thai*	❸④❸
£15+	William Curley	*Afternoon tea*	❷❸❸
	Taylor St Baristas	*Sandwiches, cakes, etc*	❷❸❸

EAST

Smithfield & Farringdon (EC1)

£70+	Club Gascon	*French*	❷❷❸
	Dans le Noir	*International*	⑤④④
	Smiths (Top Floor)	*Steaks & grills*	⑤④④
£60+	Chiswell Street Dining Rms	*British, Modern*	④④④
	Bleeding Heart	*French*	❷❷❶
	Morgan M	*"*	❶❷④
	Portal	*Portuguese*	❸❸❷
	Gaucho	*Steaks & grills*	❸④❸
£50+	Malmaison Brasserie	*British, Modern*	❸❷❸
	North Road	*"*	❶❶❸
	St John	*British, Traditional*	❷❷❸
	Bistrot Bruno Loubet	*French*	❷❷❸
	Café du Marché	*"*	❷❷❶
	Le Saint Julien	*"*	④❷❸
	Moro	*Spanish*	❷❷❸
	Hix	*Steaks & grills*	❷❸❸
	Smiths (Dining Rm)	*"*	④④④
	Sushi Tetsu	*Japanese*	❶❷❸
£40+	Brasserie on St John Street	*British, Modern*	❸❸❸
	Caravan	*"*	❸❸❸
	The Gunmakers	*"*	❷❷❸
	The Modern Pantry	*"*	④④④
	The Peasant	*"*	❸④❸
	Vinoteca	*"*	❸❷❷
	The Fox and Anchor	*British, Traditional*	❸❸❶
	Comptoir Gascon	*French*	❸❸❷
	Le Rendezvous du Café	*"*	❸❸❸
	Alba	*Italian*	❸❷④
	Fabrizio	*"*	❷❶⑤
	Santore	*"*	❷❸④
	Redhook	*Steaks & grills*	④④④
	The Gate	*Vegetarian*	❶❸④
	Burger & Lobster	*Burgers, etc*	❷❷❷
	Cicada	*Pan-Asian*	❸❸❸
£35+	Giant Robot	*American*	④④❷
	Cellar Gascon	*French*	❸④❷
	Morito	*Spanish*	❷❷❷
	Pinchito	*"*	④④❷
	Amico Bio	*Vegetarian*	④④❸
	Benugo	*Sandwiches, cakes, etc*	④④❷
	Bincho EC1	*Japanese*	④④❷
	Pham Sushi	*"*	❶④④
	Tajima Tei	*"*	❶❸④
	Busaba Eathai	*Thai*	❸❸❷
	Cây Tre	*Vietnamese*	❸④④
£30+	Smiths (Ground Floor)	*British, Modern*	④④❸
	Kolossi Grill	*Greek*	④❷❷
	Polpo	*Italian*	④❸❶
	La Porchetta Pizzeria	*"*	④❸④

	The Eagle	*Mediterranean*	❸⑤❷
	The Little Bay	*"*	④❷❶
	Tas	*Turkish*	④❸❸
	Banana Tree Canteen	*Pan-Asian*	❸❸❸
	Pho	*Vietnamese*	❷❷❷
£25+	Fish Central	*Fish & seafood*	❷❷❸
	Gail's Bakery	*Sandwiches, cakes, etc*	❸❷❸
	Look Mum No Hands!	*"*	❸④❸
	Sedap	*Malaysian*	❸❷④
£15+	Department of Coffee	*Sandwiches, cakes, etc*	❶❶❷
	Abokado	*Japanese*	④❸④
£10+	Dose	*Sandwiches, cakes, etc*	❷❷④
	Nusa Kitchen	*"*	❷④④
	Pod	*"*	❸❷❸
	Prufrock Coffee	*"*	❸❷❸
	Spianata & Co	*"*	❷❷❸

The City (EC2, EC3, EC4)

£80+	Rhodes 24	*British, Modern*	❸❸❶
	Sushisamba	*Japanese*	④❷❷
£70+	L'Anima	*Italian*	❷❷❸
£60+	The Don	*British, Modern*	❸❷❷
	High Timber	*"*	❸❸❸
	1901	*"*	④④❷
	1 Lombard Street	*"*	❸❸④
	Prism	*"*	④❸④
	Vertigo 42	*"*	④④❷
	Green's	*British, Traditional*	❸❸④
	Chamberlain's	*Fish & seafood*	❸❸❸
	Coq d'Argent	*French*	④④❸
	Lutyens	*"*	④④④
	Sauterelle	*"*	❸❷❸
	Bonds	*Mediterranean*	④④④
	Gaucho	*Steaks & grills*	❸④❸
	Goodman City	*"*	❷❷❸
	Hawksmoor	*"*	❷❷❸
	Mint Leaf	*Indian*	❸❸❷
£50+	Bread Street Kitchen	*British, Modern*	④④④
	The Chancery	*"*	❷❷④
	The Mercer	*"*	❸❷❸
	Northbank	*"*	④④④
	Rivington Grill	*"*	④④④
	Searcy's Brasserie	*"*	④❸❷
	The White Swan	*"*	❸❷④
	Paternoster Chop House	*British, Traditional*	⑤⑤⑤
	Gow's	*Fish & seafood*	❸❸❸
	Sweetings	*"*	❸❸❷
	The Royal Exchange	*French*	④④❸
	28-50	*"*	❸❷❷
	Sushinho	*Fusion*	❸④❷

	Vivat Bacchus	*International*	④❸❸
	Caravaggio	*Italian*	④④⑤
	Manicomio	*"*	❸④❸
	Refettorio	*"*	④❸⑤
	Eyre Brothers	*Spanish*	❷❸❸
	Barbecoa	*Steaks & grills*	❸④❸
	Hix at The Tramshed	*"*	❸❸❷
	Vanilla Black	*Vegetarian*	❸❷❸
	Kenza	*Lebanese*	④④④
	Cinnamon Kitchen	*Indian*	❷❸❸
	City Miyama	*Japanese*	❸④⑤
£40+	Bodean's	*American*	④④❸
	The Hoxton Grill	*"*	④❸❷
	The Anthologist	*British, Modern*	④④❸
	The Jugged Hare	*"*	❸❸❸
	Princess of Shoreditch	*"*	④❸④
	George & Vulture	*British, Traditional*	④❸❷
	Loch Fyne	*Fish & seafood*	④④④
	Orpheus	*"*	❷❷④
	Brasserie Blanc	*French*	④❸❸
	Côte	*"*	④❸④
	Browns	*International*	⑤⑤④
	Piccolino	*Italian*	④❸④
	Taberna Etrusca	*"*	④④④
	Rocket	*Mediterranean*	④❸❸
	Relais de Venise L'Entrecôte	*Steaks & grills*	❷④❸
	Chinese Cricket Club	*Chinese*	❸❷⑤
	Imperial City	*"*	❸❷❸
	K10	*Japanese*	❷④⑤
	Kurumaya	*"*	❸❸④
	Mugen	*"*	❸④④
	Gt Eastern Dining Room	*Pan-Asian*	❸❷❸
	Pacific Oriental	*"*	④❸④
£35+	Simpson's Tavern	*British, Traditional*	④④❶
	Haz	*Turkish*	④❸❷
	Bangalore Express	*Indian*	④④❸
	Thai Square	*Thai*	④④❸
£30+	Café Below	*British, Modern*	❸❸❷
	The Punch Tavern	*"*	④❸❷
	Byron	*Burgers, etc*	❸❸❸
	The Diner	*"*	④❸❷
	Natural Kitchen	*Salads*	❸④❸
	ping pong	*Chinese, Dim sum*	④④❸
	Wagamama	*Japanese*	④❸④
£25+	Hilliard	*British, Modern*	❷❷❸
	The Wine Library	*International*	⑤❷❶
	Konditor & Cook	*Sandwiches, cakes, etc*	❸④④
	Tsuru	*Japanese*	❸❸④
	Hare & Tortoise	*Pan-Asian*	❸❸④
£20+	Leon	*Sandwiches, cakes, etc*	④❸❸
£15+	Hummus Bros	*Mediterranean*	❸④④
	Taylor St Baristas	*Sandwiches, cakes, etc*	❷❸❸

	Chilango	*Mexican/TexMex*	❷❷❸
	Tortilla	*"*	④④④
	Abokado	*Japanese*	④❸④
£10+	Caffé Vergnano	*Sandwiches, cakes, etc*	④❸❸
	Fuzzy's Grub	*"*	❸❸④
	Nusa Kitchen	*"*	❷④④
	Pod	*"*	❸❷❸
	Spianata & Co	*"*	❷❷❸
	City Càphê	*Vietnamese*	❷❸⑤
£5+	Grace St Paul's	*Sandwiches, cakes, etc*	❷❷❸

East End & Docklands (All E postcodes)

£80+	Viajante	*Fusion*	❷❷❸
£70+	Galvin La Chapelle	*French*	❷❷❶
	Plateau	*"*	④❸❸
	Les Trois Garçons	*"*	❸❸❶
	Quadrato	*Italian*	④❸❸
	Roka	*Japanese*	❶❸❷
£60+	Beach Blanket Babylon	*British, Modern*	⑤④❷
	The Boundary	*"*	❸❸❷
	Gaucho	*Steaks & grills*	❸④❸
	Goodman	*"*	❷❷❸
	Hawksmoor	*"*	❷❷❸
	MPW Steakhouse & Grill	*"*	④❸④
	Bevis Marks	*Kosher*	– – –
£50+	Bistrotheque	*British, Modern*	④④❸
	The Gun	*"*	❸❸❷
	Wapping Food	*"*	❸④❶
	St John Bread & Wine	*British, Traditional*	❶❷❸
	Forman's	*Fish & seafood*	❸❸④
	The Luxe	*International*	⑤⑤④
	Boisdale of Canary Wharf	*Scottish*	④④❷
	Café Spice Namaste	*Indian*	❷❶④
	Dockmaster's House	*"*	❸④④
£40+	All Star Lanes	*American*	④❸❷
	Balans	*British, Modern*	⑤④❸
	The Empress	*"*	❷❸❸
	The Morgan Arms	*"*	❸❸❷
	The Narrow	*"*	⑤⑤④
	Whitechapel Gallery	*"*	❸❷❸
	Albion	*British, Traditional*	❸④❷
	Canteen	*"*	⑤⑤⑤
	The Grapes	*Fish & seafood*	❸❸❷
	Brawn	*French*	❷❷❷
	Browns	*International*	⑤⑤④
	Giraffe	*"*	⑤④⑤
	Il Bordello	*Italian*	❷❶❷
	La Figa	*"*	❸❷④
	Jamie's Italian	*"*	⑤④④
	Lardo	*"*	– – –

	Rocket	*Mediterranean*	④❸❸
	Corner Room	*Portuguese*	❶❷❷
	Ibérica	*Spanish*	❸④❸
	Relais de Venise L'Entrecôte	*Steaks & grills*	❷④❸
	Ark Fish	*Fish & chips*	❶❸⑤
	Pizza East	*Pizza*	❸❸❶
	Buen Ayre	*Argentinian*	❷❸❸
	Lotus	*Chinese*	④④❸
	Royal China	*"*	❷④④
	Sichuan Folk	*"*	❷❸⑤
	Yi-Ban	*"*	❸❸⑤
	Elephant Royale	*Thai*	❸④❸
£35+	Rochelle Canteen	*British, Modern*	❸❷❷
	Real Greek	*Greek*	⑤④④
	LMNT	*International*	④❷❶
	Al Volo	*Italian*	❸❸❸
	Fire & Stone	*Pizza*	④④❸
	Haz	*Turkish*	④❸❷
	My Old Place	*Chinese*	❷⑤⑤
	Little Georgia Café	*Georgian*	❸④❸
	Busaba Eathai	*Thai*	❸❸❷
	Rosa's	*"*	❸❷❸
	Viet Grill	*Vietnamese*	❸④❸
£30+	Byron	*Burgers, etc*	❸❸❸
	Story Deli	*Pizza*	❷④❸
	Wahaca	*Mexican/TexMex*	❸❸❷
	Hazev	*Turkish*	❸❷④
	Shanghai	*Chinese*	❷④❸
	ping pong	*Chinese, Dim sum*	④④❸
	Memsaheb on Thames	*Indian*	④❸④
	Itsu	*Japanese*	④❸④
	Wagamama	*"*	④❸④
	Green Papaya	*Vietnamese*	❷❷❸
	Namo	*"*	❸❸❷
	Sông Quê	*"*	❸⑤④
	Viet Hoa	*"*	④⑤④
£25+	Frizzante at City Farm	*Italian*	❷④④
	Stringray Globe Café	*Mediterranean*	④④④
	Faulkner's	*Fish & chips*	❷④④
	Mangal I	*Turkish*	❶❷④
	Clifton	*Indian*	❷❸④
	Needoo	*Pakistani*	❷❸❸
	Tayyabs	*"*	❶④❸
£20+	E Pellicci	*Italian*	④❷❶
	Franco Manca	*Pizza*	❶❸❷
	Leon	*Sandwiches, cakes, etc*	④❸❸
	Gourmet San	*Chinese*	❷⑤⑤
	Lahore Kebab House	*Pakistani*	❶④④
	Mirch Masala	*"*	❷④⑤
	Mien Tay	*Vietnamese*	❷④④
£15+	Taylor St Baristas	*Sandwiches, cakes, etc*	❷❸❸
	Tortilla	*Mexican/TexMex*	④④④

£10+	Spianata & Co	*Sandwiches, cakes, etc*	❷❷❸
£5+	Brick Lane Beigel Bake	*Sandwiches, cakes, etc*	❶❷⑤

MAPS

MAP 1 – LONDON OVERVIEW

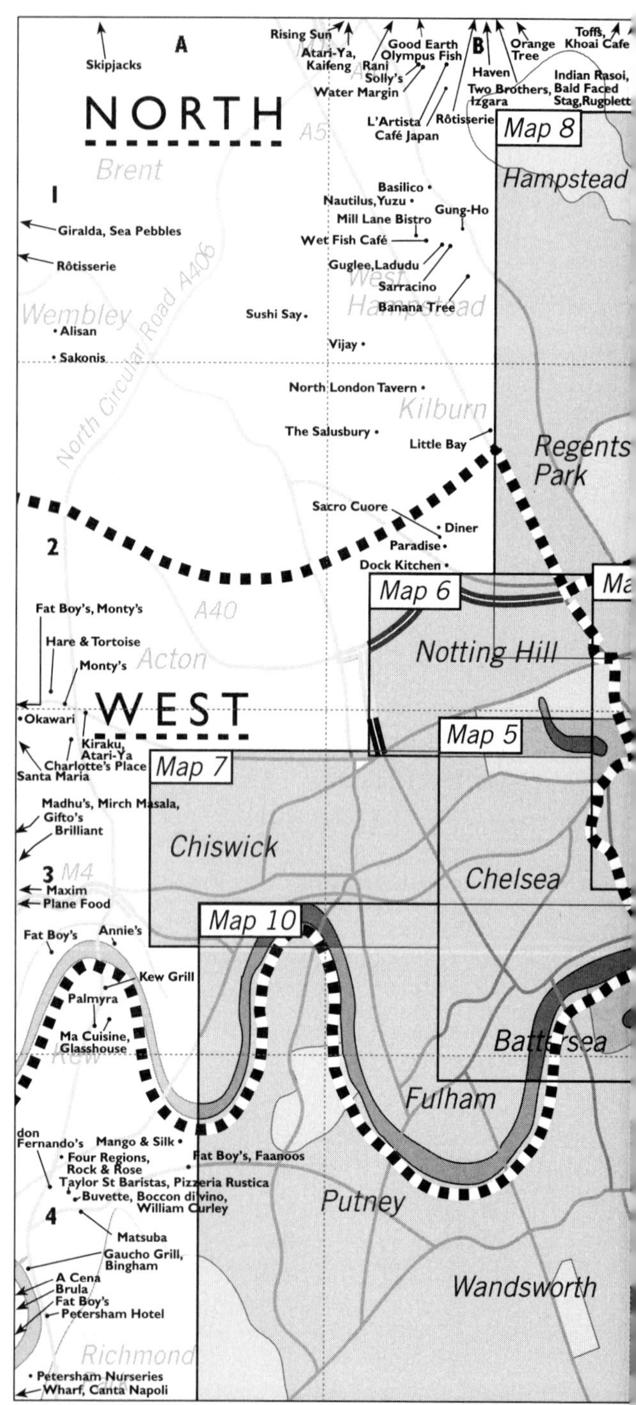

A
B
NORTH
WEST
1
2
3
4
Skipjacks
Rising Sun
Atari-Ya, Kaifeng
Good Earth
Olympus Fish
Rani
Solly's
Water Margin
L'Artista
Café Japan
Rôtisserie
Haven
Two Brothers, Izgara
Orange Tree
Toffs, Khoai Cafe
Indian Rasoi, Bald Faced Stag, Rugplett
Map 8
Hampstead
Brent
Basilico
Nautilus, Yuzu
Gung-Ho
Mill Lane Bistro
Wet Fish Café
Guglee, Ladudu
Sarracino
Banana Tree
West Hampstead
Giralda, Sea Pebbles
Rôtisserie
Wembley
Alisan
Sakonis
Sushi Say
Vijay
North London Tavern
Kilburn
The Salusbury
Little Bay
Regents Park
North Circular Road A406
A5
Sacro Cuore
Diner
Paradise
Dock Kitchen
Map 6
Notting Hill
A40
Fat Boy's, Monty's
Hare & Tortoise
Monty's
Acton
Okawari
Kiraku, Atari-Ya
Charlotte's Place
Santa Maria
Map 7
Map 5
Madhu's, Mirch Masala, Gifto's
Brilliant
Chiswick
Chelsea
M4
Maxim
Plane Food
Map 10
Fat Boy's
Annie's
Kew Grill
Palmyra
Ma Cuisine, Glasshouse
Kew
Battersea
Fulham
don Fernando's
Mango & Silk
Four Regions, Rock & Rose
Fat Boy's, Faanoos
Taylor St Baristas, Pizzeria Rustica
Buvette, Boccon di vino, William Curley
Putney
Matsuba
Gaucho Grill, Bingham
A Cena
Brula
Fat Boy's
Petersham Hotel
Wandsworth
Richmond
Petersham Nurseries
Wharf, Canta Napoli

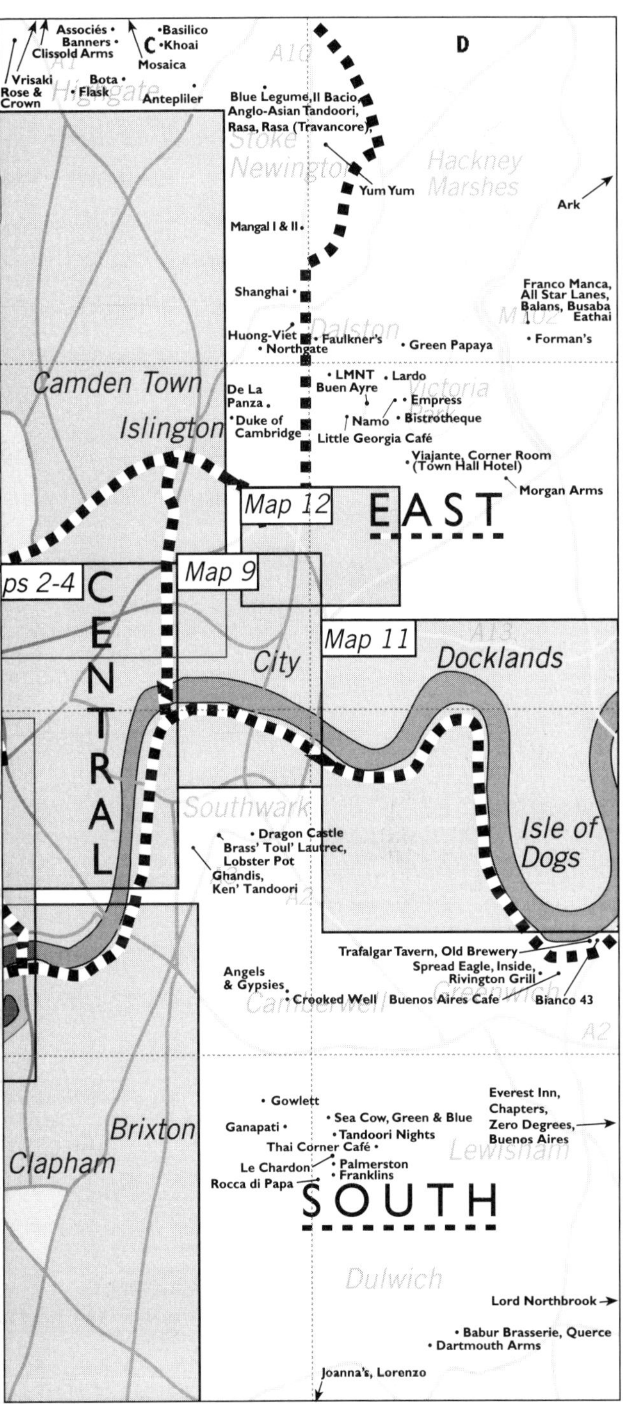

Associés
Banners
Clissold Arms
Basilico
Khoai
C
Mosaica
D
Vrisaki
Rose & Crown
Bota
Flask
Antepliler
Highgate
Blue Legume, Il Bacio, Anglo-Asian Tandoori, Rasa, Rasa (Travancore)
Stoke Newington
Yum Yum
Hackney Marshes
Ark
Mangal I & II
Shanghai
Franco Manca, All Star Lanes, Balans, Busaba Eathai
Huong-Viet
Northgate
Faulkner's
Dalston
Green Papaya
Forman's
LMNT
Lardo
Buen Ayre
Victoria Park
Camden Town
De La Panza
Duke of Cambridge
Empress
Namo
Bistrotheque
Islington
Little Georgia Café
Viajante, Corner Room (Town Hall Hotel)
Morgan Arms
Map 12
EAST
ps 2-4
Map 9
CENTRAL
Map 11
City
Docklands
Southwark
Dragon Castle
Brass' Toul' Lautrec, Lobster Pot
Ghandis, Ken' Tandoori
Isle of Dogs
Trafalgar Tavern, Old Brewery
Spread Eagle, Inside, Rivington Grill
Angels & Gypsies
Crooked Well
Buenos Aires Cafe
Bianco 43
Camberwell
Greenwich
Gowlett
Sea Cow, Green & Blue
Ganapati
Tandoori Nights
Everest Inn, Chapters, Zero Degrees, Buenos Aires
Brixton
Thai Corner Café
Lewisham
Clapham
Le Chardon
Palmerston
Franklins
Rocca di Papa
SOUTH
Dulwich
Lord Northbrook
Babur Brasserie, Querce
Dartmouth Arms
Joanna's, Lorenzo

MAP 2 – WEST END OVERVIEW

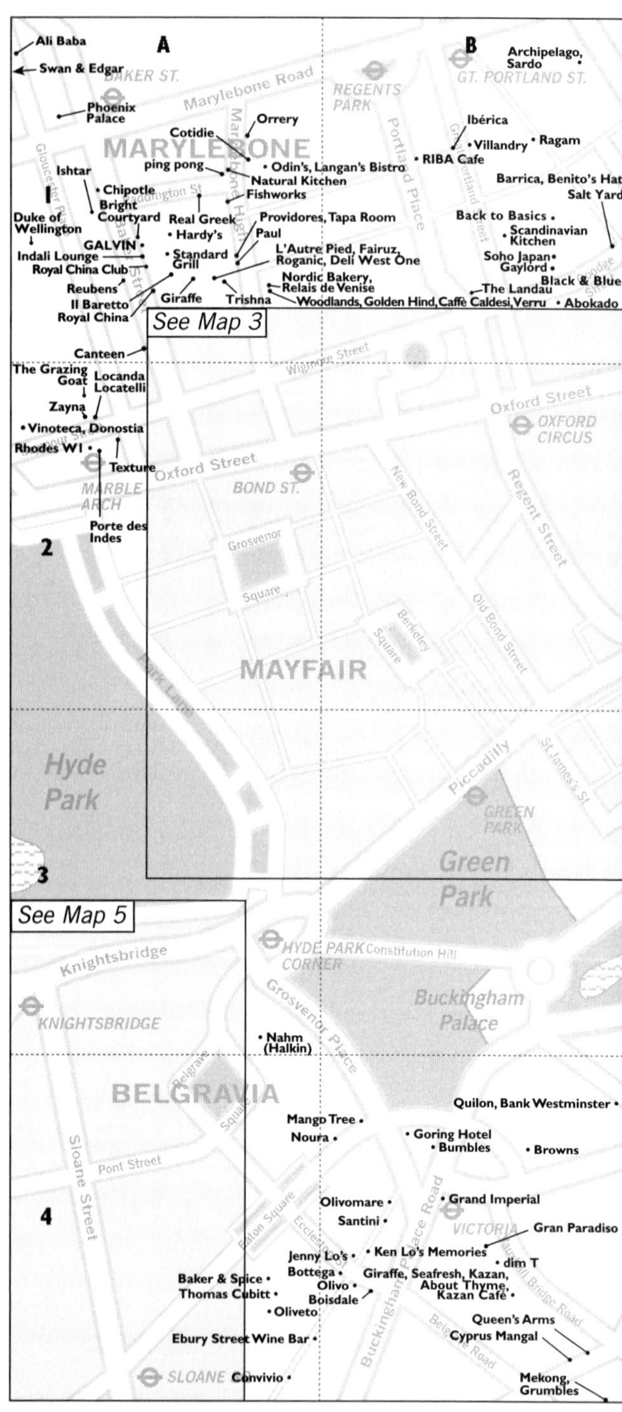

MAP 2 – WEST END OVERVIEW

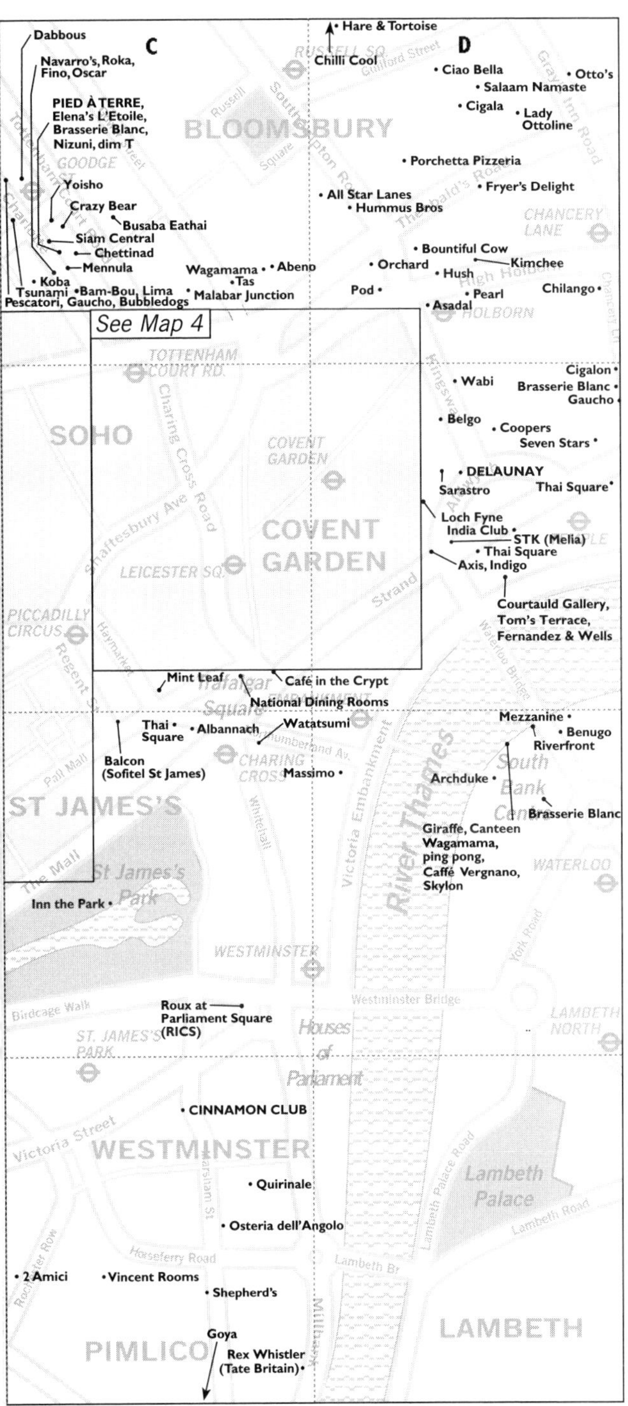

MAP 3 – MAYFAIR, ST JAMES'S & WEST SOHO

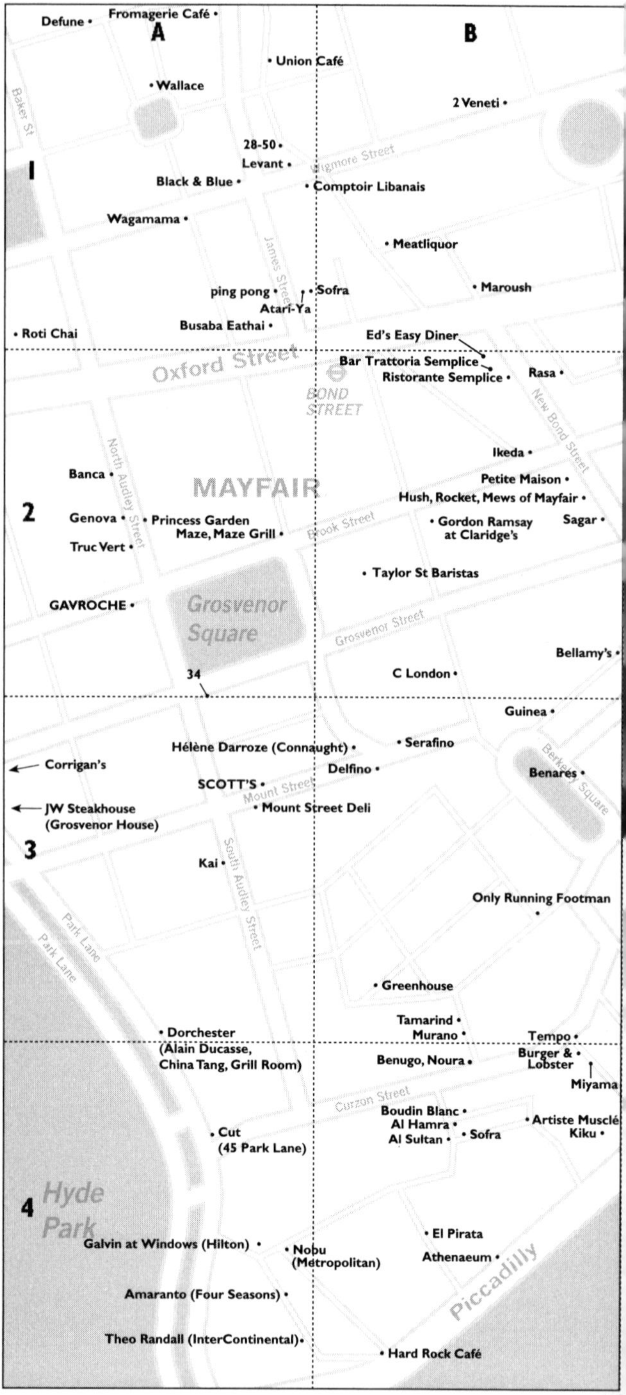

Defune •
Fromagerie Café •
A
B
• Union Café
• Wallace
Baker St
2 Veneti •
28-50 •
Levant •
Wigmore Street
1
Black & Blue •
• Comptoir Libanais
Wagamama •
James Street
• Meatliquor
ping pong •
• Sofra
• Maroush
Atari-Ya
Busaba Eathai •
• Roti Chai
Ed's Easy Diner
Oxford Street
Bar Trattoria Semplice
Ristorante Semplice •
Rasa •
BOND STREET
New Bond Street
Ikeda •
Banca •
North Audley Street
MAYFAIR
Petite Maison •
Hush, Rocket, Mews of Mayfair •
2
Genova •
• Princess Garden
Maze, Maze Grill •
Brook Street
• Gordon Ramsay at Claridge's
Sagar •
Truc Vert •
• Taylor St Baristas
GAVROCHE •
Grosvenor Square
Grosvenor Street
Bellamy's •
34
C London •
Guinea •
Hélène Darroze (Connaught) •
• Serafino
Corrigan's
Delfino •
Berkeley Square
Benares •
SCOTT'S •
Mount Street
JW Steakhouse (Grosvenor House)
• Mount Street Deli
3
Kai •
South Audley Street
Only Running Footman
Park Lane
Park Lane
• Greenhouse
Tamarind •
Murano •
• Dorchester (Alain Ducasse, China Tang, Grill Room)
Tempo •
Burger & Lobster •
Benugo, Noura •
Miyama
Curzon Street
Boudin Blanc •
• Artiste Musclé
Al Hamra •
Kiku •
• Cut (45 Park Lane)
Al Sultan •
• Sofra
Hyde Park
4
• El Pirata
Galvin at Windows (Hilton) •
• Nobu (Metropolitan)
Athenaeum •
Piccadilly
Amaranto (Four Seasons) •
Theo Randall (InterContinental) •
• Hard Rock Café

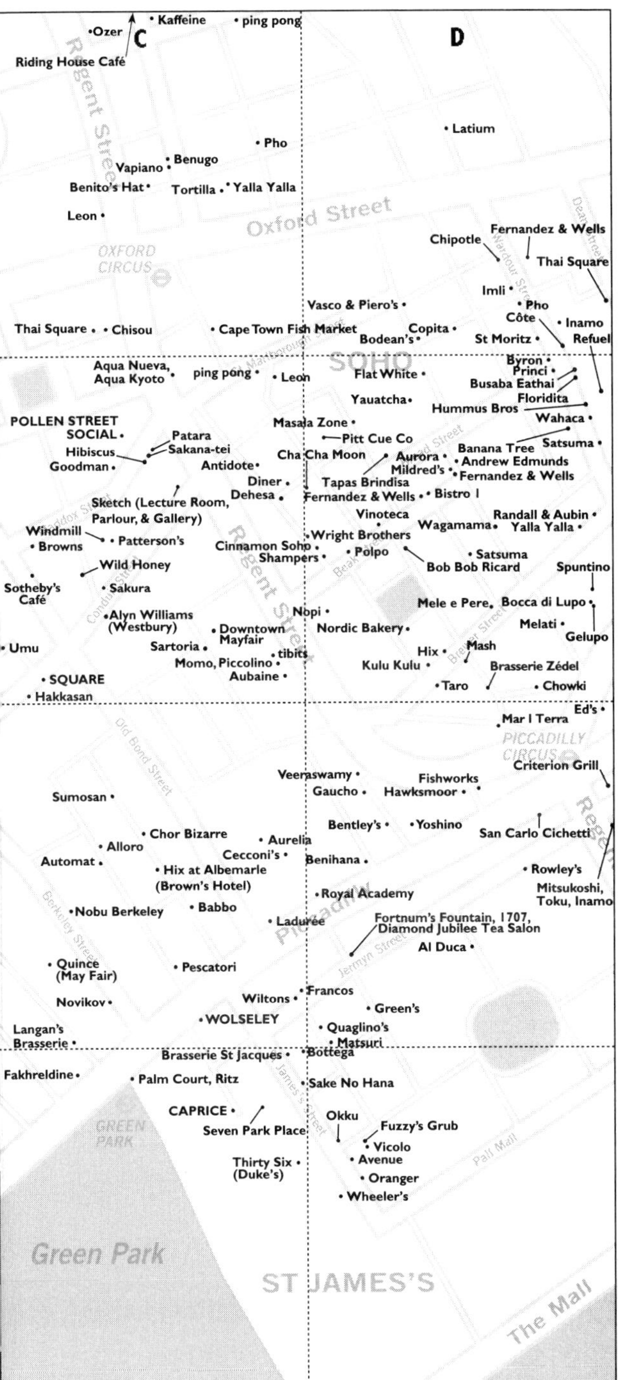

C
D
Ozer
Kaffeine
ping pong
Riding House Café
Regent Street
Latium
Pho
Benugo
Vapiano
Benito's Hat
Tortilla
Yalla Yalla
Leon
Oxford Street
OXFORD CIRCUS
Fernandez & Wells
Chipotle
Wardour Street
Thai Square
Dean Street
Imli
Pho
Vasco & Piero's
Côte
Inamo
Thai Square
Chisou
Cape Town Fish Market
Copita
Bodean's
St Moritz
Refuel
Aqua Nueva, Aqua Kyoto
ping pong
Leon
SOHO
Flat White
Byron
Princi
Busaba Eathai
Floridita
Yauatcha
Hummus Bros
POLLEN STREET SOCIAL
Masala Zone
Wahaca
Pitt Cue Co
Patara
Sakana-tei
Banana Tree
Satsuma
Hibiscus
Goodman
Cha Cha Moon
Aurora
Andrew Edmunds
Antidote
Mildred's
Fernandez & Wells
Diner
Tapas Brindisa
Dehesa
Fernandez & Wells
Bistro 1
Sketch (Lecture Room, Parlour, & Gallery)
Vinoteca
Randall & Aubin
Windmill
Wagamama
Yalla Yalla
Browns
Patterson's
Wright Brothers
Cinnamon Soho
Polpo
Satsuma
Shampers
Wild Honey
Bob Bob Ricard
Spuntino
Sotheby's Café
Sakura
Mele e Pere
Bocca di Lupo
Alyn Williams (Westbury)
Nopi
Melati
Nordic Bakery
Downtown Mayfair
Gelupo
Umu
Sartoria
Hix
Mash
tibits
Momo, Piccolino
Kulu Kulu
Brasserie Zédel
Aubaine
SQUARE
Taro
Chowki
Hakkasan
Ed's
Mar I Terra
Old Bond Street
PICCADILLY CIRCUS
Criterion Grill
Veeraswamy
Fishworks
Gaucho
Hawksmoor
Sumosan
Bentley's
Yoshino
Chor Bizarre
San Carlo Cicchetti
Aurelia
Alloro
Cecconi's
Benihana
Automat
Rowley's
Hix at Albemarle (Brown's Hotel)
Mitsukoshi, Toku, Inamo
Royal Academy
Nobu Berkeley
Babbo
Fortnum's Fountain, 1707, Diamond Jubilee Tea Salon
Ladurée
Piccadilly
Berkeley Street
Al Duca
Jermyn Street
Quince (May Fair)
Pescatori
Francos
Wiltons
Novikov
Green's
WOLSELEY
Langan's Brasserie
Quaglino's
Matsuri
Brasserie St Jacques
Bottega
Fakhreldine
Palm Court, Ritz
Sake No Hana
St James's Street
CAPRICE
Okku
Seven Park Place
Fuzzy's Grub
GREEN PARK
Vicolo
Pall Mall
Thirty Six (Duke's)
Avenue
Orangery
Wheeler's
Green Park
ST JAMES'S
The Mall

MAP 4 – EAST SOHO, CHINATOWN & COVENT GARDEN

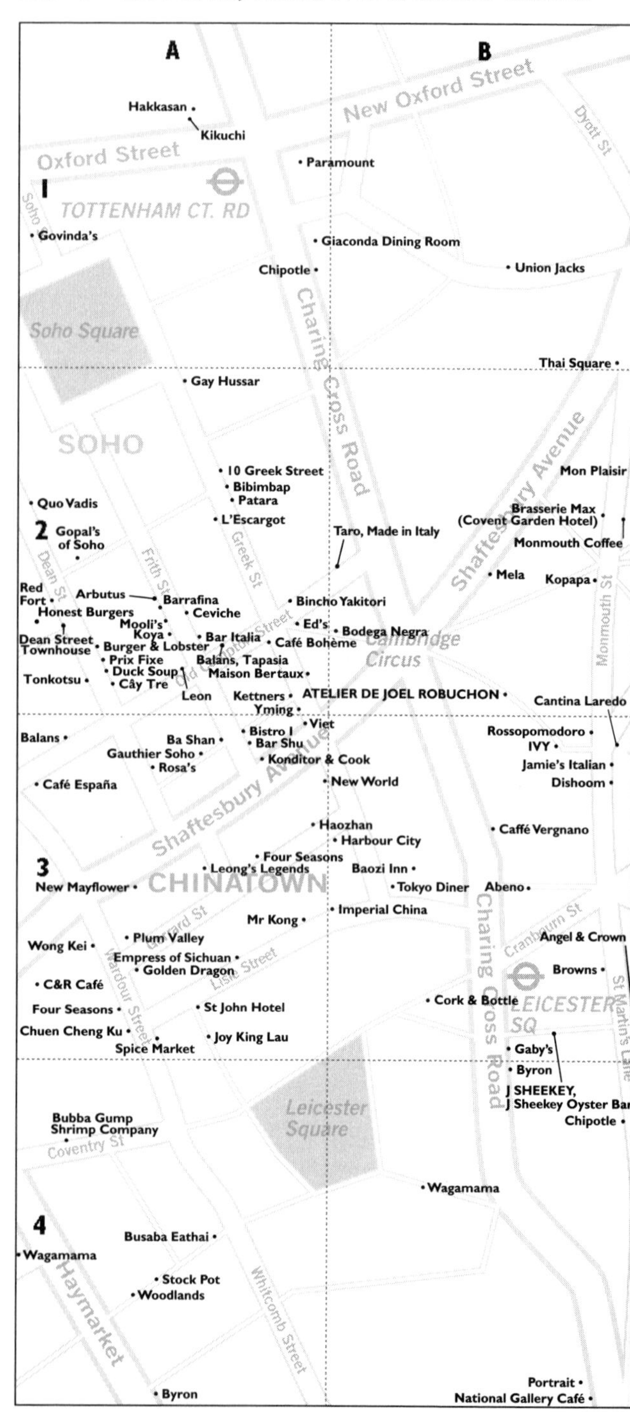

A
B
1
2
3
4
New Oxford Street
Dyott St
Hakkasan
Kikuchi
Oxford Street
Paramount
TOTTENHAM CT. RD
Soho St
Govinda's
Giaconda Dining Room
Chipotle
Union Jacks
Soho Square
Charing Cross Road
Thai Square
Gay Hussar
SOHO
Shaftesbury Avenue
10 Greek Street
Bibimbap
Patara
Mon Plaisir
Quo Vadis
L'Escargot
Brasserie Max
(Covent Garden Hotel)
Gopal's of Soho
Taro, Made in Italy
Monmouth Coffee
Dean St
Frith St
Greek St
Mela
Kopapa
Monmouth St
Red Fort
Arbutus
Barrafina
Bincho Yakitori
Honest Burgers
Ceviche
Mooli's
Ed's
Bodega Negra
Koya
Dean Street Townhouse
Burger & Lobster
Bar Italia
Café Bohème
Cambridge Circus
Old Compton Street
Prix Fixe
Balans, Tapasia
Duck Soup
Maison Bertaux
Tonkotsu
Cây Tre
Leon
Kettners
ATELIER DE JOEL ROBUCHON
Cantina Laredo
Yming
Viet
Balans
Ba Shan
Bistro I
Rossopomodoro
Bar Shu
IVY
Gauthier Soho
Konditor & Cook
Jamie's Italian
Rosa's
Café España
New World
Dishoom
Shaftesbury Avenue
Haozhan
Caffé Vergnano
Harbour City
Four Seasons
Leong's Legends
Baozi Inn
New Mayflower
CHINATOWN
Tokyo Diner
Abeno
Charing Cross Road
Gerrard St
Imperial China
Cranbourn St
Mr Kong
Angel & Crown
Wong Kei
Plum Valley
Empress of Sichuan
Golden Dragon
Lisle Street
Wardour Street
Browns
St Martin's Lane
C&R Café
Cork & Bottle
LEICESTER SQ
Four Seasons
St John Hotel
Chuen Cheng Ku
Joy King Lau
Spice Market
Gaby's
Byron
J SHEEKEY,
J Sheekey Oyster Bar
Leicester Square
Chipotle
Bubba Gump Shrimp Company
Coventry St
Wagamama
Busaba Eathai
Wagamama
Haymarket
Stock Pot
Woodlands
Whitcomb Street
Portrait
National Gallery Café
Byron

MAP 4 – EAST SOHO, CHINATOWN & COVENT GARDEN

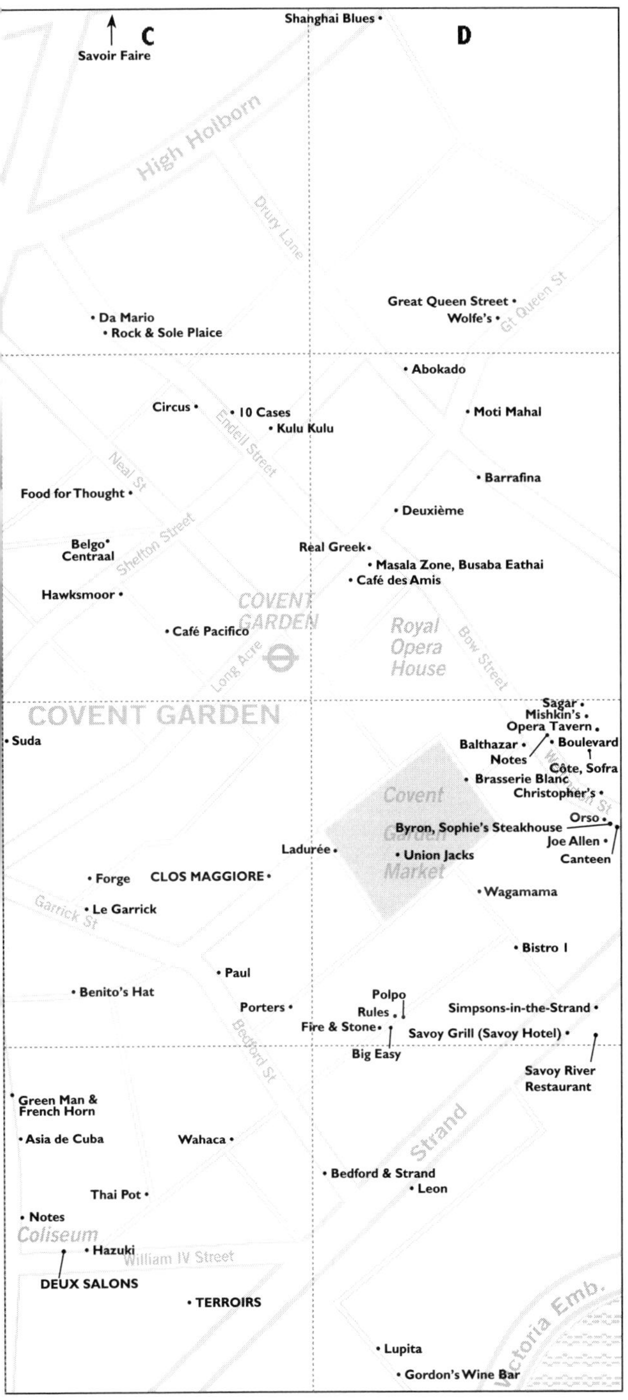
C
D
Savoir Faire
Shanghai Blues
High Holborn
Drury Lane
Gt Queen St
Great Queen Street
Wolfe's
Da Mario
Rock & Sole Plaice
Abokado
Circus
10 Cases
Kulu Kulu
Moti Mahal
Endell Street
Neal St
Barrafina
Food for Thought
Deuxième
Shelton Street
Belgo Centraal
Real Greek
Masala Zone, Busaba Eathai
Café des Amis
Hawksmoor
COVENT GARDEN
Café Pacifico
Royal Opera House
Long Acre
Bow Street
COVENT GARDEN
Sagar
Mishkin's
Opera Tavern
Suda
Balthazar
Boulevard
Notes
Côte, Sofra
Brasserie Blanc
Christopher's
Covent Garden Market
Orso
Byron, Sophie's Steakhouse
Joe Allen
Ladurée
Union Jacks
Canteen
Forge
CLOS MAGGIORE
Wagamama
Garrick St
Le Garrick
Bistro 1
Paul
Benito's Hat
Polpo
Porters
Rules
Simpsons-in-the-Strand
Fire & Stone
Savoy Grill (Savoy Hotel)
Bedford St
Big Easy
Savoy River Restaurant
Green Man & French Horn
Asia de Cuba
Wahaca
Strand
Bedford & Strand
Leon
Thai Pot
Notes
Coliseum
Hazuki
William IV Street
DEUX SALONS
TERROIRS
Victoria Emb.
Lupita
Gordon's Wine Bar

MAP 5 – KNIGHTSBRIDGE, CHELSEA & SOUTH KENSINGTON

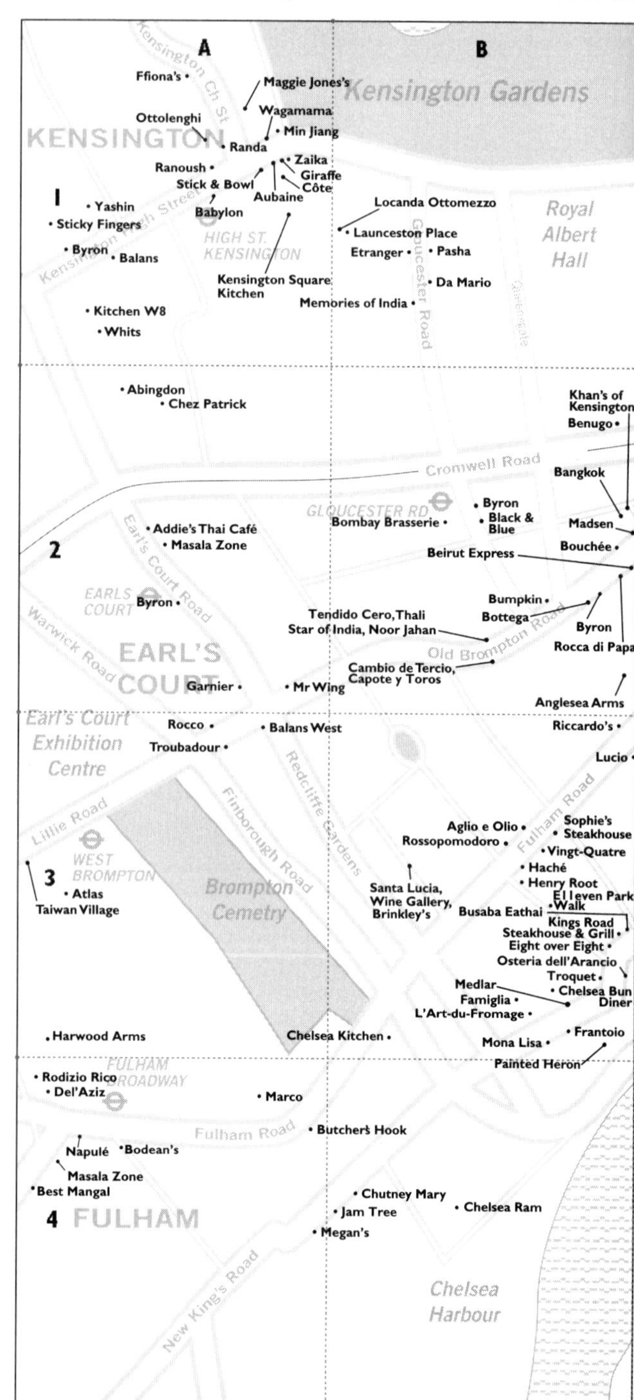

A
B
1
2
3
4
Kensington Gardens
KENSINGTON
Kensington Ch St
Kensington High Street
HIGH ST. KENSINGTON
Royal Albert Hall
Gloucester Road
Queensgate
Ffiona's
Maggie Jones's
Wagamama
Min Jiang
Ottolenghi
Randa
Ranoush
Zaika
Giraffe
Côte
Stick & Bowl
Aubaine
Babylon
Yashin
Sticky Fingers
Byron
Balans
Kensington Square Kitchen
Locanda Ottomezzo
Launceston Place
Etranger
Pasha
Da Mario
Memories of India
Kitchen W8
Whits
Abingdon
Chez Patrick
Khan's of Kensington
Benugo
Cromwell Road
Bangkok
GLOUCESTER RD
Bombay Brasserie
Byron
Black & Blue
Madsen
Addie's Thai Café
Masala Zone
Bouchée
Beirut Express
Earl's Court Road
EARLS COURT
Byron
Bumpkin
Tendido Cero, Thali
Star of India, Noor Jahan
Bottega
Byron
Rocca di Papa
Warwick Road
EARL'S COURT
Old Brompton Road
Cambio de Tercio, Capote y Toros
Garnier
Mr Wing
Anglesea Arms
Earl's Court Exhibition Centre
Rocco
Balans West
Riccardo's
Troubadour
Lucio
Redcliffe Gardens
Finborough Road
Lillie Road
Fulham Road
Aglio e Olio
Sophie's Steakhouse
Rossopomodoro
Vingt-Quatre
WEST BROMPTON
Haché
Henry Root
Atlas
Taiwan Village
Brompton Cemetry
Santa Lucia, Wine Gallery, Brinkley's
Busaba Eathai
El Ieven Park Walk
Kings Road Steakhouse & Grill
Eight over Eight
Osteria dell'Arancio
Troquet
Medlar
Chelsea Bun Diner
Famiglia
L'Art-du-Fromage
Harwood Arms
Chelsea Kitchen
Frantoio
Mona Lisa
Painted Heron
FULHAM BROADWAY
Rodizio Rico
Del'Aziz
Marco
Fulham Road
Butchers Hook
Napulé
Bodean's
Masala Zone
Best Mangal
Chutney Mary
Jam Tree
Chelsea Ram
FULHAM
Megan's
New King's Road
Chelsea Harbour

MAP 5 – KNIGHTSBRIDGE, CHELSEA & SOUTH KENSINGTON

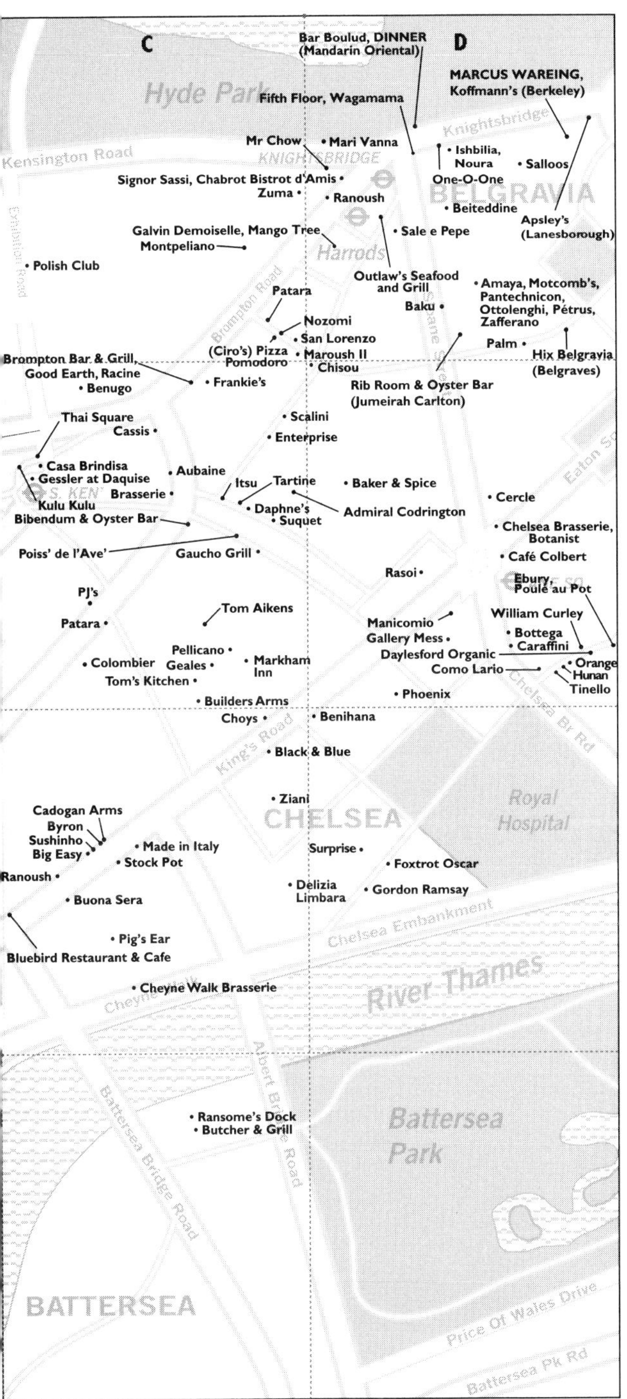

MAP 6 – NOTTING HILL & BAYSWATER

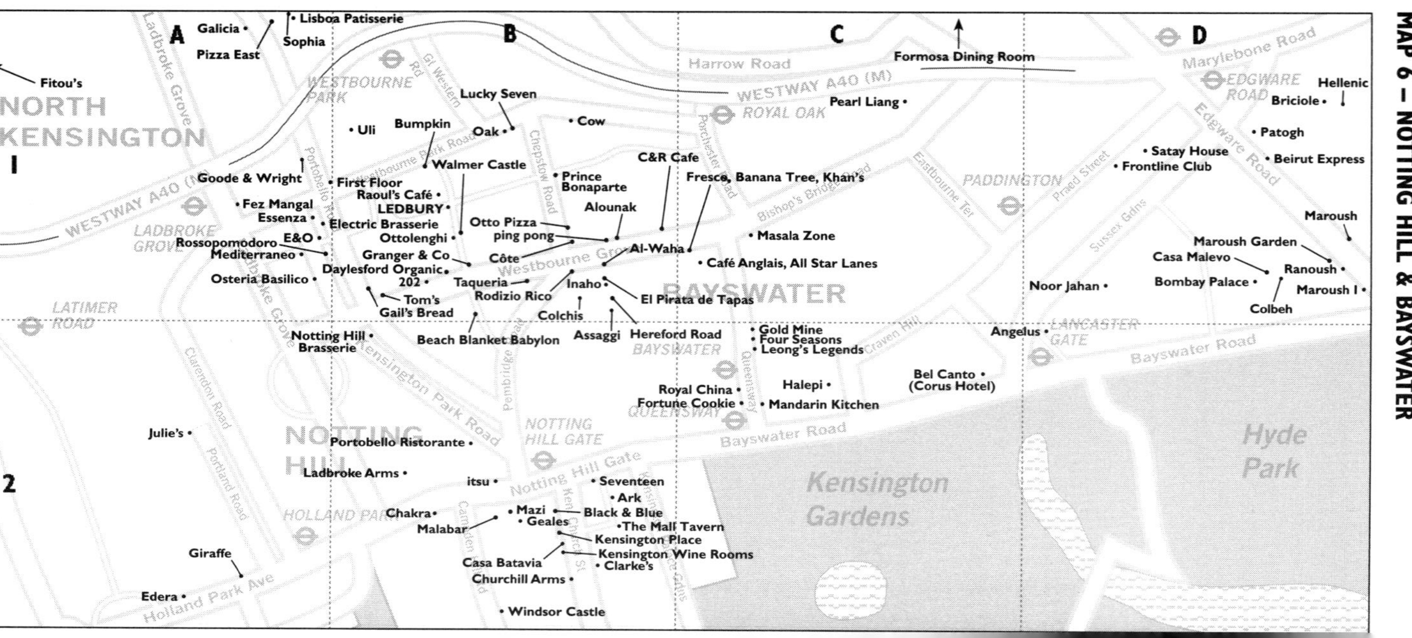

MAP 7 – HAMMERSMITH & CHISWICK

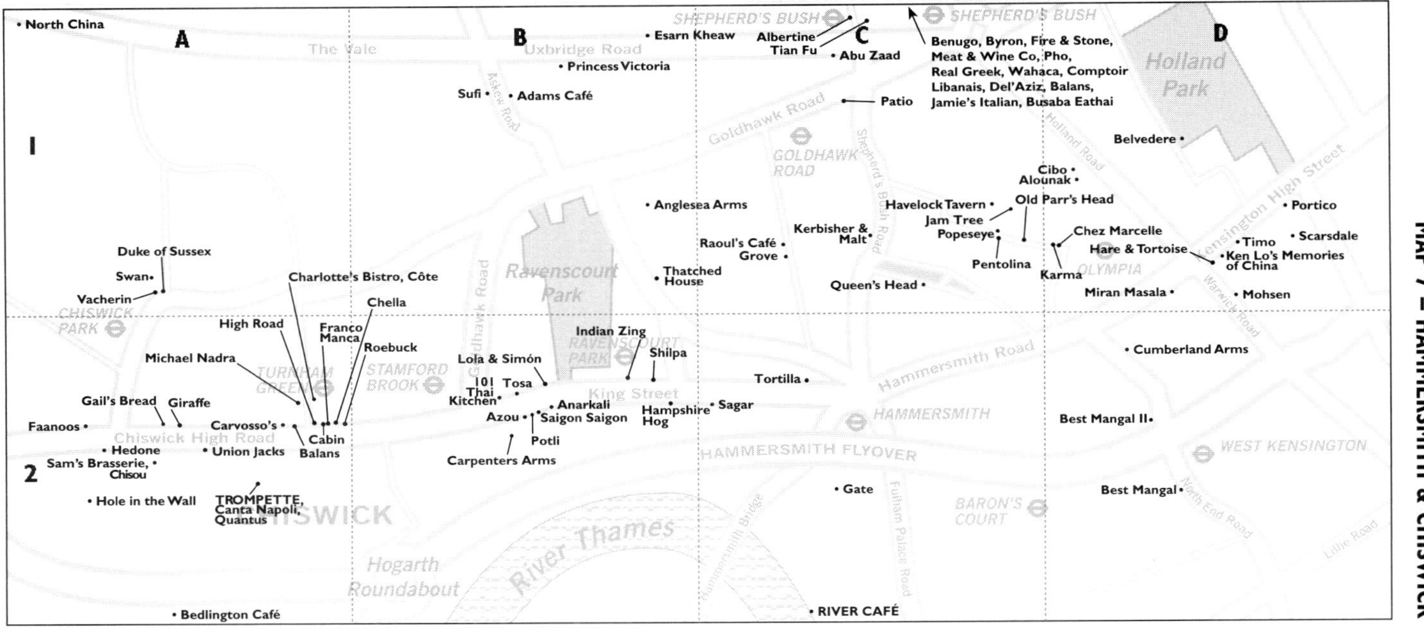

MAP 8 – HAMPSTEAD, CAMDEN TOWN & ISLINGTON

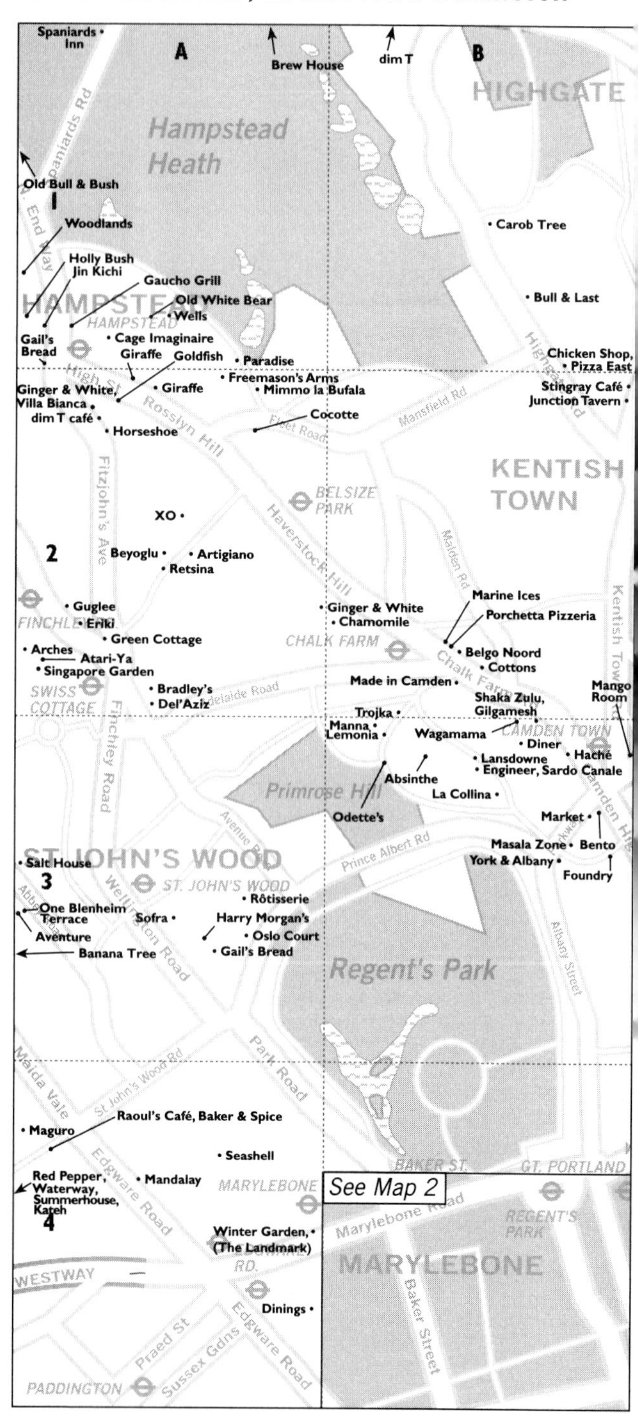

Spaniards Inn
A
Brew House
dim T
B
HIGHGATE
Spaniards Rd
Hampstead Heath
Old Bull & Bush
1
N. End Way
Woodlands
Holly Bush
Jin Kichi
Gaucho Grill
Old White Bear
Wells
HAMPSTEAD
Gail's Bread
Cage Imaginaire
Giraffe
Goldfish
Paradise
Freemason's Arms
Mimmo la Bufala
Ginger & White, Villa Bianca
Giraffe
dim T café
Horseshoe
Rosslyn Hill
Fleet Road
Cocotte
Carob Tree
Bull & Last
Highgate Road
Chicken Shop, Pizza East
Stingray Café
Junction Tavern
Mansfield Rd
KENTISH TOWN
BELSIZE PARK
Fitzjohn's Ave
XO
2
Beyoglu
Artigiano
Retsina
Haverstock Hill
Malden Rd
Marine Ices
Porchetta Pizzeria
Kentish Town
Guglee
FINCHLEY
Eriki
Green Cottage
Arches
Atari-Ya
Singapore Garden
SWISS COTTAGE
Bradley's
Del'Aziz
Adelaide Road
Ginger & White
Chamomile
CHALK FARM
Belgo Noord
Cottons
Chalk Farm Rd
Made in Camden
Shaka Zulu, Gilgamesh
Mango Room
Trojka
Manna
Lemonia
Wagamama
CAMDEN TOWN
Diner
Haché
Lansdowne
Engineer, Sardo Canale
Absinthe
La Collina
Finchley Road
Primrose Hill
Odette's
Market
Bento
Camden High St
Masala Zone
York & Albany
Foundry
Avenue Rd
Prince Albert Rd
ST JOHN'S WOOD
Salt House
3
ST. JOHN'S WOOD
Rôtisserie
One Blenheim Terrace
Sofra
Harry Morgan's
Oslo Court
Aventure
Gail's Bread
Banana Tree
Wellington Road
Regent's Park
Albany Street
Park Road
Maida Vale
St John's Wood Rd
Raoul's Café, Baker & Spice
Maguro
Seashell
BAKER ST.
GT. PORTLAND
Red Pepper, Waterway, Summerhouse, Kateh
Mandalay
MARYLEBONE
See Map 2
Edgware Road
Marylebone Road
REGENT'S PARK
4
Winter Garden, (The Landmark)
MARYLEBONE
WESTWAY
Baker Street
Dinings
Praed St
Edgware Road
Sussex Gdns
PADDINGTON

MAP 8 – HAMPSTEAD, CAMDEN TOWN & ISLINGTON

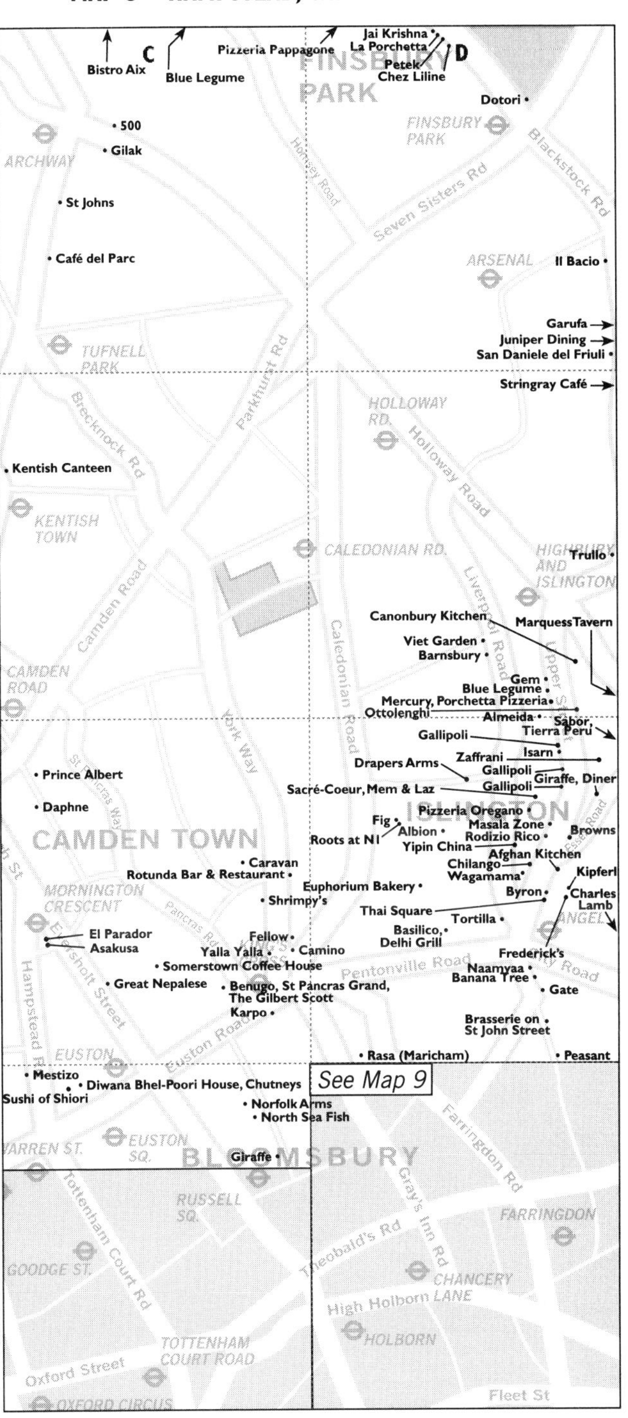

MAP 9 – THE CITY

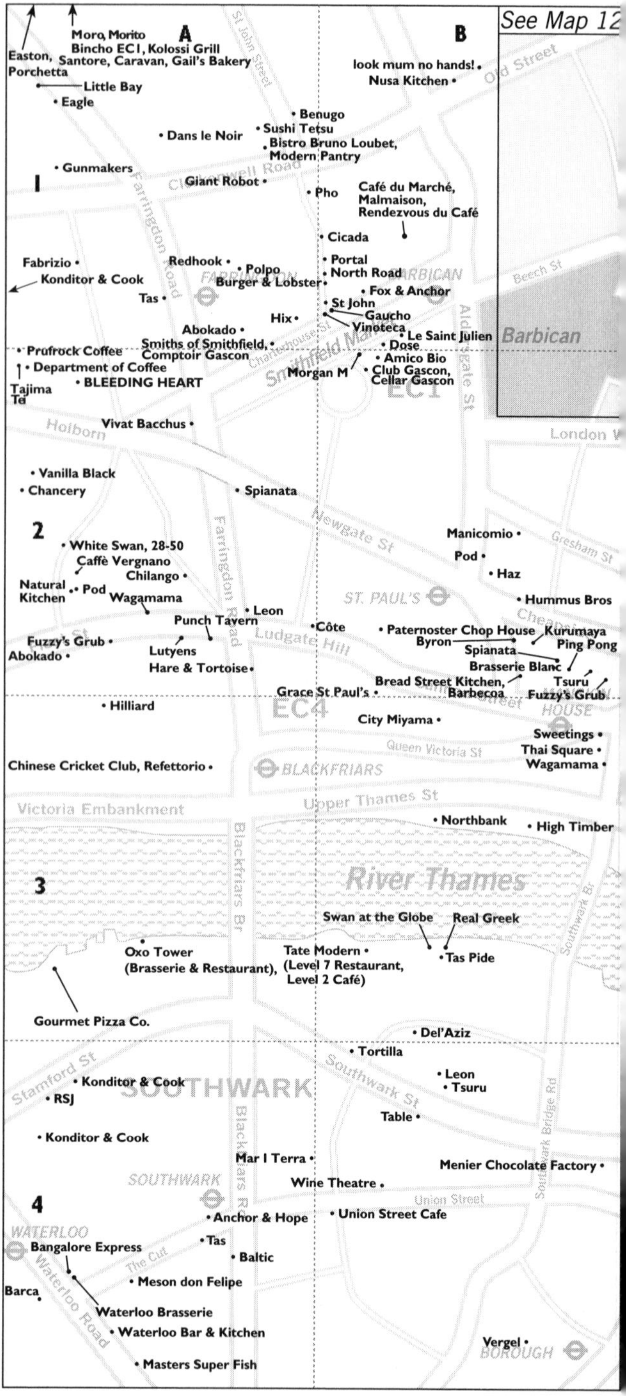

See Map 12

A

B

Moro, Morito
Bincho EC1, Kolossi Grill
Santore, Caravan, Gail's Bakery
Easton,
Porchetta
Little Bay
Eagle
St John Street
look mum no hands!
Nusa Kitchen
Old Street
Benugo
Sushi Tetsu
Dans le Noir
Bistro Bruno Loubet,
Modern Pantry
Gunmakers
1
Clerkenwell Road
Giant Robot
Pho
Café du Marché,
Malmaison,
Rendezvous du Café
Farringdon Road
Cicada
Fabrizio
Redhook
Polpo
Portal
Konditor & Cook
FARRINGDON
Burger & Lobster
North Road
BARBICAN
Beech St
Tas
Fox & Anchor
St John
Hix
Gaucho
Abokado
Vinoteca
Aldersgate St
Le Saint Julien
Barbican
Smiths of Smithfield,
Comptoir Gascon
Charterhouse St
Dose
Prufrock Coffee
Smithfield Market
Amico Bio
Department of Coffee
Morgan M
Club Gascon,
Cellar Gascon
Tajima
Tei
BLEEDING HEART
EC1
Holborn
Vivat Bacchus
London Wall
Vanilla Black
Chancery
Spianata
2
Newgate St
Manicomio
Gresham St
White Swan, 28-50
Caffè Vergnano
Pod
Chilango
Haz
Natural
Kitchen
Pod
Wagamama
Farringdon Road
ST. PAUL'S
Hummus Bros
Leon
Cheapside
Punch Tavern
Côte
Paternoster Chop House
Kurumaya
Fuzzy's Grub
Ludgate Hill
Byron
Ping Pong
Abokado
Lutyens
Spianata
Hare & Tortoise
Brasserie Blanc
Bread Street Kitchen,
Tsuru
Grace St Paul's
Barbecoa
Fuzzy's Grub
Cannon Street
Hilliard
EC4
MANSION
HOUSE
City Miyama
Sweetings
Queen Victoria St
Thai Square
Chinese Cricket Club, Refettorio
BLACKFRIARS
Wagamama
Victoria Embankment
Upper Thames St
Northbank
High Timber
Blackfriars Br
River Thames
3
Southwark Br
Swan at the Globe
Real Greek
Oxo Tower
(Brasserie & Restaurant),
Tate Modern
(Level 7 Restaurant,
Level 2 Café)
Tas Pide
Gourmet Pizza Co.
Del'Aziz
Tortilla
Stamford St
Southwark St
Konditor & Cook
Leon
SOUTHWARK
Tsuru
RSJ
Blackfriars Rd
Table
Konditor & Cook
Southwark Bridge Rd
Mar I Terra
Menier Chocolate Factory
SOUTHWARK
Wine Theatre
Union Street
4
Anchor & Hope
Union Street Cafe
WATERLOO
Tas
Bangalore Express
Baltic
The Cut
Meson don Felipe
Barca
Waterloo Road
Waterloo Brasserie
Waterloo Bar & Kitchen
Vergel
BOROUGH
Masters Super Fish

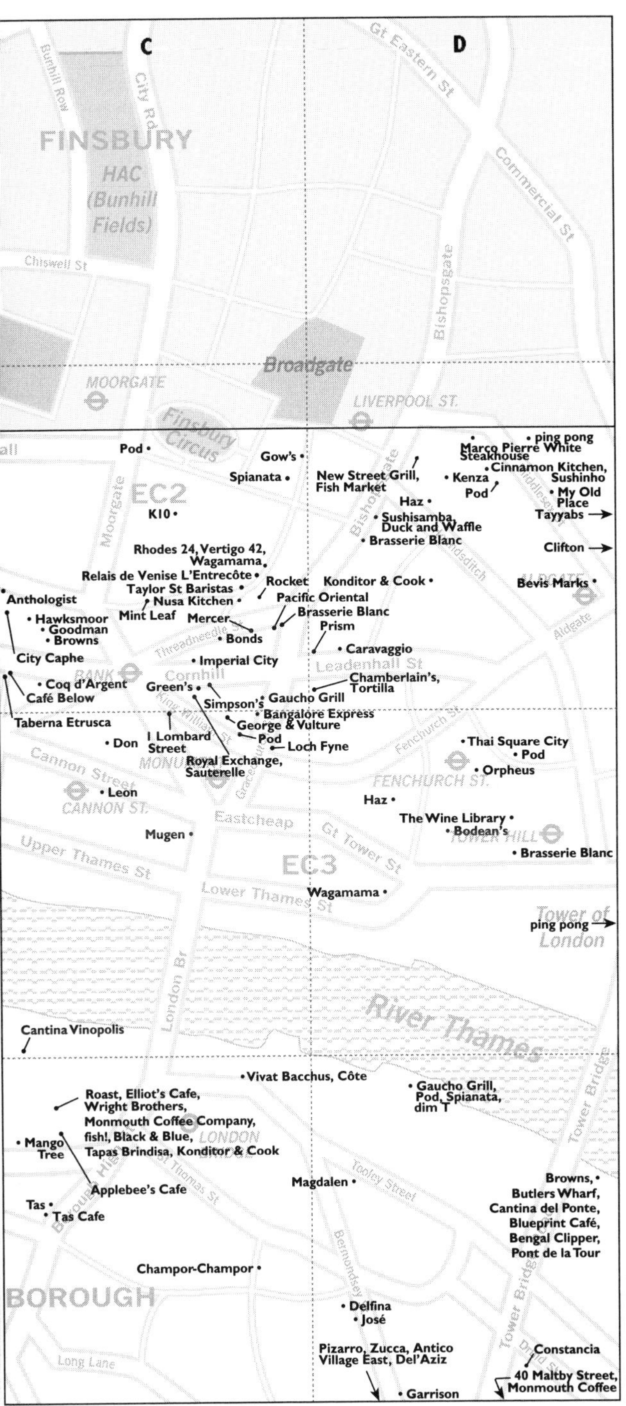
C
D
FINSBURY
HAC (Bunhill Fields)
Broadgate
MOORGATE
LIVERPOOL ST.
EC2
EC3
BANK
Cornhill
Leadenhall St
Eastcheap
Cannon Street
CANNON ST.
FENCHURCH ST.
TOWER HILL
Upper Thames St
Lower Thames St
Gt Tower St
River Thames
Tower of London
London Br
Tower Bridge
LONDON BRIDGE
Tooley Street
BOROUGH
Long Lane
Chiswell St
Bunhill Row
City Rd
Gt Eastern St
Commercial St
Bishopsgate
Moorgate
Finsbury Circus
Threadneedle St
Aldgate
Pod
Gow's
Spianata
New Street Grill, Fish Market
Marco Pierre White Steakhouse
ping pong
Cinnamon Kitchen, Sushinho
Kenza
Pod
My Old Place
Tayyabs
Haz
K10
Sushisamba, Duck and Waffle
Brasserie Blanc
Clifton
Rhodes 24, Vertigo 42, Wagamama
Relais de Venise L'Entrecôte
Rocket
Konditor & Cook
Bevis Marks
Taylor St Baristas
Pacific Oriental
Anthologist
Nusa Kitchen
Mint Leaf
Brasserie Blanc
Hawksmoor
Goodman
Browns
Mercer
Bonds
Prism
Caravaggio
City Caphe
Imperial City
Coq d'Argent
Café Below
Green's
Chamberlain's, Tortilla
Simpson's
Gaucho Grill
Bangalore Express
Taberna Etrusca
George & Vulture
Pod
1 Lombard Street
Don
Loch Fyne
Thai Square City
Pod
Royal Exchange, Sauterelle
Orpheus
Leon
Haz
The Wine Library
Bodean's
Mugen
Brasserie Blanc
Wagamama
ping pong
Cantina Vinopolis
Vivat Bacchus, Côte
Gaucho Grill, Pod, Spianata, dim T
Roast, Elliot's Cafe, Wright Brothers, Monmouth Coffee Company, fish!, Black & Blue, Tapas Brindisa, Konditor & Cook
Mango Tree
Applebee's Cafe
Magdalen
Browns, Butlers Wharf, Cantina del Ponte, Blueprint Café, Bengal Clipper, Pont de la Tour
Tas
Tas Cafe
Champor-Champor
Delfina
José
Pizarro, Zucca, Antico Village East, Del'Aziz
Garrison
Constancia
40 Maltby Street, Monmouth Coffee

MAP 10 – SOUTH LONDON (& FULHAM)

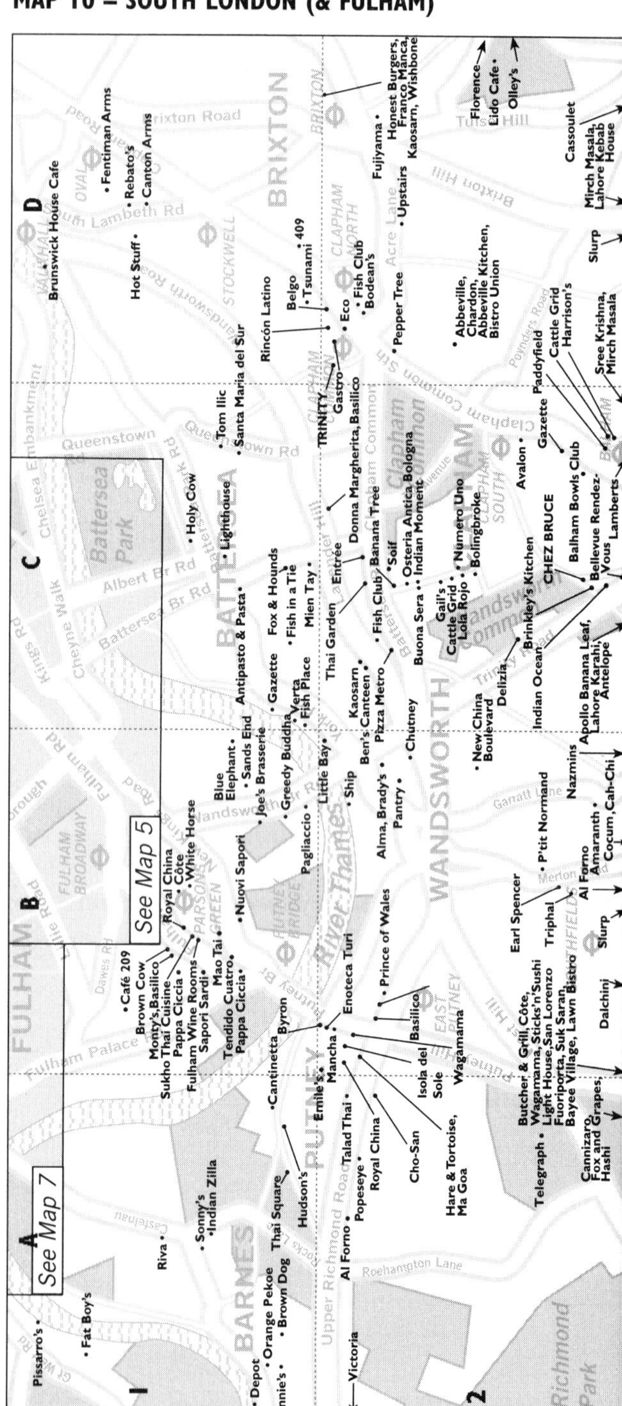

MAP 11 – EAST END & DOCKLANDS

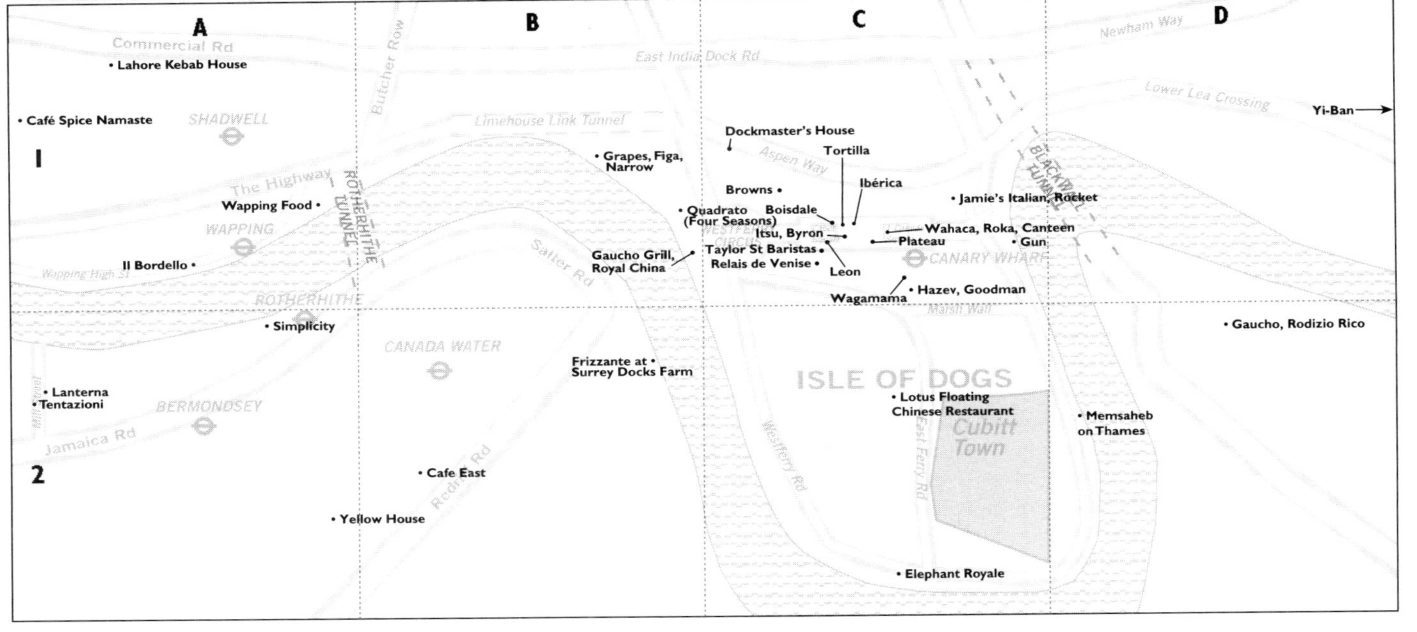

MAP 12 – SHOREDITCH & BETHNAL GREEN

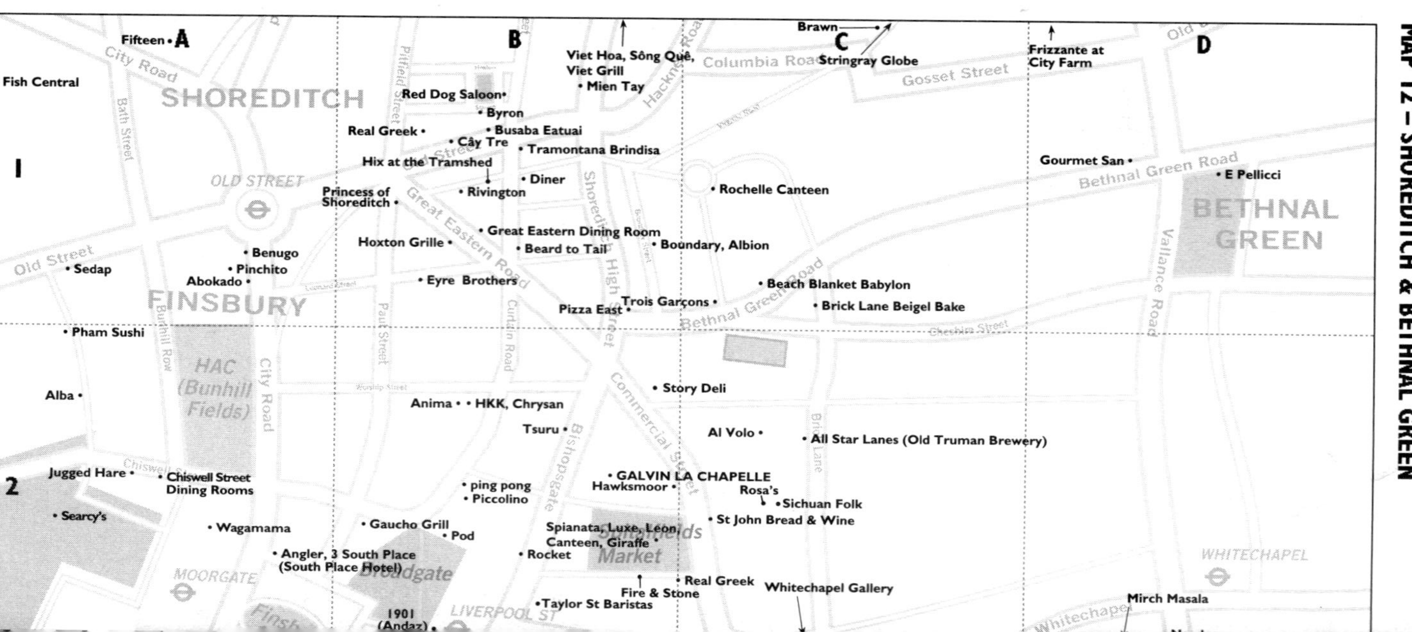